King Seneb-Kay's Tomb
and the Necropolis of a Lost Dynasty
at Abydos

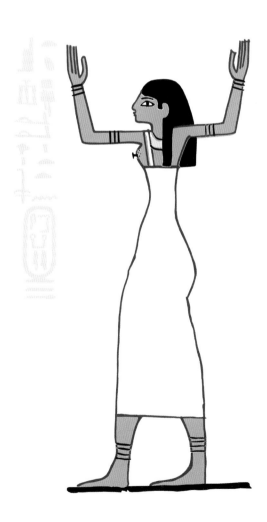

University Museum Monograph 155

King Seneb-Kay's Tomb and the Necropolis of a Lost Dynasty at Abydos

By

Josef Wegner and Kevin Cahail

with contributions by Jane Hill, Maria Rosado, and Molly Gleeson

University of Pennsylvania Museum of Archaeology and Anthropology | Philadelphia

LIBRARY OF CONGRESS CATALOGING-IN-PUBLICATION DATA

Names: Wegner, Josef W. (Josef William), author. | Cahail, Kevin, author.
Title: King Seneb-Kay's tomb and the necropolis of a lost dynasty at Abydos
    / by Josef Wegner and Kevin Cahail ; with contributions by Jane Hill,
    Maria Rosado, and Molly Gleeson.
Other titles: University Museum monograph ; 155.
Description: Philadelphia : University of Pennsylvania Museum of
    Archaeology and Anthropology, 2021. | Series: University Museum
    monograph; 155 | Includes bibliographical references.
Identifiers: LCCN 2020043117 | ISBN 9781949057096 (hardcover) | ISBN
    9781949057102 (ebook)
Subjects: LCSH: Seneb-Kay, King of Egypt, approximately 1650
    B.C.-approximately 1600 B.C.--Tomb. | Abydos (Egypt : Extinct
    city)--Antiquities.
Classification: LCC DT73.A16 W44 2021 | DDC 932/.013--dc23
LC record available at https://lccn.loc.gov/2020043117

Distributed for the University of Pennsylvania Museum of Archaeology and Anthropology
by the University of Pennsylvania Press.

Printed in the United States of America on acid-free paper.

Frontispiece Goddess on the north wall of the burial chamber with reconstruction of the hieroglyphic label: *"It is Isis who folds her arms around King Seneb-Kay."*

In memory of John Richard (Rick) Rockwell
whose interest and support of the work at Abydos
led to the discovery of Egypt's forgotten pharaoh,
Seneb-Kay.

Contents

Part 1: The Tomb of King Woseribre Seneb-Kay

Part 2: The Reused Material in the Tomb of Seneb-Kay

Part 3: The Main Tomb Cluster

Part 4: Historical and Archaeological Synthesis

Figures

Tables

Contributors

Josef Wegner is Professor of Egyptian Archaeology in the Department of Near Eastern Languages and Civilizations and Curator in the Egyptian Section of the Penn Museum, University of Pennsylvania. He received his Ph.D. in 1996 from the University of Pennsylvania. He has excavated extensively at Abydos where he is Director of the Penn Museum's excavations at the mortuary complex of Senwosret III. His publications and co-authored volumes include: *The Mortuary Temple of Senwosret III at Abydos* (2007), *Archaism and Innovation: Studies in the Culture of Middle Kingdom Egypt* (2009), *The Sphinx That Traveled to Philadelphia* (2015), and *The Sunshade Chapel of Princess Meritaten* (2017). His research interests include political and administrative organization during Egypt's Middle Kingdom.

Kevin Cahail is the Collections Manager of the Egyptian Collection of the Penn Museum of the University of Pennsylvania. He received his B.A. in Classics and Classical Archaeology in 2003 from San Francisco State University, and his Ph.D. in Egyptology in 2014 from the University of Pennsylvania. His dissertation was the result of three field seasons in Egypt, excavating tombs of royal and non-royal individuals at South Abydos. His research interests include funerary archaeology and mortuary practices of the Middle and New Kingdoms.

Jane Hill is Instructor in the Department of Sociology and Anthropology, Rowan University, and also Curator in the Museum of Anthropology at Rowan University. She received her Ph.D. in 2010 in the Department of Near Eastern Languages and Civilizations, University of Pennsylvania. She also holds degrees in Anthropology and Art History from the University of Memphis. She is author of *Cylinder Seal Glyptic in Predynastic Egypt and Neighboring Regions* (2004) and co-editor of *Experiencing Power, Generating Authority, Cosmos, Politics and Ideology of Kingship in Ancient Egypt and Mesopotamia* (2013). Her research interests include urbanism in Upper Egypt's formative period, and the emergence of Egyptian administrative and writing systems.

Maria Rosado is Professor of Anthropology in the Department of Sociology and Anthropology at Rowan University, and Adjunct Investigator of Physical Anthropology at the Museo Arqueológico de la Serena, Chile where she has on-going projects in bioarchaeology, skeletal conservation, and forensic anthropology. She received her Ph.D. in 1994 from the Department of Anthropology, Rutgers University. Dr. Rosado's research in bioarchaeology focuses on paleopathology, intentional cranial modification, and the bioarchaeology of care. Dr. Rosado is Curator in the Museum of Anthropology at Rowan University (MARU).

Molly Gleeson is Schwartz Project Conservator in the Conservation Department of the Penn Museum, University of Pennsylvania. She is also project conservator for the Egyptian and Nubian collections of the Penn Museum. She received her B.A. in 2002 from the University of Delaware. She worked on contract in Southern California and as a Research Associate on the UCLA and Getty Conservation Institute feather research project. She completed her M.A. in 2008 at the UCLA/Getty Master's Program in the Conservation of Archaeological and Ethnographic Materials. She is co-editor of *Engaging Conservation: Collaboration Across Disciplines* (2017).

Acknowledgments

We would like to express our appreciation to the numerous colleagues, friends, and supporters who have had a role in the discovery and excavation of the tomb of Seneb-Kay. The work would not have occurred without the continuing support of the Egyptian Ministry of State for Antiquities (MSA). In Cairo, we are indebted to the members of the Permanent Committee of the Ministry of Antiquities, in particular: Dr. Mohammed Ibrahim; Dr. Mamdouh Mohamed el-Damaty and Dr. Khaled el-Enany (Directors of the MSA during the period of research discussed here); Dr. Mohamed Ismail Khaled, Mr. Hany Abou el-Azm and Dr, Nashwa Gaber (in their capacity as Director of Foreign Missions). In Cairo we are also indebted to the staff of the American Research Center in Egypt (ARCE) for their assistance to the research. In particular we would like to mention Mme. Amira Khattab and Mary Sadek (past and current ARCE deputy directors for government affiliations).

In Sohag, we wish to acknowledge the efforts of the Sohag and Balliana Inspectorates of the MSA. Particular thanks are due to Mr. Gamal Abd el-Nasser (former Director General of the Sohag Inspectorate), Dr. Federica Hasan (Director, Sohag Inspectorate), Mr. Ashraf Okasha (past Director of the Balliana-Abydos Inspectorate and current Director of the Sohag Inspectorate), and Mr. Tal'at el-Madah (general director of foreign missions for the Sohag archaeological region). Thanks are also due to Ms. Aziza el-Sayed Hassan, Mme. Sana Samy, and Mr. Hazem Salah Abdullah of the Balliana Inspectorate.

In Abydos itself, the work has benefitted from the expertise of the archaeological inspectors who have worked with us during excavations in the Second Intermediate Period royal necropolis. These include Mr. Ayman Damarany and Mr. Ahmed Ibrahim Abu Ganeb (2013–2014); Mr. Mahmoud Amr Ahmed and Mr. Mahmoud Abu Zeid (2014 and 2015), Mr. Barakat Eid Ahmed Eid and Mr. Ahmed Hammad Ismail (2014–2015); Mr. Ahmed Hammad Ismail (2014 and 2016); Mr. Hany Mohamed Ahmed (2015); Mr. Mohamed Ahmed Rahman El-Khateeb and Mr. Mohamed Hussein Ahmed (2015–2016), Mr. Ahmed Abd el-Kader Abd el-Latif (2015–2016); Mr. Mena Aziz (2015–2016); and Ms. Reham Mahmoud Kamil (2015–2016). Conservation work on the tomb of Seneb-Kay in 2015–2016 has included the collaboration of MSA conservators including Mr. Sayid Diyab, Mr. Yahya Mohamed Gelal, and Mr. Omar Diab Ali.

Much of the success of the excavation work is due to the dedication and fine attention to detail of our excavation staff including our Guftis. We wish to particularly acknowledge excavation foreman, Rais Ibrahim Mohamed Ali, and other Guftis who have worked on the tomb of Seneb-Kay including Mr. Ashraf Zaidan Mahmoud, Mr. Badry Mohamed Aly, Mr. Abd el-Rasul Mahmoud Hussain (Sabir), Mr. Wadjih Hamid Aly, and Mr. Hamdy Abd el-Ghany Helal. The excavations were completed by men from the towns of Beni Mansour, el-Arabeh, and el-Ghabat whose friendship and efforts are appreciated by the team members. At Abydos, we are also indebted to the work of the Manager of the American Mission excavation house, Mr. Ahmed Ragab Ahmed, as well as the work of the house staff including Mr. Sinjab Abd el-Rahman Shehab and Mr. Hassan Mitwally.

Aside from the principal authors, members of the archaeological and conservation team in 2014–2016 have included Dr. Jennifer Houser Wegner, Dr. Jane Hill, Dr. Maria Rosado, Dr. Rasha Soliman, Dr. Lisa Haney, Dr. Shelby Justl, Dr. Leah Humphrey, Valentina Anselmi, Matthew Olson, Paul Verhelst, James Kelly, Molly Gleeson, Daniel Doyle, Lucy-Ann Skinner, and Alexander Wegner. We would like to thank

Dr. Robert Ritner for helpful for helpful comments, as well as Dr. Dawn McCormack for her associated research that has examined the neighboring 13th Dynasty tomb, S9, at South Abydos. For her contribution of time in drafting artistic reconstruction sketches of Seneb-Kay and other individuals at South Abydos (not included in this volume but published elsewhere), we would like to acknowledge Mireya Poblete Arias, of the Policia de Investigaciones, Puerto Montt, Chile. In the preparation of this volume, we would like to thank the following individuals for their assistance in providing images from museum collections that relate to the discovery of Seneb-Kay: Dr. Janice Kamrin (Metropolitan Musuem of Art); Dr. Marcel Marée (British Musuem); and Dr. Fred Vink for his photographs of the Seneb-Kay birth wand included here.

At the Penn Museum, the work at South Abydos has benefitted from the support of Dr. Julian Siggers (Williams Director of the Penn Museum), Amanda Mitchell-Boyask (Director of Development), Dr. David Silverman (Coxe Professor of Egyptology), and Dr. James Mathieu (former Director of Publications).

Thanks to Pam Kosty (in her former capacity as Director of Public Information) for her efforts regarding public interest in the discovery of Seneb-Kay. Funds for the work have included support from the Director's Field Fund of the Penn Museum under the oversight of Dr. Stephen Tinney (Deputy Director). For her editorial expertise and work in the design and production of this volume, as well as her valuable comments on the osteological sections of the book, we are indebted to Dr. Page Selinsky, Director of Penn Museum Publications.

Funding for the work at South Abydos has also come from the National Geographic Society. For site management and conservation work, funds have come through support from the Antiquities Endowment Fund (AEF) of the American Research Center in Egypt (ARCE). Dr. Charles K. Williams II and Elizabeth Jean Walker have been instrumental in the scientific results we have achieved in recent years. Most particularly we wish to acknowledge, for his encouragement and support, Mr. Rick Rockwell, to whom this book is dedicated.

Glossary of Place Names and Terms

Avaris (Greek, from Egyptian *Ḥwt-wꜥrt*) Capital of the Hyksos Kingdom located on the Pelusiac branch of the Nile in the northeastern Nile Delta.

Coffin Texts (abbr. CT) Corpus of Egyptian funerary texts that emerge in the late Old Kingdom ca. 2300 BCE and develop into the Second Intermediate Period when their use declines.

Deir el-Bahri (Arabic) Modern name for the desert bay on the west bank of Thebes forming part of the Theban necropolis. Location of cemeteries of the Middle Kingdom and Second Intermediate Period.

Dra Abu el-Naga (Arabic) Modern name for area of the Theban necropolis that includes many of the royal tombs of the late Second Intermediate Period.

el-Kab (Arabic, Egyptian *Nḫb*) Modern name for the settlement and temple site of the goddess Nekhbet in the 3rd nome (province) of Upper Egypt. Location of cemeteries and rock-cut chapels of the Second Intermediate Period.

gebel (Arabic) "Mountain" refers to the high desert cliffs that flank the Nile Valley in Upper Egypt.

Head of the South (Egyptian, *tp-rsy*) Ancient Egyptian geographical and administrative term for the southern eight nomes (provinces) of Upper Egypt stretching from Elephantine to Abydos.

***hetep-di-nisut* formula** (Egyptian, *ḥtp-dỉ-nswt*) Standardized offering formula used on mortuary equipment including stelae, statuary, false doors and funerary architecture.

Hyksos (Greek, from Egyptian, *ḥkꜣw-ḫꜣswt*) Greek term for the "rulers of foreign lands" used in Egyptian texts to refer to the kings of the 15th Dynasty who ruled Lower Egypt during the late Second Intermediate Period.

Itj-Tawy (Egyptian, *Ỉt-tꜣwy*) Royal residence city founded by Amenemhat I (ca. 2000 BCE) and used as the capital during the 12th and 13th Dynasties (ca. 2000–1650 BCE).

Kerma Modern name for the town in Upper Nubia which formed the political center of the Nubian Kerma Kingdom during the Second Intermediate Period.

khat (Egyptian, *ḫꜥt*) Form of royal headdress characterized by a bag-shaped profile.

khekher (Egyptian, *ḫkr*) Decorative frieze showing rows of bundled plants frequently used for the tops of walls in Egyptian funerary and religious architecture.

Kom es-Sultan (Arabic) The "mound of the ruler" refers to the walled area that encompasses the main town and temple of Osiris at North Abydos.

Lisht Location of the pyramids of Kings Amenemhat I and Senwosret I near the residence city of Itj-Tawy, location of private cemeteries of the Middle Kingdom and Second Intermediate Period.

mahat (Egyptian, *mꜥḥꜥt*) Egyptian term denoting a mortuary building with a primarily commemorative function that was devoid of an actual burial, sometimes translated as "cenotaph."

mastaba (Arabic) Modern word commonly used for the rectangular, flat-topped mortuary superstructures that predominate in early Egyptian cemeteries.

Medamud (Egyptian *Mꜣdw*) Settlement and temple site dedicated to the god Montu in the Theban nome, ten kilometers north east of the temple of Karnak.

Mirgissa (Egyptian *Ikn*) Modern toponym for the Egyptian fortress and community near the Second Cataract in Lower Nubia, location of cemeteries of the late Middle Kingdom and Second Intermediate Period.

nemes (Egyptian, *nms*) Royal crown characterized by lappets that extend down over the shoulders and a decorative treatment of stripes of alternating colors.

per-nu (Egyptian, *pr-nw*) Term for the symbolic shrine of Lower Egypt that is adapted into funerary equipment such as coffins and canopic boxes.

rishi (Arabic) "Feathered," refers to the style of sarcophagus decorated with bird wings. The style is particularly diagnostic of the Second Intermediate Period and early New Kingdom.

serekh (Egyptian, *srḫ*) Paneled architectural design derived from royal palace architecture and adapted for symbolic use on coffins and funerary art.

tafla (Arabic) Compact clay-like material encountered in the desert subsurface.

Thebes (Greek, Egyptian *Wꜣst*) Capital of the 4th nome (province) of Upper Egypt; during the Second Intermediate Period political center of the Theban Kingdom (the 16th and 17th Dynasties).

Thinis (Greek, from Egyptian *Ṯni*) Capital of the 8th nome (province) of Upper Egypt. Located northeast of Abydos but not archaeologically identified.

Umm el-Qa'ab (Arabic) Modern name for the Predynastic and Early Dynastic royal cemetery at Abydos, necropolis of the earliest Egyptian pharaohs and symbolic burial place of Osiris.

uraeus (Greek, from Egyptian *iꜥrt*) Hooded cobra, symbol of royalty and dominion associated with Wadjet of Buto, the symbolic goddess of Lower Egypt.

wedjat (Egyptian, *wꜣḏt*) The eye of Horus or "sound eye" commonly used as symbol of bodily well-being in Egyptian funerary iconography.

wesekh (Egyptian, *wsḫ*) Beaded broad-collar which forms part of the assemblage of jewelry and amulets included in Egyptian funerary practices.

Part 1

The Tomb of King Woseribre Seneb-Kay

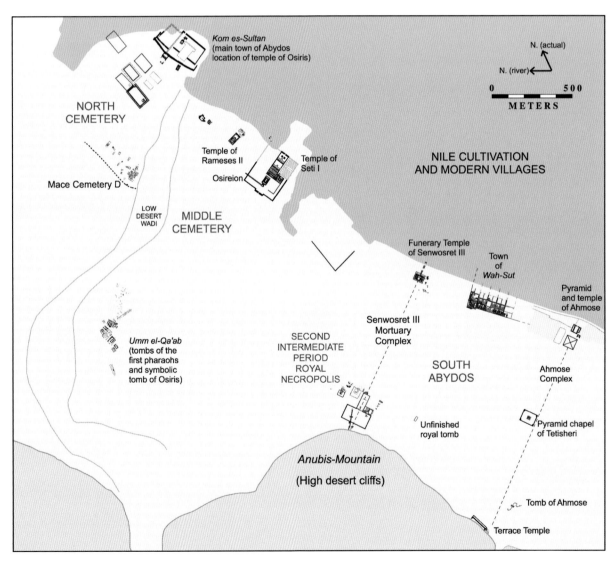

Fig. 0.1 Plan of greater Abydos showing the location of the late Middle Kingdom and Second Intermediate Period royal necropolis at the base of the cliffs at South Abydos.

Introduction

Between approximately 1650–1600 BCE, at the height of Egypt's Second Intermediate Period, an Egyptian king named Woseribre Seneb-Kay was violently killed in a military encounter. Covered in the traumatic wounds that accompanied his death, his body was mummified and buried in a hastily constructed tomb at the site of Abydos in Upper Egypt. The location chosen for his burial was the foot of the high desert cliffs of South Abydos where a group of three large tombs that we now attribute to the Middle Kingdom pharaohs Senwosret III, Neferhotep I, and Sobekhotep IV formed a royal burial ground known to the Egyptians as *ḏw-Inpw*, the *Mountain-of-Anubis* (Wegner 2009). Seneb-Kay's own tomb was inserted alongside these earlier, larger burial monuments dating the late Middle Kingdom (Fig. 0.1 and 0.2).[1]

Although Seneb-Kay's tomb was constructed quickly at modest scale (measuring just 13.5 meters in overall length), the builders took the time to decorate his burial chamber with painted funerary imagery and hieroglyphic texts. This decoration records his identity as the *Good-God, Lord-of-the-Two-Lands, Lord-of-Ritual, King of Upper and Lower Egypt, Woseribre Seneb-Kay*. Perhaps surprisingly, his decorated burial chamber is the first one belonging to a king in pharaonic history that contains painted wall imagery. It is thanks to the survival of that decoration that we are able to identify the tomb's owner, a king who would otherwise remain effectively lost to history. Apart from his tomb, archaeology has revealed no known monuments relating to this ruler. There exists only a single inscribed object, bearing

his misspelled birth-name, or nomen, in the form "Seb-Kay," that we can attribute to his reign. Who was King Woseribre Seneb-Kay and why was he buried at South Abydos? This volume examines those questions in light of his tomb and its contents.

Seneb-Kay's tomb was discovered in 2014 as part of the Penn Museum's excavations at South Abydos. Among the fragmentary remains of his burial assemblage, we recovered the body of Seneb-Kay himself still substantially articulated but discarded on the floor of the tomb by ancient robbers. Osteological analysis testifies to the extent of the traumatic wounds that led to Seneb-Kay's death. He is at present the earliest documented Egyptian king whose physical remains show he died in the midst of battle. Moreover, features of his skeleton indicate a man whose life included a specific regimen of physical and martial activities, a man who appears to have risen to power from the military elite of the Second Intermediate Period. Part 1 of this volume discusses the tomb of Seneb-Kay and its contents.

The discovery of this previously unknown ancient Egyptian king has opened a new window onto the practice of kingship during one of the most fragmented eras of Ancient Egypt: the late Second Intermediate Period, or "Hyksos Period." During this time period, Egypt was divided among multiple rival kingdoms (Fig. 0.3). These dynasties include the final pharaohs of the 13th Dynasty, ruling from the city of *Itj-Tawy*; the 16th and 17th Dynasties, ruling sequentially from Thebes in Upper Egypt; and the Hyksos or 15th Dynasty, a line of kings of Levantine origin who, after

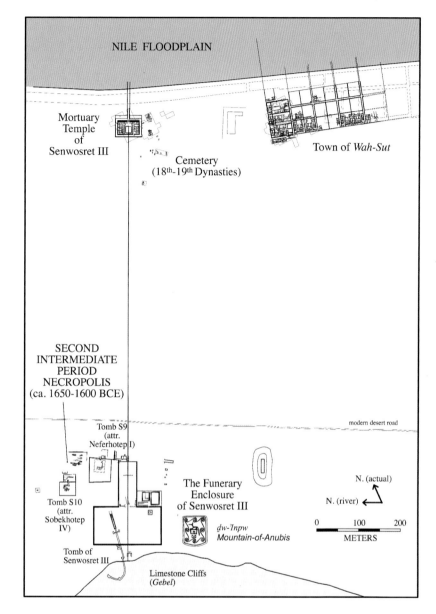

NILE FLOODPLAIN

Mortuary
Temple
of
Senwosret III

Cemetery
(18th-19th Dynasties)

Town of *Wah-Sut*

SECOND
INTERMEDIATE
PERIOD
NECROPOLIS
(ca. 1650-1600 BCE)

Tomb S9
(attr.
Neferhotep I)

modern desert road

Tomb S10
(attr.
Sobekhotep
IV)

The Funerary
Enclosure
of Senwosret III

N. (actual)

N. (river)

Tomb of
Senwosret III

ḏw-Ỉnpw
Mountain-of-Anubis

0   100   200
METERS

Limestone Cliffs
(*Gebel*)

Fig. 0.2 The environs of the mortuary complex of Senwosret III showing the primary known structures and location of the Second Intermediate Period necropolis.

set of evidence by Detlef Franke in 1988.[2] The possibility of an "Abydos Dynasty" was then more fully developed by Kim Ryholt and presented in his 1997 volume, *The Political Situation in Egypt during the Second Intermediate Period c. 1800–1550 B.C.*, as part of his broader model of the dynastic and political structure of the period. The idea of the Abydos Dynasty was subsequently dismissed by the majority of Egyptologists. Seneb-Kay and the seven tombs of his close contemporaries provide new evidence for the existence of an Abydos Dynasty (Wegner 2014, 2018a).

After the initial discovery of Seneb-Kay's tomb, work continued during 2015–16 with an expanded investigation of the surrounding landscape. The goal of this work has been defining the relationship of Seneb-Kay's tomb

taking power following an earlier line of 14th Dynasty Delta kings, ruled from their capital at Avaris, the modern site of Tell el-Dab'a in the north-eastern Nile Delta. As we examine in this volume, there is no evidence indicating that Seneb-Kay belonged to any of these dynasties. His tomb and a group of seven other tombs of similar design near that of Seneb-Kay appear to belong to a succession of Second Intermediate Period kings whose names were edited out of the later pharaonic kinglists: a lost dynasty. The existence of such a line of monarchs ruling from the Abydene and Thinite region had first been hypothesized on a slim

to adjacent structures. Identification of the ownership of Seneb-Kay's tomb in 2014 immediately shed light on a group of tombs of nearly identical design close to that of Seneb-Kay. Long before our recent excavations, Arthur Weigall, working in 1902 for the Egypt Exploration Fund, located and examined three mysterious tombs at South Abydos which, lacking dateable inscribed material, he chose to simply classify as "Late" tombs (Ayrton, Currelly, and Weigall 1904:17–18). Until the present time, these structures remained of unknown date and with no obvious architectural parallels at Abydos or elsewhere in Egypt.

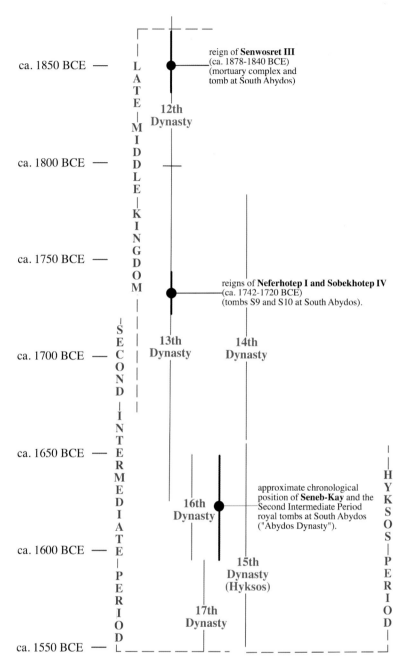

ca. 1850 BCE —

reign of **Senwosret III**
(ca. 1878-1840 BCE)
(mortuary complex and
tomb at South Abydos)

**12th
Dynasty**

ca. 1800 BCE —

ca. 1750 BCE —

reigns of **Neferhotep I and Sobekhotep IV**
(ca. 1742-1720 BCE)
(tombs S9 and S10 at South Abydos).

**13th
Dynasty**   **14th
Dynasty**

ca. 1700 BCE —

ca. 1650 BCE —

approximate chronological
position of **Seneb-Kay** and the
Second Intermediate Period
royal tombs at South Abydos
("Abydos Dynasty").

**16th
Dynasty**

ca. 1600 BCE —

**15th
Dynasty
(Hyksos)**

**17th
Dynasty**

ca. 1550 BCE —

Fig. 0.3 Chronology of the late Middle Kingdom and Second Intermediate Period showing the position of Seneb-Kay and the other kings whose tombs are located in the royal necropolis at South Abydos.

"CS" designations for "Cemetery S" deriving from an earlier convention that Weigall had used for the Senwosret III mortuary enclosure.[3] Tombs CS4, CS5, CS6, CS7, and CS8 were excavated in 2013.[4] Three of these (tombs CS4, CS7, and CS8) we immediately identified as the tombs that Weigall had opened, while two others, CS5 and CS6, had been untouched by Weigall. CS6 presented us with a surprising new discovery.

Based on its location and brick architectural elements, CS6 was contemporary with the other tombs. Uniquely, however, this tomb made use of a reused, monolithic quartzite burial chamber, weighing approximately 50 tons and originally of 13th Dynasty date. From their scale and common design elements it was evident that all five of the tombs known at that point were closely contemporaneous and of elite status. However, no additional diagnostic artifacts emerged in 2013 with which to anchor their date. At that stage, the evidence included the puzzling phenomenon of the reuse of an abandoned or relocated 13th Dynasty royal burial chamber. The discovery of Seneb-Kay's tomb in 2014, designated as CS9, close to these other five tombs finally provided a clear basis for dating the entire group to the Second Intermediate Period. Moreover, the status of Seneb-Kay's tomb as the burial of a king, along with the presence of the preexisting late Middle Kingdom royal tombs

While the tomb of Seneb-Kay itself was discovered in 2014, work on the Second Intermediate Period royal cemetery discussed in this volume began the year before, when we initiated a survey of mortuary activity, the South Abydos Tomb Census (SATC). The initial goal of this work was searching for late Middle Kingdom private tombs at South Abydos. During this work we relocated and reexamined the three tombs that Weigall had previously encountered. At that point the tombs were assigned at the site, suggested the likelihood that many or all of these tombs belong to Second Intermediate Period kings who had made use of this same mortuary landscape at South Abydos. The tombs show intriguing patterns of architectural copying but also reuse of materials from the preexisting 13th Dynasty tombs at the site, a phenomenon which we will explore throughout this volume.

During continued work in 2014 and 2015 we expanded excavation into unexplored areas between the known tombs and also around the periphery of the Second Intermediate Period cemetery. Primary goals of that work included the retrieval of new dating evidence for the necropolis as a whole and the identification of additional tombs that—like Seneb-Kay's—might yield evidence for specific ownership. This work led to the discovery of two additional tombs, CS10 and CS11, as well as a group of three brick shafts labeled CS12–14. Tomb CS10 is the largest and architecturally most impressive of the entire group of Second Intermediate Period tombs. The substructure has similarities with CS6 in its use of a single, monolithic burial chamber, but in this case incorporated within a structure that descends to over twice the depth of Seneb-Kay's tomb. Although it had been robbed, the excavation of CS10 recovered a substantial proportion of the skeletal remains of a single, adult male occupant, the analysis of whose skeleton complements the better-preserved remains of King Seneb-Kay. However, like the other tombs, it bore no decoration and the name of its likely royal occupant remains unknown. Similar results applied to the final tomb identified, CS11.

This group of tombs, CS4 to CS11, apart from Seneb-Kay we discuss here as constituting the "Main tomb cluster" (Part 3 of this volume). These structures and their contents add crucial information to our understanding of this necropolis and the social status of the individuals buried within it. Together they form a group of eight closely related tombs of the Second Intermediate Period. Seneb-Kay is the only one of these that can be identified by name. As we examine in this volume, these tombs appear to comprise a royal cemetery of the Second Intermediate Period that includes burials for at least eight kings dating between ca. 1650–1600 BCE (Fig. 0.4).

The discovery of the tomb of Seneb-Kay, containing the body of the king alongside remnants of his funerary assemblage, furnishes crucial new evidence on Egypt's Second Intermediate Period. Even more fortunately, the tomb has rewarded us with a goldmine of other information. Because Seneb-Kay's tomb was built both quickly and economically, the tomb builders made extensive use of *spolia*: reused blocks and materials taken from other structures at Abydos. The king's limestone burial chamber was constructed from blocks that had originally belonged to one or more funerary chapels built at Abydos ca. 1750–1700 BCE by a powerful Theban family who were closely linked to the 13th Dynasty pharaohs Neferhotep I and Sobekhotep IV. The blocks commemorate the family of a man named Dedtu who served in the high-ranking office of *Overseer of Fields*, his son Ibiau who was the *Master of Offering Tables of Amun* at Thebes, along with their wives, Abeteni and Nekheteni, and other family members. The carved scenes and texts were attacked through a vicious *damnatio memoriae* and were later reused in Seneb-Kay's burial chamber. Despite the damage to their decorated surfaces, these reused blocks provide a significant new window onto elite society of the 13th Dynasty during the century that preceded the lifetime of Seneb-Kay.

Capping Seneb-Kay's burial chamber were roof blocks that the tomb builders had also taken from earlier structures at Abydos. These blocks included a royal false door belonging to one of the Sobekhotep kings of the 13th Dynasty, and possibly attributed to Sobekhotep IV (ca. 1732–1720 BCE) whose own tomb may lie adjacent to Seneb-Kay's at South Abydos (tomb S10). Another block, the earliest object recovered at the site, dates to the beginning of the 11th Dynasty, ca. 2100 BCE, over four centuries before the reign of Seneb-Kay. This is a commemorative stela belonging to a Nubian ruler, the *Foremost-one of the chiefs of Wawat*, named Idudju-iker. All of these reused materials make the tomb of Seneb-Kay an exceptionally rich source of new historical information, not just relating to the era of Seneb-Kay's own life, but also for the early and late Middle Kingdom. We examine the reused materials in Part 2 of this volume.

While the exact historical and political parameters of King Seneb-Kay and the neighboring tombs in the Second Intermediate Period cemetery remain open to discussion, there is one crucial aspect of the archaeological evidence that remains overwhelmingly clear. The tomb provides explicit archaeological testimony to the scope of political and social conflict that reverberates through Egypt's Second

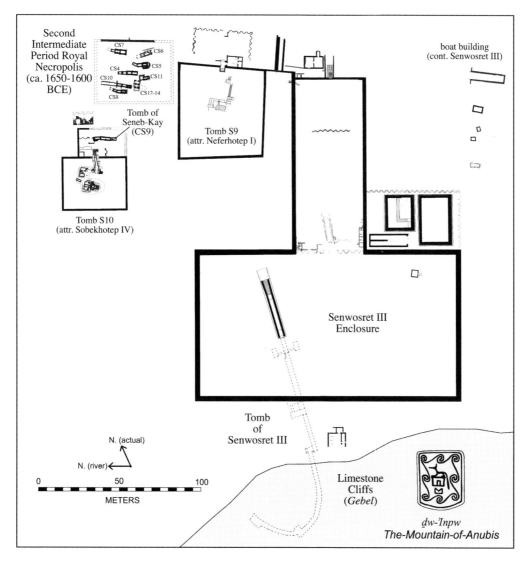

Fig. 0.4 The funerary enclosure of Senwosret III showing the location of the Second Intermediate Period necropolis on the northwest side and adjacent to the 13th Dynasty royal tombs.

Intermediate Period. Some form of dire political vendetta that may have wider political ramifications is embedded in the vicious attack witnessed on the reused 13th Dynasty chapel blocks. Separately—but perhaps not entirely unrelated to the historical phenomenon of this *damnatio* directed against 13th Dynasty monuments—Seneb-Kay's body testifies to the warfare and violence that characterized the age in which he lived. His savage death in battle, with multiple battle axe impressions embedded in his skull, is likely to be symptomatic of the territorial conflicts that, around 1600 BCE, brought an end to the brief-lived kingdom over which he ruled.

The Second Intermediate Period tombs at South Abydos were large and richly equipped for the era to which they date. However, the phenomenon of copying of earlier late Middle Kingdom architecture, along with reuse of building materials and even tomb equipment, belies the pervasive poverty that gripped Upper Egypt at the height of the Second Intermediate Period. It is likely that the economic and political pressures of the age combined to drive the blossoming of a prevalent military culture, which many scholars have observed to be a defining feature of the era. Based on analysis of their skeletal remains, the bodies of Seneb-Kay and the unknown king buried in tomb CS10 provide indications that these rulers rose to power from military backgrounds and lived and died as military leaders, as "warrior kings." This was an era of innovations in military technology and tactics that accompanied the Hyksos Period. Through the evidence of musculoskeletal stress markers, we see indications that Seneb-Kay and the rulers buried at Abydos were integrally involved in the martial practices and territorial conflicts that appear to have dominated their era.

Despite the fact that we have recovered his tomb and skeletonized mummy—the earliest, substantially preserved physical remains of an Egyptian king to survive in the archaeological record—Seneb-Kay remains a shadowy figure. Apart from his tomb, we have no architecture, stelae, statues, or inscribed stone monuments bearing his name. While he died at about 35–45 years of age, how long he reigned prior to his death in battle remains unknown. There is, however, one object today in the collection of the Egyptian Museum, Cairo, that establishes an intriguing link between Seneb-Kay and another object, a stela from Abydos today held, coincidentally, in the collection of the Penn Museum.

In 1900, the British archaeologist Arthur Mace discovered the only artifact that likely names King Seneb-Kay, an ebony apotropaion or "birth wand" found in a tomb at North Abydos. From the same tomb as the wand came the stela now in Philadelphia (Penn Museum E9952) that commemorates a military official, the *Commander of the Crew of the Ruler*, Sobekhotep, and his wife, the *Lady of the House*, Neferuptah. Aside from affirming the close connections of Seneb-Kay with Abydos, the wand suggests some form of personal or familial association that Seneb-Kay held with Sobekhotep and Neferuptah. Possibly these people were family members or even parents of the man who became King Woseribre Seneb-Kay. Here we may have evidence for the derivation of Seneb-Kay from an elite, military family, as well as more broadly a reflection of the altered practices of kingship in the Second Intermediate Period. Kings of the era did not typically follow the more familiar mode of father to son succession seen in most periods of pharaonic history. Rather, they ascended to the throne from a variety of different elite lineages. Possibly we see in this evidence further indications for Seneb-Kay's rise to rulership as the scion of an elite, Abydene military family. We will explore this

possibility in Part 4 of this volume, along with consideration of the wider political and historical context of his reign.

In the writing of the present volume, the principal author has benefitted from the scholarly expertise of the other contributors. Work on the canopic chest of Seneb-Kay and the complex set of alterations associated with it is the product of coauthor, Kevin Cahail's detailed analysis (Chapter 4). Kevin Cahail has also undertaken detailed chronological and historical study of the individuals recorded on the reused 13th Dynasty chapel blocks (Chapter 10). Preliminary results of this analysis had been presented elsewhere but are now superseded by the final publication of the reused blocks in Part 2. Molly Gleeson of the Conservation Department at the Penn Museum has completed restoration on the paintings of Seneb-Kay as well as other archaeological materials at South Abydos. An overview of the conservation work on the tomb is included here in Chapter 6.

Documentation and osteological analysis of the skeletal remains of Seneb-Kay and the other individuals buried at South Abydos was completed by Jane Hill and Maria Rosado, Department of Anthropology and Sociology, Rowan University. Their analysis forms the basis for Chapters 5 and 13. The insights of the osteological analysis provide a valuable window into the life experience and social context of the Second Intermediate Period rulers buried at South Abydos. The text of Chapters 5 and 13 has been substantially structured by the principal author and any errors or omissions are his responsibility.

NOTES:

0.1 Throughout this book we will employ the term "*late Middle Kingdom*" to encompass the period from the reign of Senwosret III (ca. 1850 BCE) through the 13th Dynasty (ca. 1800–1675 BCE). The term "*Second Intermediate Period*" refers broadly to the period of the final decline of the Middle Kingdom state—including the final phase of the 13th Dynasty—up to the reunification of Egypt by the 17th Dynasty Theban king, Ahmose (ca. 1550 BCE). The use of these broader historical phases is inexact (Müller 2018:199–216) and complicated by the evidence that the final phase of the 13th Dynasty overlapped with the rise of the Hyksos 15th Dynasty, as well as the early phase of the Theban Kingdom (Dynasty 16). Some scholars choose to include the entirety of the 13th Dynasty within the Second Intermediate Period. Here we also use the term *"late Second Intermediate Period"* to specify the century immediately preceding the reunification of Egypt under Ahmose (see Franke 1988:245–274; Ryholt 1997:311–312; Schneider 2006:168–170). This phase of time is also usefully designated as the *"Hyksos Period"* recognizing the territorial division of the country that accompanied the period of rule of the Hyksos 15th Dynasty in the Nile Delta. It is to this period that we can date the reign of Seneb-Kay and the associated royal tombs at South Abydos (see Fig. 0.3).

0.2 The site of Abydos is located on the western side of the Nile in the 8th nome of Upper Egypt. Abydos was closely related to the nearby provincial capital of Thinis. Thinis has never been identified archaeologically although the disposition of ancient cemetery sites suggest its location at the edge of the Nile to the north-east of Abydos (Brovarski 2018:51–57). In this context, we use the terms "Abydene" and "Thinite" with the same broader geographical reference. During the Second Intermediate Period the political center of the region was likely located at Thinis while Abydos served as the primary cemetery and ceremonial center of the funerary god Osiris.

0.3 Tomb numbers discussed in this volume that are preceded by the "S" follow the designations originally assigned by Weigall (principally here the 13th Dynasty tombs S9 and S10). Tomb numbers with the "CS" prefix are structures discovered and numbered since 2013 (including CS1 to CS14. To clarify this distinction at the outset, tombs S9 and S10 (the large royal tombs dating to the middle 13th Dynasty) are different than CS9 and CS10 (Second Intermediate Period tombs of Seneb-Kay and a close contemporary of unknown name).

0.4 The structures designated CS1–3 are located on the opposite side of the tomb enclosure. They belong to the original funerary ceremonies associated with the tomb of Senwosret III (Wegner 2017a:5–30) and are unrelated to the group of Second Intermediate Period tombs discussed here.

1

Excavation and Architecture of the Tomb of Seneb-Kay*

The tomb of King Woseribre Seneb-Kay (tomb CS9) was discovered and excavated in 2014. Seneb-Kay's tomb, situated in close proximity to the 13th Dynasty royal tomb S10, was deeply buried beneath extensive debris mounds flanking the front of that larger, earlier structure. Following the excavation of the main tomb cluster in 2013, work was expanded southwards towards S10 with the goal of generating more evidence on the date and attribution of that group of tombs. The resulting removal of the debris mounds fronting S10 defined the denuded remnants of a rectangular enclosure with interior dimensions of 16.2 by 28 m situated against the north (Nile facing) side of S10. This enclosure, labeled "Enclosure B" (Fig. 1.1) contains remnants of a group of thin walled structures including a set of sinusoidal walls that frame the major original feature within Enclosure B: the entrance staircase into tomb S10. The tomb of Seneb-Kay is positioned inside this earlier enclosure and only 5 m from the entrance to tomb S10.

Based on the complete exposure of this area, it is apparent that the builders of Seneb-Kay's tomb made intentional use of the existing terrain and still standing 13th Dynasty enclosure walls as a site for the king's tomb (Figs. 1.2 to 1.5). This pattern of reuse of a preexisting enclosure directly parallels the repurposing of another enclosure, the abandoned "Enclosure C" for the main group of Second Intermediate Period tombs. An advantage to the particular location chosen for Seneb-Kay's tomb is that the enclosure originally formed a discrete, elevated terrace with a compact floor surface. The relatively level floor would

have provided a convenient location for cutting a trench into the subsurface while also being protected from the wind by still standing enclosure walls. The tomb of Seneb-Kay follows the same orientation as the surrounding 13th Dynasty architecture and was carefully situated in the middle of the enclosure. The 13.5 m long tomb was centered between the brick entrance staircase of S10 and the northern wall of the enclosure. The position makes it clear the builders of Seneb-Kay's tomb were aware of the entrance into S10 which appears likely to have been accessible during the construction of his tomb. These spatial relationships corroborate the evidence discussed in Chapter 4 for the reworking of cedar boards from the painted coffin of a king Sobekhotep to form the canopic chest of Seneb-Kay. It appears possible these boards had been taken from tomb S10 in a form of state-sponsored tomb robbery that accompanied the construction and furnishing of Seneb-Kay's tomb.

The location of Seneb-Kay's tomb inside Enclosure B creates a distinct spatial separation between it and the main cluster of Second Intermediate Period tombs. There is a distance of 25 m between the tomb of Seneb-Kay and CS8, the southernmost tomb in the main cluster. Given the close architectural similarities that exist among the tombs it was initially surprising during excavations completed in the intervening area in 2014–2016 that there does not exist a continuous spread of tombs from Seneb-Kay northwards to CS6 and CS7 at the northern end of the Second Intermediate Period group. The probable explanation for this separation is that the position of

* This chapter written by Josef Wegner.

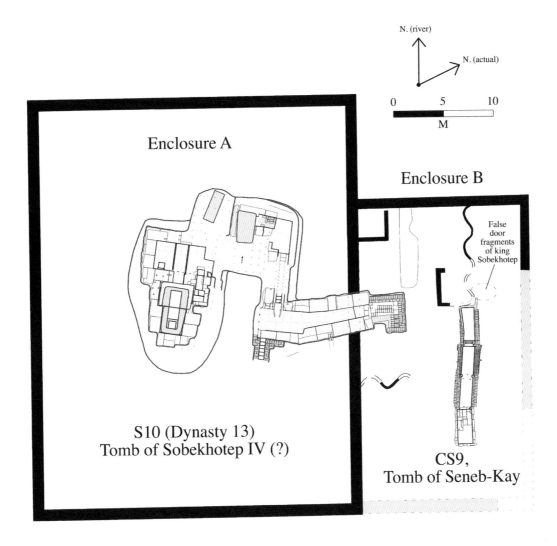

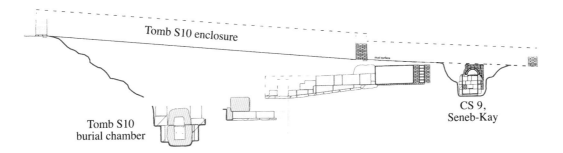

Fig. 1.1 Plan and sectional view showing the location of the tomb of Seneb-Kay (CS9) relative to the earlier 13th Dynasty royal tomb S10.

Fig. 1.2 View looking southeast over the tomb of Seneb-Kay (CS9) showing the disposition of the tomb relative to the enclosure wall of tomb S10.

these tombs reflects the locations of still extant 13th Dynasty enclosure walls at the time the tombs were constructed. Whereas Seneb-Kay's architects made use of the relatively smaller area of S10's entrance enclosure, the rest of the known tombs took advantage of what appears to have been a larger walled space: an abandoned 13th Dynasty royal enclosure to the north of S10 (for which see the discussion below in Chapter 11). The 25-meter gap between Seneb-Kay and CS8 reflects the relative positions of these two different walled enclosures.

TOMB DESIGN

The tomb of Seneb-Kay is a passage-style tomb measuring 13.5 m in total length (Figs. 1.6 to 1.8). The tomb has four primary elements: (1) a walled entrance ramp leading down to a doorway fitted with a limestone portcullis, (2) a pole-roof chamber (Chamber 1) covered with a flat roof of wooden beams; (3) a brick vaulted antechamber (Chamber 2); and (4) the stone-built burial chamber (Chamber 3). From the upper rim of its entrance ramp to the floor of the burial chamber the tomb has a vertical descent of 2.85 m. Apart from its unique use of a burial chamber composed of reused limestone masonry, Seneb-Kay's tomb is remarkably similar to the main group of Second Intermediate Period tombs in all aspects of its design and construction techniques. Particularly notable is use of the same architectural sequence of unroofed entrance ramp, pole-roof chamber, vaulted antechamber, and burial chamber in a predominantly linear descent. A summary of the tomb's major components and the excavation of these elements follows here. The architecture and decoration of the burial chamber are discussed in detail in the next chapter.

Fig. 1.3 Overview of the tomb of Seneb-Kay (CS9) showing the enclosure wall and entrance leading into tomb S10.

Fig. 1.4 The substructure of tomb S10 showing the position of the tomb of Seneb-Kay (CS9) with its burial chamber covered by the wooden structure at upper left (view looking east in 2015).

Fig. 1.5 View looking east over the tomb of Seneb-Kay (CS9) showing the full exposure in 2015 of the surroundings with the tombs of the main cluster on the upper left.

Fig. 1.6 Overview of the tomb of Seneb-Kay (view looking east after the end of the first season of excavation in January 2014).

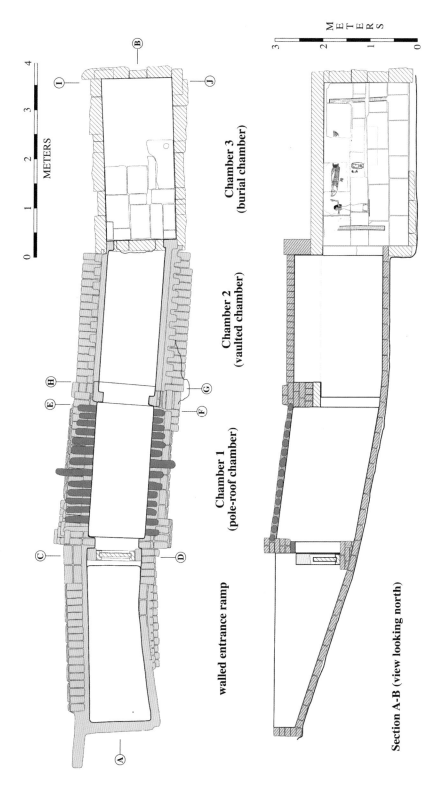

Chamber 1
(pole-roof chamber)

Chamber 2
(vaulted chamber)

Chamber 3
(burial chamber)

walled entrance ramp

METERS

Section A-B (view looking north)

Fig. 1.7 Plan and section of the tomb of Seneb-Kay showing the roofline reconstructed to its original height.

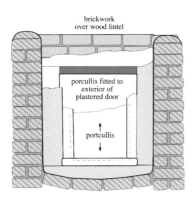

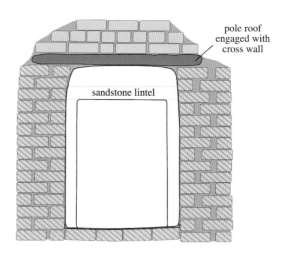

Section C-D
(section through entrance ramp
looking east to porcullis)

Section E-F
(section through Chamber 1 looking
east to doorway into Chamber 2)

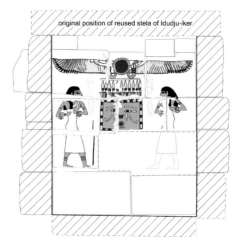

Section G-H
(section through Chamber 2 looking
west to doorway into Chamber 1)

Section I-J
(inner wall of the burial
chamber, view looking east)

Fig. 1.8 Cross sections through the primary elements of the tomb of Seneb-Kay.

ENTRANCE RAMP AND PORTCULLIS

The brick entrance ramp (Fig. 1.9) measures 3.55 m long by 1.28 m at its widest point. The structure is constructed on a 0.48 m wide base of brickwork (composed of one row of headers and one row of stretchers, but the brickwork is irregular and steps up towards the west end where the rim of the ramp is only 0.22 m wide (a single brick width). On the south side, the upper part of the ramp is completed with bricks laid as stretchers forming a thin, 0.22 m wide wall. The ramp's south side has a significant inward bow which appears to have occurred during the construction process. This curvature is not intentional but is the result of excess weight against the wall when it was still not fully hardened. Like the rest of the tomb, the entrance ramp was built in a trench cut down from the surface. When the exterior of the construction trench was filled in, the relatively thin format south wall bowed inwards through the weight of the material on the outside causing this deformation.

The ramp has a bricked and plastered floor that descends at slope of -18°. At the lower end of the ramp is a 0.56 m wide brick threshold beyond which are two 0.2 m wide brick jambs forming a doorway 0.92 m in width. The jambs were capped by a wood lintel, 0.23 m in width and 10 cm thick that supported brickwork above that engaged with the roof of Chamber 1. This brickwork was plastered on the west side forming a smooth exterior face. Set on top of the outer part of the threshold and mortared against the jambs of the 0.92 m wide door is a limestone portcullis. The portcullis consists of a base slab 0.21 m wide, 0.82 m long, and 0.11 m thick with a grooved surface to receive the sliding slab. Mounted against the sides are C-shaped channel blocks containing a limestone slab 7 cm in thickness. The frame of the portcullis is 0.82 m wide and is fitted by means of secondary brick jambs which were appended against the outer face of the already plastered inner jambs. The brickwork used to install the portcullis was left unplastered. The limestone slab would have slid upwards against the exterior face of the doorway lintel. However, there is a substantial gap of some 8 cm between the portcullis slab and the exterior face of the lintel which must have been sealed on the top by some other means.

The architecture of the entrance clearly shows two phases of construction: (1) an original doorway composed of inset jambs that supported the wood lintel above, followed by (2) the insertion of the brick threshold and limestone portcullis against the outer face of the original door jambs (Fig. 1.10). Once added,

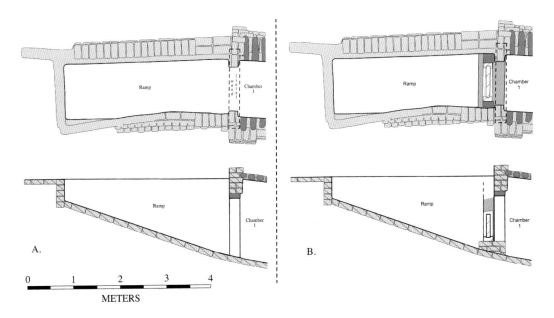

Fig. 1.9 Detail of the entrance ramp and doorway into Chamber 1 showing the original structure (A) and alteration of the entrance with the addition of threshold and portcullis (B).

Fig. 1.10 View of the outer side of the portcullis showing the original robbers' break through the top of the portcullis.

THE POLE-ROOF CHAMBER (CHAMBER 1)

From the brick threshold supporting the portcullis there is a 0.28 m drop down to the floor of the first internal space, the pole-roof chamber (Chamber 1). The pole-roof chamber of Seneb-Kay's tomb measures 1.18 m wide and 2.75 long. The chamber floor is composed of brick with a layer of mud plaster and whitewash. It descends 0.5 m over the length of the chamber. Beneath the secondary brickwork of the threshold, the bricked and whitewashed floor continues uninterrupted from the ramp into the pole-roof chamber. There is a diminution of the angle of descent of the floor from -18° in the ramp to ca. -10° in Chamber 1. When discovered in 2014, Chamber 1 presented us with the only architecturally intact example of the pole-roof chamber, a feature that occurs in many of the other Second Intermediate Period tombs at South Abydos (CS4, CS8, CS10, and probably also CS7). Choice of the pole-roof format rather than a vault for the initial chamber likely reflects the relatively higher elevation of this initial part of the tomb interior. Use of the pole-roof permitted construction of a chamber slightly below ground level with a roof system that did not protrude as a vaulted roof would at this shallow depth.

Because the roof was found intact (Figs. 1.12 and 1.13), Chamber 1 preserves the full chamber height: 1.7 m at the west end, rising slightly to 1.82 m at the inner end. The roof consisted of fourteen parallel wood poles. Unlike the wood lintel that capped the entrance into the chamber, these poles were trimmed of branches but not substantially squared or dressed. The poles average 0.15 m in diameter and include two different wood species. The roof is composed of alternating use of palm wood, probably Dom palm, *Hyphhaenae thebaica*, along with a more compact form of acacia or sycamore, probably *Ficus sycamorus*. It is unclear why the two different wood species were employed together but the wood certainly reflects the reliance on locally available building materials. The poles were coated on the upper surface with a layer of Nile mud. The ceiling of the chamber was originally plastered smooth and whitewashed. This is indicated by a slight inward lip of the plaster on the

the portcullis and surrounding brickwork would have substantially narrowed the width of the main entrance into the tomb from 0.92 m to 0.6 m. It seems likely the wider opening was maintained during the plastering and decoration of the tomb interior and the portcullis was added as a final step, just prior to, or even after the installation of the king's burial.

The vertically sliding limestone slab is insubstantial and the door would have functioned as only a minor deterrent to anyone who wished to break into the tomb. Although still in situ when exposed in 2014, the portcullis was found with the upper half of its slab and frame torn away (Fig. 1.11). It is clear that the initial robbery of Seneb-Kay's tomb occurred through the portcullis, which was simply broken through at the top permitting access to the tomb's interior. The robbers' opening between the base of the wood lintel and top of the broken portcullis block is 0.38 m at its maximum which would have created sufficient space for people to climb in and despoil the tomb's interior. Physical evidence for the use of this access point during the robbery process occurs in the pole-roof chamber.

Fig. 1.11 The inner side of the portcullis. The unplastered brickwork represents the addition of the portcullis to the tomb's entrance.

Fig. 1.12 View looking north showing the intact wooden roof of the pole-roof chamber prior to removal of the central section.

Fig. 1.13 View looking south showing the intact wooden roof of the pole-roof chamber.

top of the walls of the pole-roof chamber. The mud layer on the exterior would have bonded through the crevices between the poles with the plastering of the chamber's ceiling.

When the wooden pole-roof of Chamber 1 was first exposed in 2014, it was found to be intact: the only chamber of the tomb of Seneb-Kay with its roof still in situ. Although the wood poles and exterior mud coating were still in place, the roof was pitted in many areas and the wood had decayed. The original interior plastering on the ceiling was gone. The lack of resiliency of the wood meant that excavation of the interior of Chamber 1 was not possible without removal of the central portion of the roof. When it was determined that there were indications for preserved funerary equipment and human remains inside Chamber 1 we made the decision to remove the central part of the pole-roof. The wood was cut flush with the inner face of the chamber's side walls leaving the ends of each beam in place on the side walls (Fig. 1.14). Excavation of Chamber 1 was then completed.

THE EXCAVATION AND CONTENTS OF THE POLE-ROOF CHAMBER

During the excavation of the interior of CS9 we first dug to floor level in the tomb's unroofed components: the entrance ramp along with the burial chamber and vaulted antechamber where the roof had been broken away in ancient times. Although no original artifacts remained inside the burial chamber itself, the excavation of the vaulted antechamber showed that there were multiple elements of the king's funerary assemblage scattered on the floor at the western end of the antechamber and extending into the pole-roof chamber. As the final stage of excavation inside the tomb, we then exposed Chamber 1's interior by cutting out the central portion of the decayed pole-roof, a necessary procedure that prevented the disintegrated roof from collapsing onto the delicate remains of Seneb-Kay's burial equipment that lay below (Fig. 1.15).

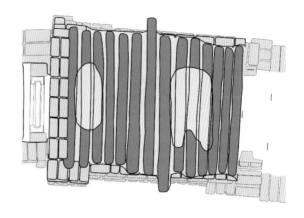

Fig. 1.14 (right) Detail of the pole-roof chamber, with wood roof in situ (above) and after removal of the central portion of the roofing (below).

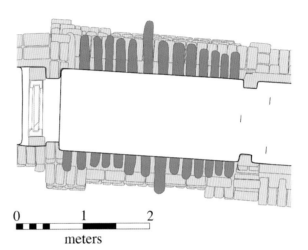

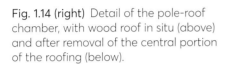

Fig. 1.15 (below) Overview of the remains of the body of Seneb-Kay and his funerary equipment on the floor of the pole-roof chamber.

Chamber 1 was filled with undifferentiated windblown sand down to an elevation ca. 0.7 m above the floor. At this level, we encountered the top of the still articulated canopic box (Fig. 1.16). The box was positioned on its side with its opening oriented toward the tomb's entrance and base toward the burial chamber. At a slightly lower elevation and extending through the doorway into Chamber 2, we exposed remnants of the rectangular ends of the lid of the king's painted outer sarcophagus (Lid Fragments 1 and 2). In the middle of the west end of the chamber, we found the majority of the lid of the canopic chest (canopic chest lid A). One of the rectangular ends had been broken off the lid but we found this element sitting against the north wall just inside Chamber 2 (canopic chest lid B). Beneath the canopic box in the middle of Chamber 1, we exposed multiple fragments of a polychrome *rishi*-style plaster cartonnage funerary mask. Many of these fragments lay directly at floor level. Also scattered in the area of the canopic box were a small group of fragments of a polychrome painted wooden anthropoid coffin. Several small pieces of gold leaf were also recovered in the debris on the chamber floor indicating the original presence of gilded elements of the funerary assemblage.

In the middle of the chamber, we found the remains of CS9's original occupant: the skeleton of Seneb-Kay (Figs 1.17 and 1.18). The fact that this skeleton is that of the king himself and not an intrusive burial, is conclusively demonstrated by the fact that the body lay interwoven with debris from his burial equipment. Like the cartonnage mask fragments, the skeleton lay on a thin layer of sand directly atop the chamber's brick and plaster floor. The postcranial skeleton remained substantially articulated. The body was in a somewhat contorted, semi-contracted position, lying on the left side with the right arm having fallen behind the back on the body's right side. The left arm was in front of the body with the hand near the flexed knees. Significantly, the main part of the canopic box lay directly atop Seneb-Kay's left arm, indicating that the body had been rifled and removed from the sarcophagus before the canopic chest was taken out of the burial chamber. The cranium, along with several thoracic vertebrae and ribs had separated from the lower body and were lying on the south side of the chamber.

Fig. 1.16 View into the pole-roof chamber showing the remains of Seneb-Kay's funerary assemblage delineated in situ but prior to excavation of the deposits.

The body of Seneb-Kay is substantially skeletonized but there are preserved areas of soft tissue, skin, and hair on the cranium, as well as patches of linen overlying darkened areas of tissue that had been treated with embalming oils and possibly resin used to coat the body. Therefore, it is clear the body was originally mummified but most of the soft tissue and linen had substantially decayed, a process that would have been accelerated by exposure of the body during the robbery. The fact that the skeleton was still substantially articulated after having been dragged out of the burial chamber also reflects the original mummified state of the body. During robbery, the body was likely stripped of its linen wrappings to the point where any valuable jewelry or funerary amulets

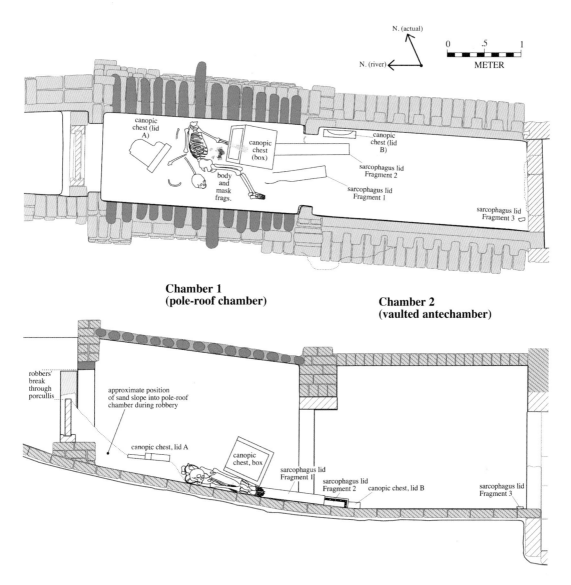

Fig. 1.17 Disposition of debris from the burial of Seneb-Kay in CS9 (Chambers 1–2).

could be removed. This allowed the limbs to hinge at the joints contributing to the contorted position in which we found the body. The disposition of the remains suggests that once the tomb robbers gained access to the king's mummy, they pillaged the body in situ, likely within the burial chamber, or perhaps in the antechamber. The body was then pulled out of the inner tomb and discarded, largely still articulated on the floor of the pole-roof chamber (Fig. 1.18).

Additionally, the manner in which we found the body, contorted and slightly flexed, suggests the remains of Seneb-Kay were thrown with significant force against a slope of sand at the west end of the pole-roof chamber. This slope of sand likely accumulated in the western end of the chamber when the robbers broke through the top of the portcullis. The robbers may have tracked sand well into the tomb, but the primary accumulation initially did not extend past the midpoint of the pole-roof chamber since the king's skeleton and cartonnage fragments in the middle of that space sat directly at floor level. However, the lid of the canopic chest close to the entrance sat on a layer of sand ca. 16 cm at its deepest. Consequently, it appears there was a sand slope coming down from the break in the portcullis at the natural angle of ca. 45° but reaching floor level at the

Fig. 1.18 View of the postcranial skeleton in situ in Chamber 1 showing superimposition of the canopic box over the body. The rib cage is visible on the left, with lower limbs and feet being exposed by excavator.

location of Seneb-Kay's body. The body appears to have been thrown against the base of this sand slope leading to the contortion and flexing of the postcranial skeleton. It may well be the skull broke away at that point and rolled slightly to the south, along with several other bones from the upper body. However, it is probable that protruding elements of the body were broken off as the tomb robbers continued activities within the burial chamber, trampling over the body and further pulling sand down into the pole-roof chamber as they passed in and out through the break in the portcullis.

As stated above, we recovered the canopic chest in three parts. The box was sitting at the highest elevation in the middle of the chamber, directly above the cartonnage mask fragments and over part of the king's skeleton. The lid had been broken into two parts. We found one of the rectangular ends at floor level in the northwest corner of the antechamber (canopic lid B). The main part of the lid was located

at the far end of the pole-roof chamber where it sat substantially elevated on ca. 16 cm of sand (canopic lid A). These spatial relationships show clearly that the canopic chest was the final element to be robbed and discarded. Therefore, the canopic chest must have originally occupied the innermost (east) end of the chamber and was broken into after the burial itself had been despoiled and removed. The main part of the lid was tossed to the far end of the pole-roof chamber where it landed just beyond the position of the king's discarded body on the sand slope from the breached entrance. The lid landed directly atop a small fragment of painted wood that derived from the inner wooden coffin that had already been torn apart, another spatial relationship reflecting the order in which the robbers plundered the funerary equipment. In this location, the canopic lid may have served as a convenient solid surface for the robbers to step on while ascending the soft sand to climb out of the tomb.

During the excavation of the canopic box an intriguing set of evidence relevant to the robbery process occurred in the form of a concentration of small charcoal fragments that had collected inside the box. Charcoal fragments were recovered scattered in other parts of the tomb's loose sand-filled interior, but it appears the box, turned on its side with its opening towards the doorway, may have secondarily collected a group of charcoal fragments. One possible explanation for the presence of the charcoal is that during the original robbery of Seneb-Kay's tomb most of the wood elements of the burial equipment were taken out through the break in the upper half of the portcullis whereupon they were burned on the surface immediately outside the entrance. The burning of both mummies and funerary equipment is discussed as a technique employed by tomb robbers in Papyrus Leopold II-Amherst and other sources. This robbery technique may have been a way to easily recover gold from funerary equipment. Given that the predominant desert winds at Abydos blow from the local north, it appears possible that fragments of the burned funerary equipment blew back in through the robbers' hole. The position of the canopic box on its side may have acted as a catch point for small charcoal elements blowing back into the tomb.

Despite the fragmentary nature, and disturbed context of these remnants of Seneb-Kay's burial, the excavation of Chamber 1 provides a crucial set of evidence relating both to the robbery process and to the original disposition of the king's body and funerary equipment within the burial chamber. The broad strokes of the robbery of the tomb can be summarized as follows. Ancient tomb robbers broke into the tomb via the limestone portcullis and gained access to the burial chamber through the pole-roof and vaulted antechamber. The robbery must have occurred within a relatively short period after the original interment because the tomb's roof was fully intact and the floor was unencumbered by debris at the time. In the process of breaking through the portcullis and entering the tomb from the desert surface, a sand slope was formed at the western end of the pole-roof chamber, and sand was tracked partially over the floor of the chamber. It was over that accumulating sand layer that the robbers discarded unwanted elements of the plundered burial assemblage of Seneb-Kay.

Upon entry to the burial chamber the robbers attacked first the king's burial proper. They broke apart the lid of the rectangular outer sarcophagus discarding the two rectangular ends of the sarcophagus lid (Lid Fragments 1 and 2) on the floor of the antechamber. They then tore apart the inner coffin and cartonnage funerary mask to gain access to the linen-wrapped mummy of Seneb-Kay. Most of this material was taken out of the tomb, likely due to the presence of gilded elements on the inner burial equipment, but not without leaving some crushed remnants of the mask, and splinters from the anthropoid coffin on the floor of the pole-roof chamber. After pulling open the linen wrappings and removing any valuables from the body itself they then threw the king's body against the base of the sand slope at the far end of the pole-roof chamber where it lay alongside elements of the inner coffin and crushed fragments of the funerary mask. As a next step they proceeded to rifle the canopic chest which was discarded atop the body of the king.

During this robbery process, a majority of the wooden elements had been removed from the tomb. In view of the retrieval of small fragments of gold leaf, parts of the burial equipment must have had gilded surfaces. The funerary mask and anthropoid coffin appear likely to have had gilded elements and the burning of these would been one easy technique to consolidate and remove the gold leaf. It may have been this activity that resulted in charcoal fragments blowing back into the tomb's interior. The robbers appear to have passed through the pole-roof chamber multiple times, pulling in more sand and likely trampling the body of the king leading to disarticulation of the cranium and other damage. Subsequent to the robbery the pole-roof chamber would have filled in rapidly with windblown sand via the break in the portcullis. The space appears never to have been entered again and the extensive damage to the masonry of the burial chamber, as we discuss below, postdated this initial robbery of Seneb-Kay's tomb.

The excavation of these floor-level deposits inside the pole-roof chamber and extending partially into the vaulted antechamber has provided us with the bulk of the evidence for the burial and funerary assemblage of Seneb-Kay. Perhaps most fortunately, the king's body had not been removed and destroyed but was left inside the tomb among residue of his robbed funerary assemblage. We will examine in detail the evidence provided by the burial equipment (Chapter 3); the canopic chest (Chapter 4), and the body of Seneb-Kay (Chapter 5) further below.

THE VAULTED ANTECHAMBER (CHAMBER 2)

At the inner end of the pole-roof chamber, a doorway measuring 0.96 m wide and 1.25 m in height leads into a room (Chamber 2) that is roofed by a brick vault (Fig. 1.19). The doorway between Chamber 1 and 2 is framed by brick jambs capped by a sandstone lintel with a width of 0.52 m and thickness of 0.15 m. The lintel projects 0.31 m inwards (east) from the brick jambs that divide the two chambers. The ends of the lintel are engaged in the side walls and support five courses of brickwork above that are also bonded into the adjacent walls. The west face of the brickwork above the lintel forms the inner end of the pole-roof chamber while the opposite (east) side forms the west end of the brick vault of Chamber 2. The vault itself is an incline vault with the vault bricks angled against the brickwork above the sandstone lintel. This aspect of CS9's construction is slightly different than the other Second Intermediate Period tombs in the main cluster in that vault construction typically leans inwards rather than outwards. In Seneb-Kay's tomb, the use of the limestone block construction for the burial chamber altered this formula and they reversed the direction of the coursing in the incline vault.

The roof of Chamber 2 is a single-ring brick vault. The vault is mostly destroyed but the surviving brickwork above the sandstone lintel preserves the full curvature of the vault. The height of the chamber to the top of the vault in this location was 1.88 m. The vault has a smooth transition from the chamber's side walls and lacks the projecting ledge which occurs in the vaulted chambers of many of the other Second Intermediate Period tombs (for discussion of which see Chapter 11). However, in all other respects the vault construction is identical to that of the other tombs including the use of the initial course of projecting bricks laid on their side in alternate courses creating the distinctive dentil effect on the exterior base of the vault (Fig. 1.20).

Fig. 1.19 The interior of the vaulted chamber (Chamber 2) looking west through the pole-roof chamber to the portcullis.

Fig. 1.20 Overview of the vaulted chamber (Chamber 2) and the burial chamber (Chamber 3) showing the incline vault and dentil effect of the vault bricks on the exterior.

The brickwork composing Chambers 1 and 2 is fully bonded and the two chambers form a single construction unit which abuts the masonry of the burial chamber. The orientation of the two chambers is rotated 5.5° north (clockwise) relative to the burial chamber. This rotation of Chambers 1 and 2 is relatively minor and may have no particular significance, but it is intriguing. The direction of rotation follows the predominant pattern of many of the nearby Second Intermediate Period tombs in which the entrance is angled toward the northeast. Because Chamber 2 abuts the burial chamber at this slightly skewed angle, the chamber has irregular dimensions: the width is 1.18 m; the length between the brick jambs is 2.87 m on the north side and 3.05 m on the south side. The vault itself is 2.58 m long due to the inward projection of the sandstone lintel.

The brickwork of Chamber 2 directly abuts the limestone masonry of the burial chamber. Demarcating the two chambers are two plastered, brick door jambs identical in format to those that divide the other architectural spaces. These are 16 cm wide (south) and 18 cm wide (north) and create a 1.02 m

doorway between the vaulted antechamber and the burial chamber. The jambs sit directly on top of the base course of limestone masonry that composes the west wall of the burial chamber. Like the jambs, the bricked and plastered floor of the vaulted antechamber also extends directly over the top of this masonry. The chamber's floor is perfectly level, which contrasts with the significant slope of the ramp (-18°) and the pole-roof chamber (-10°).

Interestingly, despite the excellent preservation of the doorways separating the three chambers of Seneb-Kay's tomb, there are no indications of any type of closure that sealed these chambers from one another. This is especially striking in the case of the doorway between the antechamber and burial chamber, a location where one might assume that a system of closure would have been desirable. It is possible the burial chamber may have been sealed by a stacked brick blocking of the type seen in some of the other tombs at South Abydos. However, no residue (mud plaster or impressions of bricks) of such a closure remains on the whitewashed jambs or floor. Therefore, it appears likely that once tomb robbers had broken through the insubstantial limestone portcullis there was straight, unhindered access through into the burial chamber itself. Consequently, we use the term "antechamber" here for the vaulted space of Chamber 2 due to this fact that it appears to have opened directly and without any form of closure, into the burial chamber itself.

As discussed in the previous section, surviving elements of the funerary assemblage of Seneb-Kay that were discarded primarily in the pole-roof chamber extended partially into the vaulted antechamber. Within the antechamber we excavated Fragment B of the canopic lid as well as the small fragment (Fragment 3) of the polychrome sarcophagus lid. Otherwise the deposition inside Chamber 2 was largely clean windblown sand. In the center of the chamber and close to floor level, we recovered in fragments a roughware bowl of Nile silt (Fig. 1.21). This object could potentially belong to the original funerary assemblage although its disturbed context in the chamber makes its attribution uncertain.

THE BURIAL CHAMBER (CHAMBER 3)

From the vaulted antechamber there is a 0.54 m drop down to the limestone-paved floor of the burial chamber. The burial chamber measures 1.5 m by 3.32 m. None of the original roof is preserved in situ but the original wall height is preserved in all four corners of the chamber. The height of the chamber is 1.8 m, very close to that of both the pole-roof chamber and vaulted antechamber. Whereas the outer parts of Seneb-Kay's tomb were built of mudbrick with limited use of stone fittings, the burial chamber stands out among the Second Intermediate Period tombs at South Abydos through its use of limestone blocks. The entirety of the structure is composed of reused limestone blocks—many bearing decoration—that originated in other parts of Abydos. It is this phenomenon of reuse that makes Seneb-Kay's burial chamber such a rich source of historical information, not just

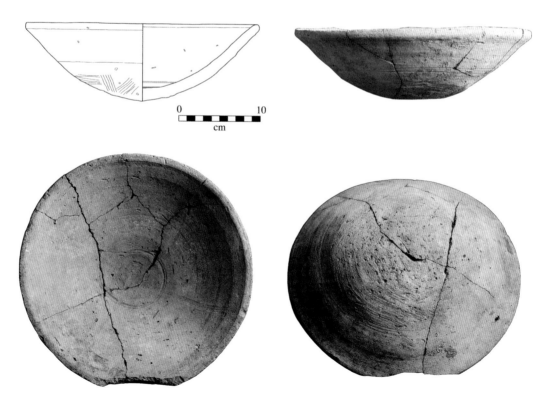

Fig. 1.21 Silt bowl recovered in fragments near floor level in Chamber 2.

on the Second Intermediate Period, but for earlier eras. The details of the architecture and decoration of the burial chamber are discussed in the next chapter, while the analysis of the reused blocks dating to the 11th and 13th Dynasties are presented in Part 2.

When the interior of the burial chamber was excavated in 2014, it was immediately clear that, while substantially preserved, the chamber was badly damaged, not primarily through the actions of the original tomb robbers, but through later removal of all of the roof blocks, as well as significant amounts of the masonry from the floor and walls (Fig. 1.22). This damage resulted in the loss of much of the upper half of the chamber's south wall. Targeted removal to the masonry occurred in the inner end of the chamber where blocks at the bottom (base course) of the side walls had been pulled out, along with all of the floor blocks from the chamber's inner half. Also pulled out of the east wall were two blocks from the middle (second course) and one block from the third course. The block from the third course was found in the

sand inside the burial chamber and was restored to its original location. We recovered no remains of the blocks from the second course.

These damage patterns show that someone had located the chamber and methodically searched behind the walls and floor at the inner end for connections to hidden spaces. The damage is unlikely to have occurred during the initial tomb robbery since that group of robbers would have been presented with an intact, royal burial assemblage and after despoiling the contents of the chamber it appears less likely they would have continued to the stage of pulling up the floor and walls. Therefore, we ascribe this damage to a second and much later phase of robbery. The removal of stone blocks and probing of the burial chamber for valuables is perhaps broadly contemporary with the wider pillaging of masonry that occurred in the large neighboring 13th Dynasty royal tombs (the tombs numbered S9, and S10, as explained in the Introduction), as well as the tomb of Senwosret III: activity that occurred in the late Roman and Byzantine Periods.

Fig. 1.22 View of the burial chamber when first discovered in January 2014, showing the missing masonry in the walls and floor (view looking east).

The burial chamber's interior contained undifferentiated windblown sand down to the stone floor, its original furnishings removed, remnants of which were scattered on the floor of the pole-roof chamber. What we did recover were dislodged elements of the decorated walls including the block from the east wall noted above, as well as a smaller component of the prenomen of Seneb-Kay that once decorated the south wall (discussed in Chapter 2). The primary discovery within and adjacent to the burial chamber were dislodged fragments of one of the smashed roof blocks, a reused 11th Dynasty biographical stela belonging to Idudju-iker. Sitting atop the east wall, we encountered one large fragment of the stela, while the largest fragment lay inside the chamber close to floor level. Other smaller fragments were retrieved from the sand in and around the burial chamber. The stela of Idudju-iker is discussed in detail in Chapter 7.

THE EXTERNAL CONSTRUCTION TRENCH

Like the other Second Intermediate Period tombs, the tomb of Seneb-Kay was built within a trench cut down into the compact desert subsurface. This exterior area of most of the tombs has not been fully investigated due to the structural problems that can arise in fully exposing these delicate mudbrick buildings. However, in the case of Seneb-Kay's tomb we decided it was of particular interest to fully excavate the tomb's exterior. Therefore, following completion of the tomb's interior in January of 2014, we excavated down to the compact subsurface. This work, conducted during May 2014, exposed the original construction trench defining the ancient cutting inside which the tomb had been built. The edges of the construction trench are irregular. At the tomb's inner (east) end, the burial chamber runs up very close to the trench leaving only 0.3 m which had been filled with loose limestone flakes and broken brick fragments. The trench is wider on the long sides of the burial chamber, averaging 0.5 m on the south and 0.75 to 1.2 m on the north side. The edges of the pit step outwards and upwards, showing how the builders created a pit into the compact desert subsurface with roughly stepping sides.

At the lowest levels of the trench on both sides of the burial chamber, loosely piled bricks had been used as fill material (Fig. 1.23). The bricks are reused from the enclosure wall of neighboring tomb S10, clearly scavenged by Seneb-Kay's tomb builders for the purpose of quickly filling in the construction trench. On the chamber's south side, the bricks were stacked in two rows inside the narrower space while in the wider trench on the north side they were simply thrown into the cavity.

During work on the surroundings of the tomb, we removed these brick stacks. On the north side,

Fig. 1.23 Bricks used as fill in the construction trench on the north side of Seneb-Kay's burial chamber.

this exposed a complete, discarded jar (Fig. 1.24). This vessel is of the same type encountered in the fill surrounding several other Second Intermediate Period tombs in the main tomb cluster (CS6 and CS8). These vessels are ovoid, roughware jars in Nile silt with chaff temper (Nile C fabric). The form has a flattened base and simple unworked rim and string

impressions around the lower body used to support the vessel during the drying process. This particular vessel (SA2548, Fig. 1.25) has areas of gypsum mortar on its interior and mouth and was evidently discarded by the tomb builders at the final stages of the masonry work and before the brick fill was thrown into the trench.

Fig. 1.24 Discarded jar used in the construction of the Seneb-Kay burial chamber.

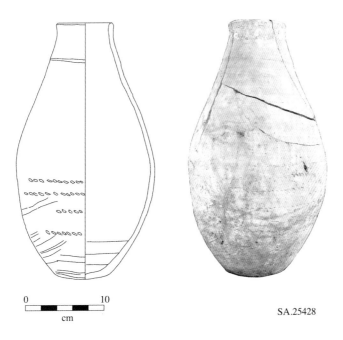

Fig. 1.25 Nile silt jar containing gypsum plaster used in the building of the burial chamber, from the construction trench of the tomb of Seneb-Kay.

0   10
cm

SA.25428

2

The Burial Chamber*

Following the architectural conventions seen in the Second Intermediate Period tomb group at South Abydos, the burial chamber of Seneb-Kay employs stone construction. This chamber stands apart through its use of limestone blocks rather than the slab-lined recess set beneath a brick-vaulted chamber that forms the typical burial chamber type in the other tombs. This use of masonry blocks necessitated that the burial chamber had a slab roof rather than the brick vault seen in all of the other tombs. A crucial aspect of the Seneb-Kay burial chamber is that the masonry employed was entirely reused from preexisting funerary structures elsewhere at Abydos. The removal of masonry from earlier structures indicates not just an economical approach to the tomb's construction, but also a need for rapid completion making use of materials culled from earlier buildings. The impetus for these quick and inexpensive building techniques is likely related to the skeletal evidence from Seneb-Kay's body showing that he died in a violent martial encounter (Chapter 5). Nevertheless, it is noteworthy that the burial chamber was stone-built and decorated with texts and imagery.

Uniquely among the known Second Intermediate Period tombs at South Abydos, Seneb-Kay's burial chamber is decorated with painted images and accompanying texts. While the tomb stands apart from the nearby tombs in this regard, in its use of decoration the tomb also diverges from the wider corpus of pre-New Kingdom royal tombs. It is a remarkable fact that the tomb of Seneb-Kay is the first known royal tomb in pharaonic Egyptian history to employ two-dimensional painted imagery in its burial chamber (Wegner 2017b:479–511). Prior to Seneb-Kay, the last known instance where two-dimensional wall imagery occurs in a king's tomb was the Predynastic Painted Tomb at Hierakonpolis dating to the Nagada IId period (ca. 3400 BCE). Therefore, while Seneb-Kay's tomb is modest, rapidly built, and sparsely decorated, it represents a crucial structure in understanding changes in royal burial practices that occurred within the fractured political milieu of the Second Intermediate Period.

CONSTRUCTION OF THE BURIAL CHAMBER

The burial chamber has internal dimensions of 1.5 x 3.32 m. Although the upper half of the south wall is badly damaged, the north and east walls are preserved close to their original height, as indicated by the position of the vertical text registers and the winged sun-disk that surmounts each wall. These elements demonstrate that the original chamber height was 1.8 m (equivalent to the chamber height of both the pole-roof chamber and vaulted antechamber). The burial chamber is built of reused limestone blocks of variable thickness. The majority, if not all, of the blocks originate from a 13th Dynasty funerary chapel or chapels associated with the family of a man named Dedtu and his son Ibiau (Chapters 8–10). The floor of the burial chamber is also constructed with

* This chapter written by Josef Wegner.

reused limestone blocks, probably taken from the same source as the wall blocks.

The wall blocks are laid in four courses. The horizontal seam for each course displays minor variations and some of the blocks have projections above or below the primary seam. On average the heights of the blocks in the courses, from bottom to top are: 0.49 m (course 1); 0.44 m (course 2); 0.36 m (course 3), and 0.58 m (course 4). Thinner in-fill blocks were used in some areas between the main courses and the top course of all three walls made use of narrow blocks to bring the masonry up to the uniform wall height of 1.8 m. Several of these thinner capping blocks remain on the east wall.

It appears probable that the height of the wall courses in Seneb-Kay's burial chamber closely reflects the original masonry coursing of the 13th Dynasty chapel architecture from which the blocks were reused. Because none of reused blocks have indications of secondary cutting, Seneb-Kay's tomb builders appear to have purposefully scavenged a set of blocks of comparable heights and trimmed smaller patch stones and shim elements as needed when laying the masonry. This explains why there are no indications of masonry construction debris in the fill surrounding Seneb-Kay's tomb. Additionally, there was no attempt by Seneb-Kay's tomb builders to cut the blocks to a common thickness. Consequently, the chamber has a ragged exterior with blocks ranging between 0.18 and 0.35 m in thickness (see Figs. 2.1 to 2.4).

The reused limestone blocks were assembled with a mortar of Nile mud rather than the standard bonding material of gypsum mortar. Where they required a thicker joint to raise blocks relative to adjacent blocks, the builders used flakes of limestone as shim. These flakes were pressed into the mud in order to prevent the weight of the blocks from pushing the mud out before it dried. This peculiar use of Nile mud for the block joints was not due to lack of access to gypsum because a skim coat of gypsum plaster was applied over the interior surface in the burial chamber—thereby concealing the mud joints. Moreover, the brick parts of the tomb are fully coated over their interior surfaces with a thick coat of whitewashed plaster. It appears possible that the use of Nile mud for the stone-built elements of the tomb reflects practices of a group of builders who were more conversant with mudbrick construction and who applied this same technique of laying the blocks to the burial

chamber as they did in the rest of the tomb's mudbrick elements. The use of small limestone flakes for filling gaps is found throughout the mudbrick architecture of the Second Intermediate Period tombs and is prevalent in the construction of the brick vaults. Altogether the technique of constructing the burial chamber, as well as the predominant reliance on reused masonry, reflects a rapid construction process.

Whereas the burial chamber's two long walls (north and south), and the inner (east) wall are constructed in four masonry courses to achieve a height of 1.8 m, the entrance to the chamber was formed by creating an opening against which the mudbrick elements of the tomb were appended. The west side (the entry wall) of the burial chamber has a low sill, 0.45 m in height, which is contiguous with the first course of the chamber's other three walls. The masonry of the long walls (north and south) extends over this base course forming the opening into the chamber. As we have seen in the previous chapter, into this opening were then inserted mudbrick door jambs projecting outwards from the limestone walls to form a 1.03 m wide door into the burial chamber. The brick flooring of the vaulted chamber (Chamber 2) originally extended directly over the limestone masonry to the inner face of the burial chamber's west wall. This created a 0.54 m drop from the floor of Chamber 2 to the floor of the burial chamber. The disposition of the architecture clearly indicates that the limestone burial chamber was the first element of the tomb to be constructed with the brick elements then added to it.

Seneb-Kay's burial chamber was originally roofed by means of three slabs of reused masonry. Remains of two of these slabs were recovered during the 2014 excavation of the tomb (see Chapter 7 for the detailed discussion of these reused roof slabs). Inside and adjacent to the burial chamber we excavated multiple fragments of a large limestone stela dating to the early 11th Dynasty. This stela, belonging to a man named Idudju-iker measures 0.26 m in thickness, 1.07 m. wide, and originally would have measured approximately 2 m in height. Two large fragments of this stela were recovered, one sitting directly above the end wall of the burial chamber, the other inside the chamber itself. It appears likely that the reused stela of Idudju-iker formed the innermost roof slab over the burial chamber with the 2 m long slab spanning the full width of the chamber and sitting over the chamber's end wall.

Fig. 2.1 Exterior view looking south showing the burial chamber when first exposed in 2014.

Fig. 2.2 Exterior view looking north showing the burial chamber when first exposed in 2014.

Fig. 2.3 The exterior of the north wall of the burial chamber showing the use of Nile mud as mortar in laying the masonry.

Fig. 2.4 View looking east showing the damaged condition of the burial chamber's south wall. The area of stacked blocks in the corner was entirely undercut by ancient tomb robbers.

Fig. 2.5 The entrance into the burial chamber with the brick elements of the tomb beyond (view looking west).

Much more fragmentary, and not recovered in the area of the burial chamber itself, are a group of fragments deriving from a limestone false door of one of the Sobekhotep kings of the 13th Dynasty (Wegner and Cahail 2015:141–148). This group, totaling fifteen fragments, was excavated in 2014 immediately adjacent to the west side of the entrance ramp of Seneb-Kay. The false door has a single preserved dimension: its thickness was 0.27 m; very close to that of the stela of Idudju-iker. The width and height can only be estimated by the scale of the text and scene elements but indicate a false door well over a meter in width and ca. 2 m in height. The scale of the Sobekhotep false door suggests it also represents one of the roof slabs reused over Seneb-Kay's burial chamber but had been pulled away and smashed during the processes of the tomb robbery. Some of the fragments of the slab were discarded near the entrance ramp into the tomb. There appear to be no other logical explanations for the reuse of such a massive royal funerary stela in the environs of

Seneb-Kay's tomb and a position over the burial chamber appears highly likely.

The width of the stela of Idudju-iker (1.07 m) along with the comparable estimate for the width of the Sobekhotep false door suggests there should have been a third roof slab of similar dimensions to complete the roofing of the 3.3 m long burial chamber. If, as seems likely, the Idudju-iker stela formed the innermost roof slab, the Sobekhotep false door would have formed either the middle or first slab. No fragments of this third roof slab were recovered and it must have been entirely destroyed in antiquity. Structurally, the westernmost of the three roof slabs would have run flush with the west end of the burial chamber masonry. The position of the top of the burial chamber walls are contiguous with the beginning of the vault of Chamber 2. This first roof slab would then have doubled both as lintel for the doorway into the burial chamber and must have supported brickwork forming the end wall of the vault of Chamber 2 (in a configuration similar to the preserved brickwork above the sandstone lintel over the doorway between the pole-roof and vaulted chambers). As already noted, the entire burial chamber must have been completed with its roofing slabs installed prior to the addition of the tomb's mudbrick components.

In view of the fact that addition of the mudbrick elements of the tomb would have created a dark, enclosed space, it appears quite possible that the painted imagery and texts in the burial chamber were finished immediately after the construction of the limestone burial chamber and prior to the addition of the mudbrick outer tomb. The decoration was clearly quickly applied, and the relatively modest decorative program represents work that could have been achieved by a small group of artists in a few days. The overall program appears quite possibly to have been attenuated, which suggests the decoration occurred under time constraints governing the completion of the tomb. Furthermore, as we consider in Chapter 3, for logistical reasons and due to its substantial size, it appears highly probable that the rectangular outer coffin of Seneb-Kay, a 1.05 m wide wooden coffin with matching lid, was installed in the chamber prior to the addition of the brick elements. Installation of the outer coffin would also have necessitated completion of the painted decoration prior to the addition of the outer chambers and entrance ramp.

THE DECORATIVE PROGRAM

The tomb of Seneb-Kay stands alone among the eight Second Intermediate Period tombs at South Abydos through the presence of painted texts and funerary imagery in the burial chamber. The use of smooth-faced limestone masonry provided the physical setting permitting application of wall decoration. There is only one other tomb in the group (CS4), which had a stone-lined burial chamber that appears to have functioned as a walk-in chamber of this type. Extensive damage to CS4's masonry leaves it unclear whether that tomb might also have had decoration in the burial chamber (see Chapter 11). All of the other tombs employed stone-lined crypts set within a vaulted brick chamber and were ill-suited for wall decoration whereas Seneb-Kay's burial chamber had flat wall faces appropriate for painted decoration. The texts and imagery are polychrome, painted

over a thin skim coat of gypsum plaster that served to smooth over irregularities in the surface and conceal the mud mortar used in the block joints.

Decoration in the burial chamber did not make use of a grid system, as generally used in Egyptian two-dimensional art. Still preserved in a number of locations are lightly painted black guidelines that delineate areas of the walls intended to receive decoration. The artists who painted the chamber appear to have blocked out areas for textual and figural elements. The decoration was then applied within those spaces without use of a grid. The imagery and texts were drawn on firstly with a thin black line, presumably by the chief artist. For the figural elements, the black line was then superimposed with a thicker, dark red-brown outline and filled in with polychrome paint. In the case of the texts, the black line was left and the body of the hieroglyphs painted in light blue. The quality of the brushwork is variable with the paint applied in many areas in a rapid and careless fashion. Indeed, some elements were rather irregularly applied to the walls. This is seen quite overtly in the eastern text band on the south wall which runs significantly askew relative to the adjacent southeast corner of the chamber. The work on the inner (east) wall appears to have been completed first and with slightly higher quality than the side walls.

It appears likely that the decoration on the longer north and south walls represents a program that was left only partially complete. On both the north and south walls are matching rectangular areas framed by black lines. These areas lack interior decoration but were framed with black lines and suggest that the process of painting the chamber was incomplete. It appears a fuller set of wall imagery was envisioned but not carried out, possibly reflecting time limitations on the artists completing the burial chamber. This is strong evidence of time constraints in the tomb construction process and that the intended decoration in was not fully complete at the time of the king's burial. The textual and figural elements in the burial chamber form a relatively sparse decorative program, but one that displays clear connections with known funerary iconography of the Second Intermediate Period. The set of elements is adapted directly from texts and imagery used on canopic chests and painted coffins of the period. The format of the program is briefly summarized in the following description and examined in more detail below.

At the center of the two long walls occurs the nomen Seneb-Kay (north wall) and his prenomen, Woseribre (south wall). The large format royal name was surmounted at the top of each wall by a winged sun-disk. At either end of the long walls occur vertical texts in blue on a black-framed yellow band. These framed text columns name the king in association with the four sons of Horus. Two goddesses appear at the west end of each of the long walls between the winged sun-disk and text band. They stand facing outwards with arms upraised with an adjacent label in blue hieroglyphs. Based on their pose, which parallels images typically applied to the ends of coffins and sarcophagi, these are Isis and Nephthys, although the deity's name does not survive in either case. The chamber's inner (east) wall is decorated with an eye panel with multicolor frame and cornice and surmounted by a *khekher*-frieze. Inside the panel are symmetrical *wedjat*-eyes flanking an offering basin and a *shen* symbol. The eye panel is likely the surviving upper element of a false door that formed the central feature of the east wall. Facing the eye panel are two additional goddesses, Neith on the left and Nut on the right, as identified by the accompanying blue-painted text labels. These goddesses have a different pose than the two on the side walls; here each has her arms bent inwards over her chest with *ankh* signs dangling from their forearms. As on the north wall, the inner wall is capped by a winged sun-disk. The content and texts of the three walls are described in more detail in the following sections.

THE NORTH WALL

The north wall was found to be substantially intact when first exposed in 2014 (Figs. 2.6 to 2.9). Only two blocks were missing from the four primary courses of limestone masonry. Missing from the upper course (course 4) is the third block from the northeast corner. This block would have included most of the right wing of the sun-disk that decorated the upper part of the north wall. Also missing from the lowest, undecorated, course (course 1) was the second block from the northeast corner. The removal of this block from the lowest course at the inner end of the burial chamber appears to be the result of tomb robbers who probed behind the walls to check whether there were any hidden spaces adjacent to

the chamber. Removal of masonry in the same relative position occurred at the base of the south wall, as well as in the middle of the east wall. There would originally have been a series of smaller blocks as occur on the east wall, that brought the chamber up to a height of 1.8 m as is preserved by the east wall masonry. The north wall includes six blocks (R1, R2, R3, R4, R12, and R13) with original, decorated surfaces and deriving from the 13th Dynasty masonry reused by Seneb-Kay's tomb builders. Blocks R2, R3, and R4 were placed with the decoration facing into the chamber. Reused blocks R1, R12, and R13 have the decoration concealed in the block seam, in all three cases placed on the west side of the block.

As on the other walls of the burial chamber, the painted decoration begins on the second course. The overall orientation of the decoration on this wall faces outwards towards the tomb's entrance (local north or true west). The texts read from left to right. In the center of the wall occurs the king's nomen in a large format cartouche. Above this occurs the winged sun-disk, 1.32 m in length and labeled as the Behdedite below its left wing. To the left of the sun-disk with her arms lifted up to the same height as the top of the disk is a goddess, either Isis or Nephthys. She stands on a thick, black ground line and measures 0.81 m to the top of her upraised arms (the same height as the goddesses on the east wall). Her black base line is also 0.81 m from the floor of the chamber which situates her at a higher position than the matching figure on the south wall. A blue-painted label which originally identified the goddess is mostly destroyed but would have matched the fully preserved labels attached to Neith on Nut on the east wall (the label is reconstructed as Isis in the cover image of this volume).

On either end of the composition are two text bands, ranging from 8.5 to 9.6 cm in width, consisting of a black, rectangular frame with light blue texts over a yellow-brown background. These labels are both set 30 cm in from the chamber corner although the inner, eastern label is somewhat askew relative to the nearby corner, an aberration seen also in the text band in the same position on the south wall. From west to east, the textual elements of the north wall read as follows:

West end text band

Nṯr nfr nb t3wy nb irt ḫt ny-swt-bity Wsribr⁢ Snb-K3y m3-ḫrw Dw3nwt.f mry, stw iry.k.

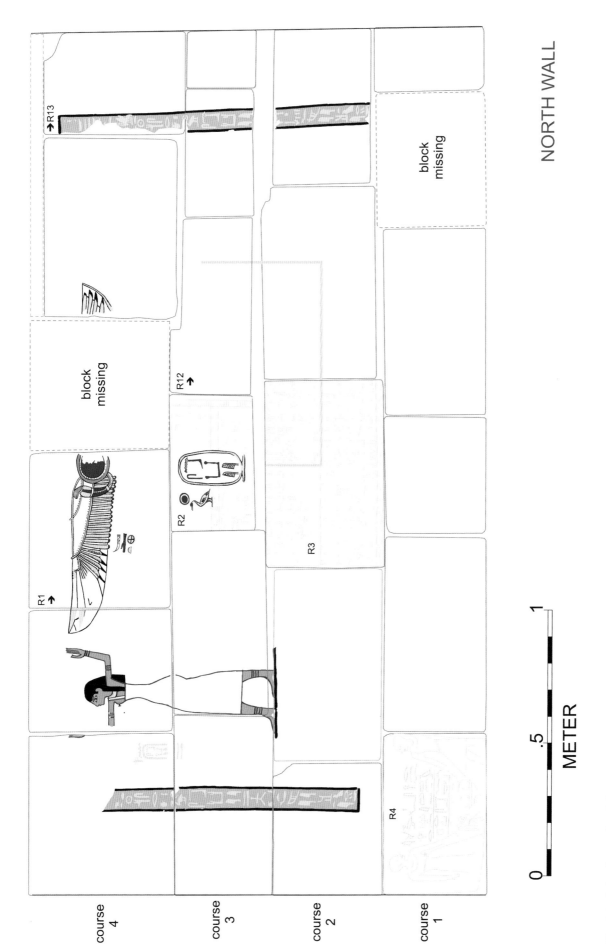

course 4

course 3

course 2

course 1

R13

block missing

R12

block missing

R1

R2

R3

R4

NORTH WALL

METER

0   .5   1

Fig. 2.6 Color facsimile of the burial chamber's north wall showing painted decoration as well as locations of reused blocks with decoration.

Fig. 2.7 View of the western end of the north wall.

Fig. 2.8 (facing) Details of the north wall: (a) goddess with upraised arms, (b) the large-format central cartouche in the middle of the wall; (c) the winged sun-disk.

(a)

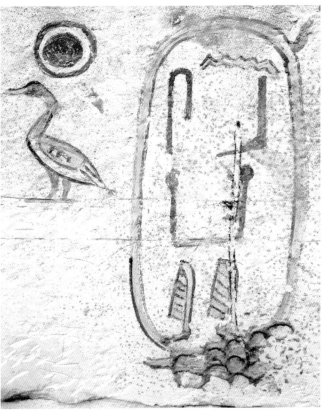

(b)

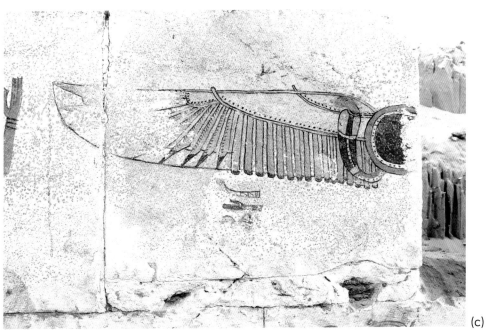

(c)

Fig. 2.9 Text band at eastern end of the north wall.

(O) Good-god, Lord-of-the-Two-Lands, Lord of ritual, King of Upper and Lower Egypt, Woseribre Seneb-Kay, true-of-voice, beloved of Dua[m]utef,[1] lift yourself up.

Label in front of goddess

[Isis or Nepthys, ḥꜣp ꜥwy] ḥrt nswt (Snb-Kꜣy) mꜣꜥ-ḥrw.

[It is Isis/Nephthys who folds (her) arms] around king Seneb-Kay,[2] true-of-voice.[3]

Beneath left side of winged sun-disk

Bḥdty

The Behdetite.

Center

Sȝ-Rc (Snb-Kȝy) [mȝc-ḫrw].

The son of Re, Seneb-Kay, [true of voice].

East end, text band

Nṯr nfr nb tȝwy nb ìrt ḫt ny-swt-bìty Wsrìbrc Snb-Kȝy mȝ-ḫrw Ḳbḥsnw.f mry, stw ìry.k.

(O) *Good-god, Lord-of-the-Two-Lands, Lord of ritual, King of Upper and Lower Egypt, Woseribre Seneb-Kay, true-of-voice, beloved of Qebehsenuef, lift yourself up.*

In addition to the completed decoration, there is an area to the right of the large format cartouche where lightly painted black lines define the base and sides of a rectangle. No upper line survives but the feature is mirrored by a similar framed area on the south wall that preserved its upper edge as well as a crude ink label on its interior (see below). This feature appears to be part of the guidelines used to frame areas of decoration, but possibly indicates an area that was never completed. Strangely, the position of the left side of this rectangle falls directly beneath the cartouche of Seneb-Kay. Consequently, a rectangle that extended upwards to the height of the line on the right would have intersected the cartouche. For that reason, it appears equally possible that the rectangle and its mirror image on the south wall may have demarcated elements of decoration that were initially planned by the artists but abandoned during the actual painting process.

THE SOUTH WALL

The burial chamber's south wall is comparatively poorly preserved owing to substantial ancient removal of the upper courses (Figs. 2.10 to 2.13). Only the two end blocks of the upper course (course 4) remain in place. The second course from the top (course 3) also is substantially damaged in its midsection with two original blocks removed from this area. Unlike the north wall, the south wall employs a base course of masonry laid flat. Beneath the inner end of the south wall (in the corresponding location to the block missing from the first course of the

north wall), tomb robbers had removed two of these base blocks in a search for concealed spaces. The blocks above were also significantly dislodged. The south wall includes five reused blocks (R5, R6, R7, R9, and R14) with decorated surfaces originating in the 13th Dynasty masonry that was repurposed for Seneb-Kay's tomb. Blocks R5, R6, and R7 are placed with the decoration facing inwards. Block R9 forms an element of the south wall's west end abutting the door into the burial chamber. It has a decorated surface facing east in the block joint. It was only documented where it projects outward on the chamber's exterior and could not be fully exposed due to the intact articulation with the jambs and brickwork of the vaulted chamber (Chamber 2). Block R14 was discovered in 2016—during the dismantling of the inner end of the tomb for restoration work—and can be identified as the base block from the innermost end of the chamber (its position is restored in Fig. 2.10).

The format of the south wall mirrors that of the north wall. Orientation of the imagery and texts faces outwards to the tomb entrance and the texts now reverse orientation, reading from right to left. Originally the wall would have had a winged sundisk but that element is entirely missing, as is most of the goddess who, although slightly lower than her counterpart on the north wall (her black base line is 0.58 m above floor) occupies the same position in the decorative arrangement. Nothing survives of the blue label that would have fronted the goddess. Best preserved are the framed text bands at the ends of the chamber. The west (outer) text names Hapi while the inner text invokes Imseti. Like those on the north side they are set in ca. 30 cm from the chamber corners but the inner label is significantly askew. The skew orientation of both of the inner bands follows the same pattern: the distance between the chamber corner and text bands widens towards the top of the band in both cases (as if the band has been rotated counterclockwise on the north wall and clockwise on the south wall). In addition to its significantly skewed orientation, there is another anomaly associated with the east text band on the south wall: the king's prenomen, Woseribre, is misspelled where it occurs as *Wsrc-ìb-rc* with an extraneous *c*.

Despite the extensive damage to the upper and central parts of the south wall, in 2014 we were fortunate to recover a component of the large-format cartouche that matches the nomen on the chamber's

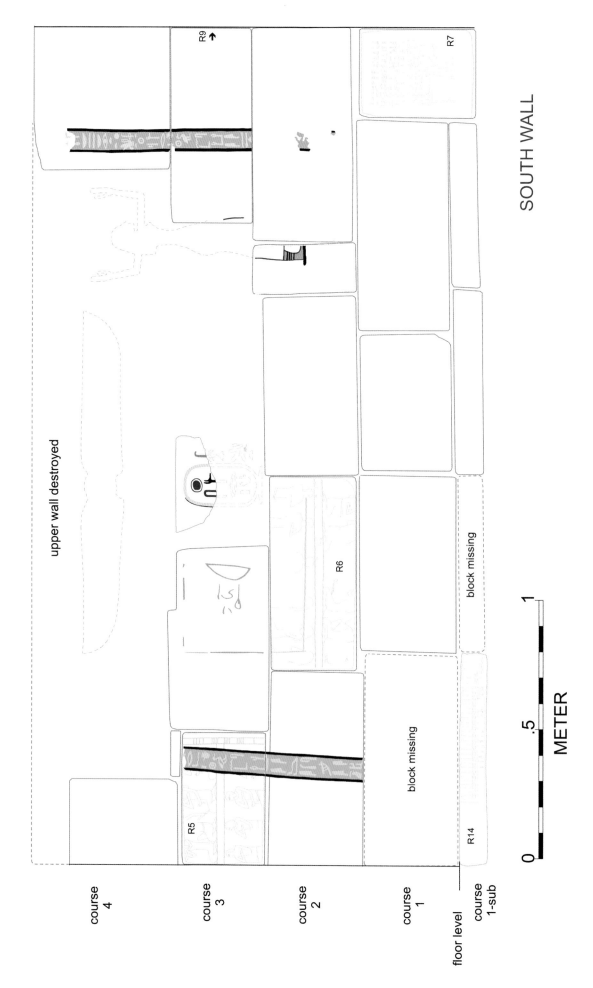

Fig. 2.10 The burial chamber's north wall showing painted decoration as well as locations of reused blocks with decoration.

Fig. 2.11 Text band, east end of south wall.

Fig. 2.12 Text band, west end of south wall.

Fig. 2.13 Details of hieroglyphs: (left) north wall, eastern text band showing use of truncated quail chick; (right) south wall, eastern text band showing name of Imseti with use of *mr* sign with double cross bars.

north wall. This fragment preserves the upper part of the king's prenomen, Woseribre, inside a blue-painted cartouche, along with a remnant of the title *ny-swt-bîty*, *King of Upper and Lower Egypt*, that would have preceded the cartouche on its right side (Fig. 2.14). The sun-disk hieroglyph is painted in the same style as occurs in the *s3-Rᶜ* title on the north wall with a disk inside of an outer circle. The head of the jackal comprising the *wsr* hieroglyph was black, a convention seen in well-preserved examples of large-format painted hieroglyphs. Although only a small part of

the overall block, the Woseribre fragment, preserves the upper, dressed surface of the block and allows us to place it with a high degree of certainty onto the south wall (the position is shown reconstructed in Fig. 2.10). This fragment confirms that the south wall mirrored the north, with the king's nomen and pre-nomen in corresponding locations on opposite sides of the chamber.

The overall sequence of text elements that would have occurred, from west to east is as follows:

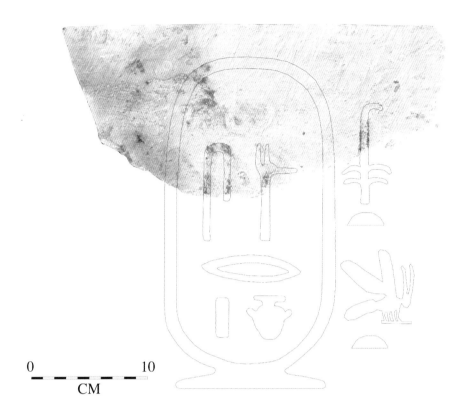

Fig. 2.14 Painted fragment originating from the south wall showing the upper part of the king's prenomen, *Wsr-ib-rˁ*, with suggested reconstruction in grey.

0 ---- 10
CM

West end, text band

Nṯr nfr nb tꜢwy nb ỉrt ḫt ny-swt-bỉty Wsrỉbrˁ Snb-KꜢy mꜢˁ-ḫrw Ḥpy mry, stw ỉry.k.

(O) Good-god, Lord-of-the-Two-Lands, Lord of ritual, King of Upper and Lower Egypt, Woseribre Seneb-Kay true-of-voice, beloved of Hapi, lift yourself up.

Label in front of goddess (text missing)

[Isis or Nepthys, ḥꜢp ˁwy ḥrt nswt (Snb-KꜢy) mꜢˁ-ḫrw].[4]

[It is Isis/Nephthys who folds (her) arms around king Seneb-Kay, true-of-voice].

Center (wall damaged, text on fragmentary block)

Ny-swt-bỉty (Wsrỉbrˁ) [mꜢˁ-ḫrw].

King of Upper and Lower Egypt, Woseribre, [true of voice].

East end, text band

Nṯr nfr nb tꜢwy nb ỉrt ḫt ny-swt-bỉty Wsrỉbrˁ Snb-KꜢy mꜢˁ-ḫrw ỉmstỉ mry, stw ỉry.k.

(O) Good-god, Lord-of-the-Two-Lands, Lord of ritual, King of Upper and Lower Egypt, Woseribre Seneb-Kay, true-of-voice, beloved of Imseti, lift yourself up.

A puzzling feature on the south wall is a hieroglyphic label or set of marks in the same black ink used for framing in the decorative zones. This area and the text within it are certainly original to the tomb chamber as are the lines that run across block seams of the laid masonry. However, the text appears to read sideways, beginning with a *nb* sign to the left followed by what looks possibly to be a *ḥpt*, oar symbol. In the center beneath the *nb*, is a sign resembling a *mꜢˁ* plough sign with the meaning "*true.*" This text could represent a builder's or artist's label, but the orientation makes its function ambiguous. It has not been possible to advance a more specific reading of this label. The fact that it was simply left on the wall, along with the matching black guidelines on north and south walls, is further indication of the speed with which the burial chamber was built and decorated.

THE EAST WALL

The burial chamber's east wall is decorated with symmetrical, inward-facing images of Neith (left) and Nut (right) flanking an eye panel and surmounted by a winged sun-disk (Figs. 2.15 to 2.20). The wall's lowest course is undecorated, and the decoration begins at the base of the second course of masonry (course 2). The figures of the goddesses are 80 cm in height. The deities have their arms bent inward over their chests with blue-painted *ankh* symbols suspended from their forearms. The *ankhs* are depicted with shortened lower straps. The eye panel measures 44 cm wide and is depicted with a polychrome border band, cornice, and *khekher*-frieze above. The panel includes symmetrical *wedjat*-eyes, flanking a basin with a *shen* symbol below. The winged sun-disk spans the full width of the wall and the base of the two uraei attached to the disk descend very close to the top of the *khekher*-frieze. The blue-painted labels in front of the goddesses read:

Label in front of goddess, north side

Nt ḥꜣp ꜥwy ḥrt [nswt] (Snb-Kꜣy) mꜣꜥ-ḥrw.

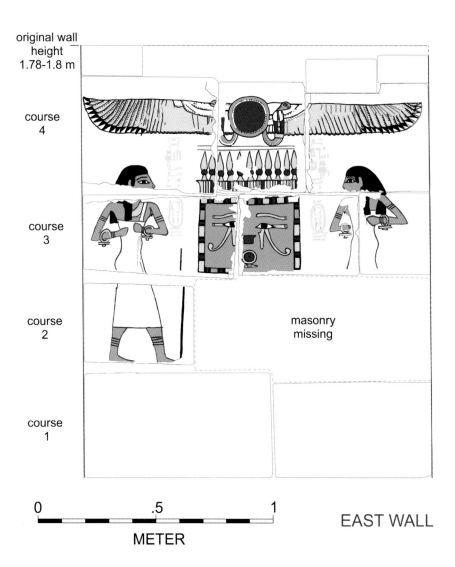

Fig. 2.15 Color facsimile of the burial chamber's east (inner) wall.

original wall height 1.78-1.8 m

course 4

course 3

course 2

masonry missing

course 1

0 .5 1

METER

EAST WALL

Fig. 2.16 The east wall after excavation, 2014.

It is Neith who folds (her) arms around king Seneb-Kay, true-of-voice.[5]

Label in front of goddess, south side

Nwt ms nṯrw ḥ3p ʿwy ḥrt [nswt] (Snb-K3y) m3ʿ-ḥrw.

It is Nut who gave birth to the gods who folds (her) arms around king Seneb-Kay, true-of-voice.

When the burial chamber was excavated in 2014, the east wall was found to have been broken through by ancient tomb robbers; evidently an attempt had been made to see whether the tomb might have additional spaces behind the chamber's innermost wall (Fig. 2.21). Masonry was missing from the second course on the wall's right side, probably originally two blocks. We encountered the central block from the third course lying at the inner end of the north wall (Fig. 2.22). This block had fallen through lack of support once the second course masonry below it was removed. The removal of blocks from the east

wall appears to have occurred at the same time as areas of damage on the inner end of the north and south walls where blocks had also been removed by ancient robbers to check whether there might be additional concealed chambers. The fallen block from the third course, which is decorated with the right side of the eye-panel and front of the body of Nut, was restored to its original position. However, we recovered no fragments belonging to the missing masonry from the second course.

The damage to the lower part of the east wall is unfortunate because this area includes not only the lower part of the body of Nut, but what is likely to have been a lower decorated panel that complemented the eye panel above to compose a false door as the focal element of the composition. On the left side of the broken area, and directly in front of Neith, is a solid, vertical black line 1.2 cm in width. This extends the full height of the block and breaks away at top and bottom where damage occurs along the block seams. On the right side of the upper part of the black line is a thinner red line confirming this is part of the wall

Fig. 2.17 The eye panel with Neith (left) and Nut (right).

(a)

(b)

Fig. 2.18a–b Details of the east wall: (a) body of Neith, (b) winged sun-disk with uraeus on right side.

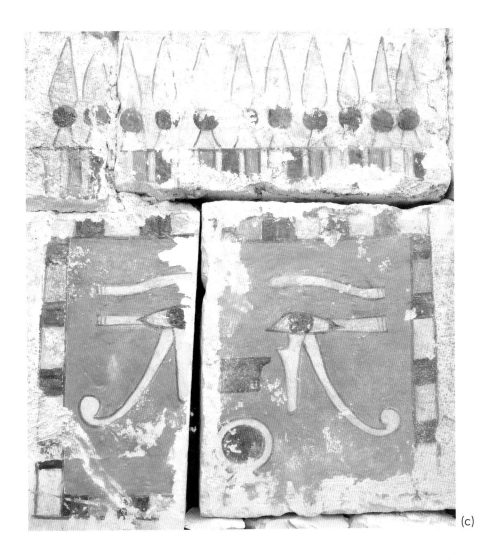

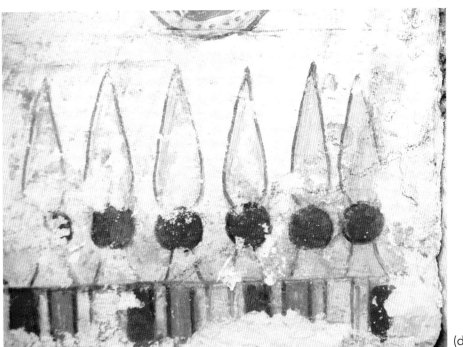

Fig. 2.18c–d Details of the east wall: (c) the eye panel, (d) the *khekher*-frieze.

Fig. 2.19 Details of the blue-painted labels in front of Neith (left) and Nut (right) on the east wall.

decoration and not merely a guideline. The position of the black line is displaced ca. 7.5 cm out from the side of the eye panel and does not represent a downward continuation of that element. Smaller areas with remnants of black paint occur directly beneath the eye panel as well as on the edge of the block with the vertical black line. Certainly, this area beneath the eye panel was not empty but contained decoration. A crucial question regarding the east wall decoration is: what was depicted under the eye panel?

It is difficult to explain the function of the heavy black line in front of Neith. The displacement relative to the eye panel suggests whatever existed in this area was not a direct downward extension of the eye panel. The width of the line is comparable to the lines framing the vertical text bands on the north and south walls making it possible there were text bands beneath the eye panel but displaced outwards. If so, we might expect the artists to have used internal color as they did with the yellow-brown background for the speech bands on the north and south walls. Another possibility is the black line is the outer edge of a larger decorative feature directly under the eye panel. The height of the space from the ground-line of the feet of the goddesses exactly matches the height of the eye panel to the beginning of the *khekher* frieze.

This raises the significant possibility that the primary element depicted in this area was the door panel that typically occurs beneath the eye panel on coffins of the late Middle Kingdom. The two panels would then be shown with the same dimensions.

Numerous variations of the eye panel atop false door occur among rectangular coffins of the late Middle Kingdom, particularly the black-type coffins of the mid-late 13th Dynasty. Coffins such as Cairo 28029 (the coffin of Senebini: Lapp 1993: pl. 34; Berlev 1974:108–109), or the coffins from the Asasif of Nefneferet (MMA 32.3.249) and Ikhet (MMA 32.3.430) illustrate this false door format well. Although the eye-panel can occur alone without the doorway panel, when it does, there is invariably something that replaces that feature: a text band or *serekh*-motif on the lower part of the coffin (Fig. 2.23). It appears highly likely that space beneath the eye panel in Seneb-Kay's burial chamber took the characteristic false door format as seen, for instance, on the coffins of Ikhet or Nefneferet. It is unfortunate that this part of the east wall is missing since, based on the format of the eye panel, this would presumably have been a beautifully rendered, polychrome version of the doorway panel (shown here, Fig. 2.24, in a reconstruction based on the parallels just mentioned).

Fig. 2.20 The king's nomen, Seneb-Kay, and funerary epithet, *mꜣꜤ-ḫrw*, *"true of voice,"* in front of the elbow of Neith (east wall).

Fig. 2.21 The condition of the east wall when first excavated, January 2014.

Fig. 2.22 The fallen central block from the third course of the east wall found inside the burial chamber.

When the decoration of the east wall was first exposed in 2014, a possible interpretation of the eye panel with flanking images of Neith and Nut was that it represents a two-dimensional depiction of the canopic chest with protective goddesses on either side. The likely position of the actual canopic chest at the inner end of the burial chamber suggested there could be a spatial relationship between imagery and

Fig. 2.23 Examples of eye panels and the false door motif on black-type coffins of the 13th Dynasty. Coffin of Nefneferet (MMA 32.4.430), upper left; coffin of Ikhet (MMA 32.3.430), upper right; coffin (MMA 32.3.431), lower left; and coffin of Entemaemsaf (MMA 32.3.428), lower right. Images courtesy of the Metropolitan Museum of Art.

the placement of king's burial equipment. However, in view of the probable existence of a lower decorated component beneath the eye panel, that initial interpretation appears less likely. A more likely understanding is that we have a rendering of the false door adapted from contemporary coffin decoration and here transferred to the actual walls of the burial chamber. The false door is the focal element of the overall burial chamber. This understanding of the east wall imagery fits with the way the figures of Isis and Nephys with upraised arms replicate the images typically used on the ends of coffins, and, as we discuss further below, the scene labels themselves copy the texts on canopic chests.

Fig. 2.24 A reconstruction of the east wall decoration showing the suggested position of the false door motif beneath the eye panel.

(masonry missing)

0   .5   1

METER

DISCUSSION OF THE TEXT PROGRAM

Apart from the large-format nomen and pre-nomen of the king, which occur in the center of the north and south walls, the primary texts in Sen-eb-Kay's burial chamber take two forms (Fig. 2.25). Immediately adjacent to the figures of the four god-desses are labels painted in light blue hieroglyphs and devoid of borders. These identify each deity with the statement that it is the goddess who enfolds her arms around king Seneb-Kay (ḥȝp ꜥwy ḥrt nswt Snb-Kȝy). These texts are direct adaptations from the spells on canopic chests in which the four protective god-desses effect corporeal protection over the deceased. Variations of this text emphasizing divine protection through enfolding of arms occur on royal canopic

chests from the late Middle Kingdom through later periods. Here we have a shortened version of the canopic chest text paired with large-scale images of the four protective goddesses.

In addition to the blue-painted labels, there are four text bands that name the four sons of Horus. These texts are enclosed within a black rectangular border and are rendered in blue hieroglyphs on a yel-low background. Unlike the unframed texts, they do not function explicitly as labels with the goddesses or other figural elements. The framed text columns employ a full invocation of the king employing both his prenomen, Woseribre, and his nomen, Seneb-Kay. These statements contain a fuller set of royal titles and epithets, being introduced by the grouping: nṯr nfr, nb tȝwy, nb ỉrt ḫt, *The Good-god, Lord of the Two-Lands, Lord of ritual*... with each text naming the king as beloved of one of the four sons of Horus. Particularly significant is the way each of these statements ends with an imperative addressed to the king in the second person: *stw iry.k, raise yourself up.*

The presence of the second person voice shows that these statements are not scene labels but are intended as speech addressed to the deceased king. Although not marked by the initial element *ḏd-mdw, words spoken,* they are clearly to be read as addresses from the respective goddesses to the king where an initial invocation of the king is followed by the divine command, *stw iry.k, raise yourself up.* The four tutelary goddesses of the canopic shrine protect the four sons of Horus who in turn protect the king's organs necessary for physical rejuvenation. Here those goddesses name the four sons of Horus in their command to the king. The statements appear to function as divine appeals to the king, calling upon the bodily elements present within the burial chamber and under protection by the four sons to permit his physical rebirth.

The positions of the text bands at the west end of the burial chamber's north and south walls fall

directly in front of the figures of Isis and Nephthys with upraised arms. The text bands on the chamber's east end, however, are located behind the figures of Neith and Nut whose images then appear on the end wall. It is conceivable there was an intention to depict additional goddesses on the two side walls facing inwards towards the text. The location of the text bands behind, rather than in front, of the goddesses at the inner end of the burial chamber does not appear to detract from their role as divine speech associated with the adjacent goddesses on the east wall. Consequently, the coordination of goddesses and the sons of Horus, which they name in their speech to the king, is as follows: Neith + Qebehsenuef; Nut + Imseti; Isis (or Nephthys) + Duamutef); Isis (or Nephthys) + Hapi.

One of the noteworthy aspects of the deities represented in Seneb-Kay's burial chamber is the occurrence of Nut in place of Selket as one of the four tutelary goddesses. The position of Nut on funerary equipment is typically associated with the interior of the lid, reflecting her role as goddess of the heavens. It is unclear why Nut occurs here in place

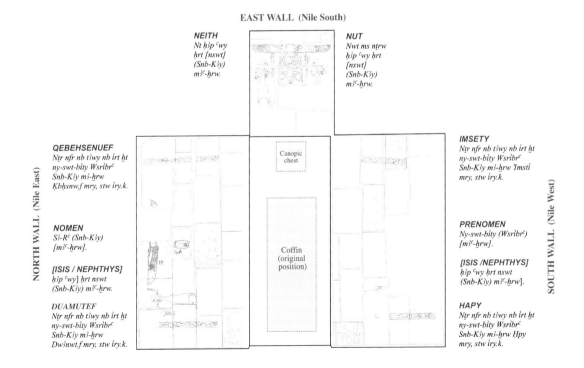

Fig. 2.25 Schematic showing the location of the texts and scene elements in the burial chamber of Seneb-Kay.

of Selket. One possibility might be the avoidance of the scorpion hieroglyph that would normally accompany Selket's name.[6] There are examples during the Middle Kingdom of substitution of other goddesses, for example at Deir el-Bersheh the goddesses Sendjet and Renenutet occur as protectresses (Lüscher 1990:17–18). Nut herself does occur on canopic texts but in positions where she is named in combination with other counterparts among the Heliopolitan Ennead: Geb (her male counterpart) and Geb and Nut's mythological parents, Shu and Tefnut. Here in Seneb-Kay's burial chamber we have a substitution of Nut in place of Selket for unknown reasons. The impetus for this change is unclear and does not appear to be attested among the known Second Intermediate Period canopic chests.

On coffins and canopic equipment from the time of the Old Kingdom, the standard correlation between the goddesses, the four sons of Horus, and the geographical and corporeal associations of funerary equipment occurs as follows: (1) Isis/feet/South paired with Imseti/liver; (2) Nepthys/head/North paired with Hapi/lungs; (3) Neith/hands/East paired with Duamutef/ stomach; and (4) Selket/West paired with Qebehsenuef/intestines (Taylor 2001b).

It is clear the relationships between goddesses and the four sons of Horus in the burial chamber of Seneb-Kay does not correlate with these typical relationships of the deities. If the goddess depicted on the south wall is Nephthys, there may be an association with Hapi as might be expected. However, the other three then do not follow the typical pairing conventions. If the placement of the texts is compared with the normal principles of Middle Kingdom coffin decoration, we also find that the burial chamber is at variance. Middle Kingdom coffins typically show Imseti and Duamutef on the east side and Hapi and Qebehsenuef on the west side. The naming of the sons of Horus in Seneb-Kay's tomb instead places Imseti and Hapi on the Nile west with Duamutef and Qebehsenuef on the Nile east.

There may exist some underlying logic behind the locations of the texts naming the four sons relative to the orientation of the tomb. The placement of Imseti on the "local south" end of the south wall and Hapi on the "local north" end of the south wall follows the ideal Nile directions of the tomb. The occurrence of Duamutef and Qebehsenuef might then reflect a notional pairing of east and west together on

the north (Nile east) wall. Ultimately, however, it appears difficult to comfortably explain the placement of the texts naming the different deities, along with substitution of Nut in place of Selket. In its particular choice of texts, the burial chamber of Seneb-Kay offers a unique Second Intermediate Period variation of the key deities associated with corporeal protection and regeneration. Given the difficulty in correlating the pairings and placement of the deities with the practices of coffins and canopic chests, it appears likely the presence of the texts and the deities named therein was more significant than their exact positions. In view of the time constraints that appear to have governed the construction and decoration of Seneb-Kay's tomb, it appears probable the artists placed relatively little emphasis on the nuances of orientation.

NOTES:

2.1 The name Duamutef is written here with the arm hieroglyph holding a *nw*-jar, rather than the normal *mwt* (vulture) hieroglyph. This variant writing avoids use of the bird hieroglyph, likely for the same reason that animal signs were truncated to render the creatures ineffectual in causing damage in the funerary setting. The writing "Duanutef" in place of "Duamutef" occurs occasionally on late Middle Kingdom/Second Intermediate Period coffins (see for example: Lapp 1993: pls.14a, 19c, 34a, and elsewhere) and canopic chests such as that of Auibre Hor (Dodson 1994:146–147).

2.2 In this label on the north wall we have partially-preserved the writing *nswt*, *king* in front of the nomen Seneb-Kay. The nomen is normally preceded by the statement *s3-Rˁ*, *son of Re*, as occurs in the large-format nomen in the middle of the north wall. This substitution of the generic word *nswt*, is paralleled by funerary texts that introduce the king's name in this way. For the Second Intermediate Period, see, for instance, the canopic chests of kings Djehuty and Sekhemre-wadjkhau Sobekemsaf of the 17th Dynasty (Dodson 1994: cat. 24 and 26 with pls. 11–15).

2.3 The text here was previously read incorrectly as *nyswt-bity*, *King of Upper and Lower Egypt*, rather than *nswt, king* (Wegner 2017:485).

2.4 No elements of this label survive, and it can only be reconstructed based on the matching labels on the north and east walls.

2.5 Both labels associated with goddesses on the east wall cross over a block seam where the element *nswt* that fronts the king's nomen is missing. This element can be reconstructed based on the available space, as well as the surviving *nswt* in the same position in the label fronting the goddess on the north wall.

2.6 In this case, the lack of Selket might parallel the motivation behind truncated hieroglyphs in avoiding images of dangerous animals in proximity to the burial. However, it would have also been possible to write Selket's name phonetically without using the scorpion hieroglyph. Moreover, Selket is not avoided on other funerary equipment of the period making this interpretation less probable.

3

The Funerary Equipment*

The burial chamber of King Seneb-Kay's tomb was severely plundered in ancient times, leaving only a fragmentary record of its original contents. Nevertheless, the objects discarded on the floor of the pole-roof chamber (Chamber 1) and extending into the vaulted antechamber (Chamber 2) provide a significant set of evidence on the characteristics of the king's burial equipment. Surviving debris recovered in the excavation of CS9 includes the lid and box of the canopic chest which was strewn atop Seneb-Kay's body as well as fragments of the containers that had once encased his burial. Along with the skeletonized remains of the king's mummy we encountered remains of three different elements of Seneb-Kay's burial equipment: (1) a polychrome painted, cartonnage funerary mask; (2) a polychrome, anthropoid wooden coffin; and (3) a rectangular outer sarcophagus employing a white background with polychrome decoration.[1] Here we examine the evidence for these three elements and the original disposition of the burial and canopic chest within the burial chamber. The details of the canopic chest, which presents its own unique set of evidence, is dealt with separately in the next chapter.

THE *RISHI*-STYLE FUNERARY MASK

Among the elements of Seneb-Kay's burial equipment scattered near floor level in Chamber 1 were fragments of the king's badly destroyed funerary mask. Numerous pieces of the mask were concentrated in a small area directly beneath the canopic box. The surviving fragments were recovered crushed together in a discrete area suggesting that a substantial portion of the mask had been pulled away and discarded together in this one location. As we have already examined in the discussion of the floor deposits in Chamber 1, the secondary depositional order appears to broadly reflect the sequence of events involved in despoiling of the burial chamber. It appears that tomb robbers opened the containers and tore apart the mask, probably removing any valuable elements, particularly the face which was almost certainly gilded. The process of stripping away the face mask was immediately followed by the pillaging of the king's body for removal of jewelry and amulets. Elements of the mask, along with the rifled body were discarded together near floor level in Chamber 1. After the burial itself was ransacked, the canopic chest, which lay at the innermost end of the burial chamber, was opened and emptied. Its lid, part of which broke away in the process, was then tossed to the far end of Chamber 1 while the box was discarded directly above the mask fragments.

The recovered pieces of the funerary mask—painted plaster fragments, primarily of small size—represent a minor percentage of the object's overall decorated surface. These fragments are insufficient to create any exact reconstruction of the mask; however, there is enough surviving evidence to indicate key decorative elements of the object. Many of these elements have parallels among late Middle Kingdom

* This chapter written by Josef Wegner.

Fig. 3.1 Scatter of mask fragments in Chamber 1 showing the impression of course linen on the back.

and Second Intermediate Period funerary masks. On that basis, we can assemble a reconstruction of the basic appearance and color scheme used in the funerary mask. This face mask was a version of a feathered or "*rishi*-style" mask with a *nemes* crown, overlain on either side of the face with wings composed of blue feathers. Due to the prevalence of the feather motif on Seneb-Kay's funerary mask, we will employ the term "*rishi*-style" mask here, although it is clear that this burial predates—if only by a short period of time—the emergence of *rishi*-style coffins, a phenomenon associated with the Theban 17th Dynasty.

A majority of the recovered mask fragments have the impression of course-woven linen on the back showing the construction was cartonnage built of a thick layer of plaster over a core of fabric (Fig. 3.1). The mask fragments can be distinguished from elements of the gessoed and painted wooden coffin through use of this linen core. Although layers of linen were used during the late Middle Kingdom over wooden anthropoid coffins (e.g., Mace and Winlock 1916:39–41), this is clearly not the case with Seneb-Kay's anthropoid coffin, a detail that distinguishes the fragments from the two different elements of the burial equipment. Surviving fragments of the wooden coffin show no remains of linen and the decoration of the coffin employed a thinner layer of gesso adhered directly to the wood. By contrast, the mask fragments have a thicker layer of plaster, which encased a central layer of linen to give the mask enhanced strength and flexibility. The linen appears to have been coated on the back (interior of the mask) by another coat of plaster. This had largely separated through flexing of

the pieces during the robbery and deterioration of the linen. The structure of the mask is likely to have been that of a "helmet" style mask (Casini 2017:56–73) in which the front and back formed a single structure and the mask was fitted directly over the head and shoulders from above.

THE MASK FRAGMENTS

The most significant group of related fragments derive from the central right side of the mask. The largest fragment (Fr. 1) derives from the area of articulation between the shoulder and the lower part of the headdress and broad collar (*wesekh*).[2] This fragment shows the following combination of features (Fig. 3.2):

(1) light blue feathers, with black tips and black cross hatching. The interstices between the feather ends are white and give way to a black lappet below.

(2) a black-painted lappet belonging to a *nemes* headdress and extending below the end of the feathers and flanked on either side by the *wesekh* collar. Together the *rishi*-style headdress and black lappet form a contiguous feature and are raised ca. 0.25 cm relative to the adjacent elements of the *wesekh* collar.

(3) curving blue and green bands on the right side indicate the upper area of the *wesekh* collar

adjacent to the shoulder. There is central red line between the two surviving bands, perhaps associated with depiction of the cordage of the terminus of the *wesekh* that has not survived.

(4)   on the left side of the lappet occur bands of alternating colors: blue, green (with black cross hatching), and light yellow (with red cross hatching). These represent the central section of the *wesekh* collar.

Significantly, Fr. 1 was found adjacent to a series of other *rishi* elements which indicate the continuation of the feather motif upwards surrounding the face. Another large fragment (Fr. 2) derived from the upper end of the feathers where they join vertically oriented lines of plumage decorated with inverted V-marks on a grey-green background. These elements occur in other examples of *rishi*-style masks and derive from the area adjacent to and below the ear (for example, Rigault-Déon 2012:96–99). The feathers then radiate outwards from this plumage. Between Fr. 1 and Fr. 2 there was an area of blue-painted feather fragments, badly decayed but with the approximate orientation of surviving elements matching the feathers emanating from the plumage

below the ear (Fig. 3.3). These fragments (not individually numbered) retain a sense of their original association, forming the lower side of the *rishi*-style headdress, and the entire scatter of elements including Fr. 1 and Fr. 2 once comprised a single, larger fragment of the mask.

One of the larger surviving elements with blue feather decoration is Fr. 3. This fragment is shown here in combination with other elements belonging to the right side of the mask (see Fig. 3.5) but is attributable to either side. Other fragments of the painted feathers and plumage of the headdress were recovered. Fragment 4 also depicts the combination of grey-green colored plumage with blue feathers and must originate from the left side of the mask. Like Fr. 2, this derives from the area adjacent to the ear. Fr. 5 indicates the probable decoration of the upper part of the funerary mask. This element shows the motif of multicolored plumage arrayed in a shingle pattern. On Fr. 5, we have a blue-painted band giving way to a single row of U-shaped plumes colored grey-green on their interiors. Above this occur multicolor plumes with red V-marks and grey-green ends. The interstices between the plumes are light blue. This motif also occurs on both the headdresses and wings on the lower body of Second Intermediate

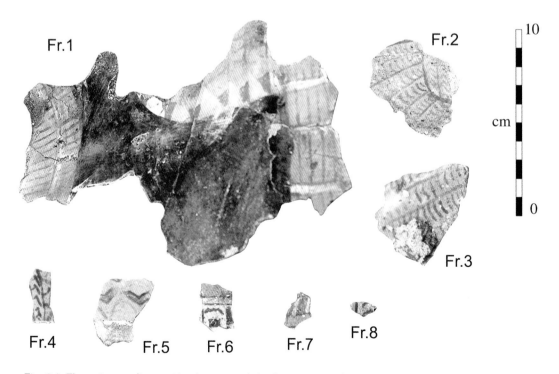

Fig. 3.2 The primary diagnostic elements of the funerary mask.

Fig. 3.3 Mask fragments 1–2 in situ with additional blue-painted *rishi* elements between.

Period *rishi*-coffins. On both coffins and *rishi*-style masks it forms the typical motif used for the upper part of the headdress. The blue band and transitional row of solid color plumes suggest Fr. 5 derives from the lower fringe of the plumed crown above the forehead.

Several fragments derive from black-painted text columns although with one exception these are too small to identify the hieroglyphs. The largest surviving text fragment is Fr. 6. This originates in a text label or panel arranged in vertical columns of black hieroglyphs. The text is framed above by a white-painted border with grey cross hatching. Above the text occurs a rectangular area of flat blue-green (no hatching or internal detail is preserved), which may represent one section of a polychrome border band that surrounds the text panel. The surviving text, *Inp*, occurs at the top of one of the columns. Certainly part of a writing for *Inpw*, *Anubis*, this fragment indicates there was a funerary text, almost certainly a *ḥtp-dỉ-nswt*, or prayer for divine offerings, as typically occurs on the lower front of funerary masks.

RECONSTRUCTION AND PARALLELS OF THE FUNERARY MASK

The surviving elements of Seneb-Kay's cartonnage mask display a number of parallels among the corpus of painted funerary masks of the late Middle Kingdom and Second Intermediate Period, particularly the "*rishi*-style" (feathered) funerary masks that have been seen as forerunners to the fuller development of *rishi*-coffins that occurred in Upper Egypt during the later Second Intermediate Period (Miniaci 2011a:136–138). In its color scheme and mode of painting, there are notable elements of similarity with the substantial group of fragmentary masks from the cemeteries at Mirgissa in Lower Nubia (Vila 1976:151–268; Rigault-Déon 2012), particularly with the later group of masks in the Mirgissa cemetery deriving principally from Cemetery X. Parallels to observe here are:

(1) the formation of the blue-painted feather design emanating from the central plumage decorated

with inverted V-marks. A nearly identical approach occurs on one of the better-preserved Mirgissa masks (Louvre E25702), which is missing most of the outer elements of the headdress but preserves the articulation between *rishi* design and face (Andreu, Rutschowscaya, and Ziegler 1997:100–102, no. 40; Rigault-Déon 2012:97).

(2)   the structure and color scheme of the shingle-pattern plumes on the upper part of the headdress. While this element occurs on virtually all examples of *rishi*-coffins, both on the chest and headdress, the style and color scheme attested by Fr. 5 appears nearly identical to examples at Mirgissa including the well-preserved Louvre E25702, as well as many others.[3]

(3)   the color and hatching details of the bands composing the *wesekh* collar have nearly identical parallels at Mirgissa with use of alternating bands of blue and green with black hatching, and light yellow bands with red hatching (Rigault-Déon 2012:42–44). No surviving fragments of Seneb-Kay's mask indicate the presence of a final band with multicolor pendant beads, but this element is so standard to the *wesekh* collar that we may regard its presence is virtually certain.

Apart from the Mirgissa masks, a smaller number of *rishi*-style masks of the late Middle Kingdom and Second Intermediate Period offer parallels to that of Seneb-Kay. The earliest of this group is a late Middle Kingdom mask with feathered headdress belonging to the commander Senu from Dahshur and dated to the late 12th or early 13th Dynasty (Yoshimura 2008:194–197, 228, no. 249). Likely post-dating Seneb-Kay are *rishi*-style masks of the later Second Intermediate Period including the mask of the *ḫkrt nswt*, Nubkherdi, from Deir el-Bahri (Cairo CG28109; Lacau 1904: pl. 23) and several unprovenanced examples of unidentified individuals with the distinctive late Second Intermediate Period feature of the proportionally reduced face (Cairo JE 45629, Manchester Acc. 7931, and Liverpool M11020; see Dodson [1998 and 2011]). A late 17th to early 18th Dynasty example with affinities to the *rishi*-mask is that of Satdjehuty (BM EA29770; Russman 2001:106). Among

these various comparanda, it is noteworthy that Seneb-Kay's mask displays the greatest similarity with the Mirgissa masks of the later group. Stylistically Seneb-Kay's mask appears to fall in the transition between the late Middle Kingdom *rishi*-style masks and predates the development of the full *rishi* coffin form during the later Second Intermediate Period.

One significant feature of Seneb-Kay's mask is the presence of a black lappet or wig element that is raised (along with the feathered section of the headdress above it) relative to the adjacent sections of the *wesekh* collar. Although it could be proposed that this shows the *rishi* headdress overlaying a black wig, there is enough preserved to show that the black-painted area is flat across its width.[4] It is clear from Fr. 1 that the cross-section of this element does not correspond with the rounded profile that would occur on a wig or a *khat* headdress. Therefore, we can be nearly certain that the black section on the Seneb-Kay mask is not part of a wig but rather belongs to the lappet of a *nemes* headdress. Use of the *nemes* occurs commonly on royal and non-royal (both male and female) *rishi*-coffins of the Second Intermediate Period. Although the *rishi* coffins post-date Seneb-Kay, they offer a useful set of comparanda for the use of a solid coloration on the *nemes*. Narrow stripes of alternating colors are typical of the *nemes,* there are also a significant number of examples that have wide black bands at the top of the lappet and in the same position as the black painted section preserved on Seneb-Kay's mask.[5]

Additional comparanda for this feature may be found on the *nemes* of the 17th Dynasty coffins of kings Sekhemre Heruhirmaat Antef (Louvre E3020) and Kamose (Cairo Temp. 14.12.27.12: Daressy 1909). The coffin of Heruhirmaat is asymmetrical and roughly decorated, but has two wider, single-tone (yellow) bands that interrupt the blue and red stripes of the lappet in the same relative position as the black area on Seneb-Kay's mask. A similar arrangement occurs on the coffin of Kamose where, again, a wide single-tone band (yellow-brown) occurs at the top of the lappet and between the alternating stripes above and below. The *nemes* of the Kamose coffin has a solid black upper section with change to colored striping occurring only lower down, although the headdress itself lacks use of the typical *rishi* design (Fig. 3.4).

Seneb-Kay's mask does not exactly correspond with the color scheme on the *nemes* of these two 17th

Fig. 3.4 Treatment of the nemes on the 17th Dynasty rishi-coffins of Kings Sekhemre-Heruhirmaat Antef (left) and Kamose (right). Images courtesy of the Musée du Louvre (left) and Merja Attia, Egyptian Museum, Cairo (right).

Dynasty royal coffins. It is conceivable that, instead of striping, Seneb-Kay's mask employed a solid black *nemes*, which thereby formed a single-tone frame for the blue *rishi* headdress. However, the fact that multiple *rishi*-coffins, including two royal examples, employ a wide band in this same position suggests Seneb-Kay's *rishi*-mask may have had a similar approach. Consequently, there may have been use of black in combination with the standard alternating bands of red and blue typically used on the *nemes*. Here we may tentatively propose a solid black upper *nemes* specifically used to contrast with the blue painted feathers framing the face. Further down on the lappets, black may have given way to stripes of alternating colors, possibly the red and blue bands that most frequently characterize the *nemes*.

The location and extent of the text elements on Seneb-Kay's mask remains speculative and is based exclusively on the small fragment that preserves the

name of the god *Inpw*. The Mirgissa masks employ text panels with a *ḥtp-dỉ-nswt* formula and the name of the deceased inside polychrome borders directly below the *wesekh* collar (Rigault-Déon 2012:48–53). We may note texts in a similar position on funerary masks such as that of Satdjehuty (BM EA 29770) dating to the end of the *rishi* tradition (Taylor 1996; Russman 2001:106). During the late Second Intermediate Period and early 18th Dynasty, the text was increasingly accommodated on a projecting tab at the base of the mask (Dodson 1998:97–99). Similarly, a central *ḥtp-dỉ-nswt* in one or two columns initiated below the *wesekh* occurs regularly on *rishi*-coffins of the Second Intermediate Period. On royal examples (Polz 2007: taf.2–9; Miniaci 2011a:268–271), the texts are normally variants of spells introduced by the term *ḏd-mdw*, *words spoken* and invoking divine protection over the deceased with the request for a good burial. However, *ḥtp-dỉ-nswt* texts also occur in the royal corpus, as for example on the coffins of Queen Ahhotep (Eaton-Krauss 1990, 2003).

The text on Seneb-Kay's mask appears to be surmounted by a border band of rectangles of alternating colors, although only green survives. Below that, the text frame itself has the additional feature of an upper stripe employing diagonal grey hatching on the same white background used for the text elements. It is unclear what the function of this hatched band might be and it does not seem to have parallels among the Mirgissa fragments or elsewhere. However, on the basis of the surviving fragment we may

tentatively locate a text panel on the lower front of the mask of Seneb-Kay in a format comparable to that known from the Mirgissa masks. Invocation of Anubis could derive from a *ḥtp-dỉ-nswt*, but, given Seneb-Kay's royal status, the god may be named as part of a funerary statement as occurs on the coffin of King Wepmaat Antef (Miniaci 2011a:268). Probably this took the form of a text initiated by *ḏd-mdw* and including the king's name and key royal titles as occur in the texts on the walls of the burial chamber. In all likelihood, the texts on the mask would have employed the same style and use of truncated

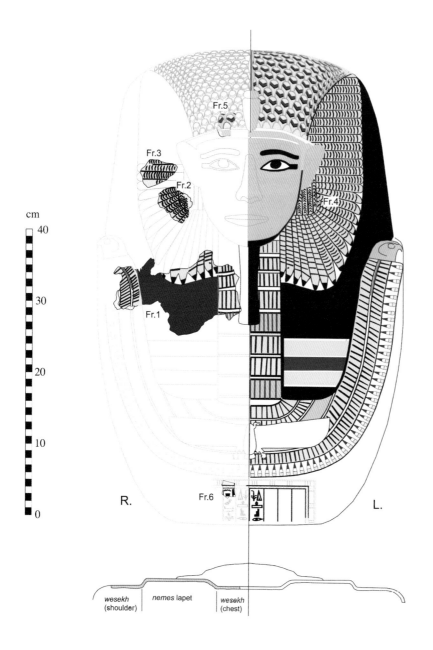

Fig. 3.5 A reconstruction of the funerary mask of Seneb-Kay based on the primary known elements.

hieroglyphs as occur on the wall texts in the king's tomb.

Based on the combination of evidence we can assemble a general sense of what Seneb-Kay's funerary mask looked like. Figure 3.5 shows the principal identified fragments positioned relative to the suggested structure of the mask on the left. On the right side of the drawing is a color reconstruction intended to impart an impression of the decoration and coloration of the mask. Despite its fragmentary preservation, what is of principal significance is the status of the mask as a "*rishi*-style" funerary mask, but one that precedes the emergence of the Second Intermediate Period *rishi*-coffins. The close similarities to be observed with the Mirgissa masks, as well as the evidence for a wooden anthropoid coffin and rectangular outer sarcophagus, suggests that the affinities of Seneb-Kay's burial equipment lie with late Middle Kingdom funerary traditions and stand apart from the Theban *rishi*-coffin tradition of the 17th Dynasty. This evidence may have implications for the chronology and historical context of the reign of King Woseribre Seneb-Kay.

THE WOODEN ANTHROPOID COFFIN

Also recovered near the canopic box in Chamber 2 is a small group of painted wood fragments originating from a wooden anthropoid coffin (Fig. 3.6). Whereas the main group of mask fragments lay together below the canopic box, the anthropoid coffin fragments were found at a slightly higher elevation between the canopic box and the north wall of the chamber. These fragments may be splinters that originated in the process of breaking up the coffin within the tomb. The original robber's hole through the limestone portcullis was less than 40 cm in height, suggesting larger elements like the anthropoid coffin and the outer sarcophagus were broken up in the tomb's interior. In connection with the removal of the coffin, as we have already discussed above, it is conceivable that an accumulation of charcoal fragments excavated within the canopic box blew into the chamber from the entrance (which faces local north and in the direction of the prevailing desert winds).

Fr.9

Fr.12

Fig. 3.6 The two largest surviving fragments of the wooden anthropoid coffin (from CS9, Chamber 1).

The charcoal may have originated in the burning of the wooden coffin to remove gilded elements.[6] Some of these smaller wood elements that collected against the wall could potentially have also blown back into Chamber 1 from the tomb's entrance.

Three fragments (Frs. 9–11) were found lying loose in the sand between the canopic box and the north wall of Chamber 2. A fourth fragment attributable to the anthropoid coffin (Fr. 12) lay immediately underneath the lid of the canopic chest. Three of the wood coffin fragments have painted decoration over a thin coat of gesso, the fourth has paint directly over the wood. There are no indications of use of a linen layer as occurs in the mask fragments. The mode of construction of the anthropoid coffin shows similarity with that seen in Second Intermediate Period *rishi* coffins in which a thin layer of gypsum directly over the wood served as the smooth coating for the painted decoration (Miniaci 2011a:24–25).

The most significant fragment (Fr. 9) is a 12 cm long section of a painted *wesekh* collar. This preserves six bands with alternating use of greenish blue, turquoise blue, and red. As occurs on the cartonnage mask, the blue and green bands have a black cross hatching. Nothing is preserved of the lappets of the *nemes* to indicate whether it employed the same configuration as the cartonnage mask. Although the width of the *wesekh* bands on Fr. 9 are comparable to those on the mask fragments, the *wesekh* on the wood is painted over a thinner coat of gesso and, as noted above, lacks the use of a linen backing. The different construction techniques clearly indicate the existence of two different components in Seneb-Kay's burial assemblage, both incorporating the *wesekh* collar: the cartonnage funerary mask and a wooden anthropoid coffin. Furthermore, it is important to note that there is a difference in application of color between the mask and the anthropoid coffin. Whereas the mask uses bands of yellow with red cross hatching in combination with the blue and green bands, the *wesekh* on Fr. 9 uses a solid red band. This common convention for depiction of the *wesekh* is attested on numerous anthropoid coffins of the Middle Kingdom and Second Intermediate Period (for example, Bourriau 1988: pl. 3:3). The change in curvature and spacing between the bands across Fr. 9 shows that the fragment originates from the area of the *wesekh* at the lower end of the headdress where the straight bands between the lappets shift to the curving bands separated by wider spacing that form the lower body the *wesekh* (Fig. 3.7).

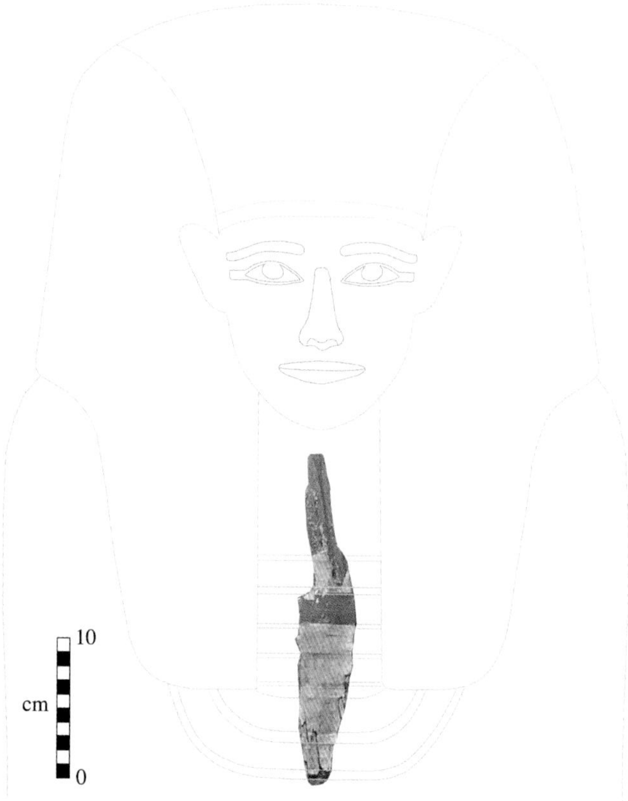

A second fragment (Fr. 10) preserves bands of turquoise blue and yellow-brown. The fragment is too small to determine its point of origin on the anthropoid coffin. A third fragment (Fr. 11) is a piece of red-painted wood with no other decorative details. The final element attributable to the anthropoid coffin (Fr. 12) is a rectangular, flat element, ca. 0.25 cm in thickness with four dowel holes through its center. This object can be identified as a dowel-pinned patch associated with the joinery of the anthropoid coffin. This piece lacks the gesso coating with paint directly on the wood but preserves a blue band with red on one side and yellow-brown above. The use of red on two of these wood fragments suggests that elements of the lower end of the lid, or possibly the coffin's box were red. Red occurs on the foot of Second Intermediate Period

Fig. 3.7 Fragment 9 showing derivation from the *wesekh* collar of the inner, anthropoid coffin.

rishi-coffins such as those of Kings Heruhirmaat Antef and Kamose. Red occasionally occurs more extensively over the lower body of the coffin lid and also can be applied to the rims of coffins and lids where it may have a protective function (Taylor 2001a:164–181). The painted patch, Fr. 12, may originate in joinery at the base or some less visually central part of Seneb-Kay's coffin that did not receive a smooth coat of gesso.

The fact that so little of the anthropoid coffin of Seneb-Kay has survived suggests that it may have included inlaid elements and use of gilding for the face and other elements. Small fragments of gold leaf recovered from the debris in Chamber 1 (not illustrated here) separately demonstrate the presence of gilded surfaces on parts of Seneb-Kay's funerary equipment. Due to the existence of a painted white-ground outer sarcophagus and canopic chest with similar surface treatment, the inner anthropoid coffin should have been the primary element of the burial assemblage that had significant use of gilding. Polychrome painting of elements like the *wesekh* collar may have been used alongside gold leaf for select decorative elements, particularly the face. Based on these considerations we can envision a vibrantly decorated coffin with dual use of painted decoration as well as elements highlighted through gilding.

It is important to note here that anthropoid coffins were certainly present in the other Second Intermediate Period tombs in the main cluster just north of Seneb-Kay. This is indicated by one of the objects that Arthur Weigall found during his 1901–1902 work. Weigall reported discovering an inlaid eye, evidently originating in an anthropoid coffin in the tomb we now designate CS8 (Ayrton, Currelly, and Weigall [1904:16], and discussed here in Chapter 11). Unfortunately, no further detail was provided, and the present location of the inlaid eye is unknown. CS8 is the southernmost tomb of the main tomb cluster and has the closest proximity to Seneb-Kay. It has the typical crypt-style burial chamber employed in most of the tombs, a feature likely designed specifically as a receptacle for a rectangular outer sarcophagus. Yet, we also have confirmation of an anthropoid inner coffin in CS8. Therefore, it appears virtually certain that not just Seneb-Kay but the other tombs of this group at South Abydos were designed to house nested burials that included an outer rectangular sarcophagus with an inner anthropoid coffin. The size of the different

components would have varied amongst the tombs and is reflected in the dimensions of the receptacles in the burial chambers designed to accommodate the outer sarcophagus. It is quite probable the burial chambers were purpose-built with knowledge of the specific dimensions of the rectangular sarcophagi they were destined to house.

Regarding the evidence for an anthropoid coffin it is significant to note that apart from the fragments themselves, an independent indicator for the existence of an inner coffin in Seneb-Kay's burial is the width of the ends of the lid of the rectangular outer sarcophagus. As we discuss in detail below, the better-preserved lid fragment (Lid Fr. 2) was preserved to its full, original width of 1.05 m (2 cubits). This width is greater than is typical of most late Middle Kingdom rectangular coffins. The width of the lid of Seneb-Kay's outer rectangular sarcophagus can be taken as an indication that it was either specifically designed (or secondarily chosen) in order that it could accommodate an inner anthropoid coffin of considerable size. This inference is complicated slightly by the possibility (discussed further below) that the outer sarcophagus was reused from a late 13th Dynasty tomb, possibly one linked with the chapel that provided the limestone blocks for Seneb-Kay's burial chamber. Nevertheless, extrapolation of the approximate size of the sarcophagus provides indications for an internal space on the order of 0.75 m by 2.1 m.

On this basis we may conclude that Seneb-Kay's anthropoid inner coffin could well have been of comparable dimensions to some of the larger Second Intermediate Period royal coffins such as those of Kings Nubkheperre Antef, Sekhemre-Wepmaat Antef, Seqenenre Tao, or Queen Ahhotep.[7] Was Seneb-Kay's anthropoid coffin one that fell within the parameters of the *rishi*-coffin tradition of the later Second Intermediate Period? Unfortunately, the paltry nature of the fragments does not provide us with sufficient evidence to address this question. However, based on the surviving fragments and decorative elements of his *rishi*-style cartonnage mask, Seneb-Kay's coffin appears likely to have incorporated some of the key elements associated with anthropoid *rishi* coffins. The date of Seneb-Kay certainly falls earlier than the 17th Dynasty emergence of the developed *rishi* coffin, but it may be an immediate forerunner to that tradition. We now turn to consider the evidence provided by the remains of the rectangular outer sarcophagus, the last element of the burial equipment.

THE RECTANGULAR OUTER SARCOPHAGUS

During excavation, two large pieces of wood were found lying on the white-washed floor in the doorway between the antechamber and pole-roof chamber (Chambers 1 and 2). These elements were found to be in a poor state of preservation, but both retained varying degrees of their original surface finish. Based on their overall size and surface features, it is clear these are the flat, batten-ends of the vaulted lid of a rectangular *per-nu* type sarcophagus.[8] The wood used for this lid was not reused cedar as occurs in Seneb-Kay's canopic box. Rather, this was an indigenous wood, likely acacia, which had been entirely reduced to frass through insect damage, accounting for the eroded condition of the lid fragments.

The first of the two fragments, Lid Fr. 1, was found in the center of the pole-roof chamber (Fig. 3.8). All that was left on its surface were small patches of white gypsum plaster adhering to the decayed wood. Damage was extensive and no decoration was preserved. The object was rectangular in cross section, measuring ca. 12 cm wide by 11 cm in height. The overall length was not preserved but the dimensions of its cross section make it clear this was the matching piece to the better-preserved Lid Fragment 2.

Lid Fr. 2 was found running approximately parallel to the other fragment in the middle of the doorway between the vaulted antechamber and the pole-roof chamber. Though also in a highly decayed state, this fragment had fared better than Lid Fr. 1 and retained a good portion of its original painted decoration. At the time of discovery, Lid Fr. 2 measured 14.7 cm wide, 11.5 cm in height, and 1.05 m in length (equaling exactly two cubits). The upper surface of the piece was almost totally decayed, and its rippled surface indicated that the wood had also deflated slightly, making the precise height of the fragment

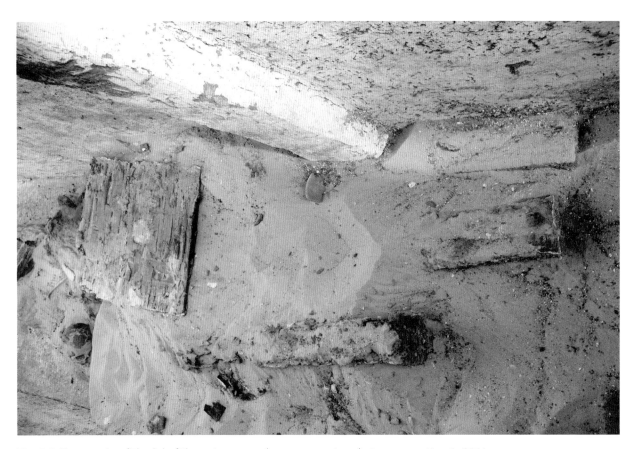

Fig. 3.8 Fragments of the lid of the outer sarcophagus emerging during excavation in 2014.

somewhat uncertain. The north-facing side of Lid Fr. 2 had isolated traces of white plaster but no visible painted decoration. This side of the block was also significantly slumped with an eroded concavity along the base. This was the result of the wood decaying around the curved mortise that had originally accommodated the woodwork that formed the convex, vaulted curve of the *per-nu* lid.

Lid Fragment 2 shows that the background color of the sarcophagus was white. Multicolored bands were preserved on the east-, south-, and west-facing sides of the fragment (Figs. 3.9 and 3.10). On the east-facing, narrow end, two vertical bands of polychrome decoration were inset 1.9 cm (equaling one Egyptian digit or finger-width) from the corners. The bands were slightly over a digit in width at 2.2 cm and consisted of two outer vertical lines and a central space divided horizontally into alternating narrow and wide rectangles, or coffers. The colors used in the coffered bands were yellow, light blue, light green, and red, with black added to define the outlines of the rectangles and edging.

A similar vertically oriented band of decoration was preserved on the fragment's south-facing long side, set 1.9 cm in from the corner (Fig. 3.10). Turning 90° to the left, the band continued horizontally and extended the length of the batten to the opposite corner. Although the top edge of the fragment is eroded, one small area was preserved, extending to about 2 cm above the top edge of the horizontal decorative band. Since this is the same distance as the one-digit space between the vertical bands and the vertical corners of the block, it is probable that this represents the full height of Lid Fragment 2. This measurement was about 11.5 cm, corresponding to exactly 6 digits or 1 Egyptian palm.

Fortunately, with Lid Fragment 2 we also had the other corner still preserved. The fragment extended close to the position of the base of the canopic box, which lay on its side with its base oriented inwards towards the burial chamber. In the process of excavating this box, the opposite end of Lid Fragment 2 was exposed revealing the same multicolor border decoration (Fig. 3.11). The length of the lid between the two short ends of the batten was measured to be 1.05 m, equaling 2 cubits. Due to its deteriorated state, a decision was made in 2014 to leave Lid Fragment 2 in situ until it could be consolidated and lifted. It

Fig. 3.9 The east-facing end of Lid Fragment 2 showing the polychrome, coffered bands with white background. The adjacent fragment is part of the lid of the canopic chest.

Fig. 3.10 South-facing side of the decorated sarcophagus fragment, Lid Fragment 1. The block of wood behind at the right is a fragment of the lid of the canopic chest (discussed below).

Fig. 3.11 The decorated east-facing end of Lid Fragment 2 (upper right), visible during the removal and documentation of the canopic box. The cartonnage mask (Mask Fr.1) is also visible (lower left) beneath the canopic box.

was thought possible that the surface sitting directly on the plastered floor might preserve additional evidence for plastered and decorated surfaces. In 2016, the fragment was consolidated and removed. This demonstrated, however, that the base surface was entirely undecorated with no indications of plastering over the wood. Consequently, Lid Fragment 2 was oriented correctly, vis-à-vis its original position on the sarcophagus lid. The undecorated lower surface is the lid base which would have sat atop the rim of the sarcophagus box.

A final sarcophagus fragment was also recovered close to floor level in CS9 near the transition between the burial chamber and vaulted antechamber (its position is shown in Fig. 1.16). Though much smaller in scale, Lid Fragment 3 has exactly the same painted decoration as Lid Fragments 1 and 2 (Fig. 3.12). Based on its location in the tomb, it probably derives from Lid Fragment 2. The small area of painted decoration remaining on Lid Fragment 3 shows the same white background as that of the other pieces. Here, it is possible to see the individual brush strokes and slight color differences between subsequent passes in the application of the white background. The polychrome coffered band has an exterior border—executed with black outlines—and a greenish-blue fill. Four smaller areas extend perpendicularly from the border line, consisting of red, green, yellow, and blue. Each of these areas are also outlined in black. This fragment illustrates the order in which the colors were applied. The white ground was painted on first, followed by the individual sections of the polychrome band. Finally, the edges of the band were highlighted with a thin black line. Together with the painted bands on the larger Lid Fragment 1, the surviving elements indicate that Seneb-Kay's burial was housed within an elaborately painted outer sarcophagus with carefully executed polychrome decoration on a white background. The time and effort evidently invested in the minor decorative detail of these polychrome borders has bearing on the nature of the sarcophagus.

Fig. 3.12 Lid Fragment 3. The coloration and patterning of this fragment is identical to that on Lid Fragment 1 and 2.

THE FORMAT OF THE RECTANGULAR SARCOPHAGUS

Despite the highly damaged condition of these elements of the lid, we have some crucial evidence on the size and appearance of Seneb-Kay's outermost burial container. Although the box must have matched the lid's 1.05 m width, we have no direct evidence for the length of the sarcophagus. However, there are limits placed on the possible dimensions of the box by the size of Seneb-Kay's burial chamber (see reconstruction drawing below, Fig. 3.15). The 1.05 m wide sarcophagus would have fit tightly into the 1.5 m wide burial chamber with only a ca. 0.22 m between the sarcophagus and the chamber's side walls. Regarding its length, the disposition of the debris in Chambers 1 and 2 indicates that the 0.41 x 0.50 m canopic chest (see Chapter 4) originally stood at the inner end of the 3.32 m long burial chamber. On this basis, we may estimate the maximum possible length for the sarcophagus at 2.9 m. This dimension would require the sarcophagus and canopic chest to be pushed flush with each other leaving no intervening space. If we allow ca. 0.2 m between the chamber walls and between the two funerary containers, we can reasonably extrapolate an estimated length of 2.3 to 2.4 m for the sarcophagus. Such a dimension appears proportional with the known 1.05 m width based on the lid.[9]

The wall thickness and internal dimensions of the sarcophagus box are unknown, but we can also derive an estimate based on the evidence of the lid battens. Structurally, the 0.15 m width of the battens served to accommodate the curved notch needed to hold the slats that composed the vault of the central part of the lid. However, the 0.15 m width would also have sat directly on the end wall of the box. A common convention in rectangular sarcophagi of both wood and stone is use of a lid batten width that matches the wall thickness of the box below. If we adopt a 0.15 m wall thickness for the box of 1.05 x 2.4 m this suggests a sarcophagus with internal dimensions of approximately 0.75 m (width) and 2.1 m (length). Building on these estimated figures and the evidence provided by the lid, we may now proceed to consider the characteristics of the decorative program on the rectangular sarcophagus.

The box and lid employed a white background and polychrome decoration. We can see from Lid Fragment 2 that the multicolor bands on the lid would have extended downwards onto both the ends and long sides of the box to frame the decorative and textual elements on its outer faces (Fig. 3.13). The format of border bands is indicated by surviving wooden sarcophagi of the late Middle Kingdom and Second Intermediate Period sarcophagi with a similar use of coffered polychrome bands. The sarcophagi of Senebini (Cairo 28029 [Lacau 1904: 77ff and pl. 15]) and

Nubkheredi (Cairo 28030 [Lacau 1904:79; Willems 1988:117, no. 280]), while employing a black rather than white background, have the same arrangement of bands on their lids and suggest the polychrome bands on the corners of the lid would have extended down to the base of the box on the longer sides with the band on the inner corner of the batten turning a 90° angle to frame the upper edge of the box. Below this, the text bands on the outer faces would likely have been framed by a separate series of polychrome borders as occurs on contemporary sarcophagi with both white and black backgrounds. On the head and foot ends of the sarcophagus, the bands likely extended straight downward, framing an internal area where similar polychrome bands formed an inverted U-shape containing text bands and likely a depiction of Isis and Nephthys on opposite ends of the sarcophagus (although different variations occur in the placement of these polychrome border bands).

In connection with the decoration on this outer sarcophagus, one of the questions that arises

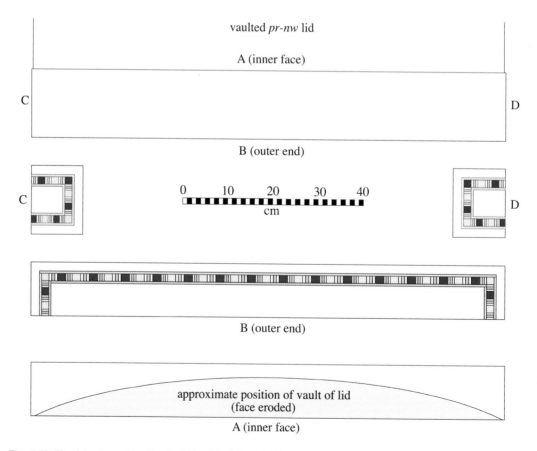

Fig. 3.13 The block end (batten) of the lid of Seneb-Kay's rectangular sarcophagus (Lid Fragment 2).

regarding Seneb-Kay's funerary equipment is: why do the walls of the burial chamber replicate texts and imagery that should have existed on the sarcophagus (and canopic chest) itself? The burial chamber contains a polychrome eye panel (likely originally with a false door below it, as discussed in Chapter 2) as the focal element of the back wall, as well as figures of Isis and Nephthys with upraised arms on the two side walls. These are elements drawn from the repertoire of coffin and sarcophagus decoration. It is a possibility worth considering that the decoration of Seneb-Kay's burial equipment was unfinished, and the requisite funerary images and texts were hastily applied instead to the inner walls of the chamber. The use of texts drawn from the corpus of spells typical of canopic chests could, by the same token, imply that the sarcophagus and canopic chest together did not bear a completed set of texts and imagery.

Although this option cannot be definitively excluded, we would suggest here that the evidence of the polychrome decoration on the lid weighs heavily against the possibility. The time-consuming artistic task of painting the complex, multicolor bands is unlikely to have been completed if other elements of the sarcophagus decoration were not painted at the same time. The bands would not have been painted first, followed secondarily by insertion of the internal imagery and texts. Rather, the whole surface would have been painted as an integrated composition. Consequently, we may be fairly confident that Seneb-Kay's outer sarcophagus bore a completed set of texts and iconography of the type attested on contemporary funerary equipment.

But, what was the nature of the decoration on the sarcophagus box itself? With a white background and polychrome decoration, Seneb-Kay's sarcophagus belongs to a small corpus of white-ground rectangular sarcophagi that can be dated to the timeframe of the late 13th Dynasty to the 16th Dynasty. These include three examples from Abydos: the sarcophagus of the *Scribe of the Temple*, Dedmut; the sarcophagus of the *Royal Ornament*, Nefretnetresi (reinscribed for the *Superintendent of the Ruler's Crew*, Sobekhotep); and the sarcophagus of the *Superintendent of the Ruler's Crew*, Amenemhat. White-ground sarcophagi from Thebes include that of Prince Herunefer and the sarcophagus of Queen Montuhotep, wife of King Djehuty (now lost but documented in watercolors of

John Gardner Wilkinson [Geisen 2004a: taf. 4]), also dated to the late 13th Dynasty (Geisen 2004b:149–157) or early 16th Dynasty (Ryholt 1997:151–160). The surviving examples of these white-ground sarcophagi show chronological and developmental overlap with Upper Egyptian wooden sarcophagi with black backgrounds. Dating to the middle to late 13th Dynasty, the black-ground sarcophagi show an evolution from use of divine speech (*ḏd-mdw*) texts and Pyramid Text spells, to the discrete group of Coffin Text spells 777–785. Where the exteriors are attested, the surviving examples of white-ground sarcophagi all employ CT spells 777–785 on their exteriors while the two Theban examples, those of Herunefer and Queen Mentuhotep also employ early versions of Book of the Dead texts on their interiors (Parkinson and Quirke 1992:37–51). This suggests the white-ground sarcophagi overlap with but extend somewhat later in time than the black-ground examples.

Interestingly, atop their white backgrounds, at least two of these sarcophagi, Herunefer and Queen Mentuhotep, employed polychrome text bands with light blue hieroglyphs painted on a yellow band.[10] This very same color scheme, as well as the use of truncated hieroglyphs that is common to this group of sarcophagi, occurs on the walls of Seneb-Kay's burial chamber suggesting not just a close contemporaneity, but the likelihood that the outer sarcophagus in his tomb employed the same layout as these other white ground sarcophagi. Consequently, the text bands on the burial chamber walls mimic the color format of contemporary white-ground sarcophagi and the actual sarcophagus in Seneb-Kay's tomb would almost certainly have followed these same conventions. We propose a sarcophagus with a decorative program akin to these other white-ground examples as well as the black-ground sarcophagi that also employ CT Spells 777–785. The box would have had a continuation of the polychrome borders we have preserved on the lid. On the head and foot ends would have been text bands and images of Isis and Nephthys framed by these borders. The sides of the box would have borne the prevalent set of Coffin Texts spells 777–785 arrayed in bands, again likely framed with the coffered borders. The box decoration likely followed the convention of nine bands on the right (back) side and eight bands along with a painted eye panel and false door below it on the left (front) of the box (Fig. 3.14).

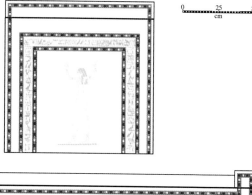

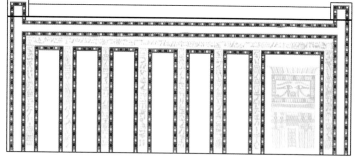

Fig. 3.14 Suggested reconstruction of the format of the polychrome borders on the lid and sarcophagus box (grey details are hypothetical and based on comparanda).

INSTALLATION AND OWNERSHIP OF THE OUTER SARCOPHAGUS

While the lid fragments demonstrate that Seneb-Kay's burial was housed within an elaborately painted, white-ground sarcophagus with polychrome decoration, there is another issue to be considered. In view of the evidence for Seneb-Kay's unexpected death in a martial encounter, paired with the rapid construction of his tomb making use of reused 13th Dynasty masonry, it appears possible that this elaborately painted rectangular sarcophagus was not made for Seneb-Kay but was appropriated from some other preexisting tomb. We might theorize that a decorated sarcophagus expressly made for Seneb-Kay under narrow time constraints may well have dispensed with less crucial decorative features such as the polychrome borders. Indeed, as we have noted, the brushwork of these borders is very well executed at small scale and does not betray any rush to finish decoration of the sarcophagus. This aspect of the painting on the sarcophagus contrasts markedly with the indications for rapid decoration of his burial chamber. Could Seneb-Kay's sarcophagus, like the repurposed cedar boards employed in his canopic box, represent another reused element of his burial assemblage?

If that is the case, the artisans who prepared the burial may simply have altered the name on an existing sarcophagus which was selected to house an anthropoid coffin that had been expressly prepared for the king. This potential reuse of the outer sarcophagus might also elucidate the texts and imagery within the burial chamber. In such a context, the artists were not reduplicating imagery on two different areas of the burial setting, but they were decorating the chamber with key funerary iconography inspired by, and drawing upon, preexisting objects at their disposal. Such a practice would have put a stamp of identity on a burial chamber and assemblage that made extensive use of *spolia* deriving from earlier tombs. However, the decoration of the burial chamber, which mimics the color scheme and elements used on white ground sarcophagi, could have been explicitly painted in a mode that complemented a repurposed sarcophagus.

Related to this question of reuse, one of the key pieces of data provided by the surviving lid fragments from Seneb-Kay's sarcophagus is that this major piece of burial equipment was 1.05 m in width. The cross section of rectangular sarcophagi is typically square or close to square at the ends, and the height of the sarcophagus box is unlikely to have been any less than the width. The opening into the burial chamber of CS9 prior to the addition of the brick chambers was 1.48 m. However, with the addition of the brick jambs against the limestone face the entrance into the burial chamber was reduced to 1.04 m. The other doorways of Seneb-Kay's tomb were yet narrower: the doorway from the pole-roof chamber into the vaulted antechamber was 0.95 m, while the main entrance into the pole-roof chamber was 0.92 m prior to the insertion of the portcullis. Once the portcullis frame was added the main entrance into the tomb was only 0.59 m.

The entirety of the mudbrick construction of CS9 is bonded and clearly built in one phase meaning that the narrowest opening (0.92 m) formed the uppermost size limit for installation of materials into the fully completed tomb. Based on these relative dimensions we can be virtually certain that the rectangular sarcophagus must have been installed inside the burial chamber prior to the completion of the tomb's brick elements. Presumably the sarcophagus, or the entrance to the burial chamber, was protected by fabric or some other material during the final construction phase.[11] The burial ceremony would then have included the deposition of the anthropoid coffin containing the king's body into the already installed outer sarcophagus, and the accompanying canopic chest at the tomb's inner end. The estimated ca. 0.22 m space between the sarcophagus and chamber walls would have been enough to allow men to squeeze into the chamber to install these and other, smaller components of the burial assemblage.

This evidence for the temporal sequence needed to install the outer sarcophagus significantly narrows the time window for preparation and decoration of the elaborately painted outer sarcophagus. This reinforces the possibility that the sarcophagus was reused, and the size of the burial chamber in CS9 was specifically adapted to accommodate the known dimensions of that crucial piece of equipment. It appears impossible to fully confirm or refute the possibility of reuse of the outer sarcophagus. However, consideration of the evidence provided by the reused 13th Dynasty chapel blocks adds further weight to this scenario as we shall consider in Chapter 10.

RECONSTRUCTION OF SENEB-KAY'S BURIAL ASSEMBLAGE

Despite the highly fragmentary state of the evidence, the data are sufficient to assemble a basic picture of the burial equipment of Seneb-Kay. Seneb-Kay

occupied a nested burial with the king's masked body laid to rest inside an anthropoid coffin, which itself sat within a rectangular sarcophagus. As we have seen, the disposition of the materials in Chambers 1–2 indicates that the initial group of tomb robbers who entered via the break in the top of the limestone portcullis first despoiled the sarcophagus and its contents. This involved breaking open the lid, which, owing to its sizeable dimensions and width that exceeded the door opening, was achieved by pulling off the rectangular battens that held the vaulted *per-nu* lid together. Once the ends were torn away, the vault of the lid itself would have disintegrated into fragments that were easily removed to provide access to the contents of the box. The bulk of this material, including the inner coffin and mask, was broken up and taken out of the tomb while the king's body was ransacked and thrown onto the floor of the pole-roof chamber.

Following the removal of the sarcophagus and its contents, they proceeded to rob the canopic chest. The canopic chest is the only part of the burial assemblage that was recovered nearly in its entirety. As the final container to be stripped of its contents, it was thrown on top of the body of the king, which had come to rest along with some discarded elements of his mask, a few splinters of the anthropoid coffin, as well as the two ends of the sarcophagus lid. These spatial patterns demonstrate that the sarcophagus occupied the outer (western) end of the burial chamber while the canopic chest sat at the inner (eastern) end. This relative position of sarcophagus and canopic chest follows the conventions seen in the earlier 13th Dynasty royal tombs (S9 and S10) at South Abydos, as well as the architectural indications from several other Second Intermediate Period tombs that the canopic chest was deposited at the inner end of the burial chamber (particularly CS 8, CS10, and CS11, see Chapter 11). In all likelihood, the body was oriented with the feet towards the canopic chest, a convention attested in late Middle Kingdom royal tombs such as that of King Auibre Hor or Princess Nubheptikhered at Dahshur (De Morgan 1895: fig. 211). Indeed, this was an arrangement for royal burials that continued into later periods.

One of the implications of the recovered elements is that Seneb-Kay's burial equipment represents a supine burial with the king's body placed on his back within the nested containers. The late

Middle Kingdom and Second Intermediate Period was a phase of change in body position that appears to be connected with the broader shift from rectangular to anthropoid coffins. This development was not unilinear. There is clear evidence for concomitant use of burials positioned on the side (following the earlier Middle Kingdom preference), as well as supine burials (Bourriau 2001:1–20). Supine burials became predominant during the late 13th Dynasty and Second Intermediate Period, a trend that appears to be associated with the growing popularity of cartonnage face masks and anthropoid coffins that substantially supplanted rectangular sarcophagi by the New Kingdom.

Particularly intriguing in the case of Seneb-Kay's burial equipment is that we seem to have the significant probability of a composite burial that made use of an earlier, reused outer sarcophagus paired with an anthropoid coffin and face mask expressly made for his burial.

While we may be virtually certain the burial was supine, this white-ground sarcophagus would—with almost equal certainty—have been decorated following the long-established convention of an eye panel and false door on the head end, notionally opposite the face of the deceased: a reflection of earlier customs of body orientation. Retention of that decorative element is attested as late as the 13th Dynasty to 16th Dynasty transition in the sarcophagus of Queen Montuhotep (Geisen 2004a). It appears quite probable the presence of the eye panel and false door at that relatively late stage was a long-engrained convention that ultimately became disassociated from the earlier position of the body on its side with the face towards the false door. Nevertheless, the use (or reuse) of a sarcophagus of this format would likely have recognized the association of the false door motif with the head of the deceased, even in the altered context of a supine burial. Therefore, the panel should have faced toward the north wall, while the opposite side of the box which would have born texts only was oriented towards the south (as reconstructed in Fig. 3.15).

Consequently, Seneb-Kay may have been buried in a supine, nested burial but making use of a reused sarcophagus decorated in a mode that derived from earlier funerary traditions of the Middle Kingdom. If so, we may find here a partial explanation for certain aspects of the wall decoration in the burial chamber of CS9 that replicated the iconography and texts of

sarcophagi and canopic chests, but with the eye panel and false door now positioned on the eastern (foot) end of the chamber. The change in burial orientation and the use of a supine mode of burial may have created an impetus for decorating the chamber with an additional false door in a location now notionally opposite the face of the deceased (see comments of Wegner 2017b:493–494).

In spite of the scant remains that have survived from Seneb-Kay's burial equipment, we have indications for the overall nature of the assemblage that allow us to consider its chronological affinities in relation to mortuary traditions of the late Middle Kingdom and Second Intermediate Period. As we have seen, the burial contained a *rishi*-style cartonnage mask that shows close similarities to late Middle Kingdom and early Second Intermediate Period painted masks, particularly those in the second phase of the Mirgissa group dating from the late 13th Dynasty through the 16th/17th Dynasties. The few fragments of Seneb-Kay's anthropoid coffin provide insufficient data to specifically address its relationship to other coffins of the era. But, judging from the style of the mask, this was likely also in *rishi*-style and may have been a forerunner to the fully developed *rishi* coffins that emerge slightly later with the Theban 17th Dynasty (Miniaci and Quirke 2008:5–25; Miniaci 2008:247–274). These elements were placed inside a white-ground, polychrome sarcophagus of a type that probably bore Coffin Texts 777–785. With close parallels at both Abydos and Thebes during the late 13th Dynasty to 16th Dynasty transition, it is the style and color scheme of this sarcophagus that appears to be emulated in the wall decoration of Seneb-Kay's burial chamber.

The practice of depositing anthropoid coffins within an outer, rectangular sarcophagus, as occurs with Seneb-Kay, appears to have been comparatively rare for the Second Intermediate Period. However, it appears this may have been more common for royal burials than is directly attested in the archaeological record.[12] We have a sizeable sample of anthropoid royal coffins for the Theban 17th Dynasty, but most of these were found out of context in the 1881 Deir el-Bahri royal mummy cache or during early 19th century excavations in Western Thebes. For the early 17th Dynasty, we find indications for a nested mode of burial in the well-known passage in Papyrus Leopold II-Amherst that records the testimony of robbers

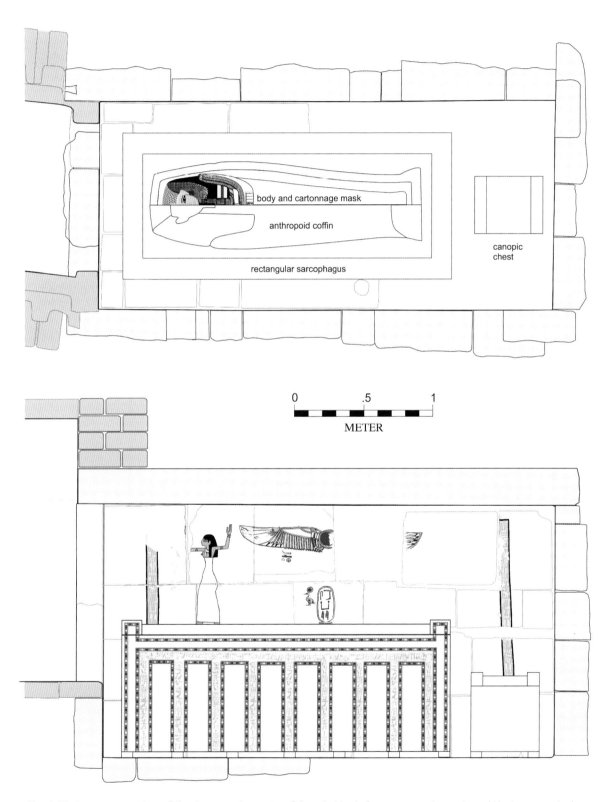

Fig. 3.15 A reconstruction of the known elements of Seneb-Kay's funerary equipment and their suggested disposition in the burial chamber.

who had despoiled the burial of Sekhemre-Shedtway Sobekemsaf II and his wife Nubkhaas (Peet 1930:45–51 and pls. 4–5). That account describes the opening of the king and queen's outer sarcophagi (*dbꜣwt*) and apparently their inner coffins (*wtw*) to reveal the mummy adorned with funerary mask (*tptyw*) and an array of amulets, jewelry, and, in the case of Sobekemsaf II, weapons.[13] The despoiled remnants of Seneb-Kay's burial assemblage broadly reflect a robbery process similar to that described in the case of Sobekemsaf II, and perhaps a similar ensemble of nested burial equipment to that listed in P. Leopold II-Amherst.

The funerary equipment of Seneb-Kay appears to reflect a unique confluence of historical, political, and economic circumstances. Taken as an assemblage, the surviving evidence appears to fit with the king's reign falling in the transitional period that accompanied the end of the 13th Dynasty and coeval with the Theban 16th Dynasty. The evidence of Seneb-Kay's tomb suggests that this same timeframe witnessed the rise to power of an independent line of kings buried at Abydos.

NOTES:

3.1 Here we use the term *coffin* for the inner, anthropoid container. *Sarcophagus* is used for the outer, rectangular case (for remarks on the terminology see Ikram and Dodson 1998:193, 244).

3.2 The *wesekh*, or "broad collar," is an element of jewelry composed of bands of multicolor cylindrical beads and a lower band of teardrop shaped beads, often with falcon-headed ends. The *wesekh* is usually depicted in painted form on coffins and funerary masks (for varying forms of the *wesekh* see Mace and Winlock [1916:64–68]). For an example of a *wesekh* from a late Middle Kingdom royal burial, see for instance the burial of Neferuptah (Farag and Iskander [1971:66–70 and pl. 40]).

3.3 For example, Louvre E25706; E26024 and E26042 (Rigault-Déon 2012, 90–91 and 172–175). The feature occurs with slight color variation on a majority of the Mirgissa masks. The plumage pattern on Seneb-Kay's mask appears to correspond to "Type 1" defined for the Mirgissa masks in which the plumes directly abut each other. Rigault-Déon (2012: 34–35) has suggested a chronological development with the closely abutted plumes typical of earlier masks (late 12th -early 13th Dynasty), but variations may be also due to other factors.

3.4 Use of black wigs alone are attested in the group of early Middle Kingdom funerary masks from the Asyut region (e.g., Louvre E 11995 [Rigault-Déon 2012:42–44] or Walters Art Museum 78.4 [Oppenheim et al. 2015:234–235]) but dating well before the advent of the *rishi*-style. Post-dating the Second Intermediate Period we may note also the solid black wig on the early 18th Dynasty coffin of Amenhotep I.

3.5 Here we may note examples such as the *rishi*-coffin of the *Lady of the House*, Reri, which has wide black bands in this same position (Miniaci 2011a: pl. 6a), or the coffin of the *Commander of the Crew of the Ruler*, Teti, with green lappets (Miniaci 2011a: pl. 2a).

3.6 The burning of coffins by tomb robbers occurs in the 20th Dynasty in the confessions recorded in P. Leopold II -Amherst (Peden 1994:248–251).

3.7 For comparative purposes, dimensions of 17th Dynasty royal coffins include the following: Nubkheperre Antef (0.58 x 1.93 m); Heruhirmaat Antef (0.48 x 1.88 m); Wepmaat Antef (0.57 x 2.00 m) and queen Ahhotep (0.66 x 2.12 m). Theban 17th Dynasty anthropoid coffins of the *rishi* type are generally assumed not to have been housed inside a rectangular outer sarcophagus (Miniaci 2011a:151–152). However, none of the royal examples were discovered in situ. Moreover, there are instances of anthropoid coffins of the *rishi* type deposited within rectangular sarcophagi, albeit late in their development (e.g., Miniaci 2011a: 277, 303). Rectangular sarcophagi were certainly in use during the late Second Intermediate Period, and it is possible that many of these royal anthropoid coffins originally had an outer sarcophagus, as we can now demonstrate occurs slightly earlier in the tomb of Seneb-Kay.

3.8 The *per-nu* sarcophagus is one that employs a vaulted lid with flat ends. This common form appears to derive from the architectural appearance of the *per-nu*, the symbolic sanctuary of Lower Egypt connected with the site of Buto and location of the cult of the tutelary Lower Egyptian deity Wadjet (Ikram and Dodson 1998:195).

3.9 There is no standard convention for ratio between length and width of rectangular sarcophagi, but they typically fall in the 2.5:1 to 3:1 range.

3.10 The color of the text bands on the Abydos whiteground sarcophagi is not explicitly recorded. In at least one case, the sarcophagus in tomb X3 (Nefretnetresi/ Sobekhotep) the black and white photograph is suggestive of blue or multicolor hieroglyphs on a yellow background (see photograph and discussion here in Chapter 10).

3.11 Due to the size of the sarcophagus receptacles and the relatively narrow dimensions of the doorways in the Second Intermediate Period tombs at South Abydos, it appears it must have been a common practice to install rectangular sarcophagi prior to completion of the tomb's brick elements. While we cannot assume use of rectangular sarcophagi in all cases this is at least confirmed in the case of CS9.

3.12 In the late 12th Dynasty, the burial of Senebtisi employed two nested rectangular sarcophagi with an inner anthropoid coffin (Mace and Winlock 1916:23–56). The practice was likely common in the late Middle Kingdom and Second Intermediate Period for elite and royal funerary assemblages.

3.13 The terminology used in P. Leopold-Amherst II is generally translated to indicate a situation of nested coffins: an outer sarcophagus and inner coffin containing the masked mummy within. The terms *ḏb3t* and *wt* may be interpreted alternatively as indicating mummy wrappings (*wt*) and a single outer coffin.

4

The Canopic Chest*

From a historical perspective, one of the most significant and intriguing objects recovered from the tomb of Seneb-Kay is the king's canopic chest, including both the box and lid that compose the chest (Fig. 4.1).[1] Like the reused masonry employed in the construction of the burial chamber itself, the cedar planks composing Seneb-Kay's canopic chest exhibit telltale markings of a complex sequence of reuse. Not only does the canopic chest hold clues to understanding the historical context of Seneb-Kay's reign, but also it contains information on earlier royal funerary assemblages of the 13th Dynasty. Some of these points have been discussed in connection to Seneb-Kay's sarcophagus. But, as we now examine, patterns of reuse represent a pervasive trait of the funerary equipment of Seneb-Kay. Here we will firstly examine the phases of use and reuse of the wood that compose the canopic chest, investigating the earlier incarnation of the wooden planks in a rectangular sarcophagus of one of the 13th Dynasty Sobekhotep kings. Secondly, we will discuss the way these planks were refashioned into a canopic chest for Seneb-Kay and consider its relationship with other known canopic chests of the Second Intermediate Period.

This chapter written by Kevin Cahail and Josef Wegner.

Fig. 4.1 (facing and left) Two views showing the disposition of the canopic box of Seneb-Kay during its excavation and removal in 2014.

PHYSICAL ATTRIBUTES OF THE CANOPIC CHEST

The canopic chest of Seneb-Kay had a rectangular footprint, with two batten legs on its base, and—like the king's rectangular sarcophagus—a *per-nu* shaped lid. The box and lid were composed of cedar (*Cedrus* sp., probably *Cedrus libani*), the natural oils of which helped to deter insect damage over the millennia (Gale et al. 2000:349–350). Nonetheless, when we discovered the box, it was in a highly friable state,

making the intact removal of the box impossible. The surface of the wood was mostly degraded and effaced, which was something of a mixed blessing. Though the surface treatment contemporary with Seneb-Kay was nearly entirely decayed, the poor state of preservation laid bare an earlier phase of decoration and use. This situation led to the unavoidable conclusion that the wood from which Seneb-Kay's canopic chest was constructed originally belonged to an object that dated to an earlier period.

As a result of the haste with which the tomb of Seneb-Kay was robbed, the canopic chest rested in three distinct pieces inside the tomb. The main body of the box was found in the pole-roof chamber (Chamber 1), near the doorway into the antechamber (Chamber 2). A large piece of the lid was also lying on the floor at the western end of Chamber 1. The final piece of the lid was discovered along the north wall of Chamber 2. Interestingly, the locations of these pieces reflect both the sequence of events that took place during the tomb's robbery, as well as the original location of the king's sarcophagus and canopic chest within the burial chamber (see the positions of the elements in Fig. 1.17).

Turning to look at the box itself, despite its poor state of preservation, we were able to record remains of blue-painted hieroglyphic texts on the exterior surfaces. Three fundamental features of these texts are of importance in understanding the history of the object. Firstly, there was a partial cartouche on the upward facing surface (Side A: Fig. 4.2). This fact demonstrates that the decoration belonged to a royal individual. Secondly, the name recorded reads *(Sbk-ḥtp) mꜣꜥ-ḥrw, (Sobekhotep) true of voice,* (with the king's nomen in cartouche) and not Seneb-Kay. Therefore, the painted texts are not contemporary with the king in whose tomb the canopic chest was used. Finally, the few preserved hieroglyphs representing animals were drawn in a truncated style—a feature which is chronologically diagnostic, placing the decoration in the 13th Dynasty or Second Intermediate Period (Miniaci 2010a:113–134).

Based solely on these three observations, it seems prudent to propose two phases in the use of the wood that composed the box. In Phase 1, the wood was part of a sarcophagus belonging to a pharaoh named Sobekhotep (N), a king who either reigned during the 13th Dynasty, when truncated hieroglyphs were common in funerary texts, or who was a close contemporary of Seneb-Kay, whose tomb also makes use of truncated hieroglyphs.[2] Phase 2 then represents a period during which the sarcophagus of Sobekhotep (N) was disassembled, and a much smaller box was built for Seneb-Kay using only a portion of the original planks from the Sobekhotep sarcophagus. We turn firstly to examine the surviving texts and their disposition on the canopic box.

PHASE I: TEXTS OF THE SARCOPHAGUS OF SOBEKHOTEP (N)

The cedar wood used to create Seneb-Kay's canopic box was formed into planks about 5 cm thick. The inner surface of this wood was unfinished but exhibited traces of black resin staining. On the exterior, three sides of Seneb-Kay's canopic box bear recognizable traces of earlier inscriptions: Side A, Side C, and the bottom of the box, Side E (Fig. 4.3). The text of Side A was the best preserved and exemplifies the features common to all of the texts. The exterior background color of the original sarcophagus was a vibrant yellow. Atop this base color, the funerary

Fig. 4.2 View of Side A of Seneb-Kay's canopic box during excavation. The original texts dating to the 13th Dynasty can be seen at the left of the box, painted in blue on a yellow background.

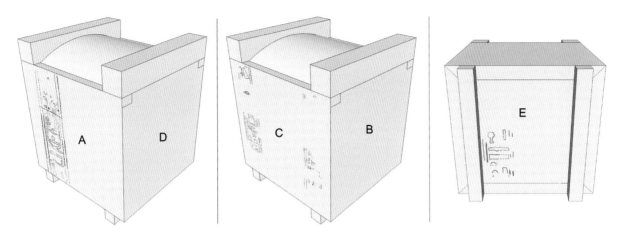

Fig. 4.3 Three views of Seneb-Kay's canopic box showing its shape, and the locations of the original Sobekhotep texts. Letters A–E have been assigned to each of the sides and the bottom.

texts were arranged in single columns with a left to right orientation. The hieroglyphs were uniformly painted in light blue, without visible highlights or corrections in a secondary color. Consequently, the text was purposefully designed to be monochromatic. The text columns were bordered on either side by bands painted light blue inside a black outline. The columns measure ca. 8 to 9.5 cm in total width from the outside of both borders, and the distance between columns on Side C is about 24 cm.

The text on Side A records a portion of royal titulary: /// ny-swt-bỉty (Sbk-ḥtp) mȝꜥ-ḫrw///,...*King of Upper and Lower Egypt, (Sobekhotep)|, true of voice...* (Figs. 4.4 and 4.5). Although damaged, enough remained of the bee hieroglyph to ascertain that it was deliberately drawn without a head. Incomplete or truncated hieroglyphs such as this, which appear in both the texts of Sobekhotep (N) and those decorating Seneb-Kay's burial chamber, were used from the late Middle Kingdom into the Second Intermediate Period on objects that were interred below ground near the body of the deceased, such as canopic chests and coffins (Miniaci, 2010a:113–134).[3]

Side C retained portions of two columns of text with the hieroglyphs all facing left (Figs. 4.6 and 4.7). As with the bee hieroglyph on Side A, the quail chick (Gardiner G43) and horned viper (Gardiner I9) in the left column were drawn in the truncated style (Fig. 4.8). The left column was the wider of the two, measuring ca. 9.5 cm between exterior borders. The right column was ca. 8 cm wide. While it is possible that this is simply the result of minor variation in the

decoration, it seems probable that the text columns alternated between wide and thin. In looking at the text itself, the left-hand column reads: /// sw //// ỉr//// rdy.ty.fy ỉp///, while the right column retains traces of //ḥw].n Ḥrw ḥ[w.tw///. Despite the highly fragmentary nature of these texts, according to R. van der Molen, there is only one attestation of the verb rdỉ in the sḏm.ty.fy form in the Coffin Texts corpus—namely CT VI:412.a (Spell 781) (van der Molen 2005:1213). Given the clarity with which the writing of the rdỉ.ty.fy and the following ỉp[.f] appear, coupled with the proximity of the //[ḥw].n Ḥrw ḥ[w.tw /// fragment in the next text column, the identification of the Side C text as CT Spell 781 is certain (Fig. 4.9). These two highly fragmentary texts are the key to identifying all the spells of the Phase I decoration as belonging to the sequence of CT Spells 777–785.[4]

The bottom of the box, Side E, retained traces of a few hieroglyphic signs and the borders of what appeared to be a narrow text column, measuring ca. 8 cm wide (Fig. 4.10 and 4.11). As with the texts from Sides A and C, the text here reads from left to right. The fragment retains the phrase: /// ḥr sštȝ ///, and belongs to CT Spell 782 (CT VI:412.j: Fig. 4.12). No other texts were preserved on the surface of the box but, given the striking similarity in the quality of the wood itself, all the planks doubtless originate from the same Sobekhotep (N) sarcophagus.

The traces of text appearing on Sides A, C, and E belong, at the very least, to CT Spells 781 and 782. All seven attestations of these two spells occur within the complete series of Spells 777–785. Consequently,

Fig. 4.4 Side A, showing the position of the original Sobekhotep (N) cartouche, which may belong to Coffin Texts Spell 780. The circular feature in the center of the drawing is a remnant of plaster and paint. The plaster dates to Phase 1 and has yellow paint on it. It was then hastily painted over with white during Phase 2, leaving a small amount of the yellow showing through.

Fig. 4.5 Detail of the original Sobekhotep cartouche on the left side of Side A.

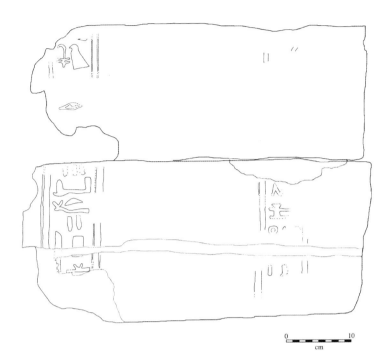

Fig. 4.6 (left) Side C of the canopic box showing the two surviving columns of text from Coffin Texts Spell 781. The left column is slightly wider than the right.

Fig. 4.7 (below) The central and lower parts of Side C showing the use of yellow background and blue painted texts still preserved from the original Sobekhotep cedar coffin.

we can safely conclude that the same group of spells originally occurred on the Sobekhotep (N) sarcophagus. This being the case, the Sobekhotep (N) source not only adds a new, eighth exemplar to the group of seven known sources, but this is also the first identifiable evidence for this textual corpus on a royal sarcophagus of the 13th Dynasty.[5]

RECONSTRUCTING THE SARCOPHAGUS OF KING SOBEKHOTEP (N)

Having gained a clearer picture of what texts originally decorated the Sobekhotep (N) sarcophagus, we turn now to examine the structure and layout of the

Fig. 4.8 Detail of the truncated hieroglyphs used in the original 13th Dynasty Coffin Texts preserved on Side C: truncated *f*-viper (left) and *w*-quail chick (right).

Spell 781

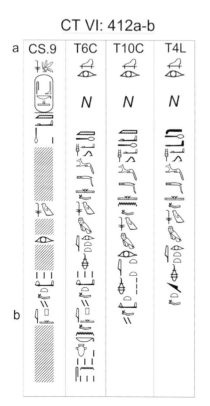

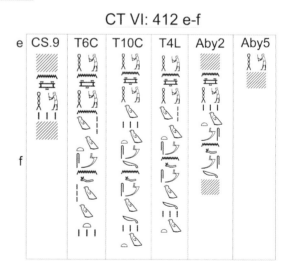

Fig. 4.9 Interlinear transcription of CTVI: 412a–b and CTVI: 412e–f comparing the position of text fragments from the Sobekhotep (N) coffin (Sides A and C, siglum CS9) against the only other known sources of CT Spell 781.

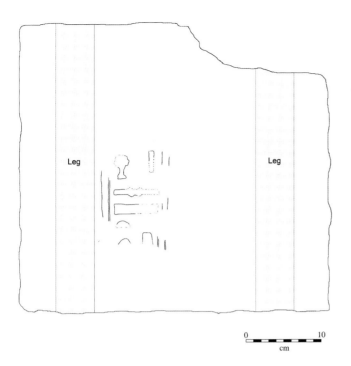

Fig. 4.10 (left) The bottom of the canopic box, Side E, showing a fragment of text belonging to CT Spell 782. The two grey areas marked "leg" are the positions of the two battens which were pegged to the bottom of the box.

Fig. 4.11 (left) View of the bottom of the canopic box during excavation showing the small preserved area of original texts from CT Spell 782.

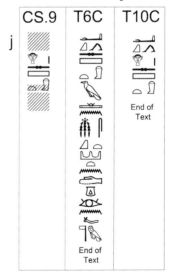

Fig. 4.12 Interlinear transcription of CTVI: 412j–k, comparing the position of text fragments from the Sobekhotep (N) coffin (Side E) against the only other known sources of Coffin Texts Spell 782.

object based on its extant fragments. For comparison we will employ the two well-preserved sarcophagi of Khonsu and Senebini from Thebes, mentioned above (T6C and T10C). Both sarcophagi are decorated with CT Spells 777–785 and follow very similar layouts in terms of the locations and order of the texts on the sarcophagi. Harco Willems and other scholars have pointed out that text bands on the exterior of Middle Kingdom coffins were meant to be legible by the deceased, thus their hieroglyphic signs all pointed toward the head end of the box (Willems 1988:119). This holds true for both T6C and T10C bearing CT Spells 777–785 (Lacau 1904: pl. XV; Grajetzki 2010a:86–87). Since all the hieroglyphs of the original Sobekhotep (N) texts are read from left to right, all of these texts must derive from the back face of the original sarcophagus.[6]

As mentioned above, close examination of the fragmentary texts from Side C of the canopic box indicates that the columns were of two slightly different widths. The column on the left was ca. 9.5 cm wide (measured from the exterior of the border bands), while the column to its right had a narrower width of ca. 8 cm. Furthermore, the distance between the two columns was ca. 23 to 24 cm. Both T6C and T10C have nine columns of text on the back, which alternate between wide and narrow format.[7] Using these measurements, and assuming that the sarcophagus of Sobkehotep (N) also had nine columns on its back (five wide and four narrow), we can extrapolate an overall exterior length of the sarcophagus of ca. 2.7 m.

Based on these comparanda, the wooden sarcophagus of Sobekhotep (N) originally had nine columns of text on its back, which alternated between wide and narrow widths (Fig. 4.13).[8] Two dark blue painted lines served as simple borders for these columns. The hieroglyphs were drawn using a lighter blue paint and were rendered in the truncated style typical of the period. The background both inside and outside the text columns appeared at the time of excavation to have been a light yellow, perhaps imitating a more expensive covering of gold foil. No indication of the lid to the sarcophagus has yet been found. This reconstruction of the Sobekhotep (N) sarcophagus correlates closely with the internal dimensions of the burial chamber of tomb S10 just south of Seneb-Kay's tomb. The sarcophagus recess in S10 measures 2.75 m long, 1.19 m wide, and 1.32 m deep. Sobekhotep (N)'s painted cedar sarcophagus would have fit quite perfectly into the burial chamber of tomb S10 for which it therefore may have been tailor-made (Fig. 4.14).[9]

DATE OF THE SOBEKHOTEP (N) SARCOPHAGUS

Published examples of the CT 777–785 group all belong to coffins originating from either Thebes or Abydos, with the majority stemming from the latter site.[10] However, with only eight known attestations—including the sarcophagus of Sobekhotep (N)—it is

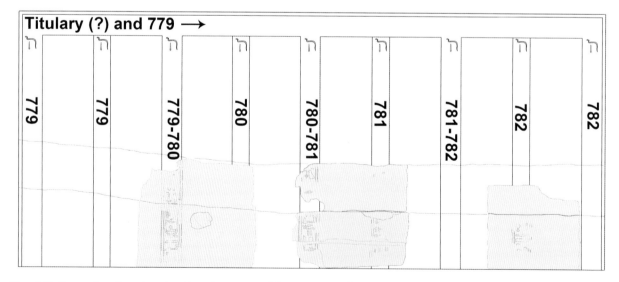

Fig. 4.13 Reconstruction showing the placement of fragments A, C, and E on the back of the sarcophagus of Sobekhotep (N). The numbers refer to Coffin Texts spells. The grey lines show the possible positions of the plank edges.

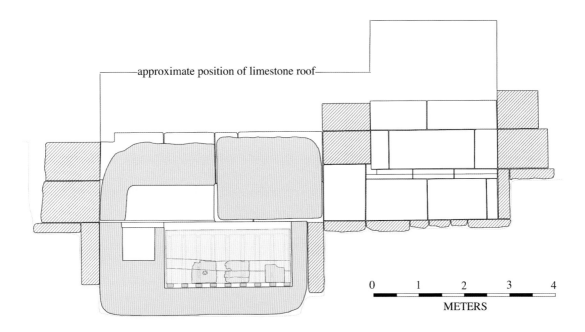

approximate position of limestone roof

0   1   2   3   4
METERS

Fig. 4.14 Sectional view of the burial chamber of tomb S10 at South Abydos showing the suggested origin of the reused planks in the painted sarcophagus of Sobekhotep (N).

tempting to see the use of the texts as belonging to a short period of time within the late Middle Kingdom or Second Intermediate Period, perhaps originating with the royal sphere before being adapted by or disseminated to a finite group of non-royal individuals.

In looking at the chronological span of these sources, Grajetzki dated the coffin of an individual he calls "Zemathor" (siglum Aby5), one of the exemplars of CT series 777–785, to the 13th Dynasty, between the reigns of Sobekhotep II to Sobekhotep IV (Grajetzki 2010a:8, 9, 94). On the other end of the spectrum, Berlev attempted to date the two Theban sources (T6C and T10C) to the reign of a very late 13th Dynasty King Sewahenre Sonebmijew (Berlev 1974:106–113). This date has also been employed to place the sarcophagus of Queen Montuhotep at the very end of the 13th Dynasty (Geisen 2004a:11–17). Grajetzki on the other hand indicated that Berlev's assertion alone was not enough to place Mentuhotep's sarcophagus reliably (Grajetzki 2010a:46–47). At the very least, little can be said about Sewahenre's position within the 13th Dynasty other than the probability that his reign occurred near the very end of the period.[11] Nevertheless, based on Berlev's dating of T6C and T10C, scholars have traditionally seen this group of Coffin Texts as a very late 13th Dynasty creation.

However, if one examines Berlev's evidence critically, there is good reason to correct his dating arguments for the late 13th Dynasty (Cahail 2015:110–112). In its broad strokes, Berlev's argument is based on his assumption that the coffin and canopic chest of the *rḫ-nswt*, Senebini, and a staff belonging to the *ḫtmty-bíty ímy-r ꜣḥwt*, Senebni, both from the purchased Golénischeff collection, belonged to the same person. Since all the objects in question derived from an antiquities dealer, and neither the names nor titles match among the sources, dating Khonsu (T6C) and Senebini (T10C) to the reign of Sewahenre is, in fact, highly unlikely.

On the other hand, a stela from Karnak now in Cairo (JE37507) mentions a daughter of the *Priest of Amun*, Senebef, who is called the *Royal Ornament*, Khonsu (Legrain 1902:213; Bazin and el-Enany 2010:1–23). This name and title are identical to those appearing on the sarcophagus CG28028 (= T6C) and canopic chest Moscow I ia 5358, which was one of the foci of Berlev's article. As we will examine in Chapter 10, Senebef's daughter Khonsu is a contemporary of the *Overseer of Fields*, Dedtu's son Neferhotep, who appears in P.Boulaq 18 (Cahail 2015). This correspondence means that Khonsu's death and burial date to the mid-13th Dynasty, around the time of Neferhotep

I and Sobekhotep IV or slightly later and not to the end of the dynasty during the reign of the unplaced King Sewahenre.[12]

Furthermore, as discussed in Chapters 9 and 10, the white-ground sarcophagi belonging to the *Superintendent of the Ruler's* Crew Amenemhat and his probable wife, the *Royal Ornament* Nefretnetresi (Abydos tomb Z2A and X3 respectively), can also be dated to a time just slightly later than Khonsu and Senebini. Amenemhat was probably the son of the *Overseer of the Offering Tables of Amun*, Ibiau, and therefore grandson of the *Overseer of Fields*, Dedtu (the two men for whom we have reused chapel blocks in the construction of Seneb-Kay's burial chamber). This correlation means that five of the eight exemplars of the CT 777–785 series are closely dateable to the reigns of Neferhotep I and Sobekhotep IV or just slightly after.

This reanalyzed date has important implications for the CT Spell series 777–785 on the sarcophagus of Sobekhotep (N) from South Abydos. Though we lack a clear picture of royal funerary texts during the 13th Dynasty, those appearing on the sarcophagus of Awibre Hor from his tomb at Dahshur certainly do not include CT Spells 777–785. Likewise, CT Spells 777–785 do not appear on sources in the late 12th Dynasty nor on any preserved sources of the later Second Intermediate Period. These facts point to the probability that kings did not employ CT Spells 777–785 until after the reign of Awibre Hor and only did so for a short period of time prior to the Theban 17th Dynasty.

Therefore, since king Sobekhotep (N)'s sarcophagus included CT Spells 777–785, the date of his burial must have occurred after that of Awibre Hor. Such a date excludes both Sekhemrekhutawy Sobekhotep I and Khaankhre Sobekhotep II as possible matches for Sobekhotep (N). Given that the other individuals who have this series of spells on their sarcophagi lived and served in royal administrative positions during the reigns of Neferhotep I and Sobekhotep IV, it is highly likely that the Sobekhotep (N) in question is none other than Sobekhotep IV himself (Wegner and Cahail 2015). Such a close contemporaneity argues for the emergence and usage of this group of spells within both the 13th Dynasty royal and elite spheres concurrently. However, only high officials and family members of the king would have been afforded access to these spells, and in the context of the political and cultural changes that occurred concomitant with

the end of the 13th Dynasty the texts did not survive into the following eras.

PHASE II: THE CANOPIC CHEST OF SENEB-KAY

Sometime after the interment of Sobekhotep (N), likely equating with Sobekhotep IV in his tomb S10 at South Abydos, that king's burial chamber was reopened, and the wooden elements of his sarcophagus removed for reuse. It remains uncertain when the burial of Sobekhotep (N) was plundered but at least a portion of the back of the wooden sarcophagus was still intact and available contemporary with Woseribre Seneb-Kay, allowing his artisans to reuse the cedar to construct his canopic box. The phenomenon of the reuse of the cedar from the sarcophagus of Sobekhotep (N) in the burial of Seneb-Kay provides a general temporal framework.

Clearly the wood must have been in reasonably good condition to have been viable for reuse in the funerary equipment of Seneb-Kay. We can see from the preservation of black resin on the interior that it must have been buried and protected both by its surface treatment as well as through virtue of being sealed in a stone burial chamber. This context would have enhanced the protection of the wood which may otherwise have been subject to insect damage. Even cedar, which is one of the most resilient woods due to its aromatic oils, can be subject to rapid decay in the cemeteries at Abydos through fluctuations in moisture near the desert surface and concomitant insect damage.[13] The deep, protected context of the 13th Dynasty monolithic burial chambers such as tombs S9 and S10 would have contributed to the viability of the wood approximately a century later. If the original royal owner of the sarcophagus of Sobekhotep (N) was Sobekhotep IV, we can estimate that a period on the order of 70–120 years had elapsed before that king's tomb was entered and the wood taken for reuse.[14]

Clearly the cedar planks that went into Seneb-Kay's canopic chest represent only a fraction of the wood that would have come from the large rectangular sarcophagus of Sobekhotep (N). The wood may have been used for multiple purposes, but some of what was generated by this form of state-supported tomb robbery was still available at the time

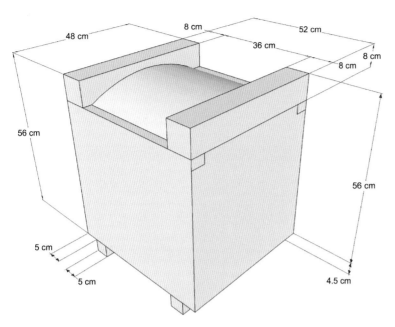

Fig. 4.15 Schematic diagram showing the dimensions of the Seneb-Kay canopic chest.

of Seneb-Kay's death and burial. We now move on to examine the specific details of the canopic chest that was formed for Seneb-Kay beginning with the its physical structure and construction methods. Due to the retrieval of the entirety of both the body and lid of the canopic chest, we have a full set of evidence on its dimensions and the carpentry techniques used in its construction (Fig. 4.15). This has permitted fabrication of a 1:2 scale replica which we illustrate here in order to help explain the details of the badly decayed elements of the canopic chest.

THE LID

In its finished form, Seneb-Kay's canopic chest consisted of two separable parts: the lid, and the box

itself. The lid took form of a *per-nu* shrine, with two rectangular ends and a curved central section connecting them. In many ways, the lid served to define the appearance of the entire container. In overall dimensions, the lid was 52 cm in length (or 1 royal cubit) by 48 cm in width (Fig. 4.15). These measurements correspond perfectly to the dimensions of the box discussed below, leaving no doubt that the two objects belonged together. The two end blocks of the lid measured roughly 8 cm square at the ends (about 4 digits or 1 palm, being 7.6 cm) and 48 cm in length. The interior faces of these two rectangular blocks had a curved rabbet cut into them to accept the three boards that composed the arched central portion of the lid. This rabbet extended roughly halfway through the thickness of the end blocks, about 4 cm (2 digits). The central curved portion of the lid was pinned to the end boards with thin dowels. These dowels were drilled at opposite angles to one another in such a way that the individual planks were locked together permanently once they were inserted without the use of adhesive.

The central portion of the lid consisted of three planks (Fig. 4.16), which were also pinned together with wooden dowels, though the technique used here was slightly different. In this case, the dowel holes were drilled perpendicular to the two faces that the carpenter wished to join. In this way, the dowels acted as floating tenons between the pieces. These dowels kept the three pieces aligned as a single unit, but it was only the dowel pins connecting the exterior planks of the center to the two end blocks that kept the entire lid together as one piece.

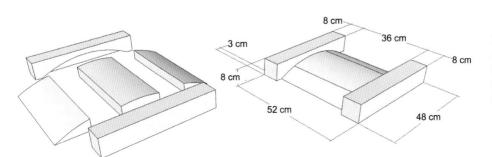

Fig. 4.16 Exploded view of the lid construction (left) and measurements of the assembled lid (right).

Fig. 4.17 The central portion of the lid as found in the pole-roof chamber (Chamber 1) with one end block still attached. Areas of plaster and white pigment still existed on the curved central portion.

Fig. 4.18 One of the two end blocks of the lid (right), lying as found in Chamber 2, next to a large fragment of Seneb-Kay's sarcophagus (Lid Fragment 2). The curved rabbet meant to accept the lid planks is clearly visible, as is the white coloring on the exterior of the box.

The three central planks were curved on their upper surfaces, creating the gentle arc of the *per-nu* shrine form (Figs. 4.17–4.18). The underside of these planks was flat, which contrasts with the common technique of using thin curved boards to create the central section. Using flat boards, which also derived from the Sobekhotep IV sarcophagus, would have been faster and easier than cutting and bending thin planks. However, making the central portion of the lid in this way meant that the edges were extremely thin and fragile. To compensate for this, these edges were set back from the full width of the end boards by about 3 cm on each side, which was enough to protect these sharp corners from being bumped and marred. Despite this feature, the overall width of the central portion of the lid still adequately covered the cavity in the box.

Despite attempts to ascertain a closing mechanism for the chest, there appeared to be no battens or pegs on the bottom of the lid meant to seat into the top of the box below. One possibility is that, in the haste to construct the chest, the craftsman never added these features. The lid would have adequately sat atop the box, as long as it wasn't inverted or bumped during transit. Another possibility is that pegs were drilled through the ends of the lid into the box, in order to permanently affix the two pieces. This situation would explain why the lid was found torn apart into two pieces in the tomb. Robbers would have pulled the lid apart by holding onto one of the two end blocks. Applying force resulted in the dislocation of one of these end blocks, allowing the robber to pry off the rest of the lid in one piece. The most plausible explanation for the deposition pattern of the lid within the tomb is that it was originally affixed to the box in some way; the robbers broke it into two pieces while attempting to open the sealed chest.

Once the five constituent lid pieces were joined with pegs, the finished lid was coated in a thin white gypsum plaster. Ostensibly, this coating was instrumental in evening out the voids and imperfections in the wood, such as grain patterns and a large knot near one thin edge of the central portion of the lid. However, it was applied over the lid's entire surface and was not meant merely as a targeted gap-filler but served as a facing for the canopic chest's eventual surface decoration. The plaster of this coating lips up from the arched central section onto the end blocks, not only filling any gaps between these pieces, but also making the lid appear as though it were carved from a single piece of wood.

At the time of excavation, this coating was solid white, without any traces of coloring. This observation leads to three viable conclusions. The first is that the canopic chest had originally been gilded, and the gilding was completely removed by tomb robbers inside the tomb without utterly destroying the box. The second is that polychrome decoration once existed on the white plaster ground, but it disintegrated over the millennia with absolutely no trace in the sandy matrix surrounding the box. And finally, the third, more viable possibility is that the canopic chest was white without any significant amount of applied decoration. The white coloring, which was still apparent at the time of excavation, represents the box's final background color. These possibilities will be explored in greater detail below, after we examine the structure of the box itself.

THE BOX

Like the lid, the box had a slightly rectangular footprint, measuring roughly 52 cm (1 royal cubit)

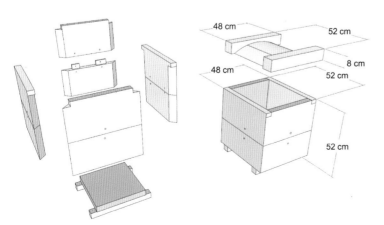

48 cm · 52 cm · 8 cm · 48 cm · 52 cm · 52 cm

Fig. 4.19 Exploded view of the box (left), and complete view of the box with measurements (right). The small circles on each face are the dowel pins which originally secured the floating tenons, visible in the exploded view at the left, background.

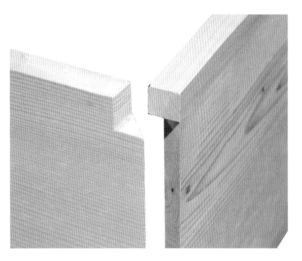

Fig. 4.20 Reconstruction of the Seneb-Kay canopic box corner joint with a butt joint over a 45° miter.

all four faces: about 28 cm up from the bottom and 20 cm down from the top edge of the box. Since the underlying painted texts belonging to Sobekhotep (N) on sides A and C were continuous columns extending across these edges, the joinery must date to the original construction of the Sobekhotep (N) sarcophagus, and not to the reuse of the wood to construct the Seneb-Kay canopic chest. The carpenter who converted the original sarcophagus planks into the canopic box made certain that each side had two pinned floating tenons in it, to assure structural stability in the resulting box (Fig. 4.19). Taken together, all these points corroborate that the box was probably made from a length of timber consisting of two narrower joined planks of cedar, which derived from one side of an original sarcophagus. The carpenter laid out the four sides along the length of this joined plank in such a way that each side of the box retained two of the original floating tenons, which may have necessitated the cutting away of a small strip of intervening wood between each of the box's sides.

Each of the four corners of the box was brought together using a simple miter joint, surmounted by a small butt joint (Gale et al. 2000:365). The advantage of this joint is that the butt joint section keeps the miter joint from slipping (Fig. 4.20). This is a very common feature of Egyptian box construction. Some examples go so far as to turn the simple butt joint

in its long dimension, and about 48 cm in width (Fig. 4.19). The height of the box was 48 cm, to which must be added the height of the two battens on the bottom of about 4.5 cm, giving the entire box (exclusive of the lid) a height of about 52.5 cm (exactly 1 cubit).

The four sides of the box (Sides A–D) were each composed of two narrower planks, joined at their edges with pinned floating tenons. The location of the joint between the two planks was the same on

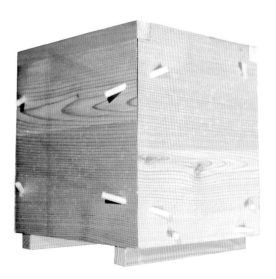

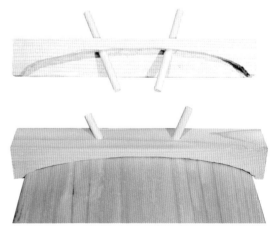

Fig. 4.21 Scale replica of Seneb-Kay's canopic chest, showing the method of angling dowel pins against one another in order to create dynamic tension in the miter joints and to keep the box together without the use of adhesive.

Fig. 4.22 Completed (1:2) scale model of the Seneb-Kay canopic chest. Once the pegs were trimmed flush with the box, the entire exterior surface was painted white. The interior was left the color of the natural wood to match the original.

into a half dovetail, locking the joint together more securely. Though this was not the case in the Seneb-Kay box, the butt joint served to add vertical stability to the otherwise weak miter joint.

In order to lock the joints in place permanently, holes were drilled through the mitered corners to accept dowel pins. At least two of these were drilled per corner, angled against each other to create dynamic tension in the joint (Figs. 4.21 and 4.23). A similar technique was also probably used to keep the lid together, although the wood was too decayed to observe exactly where these pegs were originally placed. By inserting the pegs in this way, it was virtually impossible for the two pieces of wood to separate without the removal of the dowel pins. The box would easily hold itself together without the use of glue or other mechanical fasteners.

No special joinery was employed in affixing the bottom of the box to the sides. The bottom was simply a plank of wood, cut to fit inside the already formed walls of the box. It was presumably attached to the sides with further wooden dowels, though these were not apparent on the highly damaged box. Finally, the last element of the box was the addition of two battens or feet onto the bottom. These battens were roughly 4.5 cm wide and between 4.5

and 5 cm tall and were set back from the short sides of the box by 5 cm. They extended all the way out to the edges of the box's long sides, thus bridging both the bottom plank and the edges of the two sides. Again, dowels were used to affix these battens to the bottom of the box.

The final step in the creation of Seneb-Kay's canopic box was the surface decoration. Like the lid, it was clear that the entire surface of the box had been covered in a thin gypsum plaster, overlaid with white pigment. This painted plaster was observed flaking off of the yellow background and blue hieroglyphs of the Sobekhotep IV sarcophagus decoration. The preserved areas of white pigment were scattered all over the entire surface of the canopic box (Fig. 4.24). However, in no case was any polychrome decoration apparent atop this white ground, leading to the conclusion that the canopic box was simply white when it was finished and may have lacked decoration and text. While the white background color matches the color of Seneb-Kay's sarcophagus, the lack of preserved decoration or text on the surface of the box is somewhat unorthodox. This is further evidence that the box was hastily produced. Echoing the likely unfinished nature of the burial chamber's decoration, the canopic box appears never to have received its final embellishment with texts and images.[15]

SECOND INTERMEDIATE PERIOD CANOPIC BOXES

Perhaps not surprisingly, the evolution of canopic chests during the Late Middle Kingdom and Second Intermediate Period follows directly upon that of rectangular sarcophagi. We have briefly outlined these trends above in reference to Seneb-Kay's rectangular white-ground sarcophagus. Based on the examination of his canopic chest, this object too had a white ground, matching his sarcophagus, albeit without any polychrome surface decoration.

While Second Intermediate Period wooden canopic chests are extremely rare, a few late examples belonging to kings do exist. Contemporary non-royal canopic chests seem to follow the same trends that have been discussed in terms of sarcophagus

Fig. 4.23 Side A of the Seneb-Kay canopic box. The top edge of the box is at the top of the image. Near the edges at the left and right, dowel pins can be seen, highlighted here by the white circles.

Fig. 4.24 The surface of the Seneb-Kay canopic box showing its coating of white gypsum paint (bottom) covering over the original pigmented surface of the Sobekhotep (N) sarcophagus.

evolution. The most obvious of these trends is the departure from a flat top toward the *per-nu* form in the 13th Dynasty. This point of departure is illustrated by King Awibre Hor's canopic chest, which had a flat top, while that of the Princess Nubheteptikhered was of the *per-nu* type. Interestingly, the *per-nu* shape does not seem to have been adopted as readily in the strictly royal sphere. Though badly decayed when it was discovered, the burial assemblage of Awibre Hor of the early 13th Dynasty included both a sarcophagus and canopic chest with flat lids. Awibre's set followed the late 12th Dynasty style which favored visible natural wood grain for the majority of the surface of both sarcophagus and canopic chest (De Morgan 1895: pl. 36).

Near Awibre's burial, De Morgan also discovered the intact burial of a *King's Daughter*, Nubheteptikhered. Though the texts of her burial assemblage do not indicate her relationship to Awibre, it is assumed that they were related, with many scholars identifying her as Awibre's daughter (Dodson 1994:32). Such an attribution would theoretically place her tomb assemblage slightly later in the 13th Dynasty than Awibre himself and might explain the appearance of the *per-nu* style in her sarcophagus and the canopic chest as a chronological development. On the other hand, it has been suggested that the flat lid of Awibre's set forms a deliberate archaism. In either case, while the sarcophagus and canopic chest of Nubheteptikhered are of the *per-nu* style, the arched central portion is still fairly flat suggesting only a slight movement toward the vaulted form.

The text bands of both the burial sets belonging to Awibre and Nubheteptikhered employed truncated hieroglyphs. Though this practice first appeared during the reign of Amenemhat III in the 12th Dynasty, it continues as the primary mode of rendering texts meant for tomb contexts through the 13th Dynasty and Second Intermediate Period. As discussed in Chapter 2, the decoration in the burial chamber of Seneb-Kay's tomb CS9 also employed these truncated hieroglyphs, making it highly likely that his sarcophagus and related material were also inscribed with this particular script.

Another trend that appears intermittently during the 13th Dynasty is the lack of canopic jars inside the chests. During the Middle Kingdom canopic jars were the norm, for both royal and non-royal burials alike. However, beginning in the late 12th Dynasty, while the chests themselves still normally have flat tops, individual canopic jars disappear in favor of four internal compartments within the wooden box. One such example belonged to the *Overseer*, Senbi, from Meir (MMA 11.150.17a1–3). Three virtually identical sarcophagi with the same coloration as this canopic chest are known, though, since they have slightly different names and titles and do not fit inside each other, they almost certainly belonged to different individuals (Berman and Bohač 1999:186–189). In the case of the Cleveland example (Cleveland

1914.716.a–b), the sarcophagus has a flat lid identical to that of the canopic chest and lacks Coffin Texts on the interior. Based on the style and exterior texts, the group is dated to the late 12th Dynasty reigns of Amenemhat II to Senwosret III.

With the Senbi canopic chest, the artist who fabricated it made a secondary lid, which covers four internal partitions (Hayes 1953:321). Affixed to the top of this inner lid are four diminutive carved heads, meant to replace the more traditional anthropomorphic canopic jar stoppers. The viscera would then have been placed within one of the four compartments inside the box, which would then have been sealed by means of this secondary lid, before the entire chest was closed. This layout became the standard during the Second Intermediate Period.

Recently, another canopic chest belonging to a princess of the 13th Dynasty has been found. Egyptian teams excavating at Dahshur discovered the substructure of a pyramid, whose architecture matches other known 13th Dynasty royal tombs rather well. Inside this structure, excavators found objects inscribed with the name of Ameny-Qemau, the fifth king of the dynasty and one of Awibre's predecessors. Though the lid is missing, the box has similar edge banding, tripartite text bands, and natural wood finish as that of Nubheteptikhered. Additionally, the text is written in the same truncated hieroglyphs.

By the middle of the 13th Dynasty, the *per-nu* form had become the norm for non-royal sarcophagi and canopic chests. In addition, the background color had shifted away from the natural wood to a shiny black varnish. Two canopic chests, belonging to a husband and wife and now in Moscow, exemplify this type (Moscow Ii a 5358 and Ii a 5359). As discussed above, these chests match the sarcophagi of the same individuals now in Cairo (CG 28028 and CG 28029), and can be dated to the mid-13th Dynasty, during the reign of Sobekhotep IV or slightly later (Cahail 2015:109–112). Not only do these canopic chests have much more exaggerated *per-nu* designs, they also continue the use of truncated hieroglyphs.

Other similar examples of canopic chests with black backgrounds and truncated hieroglyphs also derive from Thebes. Two such objects, now in Cairo, were published by Reisner in his *Catalogue Général* volume on canopics (Reisner 1967:362–365). The first of these is a box belonging to the *Superintendent of the Ruler's Crew,* Hemenhotep, complete with its four canopic jars (CG4727 to CG4731). Though it was purchased, the provenience was recorded as either Deir el-Bahri or Gebelein. The box has a black background with yellow texts. All four jars as well as the text on the box exhibit truncated hieroglyphs. The matching sarcophagus to this set is currently in the Field Museum (number 105215), while its lid is also in Cairo (T13C, CG28126). The box is unpublished, but the lid is decorated with Pyramid Texts sections 638a–b (Spell 368), 272–273a (Spell 252), and 275a–d (Spell 253 [Lesko 1979:103]).[16] Based on the dating of other black background sarcophagi, this set seems to date to the first half of the 13th Dynasty prior to the introduction of the CT 777–785 series.

Hemenhotep's canopic chest is of the *per-nu* type with twin batten feet on the bottom and, according to Reisner's catalogue, measuring 62.5 cm tall and 50.5 cm to a side, giving it a square footprint. The curved lid is hollow on the underside and fits into a rabbet in the top edge of the box. The two end blocks have larger pegs to secure the lid to the box. There is a thin border near the corners of the box and a chain-link design on either side of the text lines. Each side of the box has one horizontal and two vertical columns of text. In the center of each of the four sides is an image of a jackal above the *menkhet* sign and a group of plants. The jackal bears a different epigraph on each side.

There were no internal divisions within the box, indicating that the jars were meant to sit loose inside the box. All four of the jars were made of wood and had human head stoppers. The jars themselves were fabricated in two halves and then pegged together. Three or four lines of text, written in incomplete hieroglyphs, adorn the outside. The faces on the stoppers were modeled with plaster, and the flesh tone is yellow. Two of the jars were entirely empty, while the other two held only a few linen wrappings. Canopic jars dating to the mid-13th Dynasty appear to be extremely rare, and it is not entirely clear if Hemenhotep's ever held any of his preserved viscera.

Evidence for the perseverance of the black background on sarcophagi and canopic chests through the 13th Dynasty comes from another chest belonging to the *High Steward*, Khonsumes (Cairo CG 4732 [Reisner 1967:364–365; Miniaci 2010b]). Unlike the cubic box of Hemenhotep, Khonsumes's box was rectangular, measuring 35 cm tall, 46 cm long, and 33.5 cm wide. It is missing its lid, though it can be assumed to have been of the *per-nu* design (Miniaci 2010b:17). What is immediately apparent, is that this chest is much smaller than other examples of the late 12th and early 13th Dynasty. The interior space was divided into four sections by (now missing) planks set at right angles to the four walls of the box. Consequently, it is probable that the canopic box of Khonsumes was never meant to hold jars. Rather, the wrapped viscera packets would have been deposited in one of the four internal compartments.

The exterior of the Khonsumes chest is black with yellow text bands and a central panel with images of a recumbent jackal. Miniaci identifies the texts as a "garbled version of the Coffin Texts found on the rectangular coffins of the period" (Miniaci 2010b:19). He also pointed out that one of the texts is identical to that of the Senbuni canopic chest (Moscow Ii a 5358), showing some chronological affinities. Based upon numerous criteria, Miniaci concluded that the chest must date to the late 13th Dynasty into the early 17th Dynasty (Miniaci 2010b:25).

Along with the white-ground sarcophagus of the *Scribe of the Temple*, Dedmut, Peet found fragments of a canopic chest (Fig. 4.25). Like the sarcophagus, the white background of the chest was decorated with wavy chevrons, probably meant to imitate the look of a more expensive material such as travertine. The sarcophagus was decorated with the CT 777–785 series and is dated elsewhere in this volume to the mid-13th Dynasty. With this fragmentary example, we can see the move away from black backgrounds in sarcophagi was matched by canopic chests. Through the 13th Dynasty, canopic chests tended to match the sarcophagi they were meant to accompany. At the same time, these chests had their own textual programs which were seemingly independent of the textual traditions appearing on the sarcophagi.

Other isolated examples completely lack external decoration. One such example is the canopic chest of Sitre (MMA 386.1.46a/b), which is dated anywhere from the late 13th to early 18th Dynasty. It has a roughly square layout with two batten feet positioned near the edges. The lid is of the *per-nu* type, but is here constructed out of individual planks, cut to form a curve. The end boards are thin, and the central curved portion extends all the way through one of them. The other end board is an integral part of the box, showing an innovation in the way the box was constructed, and the method by which it could

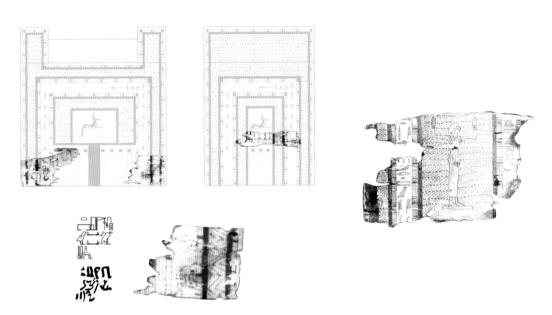

Fig. 4.25 Reconstruction of the canopic chest of Dedumut. The three fragments (after Peet 1914: pls. 13–14) are superimposed over the drawing (by author), showing their position.

be closed. There is a colored border around the edges, and the rest of the surface is white.

Rectangular coffins with white backgrounds appear at Thebes during the transition to the 16th/17th Dynasty, alongside anthropoid *rishi* coffins. These coffins are almost always uninscribed, perhaps due to the continued impoverishment of the citizenry or changing funerary beliefs. Given its unorthodox construction method and complete lack of texts, the canopic chest of Sitre may belong to this transitional period.

Three royal canopic chests can also be convincingly dated to the period between the late 13th and early 17th Dynasty, though with these examples the black coloring has disappeared in favor of either yellow or white. The first of these was originally inscribed for a king named Djehuty, but a secondary epigraph indicates that he gave it to his wife Mentuhotep (Berlin 1175). This woman was the owner of the white ground sarcophagus inscribed with CT 777–785 on the exterior and the Book of the Dead spells on the interior in hieratic. The canopic chest is of the *per-nu* design and has a yellow background. Queen Mentuhotep's sarcophagus had a white background, but for some reason she did not have a matching canopic chest. One had to be supplied for her by her husband. Presumably this chest had originally been made for him, leading to the possible conclusion that the yellow background coloring was

a royal prerogative, going all the way back to the yellow painted sarcophagus of Sobekhotep IV at South Abydos.

The canopic chest measures 44.6 cm long, by 37.6 cm wide, and 45.6 cm tall without its lid. There was no indication of original divisions in the interior, and when it was discovered by Passalacqua, it was found to contain a toilet set rather than the viscera of the deceased (Dodson 1994:39). Dodson concluded that the chest was reused at a later time and assumes that it originally held the viscera of Queen Mentuhotep.

The canopic chest belonging to the 17th Dynasty king Sekhemre Wepmaat Antef also has a yellowish exterior color (Fig. 4.26, left). Slightly smaller than that of Queen Mentuhotep, it measures 38.5 cm long, 34.2 cm wide, and 32.4 cm tall without its lid. The interior is divided into four compartments, and the lid has a *per-nu* design. The lid sockets into the box in the same way as the Hemenhotep chest, with two pegs at each end and twin rabbets along the interior edges of the long sides of the box. The texts are badly effaced, but there are images of recumbent jackals on each face of the box.

Finally, the canopic chest belonging to the 17th Dynasty king Sekhemre Wadjkhau Sobekemsaf is virtually identical, albeit with a white rather than yellow background (Fig. 4.26, right). The lid is of the *per-nu* type, the inside was originally divided into

Fig. 4.26 Canopic chests of the 17th Dynasty kings Sekhemre Wepmaat Antef (Antef V, Louvre E2538) and Sekhemre Wadjkhau Sobekemsaf (Sobekemsaf I, Leiden, AH.216). Images courtesy of the Musée du Louvre and Rijksmuseum, Leiden).

four compartments, and there were two batten feet which are now missing. The box measures 42.6 cm long, 34.2 cm wide, and 35.2 cm tall, making it somewhat squatter than the other examples. In its construction and texts, it is comparable to the boxes of Wepmaat Antef and Djehuty.

Based on the examples discussed above, a number of chronological trends are apparent. Flat tops which had been popular during the 12th Dynasty gave way to the *per-nu* type, which persisted into the Second Intermediate Period. This trend began in the non-royal sphere before becoming popular with royal canopics, hence the roughly contemporary assemblages of Nubheteptikhered and Awibre Hor have *per-nu* and flat lids, respectively. Concurrently with the introduction of the *per-nu* lid, and parallel to sarcophagus development, non-royal canopic chests also began to display black backgrounds. In the royal sphere, there is a hiatus in the record between Awibre Hor and period of King Djehuty and Queen Mentuhotep. Despite this, it seems quite probable that royal canopic chests had either natural wood or light yellow coloring. Since canopic chest decoration often matched that of the sarcophagus, the yellow background of the sarcophagus we attribute here to Sobekhotep IV hints at the probability that his canopic chest also had a yellow ground.

Around the reign of Sobekhotep IV, non-royal sarcophagi and canopic chests begin to appear with white backgrounds. This trend continues and may have influenced the royal sphere, since the canopic chest of King Wadjkhau Sobekemsaf also has a white background. Hence it is not surprising that Seneb-Kay's canopic chest, formed from reused wood, was painted to match the white background of his also probably usurped mid-13th Dynasty sarcophagus. Its size was larger than contemporary non-royal or royal examples, perhaps indicating that it was actually designed to contain canopic jars. Although no direct evidence has survived, with so much of his burial making use of usurped objects, we may speculate that it is possible that Seneb-Kay's burial reused canopic jars associated with one of the earlier late Middle Kingdom royal tombs at South Abydos or perhaps from the 13th Dynasty elite burial from which his white-ground sarcophagus may have been taken.[17]

THE CANOPIC CHEST OF SENEB-KAY

Based on the foregoing discussion, two possibilities are open to understanding Seneb-Kay's canopic chest. One is that the chest was designed purely in accordance with designs currently in use during the period ca. 1650–1600 BCE and concurrent with the 16th Dynasty. The other is that the box was created and decorated in a purposefully antique style in order to match Seneb-Kay's usurped mid-13th Dynasty sarcophagus. In either case, the box and its lid were formed from reused cedar sourced from a royal sarcophagus originally belonging to a king Sobekhotep (N), probably Sobekhotep IV.

The only surviving background color on the Seneb-Kay canopic chest is white. Areas near the edges of the box which might have had polychrome decoration (if the box mimicked the sarcophagus) do not, suggesting that the entire box was likely plain white when it was placed in CS9's burial chamber. Only one royal canopic box, that of Wadjkhau Sobekemsaf of the 17th Dynasty, had a white background, while the other known royal canopic boxes were yellow. On background color alone, it is possible that Seneb-Kay's canopic box was intended to fit into the contemporary royal tradition.

On the other hand, the size and form of the box seem to argue against this. Not only did it lack any text or decoration that would have linked it with other royal examples, it was also significantly larger. The largest of the three 17th Dynasty examples, that of Queen Mentuhotep had exterior dimensions of 44.6 cm in length, 37.6 cm in width, and 63.2 cm in height including the lid. By comparison, Seneb-Kay's canopic box was 52 cm long, 48 cm wide, and, with its lid, had a height of 60.5 cm. Though these numbers do not appear terribly divergent, the internal volume of the two boxes is significantly different: Seneb-Kay's is 72.9 liters, while that of Queen Mentuhotep is only 49.8 liters.

Based on its size, Seneb-Kay's canopic chest could have contained four jars with maximum dimensions of 43.5 cm in height and 19.5 cm in diameter. The canopic jars of Awibre Hor measured about 38.8 cm tall with an average diameter of 19.5 cm. Though the Mentuhotep box lacks internal divisions, those of Kings Wepmaat Antef and Wadjkhau Sobekemsaf both had them. By the 17th Dynasty, the prevailing trend in the royal sphere was for small canopic boxes with internal divisions designed to hold linen packets containing the viscera. Hence, the dimensions of Seneb-Kay's canopic box argue against the theory that it was fabricated according to contemporary trends.

As we discuss elsewhere (see Chapters 3 and 10), it is possible that Seneb-Kay's outer wooden sarcophagus was usurped, possibly coming from the burial of the *Overseer of the Offering Tables of Amun,* Ibiau, or his father the *Overseer of Fields,* Dedtu (whose mortuary chapel supplied the reused limestone blocks for Seneb-Kay's burial chamber). In either case, the sarcophagus conforms to a mid-13th Dynasty high official type, consisting of polychrome decoration on a white background. The burial equipment of Seneb-Kay was hastily assembled and made extensive use of repurposed materials. However, for some reason, the tomb from which the sarcophagus was taken did not also supply a canopic box.

There are myriad explanations for this, though two seem plausible. The first is that, in accordance with changing burial practices, canopic chests had fallen out of use for the majority of burials, particularly in the non-royal sphere. This idea would seem to explain why Queen Mentuhotep's husband Djehuty had to provide her with a chest originally designed and fabricated for his use, with a royal yellow background. The second explanation is that the canopic chest may have been damaged through the action of water or insects during the years between the original interment and Seneb-Kay's usurpation of it.

In either case, those responsible for the interment of Seneb-Kay found it necessary to create a canopic chest from scratch. In order to accomplish this, an artisan reused two joined planks of cedar which had been taken from the 13th Dynasty burial of King Sobekhotep (N). Almost certainly working under a deadline, this carpenter took a few shortcuts in order to create a usable box in as short a time as possible. The most significant of these is the lack of any mechanical means of connecting the lid to the box. In other examples, there are large pegs on the lower surfaces of the lid's end blocks which engage in mortises in the box. Given the thinness of the walls of Seneb-Kay's box, this method would have been difficult to achieve. Furthermore, earlier examples have two rabbets on the interior edges of the long sides of the box. The curved lid normally extends down past the end blocks, in order to engage in these rabbets. Not only does Seneb-Kay's canopic chest lack these features, the central curved portion of the lid was formed by pegging three smaller planks together. With the underside being solid and flat, the carpenter only needed to shape the upper surface. More than anything, this was a time-saving shortcut that resulted in a box with the correct *per-nu* form, but which was made in an otherwise unorthodox way.

Once the box itself was built, virtually no time was dedicated to its decoration. The traces that remain indicate that a single coat of very hastily applied white plaster and pigment was brushed onto the surface. In places, this slapdash coating even failed to cover the original yellow coloring of Sobekhotep (N)'s sarcophagus. At the very least, this white coloring would have matched the white background of Seneb-Kay's likely usurped, sarcophagus. From the outside, the box would not have been as striking as the sarcophagus with its polychrome decoration, but perhaps the important part was that it contained a set of expensive (though also possibly usurped) royal canopic jars, as opposed to simple bundles of linen wrapped viscera. On one hand, Seneb-Kay's funerary assemblage was created by appropriating elements from royal and elite burials of the 13th Dynasty. But, on the other hand, the trend in royal burials in the 13th Dynasty and after appears to favor a level of antiquarianism. Awibre Hor was buried in a flat-topped sarcophagus akin to those of the 12th Dynasty, while kings of the New Kingdom were still being buried in anthropoid coffins employing *rishi*-decoration, hundreds of years after they had died out in the non-royal sphere. In this way, Seneb-Kay's partially usurped, partially purpose-made burial assemblage fit the trend.

NOTES:

4.1 Here we use "canopic chest" to refer to the combination of box and lid, while "canopic box" designates the lower part of the container as distinct from the lid.

4.2 Of these two, the latter is the less likely since the series of texts upon the Sobekhotep (N) sarcophagus date to the mid-13th Dynasty.

4.3 It is interesting to note that Sobekhotep's name is written here phonetically, without the divine image of the crocodile god Sobek (sign I4) as it is commonly used elsewhere. Perhaps this was done in an attempt to avoid having to draw the divine crocodile in an incomplete manner. For a contemporary example in which the title *smȝyt-Ḥr* is written without the Horus falcon, see Grajetzki (2010:7).

4.4 Sources T6C and T10C follow de Buck, *Coffin Texts VI* (de Buck 1956:412), and for the original publication of these texts see (Daressy 1893:34–38), with corrections in P. Lacau, (Lacau 1904, 1906:76–78). W. Grajetzki discusses sources T4L, Aby2 and Aby5 (Grajetzki 2010a:74).

4.5 We employ the term "royal" here in the sense of pertaining only to the king. Coffin T4L, also inscribed with CT Spells 777–784, belonged to a Queen Montuhotep, wife of a king named Djehuty, who has been dated to the period between the late 13th and early 17th Dynasties (see Grajetzki 2010a:46–47).

4.6 The back of a Middle Kingdom sarcophagus is the side opposite that which is normally decorated with two eyes, called the front.

4.7 The front of both of these sarcophagi have eight columns, with the panel bearing the depiction of the two eyes in place of the ninth column. Despite its fragmentary state, the coffin which Peet found in tomb X3 also has the same layout of eight columns on the front, and nine columns on the back (Peet 1914: pl. 36 and Grajetzki 2010a:42, source siglum Aby2).

4.8 It is worth noting that the texts of T6C and T10C are not identical. In some cases, one version includes phrases and elements not included in the other, indicating that an original, "master" version of the text once existed, which was longer than either set of texts applied to T6C or T10C. Sobekhotep (N)'s sarcophagus may have made use of this text, thus filling up the longer sarcophagus more completely.

4.9 Given that the sarcophagus length matches that of the chamber so closely, we can assume that Sobekhotep (N)'s wooden sarcophagus would have been around 1.15 m or so wide and probably close to 1.30 cm tall.

4.10 At least five of the previously known sources come from Abydos, leading Grajetzki to raise the question whether CT 777–785 may have been composed at Abydos (Grajetzki 2010:103–104).

4.11 For the sources of king Sewahenre, see the discussion of Ryholt who theorizes that this king may belong to P.Turin column 8/27, reading *[s....]-n-[rʿ]*, making him the final king of the 13th Dynasty (Ryholt 1997:359). Grajetzki identifies T6C and T10C a "key group for the Second Intermediate Period," since they are linked with Sewahenre, whom he dates to the late 13th or early 16th Dynasty (Grajetzki 2010a:48).

4.12 Khonsu's mother, as recorded on JE37507, was the *smȝyt-Ḥr*, Sobekhotep. The feminine form of this title is very rare, appearing more frequently in the masculine version (*smȝ-Ḥr*, Ward Title 1292). Grajetzki erroneously believed the title to be the name of the owner of the fragmentary sarcophagus Aby5 (Zemathor), one of the exemplars of CT Spells 777–785 (Grajetzki 2010a). These fragmentary texts all break off after the title *smȝyt-Ḥr*, indicating that the actual name of the sarcophagus's owner is lost. Since only two examples of the feminine title *smȝyt-Ḥr* are known, it is possible that the owner of sarcophagus Aby5 is one and the same as the mother of Khonsu, the *smȝyt-Ḥr*, Sobekhotep (see Bazin and el-Enany 2010:10–11).

4.13 Unlike burial sites such as Dra Abu el-Naga, where the tombs are cut into limestone cliffs, separating their contents from the effects of moisture and insects, burials at Abydos tended to be in the sandy matrix of the low desert. The proximity of the funerary equipment to the soil means that most coffins and wooden objects have been consumed by termites. The S10 substructure consisted of built limestone passages surrounding the solid block of the quartzite sarcophagus chamber, replicating the conditions of rock-cut tombs at localities like western Thebes.

4.14 Assuming that Sobekhotep (N) whose name appears on the original phase of the wood's decoration was Sobekhotep IV, that king's reign can be dated ca. 1732–1720 BCE (Ryholt 1997:191–198) compared with the approximate placement of Seneb-Kay in the timeframe 1650–1600 BCE (see Chapter 14).

4.15 This is also further evidence that the sarcophagus was reused from an earlier burial since the canopic box would have taken far less time to decorate than the sarcophagus. Yet the canopic box was simply white, while the sarcophagus was carefully painted with the time-consuming technique of polychrome decoration.

4.16 This is the lid that was originally associated with Cairo CG 28030, the sarcophagus of Nubkherredi.

4.17 Fragments attributed to the travertine (calcite) canopic jars of the 13th Dynasty royal tomb S10 adjacent to Seneb-Kay (CS9) were discovered during the work of Weigall and in recent excavations (Wegner and Cahail 2015:138–141). This suggests S10 was not a source for reuse of canopic jars. It is also possible that new jars were fabricated from stone or produced in ceramic for Seneb-Kay. However, given the haste with which the rest of his burial was assembled some form of reuse in the case of the canopic jars seems plausible.

5

Osteobiography of Woseribre Seneb-Kay*

The skeletonized mummy of Seneb-Kay was discovered in the pole-roof chamber of CS9 during the 2014 excavation of that tomb. As we have seen the preceding discussion, after removing it from the outer sarcophagus and coffin, ancient tomb robbers stripped the mummy of valuable items and cast the rifled body on the floor of the tomb's outer chamber, along with other non-valuable elements of the funerary equipment. When excavated, we found the majority of the postcranial skeleton substantially articulated suggesting the body had been thrown, still largely bound together within its linen wrappings at the western end of the chamber. The cranium appears to have been detached at that time and lay in front of the body. The mandible had been smashed and was recovered in fragmentary condition.

Numerically, 79% of the skeleton's 206 bones were recovered providing a close to complete skeleton of the king (Fig. 5.1). This count includes small elements such as distal phalanges of the feet and hands. Despite the missing elements, all areas of the postcranial skeleton with the exception of a few missing vertebrae are represented almost completely.

The skeleton of Seneb-Kay is the most complete of the four skeletons belonging to original interments of the Second Intermediate Period cemetery. All of these remains belong to mature males of 30+ years of age. This skeletal sample provides the basis for a limited comparative analysis of these individuals, which we present in this volume as an osteobiography for each of the individuals. This chapter provides an osteobiography of Seneb-Kay, considering key

attributes of his skeleton, paleopathology, musculoskeletal stress markers, antemortem and perimortem trauma, and an analysis of the evidence for how he may have died. The other individuals are discussed in Part 3, Chapter 13 in connection with their location of burial in the main tomb cluster.

Seneb-Kay's skeleton is effectively, at the present time, the earliest substantially surviving skeleton of an ancient Egyptian king.[1] The preservation of Seneb-Kay's skeletal remains is outstanding due to the context of his tomb in the low desert, deeply buried within a dry sand matrix that is elevated approximately 40 m above the edge of the Nile floodplain. The remains provide a unique opportunity to examine the physical attributes and cause of death of one of the rulers of Egypt's Second Intermediate Period. Before examining the remains of Seneb-Kay in detail, we turn firstly to a brief review of the osteological methods used in the analysis of his skeleton and the other individuals discussed in Chapter 13. The remainder of this chapter then presents osteological analysis of Seneb-Kay.

OSTEOLOGICAL METHODS

Forensic anthropology and osteological methods offer the opportunity to bring together distinct, yet related, levels of skeletal analysis for the purpose of identifying and reconstructing life experiences. These approaches include osteobiography, taphonomy, anthropometry, and paleopathology.

*This chapter written by Jane Hill, Maria Rosado, and Josef Wegner.

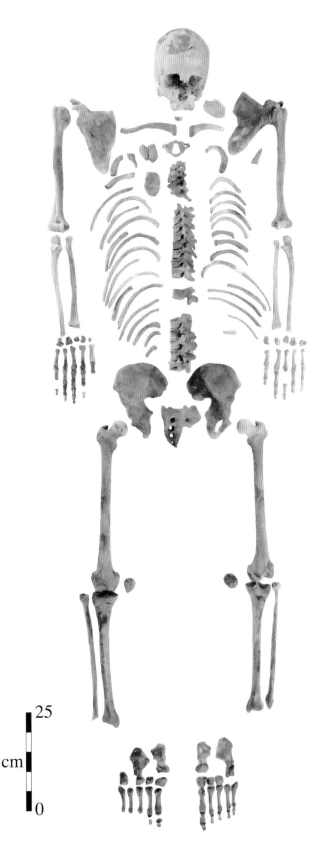

Fig. 5.1 General overview of the recovered skeletal remains of Seneb-Kay (laid out in 2014 after retrieval and prior to osteological analysis; feet, hands, and lower arm elements not in anatomical position).

25

cm

0

Collectively, the human remains excavated from the Second Intermediate Period royal cemetery are represented by cranial and postcranial bones that are remarkably well preserved given the age of the remains and taphonomic processes (e.g., burial practice, looting, weathering, and animal predation) that have acted on them. The taphonomic analysis provided details on postmortem treatment and preservation. The cranial and postcranial bones available permitted a detailed osteological analysis, enabling us to examine the sex, age, height, pathological conditions, and activity-related musculoskeletal morphology (stress markers).

For the osteological analysis of Seneb-Kay and the associated Second Intermediate Period burials we derived a skeletal blank that identified the recovered bones present, sex, age, stature, and taphonomy. From this blank we were able to identify the minimum number of individuals (MNI) present. The skeletal remains were documented using digital photography and microscopic photography (x10 magnification with Motic digital microscope camera). With this method we were able to develop a registry of bones available and a database of anomalous conditions (e.g., trauma and paleopathological markers). Anatomical features and locations on bone for identification of anomalous conditions were used for more precise descriptions.

From the mostly intact postcranial bones available in the case of Seneb-Kay and the burial in CS10, we were able to conduct a detailed analysis of activity-related musculoskeletal stress markers (MSM). The plasticity of bone results in the osseous response to continuous, repetitive stress at the point of maximum stress, causing MSM. These markers are often associated with habitual activity that induced stress (Munson 1997). The pattern of MSM of the pelvis and leg bones for both CS9 and CS10 are discussed in detail. Our osteological analysis also describes and interprets the pattern of cranial and postcranial skeletal trauma observed for CS9 and CS10, and paleopathological conditions for each individual found in the Second Intermediate Period royal cemetery (see overview in Hill et al. 2017:276–282).

DETERMINATION OF BIOLOGICAL SEX

The sex of the skeletal remains of Seneb-Kay and the other recovered occupants of Second Intermediate Period cemetery was determined using gross osteological markers on the skull, pelvis, and postcranial skeleton as described by Bass (2005), Steele and Bramblett (1988), and Krogman and Iscan (1986). The pelvis provides the most reliable features for sex determination. Seneb-Kay (CS9) and individual CS10 were estimated as clearly male based on the narrow sciatic notches and subpubic angles of their retrieved pelvises; the well-defined sexually dimorphic traits in the cranium (CS8, CS9, CS10) including large supraorbital margins, mastoid processes, and pronounced nuchal area; and robust long bones and long bone fragments (CS9, CS10, CS11). The sex estimation for all of the remains is consistent with the conclusion that King Seneb-Kay is one member of a larger cemetery dedicated to interments of mature male individuals.

ESTIMATION OF AGE

The following characteristics were used to estimate age at death for Seneb-Kay as well as the other Second Intermediate Period skeletal individuals at South Abydos: the pubic symphysis, dental eruption of third molars, dental wear, epiphyseal union of long bones, union of sacral vertebrae, arthrosis of joints and the vertebral column, and closure of cranial sutures (Bass, 2005; Steele and Bramblett, 1988; Krogman and Iscan, 1986; and Roksandic and Armstrong, 2011). For Seneb-Kay, the age determined from the pubic symphysis resulted in a score of 11 (see Stewart 1979; Gilbert and McKern 1973) which gives a range of 23–39 years. The fusion of S1 and S2 (which occurs between 30–35 years of age) is also observed for Seneb-Kay (Steele and Bramblett 1988). Further, based on Passalacqua (2009), if lipping around the auricular surface of the sacrum is evident, as well as enhanced microporosity and macroporosity, as observed for Seneb-Kay (see Fig. 5.4) then the age falls with a high degree of probability between 40–50 years old. Based on this set of features, we estimate Seneb-Kay's age at death to be between 35–45 years with indications of osteoarthritis and dental wear increasing the probability that he was at the older end of this range (Table 5.1).

ESTIMATION OF STATURE

For Seneb-Kay as well as two of the other individuals recovered in the Second Intermediate Period royal cemetery (CS10 and CS11), measurements of available long bones were used to estimate approximate living stature. For the method for approximating stature of people from antiquity to be effective, it should be calculated from genetically related populations. Therefore, the formulas for ancient Egyptian males provided by Raxter et al. (2008) were used. By this method, the average estimated stature for the skeleton of Seneb-Kay extrapolated from measurements of available bones is 168.60 cm (range 162.94–174.13 cm) (Table 5.2). By way of comparison and using the same methods for the other South Abydos skeletons (as discussed in Chapter 13), we estimate a height for

Table 5.1 Age estimate for Woseribre Seneb-Kay.

Skeleton No.	Sex	Age (y)	% of Skeleton represented
CS9	Male, determined from cranium and pelvis	35–45 determined from cranium (some closure of sutures), teeth (dental wear, enamel being lost on occlusal surface, some dentin exposed), and postcrania (full closure of epiphyseal lines of sacrum, long bones, vertebrae); pubic symphysis	79

Table 5.2 Stature estimation for Seneb-Kay based on long bone measurements (stature calculated from formulas for ancient Egyptian males provided by Raxter et al. 2008).

Bone	CS9	CS9 Stature	SEE	Range
Femur$_m$	2.257 (**47.4**) + 63.93=	170.91 cm	3.218	167.69–174.13
Tibia$_m$	2.554 (**38.9**) + 69.21=	168.56 cm	3.002	165.56–171.56
Humerus$_m$	2.594 (**32.5**) + 83.85=	168.15 cm	4.218	163.93–172.37
Radius$_m$	2.641 (**24.9**) + 100.91=	166.67 cm	3.731	162.94–170.40
Femur$_m$ + tibia$_m$	1.282 (**47.4** + **38.9**) + 59.35=	169.99 cm	2.851	167.14–172.84
Humerus$_m$ + radius$_m$	1.456 (**32.5** + **24.9**) + 83.76=	167.33 cm	3.353	163.98–170.68
Average / Range		168.60 cm		162.94–174.13

$_m$ = maximum length; SEE = standard of error estimates (Raxter et al. 2008)

CS10, 169.2 cm (range 164.53–174.97 cm); and for CS11 an estimated height of 164.95 cm (range 160.69–168.81 cm). Seneb-Kay's stature compares closely with the other males recovered in the neighboring tombs.

MUSCULOSKELETAL STRESS MARKERS (MSM)

The study of the morphology and development of areas of muscle attachment to bone at entheses, referred to as musculoskeletal stress markers (MSM), have been used to examine occupational patterns and sociocultural differences in activity in populations of the past and present. This approach is based on the understanding that strenuous and persistent muscle activity can result in bone remodeling at sites of muscle-to-bone and tendon-to-bone attachment. MSM are typically associated with habitual activity (Munson Chapman 1997; Molnar 2006; Mariotti et al. 2007; Niinimäki 2012). These markers can be identified by scoring levels of robusticity (although see Jurmain et al. [2012] for a recent discussion of limitations in the use of such markers).

In this analysis, the descriptive and photographic scoring method provided by Mariotti et al. (2007) were applied to identify levels of robusticity indicative of MSMs in the postcranial skeletal remains of Seneb-Kay. We chose this method because the descriptions are accompanied by visual markers through photographs and because of the reproducible observations. With this method, two observers identified the same level of robusticity for each bone region of Seneb-Kay's postcranium. Three levels of development correspond, in general, to low-moderate development (degree 1), high development (degree 2), and very high development (degree 3). The descriptions for each degree are as follows and were taken from Mariotti et al. (2007):

1a: slight impression; the surface is practically smooth, even though an oblique line is perceptible to the touch.

1b: low development; the insertion is marked by a line of rugosity.

1c: medium development; the line of insertion is marked by obvious rugosity, or there is a slight crest with smooth surface.

2: high development: definitive crest, possibly discontinuous, but with obvious rugosity.

3: very high development: very raised and rugose crest.

PALEOPATHOLOGY

It is a truism to say that every living person in the world today has experienced or will experience a health problem, and this is also true of ancient

Table 5.3 Paleopathological and anomalous conditions of bones and teeth, both specific and non-specific in skeleton of Seneb-Kay.

Skeleton No.	Specific (known aetiology)	Non-specific
CS9	Cribra orbitalia, osteoarthritis, dental wear, deviated septum, possible scurvy	Periosteal infection of the clavicle

populations. It can be argued that paleopathology provides a window to the understanding of past experience of disease and its impact on societies and their histories. There are a number of disease conditions that leave a mark on the skeleton and these include infectious diseases, circulatory disturbances, metabolic disorders, skeletal congenital abnormalities, skeletal dysplasias, degenerative diseases, and trauma. They can be identified through comparison to modern day samples of known aetiology (Ortner 2003). Some of these diseases are non-specific and without a known aetiology. In these cases, a disease process is still detectable (Ortner and Putschar 1981; Armelagos and Van Gerven 2003). The skeletal remains of the Second Intermediate Period royal cemetery present both specific and non-specific, paleopathological conditions. Seneb-Kay himself shows several specific pathologies (Table 5.3).

(1) Dental Wear The teeth of Seneb-Kay, like all the individuals from the South Abydos royal cemetery are worn (Fig. 5.2). According to the scoring systems provided by Schumucker (1985) and Smith (1984), Seneb-Kay's maxillary and premolars available for CS9 range in dental wear from Grades or Stages 3 to 5, where cusps are obliterated, there is exposure of the underlying dentin, and the dentin patches have coalesced. No doubt this resulted from the abrasive nature of the foods he consumed. In ancient Egyptian populations, the most abrasive materials were introduced from stone tools used in grinding grain and/or contamination of the grain with wind-blown sand (Zakrzewski 2012; Leek 1972). However, none of the maxillae or mandibles of the occupants of these royal tombs indicated evidence of dentin, apical, or peri-apical infection. This indicates that tooth wear was continuous and rapid, resulting in obliteration of possible infection foci. The kind of foods consumed determines the amount of exertion required to chew during mastication. Tough and fibrous foods require a greater amount of stress to be exerted on and by

the teeth, thus producing heavier wear on the occlusal surfaces than consuming soft refined foodstuffs would. The evidence suggests that Seneb-Kay, despite his social status, was consuming fibrous foods contaminated with particulate matter from grinding and sand. Interproximal carious lesions, dental calculus, and other varieties of periodontal disease commonly seen in ancient Egyptians (Zakrzewski 2012; Leek 1972), were not observed.

(2) Degenerative joint disease Two of Seneb-Kay's lumbar vertebrae have Schmorl's nodes—herniations of the nucleus pulposus of the intervertebral disc that penetrate the adjacent cartilaginous end plate of the vertebra (Williams et al. 2007; Dar et al. 2010). Seneb-Kay's first and second lumbar vertebrae were affected by Schmorl's nodes on the superior surface of the vertebral bodies (Fig. 5.3). The nodes can appear on any spinal vertebra but overwhelmingly affect the lower thoracic and lumbar regions. This is usually attributed to the load on the vertebrae, which increases as we descend along the spine and its curvature. The nodes themselves result from a herniation or a histological loss of nuclear material through the cartilage plate, the growth plate, and the end plate into the vertebral body. The nodes are considered a common thoracolumbar lesion, can be very painful, and are a form of lumbar degenerative joint disease. A possible reason for the development of Schmorl's nodes in Seneb-Kay's case is discussed further below.

The sacrum displays osteoarthritis of the facet joint for the fifth lumbar (L5) and first sacral (S1) vertebrae. The facets have degenerated, becoming thin and flat and the joint surfaces of the bone had direct contact (Fig. 5.4) as evidenced by lipping and mild eburnation. The right facet joint is more oblique than the left. This indicates more flexion of the right side of the lumbosacral joint. This likely resulted in lower back pain for Seneb-Kay. Facet joint osteoarthritis is an age-dependent condition, but excessive loads and flexion can exacerbate this condition (Abbas et

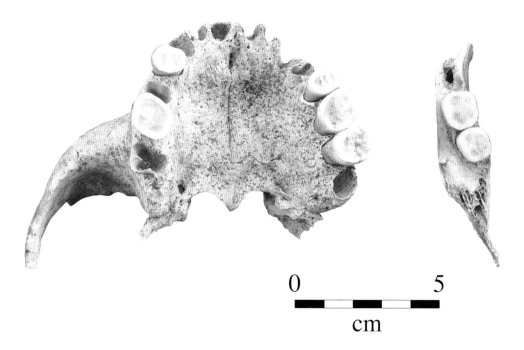

Fig. 5.2 Seneb-Kay's maxilla (left) and portion from the left side of his mandible (right); the teeth are worn: cusps are obliterated and there is marked exposure of the underlying dentin. Also note the dense porosity of the palate's surface and extending to the inferior surface of the malar, possibly indicative of scurvy.

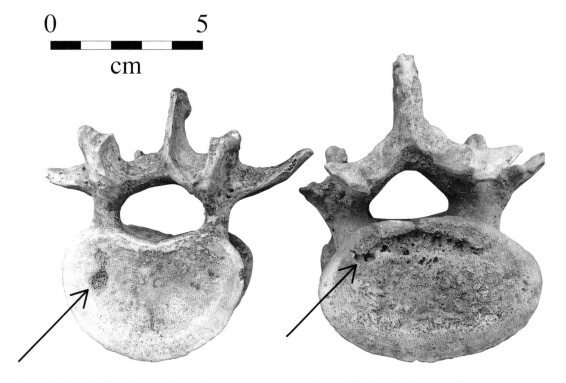

Fig. 5.3 CS9 displays Schmorl's nodes on the superior surface of lumbar bodies 1 and 2.

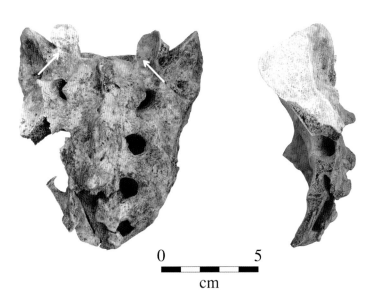

Fig. 5.4 Dorsal and side view of Seneb-Kay's sacrum showing osteoarthritis affecting the facet joint for lumbar (L5) and sacral (S1) vertebrae.

al. 2011). In our estimation, the observed osteoarthritis is not solely age dependent but also the result of some type of repetitive motion and pressure affecting the region of L5 and S1. The osteoarthritis observed here is used in conjunction with other age dependent markers for determining CS9's age estimate, and while not solely age-dependent, it does fall within the range of the other markers.

In addition to the lower back, osteoarthritic changes were evident in the sternoclavicular and manubriosternal joints. These changes were more severe in the left than in the right side as manifested by more wear (lipping around the facet) and flattening of the clavicular facet of the manubrium. Because most people are right-handed, their right sternoclavicular joint develops more osteoarthritis with age and force stress. This suggests that Seneb-Kay's dominant limb was the left. The study by Thongngarm and McMurray (2000) supports this interpretation where it was observed in modern samples that osteoarthritis lesions appear usually after age 40 and either affect both right and left sides or slightly affects more the sternoclavicular joint of the dominant limb. This indication of left-handedness may relate to evidence for the patterns of Seneb-Kay's perimortem trauma as we examine in detail below.

(3) Cribra Orbitalia and Scurvy Mild porosities in the orbital roof, known as cribra orbitalia (Ortner

and Putschar 1981; Armelagos et al. 2014), are also observed on Seneb-Kay's cranium (Fig. 5.5). The porosities of the orbit are among the most frequent pathological lesions seen in ancient human skeletal samples. They are thought to be associated with anemia, although the exact reason for the anemia is not possible to determine. The porosities are produced by the marrow expansion within the diploë of the skull that occurs as part of a systemic response to red blood cell count and hemoglobin deficiencies. Anemia-induced marrow expansion is probably a common cause of cribra orbitalia, however, other pathological processes such as those associated with scurvy, rickets, hemangiomas, and traumatic injuries can also lead to orbital roof lesions (Walker et al. 2009). Irrespective of the aetiology, the anemia observed was mild and the resulting cribra orbitalia is healed, indicating that Seneb-Kay had experienced a short episode of stress early in life. No porous lesions, active or healed, were observed on the cranial vault.

The dense porosity of the hard palatal surface of CS9 is likely indicative of a nutritional deficiency and here tentatively diagnosed as scurvy (see Fig. 5.2). Scurvy promotes bony changes marked by porosity in the skull bones, particularly in the sphenoid, the mandible, and the hard palate. An abnormal amount of porosity, as observed in Seneb-Kay's palate, almost always indicates that something is wrong with bone formation. Scurvy results from Vitamin C deficiency, which promotes subperiosteal hemorrhage as well as new bone formation. Paleopathological diagnosis of scurvy in adults is rare and remains problematic because the diagnostic lesions match closely those associated with other nutritional deficiency conditions such as rickets and osteomalacia (Armelagos et al. 2014).

(4) Nasal Septal Deviation Seneb-Kay exhibits a noticeable nasal septal deviation to the right side (Fig. 5.6). This is the deviation of the bony or cartilaginous septum that runs along the nasal aperture to one or both sides. The deviation suggests some sort of growth disjunction. One of the first causes of septal deviation is related to intrauterine pressures and trauma from birth (Gray 1978). However, humans can also develop a deviated septum in the absence of any

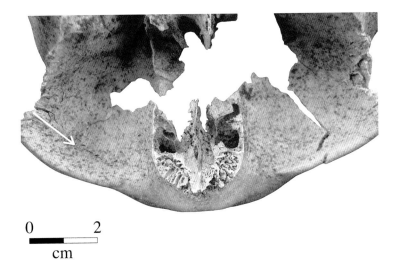

Fig. 5.5 Seneb-Kay's cranium displaying healed cribra orbitalia in the left orbit.

0   2
cm

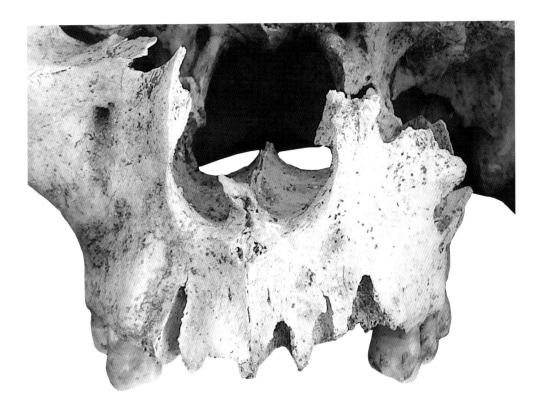

Fig. 5.6 Nasal septal deviation in the cranium of Seneb-Kay.

trauma. One possible explanation could be excess growth, causing the septum to buckle or deviate, due to the forces generated. There is no evidence of any other trauma in the area of Seneb-Kay's nasal aperture, therefore, it is entirely possible that the origin is developmental and not caused by trauma. The deviation would have likely affected the symmetry of Seneb-Kay's appearance.

(5) Clavicle Seneb-Kay exhibits a traumatic lesion of the right clavicle (Fig. 5.7). On the anterior to

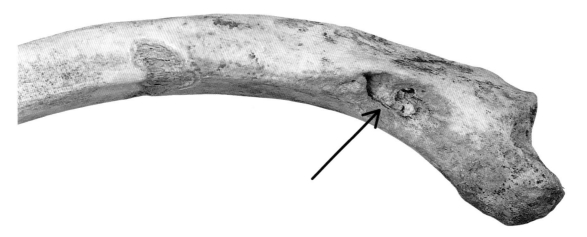

Fig. 5.7 CS9 exhibits a non-specific paleopathology in the form of a traumatic periostitis of the right clavicle.

superior surface of the clavicle there is a penetrating fracture that has pushed the bone inward (also discussed below in connection with antemortem trauma). Osteogenic repair tissue is forming from the surface of the bone. Osteogenic cells grow in the area of the fracture and, in this case, have started to form a callus of bone. The healing occurs via the bridging of the callus as it forms over the fracture's gap. However, in the process of healing an infection, has begun, possibly due to bacteria entering the wound and the bone at the fracture site (Ortner and Putschar 1981).

MUSCULOSKELETAL STRESS MARKERS (MSM)

The skeletal remains of King Seneb-Kay exhibit a particular set of activity indicators associated with contraction of muscles on their attachment sites to the bone. This pattern of activity is shared by Seneb-Kay and the male occupant of tomb CS10 suggesting that both men may have possessed a common physical regimen. In the case of Seneb-Kay, eight different sites were noted for attachments of muscles and tendons on the bones of the femora and pelvis. We interpret this to be a sign of robusticity resulting from repetitive stress placed on the pelvis and femoral attachment sites: (1) areas of insertion of gluteal muscles on the greater trochanter, (2) the linea aspera on the femora, (3) the trochanteric fossa of the femora, (4) marked iliac impressions (Poirier's

facets) on the anterior aspect of the femoral neck, (5) marked development of the adductor tubercle on the femora, (6) irregularities on the popliteal surface of the femora, (7) robust ischial spines on the pelvis; (8) strong development of the ischial tuberosity. Each of these areas is summarized and illustrated here:

(1) Gluteal attachments Seneb-Kay exhibits notable areas of insertion of all three gluteal muscles (Fig. 5.8), but especially the gluteus minimus and gluteus medius on the greater trochanter from the pulling of abductor muscles.

(2) Linea aspera The linea aspera on the femurs' posterior surfaces (Fig. 5.9) indicates repetitive stress on and development of the adductor longus muscle that inserts into the midshaft region of the linea aspera. This bone remodeling is consistent with the development of hypertrophied ligament attachments associated with the extensive use and development of the adductor muscles.

(3) Spicules on the trochanteric fossa Seneb-Kay displays development of trochanteric spicules on both femora (Fig. 5.10), as does the individual in tomb CS10. The trochanteric spicule is an enthesis at the insertion on the medial aspect of the greater trochanter of the obturator internus, a muscle important in the lateral rotation of the thigh.

(4) Poirier's facets on the femora In addition to these features, Seneb-Kay has iliac impressions (Fig. 5.11), known as Poirier's facets, on the anterior aspect of both femoral necks. Poirier's facets develop where the femur presses against the rim of the acetabulum, leaving an iliac impression.

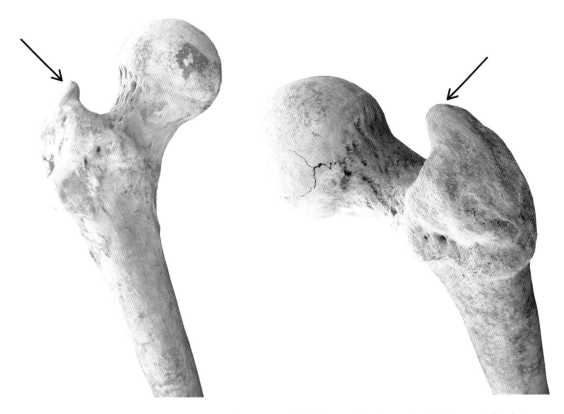

Fig. 5.8 Seneb-Kay's pronounced areas of insertion of all three gluteal muscles, but especially gluteus minimus and gluteus medius on the greater trochanter (shown on the right proximal femur anterior and posterior views; bone not in anatomical position).

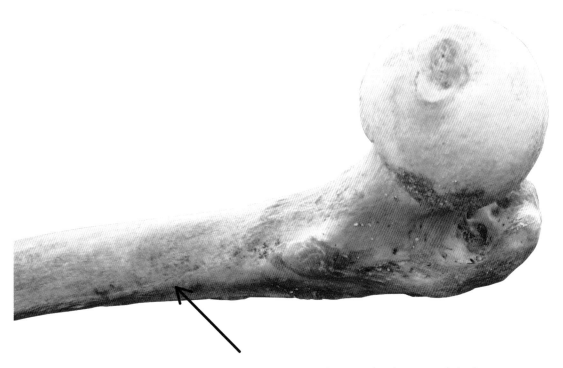

Fig. 5.9 Lateral view of the proximal end of the right femur showing development of the linea aspera.

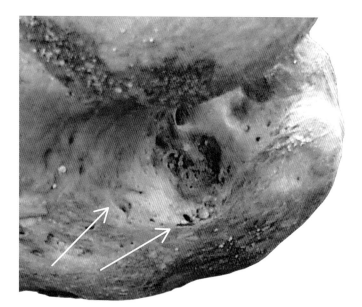

Fig. 5.10 left Seneb-Kay's skeleton has distinct spicules formed on the trochanteric fossa here shown on the right femur though also present on the left femur.

Fig. 5.11 below CS9's strongly marked iliac impressions, known as Poirier's facets on the anterior aspect of the femoral neck (right side shown).

Fig. 5.12 right The marked development of the adductor tubercle on Seneb-Kay's left femur.

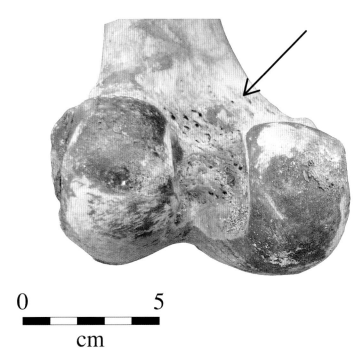

Fig. 5.13 The femur's popliteal surface (left side shown) used in attachment of the medial head of the gastrocnemius muscle is marked and irregular.

(5) Development of the adductor tubercle Adding to the areas already mentioned, Seneb-Kay displays marked development of the adductor tubercle on both sides (Fig. 5.12) for insertion of the tendon of the adductor magnus muscle. The adductor magnus is important in medial rotation of the thigh. Development of this area parallels the bone remodeling in the linea aspera and provides a signature of the hypertrophied ligament attachments associated with the use of the adductor muscles.

(6) Popliteal surface of the femora In addition to these markers, the femur's popliteal surface used in attachment of the medial head of the gastrocnemius muscle is bilaterally marked and irregular, observed to be enlarged on both sides (Fig. 5.13). The medial head of the gastrocnemius flexes the knee, and development of MSM in these areas reflect habitual physical activities that would have developed the gastrocnemius.

(7) Ischial spines on the pelvic bones Seneb-Kay's pelvic bones display evidence for habitual muscle exertion in the form of robustly developed and elongated ischial spines (Fig. 5.14). This was also seen in the CS10 individual's pelvis. Hypertrophy of the

muscles resulting from exertion of the pelvic floor during youth and early adulthood can cause elongation and posterior remodeling of the ischial spine (Antolak et al. 2002). This development in the pelvis is particularly responsive to physical activities that require consistent flexion of the hip floor muscles. The changes to the ischial spine occur during the period of development and ossification of the spinous process of the ischium. Therefore, this indicates that habitual physical activity resulting in MSM to the ischial spines spanned the period when Seneb-Kay was a juvenile and adolescent.

(8) Development of the ischial tuberosity Seneb-Kay's pelvic bones exhibit strong muscle markings of the ischial tuberosity where the tendons of the semimembranosus, semitendinosus, adductor magnus, and biceps femoris attach (Fig. 5.15). There is a correlation between the strong ischial tuberosity and the repetitive action of the adductor magnus and other muscles of the pelvic floor (Terada 2010). The adductor magnus muscle contracts and pulls the hip towards the body's midline serving to stabilize the body.

DISCUSSION OF MSM

In the analysis of Seneb-Kay's skeletal remains, one of the immediately noticeable features of his lower body occurs in the loci for muscle attachments on the femora and pelvis. We can state on the basis of eight different areas summarized above that Seneb-Kay made extensive, habitual use of the following muscles:

(1) adductor magnus (medial side of the thigh), the major muscle used in adduction (inward pulling) of the upper legs and hips.

(2) adductor longus (inner thigh ventral to adductor magnus), a muscle used primarily in lateral (outward) rotation of the thigh.

(3) biceps femoris (thigh posterior), a muscle that connects the hip and knee and is used in

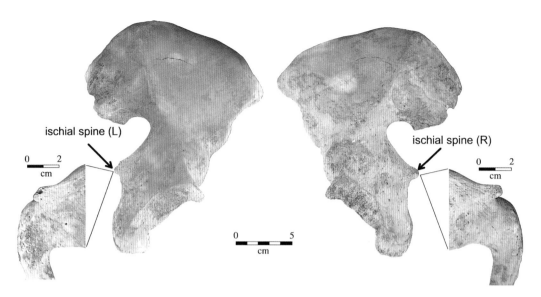

Fig. 5.14 The pelvic bones showing robust development of the ischial spines.

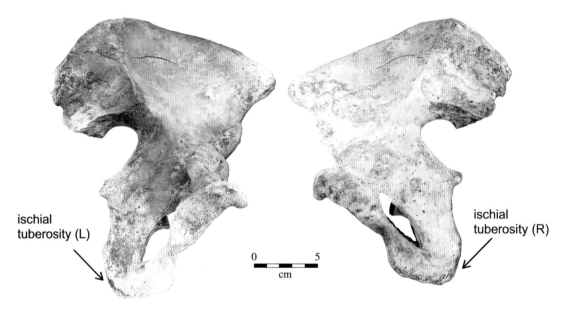

Fig. 5.15 Seneb-Kay's strong muscle markings of the ischial tuberosity.

extension of the hip and flexing and rotating the knee joint.

(4)   gastrocnemius (posterior leg, knee to heel), a two-joint muscle used in plantar flexing of the foot and flexing of the leg at the knee joint.

The MSM on Seneb-Kay's femora and pelvic bones clearly reflect long-term use of the muscles of his inner thighs and upper legs. What forms of repetitive physical activity can produce this particular constellation of muscle development? While running, jumping, and climbing can display themselves in muscle attachments to the upper legs those more standard movements associated with human locomotion do not rely on repetitive adduction and the medial and lateral rotation of the thigh that appears to be reflected in Seneb-Kay's bone signatures (Molleson and Blondiaux 1994; Blondiaux 1994). Extensive running or related activities are unlikely to have produced the type of MSM reflecting long-term use of the adductor muscles of the upper thigh.

One possibility to consider is that Seneb-Kay spent a considerable amount of time, evidently extending back to his juvenile years, as a horseback rider. The set of diagnostic features visible in Seneb-Kay's MSM has been considered by a number of different studies to be indicative of habitual equestrian activity. The bone remodeling in these areas of exertion is consistent with habitual equestrian activity (see discussions of Molleson and Blondiaux 1994; Blondiaux 1994; Ruff 1994; Erikson, Lee, and Bertram 2000; and Wagner et al. 2011). These authors identify key femoral features that characterize habitual horse riders and that are clearly evident in Seneb-Kay's femora and pelvis. Hypertrophied ligament attachments have also been noted in Native North American skeletal remains after the introduction of the horse (Erickson, Lee, and Bertram 2000). While any one of these criteria alone would not be particularly diagnostic of a specific activity, it is the full suite of elements summarized above that is highly indicative of horse riding. As Molleson and Blondiaux have stated: "the association of the three, trochanteric spicule, and gluteal and adductor development, would seem to result from habitual riding" (Molleson and Blondiaux 1994).

Relevant also is the evidence we have discussed above for lumbar joint disease and osteoarthritic changes to Seneb-Kay's lower back in the form of Schmorl's nodes and erosion to the sacral facet joints. Facet joint osteoarthrosis is an age-dependent condition, but continuous and excessive loads and flexion can exacerbate this condition. In Seneb-Kay's case, the right facet joint is more oblique than the left. This indicates flexion predominantly effecting the right side of the lumbosacral joint. The osteoarthritis of the sacral facet is characterized by lipping of articulation borders. In our estimation, the observed arthrosis is not solely age dependent, but also the result of repetitive motion and pressure affecting the region more on the right side of L5 and S1. Seneb-Kay has Schmorl's nodes on the superior surface of the L1 and L2 vertebral bodies. Schmorl's nodes in the lower thoracic and upper lumbar vertebrae of Native American males have been associated with the introduction of the horse to the North American plains (Sandness and Reinhard 1992:299–309; Reinhard et al. 1994:63–74). This evidence lends support

to the MSM evidence and the interpretation that Seneb-Kay may have practiced horse riding, where the forces exerted on the lower back contributed to the development of osteoarthritis. Although we recognize the reconstruction of human activity based on musculoskeletal stress markers is contested by some (Jurmain et al. 2012), that Seneb-Kay presents such a significant cluster of markers related to horseback riding lends weight to our interpretation. Moreover, these markers should also be considered in association with the evidence bearing on Seneb-Kay's mode of death as we discuss further below.

Egypt's Second Intermediate Period was the time period when use of the horse (*Equus ferus calballus*) was being increasingly adopted in the Nile Valley, likely in close association with military activities. Horses appear to have come into Egypt primarily as an animal valued through its martial applications. While the physical evidence is still scant, and the date of excavated remains of horses remains debated (Raulwing and Clutton-Brock 2009), it is clear that the Egyptians had substantially mastered chariot technology by the end of the Second Intermediate Period (Howard 2014). Horse-drawn chariots were in full use by the Theban 17th Dynasty during their campaigns against the Hyksos (perhaps less than a century after the death of Seneb-Kay). The use of horses in pulling chariots fundamentally relies on being able to break and ride horses. Indeed, there are indications that prior to the full mastery of complex chariot technology (which, for symbolic reasons, is textually and visually more prominent in the historical record than direct riding), horses were being ridden directly as part of military command structures and rapid movements, perhaps as early as the late Middle Kingdom (Schulman 1957:263–271). Moreover, horses appear to have had a history in gift exchanges among political elites during the Middle Bronze Age that occurred independently of their adaptation into chariot warfare (Bibby 2003:13–18).

This was a time period that predated use of the saddle, bit, and bridle (Sasada 2013:229–236). Consequently, horseback riding at the inception of equestrian practices in Egypt was necessarily a form of bareback riding, akin to the later North American Plains Indian style of riding (Bennett 1998:383–399; Dobie 1952:42–62). Such a riding technique would have been appropriate to the relatively small stature of horses that are attested for the end of the Middle

Bronze and Late Bronze Age in the Near East and Egypt (equivalent to the Second Intermediate Period and New Kingdom). Moreover, this mode of riding would have developed naturally for people used to regular riding of donkeys, although the gait and forces placed on the rider in donkey riding differ significantly from that of the horse. The biomechanics of bareback horse riding would function to enhance the muscular stressors implicated for habitual horse riding in general with need for use of muscles to grip and balance on the horse's back. The riding techniques that developed in the New World on the comparably small stature mustangs of Spanish introduction originally from North Africa (Haines 1938a:112–117, 1938b:429–437) appear to have been expressed in a similar suite of human skeletal signatures as we have detailed above.

On this basis, there appears to be a significant possibility that the MSM evidence from Seneb-Kay's femora and pelvic area indicate he was an accomplished and habitual equestrian (see also previous observations by Wegner [2015:75–78]). We cannot regard this conclusion as a certainty, but the physical evidence should also not be divorced from the historical and social context of the king's reign. The period of his life, paired with the prevalence of territorial conflict and military titles at Abydos itself during this timeframe, may imply that Seneb-Kay grew up and rose to power within the military side of the elite of Upper Egypt. In such a social context we should perhaps find physical evidence for habitual horse riding not at all surprising. Moreover, as we shall consider below, similar physical traits and additional MSM evidence suggestive of repetitive physical and military training occur in the male skeleton from tomb CS10 not far from the tomb of Seneb-Kay. In Seneb-Kay's case, his skeleton not only provides MSM evidence suggestive of habitual riding that likely started when he was still a juvenile, but there is a complementary suite of evidence for injuries relating to his death. The perimortem trauma on Seneb-Kay's body clearly indicates his death in an armed confrontation: an ambush or battle. Interestingly, the patterns of his wounds suggest he was in an elevated position relative to his assailants when he was attacked, pulled to the ground, and killed. This second, and independent line of skeletal evidence corroborates the indications for habitual equestrian activity through his MSM.

ANTEMORTEM TRAUMA

The skeletal remains of Seneb-Kay indicate that he lived a physical life that produced a set of distinctive MSM that may be indicative of his habitual involvement in martial activities. Three antemortem injuries also suggest possible warfare-related activity. These injuries were all to the upper right side of his body including fractures to his ribcage, clavicle, and zygomatic. We interpret these fractures as the result of recent trauma with the zygomatic and rib fractures having healed while the clavicle was still in the process of healing at the time of death (Fig. 5.16).

(1) Zygomatic fracture The right zygomatic had experienced a Lefort 2 separation from the maxilla (Fig. 5.17). This injury must have resulted from a significant, blunt force, impact to the right side of the face. The injury had healed but appears to have occurred within a short timeframe of the king's death.

(2) Clavicular fracture The fracture to the right clavicle was a penetrating trauma that had pushed the bone inward and become infected during healing (see Fig. 5.7). The healing of the fracture occurred via the bridging of the callus as it formed over the fracture's gap (Ortner and Putschar 1981). Based on the fact that the lesion was still healing at the time of death this appears to have been the most recent injury he suffered, and it likely occurred within a short time frame (under a year) before his death.

(3) Rib fracture The seventh right rib, superior view was fractured medially, that is towards the sternum in a hinging effect (Fig. 5.18). The injury had substantially healed but appears to have occurred during the recent life of the individual.

PERIMORTEM TRAUMA

While the areas of antemortem trauma preserved on Seneb-Kay's skeleton indicate a lifestyle that involved significant physical conflict, it is the extensive array of perimortem traumatic wounds that show how the king's life culminated in a violent and bloody death. Bones preserve enduring evidence of life experience due to biological and cultural processes that leave marks on the skeleton. Skeletal remains are, therefore, a significant source of evidence of life activity for reconstruction of historical events of archaeological sites (Licata et al. 2014). Because

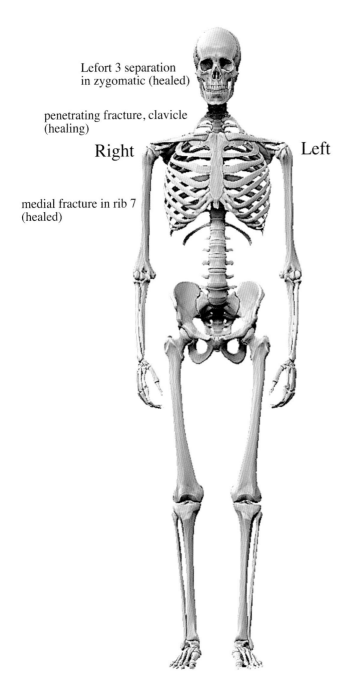

Lefort 3 separation
in zygomatic (healed)

penetrating fracture, clavicle
(healing)

Right

Left

medial fracture in rib 7
(healed)

Fig 5.16 Antemortem trauma in the skeleton of Seneb-Kay.

violence can leave indelible marks on bone, these can be documented for patterns and interpreted in conjunction with the artifactual evidence within the archaeological context. This aspect of Seneb-Kay's osteobiography has important ramifications for the social and political context of his life and death.

In Seneb-Kay's skeletal remains, trauma is represented by multiple perimortem lesions created by

bladed weapons that impacted bones from his skull to his feet. Fifteen major perimortem traumas have been documented, several of which were severe. Such a number of wounds that penetrated to the bone potentially reflects a greater extent of internal trauma to the king's soft tissues, muscles, and organs, which would leave little to no evidence on the bones themselves. The inventory of traumatic lesions (extending from the lower to upper body) are as follows (Fig. 5.19):

LOWER EXTREMITIES

(1) Feet: cuts through the left medial cuneiform and first and second metatarsals.

The center of the left foot was struck across its upper surface with a bladed weapon that cut through the medial cuneiform leaving a clean, straight cut that severed the bone (Fig. 5.20).

This bone has been cut completely across in distal to proximal direction. The angle of the cut is somewhat oblique from the dorsal surface to posterior. Based on its location and angle, the cut through the medial cuneiform is likely an extension of another cut in the dorsal surface of the proximal end of left metatarsal 1 (the upper end of the big toe). It appears a single blow sliced through the base of the toe and severed the medial cuneiform. This substantial wound would have affected the mobility of the king's left leg. The left foot was also struck in the middle with a single penetrating cut to the proximal end of the second metatarsal.

(2) Right ankle: complete cut through distal end of the right tibia and fibula.

This cut through the distal ends of both the right tibia and fibula occurred by means of a single blow, as indicated through the common plane and angle of entry of the cut to both bones (Fig. 5.21). The cut severed the medial malleolus of the distal end of the tibia and lateral malleolus of the distal end of the fibula. The cut entered just above the ankle from front to back (anterior to posterior) and with a shallow downward angle. The angle of this cut is particularly notable as, despite being very low on the body,

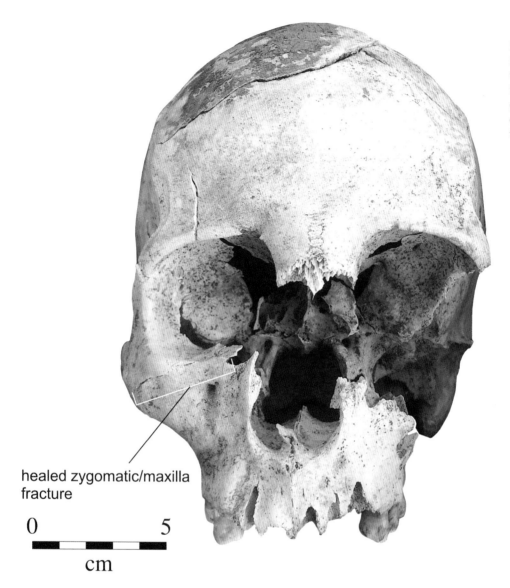

Fig. 5.17 Skull of
Seneb-Kay showing
the healed Lefort 2
fracture between zy-
gomatic and maxilla
on the right side of
the face.

healed zygomatic/maxilla
fracture

0   5

cm

it was made by a blade that struck at a nearly horizontal angle. This injury is clearly the most severe
on Seneb-Kay's postcranial skeleton. The cut would
have effectively severed the bone and arteries in the
leg and separated the junction between the lower leg
and foot, severely impeding mobility. Given the angle of entry the foot likely remained attached at the
heel but would have been effectively unusable. The
severity of the injury suggests that it was significantly
disabling injury for Seneb-Kay and would have rendered him very vulnerable to further attack.

**(3) Knees: penetrating cuts through patella and
distal end of the femur (left knee) and cut into
proximal end of tibia (below right knee).**

The evidence shows that both knees were hacked
by bladed weapons (Fig. 5.22). On the right side (the
same leg that has the cut above the ankle), there is
a single, cut to the upper end of the tibia. The more
significant injury to this part of the king's body occurred on the left side where two separate blows cut
into the knee. One major blow cut through the patella

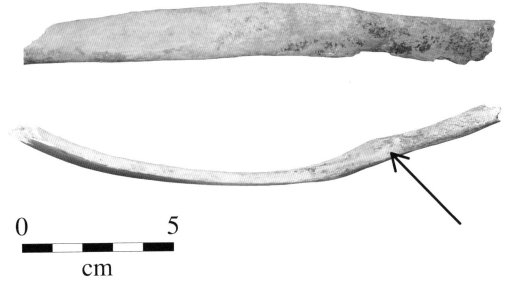

Fig. 5.18 Healed fracture in the seventh rib, right side of Seneb-Kay.

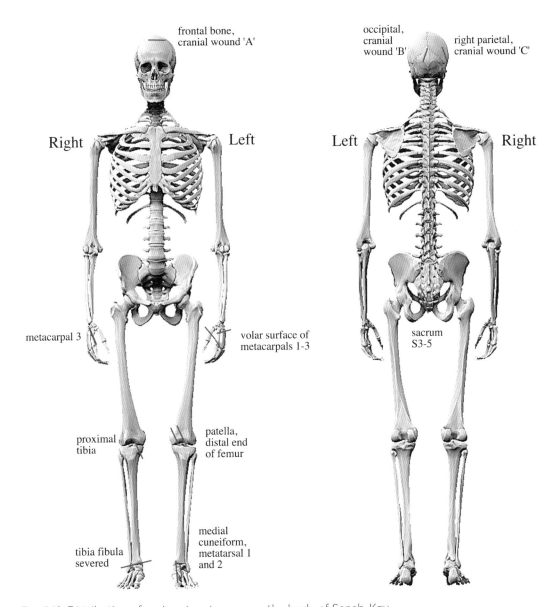

Fig. 5.19 Distribution of perimortem trauma on the body of Seneb-Kay.

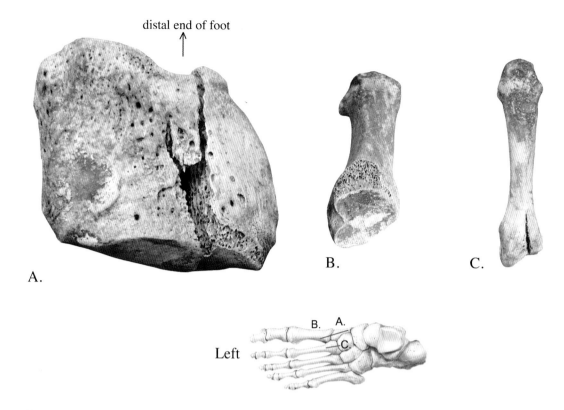

distal end of foot

A.

B.

C.

B. A.

C.

Left

Fig. 5.20 Trauma to the feet of Seneb-Kay: left medial cuneiform showing a cut across the dorsal surface of the foot (A); left metatarsal 1 (B); and left metatarsal 2 (C). Images not to relative scale.

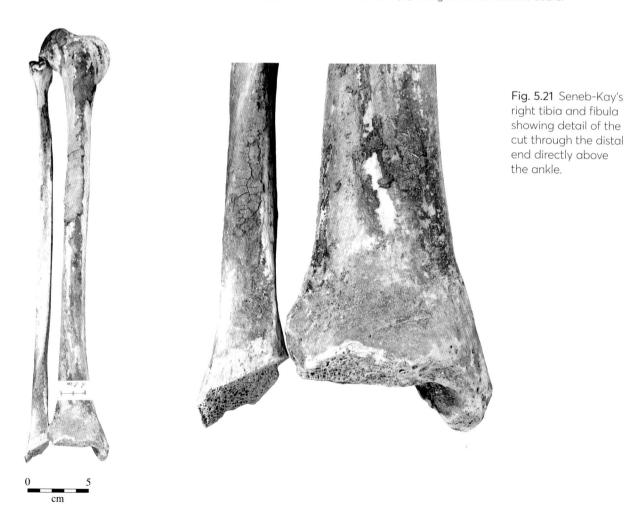

Fig. 5.21 Seneb-Kay's right tibia and fibula showing detail of the cut through the distal end directly above the ankle.

0   5
cm

and continued to terminate in the lower end of the femur's medial epicondyle. A second cut penetrated more deeply into the medial epicondyle.

(4) Lower back: two penetrating cuts through the left, posterior surfaces of the third, fourth and fifth sacral vertebrae (posterior to anterior direction).

The king's lower back was cut from behind with impact in two locations (Fig. 5.23). One cut fell directly over the center of the sacrum cutting into the lower vertebrae (S4 and S5). A second more severe blow cut through the right side of the three lower vertebrae (S3, S4, and S5). The angle of both cuts is parallel suggesting they occurred in immediate succession from the same weapon and assailant.

UPPER EXTREMITIES

(5) Hands: palmar surface of metacarpals, 3 penetrating cuts to the left hand, 1 penetrating cut to the right hand.

The king's hands were damaged by sharp bladed weaponry that left clear cuts in multiple areas (Fig. 5.24). The primary documented wounds occurred in the palmar surface of the hands. A notable pattern here is the predominance of injury to the left side. Cuts damaged the center of the left metacarpal 1 (thumb), as well as the proximal ends of the immediately adjacent metacarpals 2 and 3 (index and middle fingers). The cuts to the left hand were conducted with a sharp bladed weapon wielded with such force

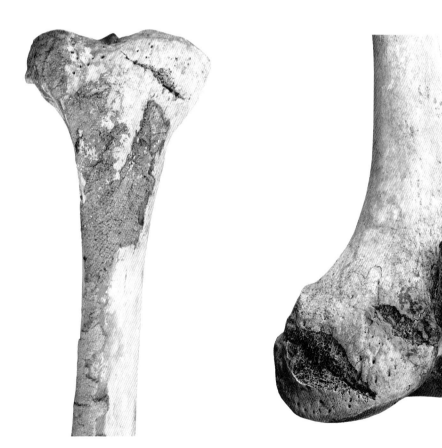

Fig. 5.22 Left photo: proximal end of the right tibia showing diagonal cut to anterior surface. Right photo: distal end of Seneb-Kay's left femur showing two penetrating wounds that severed the patella and cut into the medial epicondyle.

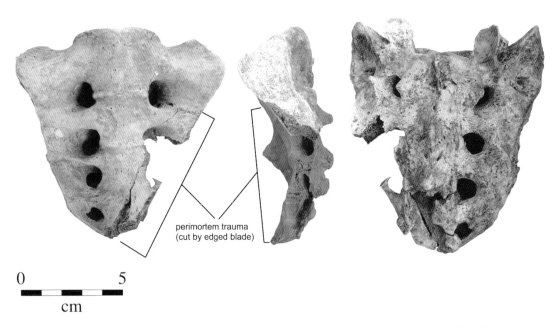

perimortem trauma
(cut by edged blade)

0   5
cm

Fig. 5.23 Seneb-Kay's sacrum showing the two parallel cuts through sacral vertebrae S3–S5.

that the bases of metacarpals 2 and 3 were practically cut off. In contrast, the bones in the right hand display minimal evidence for trauma with a single cut to metacarpal 3.

(6) Head: three traumatic blows to the cranium, one to the middle of the frontal bone (cranial Wound A), a second blow to the left side of the occipital bone (cranial Wound B), and a third one to the right parietal bone (cranial Wound C).

Among the trauma suffered in the final moments of his life, Seneb-Kay's cranium experienced the most dramatic wounds.[2] Wound A to the frontal bone consists of a sharp-force trauma created by a blade that entered Seneb-Kay's skull just above his forehead at a nearly horizontal angle. The angle of entry was from left to right. The impact of the blow penetrated the calvarium and produced three fracture lines that radiated throughout the frontal bone and stopped only when the cranial sutures were breached (Fig. 5.25). Wound A preserves the perfect impression of the curvature and profile of a battle axe measuring 4.4 cm wide and 0.25 cm in thickness on its leading edge.

Additionally, on the upper occipital bone below lambda, another sharp force traumatic blow pierced the skull (Wound B), leaving a cut approximately 4.4 cm in length which would have penetrated and damaged brain matter (Fig. 5.26). The sharpness of the instrument and its entrance angle have been imprinted in the bone as seen in the microscopy photo (Fig. 5.27). This wound was created by a weapon that struck the back of the skull from the left side. Finally, Seneb-Kay's right parietal bone was severely dented by a weapon that left a major impression in the skull (Wound C). Cranial Wound C is approximately 2 cm in length. In this case the weapon did not penetrate the skull. However, like Wound A to the frontal bone, this strike to the parietal preserves the shape of the blade that created it. The cumulative affect of the many and severe perimortem traumas to Seneb-Kay and the lack of any healing indicate death followed quickly after.

FORENSIC ANALYSIS OF PERIMORTEM TRAUMAS

The skeletal remains of Seneb-Kay are presently the oldest surviving remains of an ancient Egyptian king killed in a martial encounter. Seneb-Kay (ca. 1650–1600 BCE) predates by perhaps half a century the mummy of the 17th Dynasty Theban king Seqenenre Tao (ca. 1600–1575 BCE), who died presumably while fighting against the Hyksos. As in the case

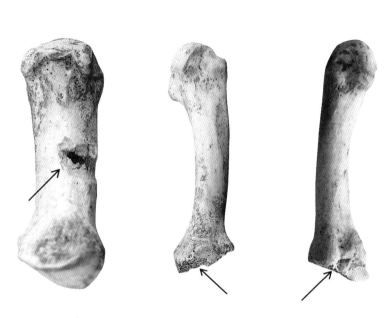

Fig. 5.24 Perimortem traumatic cuts to Seneb-Kay's left hand: metacarpal 1 (left); metacarpal 2 (middle) and metacarpal 3 (right). Metacarpals 2 and 3 exhibit trauma whereby something sharp cut the proximal heads almost completely off and left a flat surface that runs obliquely in a dorsal to palmar direction (bones not photographed in anatomical position).

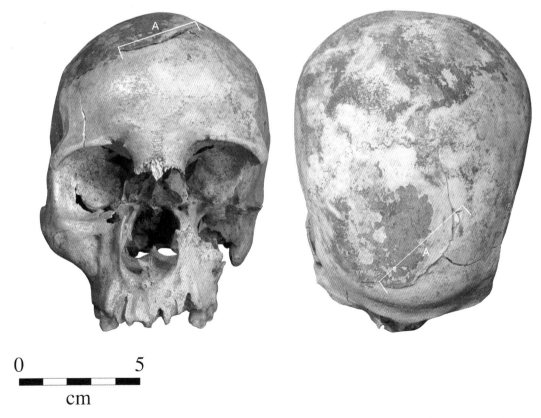

Fig. 5.25 Axe wound to middle of Seneb-Kay's frontal bone. This wound (Wound A) preserves the impression of the leading edge of a battle axe measuring 4.4 cm in width.

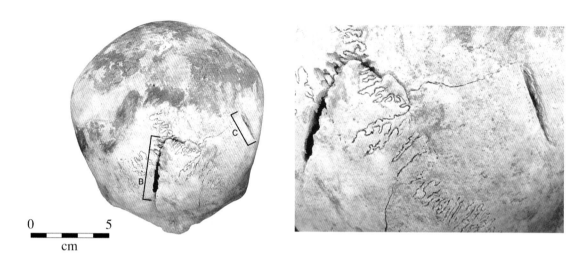

Fig. 5.26 Axe wounds to Seneb-Kay's occipital (Wound B, measuring 4.4 cm) and right parietal (Wound C, measuring 2 cm).

Fig. 5.27 Sharp force trauma on Seneb-Kay's occipital below lambda (Wound B). The clean edge indicating the sharpness of the instrument is visible as is the angle of entry from the left to right side of the cranium.

of this later Second Intermediate Period king, the violent death of Seneb-Kay represents an index to the political conflict of that phase of Egyptian history. How did Seneb-Kay die? What do the patterns of his traumatic injuries tell us? The brutality suffered by Seneb-Kay is illustrated by the scope and severity of his wounds. However, the skeleton provides evidence that allows us to go beyond a mere inventory of the perimortem trauma and make inferences regarding the nature of the king's death.

A first stage of analysis addresses the nature of the weaponry used to kill Seneb-Kay. The clearest evidence survives in the cranial wounds, one of which (Wound A) preserves a full imprint of the leading edge of the weapon that was driven into the king's skull. This wound, due to its shallow angle of entry relative to the frontal bone, preserves the entire outline of the weapon that created it.[3] An impression taken of this wound shows the weapon measured 4.4 cm across the width of the blade and was 0.25 cm in thickness. It had an excurvate leading edge with a wedge-shaped profile (Fig. 5.28).

The weapon was consistent with a battle axe of a type commonly used in the Nile Valley during the Second Intermediate Period and for which there are good surviving examples (see the historical discussion in Chapter 15). This type of blade was normally mounted in a notch cut into the upper end of the axe handle. The axe head was fastened by cordage or some other tensile material tied around two tangs that projected from the base of the blade (Davies 1987). Fastening the handle tightly on either side of the tangs compressed the sides of the notch, putting pressure on the base of the blade, while the tangs themselves prevented the blade from shifting within the notch.

In their discussion of the weaponry most likely to have killed the 17th Dynasty pharaoh Seqenenre Tao, Bietak and Strouhal (1974) provide illustrations of a variety arms, many of which were excavated at the capital city of Tell el-Dab'a/Avaris that are characteristic of the Hyksos assemblage. The measurements taken of Wound A on Seneb-Kay's frontal bone indicates that a Hyksos style battle ax with a flat or incurvate cutting edge is not the type of weapon used to deliver Seneb-Kay's fatal skull fractures (Bietak and Strouhal 1974: abb. 3–4). However, an Upper Egyptian style battle axe with an excurvate, wedge-shaped leading edge discussed here does fit the profile of these wounds. The size and curvature of the impression in Seneb-Kay's skull compares remarkably closely with preserved battle axes in royal tomb assemblages of the Theban 17th Dynasty such as the burial of Queen Ahhotep. We can conclude that Seneb-Kay cranium was struck with a weapon that would have been virtually identical to examples

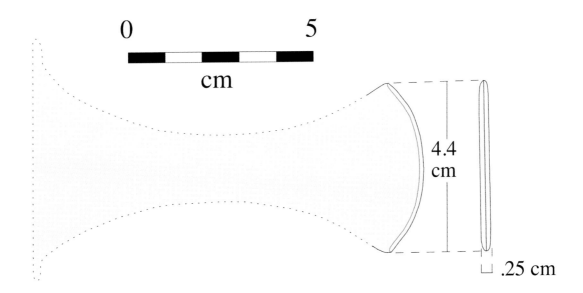

Fig. 5.28 Reconstruction of the axe blade used to create Wound A to the frontal of Seneb-Kay's cranium.

included in Ahhotep's burial such as Cairo 52646 or Cairo 52647 (Vernier 1925:207–208 and pl.44). These are relatively small and light, but lethal weapons that could be swung in one hand with considerable force. Based on the close similarity in blade size with the Ahhotep examples the weapon used on Seneb-Kay's cranium should have been approximately 40 cm in total length with a blade on the order of 10 cm long with its cutting edge of 4.4 cm (Fig. 5.29).

While cranial wound A derives from a battle axe, the other penetrating wound (Wound B) and one shallow wound (Wound C) to the back and side of his skull are less obviously attributed to that type of weapon. Nevertheless, there are good reasons for concluding that these were also created by a battle axe (Fig. 5.30). Wound B is the result of a blade that struck the back of the head at a ca. 45° angle, wielded from Seneb-Kay's left to right. This blade also struck approximately 18° off of vertical relative to the cranium itself. There is a distinctive hinging in the bone that indicates blunt force as well as a penetrating cut. Stabbing action with a sword appears unlikely to have created the level of hinging we see here, accompanied by the radiating fractures that jumped over the cranial suture lines. Implied here is a weapon that both cuts and delivers blunt force crushing action at the same time. Moreover, the ca. 4.4 cm length of Wound B conforms with the dimensions of the axe blade clearly preserved in Wound A. It is likely

Wound B was produced by the very same weapon as wound A. Wound C was created when a blade struck the right parietal at a nearly vertical angle relative to the cranium. Although the strike here was not as forceful and did not penetrate, like Wounds A and B we see diagnostic features of a wedge-shaped leading edge consistent with the form of battle axe discussed above. The implication is all blows to the head were delivered with a battle axe, possibly wielded by a single individual.

While use of a battle axe is indicated by the cranial wounds many of the postcranial injuries display evidence for longer, thinner blades than a battle axe. The clean, slicing wounds to Seneb-Kay's ankle and sacrum were delivered by a much thinner weapon with a longer cutting edge. This is particularly well illustrated by the cut above the right ankle, which severed the ends of the tibia and fibula in a single smooth cut. This kind of bone-penetrating cut was potentially caused by a spear point but appears more likely to be the result of a sword blow (compare Bietak and Strouhal 1974: abb. 2, nr. 810, 433, and 350). The extensive number of wounds, as well as clear indications for a variety of weaponry strongly suggests the king was killed by multiple assailants.

Turning to the distribution of the perimortem trauma there are some important implications to Seneb-Kay's injuries based on the location, angles of delivery, and relative severity of the individual

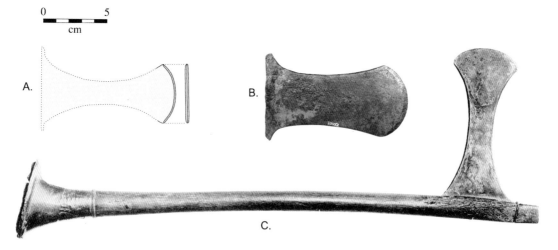

Fig. 5.29 Scale comparison of the blade impressed in Seneb-Kay's cranium (A); with an example of a preserved copper axe blade (Penn Museum E11152) showing the wedge-shaped leading edge and tangs (B); and a fully preserved Second Intermediate Period battle axe (C) from the tomb of Ahhotep at Thebes (17th Dynasty), Cairo 52646 (after Vernier 1925: pl. 44).

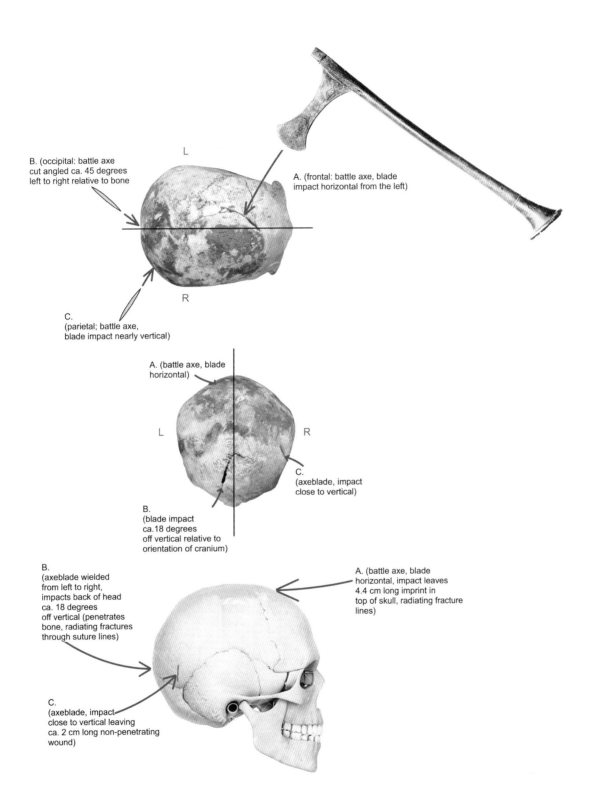

B. (occipital: battle axe cut angled ca. 45 degrees left to right relative to bone

A. (frontal: battle axe, blade impact horizontal from the left)

C. (parietal; battle axe, blade impact nearly vertical)

A. (battle axe, blade horizontal)

C. (axeblade, impact close to vertical)

B. (blade impact ca.18 degrees off vertical relative to orientation of cranium)

B. (axeblade wielded from left to right, impacts back of head ca. 18 degrees off vertical (penetrates bone, radiating fractures through suture lines)

A. (battle axe, blade horizontal, impact leaves 4.4 cm long imprint in top of skull, radiating fracture lines)

C. (axeblade, impact close to vertical leaving ca. 2 cm long non-penetrating wound)

Fig. 5.30 The three cranial wounds attributed to a battle axe showing location and angles of impact (the top and back views are photographs of Seneb-Kay's cranium, the side view shows the wound locations on a generic skull).

lesions. The king's body was subject to an astounding number of bone-penetrating injuries that extend from his feet to the very top of his cranium. While we cannot know the exact order in which the trauma occurred, the fact that some of the wounds could have proved fatal, while other wounds would have only incapacitated him allows us to make observations on the likely sequence of the assault. As we have already seen, of the three cranial wounds, the penetrating cut to the occipital (B) and massive axe blow to the frontal bone (A) are of such severity that they could have instantly rendered Seneb-Kay defenseless. Consequently, if these cranial injuries had occurred early in the confrontation there would be no reason for the large number of postcranial injuries. While we cannot discount some form of vengeful desecration of the king's body in the immediate aftermath of his death, the postcranial injuries appear logically to precede the massive cranial trauma. In all likelihood, the postcranial trauma occurred first, followed sequentially by the cranial injuries that form the final stage of the assault.

The sharp force trauma to Seneb-Kay's lower extremities appears not to be indiscriminate but rather specifically directed at his lower limbs. We may note here the cuts that targeted his feet and ankles, knees and lower back which would have effectively rendered him immobile. In particular, the conspicuous number of cuts to the lower back and legs is a physical pattern that begs for explanation. Why was there such a concentration of effort directed against the king's lower body with no detectable injuries to his torso?

If the king were engaged in hand-to-hand combat on foot, it would appear unlikely he would have accrued such a concentration of cuts to his legs with nothing whatsoever effecting his torso.[4] Analysis of Egyptian battle scenes as well as actual physical remains of soldiers who died in battle during the early Middle Kingdom show the prevalence of mid-body injuries (Winlock 1945:7–24, Sanchez 2000:143–165; Vogel 2003:239–245; Shaw 2009:165–166). Ground level combat against multiple assailants should have left a signature on the bones of Seneb-Kay's midsection, a zone of his body which is overwhelmingly free of skeletal evidence for penetrating trauma. For that reason, the concentration of cuts to the lower limbs suggests the king initially occupied in an elevated position relative to his attackers.

The possibility that the assault on Seneb-Kay started with the king in an elevated position is further suggested by the angle of entry of some of the more severe leg wounds. In particular, we would observe the nearly horizontal angle of the cut that slashed the base of his right tibia and fibula. Such an angle just above the foot is puzzling if the combatants were fighting at ground level. It would essentially require a kneeling assailant swinging a weapon close to and parallel to ground level with enough force to cut through the tibia and fibula; an unlikely physical situation in combat. However, this wound makes considerable sense if Seneb-Kay's foot were elevated at a level where an opponent was able to slash directly above the foot at a close to horizontal angle.

Higher on the leg, the severe cut to the left knee includes two blows effected probably by a battle axe that struck in rapid succession at an angle slightly off of vertical. Here we see a shift in orientation of the lesions from horizontal to vertical across the short distance of the lower leg. Again, the orientation would appear difficult to achieve in hand to hand combat unless the assailant were kneeling or seated on the ground in front of the standing king. However, if the king's knees were elevated, these inward-angled blows would make sense for an attacker striking Seneb-Kay's knees at a position above his own torso. More broadly, the wounds clearly show that Seneb-Kay was surrounded, and his lower limbs were attacked on both sides. The goal of this attention to the lower body may have been to dislodge the king from his elevated position by attacking parts of his body that would be most easily reached by his assailants' weapons. A second intent may have been to render the king immobile once he was brought down to the elevation of his attackers.

Here the intriguing patterns of Seneb-Kay's perimortem trauma converge in a suggestive way with the evidence we have discussed above for his musculoskeletal stress markers. One explanation for the king's injury patterns is that he was elevated, either on a chariot or mounted on horseback during the encounter that ended in his death. In such a scenario, he would have to be dislodged before he could be attacked and killed at ground level. The Second Intermediate Period is the very timeframe in pharaonic Egypt when horses and chariotry were being adapted into military technology (Shaw 2001:59–71). The use of chariots by the Thebans in warfare against the

Hyksos is referred to in historical sources during the reigns of Kamose and Ahmose at the end of the 17th Dynasty (Schulman 1980:105–153). Indeed, based on wound patterns preserved on the mummy of Seqenenre Tao, Bietak has proposed that king may have been riding on a chariot when he was attacked and killed (Bietak and Strouhal 1974:29–52).

While many scholars have made the assumption that horses in the Nile Valley were adapted exclusively for use as draft animals for military chariots, there is no reason to *a priori* exclude direct use of horses by military commanders. Breaking and training horses through riding is a necessary step for the development of chariotry. Consequently, there is no logical reason to exclude horse riding in military tactics over a substantial timeframe before the more complex technology of chariot warfare was fully mastered in the Nile Valley. Indeed, although the evidence remains scant, there are indications that horses may have already played a role in military tactics as early as the late Middle Kingdom with application for rapid movement of military commanders (Schulman 1957:263–271). Certainly, horses remained rare and expensive animals but would have been accessible during this timeframe in Upper Egypt only by the elite, royalty, and military segments of society. Doubt has been expressed on the use of chariots in battle prior to the end of the Second Intermediate Period and even the possibility that kings participated directly in warfare (Shaw 2009:166–174). However, this does not seem to be the case either during the Second Intermediate Period or the subsequent New Kingdom when abundant evidence demonstrates a direct role of kings in combat. While we cannot be certain whether Seneb-Kay was killed in some form of ambush rather than in the midst of conflict on the battlefield, the nature of the perimortem trauma on his skeleton weighs heavily in favor of the latter.

Let us consider the two possibilities of an elevated position on a chariot versus on horseback. If Seneb-Kay were riding on chariot when attacked, this position is not consistent with the distribution of wounds to the lower body. In a chariot Seneb-Kay would have been standing inside a carriage flanked by the vehicle's wheels and possibly standing alongside a chariot driver. The principal access to the king's body would be from behind the vehicle. Yet, the major blows to Seneb-Kay's lower body occur to the front of his limbs (feet, ankles and knees) as well

as to his lower back. These areas are precisely those that would be most easily accessible to armed men at ground level if he were mounted on horseback. Seneb-Kay was attacked by men who were able to effect cuts both vertically and laterally across the front side of his lower limbs. The clean, sweeping cut to the front of the right ankle in particular would have been difficult to inflict if he were either riding in a chariot or engaged in ground combat. If, however, Seneb-Kay were elevated on horseback it would be relatively easy for an assailant with a spear or sword to cut through the ankle joint without exposing himself to counterattack. Targeting the ankles would be particularly logical if Seneb-Kay were riding bareback with his feet angled outwards from the horse and unprotected by use of stirrups or straps.

Attacking an armed rider on horseback and particularly one that may have been accompanied by bodyguards would involve encircling the target with multiple assailants. The directionality and angle of the axe blows to Seneb-Kay's knees fit the scenario of at least two assailants on foot. Therefore, the wound patterns appear to fit well with the possibility that he was assaulted while on horseback. Evidence that suggests he was attacked on horseback is consistent with the pronounced muscle markers on his femurs and pelvis that can be interpreted independently as having developed through habitual horse riding. Effectively, two separate sets of skeletal evidence from Seneb-Kay's body appear to converge and buttress one another. We would caution that we can by no means be certain of this conclusion. However, it appears to be the best explanation for the fuller set of evidence that survives on Seneb-Kay's skeleton.

In sum, a careful reading of the wound patterns to the lower body suggests that Seneb-Kay may have been ambushed or surrounded by a group of men who attempted to dislodge him from horseback. They would likely have attacked the lower limbs of the rider as well as the mount itself to stop his progress and bring him to the ground. The goal was to incapacitate him and render him immobile and defenseless once he fell. Indeed, the scope of cuts to his feet, ankles and knees would make him unable to escape once he was brought to the ground. It appears to have been at this stage that the remaining traumatic wounds were delivered to his head and hands.

As we have seen above an additional area of injury occurs in Seneb-Kay's hands. Seneb-Kay exhibits deep cuts to the metacarpals of both hands on the palmar surface, with three traumas on the left hand and one on the right. While he was actively engaged in combat, the palmar surfaces would have been unexposed as he would have grasped weapons or other implements. Exposure of the inside of the hands is suggestive of a final defensive movement meant to ward off blows. Our interpretation is that he placed his left hand over his right, and both over his face and head in a defensive posture to fend off assault at ground level. Seneb-Kay's injuries are consistent with someone who is left-handed based on the observation that the hand with the most injuries in cases of violent death is usually the dominant one. In a study of defensive wounds in homicides it has been concluded that victims' right forearms and hands were more commonly involved in defense injuries because these are nearest the perpetrator and consistent with the preponderance of right-handed individuals in the population of homicidal deaths (Hugar et al. 2012). Seneb-Kay's defensive injuries are consistent with someone who is left-handed because the hand with the most trauma is in all probability the lead hand. Moreover, as we have seen above, moderate osteoarthritis in Seneb-Kay's left sternoclavicular joint, which indicates more stress due to asymmetrical use, also supports the conclusion that he was left-handed. The object of his final defense may have been the bladed weaponry directed against his head (Fig. 5.31).

Given the extent and severity of his lower body injuries, Seneb-Kay was probably kneeling or sprawled on the ground at the point he was dispatched by three blows to the cranium.

It is impossible to know the disposition of his head at this stage but, as we have seen above, the cranial blows delivered by a battle axe appear to have been delivered in rapid succession, and likely by the same opponent. Of the three cranial wounds, the frontal wound (A) is the most diagnostic in terms of its clear imprint and angle of entry into the bone. The axe was held nearly horizontal and entered the bone from Seneb-Kay's left side. The blow appears carefully targeted to the middle and top of Seneb-Kay's head.

If wielded by a right-handed individual the axe-blow in Wound A would be the result of a man standing directly in front of the king swinging the axe horizontally to embed itself in the left side of Seneb-Kay's cranium. A left-handed individual standing in front would have created a wound on the opposite side of the head. If the assailant were left-handed, they would have to be standing behind the king's left shoulder to achieve this angle of entry of the axe wound. Wound A is therefore almost certainly the result of a targeted blow by a right-handed individual. Moreover, the horizontal angle of the axe blade effectively necessitates that the assailant was standing in front of Seneb-Kay who at that point in time was either kneeling or prostrate with his head slightly raised at about waist level of his opponent. If both the attacker and his victim were at the same level, the blade could never have achieved this shallow angle of entry.

The axe blow to the front of Seneb-Kay's cranium is a fascinating element of his perimortem trauma that, we hypothesize here, may not be a random wound but a culturally specific reflection of ancient Egyptian patterns of warfare. Cranial Wound A displays the physical hallmarks of a symbolic death-dealing blow. The king would have been on the ground in front of an opponent who targeted the top of his head with a battle axe. The position of the blow on the top of Seneb-Kay's head appears consistent with the ancient Egyptian practice of smiting enemies. The icon of the smiting pharaoh is one of the most familiar images in the iconographic repertoire that celebrates the role of the king as warrior. The smiting scene is typically rendered in an idealized form where the king stands before his kneeling or prostrate enemies (Fig. 5.32). He grabs their head by the hair with one hand and smites the top of the head with the other. The symbolic rendering of the smiting by the hand of the king may well reflect actual military practices connected with defeat of enemies.

If Seneb-Kay was smote on the top of his head in this type of ritualized defeat, it helps to explain the way the axe blade embedded directly onto the center of his head. The victorious opponent may have grasped the king's hair with his left hand which would have steadied the head as the axe—wielded in the right hand—was swung in from the side allowing it to embed precisely into the top of the cranium. This action appears to be understandable as not just a final victory blow but also a symbolic statement of defeat. If Seneb-Kay was dealt a massive death blow in this manner, we must question why he received, in addition, two other axe blows to the back and side

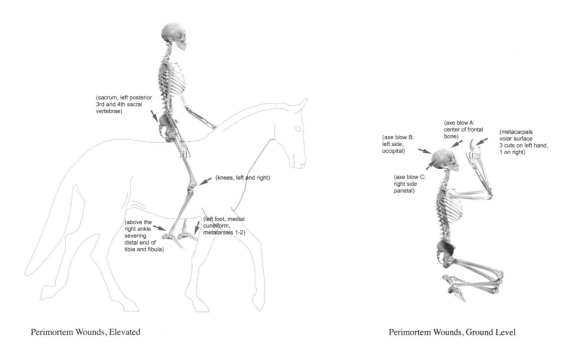

Perimortem Wounds, Elevated

Perimortem Wounds, Ground Level

Fig. 5.31 Suggested sequence of Seneb-Kay's wounds progressing from an assault while elevated (possibly on horseback) to the hand injuries and final fatal cranial blows while he was on the ground.

of his head? The penetrating blow to the back of the head (B) also displays diagnostic features: it too entered from Seneb-Kay's left to right side but made contact quite far down at the top of the occipital. The angle of entry of this wound would also be consistent with a right-handed opponent who now struck Seneb-Kay's skull with a massive blow to the back of his head. We would suggest that Seneb-Kay was first struck in his frontal bone. As the opponent removed the axe, Seneb-Kay's head fell forward and a second massive blow was delivered by the same opponent smashing into the back of his skull. Wound C, the least significant of the three, but also delivered with

a battle axe, may represent a third, glancing strike of the same weapon as the body of the king now lay prostrate.

Significantly, the frontal axe wound on the top of Seneb-Kay's head is strikingly similar to a comparable wound in the skull of the 17th Dynasty King Seqenenre Tao (Fig. 5.33). That wound, one of five in the cranium of Seqenenre, is also positioned horizontally on the frontal bone and appears to have been delivered by a battle axe (Smith 1912:4–6 and pls. 2–3). Scholars have provided various explanations for Seqenenre's frontal axe wound including the possibility of a ritual execution of the king following the

Fig. 5.32 Two examples of smiting scenes showing the ritualized defeat of enemies by the king wielding a mace (Early Dynastic Period, left) or battle axe (New Kingdom, right). Images courtesy of the British Museum (EA55586, left) and Egyptian Museum, Cairo (right).

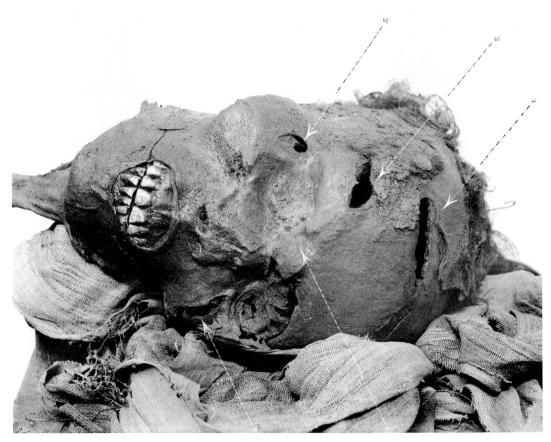

Fig. 5.33 The head of Seqenenre Tao (Cairo. CCG 61051) showing similarity of horizontal axe wound (1) to the top of the cranium with the axe Wound A of Seneb-Kay (after Smith 1912: pl. 2).

defeat of his army in battle (Shaw 2009:175–176). The parameters of the frontal axe blow of Seneb-Kay provides much more specific evidence than Seqenenre for the type of weapon, angle, and elevation at which the axe was wielded. In view of the evidence from Seneb-Kay, Seqenenre's comparable axe wound appear to fit with this same practice. It is remarkable to have physical remains of two kings of Egypt's Second Intermediate Period who died violently and with such a similar axe blow to the top of the cranium.

We might query: who was the perpetrator of such an act delivered against a king in the final throes of his defeat? It appears possible, but less likely, this was the act of a standard foot soldier, or even military commander, who happened to be there at the moment Seneb-Kay died. Rather, we might conclude these were the signature blows of a victorious ruler. If the product of one king smiting his vanquished enemy, this may suggest Seneb-Kay came face to face in his final moments with a rival king. The axe wounds

in his cranium may be read as an actual surviving example of the smiting of enemies in the context of the territorial fragmentation that predominated in Egypt's Second Intermediate Period. If so, who was Seneb-Kay's opponent and why was he so brutally butchered on the battlefield? We return to address these issues later in this volume.

POSTMORTEM TREATMENT AND TAPHONOMY

Despite the disturbed context of Seneb-Kay's burial, a taphonomic examination of the skeleton indicates that the traumas recorded predate the original deposition of the body. Due to the severe force needed to create these cuts we would not attribute any of them to damage accrued during the embalming procedure. None of the cuts to the bone resulted

Fig. 5.34 Detail showing areas of dried resin embedded in the cancellous (interior spongy) bone exposed by Seneb-Kay's wounds (left knee).

from disturbance when the burial was robbed in antiquity, or damage incurred during excavation. The color of the bone on the interior of the wound sites matches that of the non-traumatized bone. Most significantly, hardened resins from the mummification process were found on the interior of the skeletal wounds, particularly those on the knee joints (Fig. 5.34). Where mummy wrappings still adhered to bone, very little muscle or skin tissue remained between the linen fabric and bone cortex, suggesting that decay or desiccation was underway before the body was treated for burial (Shaw 2009; Smith and Dawson 1924).

The number and severity of the injuries received, particularly those in the lower extremities and skull, likely helped to accelerate internal decomposition. These also would give access to external bacteria and insect predation (Janaway et al. 2009). The condition of the body could also be an indicator of the distance traveled from the location of Seneb-Kay's death to a place where his body could be prepared for burial. The near completeness of Seneb-Kay's skeleton supports the likelihood that his body was

retrieved intact shortly after his demise. Otherwise, predation would have taken a greater toll particularly on limbs whose joints had been partially severed. As we have noted above the minor loss, numerically 21% of the skeleton, is associated primarily with smaller bones such as the distal phalanges of the hands and feet. These bones are that most likely to be missed during the excavation process. Although the body was directly redeposited from the burial chamber to the pole-roof chamber in ancient times there is a high potential for minor loss of bone material through these factors.

We may conclude that following his bloody death in a violent martial encounter, Seneb-Kay's body was retrieved quickly from the location of conflict. After some time elapsed in the process of returning his body, he was treated and mummified. Despite the decay of the mummified soft tissue, it is clear the body was fully treated to the appropriate embalming procedures. Remnants of resin and multiple layers of linen wrappings adhere to the body in many locations. The largest extant area was on the right tibia (Fig. 5.35). The surviving areas of linen show the body was wrapped in multiple layers. Many parts of the body preserve an inner layer which is black and adheres directly to the skin. This material is substantially impregnated with resin and possibly embalming oils. Superimposed over this is a layer of linen that is not discolored and retains its white color, only substantially preserved in one area on the right tibia. It appears the wrapping of the body of Seneb-Kay involved two steps: application of resin and embalming oils over which an internal layer of linen was wrapped which bonded directly to these substances. On top of that the embalmers then wrapped the body with additional outer layers of linen.

This evidence for retrieval of the body from the location of battle, perhaps at a considerable distance from Abydos, broadly parallels the well-known case of King Seqenenre Tao of the 17th Dynasty. Ultimately, we must ponder the geographical questions related to the process of Seneb-Kay's death and burial. Where did he die and against whom was he fighting? Why was he brought to South Abydos for burial? Is his burial locale a reflection of the territory

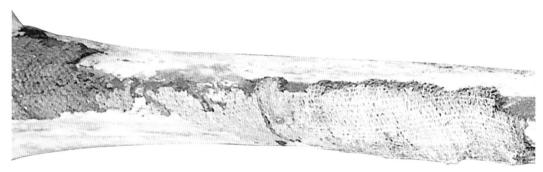

Fig. 5.35 Details of the linen wrappings preserved on the right tibia. The linen is wrapped in multiple layers with an internal layer that adheres directly to the skin (darker), overlain by an outer layer (lighter).

he controlled or was it chosen for some other reasons? These aspects of the political and historical implications of his death and burial will be taken up in the final chapter of this volume.

NOTES:

5.1 For the periods of pharaonic history predating Seneb-Kay the only burial of an Egyptian king discovered with the body in situ was the tomb of King Auibre-Hor, excavated in 1894. That body, and others of the late Middle Kingdom discovered in the Memphite necropolis was quite poorly preserved. Well preserved remains of other royalty exist for earlier periods, such as the queens of Nebhepetre Montuhotep II from Deir el-Bahri, but Seneb-Kay is the earliest well-preserved skeleton of an ancient Egyptian king.

5.2 While the term "wound" is commonly used in osteology to refer to injuries to the flesh, we apply it for ease of reference in labeling the three distinct traumatic wounds to Seneb-Kay's cranium. These were massive traumatic wounds that cut through the flesh and into the bone below.
5.3 The axe that created Wound A embedded into the skull at a shallow (nearly horizontal) angle with only the frontmost part of the curved blade piercing through the bone. Apart from where the front of the blade broke through the cranial bone, the rest of the blade impressed into the cranium leaving the imprint of the weapon's leading edge.
5.4 Wounds to the abdominal soft tissue might have occurred without leaving marks on bone. Additionally, there are two thoracic vertebrae (T11 and 12) missing which might potentially have borne evidence for cuts to

the torso. However, if his primary combat occurred in a standing position one might expect wounds to the long bones of his arms and ribcage. With the exception of the hands, evidence for lack of penetrating cuts to the arms and upper body present a striking contrast to the extent of wounds to the lower body. The hand wounds to the palmar surfaces are of someone in a defensive posture.

6

Conservation and Restoration Work*

The tomb of King Seneb-Kay provides a rare example of a royal burial dating to ca. 1650–1600 BCE, at the height of Egypt's Second Intermediate Period. The combination of information imparted by the tomb and its painted wall decoration, along with preservation of most of the king's skeletal remains, furnish a unique window into an era of territorial conflict and political flux. When the burial chamber was first exposed in 2014, it was clear that the structure had suffered considerable damage from the activities of ancient tomb robbers. The burial chamber was constructed from reused limestone blocks with a stone floor but no supporting masonry below that level. Pitting by tomb robbers had destabilized the lowest masonry courses and shattered the brittle mud mortar joints between many blocks. The overall structure was severely undermined. In 2014, we also observed that exposure of the painted decoration led to fading of the color in many areas. Subsequent to the initial reburial of the structure, we made the decision to proceed with a program of conservation and restoration to this unique structure.

With funding from the Antiquities Endowment Fund of the American Research Center in Egypt, along with additional support from the Penn Museum, we completed three seasons of work to stabilize and preserve the structure.[1] A primary goal was to undertake sufficient conservation and restoration work so that the tomb could be encased within a modern protective building that will permit it to be accessible, not as a tourist venue, but as a structure that can be seen and examined at the discretion of the

Egyptian Ministry of Antiquities. While not yet completed, we intend to return the skeleton of Seneb-Kay to the burial chamber where his remains may be visible within the conserved burial chamber.

MASONRY RESTORATION

In order to prevent progressive deterioration, the burial chamber was stabilized in the winter of 2015–2016 by reconstruction of missing blocks and the replacement of mud mortar with new gypsum mortar. Prior to this structural work, remedial conservation was carried out on the painted surfaces of the limestone blocks. Select areas of the painted decoration were consolidated with 5% Paraloid B-72 in acetone and the painted surfaces were further protected by applying a temporary consolidant, cyclododecane (CDD). Cyclododecane is a cyclic hydrocarbon and a solid wax that slowly sublimes at room temperature and with air circulation. Aluminum foil was placed over all the areas consolidated with CDD to prevent sublimation. All of the blocks from the inner (east wall) were disassembled along with the majority of blocks from the northern wall and some from the south wall (Figs. 6.1 and 6.2).

A challenge in reconstructing the chamber lay in the highly irregular width of the mortar joints. We initially mapped the chamber completely taking measurements on each joint so as to be able to recreate the position and alignment of the blocks as accurately as possible. In addition, a laser scan was

* This chapter written by Molly Gleeson and Josef Wegner.

Fig. 6.1 The disassembly of the burial chamber's north wall.

Fig. 6.2 The process of dismantling the east and south walls after resetting the masonry of the north wall.

made of the entire tomb using a LIDAR instrument (a Faro 3D Focus laser scanner). Following disassembly of the masonry, a mortared foundation was constructed in a newly cut trench immediately below the elevation of the intact floor blocks. The walls were then rebuilt with blocks restored in the missing spaces. The north wall was removed and rebuilt first followed by the east and south walls (Figs. 6.3 to 6.6). One of the issues with the burial chamber lay in the fact that it was originally somewhat irregular due to its rapid construction. As we have seen above, the burial chamber was still in the process of decoration up to the time of the king's interment and the painted imagery in the chamber appears to have been only partially completed. We did not wish to lose these aspects of the architecture. The blocks were reset to recapture irregularities in the alignment of the north wall as well as an outward widening towards the top that characterizes the east wall.

A limestone and gypsum-coated floor was added at the chamber's inner end where ancient tomb robbers had removed the floor stones (Fig. 6.7). The masonry of the burial chamber is now permanently stabilized and much stronger than it was initially due to replacement of the compromised Nile mud mortar with gypsum, as well as mortaring of the floor blocks. A fortunate result of the process of deconstruction of the masonry was that we were able to document carved relief decoration on the joints of many of the reused limestone blocks that had not been previously visible. Once the masonry was rebuilt, we completed a full program of conservation work on the painted decoration.

CONSERVATION OF THE DECORATION

Two seasons of conservation work, in the winter of 2015–16 and summer of 2016, were completed on the painted decoration in the burial chamber (Gleeson et al. 2017:57–64). As we have seen above, the limestone masonry in the burial chamber was

Fig. 6.3 Masonry restoration work on the north wall at the junction to the vaulted antechamber.

Fig. 6.4 Reconstruction of the masonry at the corner between the north and east walls.

Fig. 6.5 Reconstruction of the burial chamber's south wall.

Fig. 6.6 The exterior of the burial chamber after reconstruction (view looking south).

Fig. 6.7 Reconstruction of floor at inner end of the burial chamber (original flooring blocks are in situ in the foreground).

originally assembled with mud plaster mortar. The painted surfaces of the blocks were covered with a thin preparatory layer of gypsum, which overlay both the block surfaces and the mud mortar between the blocks. The painted texts and images were thinly applied over this ground in yellow, red, black, blue, and white paint. Most of the limestone blocks are structurally stable, but some stones were chipped and damaged and their surfaces are very pitted and uneven in places. In some areas that have seen exposure to surface moisture, the limestone is actively cracking and spalling away in layers due to salt activity. Some of the stones had small detached fragments that were found when the tomb was first uncovered.

Both the ground and the paint have been severely affected by condition problems in the limestone substrate. While in some areas the paint is well adhered and in good condition, in many places it is actively cupping and flaking and there are many losses in the painted scenes. Additionally, the paint is very fragile and susceptible to abrasion. There are small granular accretions across the surface of the limestone blocks, including in the painted areas. It is likely that the spots are related to salt activity and the salts have attracted sand accretions in these areas. There is evidence of insect activity in the tomb, not only in connection with the insect-damaged organic material found in the tomb, but also the remnant of a large hornet's nest which had developed at some point in the past over Seneb-Kay's cartouche on the north wall (Fig. 6.8).

Prior to the surface treatment, all of the blocks were fully examined and documented in written reports and photographs. When the backfill of the burial chamber was excavated and the aluminum foil was removed from the surface of the paintings, there was a considerable amount of CDD remaining on the surface of the painted blocks. Full documentation and treatment were carried out after the CDD had completely sublimed. Following documentation, all unstable, flaking, or powdering paint was consolidated using 5% Paraloid B-72 in acetone. In very fragile

Fig. 6.8 Cartouche of Seneb-Kay in the center of the north wall after removal of insect damage, consolidation, and cleaning.

areas, repeated application of the 5% B-72 solution was required to stabilize the paint. In addition to stabilization of the paint, all areas of crumbling or flaking ground and spalling stone were consolidated with the same 5% B-72 solution. There were some areas on the undecorated limestone where previous consolidation with Paraloid B-72 had caused slight yellowing. This yellowing was successfully removed using poultices of cotton with acetone. Surface cleaning was carried out using bamboo skewers and scalpels to remove the granular accretions and the remnants of the hornet's nest on the cartouche. Care was taken not to overclean, so as to avoid abrasion and loss to the surface. The use of water or solvents only softened the surface and made it further susceptible to abrasion, so only dry-cleaning methods were used. The accretions left behind brown/grey stains on the surface of the stones but removing them significantly improved the appearance of the paintings.

Two small pieces of detached painted stone elements were replaced using 40% Paraloid B-48N in acetone. Before reattachment the break edges were coated with 5% Paraloid B-72 in acetone. The repairs were further stabilized and fixed in place with gypsum mortar (locally supplied gypsum mixed with water to a desired consistency). Gypsum mortar was also used to smooth the new gypsum mortar joins between the stones (added to replace the original mud mortar as described above) and to aid with inpainting. Inpainting was carried out primarily to visually integrate images between blocks. Most inpainting was done in gouache over the new gypsum mortar between blocks (Fig. 6.9).

Additional inpainting was carried out in select areas of loss in the painted decoration. In these areas, the stone substrate was sealed with two coats of 20% Paraloid B-72 in acetone, and then the inpainting was executed in gouache (Fig. 6.10). In addition to this inpainting on and between the original blocks, a larger missing section of an image was outlined on a new block on the north wall. During the structural stabilization of the tomb, a new block was added to

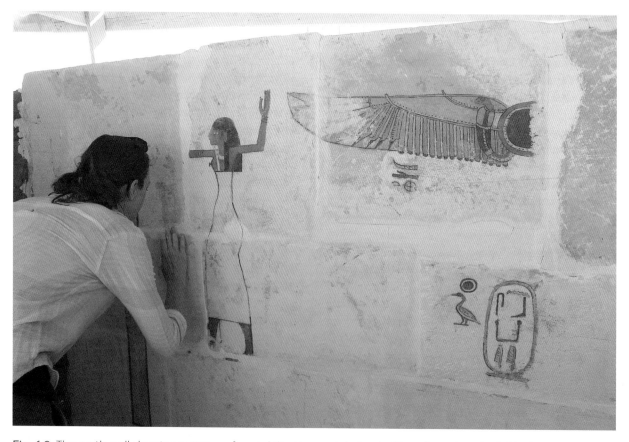

Fig. 6.9 The north wall showing painting after stabilization and during in-fill work on the rebuilt block joints.

Fig. 6.10 Overview of in-fill work on the painted decoration of the burial chamber after resetting of the masonry.

replace the missing block at the center of the north wall's upper course. This block interrupts the image of the winged sun disc that caps the center of the north wall. To reintegrate the image, the new block was given a surface wash with two coats of gypsum plaster, and the outline of the missing area of the wing was painted in gouache.

The conservation treatment carried out in the burial chamber of king Seneb-Kay was successful in stabilizing the deteriorating and fragile painted decoration on the limestone blocks. A secondary goal of reintegrating the painted images was also successful. However, based on initial documentation of the burial chamber, it is evident that significant deterioration of the paint occurred between excavation and the first conservation documentation and intervention, and likely very shortly after excavation when

the environment in the tomb changed abruptly and significantly. It will be critical to the long-term preservation of the painted decoration in the tomb to regularly monitor the condition of the tomb and to document any changes that are observed. Monitoring the environment in and around the tomb throughout the year may also assist in understanding any ongoing degradation and in future preservation strategies.

NOTES:

6.1 The conservation work has been completed by Molly Gleeson (Penn Museum Conservation Department) with financial support from David Schwartz and with assistance by conservators Daniel Doyle and Lucy-Anne Skinner. The masonry restoration work was carried out by Rais Ibrahim Muhammed Ali, Hamdy Abd el-Ghany, and Ashraf Zaidan. Laser scanning was completed by Paul Verhelst.

Part 2

The Reused Material in the Tomb of Seneb-Kay

7

The Reused Roof Blocks*

The burial chamber of Seneb-Kay was originally roofed by means of a group of limestone slabs that bridged the 1.5 m wide chamber and rested directly atop the 0.15 to 0.35 m wide masonry of the chamber's side walls. When the chamber was first discovered in 2014, no elements of this roofing remained in place. The roof blocks had been torn away in ancient times. The removal of the chamber's roof does not appear to have coincided with the initial robbery of the burial of Seneb-Kay. Due to the disposition of elements on the floor of the pole-roof chamber and the 40 cm tall hole through the top of the tomb's portcullis-style entrance (Chapter 1), the plundering of the king's burial clearly made use of the actual entrance as point of access. The removal of the roof slabs appears to be related instead to the later phase of stone removal that occurred in neighboring tombs S9 and S10 during the late Roman Period, which denuded those structures of significant amounts of their interior architecture.

The tomb of Seneb-Kay may have been uncovered during the later demolition of tombs S9 and S10. No late Roman amphorae were found in direct association with Seneb-Kay's tomb as occur in extensive numbers in S10, so this timeframe for the removal of the roof blocks remains tentative. However, the evidence we summarize below for the removal of two of the large slabs that roofed the chamber seems consistent with the patterns in neighboring S10. In the case of tomb S10, roofing blocks and the higher elevated parts of the interior architecture were extracted and hauled away leaving the lower lying

elements of the architecture in place (Wegner and Cahail 2015:132–135).

The smaller scale of the masonry elements in Seneb-Kay's burial chamber may have made it of lesser interest than the late Middle Kingdom tombs, which are built of multi-ton blocks. Consequently, removal of masonry primarily targeted the larger roof blocks. Inside the burial chamber, however, robbers at some point pulled away wall blocks at the inner end and pried up the flooring to check whether there were concealed spaces. It appears probable that this probing of the chamber, which resulted in substantial damage to the architecture, directly followed removal of the roofing. At that later stage of activity, the chamber had already been fully despoiled. Whereas the initial tomb robbers could be certain they had fully robbed the king's burial, the later gangs would have encountered an empty chamber and may have concluded there could be something of value hidden behind the walls or under the floor. This resulted in the stripping away of internal masonry to check for additional chambers.

Excavation in 2014–15 produced fragments of two different reused masonry elements that we identify as having been roofing for Seneb-Kay's burial chamber: (1) the 11th Dynasty stela of Idudju-iker, the *Foremost-one of the Rulers of Wawat*; and (2) a 13th Dynasty false door belonging to one of the Sobekhotep kings. Surviving fragments show the two slabs are of equivalent thickness (0.26–0.27 m) and were both originally on the order of 2 m in length. The width of the stela of Idudju-iker is fully preserved at 1.07

* This chapter written by Josef Wegner.

m. The width of the highly fragmentary false door of Sobekhotep (attested through a small number of fragments) is unknown but can be estimated to have been at least 1.1 m, possibly more. The interior length of Seneb-Kay's burial chamber is 3.32 m, but the roof slabs would have been required to fully cover the wall masonry from the chamber's opening to the inner end where the final roof block would have rested atop the chamber's eastern wall. This represents a total span of 3.7 m that needed roofing slabs. The combined width of the Idudju-iker stela and (estimated width) of the Sobekhotep false door is ca. 2.2 m leaving an additional 1.5 m. Quite possibly the space was covered by one additional large slab, although there might have been more than one additional block to complete the roofing (Fig. 7.1).

We discovered no remains of a third reused block and it appears that element must have been removed in its entirety. The false door of King Sobekhotep is attested only by a group of small fragments that appear to have been chipped off during that block's removal. Apparently, the rest of that substantial block was taken elsewhere for reuse. The same may have occurred to the remaining roof block (or blocks) but leaving no physical remains. The best attested of the roof blocks is the stela of Idudju-iker, which was not removed but smashed apart in situ with the two largest fragments lying astride the east wall and within the burial chamber. Here we turn to discuss the evidence of the two reused roof blocks.

THE 11TH DYNASTY STELA OF IDUDJU-IKER

The stela of Idudju-iker is a fragmentary, limestone biographical stela that dates to the early 11th Dynasty (ca. 2100 BC). The primary fragments were recovered during the initial 2014 excavation of the Seneb-Kay burial chamber while additional smaller fragments were retrieved during the subsequent 2014–2015 field season. Based on the findspot of its fragments, the stela was the innermost reused slab over the Seneb-Kay's burial chamber. It is the only one of the roof blocks that was broken apart in situ, but this does not mean all the fragments have survived. Although one of the large fragments fell into the chamber, others were clearly cast out along the

edges of the robbers' pit. Likely a substantial number of the pieces were thrown onto the surface where they subsequently decayed. The surviving fragments account for approximately half of the original stela. The process of breaking apart the inner roof block would have facilitated removal of the other roof slabs for which there were no surviving fragments in direct association with the burial chamber.

Three large, adjoining fragments (Frs. 1–3) of the stela of Idudju-iker were recovered, representing a substantial part of the upper half of the stela (Fig. 7.2). In the course of the excavations, a group of smaller fragments were recovered, some of which were joined with the larger fragments. Three of these (Frs. 4–6) do not have direct joins but can be positioned based on their content relative to the larger fragments.

Fragment 1, representing the upper part of the stela, was found in a disturbed context but sitting directly over the inner (east) wall of the burial chamber. The larger Fr. 2 was excavated inside the burial chamber itself where it was found in the sand slightly above floor level near the chamber's north wall. The smaller Fr. 3 was an outlier and was excavated unaccompanied in the sand 5 m to the north of the burial chamber. The other smaller fragments were recovered from debris inside and immediately adjacent to the burial chamber. The disposition of the fragments, particularly the location of Fr. 1 atop the inner end of the chamber, strongly suggest the Idudju-iker stela originally spanned the inner end of the burial chamber. The block was likely positioned with its rough-dressed, undecorated back forming the ceiling of the chamber and the extraneous 11th Dynasty text facing upwards.

Although recovered in a fragmentary state, the Idudju-iker stela is a highly significant historical monument in its own right, providing new information on the political and military history of the early 11th Dynasty. The stela measures 1.07 m in width and 0.26 m in thickness. The surviving fragments total 1.35 m in height but provide indications for a monument which was originally in the vicinity of 2 m in height. The stela takes the form of a "false door stela," adopting the layout of the traditional false door. However, the Idudju-iker stela has dispensed with the normal decorative elements of the false door and replaced those motifs with a lengthy hieroglyphic text. It has an outer frame measuring 7 to 9

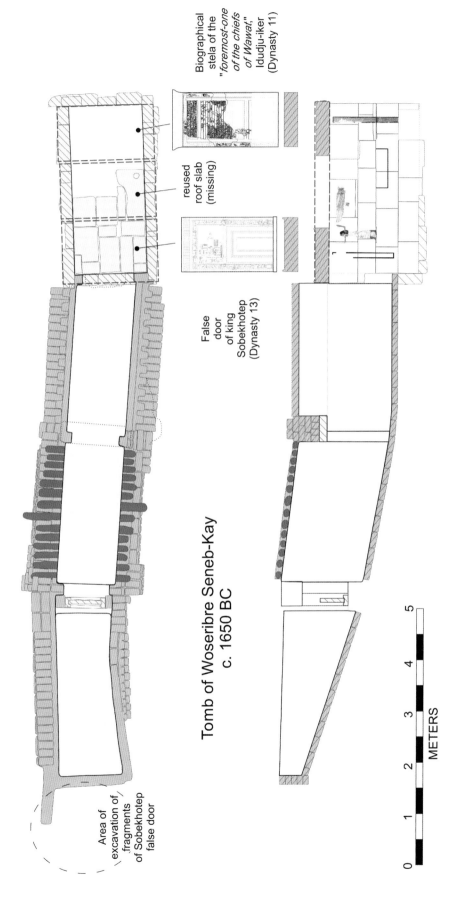

Biographical stela of the "*foremost-one of the chiefs of Wawat,*" Idudju-iker (Dynasty 11)

reused roof slab (missing)

False door of king Sobekhotep (Dynasty 13)

Tomb of Woseribre Seneb-Kay
c. 1650 BC

Area of excavation of fragments of Sobekhotep false door

METERS

0   1   2   3   4   5

Fig. 7.1 The burial chamber of Seneb-Kay with suggested position of the reused roof slabs.

Fig. 7.2 The primary recovered fragments of the stela of Idudju-iker.

cm in width, decorated in large-format hieroglyphs. Within the frame is a 7 cm wide round torus molding with two cross members that divide the upper part into two recessed panels, an "Upper Panel" (21.5 x 75 cm) and "Central Panel" (63 x 75 cm). At the bottom of the Central Panel is a rectangular cross bar below which was a "Lower Panel" of unknown height. As indicated on Fr. 5, the text continues over the cross bar and onto the Lower Panel but nothing further survives of the lower part of the stela.

The original ca. 2 m height of the stela is indicated by two complementary lines of evidence. Firstly, the reuse of the stela as a roofing block necessitates a longer dimension of at least 2 m height in order to span the width of the burial chamber and rest on the side walls. Secondly, two of the smaller fragments (Frs. 4 and 6), which derive from the stela's left side, are parts of the offering prayer which can be positioned relative to the surviving elements on Fr. 1. Together these preserve parts of the epithet of Osiris-Khentiamentiu, *m swt.f nbt nfrt wꜥbwt, in all his pure and beautiful places,* which is then followed by the invocation offering: *prt-ḫrw ḥꜣ t ḥnḳt, an invocation offering of a thousand of bread and beer.* The invocation offering must have been followed on the frame by the name and titles of Idudju-iker. We can reconstruct this part of the text based on the titles and name preserved in the Upper Panel. A minimal reconstruction of these elements demonstrates that the stela must have extended to 2 m or more. With the Lower Panel measuring approximately 0.5 m or more in height. Almost certainly the object was originally completed on the top with a cavetto cornice, a standard element of the false door (Fig. 7.3).

One of the distinctive features of the Idudju-iker stela is an area of secondary chiseling over the upper and middle parts of the Central Panel. This damage is intentional but was not directed towards the content of the text nor the name of the stela owner. This chisel damage contrasts markedly with the targeted desecration that we see on the reused 13th Dynasty chapel blocks of Dedtu/Ibiau where names and images of the chapel owners were viciously defaced (Chapter 8). Here we see instead a defined, step-shaped area that was chiseled back in a way that reflects some form of more practical alteration of the block's surface. Evidently the stela underwent an intermediate phase of reuse at some point in the ca. 450 years between its original 11th Dynasty use and its final adaptation as a roof block for the burial chamber of Seneb-Kay. The exact purpose of the step-shaped area remains obscure but is suggestive of the stela's integration into an architectural setting where a step-shaped feature lay adjacent to the stela face. An unfortunate result of the chiseled area is that significant sections of the biographical text are nearly obliterated. Although the chiseling did not absolutely erase the text—many signs and partial hieroglyphs can be discerned through the chisel marks—the damage is substantial enough to render the affected parts of the text nearly unreadable. A full translation and commentary on the Idudju-iker stela has been presented elsewhere (Wegner 2018b:157–213). Here we present the transliteration and translation of the texts.

THE OUTER FRAME

The outer frame is inscribed with three separate offering formulae. The texts are poorly preserved but consist of large format hieroglyphs with considerable internal modeling. Two separate *ḥtp-dỉ-nswt* texts occur on the left and right sides, running vertically down the frame. At the top was a third formula which began on the right side and continues into the Upper Panel since the first line of the Upper Panel is the end of the epithet of Anubis or Wepwawet, *nb tꜣ ḏsr, Lord of the necropolis.* The horizontal text on the outer frame is labeled here as Line 1 with the line numbering continuing sequentially onto the panels below. The surviving texts on the frame read:

Right. *Ḥtp-[dỉ-nswt] ꞽnpw [...] prt-ḫrw [...]*

An offering which the king gives, and Anubis, ///, [that he may give] an invocation offering...

Left. *[Ḥtp-dỉ-nswt Wsỉr nb Ḏdw Ḫnty]ỉmntỉw, nb ꞽbḏw m swt.f [nbt nf]rt wꜥbwt prt-ḫrw ḥꜣ t [ḥnḳt...]*

[An offering which the king gives, and Osiris, Lord of Busiris, and Khent]iamentiu, Lord of Abydos, in all his pure and beautiful places, that he may give an invocation offering of a thousand of bread [and beer...]

Upper (Line 1). *[Ḥtp-dỉ-nswt Wsỉr nb Ḏdw Ḫn]tyỉmntỉw, nb ꞽbḏw [Wpwꜣwt nb]...*

[An offering which the king gives, and Osiris, Lord of Busiris, and Khen]tiamentiu, Lord of Abydos, [and Wepwawet], Lord of... (text continues on Upper Panel, Line 2)

THE UPPER PANEL

The text initiated on the frame continues in the Upper Panel in three lines, 6 cm in height, of large format hieroglyphs (Fig. 7.4). This section of the stela

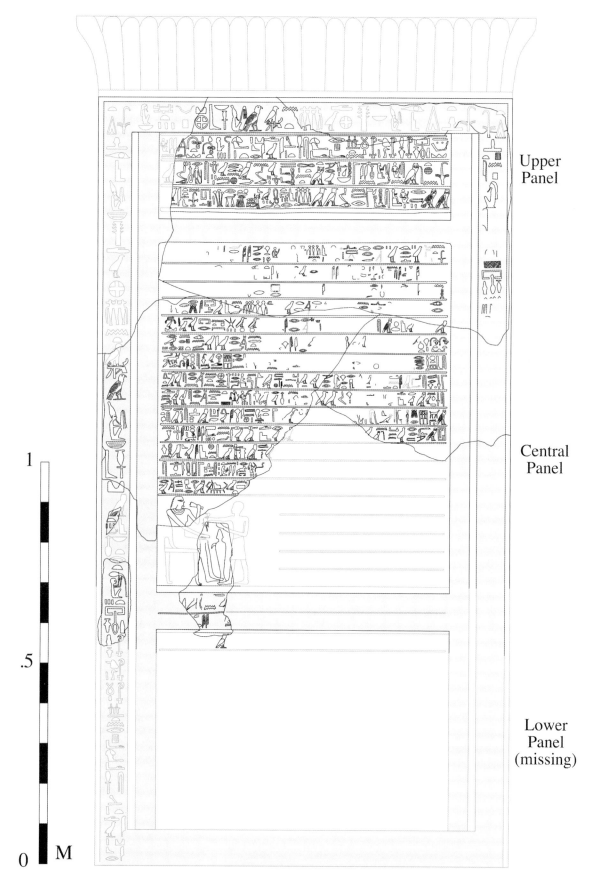

Upper
Panel

Central
Panel

Lower
Panel
(missing)

Fig. 7.3 A reconstruction of the stela of Idudju-iker showing the position of fragments that can be joined or coordinated.

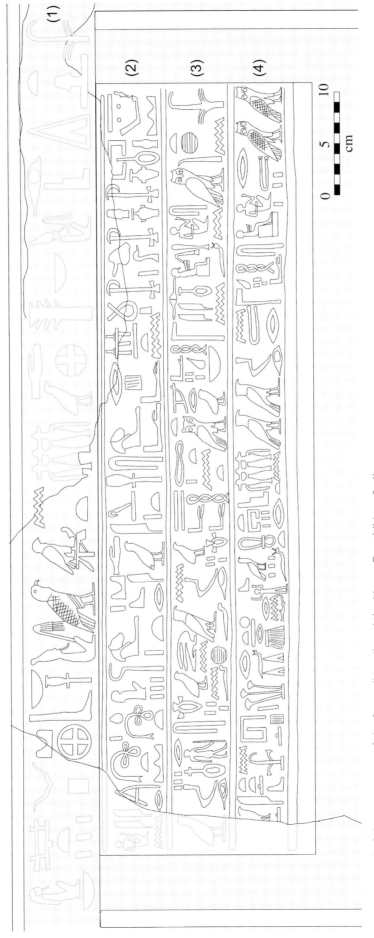

Fig. 7.4 Detail of the upper part of the frame (Line 1) and the Upper Panel (Lines 2–4).

represents a preamble to the biography and presents the name and titles of Idudju-iker, along with a lengthy set of epithets. The text here emphasizes the status of Idudju-iker effectively as a court official as he is provided the designation *iry-pꜥt ḥꜣty-ꜥ smr-wꜥty*, *Nobleman, Mayor, Sole-companion*, titles used by the highest levels of provincial and royal officials during the First Intermediate Period and early Middle Kingdom. The elaborate epithets, ten in number, emphasize Idudju-iker's devotion to the king and status as a member of the royal court. Remarkably, alongside these ranking titles and epithets Idudju-iker bears only a single functional title which occurs immediately after his name: *ḥꜣt ḥkꜣw nw Wꜣtwꜣt, Foremost-one of the chiefs of Wa(t)wat* (Lower Nubia).[1]

...**(Line 2)** *tꜣ ḏsr prt-ḥrw ḥꜣ t ḥnkt ḥꜣ kꜣw ꜣpdw ḥꜣ šs mnḥt n iry-pꜥt ḥꜣty-ꜥ smr-wꜥty Idw-ḏw-ikr ḥꜣt ḥkꜣw nw Wꜣtwꜣt mr[y n]* **(Line 3)** *nswt, ḥnms n ḥm.f, smꜣy n ḥꜥw-nṯr, nb mrwt m ḥt nyt tꜣwy, ḥꜥꜥw ibw n mꜣꜣ.f, wnḥw n.f ibw srw nfr, mꜣ3[w]* **(Line 4)** *m-m rmṯ špss ḥꜥw-nṯr, mꜣꜣ ḥnty swt r miwtiw.f, kꜣi rn ḥt tꜣ r ḏr.f, dd ḥꜣ ḥp n Šmꜥw t(w)t kiw(?) [...]*

(continues from frame inscription, Line 1)

...**(2)** *of the necropolis, that he may give invocation offerings consisting of a thousand of bread and beer, a thousand oxen and fowl, a thousand alabaster (vessels) and clothing, to the Nobleman, the Mayor, the Sole-companion, Idudju-iker, Foremost-one of the Chiefs of Wawat; one whom the king loves,* **(3)** *friend to his majesty; one who is united with the flesh-of-the-god; possessor of affection from the body of the Two-lands; one at whom hearts rejoice through seeing, one through whom goodness envelops the hearts of the officials; one who is seen* **(4)** *among the noble people of the flesh-of-the-god; one who looks beyond of the positions of his peers, one who is renowned through the land in its entirety; one who has been placed behind the law of the entirety of Upper Egypt, (?)...* (continues to Central Panel, Line 5).

THE CENTRAL PANEL AND OFFERING SCENE

The Central Panel consists of fourteen surviving lines of text with an offering scene on the lower left side (Fig. 7.5). The offering scene is only partially preserved and shows a seated man on a lion-paw chair holding a vase (*mrḥt*-vessel) to his face. There is no label, but this is almost certainly Idudju-iker himself.[2] In front of him is a standing male figure holding a jar in one hand and an object—likely a duck—towards the seated figure. Between the two figures is a large, spouted jar with a conical jar stopper. The lower part of the Central Panel adjacent to the offering scene is missing but the available space perfectly accommodates 5 lines based on the 4.2 cm text lines. We can suggest the horizontal text continued to the right of the offering scene making a total of 19 lines of text in the Central Panel (lines numbered 5–23). The text continued uninterrupted in two lines over the cross bar and directly onto the Lower Panel.

The text is highly damaged as a result of the chiseled surface in Lines 5–8. This part of the stela is written in the first person and appears to define the nature of Idudju-iker's association with the king. We have mention here of two Lower Nubian regions: Medja-land and Wawat, suggesting Idudju-iker's responsibilities encompassed both of these regions to the south of Upper Egypt. The main part of the surviving text (Lines 8–18) discusses Idudju-iker's participation in a complex series of religious celebrations in the temples of Thinis and Abydos. Notably, the events spanned several different temples in the Thinite nome including the temple of Onuris at Thinis and apparently the temple of Osiris at Abydos.[3] The last surviving line discusses the Osiris procession at Abydos and mentions the ceremonial procession of the Neshmet barque to the area named Poqer, the symbolic site of the tomb of Osiris. Throughout the text on the Central Panel is reference to Idudju-iker's activities in association with a group of other individuals, mentioned in Lines 10–11 as *wrw sbḥt ꜥꜣt, magnates of the great-portal*, and in Line 13 as the *ḥkꜣw Wꜣst, rulers of the Theban nome*. Reference to Idudju-iker's actions occurring *n.f, for him*, suggests his stela commemorates his participation in an important historical moment that included members of the Theban royal court of the 11th Dynasty and the Theban king at Thinis and Abydos. The surviving text reads as follows:

(continues from Upper Panel) **(Line 5)** *n nswt [...].wy ir(.i) r.f ḥtp.wy r mrr.f n it.n(.i) [...] st(?) ḥnt [... ...] ḥry-tp mrry.f r[... ... ...]* **(Line 6)** *... fragmentary signs ...* **(Line 7)** *... fragmentary signs...* **(Line 8)** *ir [... ... ...] n [...].n(.i)*

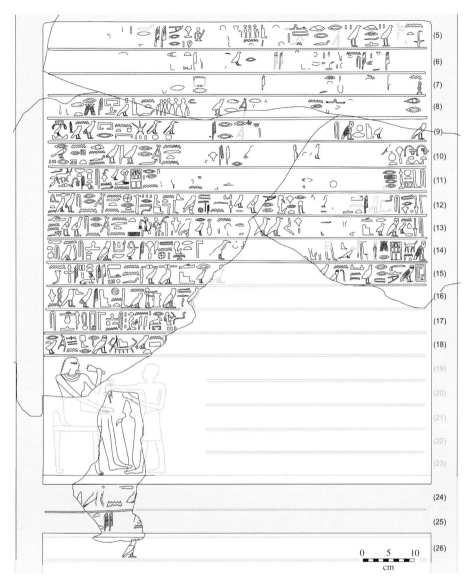

Fig. 7.5 Detail of the Central Panel with the fragmentary offering scene on the lower left.

r [... ... ...] r mrrw [...] ḫnt.f st m pr.f ìr-grt [... ...] **(Line 9)** m [... ... ...]w st ḥr m s [... ... ...] r mrrì [... ... ...] ȝḫȝḥw n pt prw n Mḏȝw **(Line 10)** Wȝtwȝt ḥr [...] //nwt [...] ry ḥr[...] n-ꜥȝt-n mrr.f w(ì) ìw ìr.n.f n.(ì) nprt r wrw **(Line 11)** sbḫt ꜥȝt rš r r [... ... ...] r r n ḥrt-ìb ḥr wdn n.f stpt nbt ìwȝw sft **(Line 12)** snṯr ḥr sdfȝ ìmn(y)t [... ... ...] r ꜣnḥrt mrrw [... ... ...] n Ṯnì [... ...] ḳnbtìw r nḏ-ḥrt(.ì) n-ꜥȝt-n mrr.sn w(ì). smt n.(ì) **(Line 13)** snṯr ȝḥw m rwdw [... ... ...] ḥr mȝȝ [...] rt n ḥr nfrw m-ìb ḥkȝw Wȝst n-ꜥȝt-n mrr.sn wì wdn.(ì) n.f **(Line 14)** m-ḥnw ḥrt-ìb grḥ [...] sꜥḳ.(ì) nṯr [...]t [... ... ...] nd[...]tìw [...] nṯrt nt Ṯnì ḥr ìw kȝ.k m ḥtp snḏm.k sty **(Line 15)** ḥwt-nṯr m-bȝḥ mrr tw dì.n.(ì) n[.f] nmw [...] rwdw smsw.n.(ì) n.f šꜥywt tw ìwn **(Line 16)** [...

... ...] [ì]w ṯsm.n.(ì) m bḫnt ìw kȝḥ n(.ì) **(Line 17)** [... ... šn]ḏtyw r ìw n ììwtyw sḥtp.n(.ì) ḥwt-nṯr mì-ḳd.s **(Line 18)** [... ... ...] Nšmt m r Pḳr n mrwt [... ... ...]

(continues from Upper Panel) **(5)** of the king (?) ... (?)... It was in accordance with that which he desires that I acted (?), without taking (?)... in front of ..., having authority over what he wishes in respect to (?)... **(6)**... **(7)**... **(8)** making... I did not take (?)... in respect of... in front of him, a seat in his house. Now moreover, ... **(9)** ... place of dwelling ... the stars of the sky, and/are(?) the ones who went forth to Medja-land **(10)** and Wawat upon (?)... inasmuch as he loves me. It was in respect *of the great ones of* **(11)** *the great portal, that he made for me an offering basin (?). It was at the entrance of ... that I rejoiced ... ... at the entrance of the central hall, making offerings for him of all meat and slaughtered oxen* **(12)** *and providing the daily offerings ... ... to Onuris, and the ones who love ... ... belonging to Thinis ... ... the council-members in order to greet me, inasmuch as they love me. I burned* **(13)** *incense, and mortuary offerings at the staircase ... ... upon seeing ... the goodness (?) through the desire of the rulers of the Theban nome, inasmuch as they love me. It was inside* **(14)** *the central hall that I offered to (for) him ... It was ... that I caused the god (?) to enter ... ... [the priesthood of ?] the goddess of Thinis greeted (me, saying): "Your person has arrived safely, you sweeten the aroma* **(15)** *of the temple in the presence of the one who loves you." I made for him a procession ... to the staircase, and presented for him cakes, gazelle (?) and cattle* **(16)** *... I constructed (it) as a pylon. I plastered* **(17)** *it ... (of) the temple staff, and the entrance to the court of the female musicians. It was in its entirety that I pleased the temple* **(18)** *... the Neshmet-bark at the entrance to Poqer, in order that ... ...* **(19–23)** *(missing).*

CROSS BAR AND LOWER PANEL

Line 24–5 (few signs preserved)

Line 26–end (upper parts of a few signs preserved, remainder entirely missing)

DATE AND HISTORICAL IMPLICATIONS OF THE IDUDJU-IKER STELA

The stela of Idudju-iker is the earliest of the re-used elements in Seneb-Kay's tomb, and indeed the oldest object excavated—albeit in altered context—in the royal necropolis at South Abydos. Although it lacks a preserved royal name, the stela can be dated with a high degree of probability to the reign of the 11th Dynasty king Wahankh Antef II (ca. 2112–2063 BCE). Numerous iconographic and paleographical features of the stela indicate an early 11th Dynasty date. These include details of the writing of the *prt-ḥrw* formula, the form of the book roll determinatives, the

use of split tail *wȝ* hieroglyphs (Wegner 2018b:177–184). The composition and style of the offering scene with central spouted jar and presence of the *mrḥt* vessel is distinctively late First Intermediate Period in character with parallels to be noted in late Herakleopolitan stelae as well as scenes in the alabaster quarries at Hatnub.

Many elements of phraseology and terminology also compare closely with early 11th Dynasty stelae such as the stela of Tjetji, chief treasurer of Wahankh Antef II, and the stela of Rediukhnum, steward of Queen Nefrukayet, the probable wife of Antef II. The treatment of the hieroglyphs compares with examples of stelae from the reign of Antef II such as the stelae of Djari from Dra Abu el-Naga, and the stela of Hetepi from El Kab. The fine quality of the workmanship and close similarities with royal stelae of Antef II including his Hound Stela and Hymn Stela suggest Idudju-iker may be tentatively dated to the second half of the 50-year reign of Antef II.

Perhaps most compelling as a dating criterion is the content of the biography itself, which, although fragmentary, recounts an elaborate series of ceremonial activities in the temples of Thinis and Abydos. The activities include the dedication of ritual equipment by the king on behalf of his court officials and associates. Idudju-iker himself had a votive object, possibly an offering basin (*nprt*, Line 11) established on his behalf. Many of the other events appear to be temple rites conducted in the company of the king and in reciprocity for the king having honored Idudju-iker with such a dedication. The description makes it clear that Idudju-iker was not in Thinis and Abydos alone but in the company of a wider delegation that included the Theban king and a group called the *ḥkȝw Wȝst, rulers of the Theban nome* (Line 13). Despite the Egyptian mode of presentation, Idudju-iker's primary title makes it clear that he himself was not a Theban or even an Egyptian. He is identified as the *ḥȝt ḥkȝw nw Wȝtwȝt, Foremost-one of the Chiefs of Wawat* (Line 2), a designation that indicates he was the highest-ranking ruler of Lower Nubia. On this basis, it appears probable that Idudju-iker was an Egyptianized Lower Nubian ruler who was involved in a political and military alliance with the Theban 11th Dynasty. Idudju-iker is likely to have belonged to the Lower Nubian C-Group, a culture that displays close interactions with Upper Egypt during the late First Intermediate Period and 11th Dynasty.

Idudju-iker may have been engaged in an alliance with the Theban king that was expressed in his formal induction as a member of the royal court. A major component of this relationship may have been the Theban interest in garnering support from Lower Nubia to strengthen their military capabilities in the ongoing conflict with the Herakleopolitan kingdom. Idudju-iker may have come to Egypt with contingents of Lower Nubian soldiers including both Wawat Nubians and the Medjau-Nubians originating from the Eastern Desert hills between Nubia and the Red Sea. This topic may have been discussed in the, unfortunately damaged, Lines 5–10 that mention Wawat and Medjau-land. Here too, the text appears to have defined Idudju-iker's relationship with the king. The implications of the stela are that Idudju-iker was present in Thinis and Abydos not as the result of a personal visit or pilgrimage, but in the aftermath of the 11th Dynasty annexation of the Thinite nome.

A substantial group of historical sources for the reign of Antef II mention the conquest of Thinis and Abydos. Stelae of individuals who participated in these events include those of Djari and Hetepi mentioned above. The conquest of Thinis is recorded in the stela of Antef II's chief treasurer Tjetji. It also is highlighted as a major political achievement of Antef II's reign in the Hound Stela from the king's tomb in the Tarif area of Thebes. Aspects of the conflict over the Thinite nome are alluded to in the literary text, the *Instruction for King Merykare*, in which the Herakelopolitan king (unnamed but presumably King Khety III) laments damage that occurred to the temples and cemeteries of Abydos.

Despite its fragmentary condition, the stela of Idudju-iker is a monument of notable scale and quality that appears to have been set up at Abydos as a way of commemorating Idudju-iker's role in the Theban victory over the Herakleopolitans in Thinis and Abydos. The stela may indeed have been set up as a dedication to Idudju-iker by the Theban ruler. In all probability it is only one of a series of such monuments that would have stood on the landscape of Abydos memorializing the individuals involved in that major military victory. Exactly where the stela originally stood and where it may have been taken from by Seneb-Kay's tomb builders is an issue we shall return to after examining the evidence for the other attested roof block, the false door of King Sobekhotep.

THE 13TH DYNASTY FALSE DOOR OF KING SOBEKHOTEP

Directly adjacent to the entrance ramp of the tomb of Seneb-Kay a discrete cluster of related limestone fragments were uncovered in 2014. These elements derive from a finely carved false door belonging to one of the Sobekhotep kings of the 13th Dynasty (see Wegner and Cahail 2015:141–146). The fragments were recovered together in the sand immediately west of the walled entrance ramp of CS9, and at the same elevation as the ramp's upper rim wall.

Fifteen fragments were recovered, several of which had joins that permitted their consolidation into eight larger elements. The surviving components include the enthroned figure of a king with right hand over his lap, left arm bent over his chest (Fig. 7.6, Fr. 1). Based on the dimensions of the throne and lower body the seated figure can be extrapolated to ca. 35 cm in height. The king wears a striated kilt and the beginning of his bull's tail is visible above his knee. Elements of piled food offerings and the scene label *nswty bd*, royal natron precede the figure. Behind the throne is a vertical pole suggesting that the left side of the scene included a Ka-figure holding a staff capped with royal crown. Two smaller fragments preserve piles of offerings that would have composed the offering scene to the right of the royal figure (Fig. 7.6, Frs. 2–3). At the base of this offering scene is a horizontal cross bar indicating the scene composed the upper panel of a false door.

Several fragments survive from the decorated frame and indicate the presence of a recessed false door panel below the offering scene. These fragments show the false door was 0.27 m in thickness and was framed by a 3.3 cm wide torus molding. Within this was a 12.5 cm wide text register with offering prayers (the *ḥtp-dỉ-nswt* formula) running down both sides. From the right side of the false door are fragments with the following text elements: *...n kȝ n sȝ-Rᶜ Sbk[ḥtp]*, *...for the ka of the son of Re, (Sobek[hotep])...* (Fig 7.7, Fr. 4); and *...snṯr...*, *...incense...* (Fig. 7.7, Fr. 5). There are two smaller fragments which, based on the orientation of the hieroglyphs, originate from the text column on the left side: *....mnḫt.... ...clothing...* (Fig. 7.7, Fr. 6) and a small remnant of the term *prt-ḥrw*, *invocation offerings* (Fig. 7.7, Fr. 7). To the left of the text frame on Fr. 4 we have preserved the inward

Fig. 7.6 left Figural fragments depicting an enthroned king seated behind an offering table.

Fig. 7.7 below Textual fragments from the frame of the Sobekhotep false door showing the raised frame surrounded by outer torus molding.

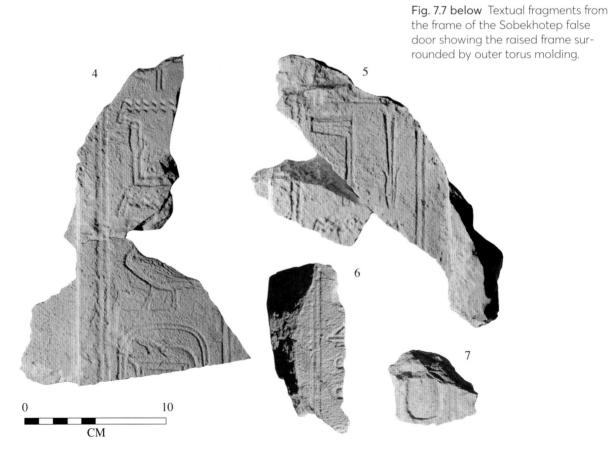

recessing of the lower panel. This represents the architectural rendering of the door panel that would have composed the lower part of the object.

The few extant fragments do not permit any detailed reconstruction of the Sobekhotep false door but there is enough to reconstruct the basic layout and approximate size of this object. Based on comparanda provided by other Middle Kingdom royal false doors, the 35 cm royal figure and associated offering scene elements suggest an offering scene of approximately 50–60 cm in height. Incorporating an offering table in the middle of the panel and a basic assemblage of piled offerings to the right would suggest a scene of at least 0.75 m in width (as shown in Fig. 7.8). We may note that this reconstruction should be viewed as minimalist. Worthy of remark here is the high quality of the sculpting of the piled food offerings suggesting there may have been a relatively detailed rendering of the offering piles on the right side. Therefore, an estimate of ca. 1 m for the offering scene width may be more appropriate. Beyond the width of the offering scene, we may project outer elements accurately based on the 12.5 cm width of the text frame and the 3.5 cm wide torus. Added to the 0.75 m minimal width for the offering scene we may suggest a width of 1.1+ m for the Sobekhotep false door. A 2:1 height to width ratio would suggest this slab, like the stela of Idudju-iker discussed above, originally measured in the vicinity of 2 m.

When the fragments of the Sobekhotep false door were initially recovered in 2014, we thought the object may have been an original fixture associated with the walled area that fronts the large 13th Dynasty tomb S10 ("Enclosure B" inside of which the tomb of Seneb-Kay was built). However, once the tomb of Seneb-Kay was excavated, it was clear that the Second Intermediate Period tomb builders had made extensive use of reused late Middle Kingdom masonry. It then appeared more likely that the Sobekhotep false door fragments could represent chips produced during the repurposing of 13th Dynasty masonry during the construction of the tomb of Seneb-Kay (Wegner and Cahail 2015:145–147). Subsequent work on tomb S10 makes it appear virtually certain that there was no standing, stone-built structure that would have accommodated the Sobekhotep false door. Therefore, the false door must have been relocated there in connection with the construction of Seneb-Kay's tomb.

Consequently, although no fragments of the Sobekhotep false door were found in direct association with Seneb-Kay's burial chamber, the estimated size and thickness of the object demonstrate with a high degree of certainty that this was one of the slabs that had been reemployed as a roof block over the burial chamber. As we have seen above, the fragments of the stela of Idudju-iker suggest that block was probably the innermost roofing element. The Sobekhotep false door may have formed the central or western slab of a probable group of three reused blocks or comparable dimensions. It appears possible that the fragments could have been produced by damage to the false door during the time of its installation by Seneb-Kay's tomb builders. A more likely scenario, is that the false door was removed from the burial chamber during the later phase of masonry removal, probably at the same time as the extensive masonry removal from tombs S9 and S10. In this case, the recovered fragments essentially represent a small group of flakes that broke off as the false door was hauled away. This explanation helps account for one of the aspects of the Sobekhotep false door fragments. Despite their high quality of carving, all of the fragments display a wind-scoured, eroded surface. This erosion occurs not only on the primary decorated face but extends as well to many of the broken edges. These fragments clearly lay on the desert surface for a period of time prior to being reburied. Therefore, it appears the reused Sobekhotep false door was removed leaving only a minor signature on site in the form of this group of accidental chips. No such remains were recovered of the probable third roof slab.

ORIGIN OF THE REUSED ROOF BLOCKS

A key question that emerges regarding the Idudju-iker stela and Sobekhotep false door is: where did Seneb-Kay's tomb builders acquire these massive blocks? These are clearly masonry elements that originated in structures that stood elsewhere at Abydos. Based on its rough-dressed back and edges, the stela of Idudju-iker must have originally been engaged in brickwork and was set up in a brick chapel. The content of the biographical text focuses significantly on the Osiris cult and procession. Therefore, an original

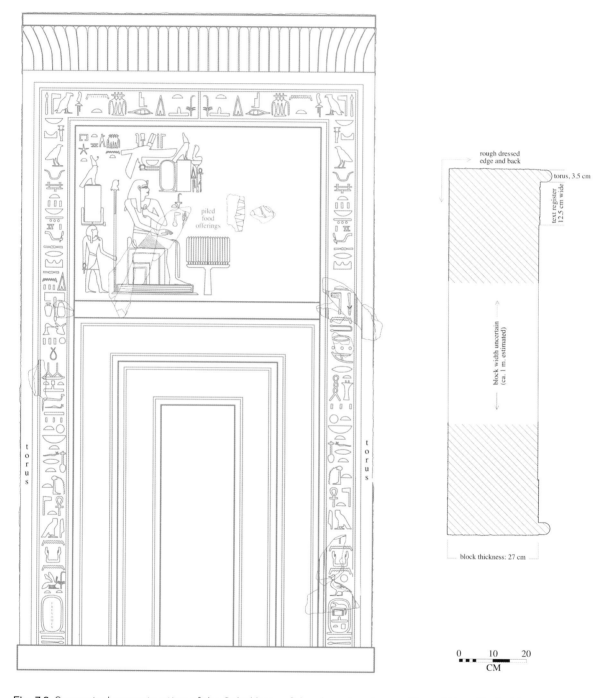

Fig. 7.8 Suggested reconstruction of the Sobekhotep false door showing position of the attested fragments.

location in North Abydos is highly probable. In all likelihood the Idudju-iker chapel stood on the desert edge behind the Osiris temple in the area of the *rwd n ntr ꜥꜣ, terrace of the great-god*, or along the processional route to Umm el-Ga'ab. However, it is also clear that the Idudju-iker stela underwent an intermediate phase of reuse prior to its installation in the burial chamber of Seneb-Kay. What was the nature and location of that intermediate phase of reuse?

The Sobekhotep false door evidently derives from a stone-built, royal mortuary building of the late Middle Kingdom. The finely dressed edges and back of the object suggest the false door originated as the fitting from a royal mortuary chapel or temple. Where at Abydos may we posit the presence of a mortuary chapel or temple for one of the 13th Dynasty Sobekhotep kings? Additionally, these roof slabs are not necessarily random objects culled from disparate locations. Is there a relationship between the provenance of the roof slabs and the group of 13th Dynasty chapel blocks commemorating the high officials Dedtu and Ibiau (see Chapters 8–10) that were used for the walls of the burial chamber?

An immediate observation to make here is the roof slabs were substantially larger and heavier than the reused wall blocks. The Idudju-iker stela was a massive object with dimensions of 0.27 x 1.07 x ca. 2 m. This block would have weighed on the order of ca. 1500 kg.[4] The Sobekhotep false door was likely of comparable or greater mass. Moving these larger blocks would have been significantly more challenging than the smaller chapel blocks, which could be handled by a few men. This raises the possibility they were taken from locations relatively close to the royal cemetery at South Abydos. Alternatively, the group of blocks may represent a more cohesive ensemble, extracted together from one location. While the origin of the reused blocks remains a matter of speculation, there are some key points of data that allow us to propose alternative possibilities. Here we define two options: (1) the blocks may have primarily originated from South Abydos and in relatively close proximity to Seneb-Kay's tomb; (2) the bulk of the blocks may have been reused from a specific, targeted area of 13th Dynasty structures in North Abydos, a locale where the stela of Idudju-iker may already have been reused.

Based on their close contemporaneity during the 13th Dynasty, there is a potential link between the Sobekhotep false door and the chapel blocks of

Dedtu and Ibiau. Although the fragments of the false door do not preserve the king's prenomen, there is a high probability this object is associated with Sobekhotep IV (Wegner and Cahail 2015:156–164), a king who along with his brother and predecessor Neferhotep I is very likely to have been buried at South Abydos. The chapel of Dedtu and Ibiau belongs to a prominent Theban family of the same timeframe as Neferhotep I and Sobekhotep IV. Possibly therefore, the Dedtu and Ibiau chapel was located in proximity to a royal mortuary building dedicated to the cult of Sobekhotep IV. A likely location for a mortuary structure dedicated to Sobekhotep IV is the desert edge of South Abydos close to the mortuary temple of Senwosret III. The existence of at least one 13th Dynasty royal cult building is proven by another object, a limestone naos with engaged figure of a seated king discovered in the 1950s by a farmer along the desert edge (Wegner 2007:44–46). This object (today set up in the forecourt of the temple of Seti) is badly damaged and only the lower parts of the text columns are preserved. However, we may observe a very similar style of carving to the Sobekhotep false door with use of an identical 12.5 cm wide text band and 3.5 cm outer torus (Fig. 7.9). The false door and naos could both derive from one, or a pair of nearby mortuary buildings along the desert escarpment associated with the 13th Dynasty royal burials in tombs S9 and S10. The exact location of these buildings is unknown but, based on the relative positions of S9 and S10, corresponding mortuary buildings should have lain somewhere just to the local north of the known mortuary temple of Senwosret III.

In this case, the chapel or chapels commemorating the family of Dedtu and Ibiau may have stood near a pair of royal mortuary buildings belonging to these prominent 13th Dynasty kings, suggesting the presence of a 13th Dynasty court cemetery or commemorative zone at South Abydos. By the reign of Seneb-Kay, the cult of these 13th Dynasty kings may have been abandoned and the chapels of these associated high officials appears to have been viciously attacked (see Chapters 8–10). Reuse of blocks originating in these 13th Dynasty royal and elite monuments may be the final step of a *damnatio memoriae* reflecting some political schism that emerged and was ultimately expressed in the rise of an independent line of kings including Seneb-Kay. This possibility would propose the chapel blocks and false door

Fig. 7.9 Late Middle Kingdom (probable 13th Dynasty) limestone naos from South Abydos with similarity of text carving and width to the Sobekhotep false door.

activity in North Abydos is the south-western edge of the North Cemetery that overlooks the low desert wadi approach to Umm el-Qa'ab. Encompassing the area of Mace's Cemetery D and Peet's Cemetery X, this was the location of one of the Neferhotep I stelae demarcating the boundary between the cemeteries and processional route of Osiris (Richards 2005). Nearby are late Middle Kingdom and Second Intermediate Period tombs including Tomb D78, the tomb of the *Superintendent of the Ruler's Crew*, Sobekhotep, and his wife the *Lady of the House*, Neferuptah (discussed elsewhere in this volume), which contained the wand with the cartouche of Se(ne)b-Kay. This elevated area, characterized by its vista looking towards Umm el-Qa'ab appears to have been a prime location for late Middle Kingdom tomb and chapel construction, as well as for reuse of elements drawn from 13th Dynasty mortuary structures during the period of Seneb-Kay. The chapel of Dedtu and Ibiau could have been set up in such a location where we would see a close contemporaneity between the commemoration of this elite Theban family and the activities of Neferhotep I and Sobekhotep IV. That chapel was later defaced and (presumably subsequently) reused by Seneb-Kay's tomb builders.

If we choose to exclusively favor either of these scenarios by itself, it must be acknowledged that we face a certain discordance in the evidence. If the bulk of the material was drawn from an assemblage of related royal and elite mortuary buildings at South Abydos the Idudju-iker stela would appear relatively incongruous. With its likely original location in North Abydos it seems unlikely that the Idudju-iker stela would have been taken to South Abydos for reuse in royal and elite buildings during that relatively affluent stage of the middle 13th Dynasty. If, however, we situate the point of origin of the Dedtu and Ibiau chapel blocks in the cemetery areas of North Abydos—possibly Mace's Cemetery D—the Sobekhotep false door then emerges as an incongruous element. The large dimensions of this object imply a substantially scaled royal mortuary chapel that supported an ongoing offering cult. A mortuary installation of this nature might have existed in North Abydos in the area of the royal Ka-chapels that flanked the main temple precinct of Osiris-Khentiamentiu (Kemp 1968:138–155; O'Connor 1992:83–98) but is not likely to have been located in the cemetery areas further westwards. The other possible location for such a

of Sobekhotep originated relatively close to the royal cemetery, a location that required moving the reused blocks only ca. 800 m (Fig. 7.10).

A second possibility is that the blocks could originate in royal and elite mortuary structures in North Abydos: buildings which again may have been specifically targeted in some form of political backlash that accompanied the end of 13th Dynasty control of Abydos. One area of notable late Middle Kingdom

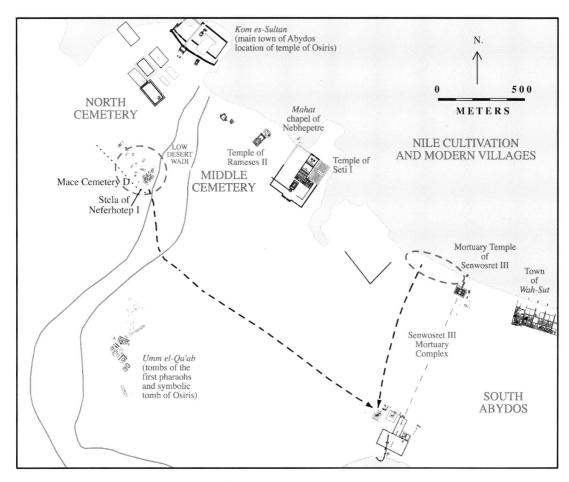

Fig. 7.10 Two alternative areas of origin for the reused blocks in the burial chamber of Seneb-Kay.

false door would be a cult building that was associated with the royal 13th Dynasty tombs S9 and S10 at South Abydos. Consequently, we may be looking at material drawn from multiple locations. Based on the existing data, the two locales proposed above appear to be the most viable areas of the Abydos landscape to have supplied the masonry reused in the construction of Seneb-Kay's burial chamber, although the builders may have availed themselves of material from other locations as well. Future excavation in these areas has the potential to add insight to the phenomenon of reuse, as well as the intimations of political dissonance which appear to be reflected in Seneb-Kay's reused blocks and other evidence from his tomb.

NOTES:

7.1 Wawat is the region of Lower Nubia between the First and Second Cataracts. On the stela it is mentioned twice, in both instances it is spelled Watwat (with an extra t).

The toponym is rendered here in transliteration as it is spelled but translated using the standard Wawat.

7.2 The offering scene is rendered in sunk relief but is somewhat effaced and has lost some of its original detail. Most of the lion-paw chair is missing but the scene may well have depicted a dog seated below Idudju-iker's chair, a common motif on stelae of the early 11th Dynasty. It is noteworthy that Idudju-iker is shown alone, without a wife, perhaps reflecting his status during his time in the Thinite nome.

7.3 The mention of the Neshmet barque of Osiris and the procession to Poqer appears to be the earliest attested occurrence of this important religious event at Abydos. If dated correctly to the reign of Wahankh Antef II, the stela may slightly predate 11th Dynasty stelae that refer to this event such as the stela of Abkau, Louvre N.169 (Oppenheim et al. 2015: 257–258).

7.4 Calculated using a figure of 2600 kg/cubic meter (Klemm and Klemm 1993).

8

The Reused 13th Dynasty Chapel Blocks*

The tomb of Seneb-Kay—tomb CS9 at South Abydos—is significant in its own right by virtue of the evidence it provides on political organization and kingship during Egypt's Second Intermediate Period. However, the historical information embedded in the tomb's architecture transcends that of a building built solely for the purpose of housing the burial of Seneb-Kay. The burial chamber itself is riddled with tantalizing traces from a period predating his reign. In 2014, partially obscured by the gypsum plaster applied by Seneb-Kay's tomb builders, we immediately observed the presence of incised decoration etched into the faces of the blocks beneath the painted images associated with Seneb-Kay. The limestone masonry of the burial chamber was not purpose-cut for the king's tomb but represents *spolia* reused from preexisting monuments elsewhere at Abydos. Many of these reused blocks are not decorated. However, a significant proportion have scenes and texts that date to the 13th Dynasty. These reused blocks derive from one or a group of associated 13th Dynasty funerary chapels. These blocks provide new evidence for private monumental construction unparalleled elsewhere at the site for the 13th Dynasty and furnish new evidence relevant to understanding the final stages of the Middle Kingdom at Abydos.

THE R-SERIES BLOCKS

During the initial excavation of the CS9 burial chamber, we documented a series of nine reused blocks in the walls and floor that had been set with their original decorated faces oriented into the chamber. That group of blocks provided the basis for a first stage of analysis and publication (Cahail 2014:172–226, 2015:93–122). In 2015, during restoration work on the burial chamber it became necessary to disassemble parts of the damaged walls that had been undermined by ancient tomb robbers and were in danger of collapse. This provided the opportunity to document four additional blocks whose decorated surfaces had been concealed in the joints, as well as two others that had been only partially documented. These additional blocks significantly augment the initial group and provide the basis for the fuller analysis of the 13th Dynasty blocks presented here.

One of the realities confronting the study of these reused blocks is that the western end of Seneb-Kay's burial chamber, which was structurally sound and also engaged with the brickwork of the vaulted antechamber, could not be dismantled in 2015. Many blocks remain (totaling 22 in situ blocks) whose full set of surfaces have never been exposed. Compounding the intact nature of the architecture is the treatment of the reused masonry by Seneb-Kay's tomb builders. As we have seen, the builders covered the wall faces with a topcoat of gypsum plaster that provided the requisite smooth surface for application of the chamber's painted ornamentation. It is clear that many other blocks bearing 13th Dynasty decoration remain obscured beneath Seneb-Kay's funerary scenes and texts. Yet, without disassembling the entire burial chamber and removing the later Second Intermediate

* This chapter written by Josef Wegner and Kevin Cahail.

Period plaster—thereby doing irreparable damage to Seneb-Kay's painted decoration in the process—these earlier carved surfaces must remain unseen. The present publication relies on those scenes that have been visible during our excavation and documentation, with the tantalizing knowledge that Seneb-Kay's burial chamber certainly conceals yet more evidence of these 13th Dynasty chapel scenes.

Consequently, although all of the masonry in CS9 is certainly reused, during the documentation of the burial chamber we have selectively applied "R" (reused block) numbers just to those reused blocks which bear 13th Dynasty decoration or possess other architecturally significant attributes. The R-series blocks, which occur in the walls and floor of the burial chamber, represent a cohesive corpus that stands apart from the larger, reused slabs used for the roof of the burial chamber (see Chapter 7). This chapter provides a detailed discussion of the individual decorated blocks (R1 to R17), as well as the smaller number of blocks that have been included in the R-series but which do not bear decoration. The reused blocks were numbered in order of identification, rather than their position in Seneb-Kay's burial chamber. In the catalogue below, they are grouped into three sections: (1) blocks originating from 13th Dynasty decorated wall faces (R1, R2, R3, R4, R5, R6, R9, R11, R12, R13, R16, and R17); (2) blocks that can be attributed to recessed statue niches (R7, R8, and R14), and (3) architecturally significant, but undecorated, reused blocks (R10, R15, R18, R19, and R20).

CHARACTERISTICS AND POSITION OF THE REUSED BLOCKS

The reused 13th Dynasty blocks are all limestone with a uniformly pure and homogeneous groundmass. Notably, the blocks are entirely free of flint nodules, a defining characteristic of limestone quarried in the Abydene area. The fine grain and uniformity of the stone indicates that it derives from a single source and the material may have originated from the Tura-Ma'asara quarries east of Memphis, suggesting that the stone was imported to Abydos at a time when long-distance trade was not hampered by political division—a point to which we will return later.

The wall blocks typically measure 24 to 32 cm in thickness and display a high degree of technical expertise in construction techniques. The blocks range between 40 to 60 cm in width and 30 to 45 cm in height. A number of the blocks retain mortises cut to accommodate butterfly tenons that had been employed in the original 13th Dynasty chapel construction.[1] Evidence for the connections of the blocks as we discuss in the next chapter shows that at least two of the mortise and tenon joints were positioned on structural corners of the primary 13th Dynasty building. The mortises are now incongruously distributed throughout the secondary context of Seneb-Kay's burial chamber where the blocks were placed in random locations, often positioned upside down or rotated relative to their original position.

NORTH WALL

The north wall includes six identified blocks bearing decoration (Fig. 8.1). Blocks R2, R3, and R4 were positioned with their decorated surfaces facing into the burial chamber. Three other blocks, R1, R12, and R13 were set with their decorated surfaces concealed in block seams. The westernmost block in the upper course of the north wall, R10, was also reused and preserves mortises for butterfly tenons at both ends but has no decoration. During restoration of the burial chamber in 2015, masonry of the north wall was disassembled from the position of R1 eastwards. This work exposed the three blocks with decoration in the joints. However, all of the eight large blocks to the west of R1 were left in situ. One of these is R4; indications are some of the other blocks at this end of the wall may also have decoration. The faces of many of these eight blocks remain heavily encrusted with the topcoat of gypsum plaster.

SOUTH WALL

The south wall is relatively poorly preserved, having lost a substantial amount of its upper two courses. The surviving wall has four reused blocks that were positioned with decorated surfaces facing into the burial chamber: R5, R6, R7, and R14 (Fig. 8.2). Also included in this group is block R9, which is engaged in the south wall masonry but set within the

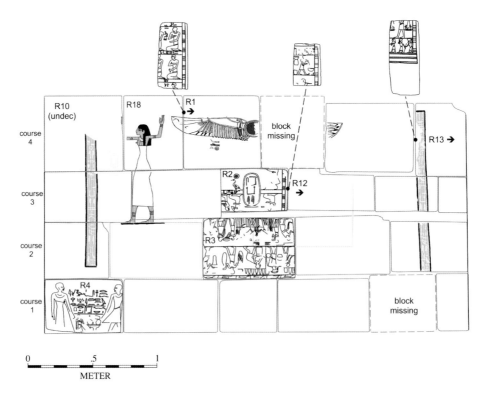

Fig. 8.1 Positions of reused blocks in the north wall of the burial chamber.

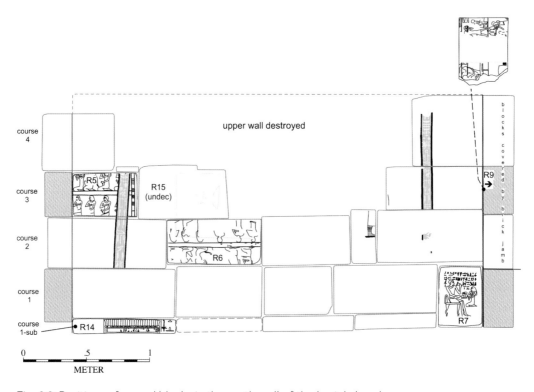

Fig. 8.2 Positions of reused blocks in the south wall of the burial chamber.

stonework that protrudes beyond the chamber's entrance where the brickwork and plaster of the vaulted antechamber were appended to the burial chamber masonry. Block R9 actually faces east and could technically be described as belonging to the chamber's "west wall." However, it is the only decorated block embedded in the door jambs at the chamber's western end and is included here as part of the south wall architecture with which it engages. Like the north wall, the blocks composing the eastern (inner) end of the burial chamber were disassembled in 2015. However, the stable masonry lying to the west of block R6 was not taken apart. Apart from decorated block R7, which is set in the first course at the wall's western end, the masonry left in situ includes nine additional blocks in the south wall proper that could have additional decorated faces. Block R15 is a reused block with a mortise and tenon joint but is undecorated.

EAST WALL

The east wall includes three reused blocks (Fig. 8.3). Facing into the chamber are blocks R16 and R17. As with much of the east wall, these two blocks are nearly completely covered by gypsum plaster associated with the Seneb-Kay wall imagery. However, outlines of 13th Dynasty decoration can be discerned at the edges and to some extent through the plaster coating. For R17, it remains impossible to trace the earlier decoration. However, for R16 the basic outlines of the decorated face can be discerned. The primary reused block documented in the east wall is R11. The decorated narrow face of this block, which was concealed in the joint abutting the south wall, was exposed in 2015 when the entire east wall was disassembled for restoration. Like R16 and R17 there are indications that the longer, inward facing surface of R11 also bears decoration, however, that face of R11 remains similarly obscured by the extant plaster and painting.

FLOOR

All of the blocks composing the burial chamber floor are reused masonry, likely stemming from the same source as the wall blocks (Fig. 8.4). The floor blocks are thinner on average, typically 15–20

cm in thickness, than those reused in the chamber's walls. Three blocks preserve significant architectural details. R18 derives from a round-topped or curving architectural feature, possibly originating in the rounded top of a limestone building, or potentially part of a limestone parapet with curved top. R19 has a rectangular, projecting frame adjacent to an inset, rough-dressed surface. R20 is the largest reused block on the floor and has a large hole that runs through the block's width.[2] The only floor block bearing decoration is R8, which was positioned with the decorated surface facing upwards. More than half of the floor area at the inner end was destroyed. This part of the chamber must have incorporated other, now-lost, reused blocks.

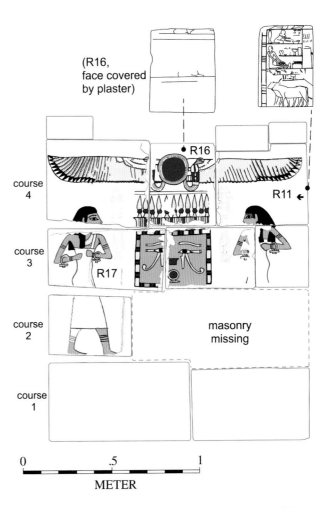

Fig. 8.3 Positions of reused blocks in the east wall of the burial chamber.

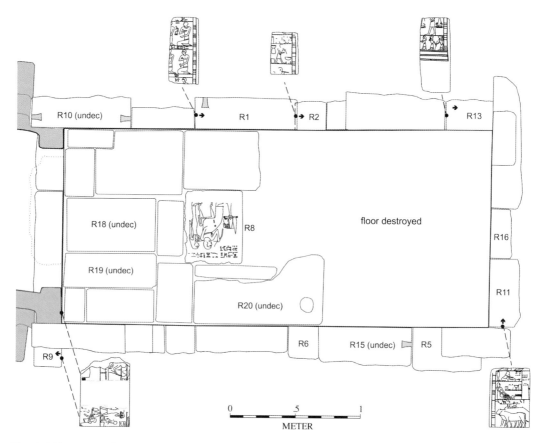

Fig. 8.4 Positions of reused blocks in the floor of the burial chamber (also showing reused blocks in the wall joints).

THE EFFECT OF THE DAMNATIO MEMORIAE

One of the commonalities of the *spolia* blocks in the burial chamber of CS9 is the overwhelming evidence for a targeted *damnatio memoriae* that had been carried out on the original 13th Dynasty building, or buildings, prior to the blocks' removal. The individual blocks attest to the malicious and comprehensive nature of this *damnatio*. Not only were the images and names of the principal figures attacked, but considerable effort went into the annihilation of the visual and symbolic role of the funerary scenes meant to ensure sustenance for the deceased. This *damnatio* may relate to political events that preceded Seneb-Kay's reign and conceivably echoes aspects of the final stages of 13th Dynasty control of Abydos. In terms of the present discussion, the effects of the *damnatio* are directly germane to the documentation and analysis of the chapel blocks.

The *damnatio* was affected primarily by means of chisels and is witnessed tangibly in the extensive damage that impacts the surface of many of these blocks. This aspect of the blocks' preservation has presented a challenge for documentation of the *spolia*. Images and texts that underwent alterations and abrasion during their repurposing for Seneb-Kay's tomb were already significantly gouged and hacked away. As we have seen, many areas of certain blocks remain further obscured by intact plaster. Therefore, for each of the blocks presented in the catalogue below we include both a photograph and line drawing. The line drawings record the decoration and texts as can be confidently traced through the damage.[3] Because the chisel marks interrupt many of the outlines of both text and figures, we present solid lines where their position is certain. However, the chisel damage itself is not rendered in the line drawings for which the associated photographs provide the best record.

Here we move on to discuss the individual re-used blocks. The catalogue that follows here includes discussion of scene and textual elements that can be related across multiple blocks that are now separated from one another in the secondary context of the Seneb-Kay burial chamber. The fuller coordination and reconstruction of the 13th Dynasty chapel scenes and architecture is presented in the next chapter.

BLOCKS DERIVING FROM WALL SCENES

BLOCK R1

This block was set in the top course of the north wall of the CS9 burial chamber. It measures 24 cm in thickness, 51 cm in height, and 78 cm in length. In its original architectural setting, R1 was a corner block with incised decoration on the narrow (left) end and a longer, undecorated, but finely dressed face. Since both of these surfaces were finished, it is clear that they were originally meant to be visible. At the top of the block and running parallel to the short, decorated face, is a half mortise that would have originally joined its mate on the adjacent block and would have been bonded by means of a butterfly tenon. The block was set into the burial chamber of Seneb-Kay with the decorated face concealed in the joint, and the longer undecorated surface facing into the burial chamber. When R1 was first identified in 2014, only a small portion of the decorated face protruded on the exterior of the burial chamber (Fig. 8.5). In 2015, when restoration work was completed, the block was removed, allowing us to document the entire deco-rated face (Fig. 8.6).

Block R1 preserves three superimposed regis-ters of kneeling figures facing left, with text bands between them. The registers are 18.5 cm in height with 18 cm tall figures (two fully preserved and three partial figures). At the bottom is the upper part of a register which is completed on the block (R5) that originally adjoined R1 below. The block spans the full height of the two registers above this. Intervening be-tween each register is a 2.5 cm wide text band that includes hieroglyphic labels connected to the fig-ures in the registers below. The registers are framed on the right side by a 2.8 cm wide vertical border

demonstrating this block formed the right corner of a decorated wall.

All the texts on this block exhibit damage, but no-tably both the male figure on the right side of the top register and his name above him were purposefully defaced with chisels. The man in the middle register was also chiseled, although his name is mainly intact. The epigraphs on the block are all names and titles. In all cases, the orientation of the texts matches that of the figures below. The titles and personal names associated with each figure are initiated within the horizontal band above. The epigraphs are separated by vertical dividing lines (less distinctly visible on R1 but more clearly seen on some of the other re-used blocks). Where the inscription could not be fully accommodated in the horizontal band the text then spills over onto a vertical column of hieroglyphs fronting the associated figure.[4]

The partial male figure at the left side of the top register has no surviving text, since the text in the band above connects with the figure at the right side. The label for the figure on the right has been chiseled over, leaving only a few signs clearly legible. Below, the figure itself has also been attacked with a chisel. The horizontal band contains his title, while his name is in the field in front of his face. Despite the damage, it is possible to read the entire text as: *s3.f 3tw-n-tt-ḥû3 'Imn-m-ḥ3t m3ᶜ-ḥrw, his son the Superinten-dent of the Ruler's Crew, Amenemhat, true-of-voice.*[5] Below is another text band which refers to the man kneeling at the right in the middle register. Neither this text, nor the individuals in the middle register were defaced as completely as was Amenemhat. The text reads from left to right: *s3.f mr.f Rdî m3ᶜ-ḥrw, his beloved son, Redi, true-of-voice.*[6] The suffix pronoun *.f* refers to the chapel owner, who, given the left-fac-ing orientation of the figures, was originally pictured somewhere to the left of block R1. Unlike his brother Amenemhat pictured above, Redi did not have a title of his own, perhaps indicating that he was a younger son and the monument in question was carved at an early stage in his lifetime.

The signs in the lowest text band on R1 are also damaged, though they do not appear to have been de-liberately chiseled over. At the left edge of the band is a trace of a vertical line, which may serve to separate two epigraphs associated with the figure at the left,[7] and the man on the right. Only the head of this man is preserved on the block, but the text identifies him as

Fig. 8.5 Block R1 as set with its decorated face in the masonry seam, protruding on the exterior of the burial chamber.

individual with a title connected with Montu of Medamud occurs on block R2. Other individuals with connections to Montu and more broadly to the Theban nome occur on several of the other reused blocks, likely reflecting the Theban associations of the family commemorated on this 13th Dynasty chapel.[10]

BLOCK R2

R2 is located in the center of the second course of the north wall of the CS9 burial chamber. The block was set upside down with respect to its original decoration, but with its carved surface facing into the tomb (Fig. 8.7). The block measures 39.5 cm wide, 25 cm high, and 24 cm in thickness. The block originally joined block R6 at the right and R11 below. Much of the face of this block is covered by the large, painted nomen, *s3-R^c (Snb-K3y)*, occupying the middle of the north wall. The coat of gypsum plaster and painting of this label significantly occludes much of the earlier incised decoration on R2. The earlier 13th Dynasty carving is primarily visible at the ends of the block.

On the block's left side is a 2.8 cm wide vertical border showing that this was a corner and the left end of a wall scene. To the right, the block preserves two registers of kneeling figures, all facing right. The upper register has four individuals, including a girl

the *sh3w ḥwt-nṯr n Mntw m M3dw, Mnṯw[-ḥtp]*, *Scribe of the temple of Montu in Medamud, Montu[hotep]*.[8] The personal name Montuhotep here is almost certain, although the name Montu alone is also viable.[9] No statement of filiation is preserved, so it is unknown if Montuhotep was the brother of Amenemhat and Redi, appearing in the registers above, or if he was connected to the chapel owner in another way. Most significantly, here we have evidence for an individual associated, both in his personal name and his priestly title, with the cult of Montu at Medamud. A second

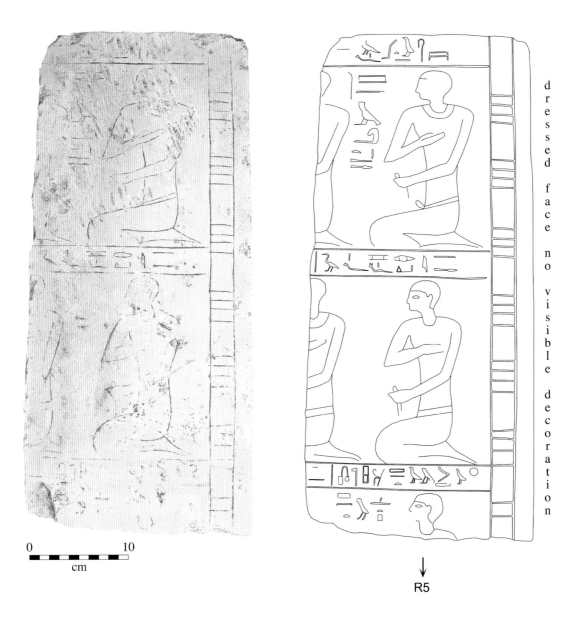

R5

Fig. 8.6 Reused block R1 (north wall, course 4).

at the far right. The girl is rendered at a smaller scale than the rest of the figures and has a side-lock composed of three braids at the back of her head.[11] Behind the girl are three adult female figures although due to the presence of Seneb-Kay's painted cartouche over the middle of this block, their forms are mostly obscured. Traces of four male kneeling figures facing right are visible in the lower register. The matching knees and legs of these same figures appears on the top of blocks R3 and R11. Details of these figures are again obscured by chisel damage and the plaster associated with the Seneb-Kay text.

One of the more significant features of R2 is the band of text between the two registers. Unfortunately, the signs are mostly concealed beneath the gypsum plaster. As we see more clearly on block R1, these intermediary text bands are typically used for the names of the figures depicted immediately below the text. Here only portions of two labels associated with men below can be discerned. The first label on the right reads *[////n/] ms.n ʾIr(?)/// -ʾImn, /// born of Ir (?)///-amun*. The man's title is unclear and the name following the statement is highly damaged. The text terminates with the element *-amun* which continues

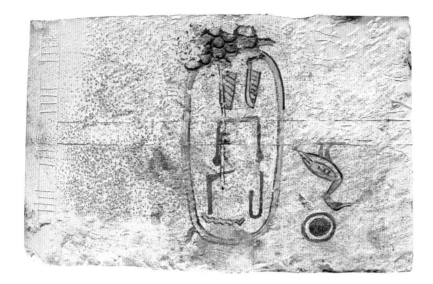

Fig. 8.7 Reused block R2 (north wall of the CS9 burial chamber, positioned upside down).

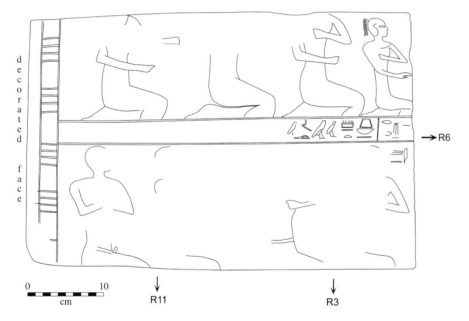

vertically in front of the figure. A vertical line separates this label from the next which although damaged can be read as: *ḫry-ḥbt n Mntw m Mꜣdw ///, the lector-priest of Montu-in-Medamud ///.*[12] The name of the individual is entirely obscured beneath the plaster as are the further names and titles to the left in the text band. The occurrence of this priestly title associated with the cult of Montu at Medamud is noteworthy in view of the presence of a scribe of the temple of Montu-in-Medamud on block R1. These priestly titles connected with Medamud, as well as the name terminating in -amun on this same block corroborate the Theban associations of the family of Dedtu and Ibiau.

BLOCK R3

One course below R2, reused in the central part of the north wall of CS9's burial chamber, was block R3 (Fig. 8.8). Like R2, this piece of *spolia* was set upside down in the wall. Block R3 is 70 cm wide, 45 cm in height, and 25 cm in thickness. In terms of its size and the variety of imagery, it is the most complex of the reused blocks. Two complete and one partial register of decoration are preserved on the block. Its decoration connects with that of block R9 on the right and R11 at the left. Prior to its reuse in Seneb-Kay's burial chamber, R3 suffered a severe

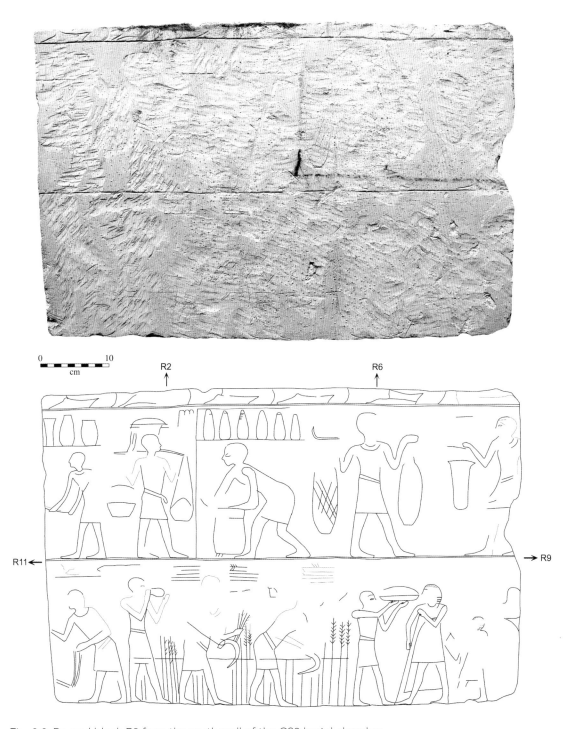

Fig. 8.8 Reused block R3 from the north wall of the CS9 burial chamber.

degree of damage through the *damnatio memoriae*. The outlines of most of the human figures were chiseled out, including a man who may represent the deceased at the bottom right of the scene. Seneb-Kay's tomb builders then appear to have sanded down the entire decorated surface prior to facing the block with a topcoat of gypsum, leaving only the deepest incised lines intact.

The uppermost register consists of a series of knees and feet of kneeling human figures. Five figures are preserved on the left facing right. One figure is preserved on the right facing left. The disposition of the figures shows that the decoration on R3 originally completed the base of blocks R2 and R6 above. The difference in orientation is a crucial aspect of the group of reused 13th Dynasty chapel blocks as a whole and suggests that R3 straddled the centerline of a large wall with a focal scene of the chapel owner above it flanked by inward-facing kneeling figures.

The middle register depicts a series of production activities. At the left is a standing figure holding tongs and engaged in some task connected with a tall capped structure.[13] The structure in front of him appears on the adjoining block R11 to the left. The feature appears to be a cylindrical kiln or furnace and the figure is shown tending the structure. One possibility is this may be a scene showing pottery firing. The possibility is emphasized by the register above, which shows a row of completed pottery vessels. The activities depicted to the right also relate to pottery production. The central portion of the scene shows a man bringing clay in baskets, strung up to a yoke toward the middle of the block. Here, enclosed by a rectangular frame is another man who bends over a large cylindrical vat. His body is contorted, and one arm evidently descends inside the vat where he works the clay. A row of pottery vessels sits at the top, possibly dried vessels ready for firing. At the right is another man with a yoke across his shoulders, but instead of raw clay he carries finished pottery vessels away in rope slings. Another man carrying objects appears at the right, facing to the left, but the specifics of his actions are unclear. He may be receiving vessels for use since the adjoining block, R9, appears to be focused on the storage and preparation of foodstuffs. The combination of elements represented in this middle register shows extremely close parallels to the smaller and more abbreviated scenes on 13th Dynasty stelae from Abydos such as the *ankh*-stela of Amenyseneb which we discuss further below.[14]

The lower register of R3 shows a ploughman at the left. He leans over a plough that he holds with his left hand while raising another object in the air with his right arm. This ploughing scene continues on block R11, where the remainder of the plough and a pair of oxen are shown. The object in the man's right arm on R11 is a branch for goading the oxen. The harvest occurs to the right of the ploughing on R3. In the center of the register, two men cut grain with sickles while a third man stands behind, drinking from a pottery vessel. Above the figures are sheaves of wheat laid horizontally representing the cut grain prior to threshing. At the right end of the field stands an individual holding aloft a large tray containing a pile of grain. He presents this to an official who stands overlooking the harvest. This figure wears a complex garment with inner kilt and outer robe. He has elaborately coiled hair which has been nearly entirely destroyed by the chisel damage. He leans on a staff that he holds in the midsection with his right hand, while grasping the top beneath his underarm with his left hand.[15] This figure is clearly a man of status who, based on comparanda from other late Middle Kingdom chapels and stelae, must be the chapel owner himself. An interesting detail of the scene is a smaller figure behind the official who is likely to be his son. The boy has vestiges of a similar hair treatment to the larger figure. The boy appears to be holding some object in front of him, but the damage makes its identification uncertain.[16]

BLOCK R4

R4 is located in the base course (course 1) at the western end of the north wall of Seneb-Kay's burial chamber. The block measures 60 cm wide, and 39.5 cm in height. It is 26 cm in thickness, closely comparable to the other reused 13th Dynasty wall blocks. The block was set into the wall with the decorated face inwards and the figures oriented upwards. The 13th Dynasty decoration was originally masked by a layer of gypsum plaster which had mostly fallen away. The decoration on R4 consists of three lines of text, flanked by images of three standing male figures: two to the left and one to the right. The legs of both of the larger standing males begin at the knee on the base of the block. The figure on the right is also incomplete indicating that R4 belonged within a larger wall scene that spread across multiple adjacent blocks.

The scene on Block 4 is remarkable for the intensity of the effort put into destroying both the text and the figures. The aggressive nature of the *damnatio*, however, is offset by the fact that the incised relief on R4 was originally quite deep. Within the chisel marks the lowest outlines of nearly all of the figures and text elements survive. Consequently, the original lines of the scene and text can be traced quite accurately as shown in the line drawing here which is paired with the photograph showing the chisel damage (Fig. 8.9).

The primary figure stands on the left side of the scene, facing right. He wears a large kilt, cinched well above the waist, which hangs down in the space between his body and his left arm. Directly to the right of the primary figure, and facing in the same direction, stands a much smaller male, in all likelihood the son of the larger figure. His left arm is crossed over

his chest and his right arm hangs behind him. In the lower portion of the scene and directly in front of the smaller male is the top of an offering table on a stand that would have originally extended to the baseline of the scene. Another adult male figure who is only slightly smaller than the primary figure stands to the right of the table, facing left. He wears a long flaring kilt with his right arm extended down over the garment and nearly touching the pile of offerings. His left arm is missing and would have been depicted on an adjacent block. All three of these figures were

Fig. 8.9 Reused block R4 (base course, northwest corner of the CS9 burial chamber).

0 ▬▬▬ 10
cm

attacked through chiseling. However, the damage affected on the left figure is noticeably more pronounced. He almost certainly represents the chapel owner and primary target of the *damnatio*.

Between the two larger males is an inscription reading from left to right. The hieroglyphs are arranged in three lines of text with a horizontal dividing line between each. The dividing line is barely visible between the first and second lines of text but better preserved between the second and third lines as well as at the bottom of the third line. The text is a variation of the *in s3.f* formula naming the son who acts to perpetuate his father's name.[17] It reads: *in s3.f sꜥnḫ rn.f ḥry ḥ3wt n 'Imn [////]tw sḥ3 (?)[////] Snb.f nb im3ḥw, It is his son who perpetuates his name, the Master of the Offering Tables of Amun,*[18] /// (title unclear), *scribe*(?) ///, *Senebef, possessor of veneration*. Due to the degree of damage to the signs after *'Imn* and before *Snb.f*, the elements after the title *ḥry ḥ3wt n 'Imn* remain unclear. There appear to be one or, more likely, two additional titles. The element *sḥ3, scribe* may be present in the badly damaged area at the beginning of the third line. These appear to be secondary titles belonging to Senebef whose name ends the inscription. The text terminates with the epithet *nb im3ḥw, possessor of veneration*, which is a rare element in the *in s3.f* formula since this type of text emphasizes the role of a living heir who keeps alive (*sꜥnḫ*) his father's name. The connotation in this context may be to mark Senebef's social status rather than a funerary epithet.

An interesting part of the scene on R4 is the presence of the third, smaller male figure directly in front of the man on the left. The three lines of the *in s3.f* formula do not appear to include reference to this individual. However, to the right of his head are very badly battered remnants of a group of smaller format hieroglyphs that may include his name. Barely discernible is the element *s3.f, his son* below which his name may have occurred in front of his shoulder. This individual may have been another one of the sons, but one who predeceased his father, and was given a place of honor accompanying him in front of his offering table. The offering table would then serve to separate the living son on the right (Senebef) from his deceased father and brother on the left.

The scene on R4 is clearly a focal offering scene. With what survives we can extrapolate the lower parts of the figures and offering table that would have extended onto the block below (Fig. 8.10). The two large figures were ca. 45 cm in height, approximately ¼ life-size, making these the largest surviving images on the reused blocks. The left arm of the figure on right, probably Senebef, can also be reconstructed as it would have extended onto the adjacent block. His arm would have hung passively at his side as there is no indication of the arm or any object held that extends over his body. The known elements of the scene were ca. 60 cm in width but there should have been additional components that made this a wider and taller scene. The name and titles of the primary figure whose identity is perpetuated by his son Senebef does not appear on R4. This text must have occurred in another scene label on an adjacent block, possibly behind the figure but more likely in a text that capped the scene. The probable format for the scene label would be a *ḥtp-di-nswt* formula, a prayer for offerings, that ended with the name and titles of the main figure. The scene as a whole may have mimicked contemporary funerary stelae where the *ḥtp-di-nswt* formula surmounted an offering scene that usually included the son of the deceased and occasionally made use of the *in s3.f* formula.[19]

Although no label survives for him, the principal figure on the left side of R4 may be the *Overseer of Fields*, Dedtu, or much more likely, the *Overseer of Offering Tables of Amun*, Ibiau. These two men—father and son—are both depicted as the focus of the mortuary cult on other reused 13th Dynasty blocks found in the CS9 burial chamber. Given the position Ibiau held as *Master of the Offering Tables of Amun*, the appearance of a son, Senebef, who has the same priestly title in the Amun establishment is suggestive of a father to son succession in this high-ranking office. Moreover, the appearance of both of the large figures on R4 as bald or with close cropped hair appears to speak to priestly status and perhaps the comparable role of both figures in temple cult. The possible relationships among these three generations of men, Dedtu, Ibiau, and Senebef, will be examined in the next two chapters.

BLOCK R5

This block is located at the east end of the third course of the burial chamber's south wall (Fig. 8.11). R5 measures 51 cm in width and 33 cm in height and was positioned right side up with the decoration facing

Primary scene label with name and titles of chapel owner
(*ḥtp-dỉ-nswt* formula?)

block missing

block missing

cm
20
10
0

Fig. 8.10 Block R4 showing completion of known figural elements that would have continued onto adjacent blocks.

into the burial chamber. At the right side, the surface is overlain with a column of painted text, belonging to Seneb-Kay's titulary. Beneath the Second Intermediate Period paint and plaster is a portion of a carved scene organized in two registers with a 2.8 cm wide border band on the right. R5 is a corner block from the right side of the original decorated wall. Block R5 connects to block R6 at the left. The decoration connects also with R1 above and R9 and R12 below.

The upper register preserves four figures all facing left in an alternating order of female, male, female, male. The two individuals at the front are musicians and represent the final figures of the troop of five musicians fronted by a harpist on adjoining block R6. The woman at the left has both arms raised up in front of her face in an attitude of clapping. The man behind her holds a long object diagonally across his chest. The details of the object are concealed beneath a patch of extant plaster but this can be identified as a long flute of a type shown elsewhere in Middle Kingdom tomb chapel scenes.[20] The musicians are followed to the right by two figures, one female and one male, in standard keeling pose, each holding a folded cloth in their left hand. The final figure, which

is substantially obscured by the painted column of Seneb-Kay, is the body of the man labeled above in block R1 as the *Scribe of the temple of Montu in Medamud, Montuhotep.*

The lower register preserves four kneeling male figures, all facing left. Between the two registers is a horizontal band of the type that was used for text labels elsewhere on the 13th Dynasty blocks. The plaster layer associated with the later painted text column of Seneb-Kay substantially covers the right side of the block and no text could be discerned. It appears likely that the majority of the band in this location was never inscribed. However, between the figures in the lower register are faint vestiges of hieroglyphs suggesting these individuals may have had their names written in front of them even if the band above was left substantially blank on this part of the wall.

BLOCK R6

This block is located in the second course of the burial chamber's south wall. It was placed with its original decoration oriented upside down. R6 is wider

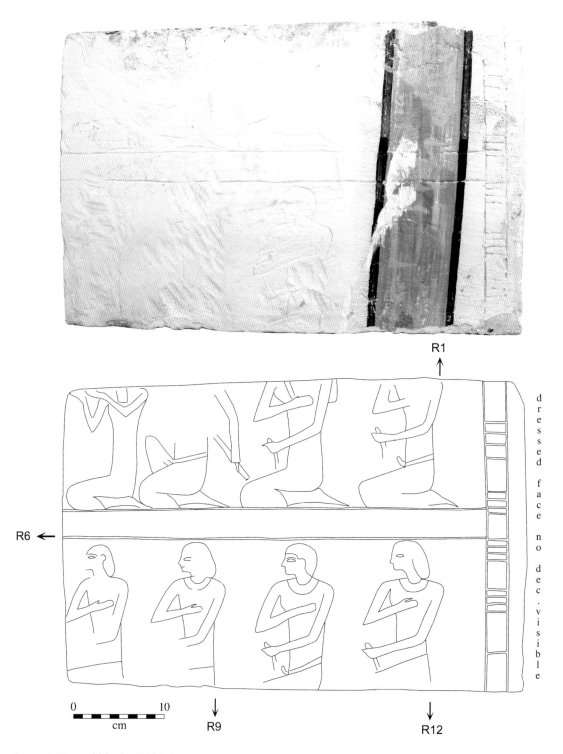

Fig. 8.11 Reused block R5 (third course, south wall).

than the other *spolia* in CS9 and measures 72 cm wide by 33 cm tall (Fig. 8.12). This block originally joined block R5 at the right and R2 at the left. The kneeling figures in the lower register are completed on blocks R3 and R9 which originally adjoined R6 below. The block preserves two superimposed registers with a text band between them. At the center of the text band, a vertical line can be discerned corresponding closely with the center of the wider wall scene. This line appears to represent the beginning of the figure labels that extend to the left. The labels on the right side do not appear to have been completed and there are no vestiges of hieroglyphs on the right side. All of the figures in both the upper and lower registers face toward the centerline marked by the vertical line in the text band. Clearly, R6 was located in the middle of a large composition with multiple registers showing kneeling attendants and musicians who face inwards towards a focal element which must have been depicted above the position of this block.

Six figures appear in the upper register. At the right are portions of three musicians, including a harpist, who all face left. On the left side are traces of three kneeling women all facing towards the right. Behind the final figure on the block occurs a large gap that separates the woman from the kneeling girl who occurs on adjacent block R2. There appears to be some feature occupying this gap, but its identity is obscure. Possibly there was an offering table in front of the girl whose arm reaches out as if to touch an offering table. This is a motif that occurs in many of the late Middle Kingdom family stelae, although none of the other kneeling figures on the reused blocks are fronted by this element. Particularly interesting, although highly damaged, is the figure of the female harpist who fronts the group of five musicians (three on R6 and two on adjoining block R5) and who and sits directly on the centerline of the composition. She cradles a harp on her lap, the base of which projects in front of her knees. The position of her arms, which are raised up over the strings, is just discernible.[21]

The lower register also has traces of six figures: three kneeling men on the left and three kneeling women on the right. They all face the center of the

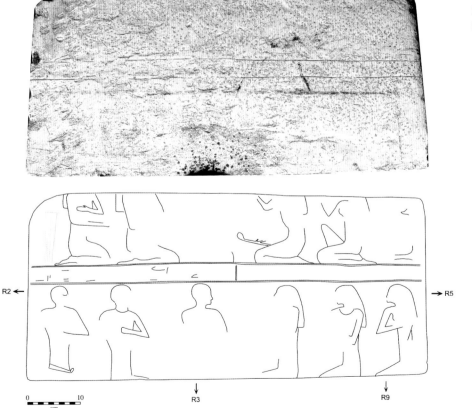

Fig. 8.12 Reused block R6.

block. As mentioned above, no text was discernible to the right of the central line. This conforms with R5 and the band in this location may not have been inscribed. However, to the left of the central line are remnants of numerous signs. The text here is essentially illegible, which is particularly unfortunate as this text band continues to the left onto block R2 where we have names and titles of individuals, one of whom at least was connected with the temple of Montu-in-Medamud. Quite possibly these individuals fall into the same geographical pattern seen on R1 and R2 commemorating people associated with the cult of Montu at Medamud with intimations of the Theban association of the family celebrated on this chapel.

BLOCK R9

The decoration on block R9 was only partially documented, owing to the fact that the stone is too deeply embedded in the architecture of CS9's burial chamber to permit its removal (Fig. 8.13). The block is set into the third course of the burial chamber's southwest corner. The decorated surface protrudes southward on the tomb's exterior, as well as into the tomb's interior, where part of the decorated face emerges on the south jamb of the chamber's entrance. The block was set with its decorated surface upside down and facing eastward. The block is 38 cm in height and approximately 52 cm wide. The left edge is chipped and damaged where it was covered by the mud mortar and plaster of the doorjamb. However, it appears the preserved width is very close to its original horizontal dimension. The block's decoration adjoins R12 and R13 on its right. Although there are no images that directly link R9 with the decoration to the left, the 52 cm width and register organization suggest it originally joined block R3 on the left side with no intervening block.

R9 preserves parts of three registers. The register widths exactly match those of R3 to the left showing these scenes relate programmatically with the series of agricultural and industrial scenes on blocks R3 and R11. The uppermost register includes the lower bodies of a series of kneeling figures facing left. These complete the kneeling figures on blocks R5 and R6 above. Below are two registers of production activities and offering bearers. On the right side

of the central register is a large figure facing left who carries trays of food on his shoulders. Behind him and facing to the right is a smaller figure who bends over what appears to be a table or rectangular feature. He appears to be related to the brewing activities shown in the connecting images on block R12. On the left side of the block is a very damaged image of a man leaning over an animal leg which is raised vertically. This is certainly an image of butchery although the finer details of the scene are difficult to discern. Above the butcher is a horizontal line above which may be containers, cuts of meat, or a combination thereof. This continues the arrangement seen in block R3 to the left where pottery vessels are shown arrayed in rows above the workers below.

The lower register preserves a man carrying foodstuffs on the right side. The man faces left holding a tray laden with three jars or vessels with his left hand.[22] In his right hand, he holds a duck by the wings. Behind his kilt is the head of the small gazelle that joins the bearer carrying four infant gazelles on block R13. On the left side of this lower register, the only surviving element is a large pillow-like feature with outward curving sides and top. It is possible this represents a granary or storage structure connected with the harvest scene that occurs to the right in this same register on block R3. However, there appears to be nothing at all above this feature making its status uncertain.

BLOCK R11

R11 (Fig. 8.14) was reused as the rightmost block of the upper course of the burial chamber's east wall. In its original 13th Dynasty context, R11 was a corner block with two perpendicular, finished faces. In the secondary context of Seneb-Kay's burial chamber, the narrower, decorated end (measuring 32 x 45 cm) formed the seam between the east wall and south wall masonry. This decorated face was concealed to view until the east wall masonry was disassembled for restoration work in 2015. The block's larger finished face (45 x 52 cm) was placed inwards and is substantially covered with a thick layer of gypsum plaster and intact painting. There is no clearly traceable decoration on this inner face, but telltale incised lines suggest there may well be 13th Dynasty decoration beneath the gypsum coating. The visible 13th Dynasty decoration preserves two registers of agricultural scenes

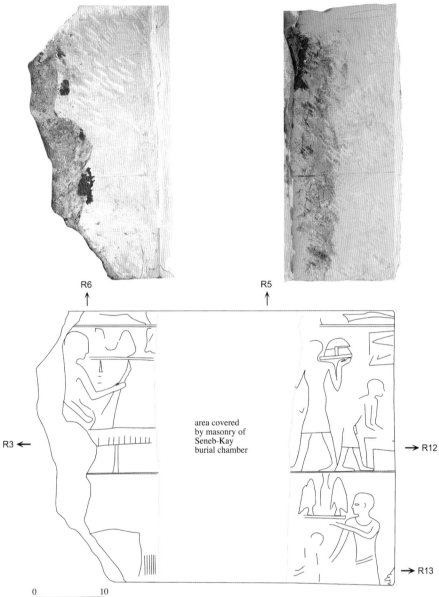

that join to block R3 on the right, as well as the feet of kneeling figures which join to block R2 above. The human and animal figures on this block were heavily damaged as part of the *damnatio memoriae* in the original 13th Dynasty chapel. As we see on most of the agricultural scenes, this appears to be an attempt to erase the efficacy of the images and hinder their ability to produce food offerings for the deceased.

On the left edge of the block, adjacent to the finished corner, is a decorative border (2.8 cm wide) that encloses the scene. The decoration to the right

of this border spans three superimposed registers and can be subdivided into five distinct areas. At the top of the block are traces of two kneeling attendants, who face right. The middle register is subdivided into three distinct production activities. At the top left is a kneeling man, who appears to be forming bread loaves in preparation for baking. In the rectangle below him is a woman facing right, kneeling on her right leg. She is grinding grain into flour on a large quern. At the right edge of the block is the left edge of the scene (continuing from R3) showing a man

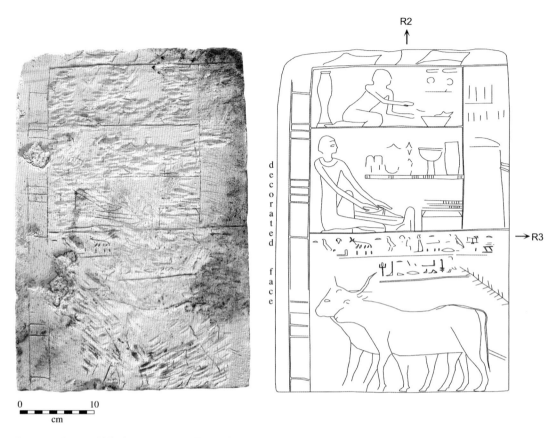

Fig. 8.14 Reused block R11 (east wall, CS9 burial chamber).

tending a cylindrical kiln or oven. Here we see the left side of his tongs held against the face of the oven. The oven itself is shown with a domed or rounded top but no internal detail. Above the oven are rows of objects laid out in parallel. The preservation is poor, but these may be cylindrical bread molds laid out cooling after the baking of bread. This group of scenes appears to include the primary steps in bread making, including grinding grain, forming of loaves, and baking. The activities sequentially follow the ploughing and harvest scenes in the register below.

The lower register of block R11 also continues the action from block R3 to its right. On R11 we have the image of a pair of oxen, shown superimposed one atop the other. A plough rope is visible extending from their hind legs off the right edge of the block. Above this is the ploughman's goad raised up over their backs. At the top of the register is a short text in two lines, badly damaged with a chisel, but partially readable. The hieroglyphs read from left to right paralleling the movement of the ploughman. The text reads: *tw(.i) ḥr ḥrp iḥw tw(.i) ḥr int drw t(ȝ) iȝbty r ꜥq sw,*

I am driving the oxen. I am reaching the eastern borderland in order to cross it. This text presents a number of noteworthy issues. The statement is clearly speech by the ploughman who drives the oxen before him. This quote appears to be the earliest surviving example of the Late Egyptian First Present verbal construction (*tw.i ḥr sḏm*), here occurring in two successive statements uttered by the ploughman (for a full discussion see Cahail [2019]). Other tomb scenes of this type dating to the Middle Kingdom have either summary statements describing the action or, in other cases, label the farmers as being the sons and family members of the deceased.[23] In this case, the text is direct, first person speech of the farmer. Such direct speech was extremely common in Old Kingdom tomb scenes (Erman 1919). The practice does reappear more sporadically in the New Kingdom but is poorly attested during the Middle Kingdom. The scene on this reused 13th Dynasty chapel block is good evidence that the practice was never really lost, but rather is less prominent owing to the more fragmentary record that has survived from the late

Middle Kingdom. Close parallels to the speech occur in decorated tombs that post-date the Middle Kingdom (Guglielmi 1973:6–28).

BLOCK R12

R12 (Fig. 8.15) is a corner block with one decorated face forming the right side of a scene and one finely dressed but undecorated surface. The block was set into the center of the upper course of the east wall of Seneb-Kay's burial chamber with the undecorated surface oriented into the chamber. The decorated face was concealed in the masonry joint and was exposed during the 2015 restoration of the burial chamber. The decorated portion of the block on its narrow side measures 21 cm wide and 31.5 cm tall. Near the finished corner occurs a 2.8 cm wide border band as attested on other corner blocks. To the left are three registers of decoration.

The top register preserves just the foot of a left-facing, kneeling figure and belongs to the first of the rows of figures that compose the upper wall scenes. This joins block R5. The two lower registers are parts of agricultural scenes. The middle register shows a man engaged in the same brewing scene which begins on block R9. Above him is a secondary ground line, upon which sit vessels and other objects, probably meant to show the products of the activity below although the items are highly damaged and hard to discern. The bottom register preserves the head and shoulders of a standing male, who carries a yoke across his shoulders and faces left. The lower portion of this man occurs on block R13. Despite its small dimensions, block R12 displays extensive chiseling of most of its elements indicating the aggressive nature of the *damnatio* that was directed against the original 13th Dynasty chapel. The piles of offering vessels and human figures were all attacked in a manner that appears intended to symbolically remove all

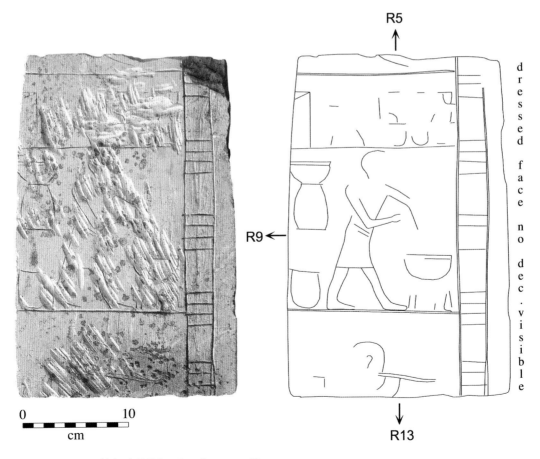

Fig. 8.15 Reused block R12 (east wall, course 3).

access by the chapel owner to the benefits of the offering cult.

BLOCK R13

Similar to the preceding two blocks, R13 is a
corner block originating in the right side of a decorated wall (Fig. 8.16). R13 was identified in 2015 in
the north wall of Seneb-Kay's burial chamber during
restoration work. The block has a narrow, decorated
side adjoining a finished corner, with a broader undecorated face. At the right of the decorated scene is
a 2.8 cm border, running down the block parallel to
the finished corner. This vertical border terminates
in three sets of double horizontal lines 24 cm above
the base. This block shows that the chapel decoration
began above a 24 cm undecorated dado and above
this border of paired horizontal lines.

The block preserves two registers of decoration
with no text. The upper register connects to R12, the
corner block above, and shows the torso and legs of
a walking male carrying a yoke. On either end of the
yoke, ropes extend down to baskets, each of which
contains a pair of juvenile antelopes. The man holds
a branch out toward the mouth of the rear-facing animal in the front basket. The basket containing antelopes on the left side extends onto block R9, which
preserves the nose and horn of the forward-facing
antelope.

In the lower register are three somewhat diminutive figures facing left, whose style and proportions
are different than the rest of the scene. The figures are
somewhat crudely proportioned with unusually large
limbs and feet, probably reflecting the fact that this is
the lowest register on the wall and the figures are of
lower status than those above. At the left is a standing male, whose hands are in front of him, holding or
manipulating some object pictured off the left edge
of the block. Behind this man are two other figures,
whose gender appears at first glance somewhat ambiguous. They wear what appear to be male kilts but
these should be taken as dresses. Both have baskets on
their heads as commonly depicted for female offering
bearers. The central figure has short hair but also has
breasts depicted on the upper body. The central figure holds a stick behind which is also grasped by the
rearmost figure on the right. This final individual has
pendulous breasts, slightly longer hair, and a hunched

posture. It might represent a corpulent, older male but
seems more likely to be an old woman who is leaning
on the stick but also touching the hand of the figure in
front. This lowest register appears to represent a frieze
of individuals carrying agricultural produce and foodstuffs associated with the activities in the scenes above.
No other blocks preserve this lowest register.

Block R13 exhibits a relatively minimal amount
of chisel damage, likely attributable to the fact that
it falls low on the wall and is relatively peripheral
to the primary scenes depicting the chapel owner
and family members. The larger figure in the upper
register, carrying baskets of baby antelopes, exhibits
chisel damage to both his abdomen and the animal
riding in the basket. Interestingly, the three smaller
figures in the lower register are completely un-
scathed, and though the entire surface of the block
appears to have been shaved down, the incised carving was left intact.

BLOCKS R16, R17, AND R18

These blocks have been assigned to the R-series
given the certainty that their inward-facing surfaces
retain 13th Dynasty decoration. However, all three
blocks are so heavily obscured by extant plaster and
painting that they contribute little to reconstructing the 13th Dynasty chapel decoration. R16 and R17
are located in the east wall. R16 measures 44.5 cm
in height and 38 cm wide. It is located in the center of the upper course (course 4) and is covered by
the center of the winged sun-disk and *khekher* frieze
of the eye panel. R17 is positioned on the north side
of the third course and is covered by the body of
Neith. R18 is in the upper course of the north wall
and the interior face is covered with the upper body
of the goddess with upraised arms (either Isis or
Nephthys). R17 and R18 preserve tantalizing indications of figures and register lines but the decoration
is too heavily coated with the gypsum layer to permit any accurate tracing (hence, no drawings of the
13th Dynasty decoration of R17 and R18 are included
here). The basic outlines of R16 can be traced, and
it is clear the block is decorated with three superimposed registers of kneeling figures, apparently all
facing left (Fig. 8.17).

The uppermost register preserves just the lower
bodies of kneeling figures facing left Most of the

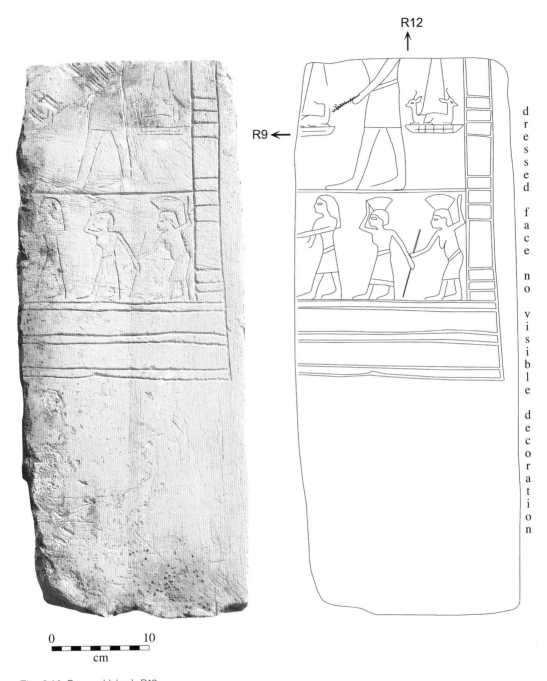

Fig. 8.16 Reused block R13.

register would have been located on the block above. Below are two further registers each separated by ca. 2.6 cm wide text bands. The central register measures 19.5 cm in height and closely matches the typical register heights on the other blocks showing kneeling figures. No figures can be confidently traced on the lowest register but the existence of the text band above it suggests it certainly would also have shown kneeling figures with the names and titles in the band above. Unfortunately, R16 cannot be directly linked to any of the other reused blocks, but the leftward orientation of the figures suggests it derives from the same decorated wall as the other wall blocks.

Fig. 8.17 Reused block R16 showing surface primarily obscured by extant plaster and paint.

BLOCKS ATTRIBUTABLE TO STATUE RECESSES

BLOCK R7

Block R7 was positioned right side up into the lowest course of masonry at the burial chamber's southwest corner (Fig. 8.18).[24] Measuring 34 cm wide and 45 cm in height, the face of the block portrays a fairly typical scene of the deceased receiving offerings. At the left is the image of a man who sits on a chair with animal-paw feet. He faces to the right, holding a jar (*mrḥt* vessel) to his nose with his left hand. An offering table is depicted in an abbreviated fashion above his knees, filling the small space between him and the image of a kneeling woman who is depicted in the same mode as the female attendants on the reused wall blocks. Both of these elements—the offering table and the woman with her epigraph—appear as if they were secondarily added in front of the male figure. As with all the other blocks, the surface of this block was substantially effaced, leaving only the deepest incisions intact. Despite the damage, areas of paint still survive in the deeper incised outlines,

particularly visible on the male figure, and in some of the hieroglyphs, which retain black paint.

Filling the space at the top of the block above the two human figures is a field of text. Two separate labels are linked with the two individuals, differentiated by the orientations of the texts which match those of the figures. The offering formula above the man reads: *ḥtp-dì-nswt Wsìr nb Ḏdw dì.f [tȝw nḏm] n ꜥnḫ n kȝ n ḥry-ḥȝwt Ib-iꜥw mȝꜥ-ḫrw ìr.n [ìmy-r ȝḥwt D]d.tw mȝꜥ-ḫrw, A royal offering of Osiris, Lord of Busiris, that he might give the sweet breath of life to the ka of the Master of Offering-Tables, Ibiau, true-of-voice, engendered of the [Overseer of Fields, De]dtu, true of voice.*[25] This text establishes clearly that Ibiau is the son of the *Overseer of Fields Dedtu*, who himself appears as the primary figure on block R8.[26] The short epigraph above the kneeling female figure identifies her as the *ḥkrt nswt wꜥtt, Nḫt.n(ì) mȝꜥt-ḫrw*, the *Sole Royal Ornament, Nekheteni, true-of-voice.*[27] The woman Nekheteni bears an extremely rare female title *ḥkrt nswt wꜥtt, Sole Royal Ornament*, attested in only one other instance.[28] The use of the term is reflective of the extremely high status of this family as we see in other evidence, and shall examine in depth in Chapter 10. Despite the statement defining her social position, it is noteworthy that the text does not include the title *ḥmt.f, his wife,* thereby raising the question of the woman's relationship with Ibiau. Moreover, Nekheteni is included kneeling at smaller scale and on a different ground line than Ibiau.[29]

Block R7 does not suffer the extreme chisel damage that occurs on some of the other blocks deriving from primary wall scenes. However, there are interesting patterns to the damage that suggest a targeted attack on the images and identity of Ibiau and Nekheteni. The faces, mouths and ears of both the man and woman were attacked. The greatest attention was given to the limbs of the male figure, particularly his forearms with the apparent motive of removing the ability of the deceased to receive the funerary offerings. Chiseling on the stomach/chest of the figure of Ibiau might be associated with the removal of the heart seen on some of the other chapel blocks. Most of the text above the figures remains intact but the name of the seated figure, Ibiau, and his father Dedtu were substantially chiseled, although the name of the wife, Nekheteni was left untouched. This suggests a targeted attack on the identity of the primary figure and the possibility that the defacing of the chapel was directed by someone who could read the texts.

The relatively selective approach to the chiseling of block R7 is consistent with another feature that sets this block apart from the main group of reused wall blocks. The edges of the block have concentrated areas of parallel finishing lines, particularly on the top, bottom and back showing the block was framed by perpendicular surfaces and mounted in a recess. This aspect of the dressing relates to another feature: the fact that the scene is substantially inset from the block's edges and does not connect directly to scene elements on adjacent blocks. The bottom of the scene begins 7 cm above the base of the block and the text and images are inset 4.5 cm from the edges on the sides and top. The composition shows the scene occupied a discrete space, that space is likely to be the side or back of a statue niche, as we examine in detail below. The same elements indicating the original placement of R7 in a statue niche apply also to the scene of Ibiau's father, Dedtu, on block R8.

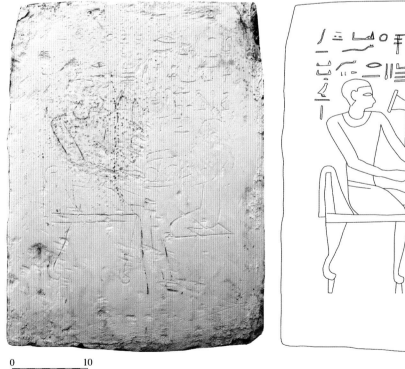

0 _____ 10
cm

Fig. 8.18 Block R7, showing Ibiau, son of Dedtu, seated at the left, and the *Sole Royal Ornament*, Nekheteni, kneeling at the right.

BLOCK R8

R8 is the only decorated block that was reused in the floor, rather than the walls of Seneb-Kay's burial chamber. This block measures 44.5 cm wide, 54.5 cm tall, and ca. 11 cm thick. It was positioned face up in the center of the western half of the chamber with the heads of the figures towards the south (Fig 8.19). Small areas of paint remain in the deeper lines: red-brown on the male figure and black at the edges of the figure's hair and in some of the hieroglyphs. The block is similar in layout and subject to R7. It commemorates Dedtu, Ibiau's father, who is mentioned in Ibiau's filiation on R7. The scene shows Dedtu seated behind a table of offerings (Fig. 8.20). He wears a *wesekh* collar, and a billowing, high-waisted kilt, fastened with a loop. He sits on a chair with lion-paw feet, holding a lotus to his nose with his right hand, and grasping a folded handkerchief on his lap in his left. Unlike R7, where the probable wife, Nekheteni, kneels in front of her husband, here Dedtu's wife, Abeteni, stands behind with her right arm on her husband's shoulder. Abeteni's left arm hangs by her side and she holds a lotus in her hand.

At the top of the block are two distinct epigraphs separated by a slight gap. In front of the seated man are two lines of text reading: *iry-pꜥt ḥꜣty-ꜥ ḥtmty-bity imy-r ꜣḥwt Ddtw mꜣꜥ-ḥrw*,[30] *the Hereditary nobleman, Mayor, Royal seal-bearer, Overseer of Fields, Dedtu, true-of-voice.*[31] Based on this group of titles, Dedtu was a central governmental official of the highest status.[32] His primary functional title, *Overseer of Fields*, was a royal governmental appointment connected with agricultural administration.[33] Following the name and titles of Dedtu, in a single line above the heads of the two figures, is the identification of the woman: *ḥmt.f nbt-pr, ꜣbt.n.i [mꜣꜥt-ḥrw]*,[34] *His wife, the Lady of the House, Abeteni, true-of-voice.* The lady Abeteni here bears the quite common title *nbt-pr, Lady of the House*,[35] but her rare personal name, attested in only three examples from the 13th Dynasty, offers a possible window into her family background.[36]

As with block R7, there are no borders around the scene and, indeed, no ground-line below the figures. The images have been purposefully placed in the center of the block devoid of direct connections with adjacent scene elements. The bottom of the scene begins a substantial 9 cm above the block base, with ca. 4 cm around the other sides of the scene and text. Around the edges of the block are pronounced parallel striations formed by the process of dressing the edges up against adjacent perpendicular surfaces. Like R7, these patterns show that R8 was housed within a recess or niche. The left facing orientation shows the slab would have formed the left side of a decorated niche. Presumably this block originates in a recess that contained a statue of Dedtu. Given R8's larger dimensions than R7, the scale of this recess would have been substantially larger than that of his son. We should also observe that whereas it appears possible the figure of the wife Nekheteni was added secondarily on block R7, Dedtu's wife, Abeteni, is an integral and original part of the scene on R8.

Paralleling the damage patterns on R7, we see a lesser degree of chiseling than occurs on most of the reused wall blocks. R8 appears to be have been more heavily effaced in association with the construction of Seneb-Kay's burial chamber, which mutes the effect of the chiseling. However, there are still discernible signs of a targeted *damnatio memoriae*. Similar to the image of Ibiau, Dedtu's arms and shoulders were chiseled, leaving only the deepest lines intact. The pattern of damage to the forearms is similar to that on Ibiau's figure on R7. Dedtu's feet and the offering table in front of him were also damaged in this way. Finally, Dedtu's eye was carved out of his head, rendering his image useless as an object of recognition for his soul. Damage to the text is less extensive but we again see indications for chiseling cutting across the signs composing Dedtu's name and titles.

Block R8 commemorating Dedtu and his wife Abeteni and the similar block, R7, commemorating his son Ibiau and wife Nekheteni are two of the crucial blocks to consider in addressing the origin of these reused 13th Dynasty chapel components. Here we have evidence for the individual commemoration of father and son in two separate statue niches of similar style. Do these blocks originate in a single funerary monument that incorporates commemoration of multiple members of a 13th Dynasty elite family at Abydos? Or, do the blocks originate in two associated but separate structures? The possible context of these blocks and the historical relationships of the lineage of Dedtu and Ibiau is discussed in detail in the next chapter.

Fig. 8.19 Block R8 in situ on the floor of Seneb-Kay's burial chamber.

0 10
cm

Fig. 8.20 Reused block R8 depicting the *Overseer of Fields*, Dedtu, seated before an offering table with his wife, the *Lady of the House*, Abeteni.

BLOCK R14

Block R14 is unique among the *spolia* from CS9 (Fig. 8.21). The block was discovered in 2015 during restoration work on Seneb-Kay's burial chamber. It was uncovered beneath the east end of the burial chamber's south wall where it had formed part of a base course of four thin slabs (labeled course 1-sub in Fig. 7.2) that underlay the larger blocks composing course 1. Originally, R14 was a lintel that spanned the top of a statue niche or recess. It measures 82.5 cm in length, 35.5 cm in width, and 13 cm thick. The block's lower surface preserves original gypsum mortar patches for edge blocks showing that it capped a niche that measured ca. 31 cm in width. The block's surface has a nearly square area painted yellow which represents the ceiling of the niche. The lintel block would have covered the entirety of the recess but was not precisely centered relative to that feature. The position of the recess is shifted right relative to the center of the block. This feature indicates clearly that the recess was engaged within a masonry-built wall, not engaged in brickwork. The narrow, decorated face of R14 preserves some of the exterior decoration associated with this recess.

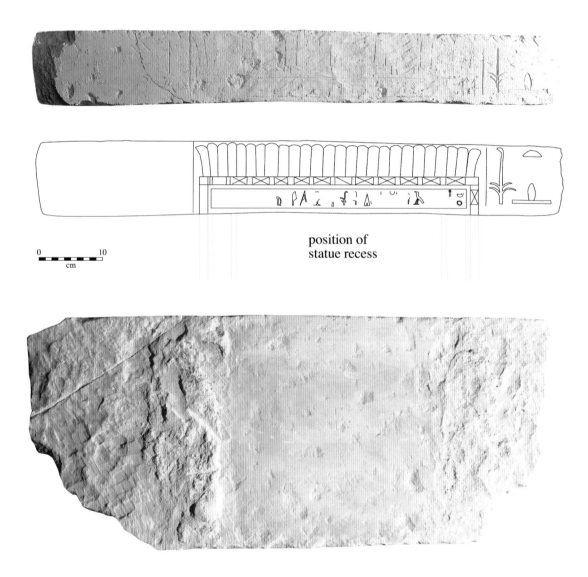

position of
statue recess

0 _____ 10
cm

Fig. 8.21 Reused block R14. The yellow painted area is the ceiling of a niche directly beneath the incised cornice on the block's face.

Although heavily damaged by deliberate chiseling (suggesting its derivation from the same chapel as the other reused blocks), the front face of the block represents the top of an incised, cavetto cornice 5 cm in height, situated between two vertical boundary lines and positioned directly above the yellow-painted area representing the ceiling of the niche. Directly below the cornice is a decorative band, composed of alternating narrow and wide rectangles. The larger rectangles each enclose a single incised "X" motif. This band simulates the appearance of torus molding but rendered here in two dimensions. At the left and right edges of the cornice, the decorative band turns down to run vertically, framing the niche. Inside the frame is a 3 cm wide band of text. Virtually all of the text has been effaced with extensive chiseling suggestive of the same targeted *damnatio* seen on the other blocks. At the center are two balanced *sw* signs (clearly preserved on the left side, barely visible on the right side) showing that two symmetrical offering formulae began at the center of the recess and extended outwards before turning down, parallel with the incised torus frieze.

A larger text in well-cut hieroglyphs begins directly to the right of the niche. This text is also the beginning of a *ḥtp-dỉ-nswt* formula oriented from left to right. The *sw* and *ḥtp* signs are clear, the *t* above the *ḥtp* sign is also present but affected by secondary damage to the block. Unlike the central text below the cornice, it appears these signs were not deliberately damaged.[37] The text measures 9 cm and is significantly larger than the surviving text on any of the other reused blocks. Based on the surviving group of three hieroglyphs, this text could have continued either vertically or horizontally. However, it would appear improbable to have a vertical *ḥtp-dỉ-nswt* text directly adjacent to the smaller *ḥtp-dỉ-nswt* on the frame of the statue recess. For that reason, these signs likely form the beginning of a horizontal text in large format hieroglyphs.

Likely what we have here is the beginning of a large-format text register that capped the primary wall scenes that extended to the right of this niche. The occurrence of large-format *ḥtp-dỉ-nswt* texts capping primary wall scenes is a common convention in Middle Kingdom tomb chapels, well illustrated, for instance, at sites such as Beni Hasan, Aswan, and el-Bersheh where nearly complete decorated chapels have survived (see for example, Newberry 1893: pls. 11–16).

Below this should occur imagery centered on the tomb owner and programmatically focused on the niche containing a statue of the deceased. Conceivably in this context there may have been a large-scale offering scene depicting the deceased as the focus of funerary offerings and located adjacent to a recess containing a statue of the tomb owner. It is puzzling that there is no indication for a symmetrical register of large format text extending to the left of this niche.

Taken together, block R14 along with blocks R7 and R8, which as we have seen can be identified as the internal decorated surfaces of statue recesses, provide evidence for the configuration and decoration of what appear to have been multiple statue niches associated with the original 13th Dynasty chapel architecture that supplied Seneb-Kay's builders. In the next chapter, we turn to the issue of reconstructing the architecture and decoration of the building—or group of buildings—at Abydos that commemorated the 13th Dynasty officials Ibiau and Dedtu and their family members.

NOTES:

8.1 The method of dovetail joinery using butterfly tenons set within mortises was quite common, occurring in both stone monumental construction (see for instance Arnold [2008:53]) and also in carpentry (Gale et al. 2000:365–366; Killen 1994:15). In masonry construction, the actual tenons were of wood (for surviving examples, see Petrie [1890: pl. ix:29]).

8.2 The large (10 cm in diameter) hole cut into R20 passes through the entire block and does not appear to be a door pivot. The original function of the hole on this undecorated block remains unclear.

8.3 The line drawings of the individual reused blocks do not show the later Seneb-Kay painted decoration, which is visible in the photographs and on the plans and elevation views of the burial chamber (Figs. 7.1 to 7.4).

8.4 This is an arrangement that occurs commonly on late Middle Kingdom private stelae where phyles of kneeling family members and associates are depicted facing the deceased. For this same arrangement on stelae compare, for example, CCG 20679 and CCG 20055 (ANOC 15.2 and 15.1h, Simpson 1974: pl. 24); and BM 238 (ANOC 54.1, Simpson 1974: pl. 76).

8.5 A man with the same name and title was the owner of a fragmentary sarcophagus found by Peet in his tomb Z2A. This important connection will be discussed in the next chapter.

8.6 Interestingly the name Redi (Ranke 1935:228.12) occurs here in the text band above the figure rather than in the field in front as happens with Amenemhat and Montuhotep in the registers above and below. This reflects the way the texts were graphically adapted by the artists depending on their length to the available space.

8.7 The figure to the left is a woman. Her body is preserved on adjoining block R5 but the upper part of the register and the text band that capped it has not survived beyond was is preserved on block R1.

8.8 This man is a *sẖȝw n ḥwt-nṯr*, *temple scribe* (Ward 1982:162, titles 1398 to 1402) specifically linked to the temple of Montu-in-Medamud (for the designation of Montu in Medamud see Leitz [2003:321]). Interestingly, the man's personal name, Montuhotep (Ranke 1935:154.21), also emphasizes an association with the cult of Montu.

8.9 Less likely, the final sign group of the man's name may be the funerary epithet *mȝꜥ-ḫrw*, *true-of-voice*, with the oar sign positioned vertically, yielding instead the translation *Montu, true-of-voice*. However, the oar was positioned horizontally in Amenemhat's name above, so it appears preferable to read the group as *hetep* here.

8.10 The god Montu is a primary deity of the Theban nome whose cult was practiced at several sites including Thebes, Armant, and Medamud. His cult center at Medamud is located ca. 5 km northeast of Thebes.

8.11 The same style of depiction of the triple braid behind the girl's head occurs on late Middle Kingdom stelae from Abydos such as ANOC 36.2 (Simpson 1974, Pl. 54) or ANOC 54.1 (Simpson 1974, Pl. 76).

8.12 The title *ẖry-ḥbt* is written with Gardiner sign W5, a writing that occurs commonly in compound versions of this title where a god is mentioned (see examples in Ward [1982:140–141]). The title *ẖry-ḥbt n Mntw m Mȝdw* occurs in this exact form on a 13th Dynasty stela in Vienna (von Bergmann 1897:36).

8.13 This scene was previously interpreted to be an image of a man chopping down a tree while acquiring wood for pottery firing (Cahail 2014:209–212). However, with the rest of the scene on block R11 discovered in 2015, it is clear the man is working in front of a cylindrical kiln. Diagonal lines that superficially resemble branches and foliage are not part of a tree but show the textured side of the kiln.

8.14 The stela of Amenyseneb can be dated to the reign of king Khendjer (Kitchen 1961:10–18, 1962:159–160). The second register on the reverse shows a remarkable similarity with the layout of activities on R3, as well as employing the juxtaposition of ploughing and harvest scenes below the production scenes (see also Oppenheim et al. 2017:268–269).

8.15 The pose and garment shown here are almost identical to images on 13th Dynasty chapel blocks from Abydos including Louvre C13 (ANOC 52.3, Simpson 1974: pl. 70), from the chapel of the reporter of the vizier, Senwosret (Oppenheim et al. 2017:260–261). A similar figure occurs also on Hermitage 1063 (ANOC 57.2, Simpson 1974: pl. 78).

8.16 Preliminary discussion of this scene suggested that the boy may be holding the hand of his father (Cahail 2015:101–103). The position of the father's hands as shown here supersedes that earlier reconstruction. The exact position of the boy's arms remains uncertain.

8.17 This type of text, which derives from Old Kingdom antecedents, typically involves the eldest living son of the deceased acting as the officiant of his father's offering cult. The person being venerated is never named in the formula which records instead the name of the son as cult officiant. See, for example, the stela of Kemes (Berlin 7287, ANOC 65.4, Simpson 1974: pl. 65) where the identity of the father occurs in the text above the scene. The *in sȝ.f* formula can occur sporadically with other individuals such as grandsons instead of sons (Säve-Söderbergh 1949:50–58).

8.18 The core title is *ẖry ḥȝwt* (Ward, 1982:116, Title 973, which he reads *ẖry wdḥw*). The full title *ẖry ḥȝwt n Imn* appears on the Juridical Stela, Cairo JE 52453, belonging to Ay, which is dated to the Second Intermediate Period (for its chronological implications see Davies [2010:223–240]).

8.19 Compare, for example, stela CCG 20515 (ANOC 30.1, Simpson 1974: pl. 46) or CCG 20571 (ANOC 30.3, Simpson 1974: pl. 47).

8.20 As discussed previously (Cahail 2014:200–202), comparable images of the male flutist here occur in the scenes of musicians in the tomb of Amenemhat at Beni Hasan (Newberry 1893: pl.12) and in the Tomb B no. 2 (Senbi's son Ukhhotep) at Meir (Blackman 1915: pl. 3).

8.21 The image of the female harpist on R6 is paralleled in other Middle Kingdom tomb scenes including Tomb 17 (tomb of Khety) at Beni Hasan (Newberry 1893: pl.16), and the configuration of the harp also has close parallels among the images of male harpers (see discussion of Cahail [2014:203–205]).

8.22 The profile of the two items on the left and right side of the tray resembles fish, however, the unnatural depiction of fish standing upright on a tray would be unparalleled. Therefore, these appear to be containers of some kind.

8.23 For example, the stela of Amenyseneb (Garstang Museum E30), discussed further below (Kitchen 1961:10–18), or the stela of Kemehu (CCG 20725, ANOC 48.1, Simpson 1974: pl. 66).

8.24 This block was previously discussed (Cahail 2015:104 and fig. 11). Recently, failing to note its excavation context at Abydos, block R7 has been associated with Thebes by Ilin-Tomich who connects it through the presence of Ibiau and Nekheteni with stela Louvre C58 (Ilin-Tomich 2018:31). Louvre C58 (which we discuss extensively below in Chapter 10) also derives from Abydos and it must be clarified that these people were Thebans who built funerary monuments at Abydos.

8.25 The text here is a characteristic 13th Dynasty writing of the prayer for offerings with several distinctive elements including use of the expression *ṯꜣw nḏm n ꜥnḫ*, *the sweet breath of life* (see Barta 1968:78, bitte 78a). Various scholars have discussed the relevant dating criteria of the *ḥtp-dì-nswt* formula during this period (Smither 1939; Barta 1968; Bennett 1941:77–82 with critical comments of Franke 2003:39–57). The formula on R7 can be compared with contemporary late Middle Kingdom examples (for which see Ilin-Tomich 2011:20–34).

8.26 The name Ibiau is a relatively common one during the period (Ranke 1935:19.4). His rare title *ḥry-ḫꜣwt*, *Master of Offering Tables*, allows us to identify both this individual and his father Dedtu on other preserved monuments of the 13th Dynasty.

8.27 The woman's personal name, Nekheteni (Ranke 1935:207.13), is written here with a seated man that is part of the word *nhi*, *to pray for* (Hannig 2006:1310). Her name is a *sḏmt.n.f* perfect relative form with the literal meaning, *the one that I prayed for*. The horizontal line and final short vertical stroke are for *n.i*, which we find written similarly in the name of Abeteni on block R8. The structure of Nekheteni's name is very similar to that of the lady Abeteni (literally, *the one that I desired*), wife of Dedtu, on block R8.

8.28 The feminine title *ḫkrt nswt*, *Royal Ornament*, is a designation of rank originating in the Old Kingdom that occurs relatively frequently among elite women in the late Middle Kingdom and Second Intermediate Period (see Ward 1982:143, no. 1234; Jones 2000:795–796, title 2900; and discussion of Stefanović 2009:85–109). The exact connotation of the title has been debated but appears to indicate a woman of elite status with connections to the royal court (also, Nord 1970:1–16; Drenkhahn 1976:59–67; Grajetzki 2009:158). The recent suggestion (Ilin-Tomich 2015:22–25), reviving older ideas that the title designates a royal concubine is extremely improbable given the married status of the majority of these women with men of rank. The addition of the element *wꜥtt*, *sole*, is extremely

rare; attested in only one other case (Stefanović 2016:92), again a mark of Nekheteni's status.

8.29 It is not clear why the woman Nekheteni does not occupy the same ground-line as Ibiau. It appears probable that her label and image were added subsequent to the main scene showing Ibiau. If we assume she was Ibiau's wife (for which, see below), they may have married after he commissioned the block, leading to her image being added afterwards in the free space in front of Ibiau. Nevertheless, there is nothing that visually or textually expresses their relationship as a couple as we see in the scene of Dedtu and his wife Abeteni on block R8.

8.30 The writing of Dedtu's titles displays several chronologically diagnostic features. In particular, the title *ḥtmty-bìty* is written with the Red Crown hieroglyph as opposed to the bee sign, a variant that appears regularly in the late Middle Kingdom stelae from Abydos (Lange and Schäfer 1925:76–77).

8.31 The name Dedtu is relatively rare (for examples see Ranke 1935:103.21). The Dedtu on R8 (and also mentioned as the father of Ibiau on R7) can be connected with a specific individual known from other 13th Dynasty monuments. Block R8 was evidently decorated after or in anticipation of his death as suggested by the funerary epithet *mꜣꜥ-ḫrw*, *true-of-voice*.

8.32 As indicated by his sequence of three rank titles (for the use of which see, Franke 1984:103–124; Grajetzki 2000:220–228). Along with the hereditary title *ìry-pꜥt* (Jones 2000:315, no.1157) he holds a succession of prefix titles commonly associated with royal officials including *ḥꜣty-ꜥ* (Ward 1982:104–105; Fisher 1985:66), and, most significantly, *ḥtmty-bìty*, *Royal seal bearer* (Fischer 1996:50–52; Quirke 2004:12), marking him as a member of the inner circle of the central government.

8.33 The position of *ìmy-r ꜣḥwt* (Ward 1982:10, no. 29) was a top tier office in royal administration during the 13th Dynasty and may derive from the earlier Middle Kingdom territorial division of this office into an overseer of agricultural lands of the north and south (see comments of Quirke 2014:91; Grajetzki 2009:86–91; and Ilin-Tomich 2015:125–126).

8.34 The final signs at the end of the text are quite eroded but are almost certainly the funerary epithet *mꜣꜥt-ḫrw*, *true of voice* (here with a feminine *.t* barely discernible in the damage), as occurs also after her husband's name.

8.35 While quite common, the female title *nbt pr* (Ward 1982:99, no. 823) denotes a woman with economic authority over an extended household. In the 13th Dynasty, the title can be held by women of the highest status including

sisters and relatives of the reigning king and queen, as
seen for instance on stela Louvre C13 (Spalinger 1980:95–
116) discussed elsewhere in this volume.

8.36 The name Abeteni literally means *the one that I desired* (Ranke 1935: no. 20) and is grammatically similar
to the name of Nekheteni on block R7 discussed above.
Abeteni is an extremely rare personal name and occurs
in three known instances during the mid- to late 13th Dynasty. A woman with this same name and also the title *nbt*

pr occurs on stela Louvre C13, which details the extended
family of Queen Nubkhaes (Spalinger 1980:95–116). Two
women named Abeteni, both members of a single family,
occur on stela Vienna 180 dating also to the mid- to late
13th Dynasty (Hein and Satzinger 1993:103–111).

8.37 The surface of the stone in this area is covered with
gypsum mortar, obscuring the signs slightly, but the chisel
marks apparent over the cornice and lintel text do not extend to this portion of the block.

9

Chapel Architecture Commemorating Ibiau and Dedtu*

One of the conspicuous aspects of the 13th Dynasty reused chapel blocks in Seneb-Kay's burial chamber is the stylistic uniformity of the texts and decoration. Equally as clear is the consistency of the *damnatio memoriae* attested on the decorated blocks. The implication is this assemblage of blocks were not collected ad hoc from a range of locations but were taken as a group, either from a single monument or a group of closely linked 13th Dynasty private funerary chapels. This impression of stylistic uniformity is borne out when one begins the puzzlework of joining the blocks. Many blocks have figures and parts of scenes that span multiple blocks. The system of register widths and border bands allows us to define the connections between adjacent blocks. In fact, nearly all of the decorated blocks discussed in the previous chapter derive from a single dismantled wall, which provides a glimpse into the primary building that supplied material for Seneb-Kay's burial chamber. We now discuss the reconstruction of this wall as well as other features, including a group of statue recesses. This provides the basis for an examination of the characteristics of this architecture associated with Ibiau and his father Dedtu and allows us to consider the question of whether we are looking at *spolia* deriving from one or multiple 13th Dynasty chapels. All of these issues have bearing on the date of King Seneb-Kay's reign as we shall explore later.

ARCHITECTURE AND DECORATION OF THE PRIMARY WALL

Nine of the decorated blocks (blocks R1, R2, R3, R5, R6, R9, R11, R12, and R13) are elements of a single decorated wall (Figs. 9.1–9.2). The wall (labeled here Wall A) measures 1.74 m in width. The surviving blocks total 1.72 m in height but originate in a wall that must have been substantially taller. The corner blocks on both sides also preserve the adjacent wall surfaces that allow us to reconstruct the architectural setting of the wall. Although extensively decorated, Wall A is clearly not the interior wall of a square or rectangular chamber. Rather, this decorated face was situated between two flanking spaces that extended laterally on either side of the decorated wall face.[1] On the right-hand side, blocks R1, R5, R12, and R15 all preserve a finely dressed face (labeled here Wall B). The Wall B surfaces are primarily covered by a thick gypsum coat associated with their reuse in Seneb-Kay's burial chamber. The nature of the decoration, if any, on Wall B remains unclear. We may be certain there was no border band near the corner as occurs on Wall A, but decoration may have occurred displaced further from the corner. On the opposite side (perpendicular to the left corner of Wall A), blocks R2 and R11 preserve the adjacent surface that

* This chapter written by Josef Wegner and Kevin Cahail.

appears to have been another wall decorated in the same mode as Wall A (labeled here Wall C). Hints of decoration survive on these two blocks suggesting that Wall C, like Wall A, had a vertical, coffered border band with horizontal registers extending over the wall surface to the left.

Wall A therefore sits between what appears to be a space (represented by Wall B) that lacks the typical framing borders of interior decorated walls and a

decorated space (represented by Wall C), possibly the interior of the chapel. As we discuss further below, the disposition of decoration relative to the architecture may reflect the origin of these blocks in a stone-built, cruciform chapel with Wall A representing the right wall of a decorated entryway that opened into an offering chamber. On this basis we can see that the majority of the masonry used by Seneb-Kay's tomb builders originated in one particular wall of a decorated 13th

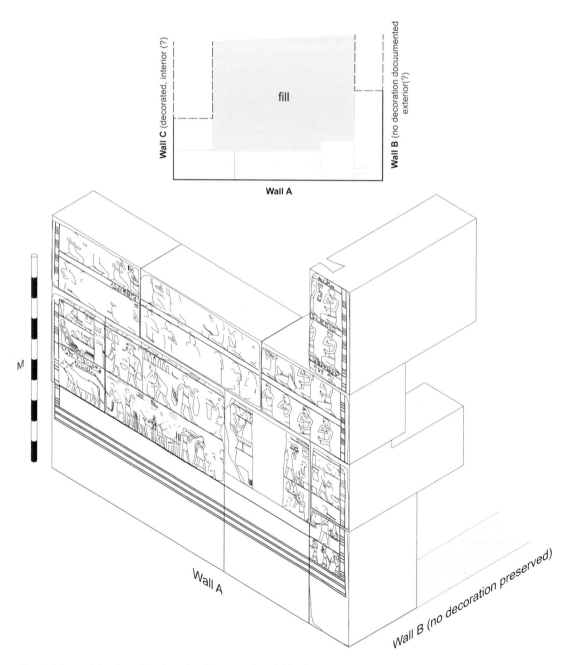

Fig. 9.1 Isometric view showing the decorated wall blocks composing Wall A with undecorated Wall B.

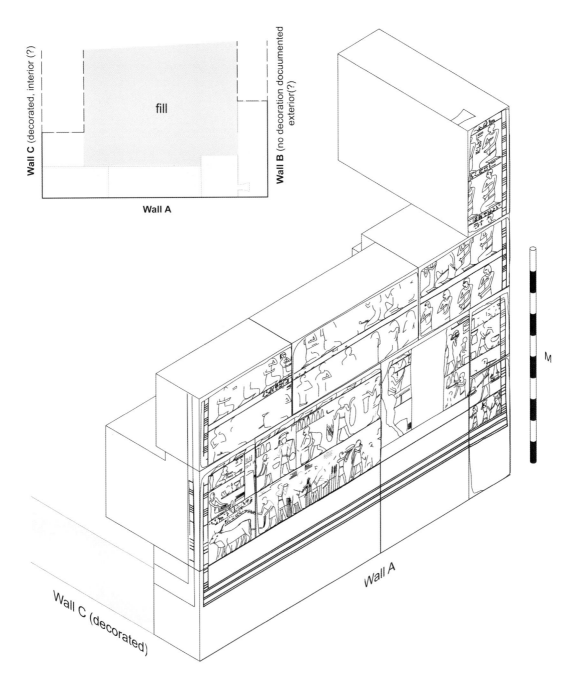

Fig. 9.2 Isometric view showing the decorated wall blocks composing Wall A with decorated Wall C.

Dynasty private chapel, although a smaller number of blocks appear to have come from other parts of the structure or adjacent structures.

The attested decoration of Wall A consists of seven registers framed by coffered border bands set in slightly from the corners (Fig. 9.3). The base of the decoration is defined by a frieze of three parallel lines above a 24 cm high undecorated dado. Register 1 is the narrowest, 11 cm in height, above which the registers are relatively uniform measuring 18 to 20 cm in height. Registers 1–3 are scenes of agricultural activity, baking, brewing, and delivery of foodstuffs. Registers 4–7 are rows of kneeling figures facing inward toward the centerline of the wall. The registers showing kneeling figures are separated from one another by 2.8 cm wide

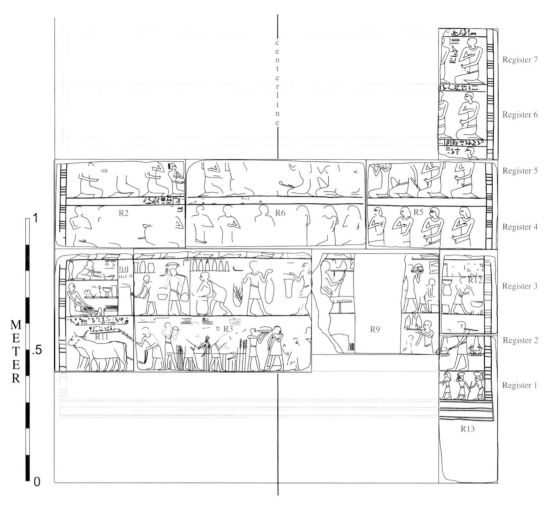

Fig. 9.3 The primary wall scene (Wall A).

bands containing the names and titles of the figures depicted below.

The surviving blocks include the base of the wall (R13) extending to a preserved height of 1.72 m (the top of block R1). The original wall stood to a greater height, but that dimension of the building cannot be established with certainty based on the surviving blocks. The upper part of the wall certainly must have included a horizontal section of the coffered band with the standard feature of a *khekher* frieze above that. If we extrapolate the wall to include just one more ca. 20 cm register, and complete the wall with border and *khekher* frieze, this would result in a wall of 2.1 m height (equaling four cubits), although the height may well have been greater (Fig. 9.4).

One of the conspicuous organizational principles of the wall is its symmetry. This is very clear in the four upper registers of kneeling figures. The full width of the wall is preserved for Registers 4 and 5 showing that there are two balanced sets of figures: seven facing left and seven facing right towards the centerline of the wall. In Register 5, the centerline of the wall corresponds with the position of the female harpist who faces left, fronting a group of musicians behind her. The position of the harpist paired with the inward orientation of the kneeling figures is likely to reflect a centrally positioned image of the chapel owner in the area above Register 5.[2] The wall organization here follows that of late Middle Kingdom family stelae where rows of kneeling figures face towards the deceased, while scenes containing harpists typically show that figure either alone or at the head of a group of musicians in proximity to the deceased.[3] Also signaling the presence of an image of the chapel owner in the center of the upper wall are the figure labels in Registers 6–7 which survive only on block

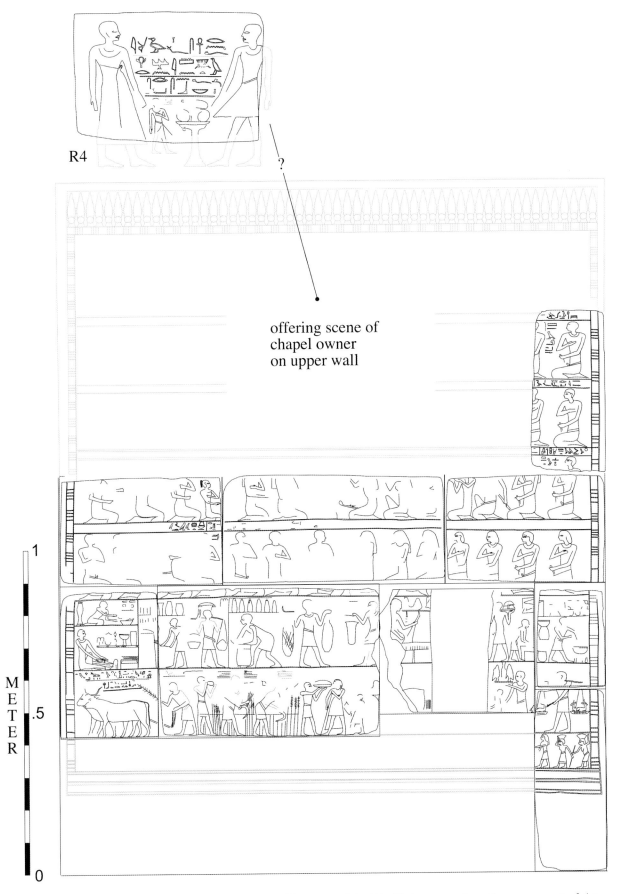

R4

?

offering scene of
chapel owner
on upper wall

Fig. 9.4 Suggested configuration of Wall A with possible origin of the R4 offering scene from the upper part of the wall.

R1. Here we have a group of men, two of whom are introduced with the title *s3.f, his son*, demonstrating that there would have been a depiction of the chapel owner immediately to the left.

Interestingly, the symmetry exhibited in the upper registers is reflected below in the agricultural and production scenes. In Register 3, there are two bearers with vessels on yokes who face each other. More overtly, in Register 2 the official who surveys the harvest stands precisely on the centerline of the wall facing left with a boy, presumably his son, behind him. In all likelihood this represents the chapel owner. The motif of the deceased surveying agricultural work on his land occurs in Middle Kingdom funerary chapels and also on 13th Dynasty monuments from Abydos.[4] Although the official in Register 2 is not labeled, the man in front of him holds a tray of grain as if offering the product of the harvest to the landowner. The central position of the man and his son might echo a larger, centrally positioned depiction of the chapel owner in the upper registers where he would presumably have been depicted facing right, flanked by kneeling family members and associates.

In view of the evidence that so many of the reused blocks in Seneb-Kay's burial chamber derive from this one decorated wall, the question arises as to whether we have blocks among the documented corpus deriving from this upper part of the wall and depicting the chapel owner. There are three blocks that potentially might be attributed to this upper part of the wall. Two are the blocks showing Ibiau (R7) and Dedtu (R8) seated behind an offering table. Both R7 and R8, as we have seen in the previous chapter, can be identified not as wall scenes but as decoration from statue recesses. It appears conceivable that the center of Wall A held a statue niche rather than two-dimensional imagery of the chapel owner. Moreover, on R7, the kneeling figure of Nekheteni directly in front of Ibiau has exactly the same style and size as the rows of kneeling figures shown in Registers 4–7, suggesting she may be the lead figure of adjacent rows of kneeling attendants.

However, the architectural configuration indicated by the blocks composing Wall A makes this possibility less likely. The evidence suggests that Wall A is not an interior chamber wall. Rather it flanks another decorated chamber, which may have been the primary offering chamber. The best explanation for the architectural evidence is that this was a side wall

belonging to a decorated, but transitional, space leading into a cruciform chapel. If so, it was not the primary focal point of the chapel and probably did not have a statue recess mounted in it. Based on the offering scene on R7, the recess containing that block does appear to have been programmatically linked with adjacent scenes that would have depicted rows of kneeling figures (culminating with Nekheteni before Ibiau), but, from what we can see of Wall A, it would appear to be a less probable setting for a statue recess.

The only other documented block that could be attributed to the upper part of Wall A is R4 depicting an unlabeled individual with his grown son in front presenting offerings along with the *in s3.f sᶜnh rn.f, making his name live* formula. This is a large-scale composition that bridged multiple blocks and would have been the central offering scene of a larger wall composition. R4 measures 26 cm in thickness: comparable to the other blocks composing this wall. The orientation with the primary figure facing right would fit with the likely position of this wall on the right side leading into an inner offering chamber (i.e., with the owner facing out from the chapel interior). A noteworthy aspect of the R4 scene is that the primary figure is not seated behind a table of offerings but is standing. Such a pose would be appropriate to the suggested architectural context of Wall A decorating the vestibule or entryway into a chapel's inner chamber. Rather than passively seated, the deceased is standing to receive offerings and visitors to his chapel. This graphic convention occurs from the time of the Old Kingdom in this same relative location, particularly on the jambs of the main entrance to funerary chapels.

The identity of the primary figure in the R4 scene remains unknown but is likely to be Ibiau based on the title of his son, *ḥry ḥ3wt n 'Imn, Master of the Offering Tables of Amun*, which is identical to that of Ibiau himself known from block R7. The figures on the block are ca. 45 cm tall and the large scale could be accommodated in a composition where the chapel owner and his son were depicted at twice the size of the adjacent registers of kneeling attendants. Despite the likely relationship of block R4 to the chapel as a whole and the strong possibility that it comes from the upper part of Wall A, the block does not preserve evidence to link it to imagery on Wall A. It remains possible that the blocks from this upper part of the wall including the primary image of the chapel owner could remain among the 22 other blocks whose surfaces have not been exposed in the intact masonry of the Seneb-Kay burial chamber.

COMPARANDA TO WALL A

Although we remain ultimately uncertain concerning the upper part of this decorated wall, what is most significant is the way in which Wall A employs imagery and themes adapted from the repertoire of Middle Kingdom tomb chapels, as well as iconography on late Middle Kingdom funerary stelae. Let us turn firstly to some of the most closely contemporary comparanda from Abydos and then examine iconographic parallels in the wider corpus of Middle Kingdom chapel decoration.

In terms of both its style and composition, one of the closest comparisons to Wall A occurs on the *ankh*-stela (Garstang Museum E30) of the *mty n sꜣ*, *phyle-overseer*, Amenyseneb from Abydos (Fig. 9.5).

The Amenyseneb stela is decorated on both sides. The front depicts two symmetrical standing figures, Amenyseneb on the left venerating Wepwawet while his father may be represented by the damaged figure on the right venerating a second deity, possibly another form of Wepwawet. His mother and two sisters appear as kneeling figures between the two men. Below are two registers only partially preserved; the upper one would have shown Amenyseneb seated behind a table of offerings on the left (broken away) with his wife, Neni, on the right side. Other family members occur as kneeling figures oriented in two groups facing towards husband and wife respectively.

Unlike the front with its images of family members, the reverse of the Amenyseneb stela is devoted to agricultural and production scenes. These compositions display a remarkable degree of similarity with those on Wall A suggesting the artists in both cases were drawing from a common set of models. Scenes of ploughing, planting, and harvesting occur in the three lower registers. The Amenyseneb stela

Fig. 9.5 *Ankh* stela of Amenyseneb (Garstang Museum, E.30). Image courtesy of the Garstang Museum, University of Liverpool.

also includes elements not seen on Wall A. Whereas Wall A has a larger harvest scene in Register 2, Amenyseneb has a reduced version of this scene with only one figure harvesting the grain, alongside other activities including threshing of the grain that do not occur on Wall A. Nevertheless, the scenes of fieldwork are closely comparable to the activities on the left side of Register 2 of Wall A. The three upper registers on the reverse of the Amenyseneb stela show the activities that followed: grinding of the grain, baking, and brewing. Many close points of similarity occur in these images with the corresponding scenes in Register 3 of Wall A. We may note very similar style in which the milling of the flour occurs, as well as the mode of depiction of the brewer with arms twisted and leaning into the vat. Also closely comparable is the depiction of the baker, holding a pair of tongs leaning towards the oven containing stacks of cylindrical breadmolds. Similarly, an almost identical image to that on the Amenyseneb stela occurs on the left side of Register 3 where we see the baking of the bread juxtaposed with the milling and preparation of bread loaves to the left. On the Amenyseneb stela, a figure of the deceased appears to have originally occupied the upper left where he stood viewing the production of foodstuffs.

Apart from its many iconographic parallels, one of the elements of close comparison between Wall A and the Amenyseneb stela occurs in the abrupt and somewhat jarring juxtaposition between the offering scenes and family images on the front, versus the agricultural and production scenes on the reverse. This strict thematic division occurs also on Wall A where we have the immediate transition between production scenes in Registers 1–3 on the lower part of the wall, to rows of family members and kneeling figures presumably centered around the chapel owner in Registers 4–7 above. In many respects, Wall A appears to bear a decorative program that forms an expanded iteration of the content of late Middle Kingdom family stelae like that of Amenyseneb. However, since we are clearly lacking the majority of what must have been a substantial funerary chapel we must be missing many more decorative elements, some of which may be indicated by other contemporary monuments.

A second 13th Dynasty funerary monument at Abydos that displays close stylistic and iconographic parallels with the decoration on Wall A is the miniature chapel of the *wḥmw n ṯ3ty*, *Herald of the Vizier*,

Senwosret (Fig. 9.6). The chapel (Louvre N170–172) may have been designed to house a seated statuette of Senwosret (Louvre N49), although the lack of evidence for the original context of these elements makes this uncertain, and the statuette may have been housed in some other feature connected with the chapel. The Senwosret chapel is one of a group of similarly structured elite monuments that include the chapels of the *Seal-bearer of the Vizier Ankhu*, Sahathor (Hermitage 1075 and 1603–4; Simpson 1974: pl. 78–79), and the chapel of Anu (MMA 69.30; Fisher 1996:123–139).

The decorative elements on the chapel of Senwosret provide points of distinct comparison with the reused chapel blocks from South Abydos. The left side has three registers each culminating in a figure of Senwosret. The differing skin tone, hair length and clothing suggest this shows the deceased over the course of the three seasons, *akhet*, *peret*, and *shomu*, of the Egyptian calendar. In front of him are rows of kneeling figures, each fronted by a miniature offering table. A troop of musicians fronted by a female harpist facing towards the deceased appears in the lowest register. This motif closely parallels the more extensive group of musicians in Register 4 of Wall A. Here, and in other examples, the orientation of the harpist is opposite the figure of the deceased,[5] thereby reinforcing the probability that the image of the chapel owner on the upper part of Wall A was depicted looking right.

The right wall of the Senwosret chapel shows the deceased standing and viewing production activities including a harvest scene similar to that on the Amenyseneb stela, as well as baking and brewing. To the right we have elements not attested on Wall A but that may have occurred elsewhere in the structure. In the upper register is a fishing and fowling scene, which is an adaptation of this motif on earlier Middle Kingdom tomb chapels. Below are boats bearing the coffin of the deceased that may depict the funeral itself or the theme of the voyage to Abydos. A small detail in the upper register that parallels the offering bearers shown in Register 1 and 2 of Wall A is the image of a man cradling a baby gazelle in his arms. While this motif is expanded on Wall A where we have a man with a yoke carrying four baby gazelles in baskets, the image adds to the thematic commonalities of the Senwosret chapel with Wall A. As occurs on Wall A, the three panels of the Senwosret chapel are framed with coffered border bands on either side

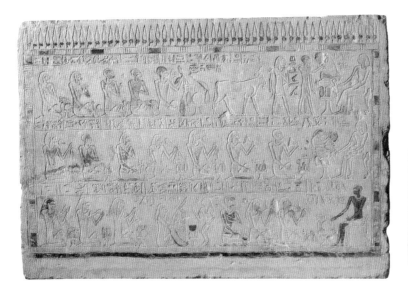

Fig. 9.6 The miniature chapel of the reporter of the vizier, Senwosret (Louvre C.16–18 = N.170–172). Image courtesy of Musée du Louvre.

and a simple border of incised bands on the bottom. The upper part of the panels is completed with horizontal coffered bands and a *khekher* frieze, the probable format we have already suggested for the upper part of Wall A.

The monuments of Amenyseneb and Senwosret just discussed have been dated to the early to middle part of the 13th Dynasty. In the case of the *ankh*-stela of Amenyseneb, a phyle overseer who is known on two other stelae (Louvre C11 and C12), each of which bears the name of King Userkare Khendjer. Although, it must be noted that the carving style of these two other stelae are noticeably different from Garstang

Museum E30 suggesting the possibility that the Amenyseneb on the *ankh*-stela could be a different man than the one who served under Khendjer. The miniature chapel of Senwosret has been dated to a similar timeframe. This is based on indications that the vizier under whom Senwosret served as herald was Ankhu, an official whose floruit occurred during the reigns of Sobekhotep II and Khendjer (Grajetzki 2000:24–26; Oppenheim et al. 2015:261).[6] Irrespective of the dating of these two monuments, we can see that the funerary chapel from which Wall A derived displays a host of stylistic and iconographic commonalities with funerary monuments being established at

Fig. 9.7 Harvest scene from the tomb Werirni at Sheikh Said (above, after Davies 1901: pl. XVI) and Intefiqer at Thebes (middle, after Davies 1920: pl. III), compared with the similar elements in the harvest scene in Register 2 of Wall A (below).

Abydos by high ranking officials of the 13th Dynasty. The decoration of Wall A draws from a common repertoire of imagery, which we see on stelae as well as other commemorative monuments at the site. What distinguishes the reused 13th Dynasty chapel blocks from these comparanda is the evident scale of the structure that they one composed.

Apart from the close parallels we find in contemporary 13th Dynasty Abydene funerary monuments we may further observe that the artists who decorated Wall A appear to have been able to draw adeptly on a corpus of motifs, iconography, and texts belonging to the wider decorative traditions of Middle Kingdom private tomb chapels. One such area of

comparison can be glimpsed in the ploughing and harvest scenes, which display use of common motifs attested in other sites. The ploughing scene on Wall A, showing a farmer goading his oxen, is a standard motif in daily life scenes at sites such as Beni Hasan (for example in the tomb of Khnumhotep; Newberry 1893: pl. 29) where we see a fuller rendition of the ploughing process. Interestingly, in the process of composing this scene the artists who decorated Wall A chose to include a speech caption for the farmer which, as we have seen above, makes use of a paradigmatic Late Egyptian verbal construction. The content of the speech incorporates terminology that survived into much later times suggesting there was a standard set of vocabulary that might be applied in ploughing scenes.

In Register 2, there are noteworthy parallels to the depiction of the field workers in the harvest scene. This composition on Wall A includes three laborers: two men cut the grain with sickles while a third figure behind them takes a rest, drinking water from a jar raised to his face. We find this identical motif in the early 12th Dynasty tomb chapel of Intefiqer and his wife Senet at Thebes (TT60; Davies 1920).[7] On the right or northern wall of that chapel's entrance passage, the scenes begin with the harvest. The scene is badly damaged but shows three men and one woman engaged in cutting and gathering grain. Two men hold sickles, another man drinks from a ceramic pot with his sickle slung over his shoulder, while the woman bends down, presumably to collect the cut grain.[8] Clearly the artists who decorated the Abydos chapel containing Wall A were fully conversant with the conventions of such scenes (Fig. 9.7). The interest in capturing the rhythms of work in the fields, with men at work alongside one resting while taking a drink, is not accidental but an expression of learned artistic conventions.

Based on the preceding discussion we can more fully appreciate the degree to which Wall A represents one part of what must have been a complex, possibly multi-room funerary chapel. While it displays many shared motifs with contemporary tomb stelae and commemorative monuments such as the miniature chapels of Senwosret and Sahathor, this appears to have been a building that represents a markedly higher order of monumental investment. Despite its sometimes less polished artistic mode, reflective of the period in which it was carved, the artisans who decorated Wall A were clearly a group of highly trained individuals conversant with the broad repertoire of funerary iconography and texts. We now turn to consider the other primary evidence provided by the reused blocks: the group of statue recesses that provide key indications for the ownership of these 13th Dynasty funerary structures.

THE STATUE RECESSES

As we have seen in the previous chapter, there are three blocks that originated from decorated statue recesses. Two of these are offering scenes

showing seated figures of Ibiau (R7) and Dedtu (R8) respectively. Based on the empty margins surrounding the scenes and dressing patterns, both blocks can be identified as the interior decoration (side walls or back walls) of statue recesses. The third block, R14, is the lintel of a statue recess with its outer face decorated with incised versions of the architectural features of the torus frame and cavetto cornice that commonly occur surrounding statue recesses, false doors, and funerary stelae. R14 provides direct evidence for the approximate scale, configuration, and setting for one of these niches.

R14 preserves a yellow-painted ceiling that measured 31 cm in width and 35 cm in depth. The approximate scale of the original recess that it covered can be estimated based on the proportions of preserved Middle Kingdom statue recesses. Proportions in the range of 2:3 to 4:5 are typical for statue recesses. Adopting the 2:3 width to height ratio we can apply the known 31 cm width of the ceiling to suggest a niche measuring 31 by ca. 46 cm in height. A recess of this scale would have accommodated a small, probably seated statuette of the deceased.[9]

The decoration on R14 also provides indications on the architectural setting of this statue niche (Fig. 9.8). Lintel block R14 preserves the beginning of a large-format (9 cm high) hieroglyphic inscription contiguous with the cornice extending to the right. This text likely capped wall scenes below. In this context, the lintel of the statue recess was at the same height as the top of the wall scene. Given the relatively small scale of the statue niche indicated by R14 vis-à-vis the clearly substantial height for the chapel walls indicated by the Wall A blocks, this elevated position is a logical location for a recess containing a statuette of the deceased. If we tentatively adopt the ca. 2.1 m wall height discussed above for Wall A this would suggest a statue niche engaged in the upper part of the wall in the vicinity between chest and head height (ca. 1.25–1.75 m).

Interestingly, the dimensions of block R7 depicting Ibiau and Nekheteni (34 cm wide and 45 cm in height) closely match the preserved depth and the estimated height for the statue niche capped by block R14. As we have noted above, blocks R7 and R8 (depicting Dedtu and his wife Abeteni), are both offering scenes that show signs of having been mounted in an enclosed space. The dressing patterns around the edges of both of these blocks strongly indicate they

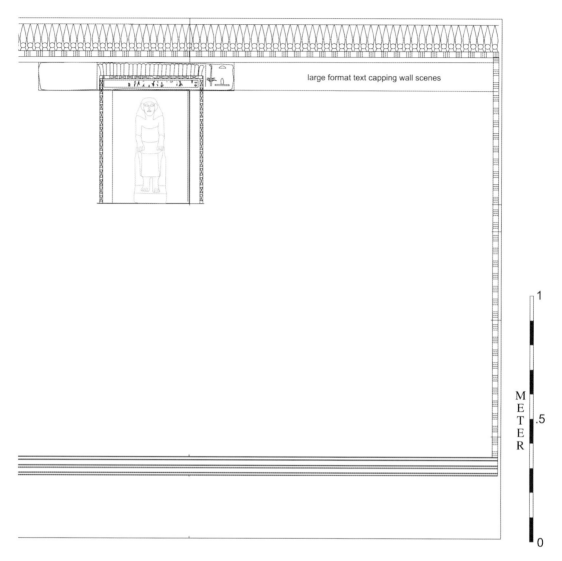

large format text capping wall scenes

Fig. 9.8 Suggested configuration of statue recess based on evidence of block R14.

Fig. 9.9 Statue recess of Amenemhat and Neferu from Deir el-Bahri (MMA 22.3.68). Images courtesy of the Metropolitan Museum of Art.

Fig. 9.10 Suggested reconstruction of the format of the statue niche with lintel (based on block R14) combined with the offering scene of Ibiau and Nekheteni (R7).

were recessed. Offering scenes of this type commonly occur inside statue niches where the deceased is shown seated, facing outwards: the two-dimensional offering scene mirroring the three-dimensional statue set within the recess. The substantial gap between the bottom of the offering scene and the block base may have been intentional allowing space to accommodate the base of a seated statue while not obscuring the imagery on the sides of the niche. A similar arrangement occurs in a closely contemporary statue recess, that of Amenemhat and his wife Neferu from Deir el-Bahri (MMA 22.3.68). The statue recess of Amenemhat and Neferu is slightly larger and more complex with a pair statue depicting the husband and wife as well as two superimposed scene registers within the niche (Fig. 9.9). Otherwise it is closely similar in its main features and style with R7 and the other reused blocks from South Abydos. Consequently, Block R7 is a reasonable candidate for one of the interior decorated sides of the recess capped by R14. The right-facing orientation of R7 suggests that block would have formed the right jamb of a statue niche with seated figure of the deceased facing outward (Fig. 9.10).

Block R8 is somewhat larger (measuring 44.5 by 54.5 cm) and it certainly derives from a bigger statue recess than the one R7 belonged to. R8 is also larger than the recess that would have been capped by lintel block R14.[10] Its leftward orientation suggests it was the left jamb of a statue recess dedicated to Dedtu. Whether or not we attribute R7 to the statue recess associated with lintel block R14, we have clear indications of the presence among the *spolia* of two different statue recesses: one commemorating Ibiau, who is depicted with a woman named Nekheteni, and a second larger recess commemorating Ibiau's father Dedtu, depicted with his (second) wife Abeteni. Both scenes are otherwise very similar in the style of their human figures and hieroglyphs.

At this juncture, we arrive at set of key questions regarding the original architectural context of the re-used 13th Dynasty chapel blocks. The majority of the reused blocks clearly derive from a single decorated wall that was targeted for removal by Seneb-Kay's tomb builders. The statue niches and other reused architectural elements logically should derive from this same chapel. Yet, we have indications for commemoration of multiple members of one family, with recesses that would have contained statues of both Ibiau and his father Dedtu. Are we looking at a single monument that commemorated multiple members of one 13th Dynasty family? Or, are we looking at fragments deriving from two separate, but adjacent structures: one dedicated to Ibiau and one to Dedtu? Can this chapel, or perhaps pair of chapels, be identified as funerary buildings connected with the actual burial of one or both of these men? Alternatively, are we talking here about commemorative *mꜥḥꜥt* structures that had dual commemorative and funerary function, but which were not associated with the actual tombs of these people? In order to address these questions, we turn now to consider the architectural evidence in more detail.

THE CHAPEL ARCHITECTURE

The reused chapel blocks provide new evidence for the existence of elite 13th Dynasty funerary architecture on a scale hitherto unknown at Abydos. While the 1.74 m width of Wall A itself is not large, we have no existing parallels for stone-built chapels of this type at the site. Indeed, there is nothing comparable that has survived for the 13th Dynasty at Thebes nor other Upper Egyptian sites. The recovered blocks from Seneb-Kay's burial chamber are insufficient to reconstruct the chapel with any degree of certainty but we can make a set of inferences based on what we have at hand. The tenon-bonded limestone walls must have rested upon a flagstone floor. The limestone wall blocks are substantial in thickness with rough dressed and irregular backs that must have been embedded in a surrounding structure, most likely of mudbrick. These features imply that we are we are looking at a masonry-built, decorated chapel interior that was encased within a brick superstructure.

Particularly puzzling is the architectural configuration in which a decorated wall face was flanked on either side, and at right angles, by a decorated wall and an undecorated wall respectively. Almost certainly the adjacent decorated face, Wall C, should represent part of an interior chamber running perpendicular to Wall A. The undecorated Wall B could represent an external wall face. If so, Wall A would be the right side of an entrance chamber or decorated vestibule leading into a cruciform chapel. This explanation presents several additional questions. If Wall A is associated with an entrance chamber, why are there no indications for a doorway in this position? Furthermore, why would an intensely decorated entrance vestibule not bear any inscriptions on its outer face? We can by no means be certain that this wall derives from this particular setting within a cruciform chapel. However, this appears to be the best possible explanation based on the surviving evidence. Proceeding from the possibility that Wall A is the right side of a decorated entrance vestibule, we may tentatively reconstruct a transverse

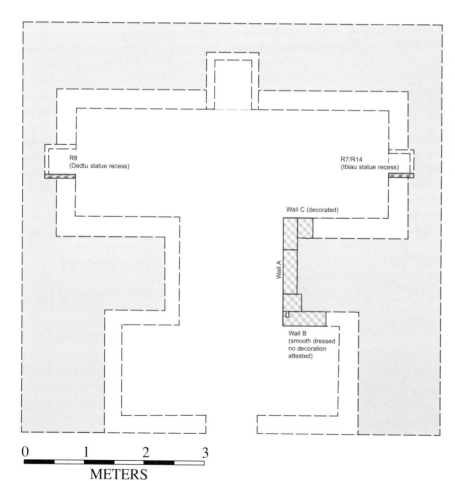

Fig. 9.11 Suggested position of Wall A in a cruciform chapel with transverse inner chamber. The statue recesses of Dedtu and Ibiau (which may originate in different chapels) are hypothetically placed here at opposite ends of the inner chamber.

R8
(Dedtu statue recess)

R7/R14
(Ibiau statue recess)

Wall C (decorated)

Wall A

Wall B
(smooth dressed
no decoration
attested)

0   1   2   3
METERS

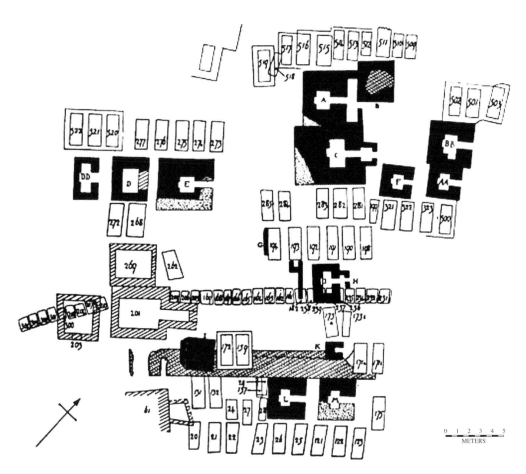

Fig. 9.12 Part of Peet's Cemetery S at Abydos showing cruciform chapels within mudbrick mastabas (after Peet 1914: fig. 8).

inner chamber and outer facade set within a brick superstructure (Fig. 9.11).

The cruciform chapel was a common architectural form during the Middle Kingdom represented at varying scales and types of construction at different sites. At Abydos itself, groups of mudbrick mastabas employing a cruciform interior were documented in the North Cemetery, in Peet's Cemetery S (Fig. 9.12).[11] The chapels are tightly clustered with a tendency for agglomeration into groups that may reflect familial or social relationships among chapel owners. The associated burials occur in shafts located to the side of the chapel. These structures can be of substantial scale, the largest being ca. 5.5 m square. However, lacking stone masonry, they represent a lower order of construction than the building from which the Ibiau-Dedtu blocks derive. The cruciform interior, sometimes expanded with entrance vestibules and transverse chambers, appears to represent variants

of the same general type of building from which the Ibiau-Dedtu blocks would have originated.

The cruciform chapel occurs during the Middle Kingdom at sites in the Memphis-Fayum region and in proximity to 12th Dynasty royal pyramid complexes. The form is attested at Lisht South as a prevalent architectural form among the tomb chapels around the pyramid of Senwosret I (Arnold 2008). While dating earlier, these elite cruciform chapels display a similar format to what we have proposed here for the Ibiau-Dedtu chapel blocks with use of limestone-built internal architecture embedded within a brick mastaba. The mastaba of Djehuty (Fig. 9.13) with a combination of columned portico and transverse inner chamber exemplifies the use of the cruciform chapel in elite funerary architecture at Lisht.

Another example of a decorated chapel with similarities to the cruciform chapels occurs in the mastaba and associated funerary chapel of Anpy at Lahun

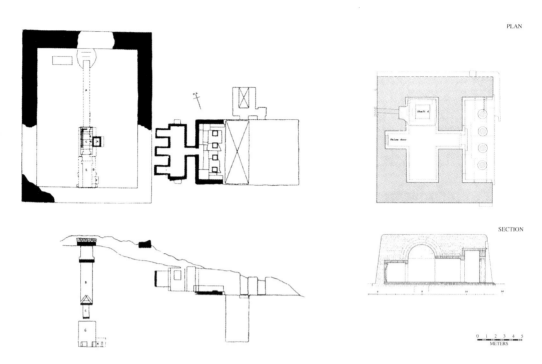

Fig. 9.13 Cruciform funerary chapels. Left: mastaba and chapel of Anpy at Lahun (after Petrie, Brunton, and Murray 1923: pl. 27; Right: Djehuty at Lisht South (after Arnold 2008: fig. 12 and pl. 96).

(Petrie et al. 1923). The tomb of Anpy includes a brick mastaba that caps the tomb itself, with the funerary chapel constructed as a separate building in front of the mastaba. The Anpy chapel is cut into the bedrock but lined in limestone masonry akin to the format of the reused blocks at South Abydos. A pillared portico leads into a transverse hall with three large chapels on the back wall and two smaller niches elevated at eye level at the ends of the transverse hall. Nearly all of the masonry had been pulled away and fragments of the decorated wall blocks, along with fragments of statuary that must have stood in the recesses inside the transverse hall, were recovered in a large shaft that fronted the chapel. The two smaller elevated recesses provide a possible parallel to the architectural setting from which the Ibiau and Dedtu statue recesses derive. While the chapel of Anpy departs from the cruciform configuration due to its use of three recesses rather than one, the layout with transverse chamber and pillared portico otherwise represents an adaptation of the cruciform chapel type.

Beyond these somewhat earlier comparanda, the primary challenge confronting an understanding of the Ibiau-Dedtu blocks is the lack of surviving 13th Dynasty elite funerary chapels whether at Abydos or

other sites. The blocks testify to a scale of elite monumental construction that we are otherwise lacking at Abydos for this period. In view of the level of investment reflected in the importation of fine limestone, the overall scale of the building or buildings represented, and the nature of the funerary imagery on Wall A, the offering scenes of Ibiau and Dedtu, as well as the unknown figure on block R4, we are confronted with the fundamental question of whether we are speaking here of commemorative chapels (*mahats*) erected at Abydos by members of one elite 13th Dynasty lineage. Or, are we looking at funerary chapels associated with actual tombs as seen, for instance, in the smaller cruciform chapels of Peet's Cemetery S?

A CEMETERY OF 13TH DYNASTY HIGH OFFICIALS?

At the beginning of this chapter, we observed the uniform characteristics of the reused wall blocks. The carving style is quite cohesive and there appear to be no stylistic traits that would indicate that any of the blocks derive from different buildings. More-over, all of the blocks are scarred with the chisel damage created through an extensive and systematically executed *damnatio memoriae*. These aspects would seem consistent with a single structure that was subject to a targeted phase of posthumous attack and subsequent dismantlement in the era of Seneb-Kay. However, in our analysis of Wall A, we have seen that there is no conclusive way of determining who would have been depicted as the primary chapel owner on the upper part of that wall. Other blocks within the reused corpus from CS9 demonstrate that we have mortuary cults represented for two, and potentially three different individuals. The offering scene on block R7 commemorates the *Master of the Offering Tables of Amun*, Ibiau, while block R8 depicts Ibiau's father, the *Overseer of Fields*, Dedtu, accompanied by his wife Abeteni. Additionally, on block R4 we have a principal figure whose identifying label is missing. Based on the occurrence of the title *Master of the Offering Tables of Amun* held by that man's son, the principal figure in that scene may be Ibiau, although we cannot exclude the possibility of yet a third man commemorated in these scenes. The existence of two, and potentially three, celebrated individuals argues against the blocks all deriving from the same chapel.

If all of the blocks are attributed to a single building, this must have been a structure with a significant degree of complexity that commemorated multiple generations of a 13th Dynasty elite family. If so, we may be looking at a monumental rendition of a late Middle Kingdom funerary stela in which an entire extended family is commemorated not just in name and image, but as parallel recipients of offering cults. A structure of this type would appear to fall under the rubric of the *mahat*: a commemorative building that was tied to the cult and offerings of Osiris at Abydos, but not the location of the actual burial.[12] On this basis, it seems possible that we are looking at a mortuary building that was built at Abydos by the scion of one prominent 13th Dynasty family—possibly Ibiau—but in which he chose to commemorate other members of his family including prominently his father Dedtu, whose titles and career mark him as one of the highest cadre of royal officials of the middle 13th Dynasty.

This line of interpretation would suggest that the primary individuals commemorated on this monument at Abydos were buried elsewhere. In view of the Theban associations of the members of the Ibiau-Dedtu family, burial at Thebes with a commemorative chapel at Abydos would appear to be a viable explanation. As we discuss further in the next chapter, an individual named the *Master of the Offering Tables of Amun*, Ibiau, occurs on a fragmentary statue base excavated in a priestly cemetery south of the complex of Nebhepetre Montuhotep II at Deir el-Bahri (Porter and Moss 1964:655 and plan V). This statue depicts a *ḥm-ntr 'Imn*, God's servant priest of Amun, [Nefer]hotep, with Ibiau listed as his father. Therefore, we appear to have commemoration of at least one of the sons of Ibiau in the Theban necropolis suggesting members of this family could be represented in mortuary contexts at both Abydos and Thebes. It appears possible both Ibiau and his son Neferhotep, prominent members of Theban civil and temple administration and descended from the *Overseer of Fields,* Dedtu, were buried in Thebes with *mahat* structures built at Abydos to celebrate the members of their family.

On the other hand, if we choose to emphasize the indications for offering cults dedicated to multiple individuals, we may conclude that the blocks derive from a group of adjacent chapels built at Abydos by members of this same 13th Dynasty lineage. The consistency of style as well as the *damnatio* could be accommodated by closely related buildings spanning a short timeframe, as well as the implication that it was not just one individual, but the entire lineage that was subject to attack. The pattern of construction in this case may parallel the organization of chapels and tombs in Peet's Cemetery S discussed above. While individual chapels were associated with multiple people, the chapels themselves cluster into groups, likely reflecting related individuals or family groupings. This is a basic pattern going back to the Old Kingdom where we have cases at Abydos of elite individuals such as Weni the elder and his father, the vizier Iuu, who constructed chapels and tombs directly adjacent to each other (Richards 2003:400–407; Herbich and Richards 2006:141–149), and conjoined funerary monuments of father and son is a not uncommon practice in sites with a long history of use by a single family. The same pattern may apply to the reused 13th Dynasty chapel blocks. In this case, Seneb-Kay's builders would have taken most of the blocks from a single wall of one of a group of chapels but augmented that material with other blocks drawn from immediately adjacent buildings. Quite possibly these same buildings were being targeted as a source of building material for other activities during the reign of Seneb-Kay as well as other rulers of his era.

It is impossible on the basis of the texts and iconography of the decorated blocks alone to distinguish positively whether this chapel or group of chapels were connected with actual tombs, or represent *mahat* buildings that lacked associated burials. Both types of structures maintained a mortuary function, and a comparable repertoire of imagery and texts would occur in either type of building. It must be noted, however, that one theme indicative of a *mahat* would be depiction of the deceased venerating a god, most likely Osiris-Khentiamentiu or one of the other principal Abydene deities. This element is a common feature of late Middle Kingdom commemorative chapels at Abydos but is absent among the surviving blocks. The lack of such a theme among the reused blocks might be viewed as consistent with the blocks' origin in one or more mortuary chapels connected with actual burials of the Dedtu-Ibiau family.

The surviving evidence is also insufficient to conclusively demonstrate derivation from one or multiple buildings. Although, the weight of the evidence appears to favor the origin of the reused blocks primarily from a single chapel that formed part of a larger grouping of related funerary chapels. What is noteworthy in this regard is the evident scale and investment in this decorated architecture commemorating Ibiau, Dedtu, and perhaps others. The enhanced level of investment at Abydos, in a period when even the highest officials were typically commemorated only by a stela or statue set within a mudbrick chapel, lends weight to the argument that these were not *mahat* structures but functional funerary chapels with associated tombs.

At first glance the possibility that a prominent 13th Dynasty lineage with Theban associations may have imported fine quality, northern limestone and built chapels and tombs for themselves at Abydos would appear relatively surprising. However, a crucial part of this equation is the fact that two of the kings of this same period constructed large, post-Hawara style royal tombs at Abydos. Tombs S9 and S10 at South Abydos are variants of the 13th Dynasty pyramid tradition and have a high probability of belonging to the middle 13th Dynasty kings Neferhotep I and Sobekhotep IV. They display physical evidence

for the burial of those two rulers beside the mortuary complex of Senwosret III (Wegner and Cahail 2015; Wegner 2019).

With the presence of tombs of two 13th Dynasty kings at Abydos, it appears increasingly likely that members of the administration and, potentially, relatives of those same kings, would have been motivated to build their own tombs at Abydos. Indeed, the construction of those royal tombs would have required the presence of royal officials as well as substantial numbers of architects and builders whose commission involved the transport to Abydos of large quantities of limestone and quartzite from northern quarries. This royally sponsored activity at Abydos is likely to have served as a stimulus for a wider range of elite activity reflected in the chapel blocks of Ibiau and Dedtu.

Despite ruling during a time when *Itj-Tawy* still served as the residence city of the 13th Dynasty, Neferhotep I and Sobekhotep IV were kings with Theban origins, descended from the *it-nṯr*, *God's father*, Haankhef, and his wife Kemi (Ryholt 1997:225–231; Wegner 2019). So too, the *Overseer of Fields*, Dedtu and his son Ibiau can be identified as members of a leading Theban family that held priestly and administrative appointments in the Amun temple, the cult of Montu at Medamud, as well as in the highest levels of 13th Dynasty royal administration. In the next chapter, we attempt to unravel the intricate historical and familial relationships of Dedtu and Ibiau, as well as the links they may have had with kings of the era including Neferhotep I and Sobekhotep IV. The *damnatio memoriae* directed against their monuments at Abydos may represent a politically motivated attack against their power and identity due to the close connections they held with these particular 13th Dynasty kings.

NOTES:

9.1 Two of the blocks on the corners also have mortises for tenons reflecting the tendency for use of tenons to stabilize the structural corners of stone architecture.

9.2 On late Middle Kingdom family stelae that employ larger, more complex, groupings of kneeling figures, there is a tendency to have their orientation facing the position of the deceased. See for instance stela CCG 20652 (ANOC 10.3. Simpson 1974: pl. 19) where the figures reverse orientation based on the position of the seated figure of the deceased above.

9.3 Compare, for instance, the left wall of the miniature statue chapel of the *Reporter of the Vizier*, Senwosret with the scenes of musicians fronted by a harpist (Simpson 1974: pls. 70–71). Also, stela Leiden V, 68 (ANOC 38.1, Simpson 1974: pl. 56), showing the harpist directly in front of the seated figure of the stela owner.

9.4 Close stylistic and compositional similarities exist between the agricultural scenes on the reused chapel blocks and two commemorative monuments from Abydos: (1) the decorated blocks of the statue chapel of the *Reporter of the Vizier*, Senwosret (Louvre C16–18, ANOC 52, Simpson 1974: pls. 70–71; Oppenheim et al. 2017:260–261); and (2) the ankh stela of Amenyseneb (Liverpool E.30: Kitchen 1961:10–18). Both of these monuments had images of the deceased surveying agricultural and productive activities.

9.5 Compare, for example, the way the harpist faces the seated stela owner, Iki, in stela Leiden V,68 (Simpson 1974: pl. 56) or the stela of Renseneb (Peet 1914: pl. 23:5).

9.6 The miniature chapel of the *Herald of the Vizier*, Senwosret, and that of the *Seal bearer of the Vizier Ankhu*, Sahathor (Hermitage 1075 and 1603–4) mentioned above are so similar they appear to have been commissioned at the same time, and likely on behalf of a specific group of subordinates of the vizier Ankhu (Franke 1984:136–137).

9.7 The tomb of the vizier Intefiqer dates to the reigns of Amenemhat I and Senwosret I. It appears to have been originally intended for Intefiqer but was reused for his wife Senet at a slightly later time and subsequent to the construction of another tomb for Intefiqer at Lisht.

9.8 Similar images of the harvesting man drinking from a vessel occur at Sheikh Said and elsewhere (Davies, 1901: pl. 16).

9.9 An example of the type of figure is the seated statue of the *Reporter of the Vizier*, Senwosret (Louvre N49: Delange 1987: 84–85; Oppenheim et al. 2017:260–261), which derived from his statue chapel Louvre C16–18 (=N170–172).

9.10 A position as the inner decorated face of a statue recess may also be feasible since the rightward orientation commonly occurs on the inner wall. If so, the width of 34 cm slightly exceeds the 31 cm width of the R14 niche.

9.11 Peet's Cemetery S is located between the Kom es-Sultan and the Shunet el-Zebib (Peet 1914:30–47). For the approximate location see the overall map of Abydos in the introduction.

9.12 The Egyptian term *mahat* is often translated with the term "cenotaph." Here we prefer to use the Egyptian term that typically designates an aboveground cult building, whereas cenotaph denotes an empty or symbolic tomb (see also discussion of O'Connor 1985:161–177).

10

The Family History of Dedtu and Ibiau*

In the preceding chapters we have looked in detail at the reused blocks which compose the burial chamber of CS9, the tomb of Woseribre Seneb-Kay. Here we will delve deeper into the history of the two principal men associated with the chapel blocks—namely the *Overseer of Fields,* Dedtu and his son, the *Overseer of the Offering Tables of Amun,* Ibiau. Who were these men, and what external dating criteria can we employ in order to contextualize them in the history of the period? Why were the names and images of these men at Abydos aggressively attacked through what appears to have been a *damnatio memoriae* directed against them and their family?

In the following sections, we will investigate the source material relating to Dedtu, his son Ibiau, as well as Ibiau's own children. Following a brief synthesis, the discussion will turn to look at the possible motivations behind the *damnatio memoriae.* Finally, we will examine the overall chronology of when the chapel was built, and when the limestone blocks were dismantled from their original building, allowing Seneb-Kay's tomb to be constructed. In attempting to answer these and other questions, it will become clear that the reused blocks not only afford a rare glimpse into the history and culture of the middle 13th Dynasty, but they are crucial in refining the chronological parameters for the lifetime and reign of Seneb-Kay.

THE OVERSEER OF FIELDS, DEDTU

To the scholar of the late Middle Kingdom, the bureaucratic history of the 13th Dynasty is simultaneously instructive and frustrating. Although the sources we have at our disposal furnish many specific pieces of information and details of the titles and careers of certain individuals, we are missing a great deal of vital information on the period, leading to an incomplete and fractured picture. First and foremost, the names and order of the pharaohs of the 13th Dynasty is still incompletely known, owing to the fact that many of these kings held power for such short timeframes. The situation with the families of high officials is also fragmentary. While we have at our disposal a rich record of family stelae and other monuments of this period, reconstruction of individual family lineages can be highly challenging. Prosopographical analysis, which examines the evidence of multiple individuals classed by social group or administrative office, is a useful approach, but ultimately incorporates a degree of generalization that becomes divorced from particular historical circumstances.

Consequently, our picture of the workings of the 13th Dynasty bureaucracy relies on tiny snapshots of individuals, often without any means of anchoring them within the overall chronology of the dynasty.

This chapter written by Kevin Cahail.

Indeed, though many of the highest officials of the 13th Dynasty are known to scholars, few of them belong to well-documented, extended families, and many cannot be chronologically anchored with certainty. One man, Dedtu, who held one of the highest cabinet positions of *Overseer of Fields*, is a rare exception to this trend (el-Rabi'i 1977:20; Franke 1984a: doss. 769; Andreu 1991:15–26; and Grajetzki 2000:135), and it is fortunate for us that he and his descendants are the people commemorated on the reused blocks from Seneb-Kay's tomb. Though his other monuments have alerted scholars to his existence, the information gleaned from the reused blocks at South Abydos greatly increases our understanding of this man and his lineage.

Dedtu was born into a family of upper-middle class, whose roots are first attested in the late 12th Dynasty. According to the stela of his father, Burekhef, found at Abydos (Cairo CG 20540; Lange and Schäfer 1908:158–161), Dedtu's grandfather was a man named Hekenu, who held the, still debated, rank title *wr mḏw Šmᶜw, Great One of the Tens of Upper Egypt*.[1] According to analysis of P.Boulaq 18, the *wr mḏw Šmᶜw* was of equivalent rank to men holding titles such as *ꜣtw n ṯt ḥqꜣ, ỉdnw n ỉmy-r ḥtmt*, and *ỉmy-r šnt* (Quirke 1990:72–75), but *wr mḏw Šmᶜw* could also be held by individuals whom we may classify as being one rung down the bureaucratic ladder (Quirke 1990:78–80). This ranking system places men like Hekenu and Burekhef who held the title *wr mḏ Šmᶜw*, potentially directly below the department heads of the outer palace who held

the ranking title *ḫtmty-bỉty, Royal Seal-bearer*. These department heads themselves answered directly to the Vizier. Therefore, Hekenu did not belong to the highest echelons of government but was perhaps only three or four layers away from the king. Hekenu's son Burekhef was born to the *Lady of the House,* Sebeket,[2] and he held the same title as Hekenu—*Great one of the Tens of Upper Egypt*—though virtually nothing is known of his career.[3] Based on the stela of Burekhef (Cairo CG 20540) and Dedtu's Odessa 52970 stela, we are able to construct a basic genealogy (Fig. 10.1).

The genealogy of this family becomes clearer from the texts of two stelae dedicated by Burekhef's son Dedtu: Louvre C58 (Awad and Ahmed 2003:43–48) and Odessa 52970 (Berlev and Hodjash 1998:41–43). The Louvre example derives from Mariette's excavations at North Abydos and, despite the fact that Porter and Moss included the Odessa stela in their Theban volume (Porter and Moss 1964:810), Berlev and Hodjash have indicated that the stela's provenance is "almost certainly Abydos" (Berlev and Hodjash 1998:41).[4] The two stelae were probably dedicated at different times, since they highlight the commemoration of two different groups of people. On Odessa 52970, Dedtu, who holds the titles *Royal Seal-bearer* and *Overseer of Fields*, is shown at the left giving offerings to a standing figure of Osiris, helping to corroborate the Abydene provenience of the piece. Below him are two registers, subdivided into smaller boxes (Fig. 10.2). At the left side of these registers are Dedtu's parents, Burekhef and Tjenetib, shown

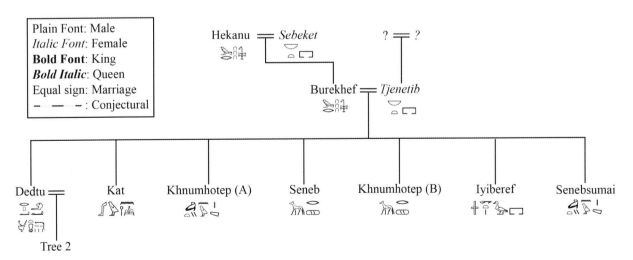

Fig. 10.1 **Tree 1**: Family tree of the *Great One of the Tens of Upper Egypt,* Burekhef, with his parents and children (based on Cairo CG 20540 and Odessa 52970).

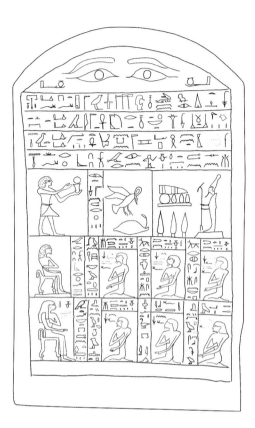

Fig. 10.2 Stela Odessa 52970, dedicated by Dedtu and commemorating his parents Burekhef and Tjenetib (line drawing by author with photo after Berlev and Hodjash 1998).

seated facing right. Kneeling on the ground and facing left toward their parents are six of Dedtu's brothers, each with his own titles. Consequently, this stela is best understood as a monument commemorating the deaths and funerary cults of Burekhef and Tjenetib, with their seven children in attendance.

The second stela dedicated by Dedtu, Louvre C58, has a similar layout in its upper portion (Fig. 10.3). The main panel shows Dedtu again giving offerings to a standing figure of Osiris. Dedtu is on the left, while the image of the god is at the right, with a pile of offerings between the two figures. The register below has a depiction of a seated woman at the left, identified epigraphically as Dedtu's wife the *ỉryt-pꜥt Ḥꜣt-špswt, Hereditary Noblewoman Hatshepsut*, while at the right, five of the couple's children kneel in attendance.[5] One of these children is the *ḥry ḥꜣwt n ỉmn ỉb-ỉꜥw, Master of the Offering Tables of Amun, Ibiau*. An identification of this Ibiau with the man pictured on reused block R7 from the tomb of King Seneb-Kay is certain, given that his name, paternity, and title match well among the sources. Just as the Odessa

stela probably marks the death of Dedtu's parents, this stela seems to highlight the funerary cult of Dedtu's first wife, Hatshepsut, and was probably set up at Abydos immediately after her death.

Dedtu and Hatshepsut had at least five sons (Fig. 10.4), and although no daughters are mentioned, this is not conclusive proof that the couple had only boys. The primary document for the children is stela Louvre C58 (Awad and Ahmed 2003: abb. 1). On this monument, the five sons appear in boxes to the right of their seated mother, Hatshepsut. Graphically, the kneeling men seem to be ranked from left to right, and top to bottom: Ibiau, Iyiberef, and Neferhotep in the top register, followed by Haankhef and Burekhef in the lower register.[6] This placement may reflect the birth order of the children, making Ibiau the eldest son of Dedtu.

A final source for Dedtu's family is the reused block R8 from South Abydos where Dedtu is depicted with a wife named Abeteni. Two facts place this source later than the two stelae discussed above. Firstly, is the dilemma of Dedtu having two wives. Concerned as it is with Dedtu's parents and siblings,

Fig. 10.3 Stela Louvre C58, dedicated by Dedtu and commemorating his first wife Hatshepsut (line drawing by author with photo after Awad and Ahmed 2003).

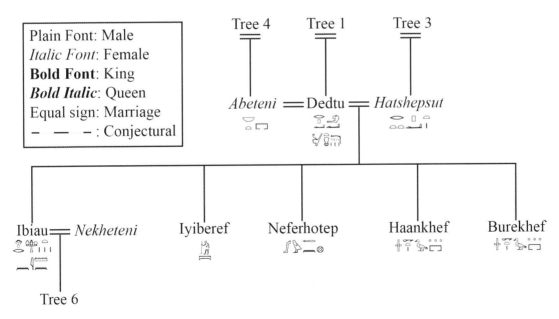

Fig. 10.4 Tree 2: Family tree of Dedtu and his children from his first wife Hatshepsut based on stela Louvre C58. The birth order of the children is reflected in a left-to-right progression.

Odessa 52970 does not include his wife. Yet, we learn from Louvre C58 that Dedtu's wife was the *iryt-pᶜt* Hatshepsut, and that she was the mother of Dedtu's children. However, the reused block R8 from South Abydos clearly records that the woman standing behind him is *ḥmt.f, his wife*, the *Lady of the House*, Abeteni. Assuming that stela Louvre C58 was meant to commemorate the death of Dedtu's first wife, Hatshepsut, it would seem that later in his life Dedtu had married a second woman named Abeteni.

Secondly, Dedtu has a longer string of ranking titles on block R8 than he does on either of his stelae. On both Louvre C58 and Odessa 52970, Dedtu is simply *ḥtmty-bity imy-r ꜣḥwt*. However, block R8 from South Abydos prefaces these titles with both *iry-pᶜt*, and *ḥꜣty-ᶜ*. A number of scholars have pointed out that during the 12th Dynasty, titles such as *iry-pᶜt, ḥꜣty-ᶜ, ḥtmty-bity*, and *smr-wᶜty* refer to a system of title ranking (Franke 1984b:103–124; Grajetzki 2000:220–228). According to this system, the title sequence *iry-pᶜt ḥꜣty-ᶜ ḥtmty-bity imy-r ꜣḥwt*, which Dedtu bears on block R8, is a higher office than the simple *ḥtmty-bity imy-r-ꜣḥwt* of Louvre C58 and Odessa 52970. However, as Grajetzki has pointed out, this system of ranking seems to have been altered during the 13th Dynasty and, according to his study, no *Overseer of Fields* ever held any rank title higher than *ḥtmty-bity* (Grajetzki 2000:138). Such a string of high-ranking titles signals strongly that Dedtu held some form of connection with the ruling family.

One person who is perhaps most integral to understanding the interconnections between Dedtu and the royal family is his first wife Hatshepsut. She held the extremely high and rare title of *iryt-pᶜt*. D. Stefanović has pointed out two main uses for the title *iryt-pᶜt*. In some cases, it may have served as a ranking title for non-royal women (Stefanović 2009:15). For instance, the non-royal wives of the governors of el-Kab employed the title (Spalinger 1980:108), but it can be deduced in most cases that their use of the title occurred in direct relation to the very high rank of their husbands. In the case of Hatshepsut, her title *iryt-pᶜt* is higher than the status of her husband Dedtu who lacks the corresponding male title *iry-pᶜt* at that stage in his career. Stefanović has also highlighted the fact that the mothers, sisters, and daughters of kings during the Late Middle Kingdom and Second Intermediate Period appear regularly with this title (Stefanović 2009:12). This opens up two possibilities:

one is that Hatshepsut was an unusually high-ranking, non-royal woman, and that the origin of her status is entirely unknown; and the other is that she was directly related by blood to one or more of the kings of the 13th Dynasty. Of these, the former seems highly unlikely, since a typical strategy for women of elite families was to marry men of equal or higher rank in order to increase family status.

To be clear, based on the sources available to us, it is currently impossible to be absolutely certain of the parentage of Dedtu's first wife Hatshepsut. However, we are left to explain why she held such a high-status title, and whether or not her higher social standing led to Dedtu's increased ranking titles at the end of his career. A small collection of circumstantial evidence allows us to construct a working hypothesis that serves to explain not only the elevated titles of Dedtu, but also the possible motivations that incited the *damnatio memoriae* wrought upon the monuments of his lineage at Abydos.

The most likely possibility open to us is to theorize that Hatshepsut was the sister of Kings Neferhotep I, Sobekhotep IV, and Sahathor (whose reign may have intervened briefly between those of his two brothers). It was during the reigns of Neferhotep I and Sobekhotep IV, a period of some 23 years, that Dedtu held his position as *Overseer of Fields*. A number of facts bolster this idea. Firstly, Hatshepsut's title of *iryt-pᶜt* may explicitly betoken her status as the sister of a king. Naturally, the counter argument may be leveled that Hatshepsut does not hold the actual title of *sꜣt nswt, King's sister*. However, there is only one attestation of her in the record: Dedtu's stela Louvre C58. The epigraph naming her is crammed into the small space between her face and the box containing her son Ibiau. Since the title *iryt-pᶜt* could convey both relationship to the king, as well as being an indicator of social rank, it perhaps superseded and replaced the use of *King's sister* in this context. Consequently, the fact that she lacks this title on the only monument known to name her does not preclude her from being the sister of Neferhotep I and Sobekhotep IV. Furthermore, as mentioned above, it is a common feature of Dedtu and his father's stelae to omit relationship statements.

The second and, in many ways, more compelling line of evidence has to do with her sons. In addition to Ibiau, Dedtu and Hatshepsut had four other sons, two of whom were named after Dedtu's brother and father: Iyiberef and Burekhef, born in that order.

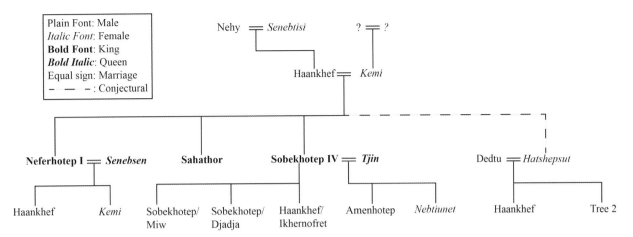

Fig. 10.5 Tree 3: Family tree showing the conjectural genealogy of the *Hereditary Princess* Hatshepsut, linking her to the family of Neferhotep I.

Tellingly, the other two sons bore the names Neferhotep and Haankhaf. Neither of these names have parallels in Dedtu's known family. The name of the father of the brother kings Neferhotep I, Sahathor, and Sobekhotep IV is known to have been Haankhef (Ryholt 1997:225). Furthermore, Neferhotep I and his Sobekhotep IV both named one of their own sons Haankhef after their father, showing that this family wished to commemorate this individual by perpetuating his name through their offspring (Fig. 10.5).[7]

While it is possible that Dedtu's sons Haankhef and Neferhotep held these names coincidentally, it is highly suggestive that Hatshepsut was also commemorating close family members. In Dedtu's case, this was his father and his brother. If Hatshepsut chose the same relations to commemorate (father and brother), then Haankhef could also have been her father, and Neferhotep her brother. The graphical birth order reflected on stela Louvre C58 also reveals a symmetry: father's brother (Iyiberef), mother's brother (Neferhotep), mother's father (Haankhef), father's father (Burekhef). In other words, Dedtu's second and fifth sons were named after his brother and father respectively, while his third and fourth sons were named after his brother-in-law, Neferhotep, and his father-in-law, Haankhef. Approximately two decades later, these two men became King Khasekhemre Neferhotep I, and the God's Father Haankhef, but, at the time Dedtu's children were named, these two men were important primarily due to their relationship to Hatshepsut.

Expanding this hypothesis further, the only title Neferhotep I's father Haankhef holds in the surviving record is the priestly title *it-ntr*, *God's father*, but his career before the accession of Neferhotep I is unknown. Since two and possibly three of his sons went on to hold the position of pharaoh, it seems logical that he was a high-ranking official before their accession to or usurpation of the royal seat. Consequently, as the third piece of circumstantial evidence, we may be justified in positing that the *God's Father* Haankhaf was one and the same as the *Overseer of Fields*, Haankhaf (Grajetzki 2000:132–133). Haankhaf was the *Overseer of Fields* in P.Boulaq 18, not Dedtu, meaning that Dedtu took up the position sometime after him, despite the fact that Dedtu's son Neferhotep already held a minor governmental position in the same document. None of Dedtu's known monuments date to a time before his was *Overseer of Fields*, but since his son was already established in the bureaucracy, Dedtu must have held a lower-ranking title previous to his tenure as *Overseer of Fields*.

If the *Overseer of Fields*, Haankhaf, was indeed Hatshepsut's father, then he would have been Dedtu's father-in-law. This situation might well explain how Dedtu himself received the high-ranking position of *Overseer of Fields*, despite coming from a family of upper-middle ranked officials who had only held the title of *wr mdw Šmʿw* for two generations. Upon the accession of Neferhotep I, Hatshepsut would have become the sister of a king, explaining her ranking title of *iryt-pʿt*. Through marriage, Dedtu would then have become the brother-in-law of the king, justifying his elevated titles on block R8 of *iry-pʿt* and *ḥꜣty-ʿ*, two titles which no other *Overseer of Fields* held during the 13th Dynasty (Grajetzki 2000:138). This hypothetical genealogy would make Dedtu's sons blood nephews of the brother kings Neferhotep I, Sahathor, and Sobekhotep IV and, therefore, members of the extended royal family.[8]

Sometime perhaps during the reign of Neferhotep I, Dedtu's wife Hatshepsut passed away, prompting him to commemorate her with stela Odessa 52970.[9] Hatshepsut's father Haankhef was raised to the title of *God's Father*, allowing Neferhotep I to appoint his brother-in-law, Dedtu, to replace Haankhef as *Overseer of Fields*. With his new-found status, coupled with Neferhotep I and Sobekhotep IV's increased interest in Abydos,[10] Dedtu dedicated at least two stelae at the site (Odessa 552970 and Louvre C58), probably located in *mahat* shrines near the votive zone.[11]

At about the same time, Neferhotep I appears to have made the decision to build his own funerary monument at South Abydos. The likely construction of a burial complex at South Abydos was motivated by a variety of factors including the Upper Egyptian/ Theban origins of the family, his expressed interest in the Osiris cult, as well as through a desire to link himself to the long and prosperous reign of Senwosret III (Wegner and Cahail 2015:159–161). Coinciding with this shift in the location of the royal burial locale, high ranking officials sought to connect their own funerary establishments to those of their monarchs. Consequently, Dedtu and his family began the construction of a tomb and chapel at North Abydos, which included images of himself and his eldest son Ibiau. However, standing behind Dedtu on block R8 is a woman with the distinction of *"his wife,"* but who it is not Hatshepsut. This woman's name was the *Lady of the House*, Abeteni.[12] Although of lower status than his first wife, Hatshepsut, Abeteni's name is rare enough to examine her possible background.

The name Abeteni is a feminine relative from the verb *3bi*, meaning *"the one* (fem.) *that I desired"* (Ranke 1935: 1.20). Apart from reused chapel block R8, there are only two sources for the name: Louvre C13 and a stela now in Vienna (ÄS 180). Both of these monuments also have connections to the royal family of the mid- to late 13th Dynasty. If one of the women named Abeteni on these stelae was married to Dedtu, it is clear that even after the death of his first wife, Dedtu was still a part of the royal sphere. The first of these three attestations of the name Abeteni appears on stela Louvre C13 (Spalinger 1980:95–116; Ryholt 1997:239–242).

This monument is dedicated to the Queen Nubkhaes and has been the subject of scrutiny for what it may convey about the royal house in the late 13th Dynasty, especially since it lacks any reference to the king and husband of Nubkahaes. The monument is intertwined with the complex genealogy of the Governors of el-Kab (Davies 2010), since Nubkhas was the mother of the *King's Daughter*, Khonsu, who was married to Ay, the Governor of el-Kab. Unfortunately, though stela Louvre C13 does include a short family group with the name of a *Lady of the House*, Abeteni, she is not linked to the family of Queen Nubkhaes in any concrete way. The final five columns of text on the stela mention the small family of the *Deputy of the Judges*, Iunef, and his wife, the *Lady of the House*, Renseneb, along with their children, the *Inspector of Scribes*, Neferhotep, and his sister the *Lady of the House*, Abeteni (Spalinger 1980: pl. 8). No husband is listed for Abeteni but given that the stela dates to the end of the 13th Dynasty or even later (Ryholt 1997:241), it is highly unlikely that this Abeteni was the second wife of Dedtu, since he would almost certainly have died long before the period represented by Louvre C13.

Another monument bears the last two occurrences of the rare name Abeteni. The stela Vienna ÄS 180 (Hein and Satzinger 1993:7, 103–107, 111) belongs to the *Sab and Mouth of Nekhen*, Khonsu, son of the *Great-one of the Tens of Upper Egypt*, Nebsumenu (ANOC 49).[13] The stela indicates that Khonsu was a contemporary of the *Overseer of the Town*, *[Vizier]*, Iuy. This man has been linked to a tomb discovered by the Metropolitan Museum of Art in 1922–1923, near the causeway of the Thutmosis III at Deir el-Bahri (Hayes 1959:57), though the fragmentary *rishi* style coffin with Iuy's name did not include the title of *Vizier*, leaving this attribution open to some question (Grajetzki 2000:22).[14] In any case, both Grajetzki, as well as Hein and Satzinger date the stela's manufacture to the late 13th Dynasty.

Two women in Khonsu's family have the name Abeteni. The first is the stela owner Khonsu's half-sister. Based on a close reading of the stela, Khonsu's mother, the *Lady of the House*, Nekheteni, appears to have had a husband previous to Khonsu's father, Nebsumenu, though the name of this man is not given. Khonsu includes three half-siblings on the stela, introduced with the phrase *sn.f n mwt.f, his brother of his mother* (Franke 1984b:21–22, 112). These individuals are the Vizier Iuy, along with a man named Saamun and a woman named

Abeteni, neither of whom hold titles. While the text does not indicate the marital status of this Abeteni, the fact that she is contemporary with the stela owner's late 13th Dynasty date also makes this Abeteni an unlikely candidate for Dedtu's second wife.

The second Abeteni on the Vienna stela is Khonsu's maternal grandmother, placing her two generations before the late 13th Dynasty and, therefore, a much more viable option for Dedtu's second wife. This Abeteni, again without title, had one sister named Nenaisi (Ranke 1935:204.20), and at least one daughter, Khonsu's mother Nekheteni. The text of the stela does not include the name of this Abeteni's husband, leaving the paternity of this branch of the family open to speculation. Consequently, it is possible that this was the Abeteni who was married to Dedtu (Fig. 10.6). In order to have born children to Dedtu late in his life, Abeteni would have been considerably younger and was probably a contemporary of Dedtu's children Ibiau and Neferhotep. Intriguingly, Abeteni's daughter was named Nekheteni and held the title *of Lady of the House*. It may be possible that this Nekheteni was named for Ibiau's probable wife Nekheteni, daughter of the *Priest of Amun*, Senebef, appearing on reused block R7 at South Abydos. If this connection between Dedtu and Abeteni is correct, then Dedtu would have been the grandfather of the Vizier Iuy, as well as Khonsu's full brother Sahathor, who held the honorific title *King's Son* (Hein and Satzinger 1993:7, 104). These high-ranking titles could have derived from Dedtu's high status and connection to the royal family, especially since Khonsu's father Nebsumenu holds the lower title of *wr mḏw Šmꜥw*.

Laying aside the genealogy of Abeteni and returning now to Dedtu, it seems plausible that he received his title of *Overseer of Fields* by virtue of his marriage to Hatshepsut and her royal connections. However, Hatshepsut's probable father Haankhef held the office of *Overseer of Fields* at the time P.Boulaq 18 was written, rather than Dedtu.[15] Since Dedtu's son Neferhotep also appears in this document, Dedtu himself must certainly have been an active member of the governmental bureaucracy by the time the document was written, but if he was not the *Overseer of Fields*, what position did he hold?

Both Dedtu's father Burekhef as well as his grandfather Hekenu held the title of *Great-One of the Tens of Upper Egypt*, leading to one possibility that Dedtu gained this same title in his early career

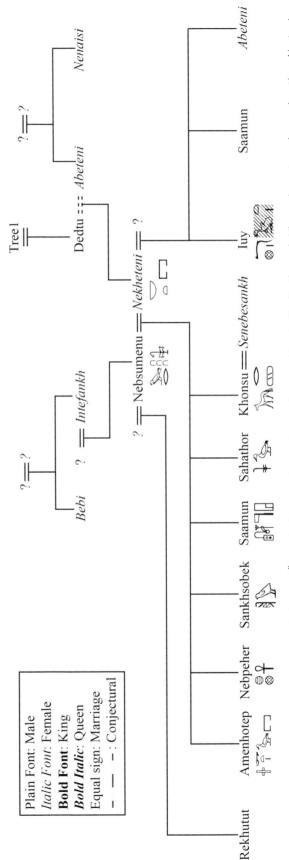

Fig. 10.6 Tree 4: Genealogy from the stela of Khonsu (ÄS 180), showing the conjectural connection to Dedtu through Khonsu's maternal grandmother Abeteni.

Plain Font: Male
Italic Font: Female
Bold Font: King
Bold Italic: Queen
Equal sign: Marriage
| — —: Conjectural

through his lineage. Though Ranke indicated that the name Dedtu was not uncommon during the Middle Kingdom, the only sources he adduced actually belong to the *Overseer of Fields* under discussion (Ranke 1935:403.21). Interestingly, another stela belonging to a man with this name was also once housed in Odessa, though it is now lost (Berlev and Hodjash 1998:43). This Dedtu held the title of *Great-One of the Tens of Upper Egypt*, precisely the same title both Burekhef and Hekenu held. Berlev and Hodjash dated the stela to the late 13th Dynasty, though they only had a secondary drawing to consult. The sole family member mentioned on the stela who is directly related to its owner is *his beloved brother Aurisu (ꜣw-rꜣsw), true of voice*, (Berlev and Hodjash 1998:43). Though this man does not appear on the stela of Burekhef (Cairo CG 20540), his epithet *true of voice* suggests that he had already died when the stela was created and may have been omitted from Burekhef's later stela.

Ultimately, there is not enough evidence preserved to make a definitive determination whether or not the two Dedtus of the Odessa stelae were the same person. However, it seems likely that the *Overseer of Fields* Dedtu held a lower position in the governmental hierarchy before the accession of Neferhotep I, holding firstly the title *Great-one of the Tens of Upper Egypt* like his father and grandfather before him. In the first few years of Neferhotep I's reign, Dedtu was appointed to the position of *Overseer of Fields*, by taking over the role from his father-in-law, Haankhef, who, concomitant with of the increased status of his son Neferhotep I in becoming pharaoh, moved into the upper levels of the administration of the Amun temple, becoming *God's Father of Amun*.

In terms of placing Dedtu into the chronology of the late Middle Kingdom and Second Intermediate Period, Grajetzki followed Franke in dating Dedtu generally to the 13th Dynasty (Franke 1984a: doss. 769; Grajetzki 2000:135). In attempting to make a closer determination based on the style of his stela Odessa 52970,[16] Berlev and Hodjash stated:

> [The stela's] dating to the period of Dyn. XIII follows from the fact of its having the scene of a worship of an idol, not found before Sobekhotep II on dated monuments (Leiden, 42), whereas the pair of eyes in the lunette is characteristic of Dyn. XIII. Moreover, the eyes without eyelashes can only be postulated for the second half

of Dyn. XIII, as well as the hands with libation vases, primarily extended by the ideograms of West and East, as in CG 20540, but stylistically the stelae bear unmistakable signs of the design which came into vogue in the times of the famous brother-kings Neferhotep I and Sobekhotep IV (Berlev and Hodjash 1998, 41).

Stela Cairo CG20540 cited in the quote above is that belonging to Burekhef, Dedtu's father, (Länge and Schafer 1908:158–161). Hence, based solely upon stylistic criteria, Dedtu and his family date to the middle of the 13th Dynasty.

Turning to other textual sources, it is possible to make an even closer determination. Franke was the first to notice that Dedtu's son, the *ꜣtw ꜥꜣ n nꜣwt*,[17] *Chief Administrator of the Town*, Neferhotep, appears in Papyrus Boulaq 18, as part of a group of officials attending the Festival of Montu (Franke 1984a: doss. 314). Franke dated P.Boulaq 18 to the reign of Sobekhotep II, but Ryholt's more recent analysis has singled out the three predecessors of Sobekhotep III—namely Kings Imyremeshaw, Antef V, and Seth—as the most likely candidates for the unnamed king alluded to in the documents (Ryholt 1997:243–245). As discussed above, since Dedtu was not the *Overseer of Fields* at the time P.Boulaq 18 was written, he must have held a lower position in the government at that time and was not at Thebes to take part in the festival. Given that Neferhotep was already active in the Theban bureaucracy in P.Boulaq 18, he was probably at least eighteen to twenty years old. Neferhotep would then have been born around the reign of Awibre Hor. Subtracting another twenty-plus years from this date places Dedtu's birthdate roughly in the opening years of the 13th Dynasty (during the reigns of Sobekhotep I or Sonebef). This theoretical lifespan would place Dedtu's sixtieth birthday during the reign of Neferhotep I. Consequently, Dedtu probably died either under Neferhotep I or perhaps lived into his seventies to see the accession of Sobekhotep IV.

MASTER OF THE OFFERING TABLES OF AMUN, IBIAU

One of the reused blocks from the tomb of Seneb-Kay, R7, extends our understanding of this 13th

Dynasty family yet further. Decorated in the same style as the Dedtu block, this limestone slab depicts the *Master of the Offering Tables of Amun, Ibiau*. This is the same Ibiau, son of Dedtu, who appears on stela Louvre C58 discussed above. Furthermore, the offering formula on R7 includes the statement that Ibiau was *engendered by the Overseer of Fields, Dedtu*, firmly stating Dedtu's paternity of Ibiau. Along with Ibiau, block R7 also depicts a kneeling adult female, labeled in the scene as the *ḫkrt-nswt-wᶜtt Nḫt.n.i, Sole Royal Ornament, Nekheteni*. As we have seen, the text on block R7 is silent as to Nekheteni's relation to Ibiau. Unlike the image of Abeteni who embraces her husband Dedtu on block R8, Nekheteni kneels in front of Ibiau, leaving her relationship ambiguous.

Women in very similar poses and positions appear on a handful of contemporary stelae from Abydos. On Louvre C18 (ANOC 52.3), for instance, the woman kneeling directly before Senwosret is said to be his sister (Simpson 1974: pl. 70). However, on the central slab of this same triptych, a woman with the same name and title is called his wife. Since the wife's name, Dita, is rare (Ranke 1935:400.27), there may be a parallel to Egyptian love poetry here which often refers to a beloved spouse or lover with the term *snt, sister*. The *Lady of the House*, Dita pictured in the two scenes with the distinctions of *ḥmt.f* as well as *snt.f* is actually the same woman.

The situation is slightly clearer on Hermitage 1063 and 1064 (ANOC 57.1–2), where the woman kneeling directly in front of the deceased and his offering table is labeled specifically as his wife (Simpson 1974: pl. 78).[18] Since none of the other sources listing Dedtu's family include a daughter by the name of Nekheteni, and by comparison to these two Abydene sources, it seems highly likely that Nekheteni was Ibiau's wife. Additionally, given her extremely rare, high-ranking title *ḫkrt-nswt-wᶜtt, Sole Royal Ornament*, the text may have omitted *his wife* in favor of a statement of her own social position. A similar situation exists with the stelae of Burekhef (Cairo CG20540) which lists his father Hekenu, but only gives his title and not the filiative statement, "his father." Dedtu even continues this tradition on his own stela Odessa 52970, where his father Burekhef's epigraph gives his title, but lacks the statement *his father*. Though some doubt may linger as to whether Nekheteni was Ibiau's wife or not, the other stelae belonging to this family regularly omit relationship statements that are otherwise commonplace on commemorative monuments.

This woman Nekheteni herself seems to have descended from a very high-ranking family centered at Thebes. Another 13th Dynasty stela (Cairo JE37507), which Georges Legrain discovered during his 1902 excavations within the Kushite Chapel of Osiris, Neb-ankh, at Karnak, is the only other source known to include a woman named Nekheteni with the title of *Royal Ornament*.[19] This woman's parents were the *ḫtmty-bity ḥm-nṯr-n-ʾImn Snb.f, ms-nswt*,[20] the *Royal Seal-bearer, Priest of Amun, Senebef, Born of the King*, and his wife, the *ḫkrt-nswt Sbk-rsw*,[21] *Royal Ornament, Sobekresu*. Bazin and el-Enany cite two other women named Nekheteni from the late Middle Kingdom, though neither one of them bore the title *Royal Ornament* (Bazin and el-Enany 2010:17–18). Consequently, there is a significant possibility that this is the same woman depicted on block R7 (Fig. 10.7).

Both the *Overseer of Fields, Dedtu*, and the *Priest of Amun, Senebef*, held the ranking title of *Royal Seal-bearer*, and, though Quirke did not include the holders of priestly titles in his discussion of bureaucracy during the late Middle Kingdom, the two men were probably of equivalent status.[22] If Ibiau's mother Hatshepsut was the sister of kings Neferhotep I and Sobekhotep IV, the marriage of Senebef's daughter to Ibiau would have increased his family's status.[23] Similarly to Dedtu, during the course of Nekheteni's life, her title was raised from *ḫkrt-nswt, Royal Ornament* (Cairo JE 37505), to *ḫkrt-nswt-wᶜtt, Sole Royal Ornament* (block R7). This elevated variant of the title is extremely rare during the 13th Dynasty and suggests that the uniting of these two elite families may have resulted in Nekheteni's increased status. This promotion also corroborates the hypothesis that Hatshepsut herself was directly related to the royal house of the period.

In addition to Dedtu's stela (Louvre C58) and block R7 from South Abydos, Ibiau is positively attested on only one other monument. During his excavations at Deir el-Bahri, Winlock found a statue base among a cluster of tombs belonging to late Middle Kingdom priests, overlooking the causeway of the Mentuhotep II temple (Winlock 1922:30–31; Porter and Moss 1964:654–655).[24] The statue depicted a seated official wearing sandals. The transition between the statue base and the front of the chair can be seen just above the eye hieroglyph in the filiation

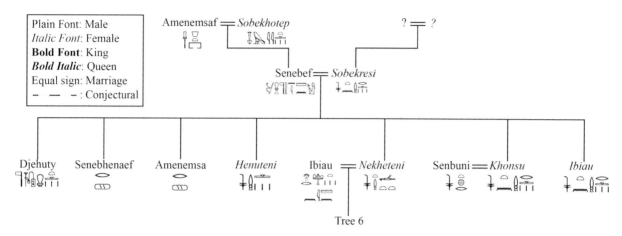

Fig. 10.7 **Tree 5**: Genealogy of Ibiau's wife Nekheteni (based primarily on Cairo JE 37507).

statement of the left text column. The text begins at the right, although the first title is broken away. The epigraph begins with a fairly clear *ḥm[////] n 'Imn.* Traces of two vertical signs to the right of the *ḥm* are the remains of a *nṯr* sign and vertical stroke, thus writing the title *ḥm-[nṯr]-n-'Imn.* During the 13th Dynasty, there was only one *Priest of Amun* at any one time, who was the highest-ranking individual connected with the temple (Bazin and el-Enany 2010:1–23; Il-in-Tomich 2015:124–125). Ibiau's wife Nekheteni was the daughter of just such a man, who also held the ranking title *ḥtmty-bity.* The layout of the statue base allows for the perfect amount of space before the title Priest of Amun for the reconstruction of *ḥtmty-bity* (Fig. 10.8).

Below the Amun group is a clear *ḥtp* with phonetic complements. Porter and Moss misunderstood the name Amun as belonging with the *ḥtp,* yielding the name Amunhotep. Since the name Amun as used here is actually part of the priestly title, we are left with an incomplete personal name. Numerous names end with the element *-ḥtp* but given the extremely tight spacing of the text at the edge of the statue base use of the name Neferhotep here seems the most likely.[25] The left column of text continues with the name of the statue owner's father. The entire text then reads: *[ḥtmty-bity] ḥm-[nṯr]-n-'Imn [Nfr]ḥtp, ir.n ḥry-ḥȝwt-n-'Imn 'Ib-iˁw, [Royal Seal-bearer, Pr]iest of Amun, [Nefer]hotep, engendered of the Master of the Offering Tables of Amun, Ibiau.*

Juxtaposed with the fine quality of the carving seen in the statue's sandal-clad feet, the text appears somewhat poorly executed.[26] The sign-forms are crude, though attributes of the text such as the three triangles on top of the offering table (Gardiner sign R1) and the wide ears on the *ḥr* sign are identical to the same signs appearing on the reused blocks at South Abydos, especially R4 and R7. Yet, one of the most glaring issues can be seen in the way Ibiau's name was written. The signs of the entire text are read from right to left in columns. At the bottom of the left column, the scribe was only able to fit the *Ib*-element of Ibiau's name before reaching the front edge of the base. He continued to write the name to the right with the reed leaf, followed by the human arm over the water sign. Even though the name is now meant to be read from left to right, he retained the orientation of the signs from right to left to match the rest of the statue. The name is spelled correctly and matches the orthography of Ibiau's name on the two other monuments mentioned above, but due to a lack of space, the name is essentially written in retrograde. This may indicate that the statue was purchased prefabricated or usurped from an earlier monument and then hastily inscribed by an artist whose skills were inferior to those who had created the statue in the first place.

This statue base demonstrates that Ibiau probably held the office of *Master of the Offering Tables of Amun* throughout his career. However, perhaps more importantly, it corroborates that Nekheteni was almost certainly his wife, since the title of Priest of Amun was passed down from Nekheteni's father Senebef, to Ibiau's son Neferhotep. Having married into the family, Ibiau may have been skipped over for this promotion, in favor of his son who was a

Fig. 10.8 MMA photo M8C 413 and line drawing with reconstruction, showing a statue base from Deir el-Bahri with the name of the *[Royal Sealer, Pr]iest of Amun, [Nefer]hotep, son of the Master of the Offering Tables of Amun,* Ibiau (photo courtesy of the Metropolitan Museum of Art, Department of Egyptian Art Archives).

blood-descendent of the previous Priest of Amun, Senebef. Nothing else is known about Ibiau's son, Neferhotep, other than the possibility that he was buried in the small group of 13th Dynasty tombs discovered at Deir el-Bahri and excavated by the Metropolitan Museum of Art (Winlock 1922:30–31).

As we have discussed above, the reused limestone blocks in Seneb-Kay's burial chamber all derived from a single 13th Dynasty funerary chapel or from a group of closely related chapels. This allows us to explore Ibiau and Nekheteni's other probable children (Fig. 10.9). Since it may show an image of Ibiau, the most instructive source to begin with is R4. This block shows the deceased on the left, his son on the right as signaled by the *in s3.f* formula: the son being the one *who makes his name live.* There is a secondary diminutive figure in front of the deceased whose name and probable filiation were originally written in a smaller label in front of his face, but which is now too damaged to read. It was argued elsewhere that the deceased individual on block R4 may represent Nekheteni's father Senebef (Cahail 2015:106–109), whose name is made to live by a son named Montu. Secondary collation of the texts on the block has shown that these readings were incorrect. While the label that identified the primary figure at the left was located beyond the preserved block (R4), the man on

the right who makes his name live is the *Master of the Offering Tables of Amun, (another title), Scribe of the (?), Senebef, Possessor of Honor.*

Assuming that these blocks all derive from the same chapel, the identity of the man on the left of block R4 is potentially either Dedtu or Ibiau. Certain circumstantial evidence leads to the probable conclusion that the man pictured at the left is Ibiau. Firstly, he is shown with a shaved head, like his son Senebef at the right. Dedtu has a long wig on both of his stelae as well as on block R7, while Ibiau's depiction on block R8 has the same bald head as that on block R4.

Secondly, though the name Senebef is fairly common during this period, Ibiau's wife Nekheteni's father was named Senebef. As we have already seen above, Dedtu named one of his sons after his father, and another after his probable father-in-law. The same naming conventions would therefore apply here, with Ibiau's son Senebef being named after his maternal grandfather, and his son Neferhotep being named for Ibiau's brother.

Thirdly, Senebef's primary title is exactly the same as that belonging to Ibiau, leading to the conclusion that his son may have taken over his role in the Amun temple at Karnak. Finally, the names of Dedtu's children by Hatshepsut are known from his

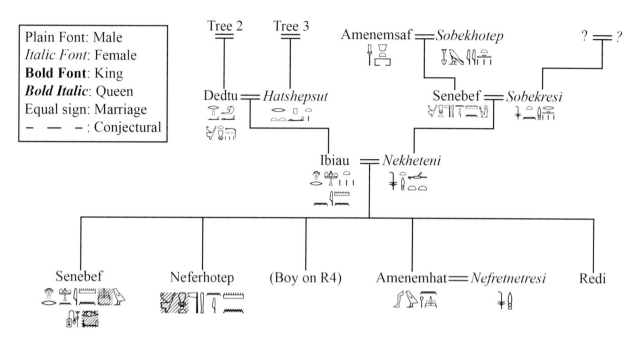

Fig. 10.9 **Tree 6**: Genealogy of Ibiau and Nekheteni's children, based on the reused chapel blocks and the statue base MMA M8C 413.

other stelae, and they do not include a son named Senebef—the man who makes the deceased's name live on block R4. Therefore, it is unlikely that Senebef is one of Dedtu's sons, but quite plausible that block R4 depicts Ibiau at the left and his son Senebef at the right. The small boy in front of Ibiau may be another of his sons, who perhaps died young. This may be the same young boy depicted with the tomb owner in the harvest scene on block R3.

Still working under the assumption that all the reused blocks derive from the same chapel, block R1 records other individuals probably belonging to Ibiau's family. The kneeling man in the center register who is named *his beloved son Redi* does not hold a title, making it virtually impossible to identify him in other sources. Ranke only lists one attestation for the bare name Redi (Ranke 1935:227.30). Therefore, the name may have been a shortened theophoric name such as Rediamun or Rediptah.

Below this man is the *Scribe of the Temple of Montu at Medamud*, Montuhotep. This man lacks a definite statement of filiation, so we cannot be sure if he was Ibiau's son.[27] If nothing else, his appearance on the block, coupled with his title, serve to link the Ibiau family with the Theban area even more strongly. Montuhotep's specific title also does not appear in

Ward's index of administrative titles, nor does Fisher include it in his supplement, as such, the identity of this man must also remain speculative until further evidence comes to light.

The final man appearing in the top register of block R1 is called *[His s]on the Superintendent of the Ruler's Crew*, Amenemhat. Following the arguments presented above, we may conclude that this is another son of Ibiau, rather than the offspring of Dedtu. Intriguingly, in his 1911–12 excavations in the North Cemetery at Abydos Peet found 13th Dynasty coffin fragments belonging to a *Superintendent of the Ruler's Crew*, Amenemhat (Peet 1914: 66, 122–123 and figs 88–89). For a variety of reasons, it is extremely likely that this is the same man listed among the kneeling family members on reused block R1. Furthermore, the existence of a rectangular wooden sarcophagus argues strongly that we are dealing with actual burials in the area, associated with the chapel blocks, rather than the building being a *mahat* without burials. We will elaborate on this individual more fully in the next section.

Having analyzed the monuments naming Ibiau, the question remains where to place his life and career within the regnal history of the 13th Dynasty. As with Dedtu, the dating of Ibiau relies heavily on the

P.Boulaq 18 correspondence with his brother Nefer-hotep. Assuming that the graphical arrangement of the children on Dedtu's stela Louvre C58 represents their birth order, Ibiau was probably a year or two older than his brother Neferhotep. Consequently, he may have been born around the reigns of Sobekho-tep II or Awibre Hor. He would have celebrated his sixtieth birthday during the reign of Sobekhotep VI. He may have died during that reign or during the succeeding reign of his namesake: King Wahibre Ib-iau. What emerges as being of crucial interest here is the strong possibility that Ibiau, and other members of his family were buried at Abydos, a geographical choice that may be reflective of the family's close personal connections with Kings Neferhotep I and Sobekhotep IV who appear to have chosen Abydos for their funerary complexes.

THE BURIALS OF IBIAU AND HIS FAMILY AT NORTH ABYDOS

In the same area that Peet discovered the frag-ments of Amenemhat's sarcophagus, he also found the fragments of another identical sarcophagus, orig-inally inscribed for the *Royal Ornament,* Nefretne-tresi.[28] Both sarcophagi were reused later, and that of Nefretnetresi was actually reinscribed in ink, some-what hastily, by the *Superintendent of the Ruler's Crew,* Sobekhotep (Peet 1914: 61, 123 and pls. 13 and 36). These sarcophagi are also discussed further in Chap-ter 14, but the information on block R1 allows us to demonstrate that Amenemhat was Ibiau's son.

The two sarcophagi of Amenemhat and Nefret-netresi are identical in decoration and textual pro-grams, down to the minutiae of how individual sign forms were created and decorated. They are so simi-lar that they were almost certainly made by the same artist. This situation leads to the conclusion that Amenemhat and Nefretnetresi were probably closely related, having purchased their burial assemblages at the same time from the same workshop. In all likeli-hood, these two individuals were husband and wife originally buried in the same tomb at North Abydos.[29] Therefore, both Amenemhat and Nefretnetresi and their sarcophagi, date to the mid- to late 13th Dynasty, with a rough date of death around 1680 BCE, during the reign of Merneferre Ay or slightly later.

The findspot of Amenemhat and Nefretnetresi's sarcophagi in the North Cemetery of Abydos lay on a hill at the south end of the cemetery overlooking the processional way to Umm el-Qa'ab. The archaeolog-ical evidence, while fragmentary, indicates this area has a pronounced concentration of late 13th Dynasty activity. Other 13th Dynasty sarcophagi were found in the area, most notably that of a woman holding the rare title of *smȝyt Ḥr* (Grajetzki 2010a). This is the same title held by Nekheteni's paternal grand-mother, and though the name of the owner of this sarcophagus is lacking, it is tempting to see it as be-ing connected to the family. Additionally, during the excavation season of 1899–1900, Arthur Mace dis-covered a tomb lying within this same portion of the North Cemetery, which he called Cemetery D. Mace's Tomb D62 contained an offering table and an ebony offering tray belonging to a *Royal Sealer, Officer of the Ruler's Crew,* Iyemiatuib (Randall-MacIver and Mace 1902:85, 100, and pl. XXXIV; D'Auria et al. 1988:129–130; Franke 1984a: doss. 23).

A number of years later in virtually the same area of the North Cemetery, John Garstang discovered another limestone object naming the *Royal Sealer, Leader of the Broad Hall,* Khonsu son of Iyemiatuib, and the *Royal Ornament,* Id (Grajetzki 2010a:8–9).[30] The same Iyemiatuib also appears on a stela from el-Mahasna, now in Würtzburg, which belonged to a relation of Queen Aya, who is named on the document (Ryholt 1997:245). This queen is the same woman mentioned in P.Boulaq 18, who was married to one of the three kings preceding Sobekhotep III.[31] Both Iyemiatuib and his son Khonsu held the ranking title *ḫtmty-bỉty,* and Khonsu's mother was a *Royal Orna-ment.* These are the same titles held by Ibiau's family members, and based on correspondences in P.Boulaq 18, Iyemiatuib was a contemporary of Dedtu's sons Neferhotep and Ibiau. The tombs of Iyemiatuib and Khonsu demonstrate that high ranking members of the governmental bureaucracy, who lived at exactly the same time as Dedtu's sons, chose to be buried in this part of the North Cemetery at Abydos.

Additionally, Randall-MacIver and Mace discov-ered a well-known boundary stela set up by Nefer-hotep I in the exact same area (Randall-MacIver and Mace 1902:93–94, pl. XXIX). Though usurped, the text is dated to Year 4 of Neferhotep I and comes from the southern extension of the North Cemetery (Mace Cemetery D), overlooking the processional way to

Umm el-Qa'ab. The very existence of this stela, demarcating the land available for new tombs corroborates that there was renewed interest in creating burials within this area during the mid-13th Dynasty. Neferhotep I and his brother Sobekhotep IV themselves were probably buried at South Abydos in tombs S9 and S10, also demonstrating enhanced royal and elite 13th Dynasty interest in Abydos during this period (Wegner and Cahail 2015). Both Ibiau and his contemporary Iyemiatuib and their families chose to be buried in this area of the North Cemetery, in an area designated by Neferhotep I for just such a purpose.

In addition to the funerary objects just discussed, Henri Frankfort found evidence at Abydos of 13th Dynasty funerary chapels which had been disassembled and reused in later periods (Frankfort 1928: pl. XXII, no. 4). While fragmentary, this evidence provides crucial corroboration of the reused chapel blocks commemorating Ibiau and Dedtu. One block shows a large-scale seated figure of the deceased drawn in virtually the same style as the images of Ibiau and Dedtu (Fig. 10.10). Frankfort stated that the image was "engraved rather than carved," (Frankfort 1928:239), which is the same technique used on the reused 13th Dynasty chapel blocks from Seneb-Kay's burial chamber. Though fragmentary, the remaining pieces of the scene are roughly 70 cm tall and too large to have belonged to a normal stela. These pieces may derive from an inscribed portcullis stone like that of Khonsu, son of Iyemiatuib, or perhaps more likely since the names of other individuals appear in the column of text at the right, once formed part of a chapel wall depicting the deceased being attended by smaller figures facing him. Lines of text which appear to record an offering formula are placed above the deceased, who faces right. His name is missing, though the name of his mother seems to terminate the line of text above his head. The scale and style of this piece argues for its origin in a tomb chapel contemporary to that of Ibiau, adducing more evidence for a mid- to late 13th Dynasty court cemetery at North Abydos.[32]

In short, it appears now that the royal burial place was transferred from *Itj-tawy* to Abydos under Neferhotep I. Reflecting an interest in connecting himself with Senwosret III, Neferhotep I constructed his tomb at South Abydos, adapting architectural elements of the earlier 13th Dynasty Memphite royal pyramids to a tomb built beside that of Senwosret III. We have indications that Neferhotep I's brief-reigning successor, Sahathor, may have initiated an abandoned complex adjacent to that of his brother (Wegner 2019). More significantly, Neferhotep I's program at Abydos was sustained during the reign of his brother, Sobekhotep IV, with the addition of his own funerary complex at South Abydos. Perhaps this choice of burial location signals the watershed moment where the 13th Dynasty, building upon the Theban origins of the family of Neferhotep I and Sobekhotep IV promoted a southward shift in the dynasty, even while *Itj-Tawy* continued to function as the primary royal residence. This move may have responded in part to the expanding territorial influence of the early Hyksos rulers, or their 14th Dynasty forerunners in the Delta. In light of the recent suggestion that the reigns of Neferhotep I and Sobekhotep IV were contemporary with the early Hyksos Period, we may see here the seeds of a territorial and administrative restructuring of the 13th Dynasty that ultimately expressed itself in a progressive subdivision of Upper Egypt from *Itj-Tawy*, resulting in the contemporaneous late 13th, 16th, and "Abydos" Dynasties.[33] Accompanying this shift in royal burial location, a court cemetery was developed in what has become known as Mace Cemetery D, serving as the burial place for many of the high officials serving under the brother kings, including that of Ibiau and his family. The boundary stela of Neferhotep I—generally viewed in broad terms as a royal proclamation preventing encroachment on the processional route of Osiris—may be fundamentally connected to these changes in royal and elite funerary activities. The very location and content of the stela may reflect the inception of a growing cemetery of royal court officials at the southern end of the North Cemetery, overlooking Umm el-Qa'ab and notionally linked to the burial locale of Neferhotep I and Sobekhotep IV at South Abydos.

In this historical context, and despite their Theban origins, key members of the family of Dedtu and Ibiau chose to be buried within this newly emerging cemetery area at North Abydos. Their interconnections with the royal family not only superseded any desire they may have had to be buried locally at Thebes, but it also allowed them access to this cemetery, and to high quality building materials like the fine-grained white limestone used to build their tomb chapels. The visible statement of 13th Dynasty royal power inherent in the tomb superstructures of Ibiau and his family may have been the main contributing factor to the downfall

Fig. 10.10 13th Dynasty chapel block found by Frankfort at North Abydos, now in the Chadwick Museum in Bolton (after Frankfort 1928: pl. XXII.4).

of the prime motivating factors for the creation of funerary chapels. Continued commemoration was seen as the most reliable way to assure a comfortable existence in the afterlife, resplendent with a multitude of comestible offerings. Images and offering spells in the tomb chapels—meant to be visited and interacted with by the living—served to propitiate the continued existence of the deceased in the netherworld. While the Egyptians may have recognized that, practically speaking, the eventual disappearance of tomb chapels from the landscape was inevitable, the hope was that this would not happen for an extremely long time. In the interval, the offerings and praise the deceased would have gained thorough the living interacting with their cult locations would increase their standing in the underworld. Conversely, the rapid removal or destruction of tomb images following the death of an individual was a powerful way of attacking them in the afterlife and censoring their ability to exist therein through a form of second death (*mwt m whm*, which could be assisted by magical rites of destruction, [Bochi 1999:73–86]). If such actions were combined with the actual destruction of their bodies, their very existence in the afterlife would have been in jeopardy.

By definition, a *damnatio memoriae* properly is the deliberate and complete erasure of an individual from history with the goal that later generations would have no idea that they had ever existed. In his useful discussion of patterns of *damnatio memoriae* in the Valley of the Kings, R. Wilkinson also highlights another type of attack which he terms "selective *damnatio*" (Wilkinson 2016:335). He uses the example of the attacks against Hatshepsut that targeted her pharaonic images, but not those which portrayed her as queen. In this case, it was not her eternal soul the attackers wished to destroy, but rather the claims to royal power, which she had made during her life. Wilkinson also highlights various types of monumental usurpation that resulted in the removal of the original owner's

of these monuments. Before moving on to consider possible motivations behind the *damnatio memoriae*, we must now turn to the details of the attack against their identity which forms such a prevalent feature of the blocks commemorating Ibiau and Dedtu.

DAMNATIO MEMORIAE ON THE REUSED BLOCKS

To the ancient Egyptian mind, having your name and image remembered by later generations was one

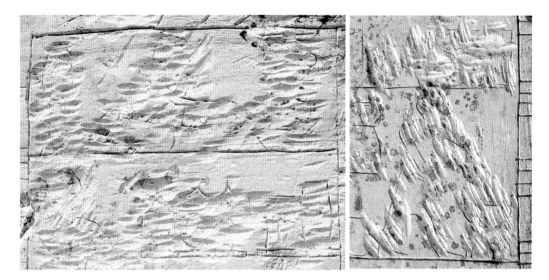

Fig. 10.11 Detail of the damage patterns on block R11 (left) and R12 (right). These marks were made with a narrow, round-nosed chisel.

names. However, since this type of destruction is not designed to remove an individual's memory but is merely the opportunistic theft of an earlier monument, this form of damage cannot strictly be called *damnatio*. With these issues in mind, let us turn to examine the specific patterns of damage on the reused 13th Dynasty chapel blocks with a view to elucidating the nature of the attack on Ibiau and Dedtu.

One crucial point to be made is that because the chisel marks cross over block joints on Wall A, we can state that the damage was directed against the building while it was still standing. The orientation and patterning of the chisel marks provide insights into the mechanics of the *damnatio*. The chisel marks suggest the primary use of two differently shaped chisels to affect the damage. One of these was a narrow chisel with a slightly rounded tip (Fig. 10.11). The individual wielding this tool appears to have been left-handed, as evidenced by the fact that the rounded-tip chisel marks predominately slant from the upper left to the lower right. In some areas the same chisel was wielded to cut horizontally, again from left to right. This damage appears to be formed by a left-handed individual holding the chisel in his right hand, while striking it with a mallet in his left.

Another set of gashes were produced by a slightly wider chisel with a square end. These chisel marks typically slant in the opposite direction from those made by the rounded chisel (Fig. 10.12, Block R4). The wider chisel appears to have been primarily wielded by a right-handed individual. The damage patterns on Wall A suggest two men working side by side to deface the decoration, although a lesser volume of marks made by a smaller chisel that also belong to a right-handed man can also be observed, likely indicating that a third individual was employed in the work. Clearly, given the rough nature of their work, a small group of men could have rapidly executed the task of defacing the chapel.

More significantly, based on the chisel patterns it appears these men were given very specific instructions. They were not told simply to target the images of the deceased. Rather, they were tasked with removing the ability for the deceased individuals to exist, eat, and breathe in the afterlife (cf. Wilkinson 2011:136). In order to accomplish this, the arms and legs of the dead were specifically targeted, rendering them incapable of eating and drinking by themselves. Ibiau and Dedtu's faces were also damaged, both to make their images unrecognizable, but also to hinder their ability to eat, drink, and breathe. Furthermore, a single chisel stroke to the heart of the figures appears intended to ritually kill them in the afterlife by destroying the seat of their soul.[34]

Images of the chapel owner and his direct family were obvious targets of the *damnatio*. Block R4, likely depicting Ibiau and his two sons, displays the most complete destruction. The chisel marks on this

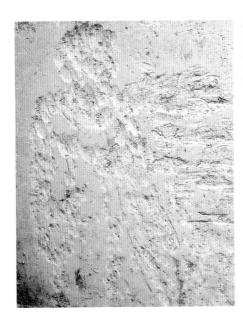

Fig. 10.12 Detail of the *damnatio* on block R4 (left), created by a wider, flat-tipped chisel; and R1 (right) created with a narrower chisel. These images illustrate the extent to which the physical identity of the figures was targeted.

block angle downward to the right and belong to the left-handed man. On the scene's left side, the outline of the primary figure was almost totally obliterated, essentially erasing him from history. The workman followed the outline of the figure, leaving the undecorated surface of the man's body intact, except for a large hole above his heart. To the right of this figure, it appears a different worker removed the central text and the image of Senebef at the right in a less complete way, using a different chisel driven in almost horizontal strokes. Damage to his chest near his heart is less severe than that on the deceased at the left, but his hands and face were almost totally removed. The same chisel was used to remove the image of the smaller boy at the bottom of the scene.

The depiction of Ibiau on block R7 was damaged in a visually subtle way, perhaps reflecting the less accessible architectural context of this block inside a statue recess (Fig. 10.13), but still indicating a desire to erase the man's physical existence. The text of the offering spell was left mostly intact, with only one chisel mark near Ibiau's name. However, two other gashes almost totally remove the first signs of Dedtu's name and his title which occur in Ibiau's filiation. Further hints of the thought process behind the *damnatio* can be gleaned from block R7. Both the eye and nose of Ibiau on this block were entirely hacked out.

There is a single chisel mark on his lower left chest, almost certainly meant to coincide with his heart. While the rest of his torso was left intact, his forearms were almost entirely cut out with the intention of precluding him from being able to raise any food or drink to his face. Furthermore, his calves are intact, but his knees, shins and feet have been targeted. Finally, the legs of his animal-paw chair were cut through by the left-handed worker. In the afterlife, Ibiau would have fallen to the ground on his broken chair, would be unable to see or speak, and would be unable to get up or find help without arms or legs. Finally, denied a heart he would have ceased to exist in the netherworld altogether. At the same time, Ibiau's wife Nekheteni also had her ear, nose, and mouth cut out, and her arms and legs were similarly sliced off. In short, the apparent goal of the *damnatio* carried out on these images was to effectively destroy the eternal souls of Ibiau and Nekheteni.

Similar damage patterns occur on block R8, depicting Dedtu and his second wife, Abeteni (Fig. 10.14). While in this case his nose and mouth appear mostly intact, Dedtu's eye has been totally removed. His right arm, left shoulder, left hand, and feet have also been chiseled in the same way as those of Ibiau. Also, the front leg of his chair has been cut, as has the base of his offering table. On the other hand, his

head was almost totally erased by the left-handed workman. Extensive damage was done to his upper arms, with the chisel gashes extending over the location of his heart at the left side of his chest. Additional gashes cut across his lap, rendering him incapable of standing up. In the register below, the deceased's son, Redi, displays minor damage to his head and right shoulder but large chisel marks directly over his heart made by the same left-handed worker. By contrast, the head of the man named Montuhotep in the lower register is mostly intact, with only minor scratches running across his name and titles.

On blocks R5 and R6, the head, arms, and legs of the unnamed kneeling figures were generally attacked, but it does not appear as though their hearts were specifically targeted as occurs with the primary figures. By contrast, the images of the unnamed individuals involved in production scenes on blocks R3, R9, R11, and R12 were almost totally removed. Here, the intention does not seem to have been to attack particular elements of the anatomy of the individual as is seen with the damage to Ibiau and Dedtu. Rather, the idea was to obliterate the agricultural workers whose symbolic role was to produce goods for the deceased. Here again, it is the ability for the deceased to eat and drink in the afterlife that was being attacked. Unlike "selective *damnatio*" or usurpation, the attempt to obliterate the eternal existence of Ibiau's family argues in favor of understanding this pattern of destruction as a full *damnatio memoriae* representing some form of politically motivated or personal attack. A close reading of the patterns of damage appearing on the reused blocks betrays the nuances of the *damnatio*. Yet the specifics of how this *damnatio* was carried out says nothing about why it was done. In many ways, this is the more interesting topic. Who attacked these 13th Dynasty scenes and texts with such an obvious degree of animosity?

wife Abeteni's outline was left intact. Her position on block R8 would have been at the interior end of the statue recess to which this block belonged and would have been relatively less visible and accessible. Nevertheless, an area of chiseling in the middle of her torso exists, showing that even in this less easily reachable location her image attracted damage, again likely meant to remove her heart.

The images of other named individuals related to the deceased tomb owner were also attacked. On block R1, Amenemhat in the top register received almost exactly the same treatment as the figure of Ibiau on block R7. Amenemhat's name and titles were damaged, but not so completely as to be rendered unreadable. His

Fig. 10.14 Detail of Dedtu and Abeteni from block R7. Dedtu's eye, shoulder and forearm have been damaged, and Abeteni has a series of chisel marks over her heart.

MOTIVATIONS FOR THE DAMNATIO MEMORIAE

One possibility to consider is that the *damnatio* preserved on the chapel blocks of Dedtu and Ibiau is part of a site-wide phenomenon directed more broadly to chapels and tombs of the middle 13th Dynasty at Abydos. The evidence supplied by numerous contemporary monuments argues against this interpretation. For instance, the offering table and portcullis slab of the contemporary Iyemiutib and Khonsu family, as well as the wall slab discovered by Frankfort (Fig. 10.10), show absolutely no signs of a *damnatio*. Indeed, among the sizeable 13th Dynasty corpus of funerary stelae from Abydos, there is nothing remotely comparable to the attack on the reused blocks from CS9. Such a situation leads to the inescapable conclusion that family of Dedtu and Ibiau was singled out and specifically targeted. Given the relatively short period of time between their burials in the mid- to late 13th Dynasty and Seneb-Kay's reuse of their tomb blocks approximately a century later, the *damnatio* itself almost certainly transpired within the historical and political context that accompanied the final stages of the 13th Dynasty.

Lacking fuller biographical evidence for the lives of Dedtu and Ibiau, it is impossible to ascertain whether or not they committed personal acts or were engaged with political actors that might have elicited such a *damnatio*. Both father and son were firmly rooted in the bureaucracy of the 13th Dynasty. Dedtu was a high-ranking official of the outer palace with seemingly no religious duties. Ibiau and his sons Senebef and Neferhotep on the other hand all belonged to the upper strata of the temple of Amun at Karnak. Ibiau's wife was the daughter of the *Priest of Amun*, Senebef, who may have been distantly related to a previous royal family by virtue of his epithet *ms-nswt*.[35] Finally, another of Ibiau's sons, Amenemhat, was a military commander during the late 13th Dynasty.

Given the Abydene location of the tomb chapel, we may also entertain the possibility that the *damnatio* might have been rooted in some way in the family's dual Theban and 13th Dynasty connections. Concomitant with the final stages of the 13th Dynasty, we have indications for the breakaway of Upper Egypt forming the independent 16th Dynasty. It was within this broader political context that the "Abydos Dynasty" of which Seneb-Kay appears to have been a member may have arisen. It is certainly viable that political friction may have arisen in this era of territorial change and animosities may have been directed against prominent families with Theban and/or 13th Dynasty associations. The timeframe for such a *damnatio* may fall in the reign of Merneferre Ay (ca. 1701–1677 BCE) or slightly later—perhaps a half a century or two to three generations before the reign of Seneb-Kay. However, this does not explain the lack of *damnatio* on other 13th Dynasty monuments at North Abydos.

Let us return to the fact that the targeted nature of the *damnatio* argues in favor of the possibility that Ibiau and his lineage were the specific focal point. Ibiau's mother was an *iryt-pꜥt*, which based on the sources we have discussed above, probably identifies her as the sister of Kings Neferhotep I and Sobekhotep IV. Consequently, Ibiau was a blood nephew of these kings, which potentially could have afforded him and his offspring a remote claim to the throne in the period after the death of Sobekhotep IV. Ibiau himself may have wielded considerable power, being the son of the *Overseer of Fields*, the son-in-law of the *Priest of Amun* at Karnak, related by blood to the royal family, and father of influential men in both the Amun establishment, as well as the central government. One possible explanation of the *damnatio* is that Ibiau's position was elevated later in his lifetime, a promotion in status that might have been accompanied by his son Senebef succeeding him at Karnak as *Master of the Offering Tables of Amun*. There are three possibilities open if we follow this line of reasoning, although each is hampered by its own set of complications, compounded by the fact that the personal name Ibiau was relatively frequent during the mid- to late 13th Dynasty.

There was an *Overseer of Fields* named Ibiau, the same title held by Dedtu, who can be dated to this time period. A remote possibility might be that Ibiau ascended to his father's administrative office. Since the only attestation of this man comes from a fragmentary black-background sarcophagus found at Thebes, this individual does not seem to fit the evidence for an Abydene burial for Ibiau (Grajetzki 2000:136). Winlock understood the text on the Theban fragment to refer to the coffin owner, precluding this Ibiau from having been buried in connection with his Abydene tomb chapel. However, since the sarcophagus was highly fragmentary, it is possible

that Winlock misunderstood the text, and it referred rather to one of Ibiau's family members who was buried at Thebes. In any case, since Ibiau is still called the *Master of Offering Tables of Amun* on his son's statue base, it does not seem likely that Ibiau became an *Overseer of Fields* like his father.

Another potential scenario that may explain an elevated status of Ibiau at the end of his life is his promotion to become the Vizier Ibiau known from this period. Although the names of the Vizier Ibiau's parents are also unknown, one problem with this attribution is that his monuments do list two different wives, neither of which is Nekheteni (Franke 1984b: doss. 64). However, among other 13th Dynasty high officials, Ibiau's father Dedtu had at least two wives during his life, downplaying this caveat. Perhaps significantly, the Vizier Ibiau had a son named Senebhenaef. Although the name was somewhat common at the time, Ibiau's wife Nekheteni had a brother who had the honorific title *iry-Nḫn, One relating to Nekhen*, named Senebhenaef, who could conceivably have been the namesake of the Vizier Ibiau's son. This Senebhenaef began his career as the *Overseer of Fields*, before becoming the *ḥrp-wsḫt, Controller of the Broad Hall* (Grajetzki 2000:135–136). The title of *Overseer of Fields* would therefore have stayed in the same family for generations, especially if we theorize that the *Overseer of Fields*, Haankhef, was Dedtu's father-in-law. The main issue here is that Ibiau's only title on the reused blocks is *Master of the Offering Tables of Amun*. The Vizier Ibiau originally held the title *imy-r ḫnrt, Overseer of the Enclosure* (Ryholt 1997:259). Consequently, since his chapel decoration at Abydos is only known to include the title of *Master of Offering Tables of Amun*, we have little concrete evidence to argue that Dedtu's son Ibiau became Vizier.

Finally, identifying Ibiau with the 13th Dynasty king Wahibre Ibiau is also a remote possibility. Being a prominent member of an elite family with members at the highest levels of civil administration and his long career in the highest ranks of the Amun establishment could potentially have made Ibiau a viable candidate to take power after the short-reigning kings Sobekhotep V and VI. None of the family members of this king are known, leaving open the possibility that Dedtu's son Ibiau became king at the very end of his life, though his burial location remains a mystery. The last two possibilities preclude the idea that Ibiau was actually buried in his Abydene tomb.

In this case, the 13th Dynasty white-ground sarcophagus which Seneb-Kay appears to have usurped (see Chapter 4) may have belonged to Dedtu, or if it was Ibiau's, it had been installed during construction of the tomb, but was never used. Returning to the notion that Ibiau held the title of *Master of the Offering Tables of Amun* throughout his life and was buried in a tomb connected with his chapel at North Abydos, there is another, perhaps more likely explanation for the intensity of the *damnatio*.

Existing discussion of the scant evidence for the successors of Sobekhotep IV suggests there were major shifts in the alliances of elite families and ruling kings during the final stages of the 13th Dynasty. Sobekhotep IV's successor was probably Merhotepre Sobekhotep V, whose father was not a king (Ryholt 1997:231–232). However, his throne name and use of genealogical seals links him ideologically with Sobekhotep III, Neferhotep I, and Sobekhotep IV. Through the reign of Wahibre Ibiau, it would seem that the high offices remained stable within the same families, perhaps indicating that the royal succession was intertwined with the families of these high officials. With the accession of Merneferre Ay and his son Merhotepre Ini, there seems to have been a change not only in royal family, but also in the elite lineages occupying the highest- ranking offices (Ryholt 1997:233). The events and genealogies surrounding the governors of el-Kab show that the office of vizier passed from the family of Vizier Ibiau and his son Vizier Senebhenaef, to Ay, the Governor of el-Kab, in Year 1 of Merhotepre Ini.

Furthermore, despite the substantial ten-year reign of Wahibre Ibiau, and the nearly twenty-four-year reign of Merneferre Ay, there is no evidence at Abydos that they attempted to follow their predecessors Neferhotep I and Sobekhotep IV, either with enhanced royal patronage of the Osiris cult, or in the continued construction of royal tombs at the site. This may simply be explained as part of the complex, and ever-shifting choices for location of the royal burial site. However, it very well may reflect the reality of a different array of ascendant elite families and political alliances that had no connections with the era of Neferhotep I, Sobekhotep IV, and their immediate successors. While Ibiau's relation to the family of Neferhotep I and Sobekhotep IV served him and his family well during their reigns, once a new royal family entered the palace, the status of Ibiau's lineage

almost certainly waned. Indeed, after the death of Sobekhotep IV, Ibiau, his brothers, and their children could all have been in a position to claim the kingship by virtue of their royal bloodline descended from the *ỉryt-pꜥt* Hatshepsut, sister of Neferhotep I and Sobekhotep IV. As such, they may have invited an unusually malicious *damnatio memoriae* that targeted their monuments at Abydos and elsewhere.

Without the discovery of further evidence, it may never be possible to understand the precise reasons behind the *damnatio*. However, the damage wrought upon these chapel blocks does seem intensely personal. If nothing else, the characteristics of the *damnatio* gives us a rare insight into Egyptian views of the afterlife during the 13th Dynasty. For whatever reasons Ibiau and his family elicited such an astonishing degree of hatred, this was not just an attack on their visible monuments, but an assault on their eternal existence. This was an attempt to extinguish the lineage of Dedtu and Ibiau. As such, we may reasonably conclude that not just Ibiau's aboveground chapel was attacked, but his burial and those of other members of his family may well have invited retribution. Assuming the burials themselves were not subject to complete destruction at the time of the *damnatio*, funerary materials that survived in good condition may have been open to reuse during an era when Upper Egypt was subject to increasing economic isolation. This raises the distinct possibility that when Seneb-Kay's tomb builders decided to reuse the 13th Dynasty chapel blocks they might have made use not only of surviving aboveground elements, but they may also have appropriated other undamaged elements of these elite 13th Dynasty tombs. Potentially this includes the white-ground outer sarcophagus which might have originated in the tomb of Ibiau or one of his family members buried at Abydos.

NOTES:

10.1 Hekenu is not specifically labeled on the stela as *ỉt.f, his father*, leading Andreu to omit him from his family tree (Andreu 1991:23). However, Burekhef is also not explicitly labeled as Dedtu's father on Odessa 52970. Given the identical titles and the place of honor Hekenu has on Burekhef's stela, it seems extremely likely that Hekenu was Burekhef's father.

10.2 There are two different spellings of this name (Ranke 1935:306, 4–5), one with the Sobek crocodile and the present instance, which is spelled out phonetically.

According to Ranke, Burekhef's stela is the only attestation of this phonetic spelling.

10.3 Burekhef's name is an early attestation of the Late Egyptian negative aorist (Cahail 2019).

10.4 Their conclusion is corroborated by the fact that the stela of Dedtu's father, Burekhef (Cairo CG20540, Franke 1984a: doss. 220), also derives from Abydos (Lange and Schäfer 1908:158–161).

10.5 Of the five children, four of them hold titles connected with either the military (Neferhotep), or various local security forces (Ilin-Tomich 2015:129–130). This may reflect the expeditionary role of the *wr mḏw Šmᶜw*, the title held by Burekhef and Hekenu (Quirke 2004:87). Ibiau is the only son who holds a religious title, but it is quite possible that the *Master of Offering Tables* was an official concerned with the supply of goods for the cult, as opposed to a strictly religious or priestly role.

10.6 Ibiau is the leftmost figure in the top register. Below him is the offering table associated with his mother Hatshepsut, placing Ibiau as the foremost of the children graphically.

10.7 This is a common naming practice which also occurs in the royally linked genealogies attested at el-Kab (Spalinger 1980:98, 105).

10.8 Block R11 contains an epigraph above the ploughing scene that employs two attestations of the Late Egyptian First Present verbal construction (*tw.ỉ ḥr sḏm*). It has been argued elsewhere that this epigraph reflects a residence sociolect or, in other words, the dialect spoken by the king and the royal family (Cahail 2019). This residence sociolect derives from a northern or Lower Egyptian dialect and would not be the normal way of speaking for a Theban family such as that of Dedtu. The use of this dialectical feature may also corroborate that Ibiau, the probable tomb owner, was a blood relation of the king.

10.9 Her death must have post-dated the accession of Neferhotep I since she held the title *ỉryt-pᶜt* on Louvre C58. Again, no monument positively states that she died at this time, but the Louvre stela was dedicated to her funerary cult, and, since no other monument names her, it is safe to assume that she probable died early in the reign of Neferhotep I.

10.10 Apart from the two 13th Dynasty royal tombs attributable to Neferhotep I and Sobekhotep IV at South Abydos there is an abundance of inscriptional and monumental evidence from North Abydos reflecting the increase in royal patronage of Abydos under these two kings. The evidence includes the Neferhotep I stela from the Osiris temple (Pieper 1929; Helck 1983:21–29); the king's boundary stela excavated near Cemetery D (Randall-MacIver and Mace 1902: pl.29; Leahy 1989:41–60); and monumental remains in the Kom es-Sultan.

10.11 Marée has put forth the idea that the dateable stelae set up in the votive zone associate chronologically with known royal visits to the site, as well as otherwise attested royal building projects at the Osiris complex (Marée forthcoming). Dedtu's stelae may have been set up at the same time as these royal visits to the site to inspect the work on the temple.

10.12 Another possibility is that Dedtu had two wives concurrently. The genealogy on Louvre C13 corroborates high ranking officials having numerous wives. However, one problem with this notion is the question of why Dedtu is only pictured with Abeteni on block R7. Following our discussion in the previous chapter on the architectural reconstruction of this block, it is possible that Dedtu was pictured with his primary wife Hatshepsut on the opposing statue niche block. However, the evidence seems to support the early death of Hatshepsut.

10.13 Simpson included two stelae in ANOC 49: Cairo CG 20093 and Avignon-Calvet 3, though the connection with CG 20093 has been shown to be incorrect (Hein and Satzinger 1993:7, 106).

10.14 On this point, it is interesting to note that the only damage to the stela Vienna ÄS 180 is a neat hole directly where the title *Vizier* should be in Iuy's name. The remaining epigraph lists only his title of *Overseer of the City*, exactly like the text, which Winlock reported finding on his coffin. From the photograph, it is difficult to say if this damage was accidental or deliberate, but the possibility does exist that Iuy was demoted from the office of Vizier later in life, leading to the removal of this title from the stela.

10.15 Ilin-Tomich briefly discusses the office of *Overseer of Fields* and comes to the conclusion that up until the reign of Sobekhotep VII—the king whose reign he believes defines the end of the late Middle Kingdom—there were two *Overseer of Fields* at any given time (Ilin-Tomich 2015:125–126). Specifically, one for the north of the country, and another for the south, whose title was *ỉmy-r-ꜣḥwt n nỉwt rsỉ, Overseer of Fields of the Southern City*. Haankhef holds this title in P.Brooklyn 35.1446, which is possibly the only attestation of it in the corpus. Dedtu only has the base title *Overseer of Fields*, but since he and his family are inextricably tied to Thebes, it seems highly unlikely that he would have served as the northern *Overseer of Fields* concurrently with Haankhef, especially since his son Neferhotep actually appears in P.Boulaq 18. Consequently, despite the theory that there were two individuals with the title *Overseer of Fields* active at the same time, Dedtu was not one of them, but instead took up his Theban position after Haankhef vacated it. Furthermore, given the southern shift seen in the burial locations of Neferhotep I and Sobekhotep IV, it is not clear to what level the 13th Dynasty government had control over the north at this time.

10.16 Malaise also discusses the appearance of divinities on Middle Kingdom stelae (Malaise 1981:259–283).

10.17 Ward reads this title *wᶜrtw n nἰwt* (Ward 1982: title 698).

10.18 On another 13th Dynasty stela belonging to a man named Amenyseneb from Abydos, the woman in this position is named as the mother of the deceased (Garstang Museum of Archaeology, Liverpool, E30). Ibiau's mother is known to have been the noblewoman Hatshepsut, so Nekheteni cannot be his mother.

10.19 Legrain reported that the stela "a été trouvée in place, debout, contre la muraille," (Legrain 1902:213).

10.20 Senebef appears on the stela to have a second name or epithet which is spelled 𓏏𓏏𓏏𓏏, perhaps reading "Mesnesut." Mesnesut does not appear as a personal name, but according to WB, II:139.7, it is an epithet used to refer to princes. The phrase is also tied up with the idea of the Heb-sed (Kaiser 1983:261–296). Bazin and el-Enany read it as one name, Senebefmes, following Clère's suggestion that the seated king is an error for Gardiner Sign B3, used as a determinative for *ms*. However, there are also no comparanda for the name Senebefmes, and while the reading Mesnesut is somewhat provisional, it has the benefit of not requiring any emendation to the text of the stela.

10.21 The name is spelled *k-b-s*, leading Bazin and el-Enany to render it as Kebesres, with references to the possibility that it was meant to be read Sobekresu (Bazin and el-Enany 2010:13). We have read the name as Sobekresu.

10.22 Though this question is outside the scope of this work, it seems that the government at this time was divided into departments, each of which was controlled by an individual with the ranking title *Royal Sealer*. Theoretically, the head of the Amun temple at Karnak was of equal standing to the other governmental departments and either directly below the Vizier or, more probably, the king himself.

10.23 What is not entirely clear is whether Ibiau entered the priesthood at Karnak due to his father's governmental connections and later married the high priest's daughter, or if Ibiau began working at the temple because he had already married Nekheteni. The latter may be the case,

since Ibiau is the only one of Dedtu's children to enter the priesthood.

10.24 According to Porter and Moss, the statue base was inscribed for the *Head of the Altar of Amun, Ibiau, and Amenhotep* (Porter and Moss 1964:655). However, consulting the original photograph (MMA photo M8C 413, Fig. 9.8) shows that Porter and Moss misunderstood the text.

10.25 Ibiau and his wife may also have followed the naming practice exemplified by Dedtu and Hatshepsut. If so, this son Neferhotep would have been named after Ibiau's brother Neferhotep. As we discuss below, Ibiau also had a son named after his wife's father, Senebef.

10.26 Most statues depicting high officials of the 13th Dynasty are shown barefoot. This statue wears sandals, and, on the stela of the *Priest of Amun*, Senebef (Cairo JE 37507), he is the only one of sixteen figures wearing sandals. He also wears a leopard skin shawl, which the statue probably also originally had. The fact that the statue is wearing sandals reinforces the identification of (Nefer)hotep as the *Priest of Amun*, like his grandfather Senebef.

10.27 This man's image was also not attacked as part of the *damnatio*, which also argues against his being one of Ibiau's offspring.

10.28 Ranke does not include this name in his work, but the pattern of names ending in –resi is a hallmark of Thebes (Ilin-Tomich 2015:121, note 7).

10.29 Compare with the similar situation of the sarcophagi belonging to the *King's Acquaintance*, Senbuni (T9C) and Nekheteni's sister the *Royal Ornament*, Khonsu (T10C), which are also so identical that they must have been made by the same artists. This fact has led most scholars to assume that the two were also married, though no document actually proves this connection conclusively.

10.30 Grajetzki calls this object a stela, but it was composed of three pieces: two side runners, and a central slab with two holes at the top. An identical stone was set into the doorway of the tomb of Seneb-Kay, employed as a portcullis. Mace also discovered identical door blocking within shaft tombs in his Cemetery D (Randall-MacIver and Mace 1902:70, pl. XXV.3). Hence the Khonsu object is probably also a portcullis, and the CS9 example may also be reused from a 13th Dynasty tomb, perhaps that of Ibiau or Amenemhat.

10.31 Mace reported finding a "fragment of paint-palette" with the cartouche of Sobekhotep III in Tomb D41, corroborating Ryholt's date of P.Boulaq 18 (Randall-MacIver and Mace 1902:99).

10.32 To this corpus one might add the large wall slabs from North Abydos Cairo CG 20724 and CG 20725, which are similar to the reused blocks from South Abydos in both scale and decorative content (Lange and Schäfer 1908:355–357).

10.33 A chronological overlap between the reigns of Sobekhotep IV and the 15th Dynasty/Hyksos King Khyan has been proposed based on the co-occurrence of seal impressions of these two kings at Tell Edfu (Moeller and Marouard 2011:87–121), although a number of scholars have cautioned against making chronological conclusions based on royal sealings that may reflect complex patterns of use over long timeframes (Porter 2013:75–79; Ilin-Tomich 2014:149–150). Regardless of the Edfu evidence, the period of Neferhotep I and Sobekhotep IV was one when the 13th Dynasty state was likely to have been increasingly circumscribed by the loss of the Nile Delta and other factors (Schneider 1998:158–159).

10.34 A similar pattern occurs later in the *damnatio* in the tomb of King Ay in the Valley of the Kings (Wilkinson 2011:129–147).

10.35 If this epithet does denote a royal relationship, it is probably to the family of a king who ruled in the years before Neferhotep I. The rapid turnover of the royal office during the 13th Dynasty meant there were probably many families who could claim royal status at one time or another.

Part 3

The Main Tomb Cluster

11

Excavation and Architecture of the Tombs*

The tomb of Seneb-Kay is one of a group of eight known tombs of similar design at South Abydos. Seneb-Kay's tomb occupies a position directly adjacent to one of the two 13th Dynasty tombs, S10, which we have tentatively attributed to Sobekhotep IV. The builders of Seneb-Kay's tomb made use of a rectangular enclosure that fronts the primary temenos surrounding tomb S10. The other Second Intermediate Period tombs, seven structures (CS4, CS5, CS6, CS7, CS8, CS10, and CS11), which we refer to here as the "main tomb cluster," compose a tightly concentrated cemetery spanning an area approximately 30 x 35 meters located to the northeast of Seneb-Kay (Fig. 11.1). This chapter examines these tombs in detail.

Modern work on the structures comprising the main tomb cluster predates the recent University of Pennsylvania excavations. In 1901–1902, as part of his exploratory season of work at the tomb enclosure of Senwosret III, Arthur Weigall discovered and excavated three tombs in this area, which he did not attempt to date, but which he briefly described in his report published in *Abydos Part III* (Ayrton, Currelly, and Weigall 1904:16). These are the tombs we designate as CS4, CS7, and CS8. As a precursor to our recent program of excavation, we conducted a magnetic survey of this area in 2002–2003. While the initial goal of the subsurface survey was identification of other structures associated with the Senwosret III enclosure, the results showed the position of the three structures Weigall had identified as well as others indicating the presence of a larger cluster of tombs. The potential for identifying the date and

status of these tombs that lay so close to the late Middle Kingdom royal tombs led to the excavations in this area beginning in 2013. Work on the main tomb cluster began in the summer of 2013 as part of a survey looking for evidence of elite, non-royal cemetery activity at South Abydos. As part of the South Abydos Tomb Census (SATC) we completed excavation of five tombs, the three previously examined by Weigall (CS4, CS7, and CS8) as well as two newly identified tombs (CS5 and CS6). The tombs were given 'Cemetery S' (CS) designations following the naming convention initially used by Weigall. Due to the heavily robbed condition of these tombs the 2013 work did not produce chronologically diagnostic artifacts to permit dating of the tombs. In the winter of 2013–2014, we began to investigate the area between these tombs and the royal 13th Dynasty tomb S10 for additional evidence. That work led to the discovery of the tomb of Seneb-Kay (CS9) in January 2014, which provided the crucial iconographic dating evidence showing that the entire group of tombs date to the Second Intermediate Period, and that at least one of the tombs belonged to a king of that era.

Following the discovery of Seneb-Kay's tomb, and with the benefit of new insights regarding the date and status of these tombs, we conducted expanded work in the area in 2014–2016. In the summer of 2014, we identified and excavated two additional tombs, CS10 and CS11, which due to their depth and overburden, had formerly been overlooked in the middle of the main tomb cluster. We also identified three associated shafts, labeled CS12–CS14,

*This chapter written by Josef Wegner and Kevin Cahail.

Fig. 11.1 General view over the central part of the main tomb cluster showing tombs CS4 (foreground), CS10 and CS8 (center) with the location of Seneb-Kay (CS9) in front of the enclosure wall of S10 (view looking south).

belonging to a still unexamined tomb (CS13). Of this more recently discovered group, CS10 forms the most significant addition to our understanding of the Second Intermediate tombs at South Abydos. It is the largest of the main cluster tombs and its architecture provides insight into the derivation of this particular Second Intermediate Period tomb type from the late Middle Kingdom royal tomb tradition. Although no further inscriptional evidence for specific ownership or royal status has emerged in these badly robbed tombs, the excavations of these structures in 2013–2014 provided a significant set of skeletal remains demonstrating the association of these tombs with single, mature male burials. The implication of the architecture in tandem with skeletal evidence suggests the majority, if not all, of these tombs, like that of Seneb-Kay, belong to Second Intermediate Period kings who used this area as a royal burial ground adjacent to the tombs of late Middle Kingdom pharaohs.

Of particular interest is the spatial distribution of the known tombs and their relationship with the preexisting 13th Dynasty royal funerary structures (Fig. 11.2). Excavation in 2013–2016 exposed the entire 25 m wide expanse between Seneb-Kay and CS8, as well as the wider area between Seneb-Kay and the west side of the enclosure wall of tomb S9. We can conclusively state that there are no further tombs in this immediate area. Although the distance is not substantial, one notable aspect of the disposition of these tombs is the spatial separation between Seneb-Kay (CS9) and the main group of Second Intermediate Period tombs. The location of Seneb-Kay relative to the other contemporary tombs appears to reflect the adaptation to and selective reuse of late Middle Kingdom structures that already occupied the landscape. Furthermore, the position of Seneb-Kay vis-à-vis the main tomb cluster may have implications for other Second Intermediate Period tombs that have not survived. We turn firstly to examine this landscape and the relationship between the 13th Dynasty and later Second Intermediate Period tombs. The remainder of this chapter presents the individual tombs in detail.

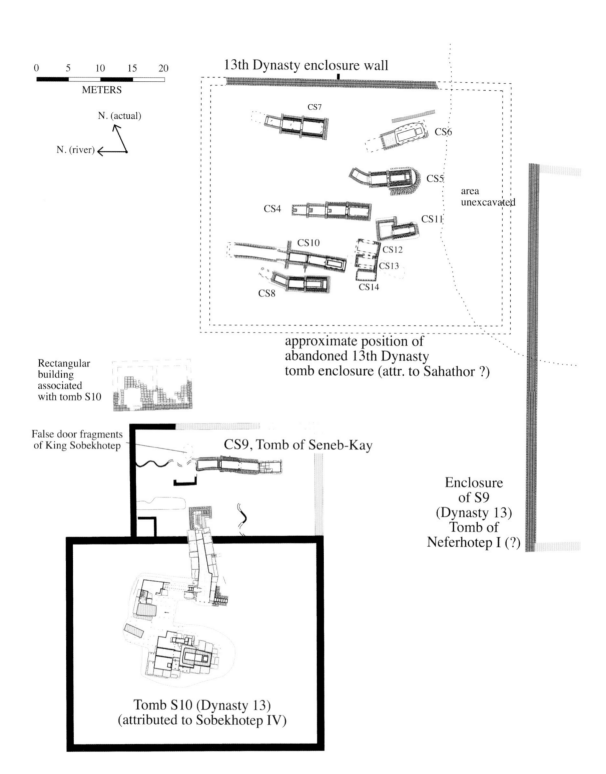

Fig. 11.2 The Second Intermediate Period tombs and adjacent 13th Dynasty structures.

Fig. 11.3 View looking west (2013 excavations) over the four tombs at the northeast corner of the main tomb cluster (CS4, CS5, CS6, and CS7), showing the reused 13th Dynasty burial chamber (CS6) and the enclosure wall of the abandoned 13th Dynasty tomb enclosure (upper right).

THE LANDSCAPE OF THE MAIN TOMB CLUSTER

During the first season of excavations of the Second Intermediate Period tombs two pieces of evidence emerged that are crucial to understanding the diachronic picture of the site's development. Forming the northern boundary of the main tomb cluster is a substantial mudbrick enclosure wall, 1.2 m wide and constructed with the same type of large format (12 x 19 x 38 cm) bricks employed in the nearby 13th Dynasty tombs, S9 and S10 (Fig. 11.3). Not known prior to 2013, this wall is preserved over a length of 45 m. It follows precisely the same orientation as tomb S10, further to the south, as well as the west side of the enclosure of S9. However, the position of the wall shows it forms a different structure than the temenos walls surrounding S9 and S10. The wall is the same thickness as the enclosure surrounding S10 and represents the denuded remnants of a third 13th Dynasty royal tomb enclosure.

The function of this enclosure wall is illuminated by specific evidence furnished from tomb CS6, discovered in the main tomb cluster in 2013. Tomb CS6

is an unusual structure in that its brick components were added secondarily to a reused 13th Dynasty royal burial crypt that is nearly identical to the two still in situ within tombs S9 and S10 (Wegner and Cahail 2014). The combination of brick enclosure wall and reused burial chamber suggest strongly that the site represents the location of an unfinished 13th Dynasty royal tomb. If this tomb had been completed, there would have been a trio of 13th Dynasty royal tombs of similar design. The unfinished tomb appears to have been in the earliest stages of its construction during which the area had been defined by a brick surface enclosure and the monolithic quartzite burial chamber had been delivered to the site. Actual construction of the tomb's substructure had not proceeded beyond that point. No inscriptional evidence has been recovered to directly date the owner of this abandoned complex. Based on the close similarity of the crypt with the two preserved in tombs S9 and S10, this unfinished tomb should date very close in time. Based on the proposed attribution of the 13th Dynasty tombs (Wegner and Cahail 2015:123–164) to the brother kings Neferhotep I (S9) and Sobekhotep IV (tomb S10) it is possible the unfinished enclosure was initiated for the short-reigning third brother, Sa-hathor, who may have reigned briefly between the long reigns of his brothers (Wegner 2019).

As a result of the recent excavations, we have five known enclosures associated with three 13th Dynasty royal tombs at South Abydos (Fig. 11.4). Two of these, Enclosure A and Enclosure B, belong to tomb S10: Enclosure A forms the main tomb enclosure with Enclosure B appended to the front demarcating the area of the tomb's entrance and ancillary structures on the north side of S10. Enclosure C forms the te-menos for the unfinished tomb of which only part of the north wall has survived. Enclosure D is the main enclosure surrounding tomb S9, while Enclosure E

is appended to the north side of Enclosure D in the same relationship as occurs between A and B. Enclo-sure E uniquely in this group is bounded by sinusoi-dal walls and demarcates the location of the entrance into S9 as well as a brick funerary building that flanks the entrance (McCormack 2014:16–18).

The positions chosen for building the Second Intermediate Period tombs appears to have been substantially determined by the disposition of these preexisting 13th Dynasty structures. While Sen-eb-Kay's tomb was situated within the walled enclo-sure (Enclosure B) on the north side of S10, the main group of tombs appears to have taken advantage of still standing brick walls belonging to the unfinished

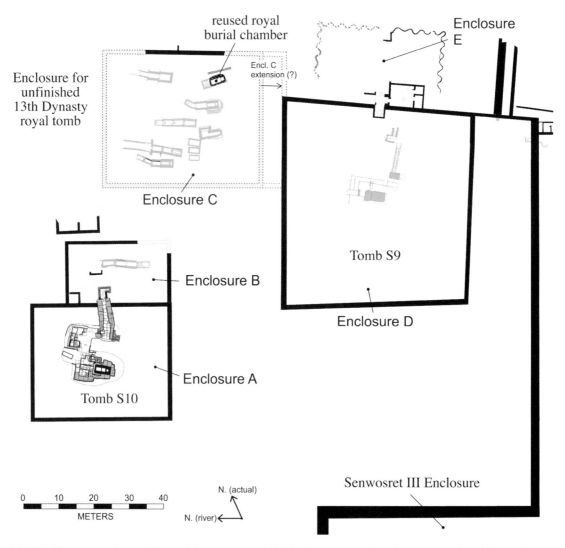

Fig. 11.4 The suggested position of the abandoned 13th Dynasty tomb enclosure based on the position of the intrusive Second Intermediate Period cemetery.

tomb (Enclosure C). The position and distribution of these tombs likely reflects the original interior of the enclosure belonging to this abandoned 13th Dynasty royal tomb. Moreover, the relationship of the main tomb cluster with this third tomb enclosure explains the spatial disjunction between Seneb-Kay and the main tomb cluster. These tombs were not placed indiscriminately in any location on an open desert landscape, but rather were specifically housed within the walled areas that already existed on the site. The Second Intermediate Period tombs were opportunistically appropriating mortuary space from the late Middle Kingdom royal structures, both finished and unfinished, at South Abydos.

Due to the fact that two of five 13th Dynasty enclosures were adapted as locations for tomb construction in the Second Intermediate Period an implication of our current evidence is that Seneb-Kay and the main tomb cluster may not represent the full roster of Second Intermediate Period tombs that once existed on the landscape at South Abydos. The two primary enclosures surrounding tombs S9 and S10 may have formed attractive locations for secondary tomb construction. While these enclosures may have originally contained some form of superstructure over the original 13th Dynasty tomb itself, substantial areas of both Enclosure A and Enclosure D could potentially have contained intrusive construction in the same way that Enclosure C did. Unfortunately, the extensive demolition of the substructures of both S9 and S10 during the late Roman and Byzantine Periods occurred on such a scale that the majority of the interiors of both enclosures was destroyed. The massive pits that cut down into the substructures would have demolished any smaller tombs that lay above within the two enclosures. Enclosure E fronting tomb S9 is another potential location for outliers to the main tomb cluster and it has only been partially investigated. But, the less substantial screen walls demarcating its north side suggest this are may have been less desirable as a walled tract of desert terrain for tomb builders in the Second Intermediate Period.

The 13th Dynasty enclosure wall exposed in 2013 is heavily eroded and preserved only to a maximum height of two brick courses. The wall sits slightly below the modern surface. Continued work in the area in 2014–2016 has attempted to locate additional surviving sections of the enclosure, particularly any

elements belonging to the other three sides of what was presumably a rectangular enclosure encompassing a similar area to those of S9 or S10. Although faint, linear anomalies on the 2002 magnetic survey map suggested the presence of further elements of the enclosure, direct excavation has not exposed additional surviving elements. At the present time, we may be certain that no stretches of this enclosure exist on either the south or west sides.

Although there is no conclusive confirmation for the position of the rest of the third 13th Dynasty enclosure, there appears a strong likelihood that the dense nucleation of the main Second Intermediate Period tomb cluster reflects the approximate position of the enclosure walls at the time those tombs were built. The tombs cover an essentially square area 30 m (north-south) x 35 m (east-west) with the northernmost tombs, CS6 and CS7, only 5 m from the inside of the enclosure wall. The size of this area is comparable to the 30 x 38 m interior of tomb S10's main enclosure (Enclosure A) implying the enclosure associated with the unfinished tomb was of comparable dimensions to S10. Following the 5 m displacement between tombs CS6 and CS7 from the south/inner face of the north side of the enclosure wall we may tentatively extrapolate a ca. 35 x 40 m enclosure wall running 5 m west of the entrance ramp to CS10, and 5 m south of CS8.

On the east side and adjacent to S9, there remains potential for segments of the enclosure wall to have survived beneath unexcavated debris mounds that encumber the northwest side of the tomb S9. At the present time the area between the known Second Intermediate Period tombs and the S9 enclosure wall is unexamined. The area remains encumbered by deep debris mounds (area delineated and labeled "unexcavated") and received lower priority in the excavation program during 2013–2016 because it was considered more likely that additional tombs might occupy the intervening terrain between Seneb-Kay and tomb CS8. Now that the patterns of purposeful insertion of the Second Intermediate Period tombs into the existing 13th Dynasty enclosures has become clear, it appears possible that additional tombs could exist in this area extending directly between the main tomb cluster and the S9 enclosure wall.

One of the implications of the distribution of Second Intermediate Period tombs in the unfinished 13th Dynasty enclosure is that the enclosure's east wall must have run extremely close to the western side of the tomb S9 enclosure. It is notable that the newly identified enclosure wall follows the same orientation as the S10 enclosure, as well as running perpendicular to the western wall of tomb S9. Given the proximity to S9 and use of the same system of orientation, there appears a possibility that the enclosure for the unfinished tomb did not run parallel and independently of S9 but abuts the northwest corner of the S9 enclosure. Particularly if the two tombs followed each other closely enough in time, there may have been an interest in abutting the enclosures. Consequently, the walls of the third enclosure may have projected eastwards abutting the western face and northwest corner of S9 (area labeled "Enclosure C extension" above). In this wider format for Enclosure C, there may be a nearly 20 m area of terrain that could include additional tombs. At the time of writing, this possibility remains yet to be investigated although appears to be less probable.

Based on the preceding discussion, there is a significant possibility that the five walled enclosures associated with the 13th Dynasty tombs attributed here to Neferhotep I, Sobekhotep IV, and Sahathor may once have contained additional intrusive tombs of the type represented by Seneb-Kay and the structures in the main tomb cluster. There also remains a possibility that additional Second Intermediate Period tombs may yet be located in the unexcavated area flanking tomb S9 or even in the partially explored Enclosure E in front of it. However, at the present time, the seven tombs forming the main tomb cluster represent our principal evidence that Seneb-Kay was not an aberration, but part of a larger phenomenon of reuse of these earlier royal enclosures for a burial ground of the later Second Intermediate Period.

It is the existence of eight known tombs of comparable size, architectural form and location that suggests we may have the remains of a dynastic necropolis of a distinct succession of Second Intermediate Period kings. In the following, we examine the main cluster tombs (Fig. 11.5) in detail. The tombs are discussed here in order of numbering: CS4, CS5, CS6, CS7, CS8, CS10, and CS11. We also discuss the evidence of the trio of shafts, CS12, CS13, and CS14, which appear to represent another contemporary burial type in the cemetery. Issues of internal development and horizontal stratigraphy of the main cluster will be addressed in the next chapter. The

evidence provided by the skeletal remains recovered for these tombs is presented in the final chapter on the main tomb cluster (Chapter 13).

TOMB CS4

GENERAL DESCRIPTION

CS4 is one of the three largest tombs (including Seneb-Kay [CS9] and CS10) in the cemetery. It is situated in the center of the tomb cluster in close proximity to CS11, the corner of which lies just 1 m southeast of CS4's burial chamber (Fig. 11.6). The tomb has a total length of 12.1 m and follows the typical sequence found throughout the cemetery consisting of: (1) walled entrance ramp; (2) pole-roof chamber; (3) vaulted chamber; and (4) stone-lined, brick vaulted burial chamber. Unlike some of the other tombs, which employ a rotation of the entrance towards the northwest, CS4 is strictly linear with only minor differences in orientation between the successive chambers. CS4 is the closest in overall scale and design to the tomb of Seneb-Kay. However, unlike Seneb-Kay, CS4 follows the predominant practice of the cemetery and has a brick burial chamber with and internal lining of limestone slabs. This burial chamber has some unique attributes suggesting the possibility that like Seneb-Kay it may originally have been decorated.

CS4 is one of the three tombs (including CS7 and CS8) that Weigall located and examined in his exploratory season of 1901–1902. He described the tomb as follows:

The middle tomb contained four chambers. The first sloped down from the desert surface for 7 ft., being about 4 ½ ft. wide, and having two small steps at the mouth. The second chamber was the same width, and sloped for 8 ft., at the end of which was a doorway, barred with limestone, led into a barrel roofed chamber, 9 ft. long and 4 ½ ft. wide. Through this a second doorway opened on the sarcophagus, constructed as before of loose limestone slabs, in which a few male bones were found. All the walls of the chambers were whitewashed (Weigall in Ayrton et al. 1904:18).

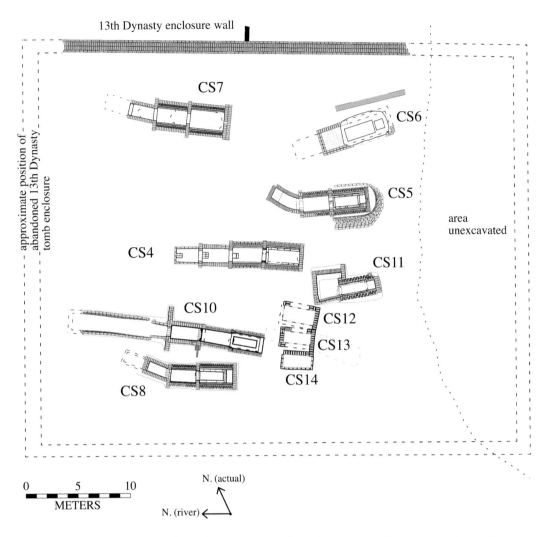

Fig. 11.5 The Second Intermediate Period main tomb cluster, showing the seven tombs and three shafts occupying the area of the unfinished 13th Dynasty royal enclosure.

We relocated the structure in 2013 and completed an excavation of the substructure (Figs. 11.7 and 11.8). We then reopened it for further documentation in 2014. As with the two other tombs that Weigall had examined, CS4 produced a meager set of artifactual remains and no diagnostic objects related to its original burial assemblage.

ENTRANCE RAMP

The entrance ramp measures 1.3 by 2.1 m. It has low walls of a single brick width and a brick floor with a set of two steps set against the ramp's end wall. The walls of the ramp of CS4 have certainly lost a substantial number of courses and probably originally rose to the height of the roof of the tomb's first chamber. No other tombs preserve steps at the mouth of the entrance ramp. By comparison, the much deeper entrance ramp of Seneb-Kay, which is preserved to its full original height, lacks the use of steps. Therefore, it is likely the level of the surrounding terrain was substantially higher than at present and the steps facilitated the step downwards to the floor of the ramp. The use of brick steps is a unique feature of CS4 and is replicated in the tomb's interior chambers.

Fig. 11.6 CS4 (view looking southwest) with adjacent tombs: CS8 and CS10 to the south (behind) and CS11 and shafts CS12–14 to the east (left).

Fig. 11.7 Overview of CS4 (view looking west).

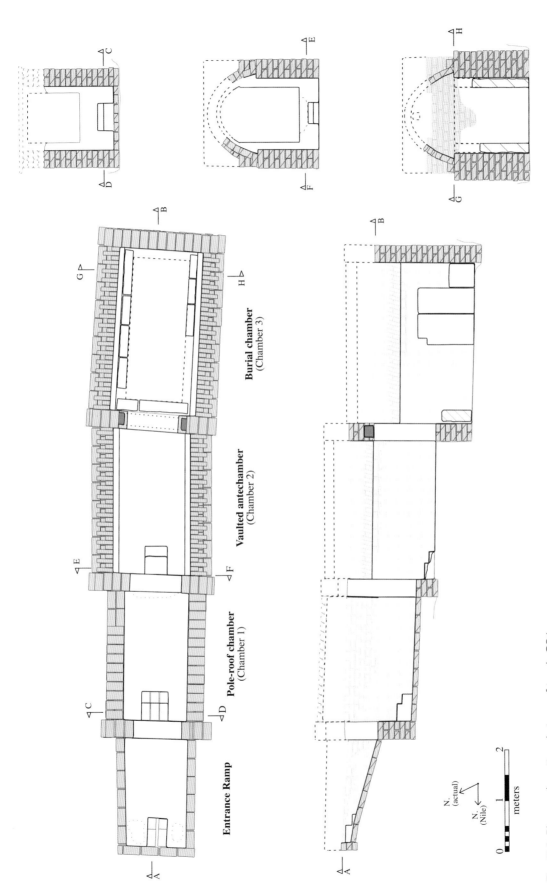

Fig. 11.8 Plan and sectional views of tomb CS4.

Fig. 11.9 The brick steps leading from the entrance ramp into the pole-roof chamber.

POLE-ROOF CHAMBER (CHAMBER 1)

The interior of Chamber 1 is well-preserved (Fig. 11.9) although the upper walls lack remains of the original pole-roofing as occurs in other tombs (e.g., CS9, CS10). The space measures 1.3 by 2.45 m. The walls are preserved to a maximum height of 1.5 m. The chamber appears to have lost several courses of brickwork due to the relatively high elevation of this tomb. Chamber 1 is likely to have risen somewhat further to ca. 1.8 where it was completed with a pole-roof as used for the initial chamber throughout the cemetery. Use of a pole-roof is indicated by the narrower format of the walls of Chamber 1 as well as the proximity to the surface which would have precluded use of a vault. A set of brick steps are preserved against the chamber's entrance from the walled ramp where there is a substantial .7 m drop from the ramp to the floor of Chamber 1. The chamber has a brick floor and whitewash preserved on walls and floor.

Weigall's description of this tomb mentions the presence of a limestone closure ("barred with limestone") at the inner end of this chamber (the doorway between Chamber 1 and 2). No evidence was found in 2012–2013 of a limestone door in this position. It

is possible that Weigall encountered loose limestone slabs in this vicinity that had been dislodged from the badly damaged burial chamber. However, it does appear possible that a limestone portcullis-style door may have been extant in this location at the time of Weigall's work. Doorways of this type appear to have been standard elements throughout the necropolis, the entrance into the pole-roof chamber of Seneb-Kay being the only surviving example. Weigall may well have observed remains of such a closure in CS4 but subsequent damage to the masonry may have resulted in the limestone being removed. The brickwork of the threshold between Chambers 1 and 2 is damaged creating a non-original stair-like feature. Due to this damage, it is quite possible there was originally a limestone threshold and associated elements for a stone closure system as stated by Weigall. Preserved against this doorway inside Chamber 2 are remains of another set of steps like those at the west end of Chamber 1.

VAULTED ANTECHAMBER (CHAMBER 2)

The central chamber measures 1.3 by 2.8 m and has a vaulted brick roof. It has a badly eroded set of brick steps set against the doorway from Chamber

Fig. 11.10 Wood lintel set into the brickwork of the doorway between Chamber 2 and the burial chamber.

Fig. 11.11 The burial chamber of CS4 showing the in situ blocks against the chamber's western end (view looking west).

Fig. 11.12 View of the surviving limestone wall slabs in the burial chamber of CS4 (view looking east).

1. Unlike the entrance ramp and Chamber 1, which both have brick floors, the floor of Chamber 2 is set directly on the compact desert subsurface and slopes downward slightly towards the inner end. The floor was plastered and whitewashed but is now substantially pitted. The side walls of the chamber rise to a height of 1.3 m where there is a 0.12 m wide ledge on either side at the point where the vault begins. Only the lowest two courses of the vault are preserved. On the exterior are several courses of mortared stacks of bricks laid parallel to the vault that served to counteract the outward force exerted by the lower part of the vault.

The doorway between Chamber 2 and the burial chamber measures 1.05 m wide and is preserved to its original height of 1.3 m (equivalent to the height of the ledge). On top of the projecting door jambs on both sides are remains of a wooden lintel measuring ca. 25 by 25 cm set into the brickwork (Fig. 11.10). There are no clear indications of use of stonework or other elements flanking this doorway but again this may be a viable location for a portcullis-style closure system as suggested by Weigall's description of the preceding doorway leading into Chamber 2.

BURIAL CHAMBER (CHAMBER 3)

The burial chamber of CS4 is a vaulted brick chamber with an internal lining of limestone slabs comparable in construction to other burial chambers of the main tomb cluster (Fig. 11.11). However, the architectural arrangement of the chamber has some notable differences that suggest the original form of the chamber may not have been a brick vault containing a stone-lined receptacle in the floor for the sarcophagus. Rather, the burial chamber of CS4 appears more likely to have been a walk-in chamber akin to that of Seneb-Kay.

The brick construction of the burial chamber is identical to that of the other tombs: a barrel vault is set atop vertical side walls with the vault's brickwork inclined against the chamber's end wall. The chamber interior measures 1.5 x 3.2 m. A ca. 0.12 m wide ledge occurs on either side formed at the junction between the walls and the base of the vault. Unusually, the height of the side walls rises to 1.5 m where the ledge and transition to the vault occur. The substantial height of the chamber is particularly noticeable since the drop into the burial chamber from the floor

Fig. 11.13 Detail of the stone lining showing use of mud mortar with gypsum coating still preserved in the block joints.

of the preceding chamber (Chamber 2) is only 0.6 m. This means is that one did not enter the burial chamber at an elevation above the limestone sarcophagus recess as occurs in other tombs such as CS5, CS8, and CS10. Rather, access to the chamber occurs only slightly above the floor level of the stone-lined crypt itself.

The limestone lining is, unfortunately, badly damaged (Fig. 11.12). Nine orthostats, whole and damaged, remain in situ along the two long walls (north and south) and the west wall directly in front of the doorway leading in from Chamber 2. The blocks were installed with joints which, as occurs in Seneb-Kay's burial chamber, consist of a Nile mud mortar that was faced with a gypsum whitewash. The gypsum coat still adheres over the mud mortar on a number of these block seams (Fig. 11.13). The surviving masonry averages 0.2 m in thickness, and the scale of the blocks is more substantial than occurs in any of the other stone-lined burial chambers. Moreover, the dimensions of the internal space are greater. Although the slabs lining the chamber's inner (east) wall are missing, we can estimate their width

at approximately 0.2 m based on the blocks in situ. The interior of the stone-lined space is 1.2 x 2.8 m. By comparison, the stone-lined crypts of CS5 and CS8 measure only 0.8 by 2.2 m. There are no surviving indications at the inner end of CS4's burial chamber for the separate canopic recess, which we see in several tombs (CS5, CS8, and CS11). The wall blocks extend all the way to the back wall suggesting the chamber was characterized by a single, unbroken stone-lined space. The interior of the stone-lined space is marginally but not substantially smaller than the burial chamber of Seneb-Kay (which measures 1.5 x 3.2 m), and which has a similar 0.6 m drop from antechamber to floor of the burial chamber.

It is further intriguing that there is no indication on the well-preserved face of the whitewashed brick walls of any mortared joint deriving from the capstone edging that should have formed the top of the vertical stone slabs. Therefore, in all likelihood the wall blocks rose with additional courses of masonry to the full height of the brick ledge: 1.5 m above floor level. Indeed, residual gypsum from the joints of additional blocks placed above is preserved on the top of the fully preserved orthostats on the chamber's south side. This height of 1.5 m for the stone lining of the burial chamber is much greater than any of the other stone-lined sarcophagus recesses. By comparison, the stone-lined burial recesses of CS5 and CS8 are only 1 m in height and the sarcophagus recess in the monolithic crypt of CS10 is 0.86 m deep. The vaulted roof of the CS4 burial chamber would have risen another meter beyond the ledge making the entire chamber nearly 2.5 m in height. It appears possible therefore that CS4 employed a hybrid version of the burial chambers seen in the other tombs: a stone lining that formed a walk-in chamber set within the brick-vaulted structure.

Given the large scale, and apparent walk-in format of CS4's burial chamber, it appears possible that this tomb might once have been decorated. Seneb-Kay's burial chamber is the only one of the Second Intermediate Period tombs at South Abydos positively known to have decoration on the walls. However, it is also the only one specifically known to have had an open chamber format instead of the stone lined sarcophagus receptacle that predominates throughout the cemetery. If CS4 also had an open-chamber format, this raises the possibility that its walls may once have borne painted decoration.

Fig. 11.14 Reused blocks lining the north wall of the CS4 burial chamber. The block in the center has a worked corner deriving from its original use in some earlier building at Abydos.

Like Seneb-Kay's masonry-built burial chamber, CS4 makes extensive use of reused stone. Four of the wall slabs have clear indications of having belonged to some other building prior to their use in CS4. In several locations, there are incised mason's lines that do not appear related to the construction of CS4 itself. One of the blocks appears to be a pavement block with an inset surface and raised surface with straight chiseled edge or corner that may represent the transition from floor to base of a wall (Fig. 11.14). There are no remains of earlier decorated surfaces, as occurs in Seneb-Kay's tomb, nor any surviving decoration associated with the CS4 burial chamber. In the case of painted decoration, one possibility is that due to the severe damage to the chamber all remnants of the gypsum coating over the blocks has eroded away taking any surface decoration with it. Gypsum mortar survives in CS4 only in the block joints but not on the surfaces. Given the number of missing blocks the chamber is likely to have stood open to the elements for an extensive period of time and we may conclude that exposure could easily have eroded any painted

decoration as well as the gypsum surface that served as substrate for the painting.

Although it remains uncertain whether CS4 would have had a decorated burial chamber, the architecture of the space suggests that this tomb is transitional between the standard form of stone-lined burial crypt that predominates in the main cluster tombs and the open chamber form of Seneb-Kay where sarcophagus and canopic chest would have been deposited on the floor of the chamber itself.

TOMB CS5

GENERAL DESCRIPTION

CS5 is one of a group of three slightly smaller tombs including CS6 and CS11 that predominate in the northeastern corner of the main tomb cluster. The tomb sits between CS11 located to its south and CS6 on its north. The structure consists of two chambers

Fig. 11.15 CS5 with neighboring tomb CS6 visible at upper left (view looking east).

covering a length of 7 m, fronted by a 3 m long entrance ramp (Figs. 11.15 and 11.16). As occurs in several of the tombs, the entrance ramp is angled toward the northwest. CS5 was first identified and excavated in 2012–2013. Despite this tomb's high elevation on the terrain, Weigall missed CS5 in his exploratory work of 1901–1902. We found the architecture to be in excellent condition, with the majority of the masonry composing the stone-lined burial chamber still intact.

The brickwork of this tomb, uniquely in the cemetery, displays extensive use of a common brickmaker's mark throughout the structure. Many of the bricks are impressed with either a single or double finger impression (Fig. 11.17). The impressions appear to correlate with the size and use of the bricks. The single dotted bricks are somewhat larger in format (averaging 35 x 16 x 9 cm) and were used for the primary walls. Double dotted bricks are thinner (29 x 14 x 7.5) and appear to have been purpose-made for the vault construction. Such a differentiation of thinner vault bricks occurs in some of the other Second Intermediate Period tombs and also among the New Kingdom tombs at South

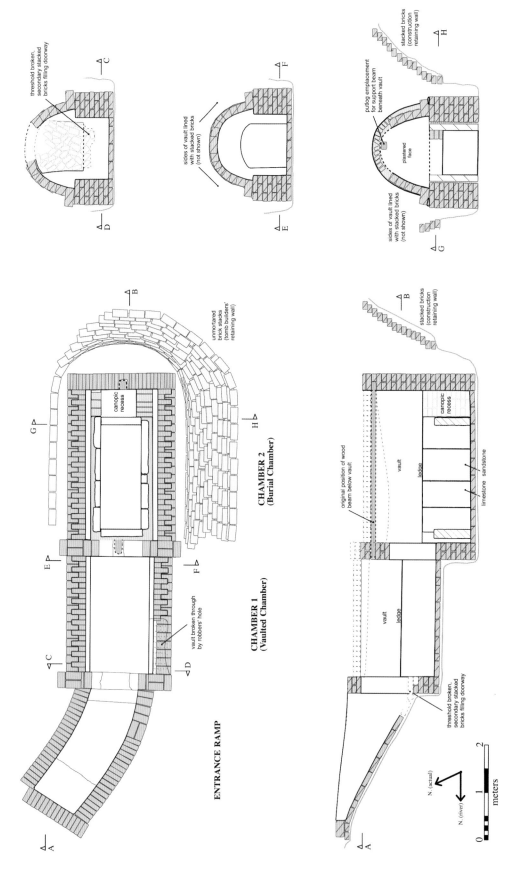

Fig. 11.16 Plan and sectional views of tomb CS5.

Fig. 11.17 Impressed marks on the bricks of CS5.

Fig. 11.18 The loose brick blocking in the doorway into Chamber 1 (view looking west).

Fig. 11.19 Chamber 1 with the arched doorway leading into the burial chamber (view looking east).

Abydos. However, none of the other tombs in the main cluster show use of brickmaker's marks.

THE ENTRANCE RAMP

The walled entrance ramp of CS5 is a variant of unroofed ramped entrances in the Second Intermediate Period tombs. The ramp is 1.1 m wide on its interior with a bricked and whitewashed floor and a steep angle of descent (ca. -25°) over a short 2.8 m span. The walls are 0.35 m in thickness (one-brick length); more substantially built than the normal ramps which are composed entirely of courses of bricks laid as stretchers with a thickness of ca. 0.14–0.16 m. Unusually, the ramp has curving walls, which accentuate the turn in orientation of the tomb's entrance towards the northwest. Most of the bricks were laid as headers that helped the builders create a curved shape to the ramp. Whereas the two inner chambers of CS5 are in perfect alignment with each other, the entrance ramp turns away at a substantial

35° angle. While use of the skewed entrance does not characterize all of the tombs, the occurrence of this purposeful shift in alignment (seen also in tombs CS7 and CS8) suggests that there may have been some underlying interest in positioning the tombs' entrances towards the northwest.

CHAMBER 1

With a two-chambered layout, CS5 lacks the common element of the pole-roof chamber. The walled ramp leads directly through a low, arched doorway (1.1 m wide and ca. 1.05 m high) into a barrel-vaulted chamber (Fig. 11.18). In 2013, the doorway was found to be blocked with a loosely stacked pile of mudbricks. This roughly stacked blocking is clearly secondary and is not the original closure of the tomb. The bricks, many of which are eroded, are laid in a haphazard arrangement. There is no use of mortar and the outer face lacks mud plaster. By comparison, an intact brick blocking with mud-plastered face is still preserved in the doorway into the burial chamber of CS8. Additionally, the brickwork of the threshold between the entrance ramp and Chamber 1 is broken, and the brick stacks were added atop this already damaged doorway. Originally there was a 0.6 m drop down from the threshold to the floor of Chamber 1. It appears likely that the blocking was an impromptu addition by tomb robbers who stacked a loose array of bricks into the opening to prevent sand flowing from the entrance ramp into Chamber 1. The tomb's entrance would originally have been blocked by other means.

Chamber 1 is a small version of the vaulted antechamber found in the majority of the tombs. It measures 1.3 by 2.46 m. The chamber's side walls rise to a height of 0.72 m, where there are ledges ca. 0.12 m that widen out to the beginning of the vault (Fig. 11.19). The roof is single-ring brick vault with loosely laid stacks of unmortared bricks along the exterior to counteract the outward force at the base of the vault. The floor is bricked, plastered and whitewashed. The inner end preserves, still standing, an arched doorway, 0.9 m wide and ca. 1 m in height, which leads into the burial chamber. The upper part of the cross wall above the tympanum retains an emplacement for the end of a wood beam that originally engaged in the brickwork above the arch from the burial chamber beyond. The surviving architecture of the doorway from the entrance ramp into Chamber 1 shows that no wooden beam was employed below its vault, which was smaller than the one over the burial chamber.

THE BURIAL CHAMBER (CHAMBER 2)

The burial chamber of CS5 is in an excellent state of preservation (Fig. 11.20). The majority of the stone-lined crypt is intact, as well as the entirety of the back wall which retains the full curvature of the vaulted roof. Like the rest of CS5, due to the fact that the chamber's floor does not reach the compact desert subsurface, the chamber has a bricked and whitewashed floor. The interior of the brick chamber measures 1.4 x 3.2 m. Its original height to the top of the vault was 1.95 m. The chamber's vertical side walls rise to 1.05 m where there is a 0.15 m ledge extending out to the beginning of the vault. The vault was originally 0.95 m high and constructed of a single ring of bricks inclined slightly against

Fig. 11.20 View from the burial chamber through the arched doorway into Chamber 1.

Fig. 11.22 Burial chamber of CS5. View looking north.

Fig. 11.21 Burial chamber of CS5. View looking south.

the end wall. A putlog hole at the top of the back wall measures 0.1 x 0.13 m and originally supported the wood beam that extended the length of the burial chamber with its other end engaged above the arched doorway connecting Chambers 1 and 2. The use of wood beams is attested in other tombs where the end walls have been preserved to their full height (CS7 and CS8). These beams evidently served only during the tomb's construction. It appears the beams were cut off at the wall face at the stage of construction when the vaults were plastered at whitewashed. Erosion of the wall plaster and decay of the residual wood stubs embedded inside the walls has opened up the emplacements as we see in CS5.

The stone-lined burial crypt (Figs. 11.21 and 11.22) has interior dimensions of 0.9 x 2.25 m and a height of 0.95 m. These dimensions are almost identical to the sarcophagus recess in CS8. The walls are constructed partially of limestone and partially of sandstone slabs which extend up to a height contiguous with the ledges of the side walls. The masonry lining preserves eleven blocks in situ averaging 12–15 cm in thickness. On the north side, the wall is composed of four orthostats that extend the full 0.95 m height contiguous with the brick ledge. On the south side, there are two vertical orthostats and the rest of the wall is composed of two blocks laid on their side. The narrower end walls each preserve a single slab that does not reach the full height of the side walls. There must originally have been an additional block on each of these end walls to complete a sarcophagus recess with a rim of uniform height.

Unlike the similarly built CS8 where there was a top course of capping blocks that completed the edges of the sarcophagus recess, CS5 lacks this element. On the south side above the horizontally laid slabs, the edge was completed by a row of bricks. The gaps between the slabs and the chamber's brick walls were filled with loose debris and covered with a layer of mud plaster and whitewash. These construction techniques represent a more economical approach than that seen in CS8, which is otherwise the tomb most similar to CS5. In general, echoing its smaller overall size, the quality of the construction in CS5 is somewhat lower than the other tombs in the main cluster.

An interesting feature of CS5's burial chamber is the use of both limestone and sandstone. Seven of the slabs composing the crypt walls are limestone while three are a violet colored sandstone. Use of sandstone also occurs in the tomb of Seneb-Kay (CS9) for the door lintel between Chambers 1 and 2. A sandstone slab of similar color but not in situ was also found in the very damaged tomb CS7 where it may have originally formed part of a lintel or threshold or part of the lining of the burial chamber. In CS5, the color variation between the limestone and sandstone was concealed by use of a skim coat of gypsum whitewash over the masonry. The apparent intention was to mimic the appearance of a single, monolithic crypt of the type preserved in CS10.

One of the significant architectural details of the burial chamber of CS5 is the excellent preservation of a 0.6 x 0.8 m loculus or receptacle at the inner end behind the stone lining of the sarcophagus recess (Figs. 11.23 and 11.24). Variations of this element were present in most of the other tombs but were not as well preserved as occurs in CS5. Behind the stone lining, both sides of the space were filled with mortared bricks that created two wide, projecting ledges contiguous with the ledges at the base of the vault. These extended ledges (0.33 m on the north and 0.44 m on the south) were plastered and whitewashed on their tops and sides, creating an independent receptacle behind the sarcophagus recess. We may identify this space as the canopic recess. The location corresponds with similar features in many of the other tombs as well as the evidence from the burial equipment in Seneb-Kay's tomb that the canopic chest was placed at the inner or foot end of the burial chamber. This customary location of the canopic chest seen in the 13th Dynasty royal tombs was replicated in all of the Second Intermediate Period tombs. In CS5, both the sarcophagus and canopic recesses could presumably have been closed and sealed by slabs or lid stones that bridged the two receptacles. No remains of any stone slabs used for covering were found in CS5. However, the system may have resembled that of CS10 where two purpose-made lid blocks originally covered the sarcophagus recess.

EXTERNAL BRICK RETAINING WALL

A prominent feature associated with CS5 is extensive stacks of bricks in a horseshoe shape ringing the position of the burial chamber. While many of the main cluster tombs have brick stacks immediately flanking the sides of the vaults, no other tombs have an equivalent situation with carefully stacked, but unmortared, bricks encircling the broader area of the tomb. The disposition of CS5's substructure relative to these bricks shows that they are not secondary, nor were they created by tomb robbers. Rather, they form a retaining wall used in the tomb construction process. The bricks are not eroded or reused and must have been laid not long after they were produced. The retaining wall bricks were not marked by the finger impressions visible in many of the construction bricks used in CS5, but they employ comparable dimensions of ca. 36 x 16 x 9 cm. Because CS5 was built at a relatively high elevation and the compact desert subsurface lay much deeper, it was necessary to surround the

Fig. 11.23 The canopic recess in CS5, view looking northeast.

Fig. 11.24 The canopic recess in CS5, view looking southeast.

Fig. 11.25 Overview of CS6 after completion of excavation in 2013 (upper left) and CS5 (right). View looking east.

construction pit with a retaining wall that rested on the more compact desert sand below and held back the deep overburden of loose windblown sand. The stacks may have originally extended along the full length of the tomb's periphery but are now preserved adjacent to the burial chamber where the stacks reached the greatest depth. Once the tomb was completed, the stacks were simply left in place and buried with sand.

TOMB CS6

GENERAL DESCRIPTION

CS6 is the most unusual of the tombs in the Second Intermediate Period cemetery. The tomb

occupies the northeastern edge of the main tomb cluster. The structure stands apart from the other tombs through its reuse of a 13th Dynasty royal sarcophagus chamber in place of the standard brick and slab-lined burial chamber (Fig. 11.25 and 11.26). The reused chamber is a monolithic crypt originally intended to form the core of a 13th Dynasty royal tomb (Wegner and Cahail 2014). As we have discussed at the beginning of this chapter, the ca. 23 m long section of late Middle Kingdom enclosure wall to the north of the Second Intermediate Period cemetery indicates the approximate position of this abandoned royal tomb, which would have been situated immediately west of S9 and north of S10. The entire area of this unfinished 13th Dynasty complex was secondarily used for the Second Intermediate Period cemetery while CS6 itself made use of the quartzite

Fig. 11.26 Overview of CS6 after completion of excavation in 2013. View looking west.

chamber, which appears to have been intended for this unfinished complex.

CS6 was constructed by fitting a brick vault to the top of the quartzite crypt, accessible by an entrance on the local north side (Fig. 11.27). The combination of elements, while unique, follows the essential orientation and architectural layout seen in the other Second Intermediate Period tombs. CS6 was discovered and excavated during May of 2013. Unfortunately, very little remained of the tomb's brick elements. This poor state of architectural preservation is likely a result of the relatively high elevation of the tomb's vault and outer brick components. CS6, like tomb CS7 just ten meters to the west, is positioned very close to the south side of the preexisting 13th Dynasty enclosure wall. It appears that the entire cemetery made use of this enclosure as a funerary precinct and the north wall was likely standing to a

significant height at the time these tombs were built. The relative elevation of both CS6 and CS7 suggests that there was significant sand accumulation against the southern face of the enclosure wall at that time. Subsequent removal and decay of enclosure's brickwork has resulted in a substantial deflation at this northern end of the site and led to the relatively poor state of preservation of tombs CS6 and CS7. We might observe that CS5 which is also built high on the terrain survived in better condition probably owing to factors of differing sand deposition and deflation over relatively localized areas of the site. As a result of the poor preservation of the brick elements of CS6, we cannot be absolutely certain of the original appearance of this tomb. In the following, we examine the surviving elements along with observations of the possible disposition of the brick elements that were added atop the quartzite chamber.

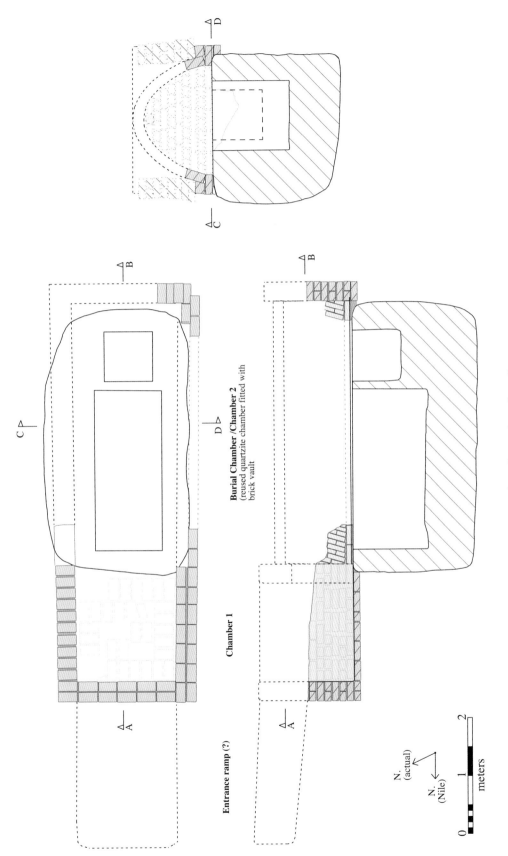

Fig. 11.27 Plan and sectional views of tomb CS6 showing suggested configuration of vault.

CHAMBER 1

The best-preserved component of the brick architecture of CS6 was a small rectangular chamber or shaft fitted to the west end of the reused chamber. This feature, Chamber 1, has well-built walls and a brick floor which originally extended over the upper end of the quartzite chamber. Chamber 1's walls are preserved to a height of 0.85 m, and the feature has a north-south width of 1.75 m. The lower courses of the brickwork were preserved on the south, north, and west sides. The eastern side and articulation with the vaulted chamber (Chamber 2) behind is not preserved. However, a shift in the brick patterns of the floor indicates the possible position of a dividing wall between Chamber 1 and the burial chamber, similar to the walls that separate the successive chambers in the other Second Intermediate period tombs. A wall in this location appears to have been positioned immediately in front of the outer edge of the quartzite sarcophagus, mirroring the position of the back wall of the vaulted chamber slightly beyond the chamber's eastern end. The wall presumably would have had a doorway, arched or with a wood lintel, that led into the burial chamber.

Given its small dimensions, we cannot be absolutely certain that Chamber 1 represents a chamber proper. Instead it might be a shaft or entrance chamber akin to the larger square feature that fronts the burial chamber of tomb CS11. However, we would note that what survives is quite well-constructed with perfectly vertical walls and brick floor. It does not correspond with the entrance ramps seen in most of the other tombs. Therefore, the construction may have been a small pole-roof or vaulted antechamber that opened into a larger vaulted space that capped the reused quartzite chamber. Moreover, given the relatively shallow depth of the structure as a whole, the use of a vertical shaft would appear improbable. Eroded areas of decayed brickwork were excavated in 2013 west of Chamber 1, and it appears probable there were additional elements to this tomb, possibly including a walled entrance ramp providing access from the local north. Most likely CS6 was a variation of the passage-style format seen in the better-preserved examples in the main tomb cluster, but

Fig. 11.28 The quartzite chamber showing the remains (lower left) of the inner end of the brick vault (view looking west).

THE BURIAL CHAMBER VAULT

Only vestiges of the burial chamber vault remained in 2013. Enough was preserved to indicate the position and approximate dimensions of the vault (Fig. 11.28). Brickwork at the southeast corner preserved the tomb's east wall which was set just outside the end of the quartzite chamber, as well as elements of the incline vault that was set against this wall. The vault's south side aligns with the wall of Chamber 1. A small section of brickwork from the vault also survived at the junction between Chamber 1 and the burial chamber. Based on the surviving brickwork, we estimate the vault to have been approximately 4.7 m long with a width at the base of 1.9 m. Using an average ratio for the height to width of 2:3 based on the better-preserved vaults in the cemetery we estimate

the vault to have risen ca. 1.2 m above the top of the quartzite chamber. Given the substantial size and depth of the sarcophagus recess (1.32 m), a vault of this modest height would have created a quite spacious burial chamber with the vault rising some 2.5+ m above the floor of the sarcophagus recess.

A notable result of the reuse of the 13th Dynasty quartzite chamber in CS6 is that the relative position of the sarcophagus and canopic recess matches not only the two identically configured 13th Dynasty royal tombs, S9 and 10, but also the Second Intermediate Period tombs that emulated this same layout. In all cases, the burial chamber is oriented local north-south (true east-west), with the burial recess at the local north end and the canopic recess at the burial chamber's inner end. It is striking how consistent this orientation is among all tombs in the necropolis. The question arises as to whether the abandoned quartzite burial chamber was already in this position when it was reused, or whether it had to be moved or rotated to achieve this orientation. We consider this issue further below in considering the date and function of the retaining wall that flanks the north side of CS6.

THE REUSED 13TH DYNASTY ROYAL CRYPT

The reused 13th Dynasty royal burial chamber incorporated into CS6 is a monolithic feature, carved from a block of red-orange quartzite with striations of white, yellow, and purple. The material and dimensions of the chamber are extremely similar to the burial chamber still in situ within tomb S9, as well as that discovered in 2015 in situ in tomb S10. The chamber's exterior dimensions are 4.7 m long, 2.55 m wide, and 2.25 m high. The exterior is rough with a bulging, convex profile on all sides, particularly pronounced on the north. The rough exterior reflects the fact that the chamber was designed essentially to be a crypt embedded beneath surrounding masonry just as occurs in tombs S9 and S10. Following the configuration in S9 and S10, the crypt would have been fitted with a monolithic lid-stone with a vaulted interior that was mortared into place over the back end of the chamber and extending halfway over

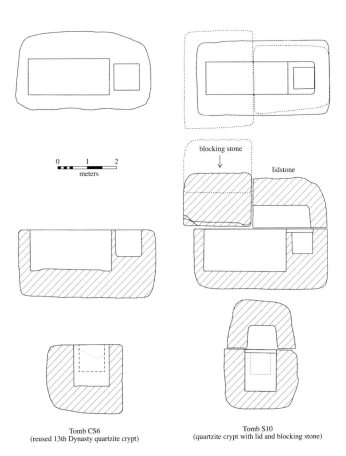

blocking stone

lidstone

0   1   2
meters

Tomb CS6
(reused 13th Dynasty quartzite crypt)

Tomb S10
(quartzite crypt with lid and blocking stone)

Fig. 11.29 Scale comparison of the reused quartzite crypt in CS6 and the in situ crypt and lid system of tomb S10.

the sarcophagus recess (Fig. 11.29). A separate port-cullis block that covered the front half of the crypt would have been lowered into place once the burial had been installed. The top surface of the crypt, onto which this closure system would have been low-ered, as well as the recesses for the sarcophagus and canopic chest are finely dressed. The sarcophagus recess is 2.76 m long, 1.18 m wide, and 1.32 m deep. The smaller canopic recess measures 0.855 m cubi-cally and is separated from the sarcophagus recess by a 0.15 m wide dividing wall.

The chamber reused in CS6 is slightly larger than those still in situ inside tombs S9 and S10. Examina-tion of the quartzite made in 2013 confirms the ori-gin of the chamber in the northern quartzite quarries of Gebel Ahmar. Magnification of the stone under a 60x lens shows the combination of rounded sand grains with chert, a composition that occurs only at the Gebel Ahmar, and not in the southern quartzite quarries near Elephantine. This follows the wider patterns of late Middle Kingdom royal mortuary structures at South Abydos where it appears all of the quartzite originated in the Gebel Ahmar quarries.

Comparison of the reused crypt with the installed example in situ inside of tomb S10 presents some use-ful observations. It is noteworthy that the sarcopha-gus recess of the CS6 crypt is identical in length (2.76 m) to that in S10 but somewhat wider (1.18 m as op-posed to 1.06 in S10). The depth of the recess is not as great and, while S10's crypt has a smooth floor, that of CS6 retains a raised central surface that is still rela-tively rough, surrounded by a more deeply cut trough around the inner walls of the recess. This suggests that the sarcophagus recess had been nearly finished but still awaited smooth dressing of the floor. The ex-terior of the S10 sarcophagus is also roughly dressed but the overall contours are closer to rectangular than the bulging exterior profile of the CS6 crypt. These aspects suggest the chamber later reused by tomb CS6 was close to finished but was still awaiting a fi-nal stage of internal dressing and external trimming: work that would have accompanied the installation of the crypt into the tomb's substructure.

In its present state, the crypt has several signif-icant cracks running through the block. The largest crack runs through the narrow end of the sarcophagus recess (close to the northwest corner) and continues lengthways along the lower north wall of the sarcoph-agus recess (see Figs.11.27–28). Another crack runs

between the northeast corner of the canopic recess and the exterior of the block. There are other second-ary cracks. One possibility to be considered is whether the block was abandoned during the 13th Dynasty due to these flaws, which may have developed subsequent to the block's delivery to the building site at South Abydos. Alternatively, the block may have suffered damage later in the Second Intermediate Period in the process of relocating it for reuse in tomb CS6. While it is difficult to determine the relationship of the cracks in the chamber relative to the primary and secondary phases of its use at the site, we may note that the ma-jor defect is likely to have resulted from considerable force effecting the chamber's north side. Given the mass of the stone, such cracks almost certainly cannot have been produced from any implement. The likely source of such crack would be the weight of the ca. 50-ton chamber bearing down on the weaker points of the walls or corners while the object was turned on its side or top, possibly while being rolled.

When we first discovered the quartzite chamber of CS6 in 2013, the lack of an identified burial chamber at that point within nearby tomb S10 suggested the possibility that the chamber may have been extracted from that structure.[1] The cracks appeared explicable as damage caused during the removal and relocation of the chamber to its present location in CS6. How-ever, in 2014–2015, full excavation of S10 revealed not only the in situ chamber within that structure but the inherent unfeasibility of extracting a massive cham-ber of this scale from such a depth (10 m below the desert surface). These results suggest that if the CS6 chamber was moved from some other location during the Second Intermediate Period, that location is un-likely to have been very far from its current position. Indeed, the presence of a well-built retaining wall ad-jacent to the chamber suggests it was not relocated at all but was repurposed in the very same position in which it was abandoned during the 13th Dynasty. The origin of the cracks remains ambiguous.

SUBTERRANEAN RETAINING WALL

Unlike any of the other Second Intermediate Pe-riod tombs, CS6 is flanked on its north exterior by a well-constructed, brick wall, today preserved to a maximum height of 2.1 m. The wall has a preserved length of ca. 6.5 m but has ragged ends and may be reduced from an originally longer wall. The bricks measure an average of 10–12 x 16–17 x 36–38 cm. At its lowest elevation, the base of this wall sits at the same level as the bottom of the quartzite chamber, however the base is not level and slopes downwards from the east. The wall rises up to essentially the same height as the top of the quartzite chamber. The brickwork is carefully mortared with a slight outward batter towards the north. Although well-built, this wall was never plastered or whitewashed. It runs very close to the northern side of the chamber (ranging between 0.8 and ca. 1.2 m from the chamber), but its orientation is slightly skewed, rotated approximately 10° further north (clockwise) relative to the quartzite chamber. This orientation does not match that of the 13th Dynasty enclosure wall, which sits slightly further north, nor does it appear to relate directly to any other architectural elements in the cemetery. At the wall base between the quartzite chamber and wall face, a complete roughware Nile jar was exposed (Fig. 11.30). Like other roughware jars on the exterior of the tombs this appears to be related to the construction process.

It is clear this wall is related to the position of the sarcophagus chamber, but the question arises as to whether this is a remnant of the abandoned 13th Dynasty construction project or whether the wall was built in conjunction with the Second Intermediate Period reuse of the quartzite chamber to create tomb CS6. Given the size of the chamber, it appears quite possible it was never moved from the location where it was abandoned during the 13th Dynasty. The wall may belong to the initial process of cutting into the desert subsurface and situating the chamber in what would eventually become the core of the royal tomb. In this case, the chamber was rediscovered during the Second Intermediate Period—still in its existing position—where it was then adapted for reuse with the addition of the brick shaft and vault. Alternatively, the retaining wall may be a result of a secondary process of moving and resetting the chamber

Fig. 11.30 Roughware jar (Nile C fabric) from base of the retaining wall adjacent to CS6.

from some other location. The purpose of the wall may have been to act as a support and retaining structure for the nearby enclosure wall which occupies an elevated position and which was presumably still standing to significant height during the Second Intermediate Period.

When tomb CS6 was first discovered and excavated in 2013, we initially theorized that the quartzite chamber had been reused from tomb S10 further to the south. The reason for this supposition was the 1901–1902 work of Weigall had failed to locate a burial chamber in S10. His report suggested the possibility that the burial chamber had been removed from S10 and, therefore, might be located in the vicinity. Consequently, an attractive hypothesis was that CS6 was created by the extraction of the burial chamber from S10 and removal to its current location. However, as we have noted above, the excavation of the interior of S10 completed during 2014–2016 has now disproven this possibility. The work in S10 has revealed the well-preserved substructure of S10 including the in situ chamber with its lid and blocking stone in place. Moreover, exposure of the massive internal architecture of both S9 and S10 in recent years has emphasized the unfeasibility of the deconstruction and extraction of these massive burial chambers. The reused chamber in CS6 is a third royal burial chamber that has no association with tomb S10 but belongs to an abandoned late Middle Kingdom royal tomb initiated in the area north of S10.

As a result, it appears much less probable that the reused chamber of CS6 was ever moved from its original position. Given the ca. 50+ ton weight of the feature, and the difficulty that would accompany its movement across the soft desert sand, it appears highly likely that it remains in the very position where it was abandoned during the 13th Dynasty. Moreover, we must observe the variant orientation of CS6 which is rotated substantially (ca. 18°) counterclockwise relative to the predominant east-west (local north-south) orientation of the Second Intermediate Period tombs. If the chamber had been purposefully repositioned they might have achieved a comparable orientation to the other main cluster tombs.

On that basis, the retaining wall appears to have served as part of the original process of lowering the chamber into position in the desert subsurface. The intent may have been to lower the chamber to a depth equivalent to that in tomb S9 and S10 (ca. 10 m below desert surface) and in the center of the enclosure. However, the chamber never reached its intended final location, which should have lain substantially south of the enclosure wall. The size of the bricks used in the retaining wall is smaller than the large format 12 x 19 x 38 cm bricks used in the 13th Dynasty enclosure wall. However, bricks of comparable dimensions also occur in various ancillary walls around the masonry-built interior of tomb S10 suggesting they may have served comparable functions in the process of building the subterranean architecture. On this basis, as well as the fact that none of the Second Intermediate Period tombs have indications for use of such mortared retaining walls, we would conclude the higher probability is that the wall is a residual feature of the unfinished 13th Dynasty royal tomb.

TOMB CS7

GENERAL DESCRIPTION

Tomb CS7 is located just 4.5 m south of the 13th Dynasty enclosure wall and 8 m west of CS6 (Figs. 11.31 and 11.32). The brickwork of CS7, like that of CS6, is substantially eroded and indicates that the ground level in this area of the site was originally higher than it is now. It appears that at the time of construction the nearby 13th Dynasty enclosure wall may have been standing to significant height. Both of these tombs were likely buried beneath sand that had accumulated against the south face of the enclosure wall. The area appears to have suffered substantial wind deflation and the 13th Dynasty wall is now reduced to a single course over most of its length. As a result, these tombs, with their entrances at higher elevation and originally protected by sand accumulation against the enclosure wall, are both the least well-preserved in the main tomb cluster. Although the back wall of the burial chamber of CS7 is preserved to its original height, the tomb as a whole has suffered considerably and preserves none of the stone lining of the burial chamber. The two outer chambers are heavily eroded and have lost much of the upper parts of their walls.

The tomb was excavated in the summer of 2013. At that point, based on the plan and description published by Weigall, it was immediately clear that CS7 is the northernmost of the three tombs he had

Fig. 11.31 Overview of CS7 with the 13th Dynasty enclosure wall (left) and tombs CS6 and CS5 behind (view looking east).

encountered in his 1901–1902 season. His brief description of the tomb is as follows:

> The last of the three tombs had only three chambers. The first was 3½ ft. wide and ran down for 10 ft. to the next division, 4 ft. wide and 9 ft. long and roofed as before. Again a door blocked with a limestone slab led to the burial, in a room 10 ft. by 5½ ft, roofed, and containing the remains of a sarcophagus similar to those described above (Weigall in Ayrton et al. 1904:16).

In its current state of preservation, CS7 resembles a slightly simplified version of the Second Intermediate Period tombs employing a two-chamber interior fronted by an entrance ramp. However, what now appears to be an entrance ramp is certainly the remains of the tomb's pole-roof chamber, this feature having been reduced to a height of only a few courses. CS7 in all likelihood employed the same standard set of chambers seen in the other tombs and once would have had an entrance ramp extending west from the pole-roof chamber.

The three surviving elements are the pole-roof-chamber (Chamber 1), the central vaulted chamber (Chamber 2), and the burial chamber (Chamber 3), together extending over a length of 9.6 m. The tomb makes use of two different sizes of brick: the standard wall bricks measure 30 x 16 x 9 cm, while slightly thinner bricks, measuring 30 x 16 x 7 cm, occur in the vaults. Due to the elevation of its construction, CS7 is not cut down into the solid, desert subsurface but is built in the looser sand. As a result, like CS5, the chambers all have built brick floors with no use of

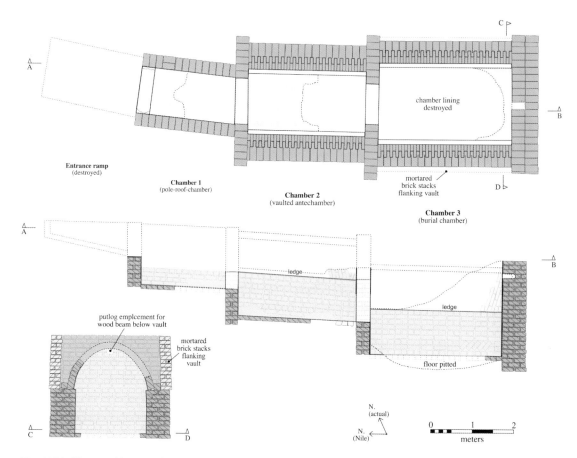

Fig. 11.32 Plan and longitudinal section of tomb CS7.

the plastered desert subsurface as occurs frequently elsewhere in the cemetery. Although the two vaulted chambers form a linear grouping, the orientation of the pole-roof chamber employs the slight turn towards the northeast also seen in CS8. The angle of rotation is slightly lower than occurs in CS8 but betrays the same intention of orienting the tomb's entrance and outer sections towards the northwest.

CHAMBER 1
(PROBABLE POLE-ROOF CHAMBER)

The tomb's first chamber is badly destroyed. The side walls survive to a height of only four brick courses. The chamber's interior measures 1.1 m wide by 2.1 m in length and is rotated 7° north (clockwise) relative to the tomb's inner chambers. The floor is bricked and coated with mud plaster. No original whitewash survives. One of the crucial details to this

chamber is its construction with walls of alternating courses of headers and stretchers composing a wall thickness of one full brick length (36 cm). This is the standard mode of construction for vertical chamber walls throughout the Second Intermediate Period tombs at South Abydos. The walled entrance ramps, which survive on several tombs such as CS4 and CS9 (Seneb-Kay), are typically constructed of thin rim walls, only a single brick width (ca. 15 cm). Even the unusually long walled approach to CS10 is flanked by walls of only a single brick width. This part of CS7 is more robustly built and evidently composes a subterranean chamber rather than an open ramp. Moreover, the floor in the chamber slopes only slightly inwards unlike the steeper downward gradient that typically occurs in the entrance ramps. We may be virtually certain that a walled ramp originally provided access to this chamber, which, due to its elevation, probably followed the format for the initial chamber and had a flat, wooden pole-roof.

CHAMBER 2 (VAULTED CHAMBER)

The central vaulted chamber measures 1.3 by 2.85 m. The floor is bricked and plastered. The edges of the vault survive with mortared brick stacks flanking the vault's exterior and a ca. 0.15 m ledge on either side of the interior (Fig. 11.33). An interesting construction detail of Chamber 2 is the fact that the vault bricks are not inclined towards the interior of the tomb, as normally occurs, but rather they incline outwards leaning against the cross wall that separates Chambers 1 and 2. This provides an additional structural clue that Chamber 1 was a fully roofed chamber and not an unwalled entrance ramp, which was appended to the face of the outermost chamber

During the 2012–2013 excavation of Chamber 2, a substantial slab of violet colored sandstone measuring 0.43 by 0.88 m and 0.15 m in thickness was exposed loose in the sand fill slightly above floor level. The block has remnants of a line of mud mortar adhering to its surface indicating it originally was engaged into the building and abutted by other masonry or a mud-mortared wall face. It is possible this block derives from the stone blocking that Weigall described at the doorway into the burial chamber of this tomb (although stated to be limestone not sandstone), possibly indicating use of a portcullis-style entrance like that preserved in Seneb-Kay's tomb and indicated by emplacements in two locations in tombs CS10. Alternatively, the block could be a lintel from one of the two interior doorways in the tomb. The door into the vaulted antechamber in the tomb of Seneb-Kay preserves an in situ sandstone lintel, mortared and plastered with gypsum whitewash. A similar use of sandstone could occur at this position in CS7. Another, perhaps more likely, option is that the sandstone may be part of the stone lining of the burial chamber. Although the stone-lined crypts in the cemetery predominantly use limestone, tomb CS5 which is close to CS7 at the northern end of the main tomb cluster uses the same violet colored sandstone in combination with limestone. The proximity of CS7 to CS5 could reflect a close contemporaneity and use of the same materials in the burial chamber lining.

BURIAL CHAMBER (CHAMBER 3)

At the level of the wall base, the burial chamber measures 1.65 by 3.18 m. The chamber employs the

Fig. 11.33 The central vaulted chamber (Chamber 2) and the burial chamber of CS7 (view looking east).

Fig. 11.34 Detail of the inner wall of CS7's burial chamber with preserved brickwork and plaster of the vault (view looking east).

standard format of vertical side walls supporting a barrel vault, the face of which is set back creating ca. 0.15 m ledges on both sides. Although the chamber lacks any surviving stonework, the preservation of the eastern wall is sufficient to preserve parts of the vault and the full height and curvature of the vault's articulation with the back wall (Fig. 11.34). The wall height from floor to the ledge is 1.05 m and the height from floor level to the interior of the vaulted roof was slightly over 2 meters. The chamber is entirely denuded of its stone lining. Although Weigall mentioned seeing remains of the stone-lined burial recess (described as "remains of a sarcophagus"), any surviving masonry appears to have been removed subsequent to his work in 1901–1902. This suggests the tomb may have been left substantially open and suffered modern damage that occurred after the end of the Egypt Exploration Fund work. The 1.05 m height of the burial chamber's side walls suggests the format of the burial chamber was quite similar to CS8 where a stone-lined crypt extended up to the height of the ledge and formed a ca. 1 m deep recess.

The vault's brickwork is laid in inclined courses and leans against the back wall. In the upper part of the inner wall are denuded remnants of a putlog emplacement for a wood beam that originally ran the length of the chamber immediately beneath the vault. Small areas of mud plaster and whitewash, completely eroded elsewhere throughout the tomb, adhere to the inner face of the vault. Linear stacks of mortared bricks line the exterior of the vault providing mass against the outward force of the vault. Unusually, these stacks are mortared to the back wall, which rises up to square corners aligned with the exterior of the brick stacks.

Despite its highly eroded condition, CS7 provides some intriguing architectural indications for the possibility, also discussed below in the case of CS10 and CS11, that some of the Second Intermediate Period tombs may have had aboveground superstructures. What appears notable about CS7's brickwork is the way the external brick stacks flanking the burial chamber are carefully laid and mortared, engaging with the back wall, which rises up to form corners at the back of the tomb. At the front of the burial chamber, the mortared brick stacks are also bonded to the cross wall separating Chambers 2–3, which steps outwards on the desert terrain in a way that appears similar to the construction of the spur walls at the front of tomb CS10 (see discussion below). The mortared brick stacks also flank Chamber 2 with the same care in laying the courses. None of the other tombs display this particular level of effort in the construction of the brick stacks, which are typically loose piles of bricks laid alongside the sides of the vault.

The essential result of this mode of construction is that the brick stacks flanking CS7 form solid brick walls above the level of substructure. Perhaps this is simply a more careful mode of construction akin to the loose brick stacks found in the other tombs and intended to address the lateral force exerted by the vaults. However, the brick stacks appear quite possibly designed here to serve a dual purpose: (1) to stabilize the sides of the vaults, and (2) to provide the foundation for aboveground features that rose up over the tomb. The construction technique seen here is comparable to examples of New Kingdom private tombs at North Abydos where single vaulted chambers were capped by brick-built pyramids. We will return to consider the issue of superstructures on the Second Intermediate Period tombs in the next chapter.

Given the robbed and highly damaged nature of the burial chamber of CS7, it is not surprising that we found no original contents within the chamber itself. However, in the debris on the south side of the chamber a painted coffin fragment was recovered which potentially derives from the original burial (Fig. 11.35). This is a fragment of a cedar wood, polychrome coffin with yellow background. The similarity here is notable to the decorative treatment of the Sobekhotep (N) sarcophagus refashioned to form the canopic

0   2
cm

Fig. 11.35 Cedar coffin fragment with yellow ground found in debris on the south side of CS7.

box of Seneb-Kay. The fragment has painted blue border bands, but no text elements survive. Given the disturbed context, the origin of the fragment remains uncertain, but it is possible it derives from the CS7 burial equipment. The fragment perhaps indicates reuse of cedar wood funerary equipment in CS7 paralleling the case of Seneb-Kay.

TOMB CS8

GENERAL DESCRIPTION

CS8 is the southernmost tomb in the main cluster (Figs. 11.36 and 11.37). In the construction techniques, dimensions, and architectural details of its burial chamber and vaulted antechamber, CS8 is almost identical to CS5. However, CS8 differs from CS5 in the addition of a pole-roof chamber as the first internal space. The structure lies extremely close to CS10 but was built at a significantly higher elevation than CS10. The entrance ramp that once fronted the first chamber is now missing but small stubs of brickwork projecting from the well-preserved walls of the pole-roof chamber show where this ramp bonded with the walls of the pole-roof chamber. Exposure of the compact subsurface in this area indicates the general position of the ramp, which was approximately 2 m in overall length. Apart from the now-missing entrance ramp, CS8 includes three chambers covering a total length of 9.5 m: (1) a pole-roof chamber (Chamber 1); (2) a brick vaulted central chamber (Chamber 2); and (3) a limestone-lined, vaulted burial chamber (Chamber 3).

Tomb CS8 is not absolutely linear but displays a similar feature to CS5 and CS7: use of a skewed entrance where the walled ramp and first chamber have been rotated off the axis of the burial chamber to achieve a northwesterly orientation. In CS8, the first chamber (Chamber 1) is angled northwards of the main axis by approximately 26°. There appear to be no physical reasons why these tombs should not be absolutely linear. It appears possible that this northwest orientation of the entrance has a symbolic or conceptual basis. However, if so, the principle was inconsistently applied and some of the tombs including CS4, CS9 (Seneb-Kay), and CS10 lack this shift in orientation. The use of the skewed orientation could

Fig. 11.36 Overview of tomb CS8 (view looking west).

indicate a close chronological relationship for the tombs that show it: CS5, CS7, and CS8.

CS8 was excavated in the summer season of 2013 and reopened again in the summer of 2014. CS8 is certainly one of the three tombs in the Second Intermediate Period cemetery that Arthur Weigall encountered and excavated in 1901–1902. The relatively high elevation of the tomb explains why he found it, but not the larger structure of CS10, which sits only a few meters away but buried at significantly greater depth. Of the three tombs that Weigall examined, he

considered CS8 to provide the best architectural example of the tomb type and he gave this tomb the longest description in *Abydos, Part III*:

To the north of S10 and S9, there are three smaller tombs constructed upon a uniform plan. The most westerly of the three runs down from the surface as a sloping passage or chamber of whitewashed brick, 3 ft. wide and 10 ft. long. At the bottom a limestone slab fixed into a brick doorway originally blocked the way. This was the entrance to

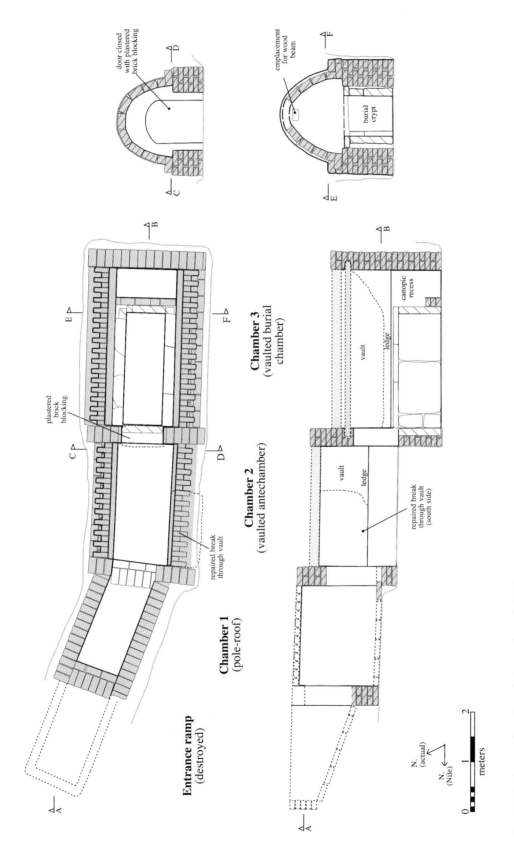

Fig. 11.37 Plan and sectional views of tomb CS8.

a second chamber with a barrel-shaped roof of whitewashed brick, which had, of course, had fallen in. The chamber was 4 ft. wide and high enough in the centre for a person to stand upright. It was 8 ft. long and ended against another limestone slab. Behind this was a clean drop of a couple of feet into the burial chamber, which had originally been roofed like the second chamber. It was 10 ft. long, 4 ½ ft. wide, and about 8 ft. high, the walls whitewashed. Four slabs of limestone seem to have encased the coffin, and there may have been a fifth placed across them as a lid. One inlaid eye from a coffin was the only fragment of burial that remained (Weigall in Ayrton et al. 1904:16).

The work of 2013 produced very few artifacts that might be attributable to the original burial. From this tomb, we recovered a small sample of skeletal remains, insufficient evidence to address the interment proper. The fact that Weigall had entered the tomb previously explains the lack of material finds. The location of the inlaid coffin eye he mentions in his report remains unknown. Weigall's description of limestone slabs between the successive chambers is considered further below in the detailed discussion of the tomb's architecture.

POLE-ROOF CHAMBER (CHAMBER 1)

The pole-roof chamber measures 0.9 m wide and ca. 2.1 m in length, although the chamber's dimensions are irregular as a result of the change in orientation of the tomb at the junction between tomb's first two chambers. Chamber 1 preserves the brick threshold at both ends and whitewash on its walls. The floor was originally bricked, plastered, and whitewashed, but only a single row of bricks survives at the chamber's inner end. The chamber does not preserve the original wooden pole-roof although the uppermost course of brickwork has patches of wood staining adhering to the surface indicating the extant walls are at their full height (1.7 m). This evidence corroborates the lack of a brick vault and makes it clear that CS8 followed the typical arrangement of the other Second Intermediate Period tombs with a wooden pole-roof over the initial chamber.

CENTRAL VAULTED CHAMBER (CHAMBER 2)

The central chamber is vaulted, measuring 1.15 by ca. 2.4 m, although again the shift in orientation makes the lengths of the two side walls slightly different. The floor steps down 0.45 m from the threshold leading in from the tomb's first chamber. Like the outer chamber, the floor of Chamber 2 is destroyed. Originally, it was constructed of laid brick, plastered and whitewashed. Floor bricks are still preserved along the edges of the chamber's inner end. The chamber employs the standard format of a vault outset (0.15 m) from the wall faces creating a ledge at a height of 0.6 m from the wall base and extending along the two sides of the chamber. The vault is badly damaged on the chamber's north side but preserved to nearly its original height of 1.6 m on the south side.

The better-preserved south side of the vault provides an important piece of evidence regarding the history of the burials in the Second Intermediate Period cemetery (Fig. 11.38). The western end of the vault's south side shows clear indications of having been broken through and repaired. The brickwork in this section of the vault is not laid in the normal system but uses stacks of horizontally set bricks. Mud plaster bonds these horizontally laid courses to the adjacent vault brickwork. It is clear the vault was penetrated at some stage creating a substantial hole in the front two-thirds of the vault's southern side. The vault was then quickly repaired without bothering to replicate the complicated vault structure. The tomb's entrance must have been reopened at that stage to allow the inner surface of the repair to be mud plastered. Interestingly, there is a similar robbers' hole that punctured the south side of the vault of tomb CS5 in this same relative location suggesting multiple tombs were targeted in this way. The structural evidence from CS8 provides strong indications for tomb robbery that occurred at a point in time when the cemetery was still in active use. It appears likely that the robbery process was halted and the tomb repaired and reburied. Although, it is conceivable that the penetration of the central vault of CS8 resulted in the complete robbery of its original burial. If so, repair to the vault of the central chamber could be interpreted not as the resealing of the tomb after a failed robbery attempt, but rather an indication of use of the tomb for a secondary interment.

Fig. 11.38 The central chamber (Chamber 2) showing the repaired break in the south side of the vault.

In view of the evidence for penetration through the central vault of CS8, it is interesting that the opening between Chamber 2 and the burial chamber preserves in situ a roughly laid mudbrick blocking (Fig. 11.39). This consists of loose stacks of bricks set with their longer dimension paralleling the tomb's axis and coated with mud plaster on the outer face. The stacked bricks and mud coating sit directly on remnants of the chamber's floor bricks still preserved at the inner corners of the chamber. The blocking is preserved to a height of nearly 1 m. Given its rudimentary nature, this closure does not appear to belong to the tomb's original interment. The blocking was evidently laid very quickly suggesting it represents a resealing of the burial chamber connected with the penetration through the vault of Chamber 2. It appears that a robbery attempt was made not long after the primary interment. But, in all likelihood, this initial entry failed to fully despoil the tomb's contents, and repair and resealing of the structure then occurred. Presumably the tomb was thoroughly plundered at a later point in time.

THE BURIAL CHAMBER (CHAMBER 3)

The burial chamber of CS8 is a well-preserved example of the stone-lined crypt found in most of the Second Intermediate Period tombs at South Abydos (Figs. 11.40 and 11.41). The interior of the brick chamber measures 3.15 x 1.23 m. The vault sits atop the chamber's side walls with a ca. .12 m outset on both sides forming a plastered ledge along both sides of the vault. The chamber employs a brick vault that rises to a height of 2.3 m. The inner wall is preserved almost to its original height and has an emplacement for a wood beam (ca. 0.12 x 0.23 m) that once ran the length of the chamber directly beneath the top of the vault. This beam, like other examples (CS5, CS7), appears to have been used as part of the vault construction and was removed and the recess plastered over upon completion of the vault.

The chamber interior is divided into a 2.4 m long front section lined with mortared limestone

was meant to mimic the style of a monolithic stone burial chamber such as that used in CS10. Whereas CS10's crypt is actually composed of a single ca. 7-ton block of stone, the burial chamber of CS 8 only emulates the appearance of a monolithic stone chamber.

Behind the stone-lined crypt is a low dividing wall of mud-brick and a space measuring 0.58 m deep extending the full width of the chamber. There is no preserved stone lining beyond the receptacle for the sarcophagus. However, the plaster and whitewash on the chamber's inner wall does not continue lower than the elevation of the ledge suggesting there was originally a brick-edged receptacle or loculus in this area, which was torn away with the exception of the lower brickwork at the back of the sarcophagus recess. Although it is more heavily damaged, the configuration of this space appears to have been nearly identical to that which is better preserved in tomb CS5. The space constitutes a receptacle similar to those in other tombs and likely designed for interment of the canopic chest.

One question regarding the burial chamber of CS8 is whether the stone-lined crypt would have been sealed originally with a slab covering like that recovered in neighboring CS10. No evidence was recovered of fragments that could be attributed to such a covering. However, the architectural attention to creating a sarcophagus receptacle with a continuous

blocks that form a burial crypt. The crypt's internal dimensions are 0.8 (width) by 2.26 (length) and 1 m (height). It is composed of vertical slabs or orthostats on top of which are set horizontal slabs directly abutting the plastered brick ledges of the vault. The floor is unlined but was cut into the compact desert subsurface, which was plastered with gypsum whitewash, still preserved in many areas. The dimensions of the sarcophagus recess are nearly identical to the burial chamber of CS5. In the case of CS8, the preservation is sufficiently good to appreciate how the configuration of this type of slab-lined burial crypt

Fig. 11.40 The stone-lined burial crypt of CS8 (view looking north).

Fig. 11.41 The stone-lined burial crypt of CS8 (view looking west).

Fig. 11.42 Roughware jar in situ on south exterior side of Chamber 2.

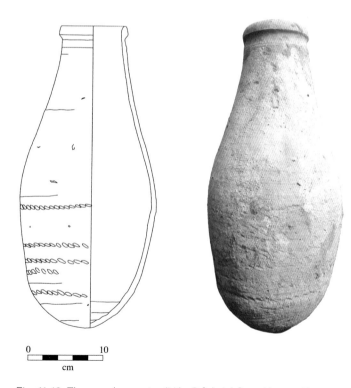

0   10
cm

Fig. 11.43 The roughware jar (Nile C fabric) from the south side of tomb CS8.

flat ledge, formed by narrow blocks set atop the vertical wall slabs, suggests strongly that the chamber was designed to have such a covering. It is interesting that the loose-stacked, mud plastered brick blocking in the door of the burial chamber extends all the way up to the very edge of the crypt, even projecting slightly over the inner face of the crypt. This suggests that the brick blocking may be secondary, perhaps added at the same time as the repair to the break through the roof of the central chamber. On that basis, the burial chamber may have been entered and the original blocking damaged or removed during the robbery process. Potentially the lid stones themselves were partially or wholly removed already at that point in time. Installation of a secondary blocking indicates either that the complete plundering of the burial was interrupted. A less likely possibility is that a secondary interment occurred inside an already plundered tomb.

MATERIAL REMAINS

Excavation of CS8 produced few artifacts, and the association of those encountered inside the tomb is ambiguous due to the fact that Weigall clearly substantially cleared this tomb. Fragmentary stone and ceramic vessels were recovered from the interior of the tomb in 2012–2013. These include: a rough limestone bowl and a thin-walled stone vessel of marble or white breccia with dark veining. From debris inside of Chamber 2 was recovered a shallow, red-slipped bowl with white cross-line decoration applied on the exterior. When CS8 was reopened in 2014, further exposure was made of the tomb's exterior. A complete Nile silt jar was found at high elevation in the sand fill on the south side of Chamber 2 (Fig. 11.42).

The vessel is flat based with a simple neck (Fig. 11.43). This jar does not belong to the burial assemblage but is connected with the tomb construction and was discarded in the fill surrounding the structure. This follows the pattern seen around the tomb of Seneb-Kay where vessels of this same type were recovered in the fill surrounding the burial chamber. It is likely full excavation of CS8's exterior would reveal further ceramics connected with the tomb construction. Near floor level in Chamber 1 was a small fragment of gilding attached to white gypsum plaster. The fragment (not illustrated) was too small to provide significant information but likely derives from a gilded coffin, canopic chest, or funerary mask. The object generally follows the pattern of neighboring tombs indicating the high status of the burials in the Second Intermediate Period cemetery.

HUMAN REMAINS

Disarticulated human remains were recovered in the central vaulted chamber of CS8. Near the doorway between Chamber 1 and 2 a human scapula was recovered. A mandible was recovered in the same vicinity and these elements appear to derive from the original occupant. More significantly, loose in the sand fill adjacent to the upper preserved areas of the burial chamber, two skulls were recovered. Subsequent excavation of the closely adjacent tomb CS10 recovered more extensive skeletal remains from that tomb's burial chamber. This includes a mandible that derives from one of these two skulls and shows that it belongs

to the burial of CS10. The other skull which pairs with the mandible found inside CS8 is associated with the CS8 burial itself. The two skulls originating from CS8 and CS10 respectively had been disturbed by ancient robbers and Weigall's later examination of tomb CS8. While only representing a small segment of the CS8 individual, the surviving osteological evidence provides some evidence for the occupant. Tomb CS8 follows the predominant usage pattern of the Second Intermediate Period tombs with remains of a single adult male burial, a man who died at ca. 50+ years of age. We examine the CS8 skeletal evidence in Chapter 13.

TOMB CS10

GENERAL DESCRIPTION

CS10 occupies the center of the main tomb cluster. The structure is flanked closely on its south side by CS8 (Fig. 11.44) and on the east by the group of three brick-lined shafts (CS12–14). Tomb CS10 is the largest and deepest of the tombs in the Second Intermediate Period cemetery. Although it follows the same basic architectural format as the other tombs, it displays a number of unique construction features. The structure descends to a depth of more than 5 m below the desert surface: approximately twice the depth of the shallower tombs. Despite its significant size, and the fact that its entrance ramp lay quite close to the surface, the tomb was entirely missed by Weigall who managed to work on the adjacent tombs CS4 and CS8 while not noticing CS10. The location of the tomb was detected in the 2002–2003 magnetic survey, which identified the higher elevated brickwork belonging to the walled entrance ramp and the tomb's west-facing facade. Excavation was conducted during the summer of 2014.

The tomb incorporates an architectural sequence comparable to that seen in other tombs: (1) a brick-edged entry ramp; (2) a flat-roofed wooden pole-roof chamber forming the first internal space; (3) a brick-vaulted antechamber leading to (4) a vaulted burial chamber with stone crypt (Figs. 11.45 and 11.46). However, the scale of construction that occurs in CS10 distinguishes this tomb as one that was built substantially ahead of the death of its occupant, and with considerably greater investment of time and

Fig. 11.44 Overview of the deeply set chambers of CS10 (foreground) with CS8 behind (view looking south).

materials. Particularly notable is the use of a mono-lithic limestone sarcophagus chamber weighing ca. 7 tons which was maneuvered to a considerable depth. This limestone crypt was fitted with a brick vault that displays a unique mode of construction. The tomb proper measures 9.2 m in length, but the ramped ap-proach fronting the entrance is considerably larger: 1.5 m wide and preserved to a length of more than 8 m. Therefore, the entire tomb measures over 17 m in length with a predominantly linear orientation and only minor differences in orientation between the successive elements.

THE WALLED ENTRANCE RAMP

The entrance ramp fronting CS10 is significantly larger than that of any of the other tombs in the Second Intermediate Period necropolis (Fig. 11.47). Whereas the typical entrance consists of a walled trough-like feature with a brick floor, CS10 has a walled approach nearly 10 m long with a sand floor.

Moreover, the entrance system shows clear indica-tions of two separate phases, strongly suggesting the completion of this tomb well in advance of the burial.

The ramp consists of four separate wall seg-ments. The two longest wall sections (A and B) sit 1.5 m apart and are preserved out to a distance 8.5 m from the tomb's entrance where they break away. These walls would originally have extended some-what further and, in all likelihood, were completed at the outer end by a narrow end wall as occurs in the smaller ramps in the cemetery. The walls are a single brick in width (20 cm) and extend to within 1.7 m (north side) and 1.4 m (south side) of the tomb entrance, where they break off. The walls sit on the compact desert subsurface and are battered out-wards acting as retaining walls for the loose desert sand behind. The walls' inner faces are smoothed with mud plaster but preserve no whitewash; the ex-terior face built against the desert was unplastered. In the space between these longer wall sections and the front face of the tomb, there are two shorter wall sections (C and D) built not on the desert subsurface

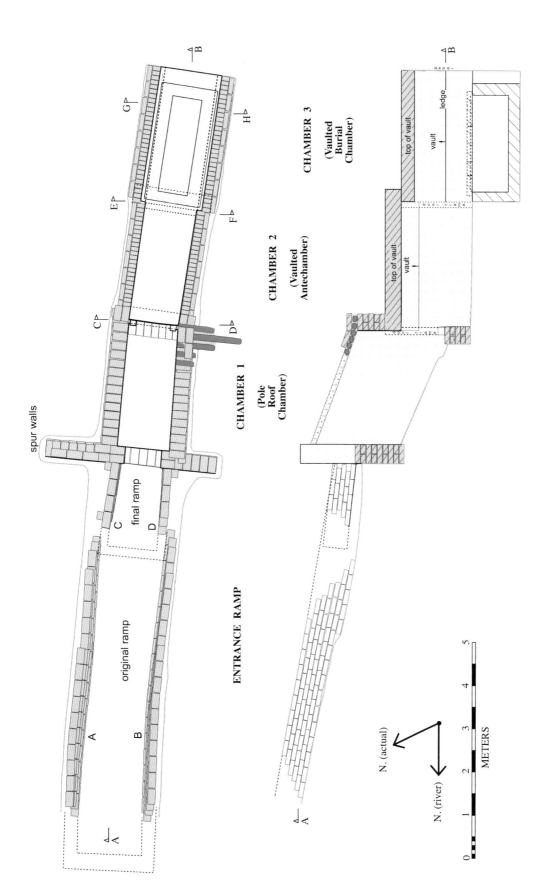

Fig. 11.45 Plan and longitudinal section of tomb CS10.

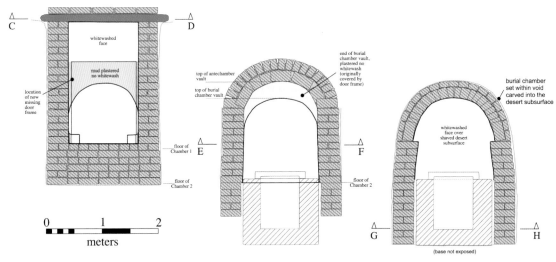

Fig. 11.46 Sections through tomb CS10.

but on loose sand with their base at higher elevation (Fig. 11.48). These walls abut the entrance and are 0.95 m apart at the entrance widening slightly to 1.1 m at the outer end. Like the longer sections, the walls were smoothed. Whitewash from the jambs of the tomb entrance extends slightly out onto the inner face of the walls indicating they are contemporary with the plastering of the tomb itself.

During excavation, it first appeared likely that the secondary phase of the wall system was sitting on top of and sealing in beneath it the extension to the original 1.5 m approach. The two shorter sections, C and D, were then removed to reveal this articulation. However, it was found that the longer sections break off as described above, before reaching the face of the tomb. The disposition of these wall segments indicates that CS10 was originally built with a 1.5 m wide and 8+ m long walled ramp. However, it appears that something must have happened to the inner end of the ramp where it originally articulated with the entrance to the tomb. Secondary walls were then added forming a narrower approach 1 m wide.

One explanation is that the tomb was originally fitted with the longer walled approach, which sat unused for a substantial time period and which became sanded up and partially damaged, prior to installation of the burial. When then burial was installed, rather than emptying a now extensively sanded approach, the tomb's entrance was fitted more expeditiously with a narrower and shorter walled access ramp. Construction of this secondary walled

approach likely reused bricks from the inner end of the original wider approach. It is difficult to estimate how long the tomb may have sat empty prior to installation of the burial. Certainly, the local north-facing entrance of CS10 would have easily sanded up quickly. However, the fact that the walled approach underwent this secondary phase of alteration implies a significant interval between completion of the tomb and installation of the burial.

THE POLE-ROOF CHAMBER (CHAMBER 1)

From the threshold forming the entrance into CS10, there is a sharp drop of 1.07 m to the floor of the first chamber. This initial chamber is a steeply descending space measuring 2.92 m in length and 1.19 m wide at the upper end, narrowing slightly to 1.12 m at its inner end (Fig. 11.49). The chamber floor descends 1.1 m over its length (a -22.5° angle of descent). The chamber is still preserved to its full height of 2.1 m. The tops of the walls preserve remains as well as impressions of wood logs forming a flat pole-roof, identical in technique to that preserved in the tomb of Seneb-Kay (CS9) and several other tombs in the cemetery.

At the time of excavation, two well-preserved wood beams were still in situ on the southeast side (inner end) of the chamber. The beams sat atop the brickwork, extending out over the compact desert

Fig. 11.47 View of the first phase (segments A–B) of the walled entrance ramp of CS10 (view looking east subsequent to removal of the smaller wall segments C–D).

subsurface. Indications of other wood roofing beams occur embedded in the mud mortar showing the entire chamber and the door lintel between Chamber 1 and 2 was capped by the wood roofing. The innermost beam extended a significant length of 1.54 m beyond the chamber, almost reaching the location of tomb CS8 just to the south side of CS10. It is interesting that the wood beam would not have been trimmed to a shorter length. Conceivably the wood framing of the roof also served as underlayment for the fill of a possible superstructure that articulated

with the two spur walls forming the front face of the tomb. The use of beams that extended a substantial distance beyond the chamber walls would have served to strengthen the roof structure when first installed, since the outer ends of the beams would have been weighed down by fill above, thereby reducing the flex of the beam as a whole.

The inner end of the pole-roof chamber is formed by a 0.4 m thick wall that is fitted directly over the outer end of the vaulted roof of Chamber 2. The vault end is bonded into the end of Chamber 1 creating an arched

Fig. 11.48 The second phase of the walled ramp with ramp segments C–D (view looking north).

doorway. The height of the opening from the threshold to the top of the vault was only ca. 1.05 m. The brick-work above the arch was still intact when first exposed. Whitewash had been applied to the upper part of this inner end wall above the doorway, but the wall face was unplastered across the full width of the chamber to a height of 30 cm above the arched entrance (Fig. 11.50). It is clear there must have been a now-missing architectural feature fitted to the inner end of the pole-roof chamber, likely some type of doorway, possibly of wood or stone. Given the space constraints it appears quite likely there was a sliding portcullis system as oc-curs on the entrance to the pole-roof chamber in the tomb of Seneb-Kay. Such a portcullis would have been appended to the outer face of the opening in a similar configuration to that in Seneb-Kay's tomb.

Beneath the arched doorway between Chambers 1 and 2 is a brick threshold that preserved two narrow, plastered jambs abutted on each side by two cube-like limestone blocks, each measuring 14 cm square. The blocks are smooth dressed and are bonded to the floor and also plastered with gypsum on their inner faces, which are flush with the inner face of the threshold that also forms the west (outer) wall of Chamber 2 (Fig. 11.51). The blocks protrude slightly (5–6 cm) into the pole-roof chamber and project be-yond the face of the doorway. Therefore, it appears virtually certain that the two blocks are part of a door framing system as indicated by the non-whitewashed area above the doorway. They may have served as set-ting blocks for now missing wood or stone framing, probably capped with a lintel that covered the wall face above the arched doorway.

SPUR-WALLS AND POSSIBLE SUPERSTRUCTURE

A unique feature preserved in CS10 is an exter-nal tomb facade composed of two spur-walls run-ning perpendicular to the tomb's axis and extending outward from the main entrance. The spur walls are structurally bonded to the main walls of Chamber 1 and built on a solid base measuring a full brick length

Fig. 11.49 The pole-roof chamber of tomb CS10 (view looking east).

exterior facade and one that, due to its high elevation, is likely to have been visible aboveground.

Of particular interest here is the possible function of these spur walls and their architectural relationship with the pole-roof chamber. Spur walls flanking the entrance to subterranean buildings at South Abydos have been identified in two other cases, although not contemporary with the Second Intermediate Period tombs. One of these is a large vaulted, subterranean boat-building dating to the 12th Dynasty and associated with the tomb and enclosure of Senwosret III (Wegner 2017a:5–30). This structure had an arched entryway flanked by spur walls that rose to ground level as they extended outwards from the building. That building had a massive 4.1 x 20 m subterranean vault. The vault rose to a height of 5 m and the area adjacent to it was filled with limestone boulders and debris. In this case, the spur walls appear to have served as a front retaining wall system for the material that covered the vault below. A comparable system occurs in a subterranean building of unclear function dating after the New Kingdom. This structure, a double chambered, vaulted building with a ramped approach had spur walls that again appear to have served a retaining wall for the fill that covered the structure's vaults.

CS10 employs a similar system to these two other buildings but whereas the spur walls served as retaining walls for fill in the examples just mentioned, the spur walls of CS10 rise above the height of the tomb's architecture and would likely have been visible aboveground. The spur walls might have formed a simple facade against the back of which the fill material that buried the tomb chambers was thrown. However, it would appear strange if the builders put considerable effort into creating a smooth plastered, whitewashed facade on one face and a ragged, unplastered face behind. Due to the elevation reached by the spur walls relative to the rest

(38 cm) in thickness. This wall is unplastered and rough on the interior (east) but smoothed and whitewashed on the outer (west) face. The wall base on both sides steps upwards on the desert as it moves away from the tomb proper. Both of these walls are broken at their outer ends. On the north side, the spur wall extends 1.9 m before breaking away. On the south side, the wall is preserved to 1.3 m. These walls are slightly battered and, significantly, like the interior of the tomb are whitewashed on the exterior face. CS10 is, therefore, the only tomb of the Second Intermediate Period group that preserves a form of

Fig. 11.50 The doorway between Chambers 1 and 2 with stone blocks and impression of a now-missing closure that was fitted to the opening (view looking east).

bonded to the deeper walls of the substructure and ran across the brickwork forming the lintel of the front doorway. The other three sides would have been built near surface level and have been entirely destroyed as part of natural erosion and activities of tomb robbers that undermined the roof of the pole-roof chamber and anything above it. If so, the 1.9 m length of the northern side provides a minimum estimate of 4.6 m for the front of the tomb facade. Projected backwards (east-west) an equivalent distance, a possible superstructure might have taken the form of a square debris-filled platform that surmounted Chamber 1 and the western half of Chamber 2.

Such a brick-edged platform could have served as the base for a small brick pyramid or some other form of superstructure that has not survived. Although CS10 is unique in providing possible evidence for a superstructure, it would appear that all of the tombs were marked by some form of aboveground feature, possibly small brick-built pyramids. The period of Seneb-Kay and the other likely royal burials of the main tomb cluster at South Abydos is both preceded and succeeded by the continuation of the pyramid tradition for royal burials. Pyramids, albeit incomplete, are well attested during the 13th Dynasty, including the two adaptations of that architectural tradition, S9 and S10 at South Abydos (Wegner and Cahail 2015:123–164) as well as during the later Second Intermediate Period at Thebes. During the 17th Dynasty, we have both textual sources (such as P.Leopold-Amgerst II [Peet 1920:45–51]) and archaeological evidence for use of pyramid superstructures surmounting royal tombs. The best documented example is the pyramid of Nubkheperre Antef at Dra Abu el-Naga which measured ca. 9 m on its base and was nearly entirely obliterated through the depredations of tomb robbers and other factors (Polz and Seiler 2003:14–20).

If a variation of the pyramid were used at Abydos over the Second Intermediate Period royal burials, these were evidently modestly scaled variants of the architectural form and, like the Theban example of Nubkheperre Antef, subject to erasure from the

of the tomb, these may be part of a retaining wall for a formal superstructure that once surmounted the fill above Chamber 1. Indeed, as mentioned above, the peculiar 1.5 m extension of the best-preserved roofing beam beyond the wall of Chamber 1 could reflect structural preparations for an aboveground superstructure that covered a wider area over Chamber 1.

While the spur walls do not preserve evidence for corners, it appears possible the walls extended outward close to surface level where they turned a corner articulating with additional walls to create a square or rectangular structure at surface level. Essentially the western side is preserved because it was

Fig. 11.51 The threshold between Chambers 1–2 showing the limestone blocks that supported the jambs of a now-missing closure system (view looking west).

landscape in the last three and a half millennia. If they were completed essentially as surface structures and of modest scale, such a mode of construction would explain why these superstructures have not survived. In the case of neighboring tomb CS8, the substructure shows evidence for very earlier penetration by robbers into the south side of the first vaulted chamber. This damage was repaired indicating the early date of intrusion possibly occurring during a period when a superstructure may have still been present. The presence of superstructures might have served as an indication for robbers, not just for locating the tombs' original entrances, but as a guide for the approximate position of the substructures which could easily be targeted by tearing away the superstructure itself. The spur walls on the upper part of CS10 remain inconclusive but provide the most likely evidence for these tombs having been capped by superstructures.

VAULTED ANTECHAMBER (CHAMBER 2)

From the threshold separating Chamber 1 and 2 the tomb steps down a further 0.34 m to reach the plastered floor of Chamber 2. This chamber is 1.2 m wide and 2.88 m in length. It has vertical side walls rising to 1.3 m where the vaulted roof begins: a double-ring vault that rises up to reach 1.7 m in between the floor and the upper curve of the vault. The vault was 0.4 m thick, composed of an inner ring of bricks placed edgeways and an outer ring of bricks placed flat.

As occurs with the junction between Chambers 1 and 2, the connection between Chamber 2 and the burial chamber (Chamber 3) was created by fitting the vaulted roof of the antechamber directly over the outer end of the vault of the burial chamber. The vault of the burial chamber was ca. 0.3 m lower than the vault of Chamber 2. A cross wall was fitted over the exterior (west) end of the burial chamber vault. This dividing wall served as the inner support wall for the incline-vault construction of Chamber 2. When excavated, this articulation between the vaulting of Chambers 2 and 3 was still intact. Due to the degree of damage to the vaults of both adjacent chambers, it collapsed but the remaining brickwork stood long enough to record its height and details of the construction.

The vault of the burial chamber extended flush with this inner cross wall of Chamber 2 forming an arched opening. The wall face above created a crescent-shaped tympanum bounded above by the vault of Chamber 2 and below by the vault of Chamber 3. The face of this tympanum shows no evidence for white gypsum coating over the mud plaster (Fig. 11.52). Aligned with the inner face of the tympanum are two vertical bands on the chamber walls that lack whitewash. On the north side, this forms a vertical, uncoated band ca. 10 cm wide. Directly opposite on the south side is a slightly wider uncoated band ca. 12 cm wide. It is evident that there must have been vertically oriented elements abutting the walls on either side of the opening in place at the point the tomb was whitewashed. This feature extended upwards and also covered the tympanum above the opening into the burial chamber.

The patterns of the plastering and whitewashing show that the doorway between Chamber 2 and the burial chamber—like the opening between Chambers 2 and 3—had a closure system that was entirely torn away by tomb robbers. Such doorways may have been of stone or wood, although use of the limestone support blocks in the Chamber 1–2 doorway suggests the use of stone. Again, given the space constraints, this would likely have been a portcullis-style doorway akin to that used in the tomb of Seneb-Kay. The portcullis would have slid upwards against the face of the tympanum. Because the ceiling above in this location was a vault, we can infer that the portcullis slab must have had a rounded top in order to slide up into the space below the vault of Chamber 2.

Fig. 11.52 The inner end of Chamber 2 during excavation showing remains of the vault and plastered, crescent-shaped tympanum above the doorway into the burial chamber (view looking east).

CHAMBER 2 FLOOR DEPOSIT

Tomb CS10 was extensively plundered, providing little evidence for the nature of its original funerary equipment. Lying askew in the middle of Chamber 2, we uncovered a large section of the limestone lid stone that covered the sarcophagus recess in the burial chamber (discussed below, Fragment D). This must have been torn away by the initial group of tomb robbers and was probably secondarily moved by other plunderers who broke through the vaulted antechamber leaving the lid stone sitting in the middle of the smashed vault. Beneath this lid fragment, the chamber interior was filled with windblown sand down to the floor where we exposed an ensemble of objects sitting immediately in front of the entrance into the burial chamber (Fig. 11.53).

Lying atop the plastered floor were the following items:

1) two flat-based baskets (both ca. 36 cm in diameter).

2) a group of three shallow footed offering dishes or lids with a white slip.

3) three small jars with cylindrical bodies and white slip, associated with date pits.

4) a diorite stone pounder.

5) ten small fragments of gold leaf.

6) small painted wood coffin fragments.

Fig. 11.53 Artifact deposit on the floor of Chamber 2 (immediately in front of the doorway into the burial chamber (view looking east).

7) a faience bead.

8) human bone elements including human ribs and a medial cuneiform of a right foot.

Although deposited directly on the floor of the antechamber, it is unclear whether this small artifact assemblage represents objects in primary position as part of an original funerary deposit, or objects that were relocated during the initial phase of ancient robbery of CS10. The fact that the objects are on or near floor level is not a conclusive indicator that they remain in their original position, undisturbed by tomb robbers. It appears probable that CS10 was originally entered via the tomb's entrance at a stage when Chamber 2 was unencumbered with debris. Robbers may have entered through the main entrance and then broken through the now-missing door closures to despoil the burial. The pounding stone possibly is an impromptu tool used in the robbery process. The combination of gold leaf and small painted wood coffin fragments certainly derive from the process of

despoiling the burial. The white slipped ceramic vessels and baskets are certainly original tomb contents, but they may have been relocated from the burial chamber or other interior spaces. Consequently, a viable interpretation is that this chamber was a location for stripping the burial of its valuable items leaving a small range of fragments and abandoned objects scattered on the floor.

An interesting feature of the pottery vessels is the use of a white coating on the exterior of all four of the small jars, as well as on the bases of the small dishes (Fig. 11.54). Residual gypsum is often attested on vessels associated with construction activity including examples recovered from some of the other Second Intermediate Period tombs including that of Seneb-Kay. However, these vessels clearly do not represent remnants of construction activity and the white coating is carefully applied to cover the entire exterior. They may be ritually coated containers for funeral offerings. It seems likely these were vessels belonging to CS10's burial assemblage, discarded through their lack of value by tomb robbers.

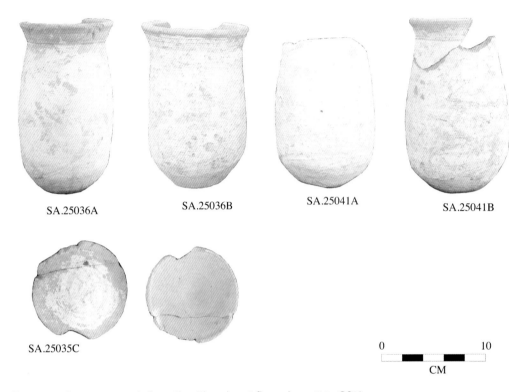

SA.25036A SA.25036B SA.25041A SA.25041B

SA.25035C

0   10
CM

Fig. 11.54 Ceramic vessels from the Chamber 2 floor deposit in CS10.

BURIAL CHAMBER (CHAMBER 3)

The burial chamber of CS10 is unique in terms of its considerable depth—approximately 5 meters below surface level—and its form of construction (Fig. 11.55). The chamber includes a monolithic limestone crypt of a type that echoes the in situ quartzite burial chambers of the 13th Dynasty tombs S9 and S10 at South Abydos and the reused 13th Dynasty chamber of CS6. The CS10 crypt is a single limestone block measuring 1.3 m in width and 2.7 m in length. The recess for the sarcophagus measures 0.7 by 2.24 m with a depth of 0.86 m. The stone is a fine, dense limestone, and the weight of the crypt can be estimated to weigh ca. 7,200 kg.[2]

The burial crypt is set into the floor of a brick-vaulted chamber that, notably, made use of the compact desert subsurface for its back wall, rather than the normal use of a brick built inner wall (Figs. 11.56 and 11.57). Against the carefully trimmed desert end wall the builders constructed a double-ring brick vault set atop vertical walls. Using a mode of construction that occurs also in neighboring CS8, they set the vault back from the inner face of the

vertical walls forming a 10–12 cm wide ledge on either side. The considerable depth and complexity involved in maneuvering the approximately 7 ton burial crypt into the space and then encasing it with a double-ring vault indicate an investment of time and labor well beyond that in any of the other tombs including that of Seneb-Kay. Given the penchant for reuse of materials visible in the Second Intermediate Period tombs at South Abydos, it appears possible the limestone burial crypt in CS10 might originate in some other structure. However, even if reused, the transport and installation of the chamber alone is a process that marks CS10 as the largest and most labor intensive of the Second Intermediate Period tombs. The chamber represents the architectural ideal of a monolithic burial chamber that the other tombs aspired to but could only achieve by means of slab construction.

THE LID STONE

The excavation of the interior of CS10 produced a group of four fragments deriving from the limestone

Fig. 11.55 above The monolithic lime-stone burial crypt of CS10 with brick vaulted chamber constructed above it.

Fig. 11.56 left The inner end of the burial chamber showing the use of the desert subsurface as the inner end of the chamber (note the white plaster adhering to the vertically shaved subsurface).

Fig. 11.57 The limestone burial crypt looking back through the antechamber (Chamber 2) and pole-roof chamber (Chamber 1).

suggested by the floor deposit in the vaulted antechamber and position of lid Fragment A. Later plunderers were likely responsible for breaking through the tomb's vaulted roofing and combing the debris for any remnants left by the original robbers.

The lid is a 12 cm thick, rough-dressed, limestone cover with overall horizontal dimensions of 0.88 by 2.42 m (Fig. 11.60). The lid was not a single stone but composed of two adjacent blocks: a smaller one 0.46 m in length (Lid A) and a larger slab (Lid B) originally 1.96 m in length. The larger block (Lid B) was broken into multiple fragments of which we recovered three pieces in 2014 (Fragments 2–4) permitting a reconstruction of the entire cover stone (Fig. 11.61). The lid stones have a 12 cm wide edging that projects 4 cm creating a raised frame that sat on the top of the four sides of the burial recess. The inner dimensions of this projecting frame are nearly identical to the 0.7 x 2.24 m sarcophagus recess making it clear the two lid blocks were positioned end to end with the projecting edging placed flush with the edges of the recess. In all likelihood, the system of closure involved installation of the longer block over the inner end of the burial recess. The smaller block then completed the cover and the front end of the chamber. As we have seen, the smaller block appears to have been pulled off first by ancient robbers who discarded it on the floor of the pole-roof chamber.

These cover blocks from the CS10 burial chamber are comparatively insubstantial and would have been easily torn away by tomb robbers. During excavation of the burial chamber, two sections of mudbrick were found sitting on the short ends of the limestone crypt. Although not mortared into place, it is possible these bricks are remnants of a loose brick fill that was installed directly on top of the lid stones. The limestone cover may have closed the burial within the crypt but also then supported a brick packing that further protected the burial within the vaulted chamber. Once the chamber was penetrated, robbery would have been relatively simple with removal of any fill material, followed by the limestone lid stones below. Interestingly the smaller block, Fragment A, was complete and would have been pulled away intact. The larger lid stone was

covering that originally enclosed the burial crypt. The fragments were found in the two outer chambers (Chambers 1–2). One of these fragments (Fragment 1) was found near floor level just inside the pole-roof chamber (Fig. 11.58). It may have been discarded in that location by the original tomb robbers who would have pulled away the lid to gain access to the burial recess. The other fragments (2–4) including the largest (Fragment 4) were encountered at higher levels (Fig. 11.59). While the original robbers must have broken through and dislodged these lid stones, many of the fragments appear to have undergone a secondary phase of relocation. This implies CS10 was entered multiple times. The initial robbers appear likely to have gained access through the main entrance as

Fig. 11.58 Lid fragment 1 as found inside Chamber 1. Skeletal remains attributed to the original CS10 burial are visible adjacent to the lid fragment.

Fig. 11.59 Lid fragment 4 as excavated inside Chamber 2.

Fig. 11.60 The limestone lid of the burial crypt of CS10 (interior view).

broken into multiple fragments, reflecting a solid blow in the block's center. It appears the burial was entered by smashing this block in its middle, which then permitted easy removal of the fragments and access to the burial recess.

As we discuss in the next chapter, the use of a monolithic burial crypt in CS10 may be derivative from late 13th Dynasty royal funerary architecture, including prominently the chambers of S9 and S10 as well as the reused 13th Dynasty royal crypt (tomb CS6) at South Abydos. However, one notable difference is the absence of a separate canopic recess inside the monolithic chamber. This raises the question of whether the recess housed both sarcophagus and canopic chest together, and whether the crypt was intended as a receptacle for a rectangular outer sarcophagus. It is possible both the sarcophagus and canopic chest might have been accommodated together within the single 0.7 by 2.24 m recess. If we adopt the known dimensions of Seneb-Kay's canopic box (0.69 cm square), it appears likely that inclusion of the canopic box within the rectangular recess would have reduced the length available for the sarcophagus to something on the order of 1.5 m which would appear too short either for an anthropoid coffin alone, or a nested arrangement of rectangular sarcophagus and inner anthropoid coffin. Therefore, the canopic box would have been set at the inner end of the chamber as for Seneb-Kay and also implied by the inner loculus in some of the other main cluster tombs including CS8 and CS11. If so, the 0.7 x 0.86 x 2.24 m recess appears well proportioned to contain a rectangular outer sarcophagus that could then have enclosed an anthropoid inner coffin.

REMAINS OF THE CS10 BURIAL

Although CS10 was extensively plundered like the other Second Intermediate Period tombs at South Abydos, excavation of the debris in the tomb yielded a significant set of skeletal remains, which can be identified as the remains of the tomb owner. The bone material was found scattered throughout the debris, but a primary concentration came from the lower elevations within the burial chamber (Chamber 3) and the vaulted antechamber (Chamber 2). A significant amount of the skeleton was found inside the sarcophagus recess itself (Fig. 11.62).

Also scattered through the debris in and around the CS10 burial chamber were numerous small fragments of linen. Similar fragments were recovered in most of the other Main Cluster tombs. The best preservation of linen fragments occurs in CS10 and neighboring CS11 due to the fact that these two tombs had not been identified and disturbed during the work of Weigall. The relatively greater depth of CS10 also contributed to the preservation of the fragments. The linen derives nearly certainly from the mummy wrappings. In CS10, there are two different grades of linen, fine and course (Fig. 11.63). The finer grade displays a thread count in the range of 24 (warp) and 42 (weft) threads per centimeter (equaling a "thread count" of ca. 160 TPI of threads per inch). The coarse linen has a thread count approximately one-third of that. It appears likely the finer linen was used for the wrapping of the body. Small areas of the surviving linen wrappings adhering to then skeleton of Seneb-Kay from CS9 (see Fig. 5.37) display the same high-quality weave as the finer

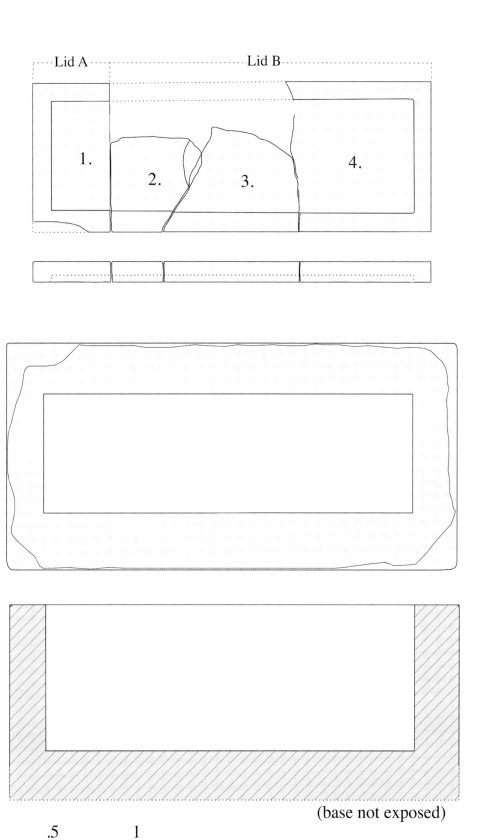

Lid A   Lid B

1.   2.   3.   4.

(base not exposed)

0   .5   1
METER

Fig. 11.61 The limestone crypt and lid of CS10.

Fig. 11.62 Parts of the male skeleton (here the left pelvis) recovered in disarticulated form in the interior of CS10.

linen grade from CS10. The course linen may derive from other fabric elements of the burial assemblage, although the small size of the fragments makes this less certain.

The bone material all derives from a single individual, a male, aged 35–45 years. There are no indications of secondary burial activity in the tomb. A significant find among the skeletal elements in and around the burial crypt was the complete mandible belonging to one of the two skulls that were recovered at higher elevation adjacent to tomb CS8 (see discussion above). That indicated the skull derived from the CS10 burial and allowed retrieval of a large percentage of the skeletal remains associated with CS10. Despite the dislocation of the cranium, the fact that CS10 had not been previously entered by Weigall means that the tomb contents had not been subject to modern disturbance as occurred with the three tombs that he examined (CS4, CS7, and CS8). Consequently, there is a high probability the individual recovered is the original occupant of CS10. With nearly 50% of the skeleton of this individual recovered, the

burial associated with CS10 provides the most significant set of osteological remains apart from Seneb-Kay. We shall turn to examine the CS10 skeletal remains in detail in the next chapter.

TOMB CS11

GENERAL DESCRIPTION

CS11 is the smallest of the tombs in the Second Intermediate Period cemetery (Figs. 11.64 and 11.65). The tomb is positioned due south of CS5. On the west side, the structure of CS11 falls very close to CS4 and the group of three shafts (CS12–14). CS11 was first identified and excavated in the summer of 2014. The tomb had been extensively plundered but provided remnants of painted and gilded funerary equipment, as well as a set of skeletal remains. CS11 measures only 6.4 m in total length. The tomb lacks the normal sequence of descending chambers entered by a

Fig. 11.63 Examples of linen fragments recovered from tomb CS10 showing the finer grade of fabric (left) and courser grade (right), likely attributed to different elements of the burial assemblage.

walled ramp. Instead it employs a stone-lined burial chamber (Chamber 2) entered via a large, square (2.5 x 2.5 m) brick chamber (Chamber 1). This square chamber could be identified as an entrance "shaft" but is disproportionately large relative to the modest dimensions of the burial chamber. In other tombs in the cemetery, the width of the entrance ramp is commensurate with the width of the inner chambers. Here, Chamber 1 is square and extends to twice the width of the burial chamber, leading to questions about the function of this structure in relation to the burial chamber. Despite the overall variation of the layout of CS11, the architecture and construction techniques are closely comparable to the other Second Intermediate Period tombs.

SQUARE ENTRANCE CHAMBER (CHAMBER 1)

Chamber 1, with interior dimensions of 2.4 x 2.5 m, sits on a high area of compact desert subsurface that rises up on the west side and falls away to the east in the direction of the burial chamber (Fig. 11.66). This projecting subsurface was trimmed back on all sides to form the lower face of the walls of Chamber 1. The walls are well constructed and plastered on the interior, but the structure is somewhat irregular, apparently influenced by the nature of the subsurface as well as its location adjacent to preexisting structures particularly the three shafts CS12–14. The walls are 38 cm thick (one brick length) at their base. On the north and east walls, this width is maintained to the surviving height of the walls. On the south wall and southern end of the east wall, the format shifts in the upper part to construction of stretchers alone and thickness is reduced to 19 cm. This reduction in

thickness may relate to the presence of shaft CS12 directly abutting the southwest corner of Chamber 1. On this basis, the shafts CS12–14 appear to predate CS11. Despite the shifts in wall thickness, from the bonding patterns it is clear the burial chamber and Chamber 1 were built together as a single structure. Because the interior of Chamber 1 is relatively large, it was a convenient location for tomb robbers to discard material stripped from the burial chamber. Inside Chamber 1 we found four large elements of the limestone slab lining which had been torn away from the burial chamber (Fig. 11.67).

A primary issue regarding CS11 is the function of this unusually wide, square entrance chamber. The width does not appear to indicate the structure of Chamber 1 was conceived as an entrance shaft. With no indications of vaulting, roofing of the 2.5 m span of the chamber would likely have used wooden beams, although the width here is twice that of the pole-roof chambers found in many of the other tombs. If this structure were roofed there would have been no means of reentry into the substructure suggesting the alternative that the chamber may have been filled with debris and sealed from above. In this case, the square format may represent the base of an aboveground architectural element that once capped the tomb. It appears conceivable that Chamber 1 was capped by a brick-built pyramid and the structure may provide a further hint to the presence of now-missing superstructures that we have considered already in the case of the spur walls fronting tomb CS10 and the mortared external walls of CS7. If so, the structure was not intended to protect the burial as the burial chamber extends to the east and could have been robbed simply by digging down from the surface on the east side of Chamber 1.

Fig. 11.64 CS11 (foreground), with the brick shafts (CS12–14) left, CS 4 (right), and CS8 and CS10 (center). View looking west.

BURIAL CHAMBER (CHAMBER 2) AND CANOPIC RECESS

The burial chamber is a brick vaulted room forming a variant of the stone-lined burial crypt seen in the other main cluster tombs (Fig. 11.68). The chamber measures 1.1 x 3.48 m. It has a maximum height of 2.05 m. The side walls have a projecting brick ledge at the base upon which were set limestone slabs to compose the burial recess. At the inner end of the chamber, there is a vaulted recess 0.8 m deep and 0.78 m wide. In this location, the brick walls of the chamber itself project inwards 18 cm and the vault itself lowers relative to the height of the main vault over the chamber. The limestone lining of the sarcophagus recess would have abutted the projecting brickwork on either side of this inset vault. Preserved areas of whitewash on the vault and upper walls show the original location of now-missing wall slabs that framed in the sarcophagus recess. The block forming the end wall

of the slab-lined sarcophagus recess would have been placed against the projecting jambs of the inset vault at the back of the chamber. Although the majority of slabs forming the burial receptacle are now missing the surviving evidence shows that the recess was originally ca. 0.82 x 2.36 m.

One of the most interesting architectural elements of CS11 is the 0.78 x 0.8 m vaulted receptacle at the inner end of Chamber 2 and behind the lining of the sarcophagus recess. The location of this feature at the inner end of the burial chamber conforms with the evidence from tomb CS8 for a loculus behind the sarcophagus recess intended for placement of the canopic chest. In the case of the tomb of Seneb-Kay (CS9), we have also discussed evidence that the canopic chest was placed at the inner end of the chamber. Despite its relatively modest scale, CS11 shows the most specific architectural evidence for the placement of the canopic chest at then interior end of the burial chamber.

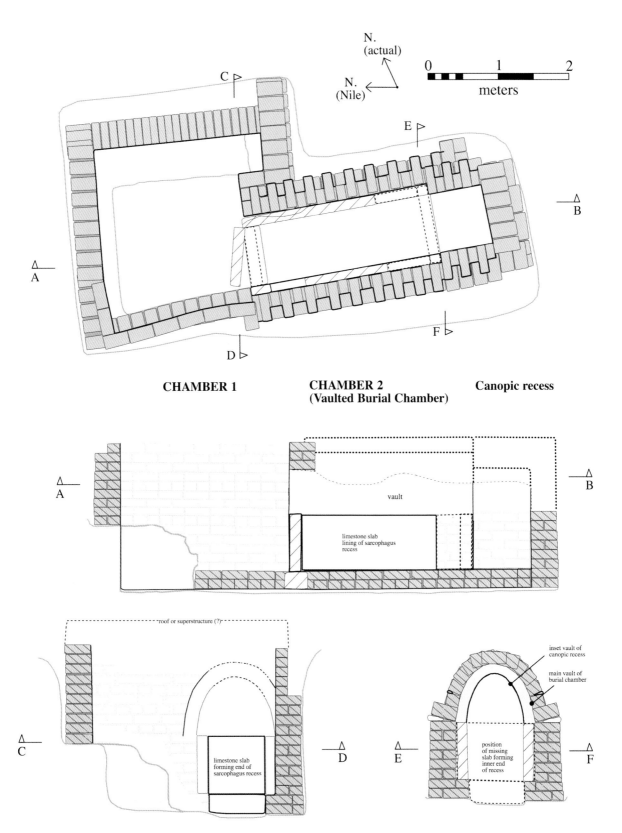

CHAMBER 1 **CHAMBER 2** **Canopic recess**
(Vaulted Burial Chamber)

Fig. 11.65 Plan and sectional views of CS11.

Fig. 11.66 CS11 showing the dislodged masonry inside Chamber 1.

Fig. 11.67 Excavation inside Chamber 1 of CS11 (view looking south).

Fig. 11.68 Exterior view of the burial chamber of CS11 showing slab lining and the inset vault of the canopic recess (view looking north).

SKELETAL REMAINS AND ELEMENTS OF THE BURIAL ASSEMBLAGE

CS11 was thoroughly plundered with almost nothing remaining of its burial assemblage. The excavation produced numerous pieces of gold leaf indicating, as with the other main cluster tombs, the presence of a richly equipped burial. At the inner end of the burial chamber and concentrating in the canopic recess, we retrieved a set of skeletal remains, as well as numerous small splinters of painted wood originating from a decorated sarcophagus and/or coffin and canopic box. These are not illustrated due to the small size, and lack of specific indications they provide for the burial equipment. The primary concentration of skeletal remains in the back of the chamber suggests the original burial was stripped on site and discarded within the tomb itself. The remains indicate CS11

was used for a single interment of a mature male as we shall comment on further in Chapter 13. Numerous fragments of linen were also found in and around the burial chamber's inner end and derive from the mummy wrappings. The plundering of CS11 evidently occurred on multiple occasions producing the highly fragmentary set of physical remains recovered in 2014.

SHAFTS CS12–14

Directly east of CS10 and abutting the southwest corner of CS11 is a group of three shafts, CS12, CS13, and CS14 (Figs. 11.69 and 11.70). The existence of these structures was indicated on the 2002 magnetic map, but they were not examined until 2014. The shafts occupy a highly elevated area of compact desert subsurface. The structures were cut down into the subsurface and capped at the mouth with a rectangular brick collar. The interior dimensions are

Fig. 11.69 View looking west with the three shafts, C12 (left), C13 (center), and C14 (right) in the foreground. The neighboring structures are tombs CS8 (upper left), CS10 (directly behind), CS4 (upper right), and CS11 (lower right).

1.34 x 2.94 m (CS12); 1.05 x 2.94 m (CS13), and 1.05 x 2.65 m (CS14). The brickwork makes use of the same 19 x 38 cm bricks seem elsewhere in the Second Intermediate Period tombs. The surviving brickwork is bonded at the lower levels showing that all three are connected and were built at the same time.

When we exposed these structures in 2014, we found that the brickwork of the top of the shafts had been trenched through in a north-south direction at some point, quite possibly during the 1901–1902 exploratory work of Weigall. We found the longer side walls were mostly destroyed, leaving the shorter end walls unsupported atop the mouth of the shaft. Moreover, during their original construction, the brick collars were not founded directly on the compact subsurface but sit on a loose sand stratum overlying the subsurface. The compromised brickwork had to be shored up with wood, as well as supported beneath with new brickwork to fill in the loose sand stratum to permit work in the shafts below.

Despite the fact that they are conjoined features and appear nearly identical at surface level, the three shafts are quite different (Fig. 11.71). CS14 is a shallow structure that descends slightly over a meter and terminates. CS12 and CS13 both form proper shafts that descend into the subsurface. Although cut through the relatively soft matrix of the desert subsurface, the two shafts are carefully squared with perfectly straight walls. CS12 descends to a depth of 3.3 m from its brick rim and ends without any subterranean chamber. The central shaft, CS13 descends to a depth of 5.45 m. At its base, CS13 opens westward and eastward into two chambers. On the west is a roughly cut chamber measuring 1.8 m in length (Chamber 1). The inner end of this chamber extends so close to the burial chamber of CS10 that there is a small opening that connects the two in the northeast corner of CS10's burial chamber. On the east side of CS13, the shaft opens into a much larger chamber, ca. 5 m long and 2 m wide cut into the desert subsurface

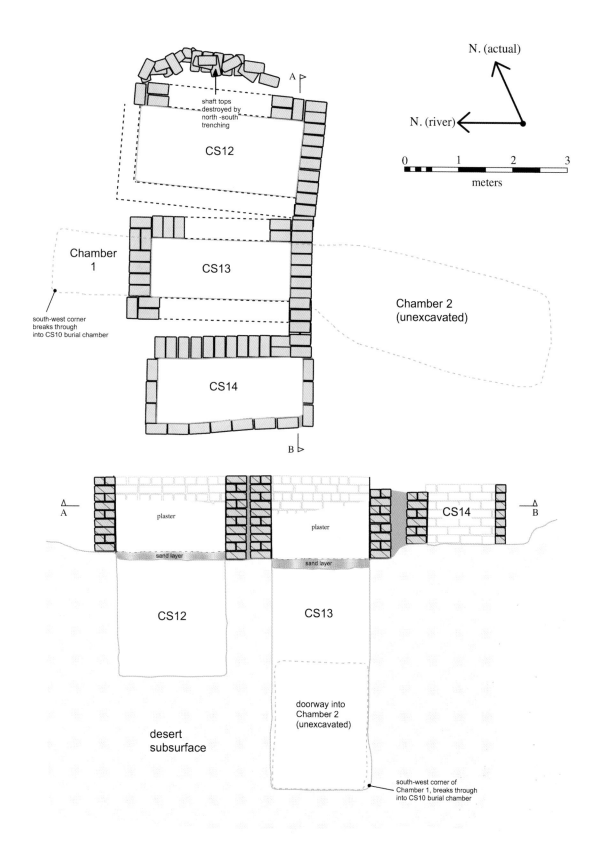

Fig. 11.70 Plan and section of the shaft group CS12, CS13, CS14.

(Chamber 2). This chamber runs slightly askew relative to the shaft itself and extends in a southeasterly direction with an orientation that closely matches that of the neighboring CS10 burial chamber. Therefore, CS13 appears to be a functional tomb whereas the two structures flanking it, CS12 and CS14, were either incomplete or ancillary structures associated with the primary shaft in the middle of the group.

At the time of its discovery in 2014, Chamber 2 in CS13 presented a physical obstacle to excavation (Fig. 11.72). The chamber was full of sand with stray bricks visible against the rough-cut walls. It appears quite probable there was originally a brick-lined chamber that had been constructed within this subterranean cavity. However, any chamber that filled the space was clearly significantly damaged, leaving a void within the desert subsurface. Given its large dimensions, and the soft matrix into which it was built, we deemed Chamber 2 to be too dangerous to excavate and the work was ended with it unexplored. Consequently, the date and characteristics of this tomb remain unclear.

Shaft group CS12–14 remains an enigmatic element within the main tomb cluster. The structures differ from the standard passage-style tomb architecture of the known tombs. Indeed, we have no other known examples at South Abydos of tombs entered via vertical shafts, which was a more standard mode of construction in the cemetery areas in North Abydos. The work produced no artifacts to conclusively date the shafts, but the brickwork appears identical to that in the adjacent Second Intermediate Period tombs. It is also noteworthy that despite the different

Fig. 11.71 The three conjoined shafts CS12, CS13, and CS14 (view looking south).

Fig. 11.72 View into the central shaft, CS13, showing the entrance to the unexcavated chamber (Chamber 2) opening off of the base of the shaft (view looking east).

entrance system, what appears to be the main burial chamber (Chamber 2) opens towards the east following the orientation of the Second Intermediate Period passage-style tombs at South Abydos. It appears possible that CS13 represents some form of satellite tomb linked with one of the neighboring tombs, possibly CS10, which it not only abuts, but to which it shows possible connections in location, orientation, and depth of the burial chamber. Any definitive statement on its date or ownership depends on future examination of the unexplored contents of Chamber 2.

NOTES:

11.1 In his initial excavation of the 13th Dynasty royal tomb, S10, Weigall entirely missed the burial chamber which was located below the depth of his excavations. We discovered S10's burial chamber with its two lid stones still in place in 2015.

11.2 Employing an estimated overall height of 1.2 m, the block has a volume of ca. 3 cubic meters of limestone. Based on 2,400 kg per cubic meter for fine, dense limestone, the total weight is approximately 7,200 kg.

12

Architectural Traditions in the Second Intermediate Period*

The eight tombs at South Abydos provide a rare example of Upper Egyptian funerary architecture of the Second Intermediate Period. As we have discussed throughout this volume, these tombs can be broadly classified as "royal," certainly in the case of Seneb-Kay, and likely also for the seven other tombs. Although there is significant variation in the size of these structures, the group is quite cohesive in terms of architecture and construction methods. Techniques of brickwork, vault construction, and stone lining within the burial chambers are similar. The ideal sequence progressing from open entrance ramp, to pole-roof chamber, to vaulted, stone-lined burial chamber occurs throughout the main group (excluding shafts CS12–14). All of the tombs employ the same orientation.

The Second Intermediate Period tombs at South Abydos lack direct parallels in their architectural idiom. Nevertheless, these tombs show some similarities with late Middle Kingdom and Second Intermediate Period (MB IIA–IIB) tombs in the Nile Delta, including those associated with Hyksos sites such as Tell el-Dab'a (Van den Brink 1982; Forstner-Müller 2002:163–184). Similarities occur in the construction of the larger late Middle Kingdom and Hyksos Period chamber tombs that employ a burial chamber with a brick barrel vault set atop brick side walls. These tombs typically have a vault constructed with the brick courses inclined against an inner supporting wall. The brickwork employs the same principal where alternating courses of the vault have an angled, projecting base creating an external

dentil effect along the base of the vault. This form of vault construction has been documented now extensively in the Nile Delta at Tell el-Dab'a (van den Brink 1982; Schiestl 2009:35–67), Tell el-Maskhuta (Holladay 1982:44–47), and other sites. Rather than being a hallmark of the Middle Bronze culture in the Delta, the lack of parallels to this construction in the Levant and Syria suggest the vault form derives from indigenous Egyptian construction practices (Schiestl 2008:246–249). The South Abydos tombs now confirm the wider use of comparable vaulted tombs in the Nile Valley during the Second Intermediate Period.

While the vault architecture shows distinct similarities with construction practices in the Nile Delta, the overall architectural form of the South Abydos tombs differs in significant ways from these contemporary traditions in northern Egypt. The MB IIA–B vaulted chamber tombs in the Delta are primarily single or double chamber tombs without the linear chamber sequence that predominates in the Abydos group. The closest parallel occurs in tombs that have a square or rectangular entrance shaft (Type 10 of Schiestl 2009:53–55): a comparable arrangement could perhaps be seen in the two South Abydos tombs (CS6 and CS11). Entirely lacking in the Delta is the use of stone lining for the burial chamber as occurs in different forms at South Abydos. The parallels in the Nile Delta show similarities in brick construction techniques and vaults, but little commonality in other design elements. It is unfortunate that so few tombs of the Second Intermediate

*This chapter written by Josef Wegner.

Period have been documented in Upper Egypt, but it seems likely the South Abydos tombs could incorporate elements of more widely practiced elite mortuary traditions of that period. However, in terms of the surviving evidence, the most significant aspect of these Second Intermediate Period tombs is their evident derivation from 13th Dynasty precursors at Abydos itself.

ADAPTATION OF 13TH DYNASTY ARCHITECTURAL MODELS

One of the consistent features of the architecture of the Second Intermediate Period tombs at South Abydos is the use of a predominant orientation paralleling the Nile with the tomb interior running from local north to south. In all instances, the burial chamber is entered from the (local) north with the sarcophagus recess itself following this north to south orientation. Despite the variations in other features of these tombs, the orientation of the burial chamber and the spatial sequence of sarcophagus recess and canopic loculus (where preserved) is consistently applied. It is probably not coincidental that the orientation of the burial crypts of both of the completed 13th Dynasty royal tombs, S9 and S10, at South Abydos follows this same north to south orientation, with the sarcophagus recess forming the first element of the burial chamber, and the canopic recess forming the innermost element. The abandoned 13th Dynasty burial chamber reused in tomb CS6 also follows this same orientation. That structure appears unlikely to have been shifted significantly, if at all, from the position it was left in during the 13th Dynasty.

Paired with the commonality in orientation is the fact that a majority of the Second Intermediate Period tombs employ a crypt-style burial that closely mimics this same component in the earlier 13 Dynasty tombs. While the massive masonry elements and protective devices employed in the 13th Dynasty royal tombs have been abandoned in favor of simpler, more economically built architecture, we see the same concept of a burial chamber that essentially consists of a recess for the sarcophagus with space for the canopic interment behind. Whereas the builders of CS6 simply repurposed a 13th Dynasty burial chamber, the other tombs appear to be fundamentally derivative of the prior architectural concept. The tombs in which the sarcophagus recess is set below floor level—CS5, CS7, CS8, and CS10—show the closest similarity with their forerunners. The masonry slab lining used in most of these tombs is an economical way to create a burial recess akin to that of the monolithic 13th Dynasty crypts.

The largest of the Second Intermediate Period tombs, CS10, is even more explicitly imitative of the 13th Dynasty tombs in its use of a monolithic limestone crypt. In CS10, the sarcophagus recess was sealed with a slab covering and the other tombs may have had a similar system for closing the burial recess. As we have already discussed, some of the tombs, including Seneb-Kay (CS9), CS4, and CS11, differ slightly with burial chambers that were entered at or slightly above floor level, rather than employing a burial loculus recessed into the floor. Nevertheless, in other ways they fall solidly within the same architectural tradition.

We suggest that the Second Intermediate Period tombs at South Abydos are not only located adjacent to the earlier 13th Dynasty royal tombs but are conspicuously derivative from them (Fig. 12.1). This relationship may indicate: (1) the continued practice of late Middle Kingdom modes of royal burial at Abydos, possibly extending into the funerary assemblage and corpus of funerary texts applied to the burial equipment; (2) it may indicate that the builders of these tombs had direct knowledge of, and access to, the interiors and contents of the 13th Dynasty tombs. As we have explored in Chapter 5, a major insight from the contents of the tomb of Seneb-Kay is that carpenters who created that king's canopic box carefully reused cedar coffin boards originating from the painted rectangular coffin of one of the 13th Dynasty Sobekhotep kings. Furthermore, among the reused masonry associated with Seneb-Kay's burial chamber is a large (ca. 2 m tall) false door, also of one of the Sobekhotep kings. While the phenomenon of reuse of these elements indicates a highly developed, state-supported level of tomb robbery, it becomes an unavoidable reality that royal funerary monuments of the 13th Dynasty were open, and being stripped of usable materials, at the time of Seneb-Kay. It appears that the opportunity existed to directly mimic, or even co-opt, the architecture, contents, texts, and materials that characterized the earlier royal tombs.

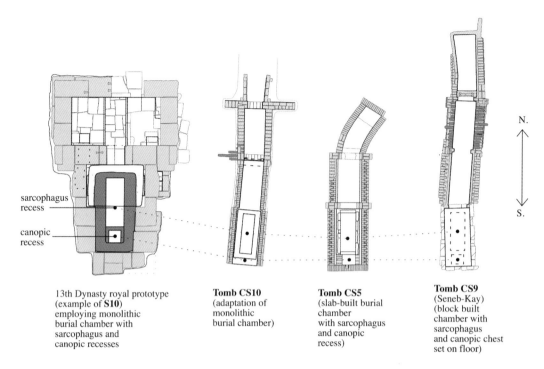

sarcophagus
recess

canopic
recess

N.

S.

13th Dynasty royal prototype
(example of **S10**)
employing monolithic
burial chamber with
sarcophagus and
canopic recesses

Tomb CS10
(adaptation of
monolithic
burial chamber)

Tomb CS5
(slab-built burial
chamber
with sarcophagus
and canopic
recess)

Tomb CS9
(Seneb-Kay)
(block built
chamber with
sarcophagus
and canopic chest
set on floor)

Fig. 12.1 Suggested derivation of Second Intermediate Period tomb design at South Abydos from 13th Dynasty royal prototype.

CHRONOLOGICAL DEVELOPMENT OF THE ARCHITECTURAL FORMS

As we have seen above, the tomb of Seneb-Kay along with the seven other, Second Intermediate Period tombs compose a quite cohesive architectural ensemble. It appears likely the period of time represented by this group of tombs is comparatively short, perhaps on the order of a few decades. While the cemetery is too small to permit an analysis of horizontal development, we may group the tombs usefully in terms of common architectural features, which might signal chronological proximity. Based on the discussion above, the tomb that stands apart from the others in the main cluster is CS10, on the basis of its depth and use of a monolithic burial chamber. While we cannot be certain whether the limestone chamber was reused or quarried for CS10, these features ally it most closely with the 13th Dynasty prototypes and imply it may be relatively early in the developmental sequence. Other tombs employing the slab-lined chambers that mimic the combination of

sarcophagus recess and canopic recess appear to be more economical versions, and possibly derivative, of the chamber type seen in CS10. Here we may group CS5, CS7, and CS8 through their close similarities. Another feature that suggests chronological proximity of these three tombs is the use of the rotation of the walled entrance ramp towards the northwest. This element was explicitly employed in these three tombs but not in the others.

The tomb of Seneb-Kay stands apart from all of the main cluster tombs, not just through its situation within a different enclosure, but in its use of a block-built burial chamber. In this instance, we must also factor into consideration the evidence that Seneb-Kay died unexpectedly in battle. Construction techniques applied to his tomb may have been influenced by the timeframe required for completion of his burial. As we have discussed above, the tomb that shows the greatest similarity to Seneb-Kay is CS4. Both employ the same direct linear descent without rotation of the entrance. CS4 also shows indications of a development away from the sarcophagus recess to use of a slab-lined chamber that was now entered as a walk-in space. Potentially CS4 is chronologically transitional between the (earlier) crypt-style burial chamber to a fully-fledged burial chamber that may have borne wall decoration.

Tombs CS6 and CS11 each present unique features that make it difficult to group them based on specific attributes. The fact that CS6 reused an abandoned 13th Dynasty crypt of a form that was also being emulated in the architecture of these tombs might imply that tomb played a role in the early choice of architectural form. But, the poor preservation of the brick components makes it difficult to propose any specific relationships with others in the group. To some extent both CS6 and CS11 appear to be reduced versions of the standard combination of chambers we see predominating in the other tombs, but whether this has any chronological significance is difficult to ascertain.

Based on this line of reasoning we tentatively propose a chronological sequence in which the tomb design evolved from a direct copying of the 13th Dynasty monolithic crypt on an ideal north-south orientation, towards the use of an open-style burial chamber where sarcophagus and canopic chest sat directly on the floor rather than within recesses. This could suggest CS10 may be the earliest, followed by CS5, CS7, and CS8, and then by CS4 and CS9 (Seneb-Kay). If this analysis holds, the architecture would appear to indicate that Seneb-Kay is the latest tomb among the eight identified at South Abydos. Clearly, there may be other factors at play in the choice of architectural elements and the apparently short timeframe represented by the necropolis could be accompanied by a more varied sequence.

BURIAL CHAMBER DESIGN AND FUNERARY EQUIPMENT

Excavation of the main cluster tombs provides a certain degree of evidence for the characteristics of the burial equipment that went into these tombs. Due to constraints created by chamber and door sizes, there are implications for the spatial and temporal relationships between tomb construction and the funerary equipment used in these burials. One of the likely indications of the use of the sarcophagus recess is that the chambers were designed to accommodate nested burials: i.e., the recess was intended

for a rectangular outer sarcophagus within which there would have been an anthropoid inner coffin. This is the burial format we have attested from the fragments in the tomb of Seneb-Kay. The crypt-style chambers appear specifically linked to this form of burial. The burial recess is not a substitute for the outer rectangular sarcophagus itself but would have been designed to accommodate a system of coffin nested within an outer sarcophagus. We see the burial equipment as deriving, like the chamber design itself, from 13th Dynasty royal forerunners. Moreover, one of the few objects mentioned in Weigall's description of the tombs he examined was an inlaid eye from tomb CS8, demonstrating the use of an anthropoid coffin.

The specific dimensions of the burial receptacles must have been determined based on known dimensions of the sarcophagi they were designed to house, suggesting that the tombs were built in parallel with preparation of the burial equipment. As summarized in the table below (Table 12.1), for the tombs employing the adaptation of the 13th Dynasty burial chamber (CS10 and the slab-constructed chambers CS5, CS8, and CS11) there is a tight size range in the dimensions of the sarcophagus recess.

POSSIBLE USE OF SUPERSTRUCTURES

The Second Intermediate Period tombs at South Abydos survive as empty shells, largely denuded of their contents and, due to their relative proximity to the desert surface, often eroded below the original roof level of their uppermost architecture. These tombs, as well as the 13th Dynasty tombs that preceded them on the site, present questions regarding the architectural forms that existed aboveground as well as belowground. The two 13th Dynasty tombs employ versions of the post-Hawara style royal pyramid interior, which characterizes all of that period's royal pyramids known from sites in the Memphite region including Dahshur, Mazghuna, and south Saqqara.[1] But there are no surviving indications for use of pyramids atop these 13th Dynasty royal tombs at Abydos.

Similarly, for the Second Intermediate Period tombs which appear to be derivative of 13th Dynasty

Table 12.1 Dimensions of the sarcophagus recess and burial chamber in the eight Second Intermediate Period tombs.

| Tomb | Burial Chamber | | | Sarcophagus Recess | | |
	width (m)	length (m)	height (m)	width (m)	length (m)	height (m)
CS4	1.5	3.2	ca. 2.5	1.2	2.8	1.5
CS5	1.4	3.2	1.95	0.9	2.25	0.95
CS6 (reused 13th Dynasty crypt)	1.9	ca. 4.7	ca. 1.2 (vault)	0.9	2.25	0.95
CS7	1.65	3.2	ca. 2.1	-burial chamber lining destroyed-		
CS8	1.23	3.15	2.3	0.8	2.26	1.0
CS9 (Seneb-Kay)	1.5	3.32	1.8	-stone block chamber, no recess-		
CS10 (limestone crypt)	1.32	3.1	1.4 (vault)	0.9	2.25	0.95
CS11	1.1	3.48	2.05	0.82	ca. 2.3	ca. 0.8

models we have no clear evidence for superstructures. The question is a consequential one as the late Second Intermediate Period was the final era in the development of the royal pyramid form. Indeed, the last known royal pyramid in Egypt was built by Ahmose at South Abydos (Harvey 1998:126–137). Was Ahmose's pyramid complex preceded at the site not only by 13th Dynasty pyramids, but also by later Second Intermediate Period royal tombs capped with pyramidal monuments? Did these structures employ some other form of aboveground superstructure? Or, were they built exclusively as subterranean burial structures devoid of aboveground elements?

As we have seen in the discussion of the individual tombs, there are hints in the surviving architecture that some or all of these tombs may have been capped by superstructures. The highest standing elements of CS10, the spur walls that extend laterally from the tomb's entrance, are plastered and whitewashed on their outer face and rise to an elevation that may have been visible on the surface. These spur walls may have extended a greater distance and could have been part of a brick retaining wall forming the base of a superstructure.

Additionally, we have seen in the case of CS7 that the system of mortared brickwork external to the two vaulted chambers is carefully constructed and bonded with the back wall of the tomb. This mode of construction appears to exceed the requirements of providing mass along the sides of the vaulting but may indicate the function of these walls as a base

for an aboveground structure. We may observe that the structure of CS7 is very similar to examples of vaulted tombs at Abydos and other slightly later sites, during the New Kingdom, with brick-built pyramidal superstructures (Cahail 2014:399–416). One of the clearest cases is tomb Y9 (Peet Cemetery Y) at North Abydos where a vaulted superstructure was capped with a brick pyramid engaged with the end walls of the vault. This structure was a relatively small (just 1.55 m on a side), brick-faced pyramid, resting on a single layer of bricks above the vault. The brick walls contained a debris fill (Peet 1914:85–86). The disposition of elements in Y9 appears similar to tomb CS7 with its square back wall and mortared external walls flanking the vaulting. Peet concluded that most or all of the vaulted substructures at North Abydos were originally capped by superstructures of similar type to Y9, but that erosion had eradicated the majority of evidence for superstructures of this type.

Aside from these architectural clues from the main cluster tombs at South Abydos, there is the evidence for robbery and repair in the cases of tombs CS5 and CS8. Both of these tombs were broken into, apparently not long after their construction, through penetration of the south side of the vaulted antechambers. In the case of CS8, this was repaired, suggesting the robbery was interrupted and the tomb resealed. The ability of tomb robbers at an early stage to dig down and accurately penetrate the subterranean vaults from the side suggests that they were able to pinpoint the location of the substructures through visible elements aboveground. This mode of tunnel-ing into subterranean substructures is recounted in the late Ramesside tomb robbery papyri including P. Leopold II-Amherst, which we have mentioned for its description of the robbery of Second Intermediate Period royal burials.

An additional point of discussion relevant to South Abydos is the continuity in the use of the pyr-amid form in association with royal tombs in Upper Egypt during this timeframe: attested both through archaeological remains and textual sources. Archae-ological remains of royal pyramids of modest scale occur in Dra Abu el-Naga and the Assasif (western Thebes) during the 17th Dynasty. The pyramid of an unknown Second Intermediate Period ruler was excavated by Winlock in the eastern Asasif (Polz 2007:138–160), a ca. 8.2 x 8.2 m pyramid set within a surrounding walled complex. The best-known ex-ample is the pyramid of Nubkheperre Antef, a struc-ture measuring approximately 9 m on its base, which covered the subterranean rock-cut burial chamber (Polz and Seiler 2003:14–20; Polz 2007:116–132). The brick-built superstructure was almost entirely de-stroyed through a variety of factors including rob-bery, surface erosion, and later activity in the area. The pyramidion of Wepmaat Antef has also survived suggesting his pyramid tomb lay in Dra Abu el-Naga. The P. Leopold II-Amherst records the plundering of the pyramid of Sekhemre-Shedtway Sobekemsaf II. And, P. Abbott (Peet 1930:1–45), which also mentions the pyramid of Sobekemsaf II, enumerates other pyr-amid tombs of 17th Dynasty Theban rulers including Sekhemre-Wepmaat Antef, Seqenenre Tao II, Ka-mose, and Ahmose-Sapair.

The location and characteristics of the tombs of the 16th Dynasty Theban kings remains unknown. However, it is quite probable that these would have been forerunners to the 17th Dynasty examples. Our chronological evidence shows that Seneb-Kay and the other individuals (presumably also kings) buried in the main tomb cluster were contemporaries of the Theban 16th Dynasty. On the basis of the late Second Intermediate Period practice of pyramid construc-tion at Thebes, we hypothesize that at Abydos royal

tombs of this era also employed pyramid superstruc-tures. Through the persistent environmental impact of wind erosion, the low-desert environment of Aby-dos is ill-suited to long-term preservation of exposed, standing buildings, particularly modestly scaled structures of less-resilient materials such as mud-brick and plaster. Structures that were not sanded over were subject to natural erosion or eventual re-moval through human agency. The situation at the base of the high desert cliffs at South Abydos is even more destructive to surface structures than parts of the site closer to the floodplain. Consequently, just as Peet had long ago concluded regarding the disap-pearance of substructures in North Abydos, the Sec-ond Intermediate Period tombs may well have been capped by superstructures, of which pyramids would be the most probable form. These have vanished through a combination of natural and human agency.

We may finally observe that at the point of tran-sition between the Second Intermediate Period and early 18th Dynasty, South Abydos was the location of at least two pyramids of 17th Dynasty royalty: the pyramid of Ahmose and the commemorative pyr-amid chapel dedicated to Queen Tetisheri. In all likelihood, there was also a third pyramidal monu-ment dedicated to Queen Ahnmose-Nefertari (Har-vey 2004:3–6). Possibly these pyramidal structures were added to a mortuary landscape at South Aby-dos, which at that point in time still displayed visible pyramidal structures of Second Intermediate Period rulers who had been buried in the necropolis that had developed adjacent to the subterranean tomb of Senwosret III.

NOTES:

12.1 The substructures of known royal pyramids after the late 12th Dynasty reign of Amenemhat III follow the de-sign established by Amenemhat III's pyramid at Hawara. The system of counterclockwise, inward turning passages interrupted by portculli and terminating in a monolithic burial chamber defines all of the 13th Dynasty pyramids and was also replicated at South Abydos in tombs S9 and S10 (McCormack 2010:69–84; Wegner and Cahail 2015:123–164).

13

The Skeletal Remains from the Main Tomb Cluster*

Despite their badly plundered condition, the tombs in the main cluster provided a valuable set of skeletal evidence for their original occupants. The human remains associated with these tombs were recovered entirely disarticulated in disturbed contexts within and around their respective tombs. None of the structures provided anything comparable to the redeposited, but substantially articulated, remains of Seneb-Kay in CS9. However, the concentration of skeletal remains within the tomb substructures allows us to attribute the bodies confidently in three cases: tombs CS8, CS10, and CS11. The predominant pattern evident in these remains—particularly emphasized by CS8 and CS10 and correlating with CS9—is the association of a single, adult male burial with each tomb. Weigall had also encountered the remains of a single male burial in his excavation of tomb CS4 (Weigall in Ayrton et al. 1904:18). The skeletal evidence corresponds with the architecture of the structures, which were specifically designed for single interments.

Here we discuss the evidence supplied by the partially preserved burials associated with CS8, CS10, and CS11. The other tombs in the main cluster also provided samples of human skeletal material but in such a minor fraction as to be of little use. Of the main cluster tombs, the burial associated with CS10 is by far the most significant. Nearly half of the skeleton (46%) was recovered, and this body provides a significant set of physical evidence for age, stature, trauma, pathologies, and musculoskeletal stress markers. The burials of CS8 and CS11 were much more fragmentary and provide more limited insights into these

individuals. We begin with the skeleton from CS10 and consider the evidence from CS8 and CS11 at the end of the chapter.

OSTEOBIOGRAPHY OF THE CS10 SKELETON

The most substantially recovered skeleton from the main tomb cluster is the individual who was buried in tomb CS10 (Fig. 13.1). Recovery of the occupant of this tomb is significant in that the structure is the largest of the Second Intermediate Period tombs at South Abydos. Its deeply set monolithic limestone chamber represents a level of investment that implies status on a par with Seneb-Kay. Therefore, it is reasonable inference that this man, like Seneb-Kay was a king. Unlike Seneb-Kay's tomb, we have indications that CS10 was built well in advance of the death of its owner. The occupant's skeletal remains provide no indications that he died unexpectedly or through violence. The skeleton of the man buried in CS10 displays features that show similarities with Seneb-Kay with regard to: (a) nutrition and dentition, and (b) musculoskeletal stress markers.

TAPHONOMY

The remains of the burial in tomb CS10 were recovered entirely disarticulated, in multiple layers

---

This chapter written by Jane Hill, Maria Rosado, and Josef Wegner.

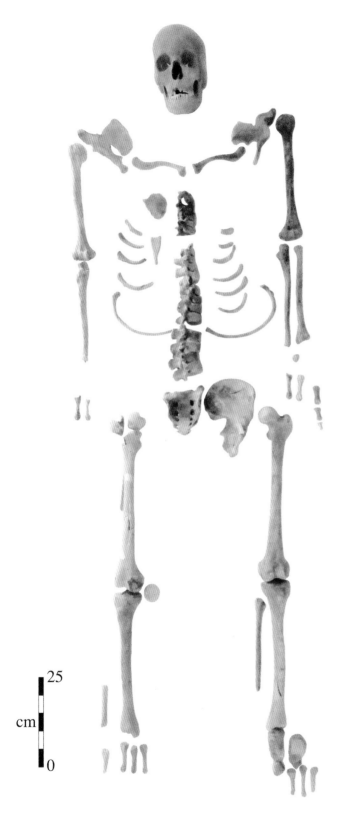

25

cm

0

Fig. 13.1 View of the recovered skeletal components of the burial from tomb CS10 (lower arm elements are not in standard anatomical position).

in the excavation of the tomb interior. A minor fraction of the bone material attributable to this burial was more widely dispersed and retrieved close to the nearby tomb CS11 (ca. 12 m northeast) while the cranium (Fig. 13.2) had been thrown to the surface and lay south near the edge of the adjacent tomb CS8. Clearly CS10 had been significantly plundered by ancient looters who disturbed the body probably on multiple occasions. Differential coloring between the skull, vertebral column, and hand and foot bones indicate that parts of the body lay exposed and suffered weathering and sun bleaching while others remained buried and well protected from the elements. There is some postmortem breakage in the long bones as evidenced in clean, white breaks in the bones' cortex seen in cross section (Fig. 13.3). This damage to the skeleton is not attributed to the excavation but likely derives from a history of multiple, forceful entries by groups of tomb robbers into the deeply buried interior of CS10.

Despite the disturbed context of the skeletal remains from this tomb, the vast majority of elements were recovered inside the tomb interior itself. Most of the elements of the skeleton were encountered in the lowest levels of the deposits, within and immediately adjacent to the burial chamber. On that basis, we can be confident in the identification of this individual as the original occupant of CS10. The CS10 body was certainly fully mummified but due to its disarticulation through robbery, no direct preservation of linen adhering to the skeletal remains occurs. As we have seen in the discussion of the CS10 tomb, linen fragments attributable to the original burial occur throughout the debris but represent fabric that had been torn from the wrapped body. Some of the bones preserve small areas of flesh adhering to the surface but the soft tissue has otherwise broken away or entirely decayed.

ESTIMATION OF AGE

As in the case of Seneb-Kay, skeletal features used for estimating age at death for the CS10 individual (Table 13.1) include arthrosis of the pubic symphysis, dental eruption of third molars, dental wear, epiphyseal union of long bones,

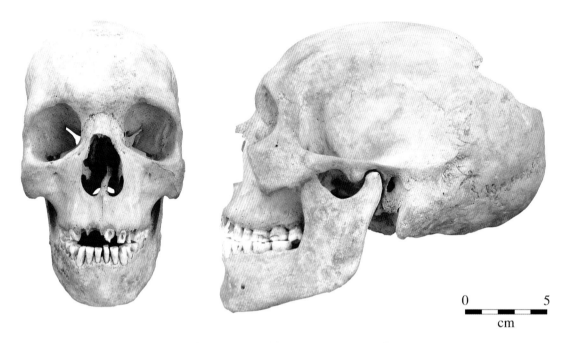

Fig. 13.2 Cranium and mandible of the individual from tomb CS10 (skull not photographed in the Frankfort plane).

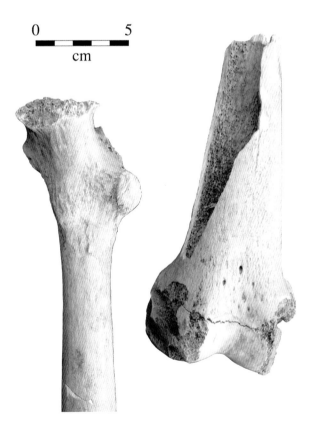

Fig. 13.3 Examples of the varied exposure and breakage of bones from the CS10 burial (medial view of the right proximal femur and anterior view of right distal femur).

union of sacral vertebrae, arthrosis of joints and the vertebral column, and closure of cranial sutures (Bass 2005; Steele and Bramblett 1988; Krogman and Iscan 1986; and Roksandic and Armstrong 2011). Scoring of the pubic symphysis resulted in a score of 11 (see Stewart 1979; Gilbert and McKern 1973) indicating a range of 23–39 years. The fusion of S1–S2 suggests an age between 30–35 years (Steele and Bramblett 1988). However, we also observed lipping around the auricular surface of the sacrum, as well as enhanced microporosity and macroporosity, consistent with a somewhat more advanced age between 40–50 years (Passalacqua 2009). Based on this set of features, we estimated the age at death for the CS10 individual to be ca. 35–45 years.

ESTIMATION OF STATURE

Although the excavations resulted in only partial recovery of the CS10 individual, nearly all of the larger bones including the limb bones were recovered. This includes the entirety of the cranium and mandible. Some of the long bones were broken or partial (Table 13.2). The estimated stature of the CS10 individual is ca. 169.2 cm (range 164.53–174.97 cm) making him

Table 13.1 Summary of skeletal attributes of CS10.

Skeleton No.	Sex	Age (y)	% of Skeleton represented
CS10	Male, determined from cranium	35–45 determined from cranium (some closure of sutures), teeth (dental wear, enamel being lost on occlusal surface, some dentin exposed), and postcrania (full closure of epiphyseal lines of sacrum, long bones, vertebrae); pubic symphysis	46

Table 13.2 Stature estimation for CS10 based on long bone measurements (stature calculated from formulas for ancient Egyptian males provided by Raxter et al. 2008).

Bone	CS10	CS10 Stature	SEE	Range
Femur$_m$	2.257 (**46**) + 63.93=	167.75 cm	3.218	164.53–170.97
Tibia$_m$	2.554 (**39**) + 69.21=	168.82 cm	3.002	165.82–171.82
Humerus$_m$	2.594 (**33.5**) + 83.85=	170.75 cm	4.218	166.53–174.97
Radius$_m$	2.641 (**25.9**) + 100.91=	169.31 cm	3.731	165.58–173.04
Femur$_m$ + tibia$_m$	1.282 (**46 + 39**) + 59.35=	168.32 cm	2.851	165.47–171.17
Humerus$_m$ + radius$_m$	1.456 (**33.5 + 25.9**) + 83.76=	170.25 cm	3.353	166.90–173.60
Average / Range		169.2 cm		164.53–174.97

$_m$ = maximum length; SEE = standard of error estimates (Raxter et al. 2008)

perhaps marginally taller than Seneb-Kay. In general, the skeletal remains from CS10 indicate a somewhat more robust individual than Seneb-Kay, although both show clear signs for having led physically active lifestyles with a set of habitual activities expressed through muscle development.

PALEOPATHOLOGY

The surviving elements of the CS10 skeleton indicate a range of pathologies as follows:

(1) Nasal Septal Deviation CS10 exhibits nasal septal deviation towards the individual's left side (Fig. 13.4). In the absence of evidence of any other trauma in the area of the nasal aperture, it is proposed, as in the case of Seneb-Kay (CS9), that the origin of the deviation is developmental.

(2) Dental Wear and Temporomandibular Osteoarthritis Moderate to severe tooth wear is exhibited in CS10 (Fig. 13.5). According to Smith's (1984) and Schumacker's (1985) dental wear grade schemes,

CS10's molars range in grade from 2–6. His mandibular molars (right and left molar 1), exhibit grade 6, where the dentin has been almost completely exposed. The stress exerted on and by the teeth, resulting in wear of the tooth enamel down to the dentin may have also contributed to osteoarthritis of the temporomandibular joint (TMJ), characterized by flattening of the anterior border of the fossa (glenoid fossa) and flattening of the mandibular condyles (minimum to maximum expressions according to Rando and Waldron's [2012] criteria for diagnosing TMJ osteoarthritis) (Fig. 13.6). Similar patterns have been observed in archaeological populations (e.g., Hodges 1991, for a British population). The moderately dense porosity of the hard palatal surface of CS10, as in CS9, is potentially indicative of a nutritional deficiency such as scurvy. Because scurvy can be accompanied by other nutritional issues including vitamin D deficiency (osteomalacia) and anemia, the task of identifying a specific nutritional disorder in dry bone is difficult in adult skeletons (Crist and Sorg 2014). Therefore, the dense porosity of the hard palate is tentatively proposed

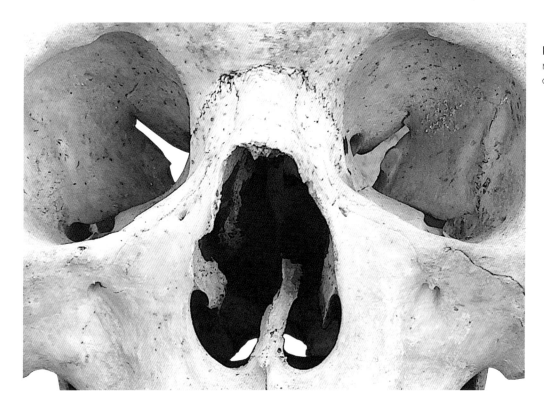

Fig. 13.4 CS10's nasal septal deviation.

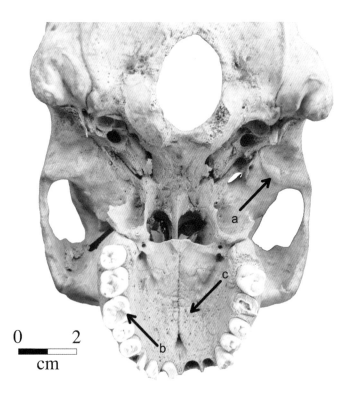

Fig. 13.5 Inferior view of the cranium and maxilla of CS10. Note flattening of the anterior border of the temporomandibular joint, the glenoid fossa (a) and dental wear of left molar 1, premolar 2, and premolar 1 (b). The moderately dense porosity of the palate (c) is possibly indicative of scurvy.

here as a diagnosis of scurvy for both Seneb-Kay and the CS10 individual.

(3) Sterno clavicular osteoarthritis The analysis of CS10's sternoclavicular joint revealed that osteoarthritic changes were considerably more severe in the left side than in the right, indicated by more wear and flattening of the clavicular facet with marginal lipping and porosity of the manubrium (Fig. 13.7). This evidence also suggests that CS10's dominant side and more heavily used arm was his left.

(4) Vertebral Osteoarthritis The majority of CS10's spinal column was retrieved allowing qualitative assessment of the long-term effects of stress on his back. All of the vertebrae from the last cervical vertebra downwards show signs of osteoarthritic changes. The thoracic vertebrae are preserved to T8 as well as lumbars 1–4. (Thoracic vertebra T9–12 were missing as was lumbar vertebra L5). All of the recovered lower back vertebrae show signs of lipping and/or pitting (grade 2; as per the categories for scoring

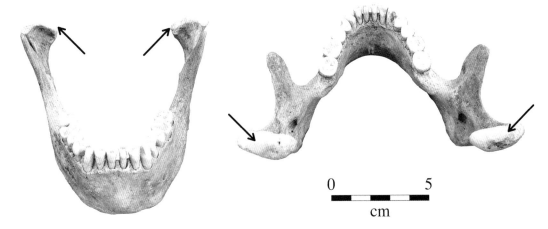

Fig. 13.6 The mandible of CS10 showing dental wear and the flattening of the mandibular condyles.

Fig. 13.7 CS10's osteoarthritic changes were more severe on the left side than on the right, indicated here by differential wear and flattening of the left clavicular facet of the manubrium.

osteoarthritis provided by Ubelaker [1999]) visible as a flattening of the body of the vertebra and extra bony growth around the rim of the vertebral bodies. No eburnation on the vertebral body rims was observed. Although L5 is missing, the articulation between L5 and the sacrum indicates grade 2 osteoarthritis, described as moderate lipping and/or pitting.

In addition, CS10 displays the development of a Schmorl's node in his thoracic vertebra T8 (Fig. 13.8), located in his lower middle back. As we have already noted in the case of the skeleton of Seneb-Kay from CS9 (see Chapter 5), Schmorl's nodes are a specific expression of degenerative change of the spine. The nodes develop as herniations of the intervertebral disk penetrating into the vertebral body (Dar et al. 2010). Again, Schmorl's nodes in association with other stress-affected pathological lesions may reflect aspects of the long-term physical behaviors of the individual.

(5) Sacral arthritis CS10 displays at least five regions of the sacrum with osteoarthritis characterized by lipping of the articulation borders and lateral right mass and deformity of lateral masses, which may be indicative of lumbarization (Fig. 13.9). For the age of this individual, 35–45 years, the osteoarthritis also indicates that heavy loads and stresses through repetitive motion were exerted on the proximal region of the sacrum. Both the right and left sides were affected. With osteoarthritis of the lumbar and sacral vertebrae, the normally soft discs between the vertebrae of the lower back gradually lose their elasticity and become progressively dehydrated beginning in the third decade, and their ability to effectively cushion the bones is reduced (Kalichman and Hunter 2007). In our estimation, the observed osteoarthritis is age dependent but also indicative of some type of repetitive motion and pressure that mostly affected the region of L5 and S1.

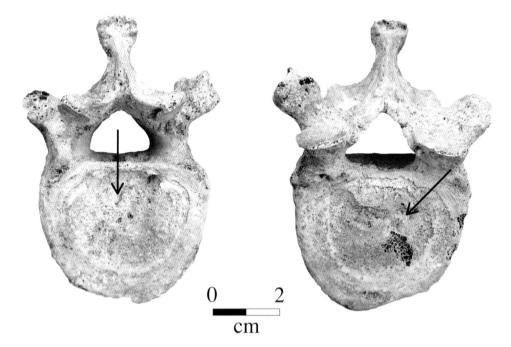

Fig. 13.8 CS10 exhibits the development of Schmorl's nodes in the eighth thoracic vertebra.

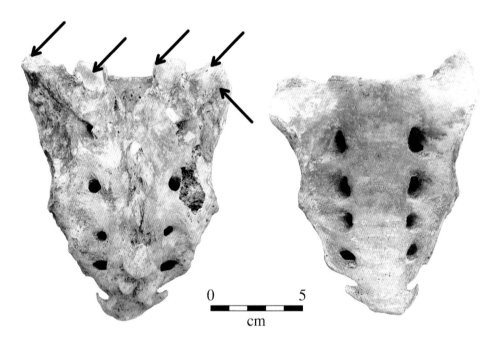

Fig. 13.9 CS10 displays at least five regions of the sacrum with osteoarthritis characterized by lipping of articulation borders and lateral right mass, and deformity of lateral masses.

MUSCULOSKELETAL STRESS MARKERS

The skeleton of the man buried in tomb CS10 displays a series of musculoskeletal stress markers (MSM) that have implications for the parameters of repetitive physical activities over the course of his approximately 35 to 45 years. Some of these markers display notable similarities with those observed in the skeleton of Seneb-Kay raising possibilities of a similar physical regimen common to these two individuals and potentially signaling the social stratum from which the two men derive, a topic that we shall examine in detail in the final part of this volume. The CS10 body displays two different sets of MSM evidence: (1) MSM related to the pelvis and lower body; and (2) evidence for habitual exertion in the left arm as signaled by joint wear as well as the osteoarthritis just discussed.

LOWER EXTREMITIES

On the lower body there are clear indications of repetitive stress and habitual physical exertion in a majority of the same diagnostic bone attachments that we have examined in the case of Seneb-Kay. These include: (1) pronounced areas of insertion of gluteal muscles on the greater trochanter, (2) pronounced linear aspera on the femora, (3) spicules on the trochanteric fossa of the femora (4) iliac impressions (Poirier's facets) on the anterior aspect of the femoral neck, (5) marked development of the adductor tubercle on the femora; (6) irregularities on the popliteal surface of the femora, (7) robustly developed and elongated ischial spines on the pelvis; (8) strong development of the ischial tuberosity. Additionally, we may observe (9) the presence of hypertrophied ligament attachment areas around the fovea capitis.

(1) Gluteal attachments on femora and pelvis CS10 displays pronounced areas for attachment of the gluteus maximus and minus on the femora and pelvis on both sides. These include the pronounced areas of insertion on the greater trochanter and posterior ilium on the pelvic bones (Fig. 13.10).

(2) Linea aspera The CS10 skeleton has robust development of the linea aspera on the femora. This attachment area corresponds to the adductor longus muscle of the inner thigh used in lateral rotation of the thigh (Fig. 13.11).

(3) Spicules on the trochanteric fossa CS10 has prominent development of trochanteric spicules (not illustrated here). The trochanteric spicule is an enthesis (stress features associated with tendon and ligament attachments) at the insertion on the medial aspect of the greater trochanter of the obturator internus, a muscle important in the lateral rotation of the thigh.

(4) Poirier's facets on the femora The femurs of CS10 have iliac impressions known as Poirier's facets on the anterior aspect of the femoral neck (Fig. 13.12). The facets develop where the femur presses against the rim of the acetabulum leaving an iliac impression and represent a response to habitual stress placed on the upper thighs and pelvis.

(5) Development of the adductor tubercle Robust development of the adductor tubercle on the distal end of the femora occurs in the CS10 skeleton and is another diagnostic indicator for muscularity

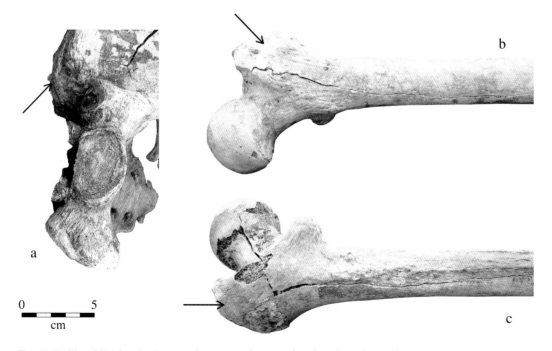

Fig. 13.10 The CS10 body shows robust attachments for the gluteal muscles on the left side of the pelvis (a) including the greater trochanter (b and c, left proximal femur).

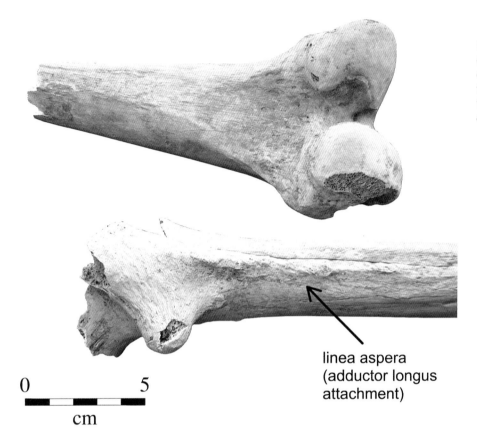

Fig. 13.11 The right femur of CS10 showing the highly developed linea aspera on the femur's posterior surface (for attachment of the adductor longus muscle).

linea aspera
(adductor longus
attachment)

in the adductor magnus muscle (Fig. 13.13). Development of the tubercle parallels the bone remodeling in the linea aspera and reflects the extensive use and development of the adductor muscles.

(6) Popliteal surface of the femora At the distal end of both femora, CS10 has irregularities in the popliteal surface for attachment of the gastrocnemius muscle (Fig. 13.14). These irregularities are a form of MSM reflecting habitual physical activities that stressed and developed the gastrocnemius used in flexing the knee.

(7) Ischial spines on the pelvic bones Perhaps the most diagnostic feature showing habitual stress placed on the pelvis of CS10 is the elongation of the ischial spines (Fig. 13.15). These spines respond to habitual exertion of the pelvic muscles and elongation indicates bone modification that has occurred over a long period during ossification of the spinous process of the ischium. This indicates that the habitual physical activities were not simply an element of the adult life of CS10 but represent a physical regimen that continued from youth into early adulthood.

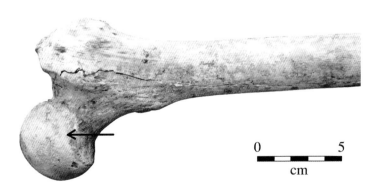

Fig. 13.12 Poirier's facets (iliac impression) on the anterior aspect of the left femur of CS10.

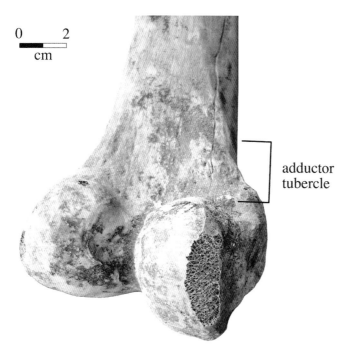

Fig. 13.13 Detail of the strong development of the adductor tubercle on the distal end of the left femur of CS10.

adductor
tubercle

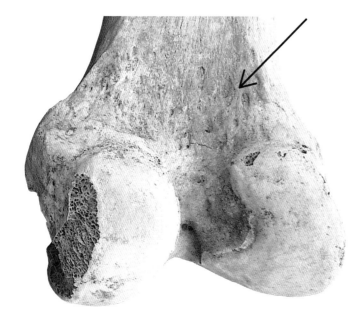

Fig. 13.14 The popliteal surface of CS10's right femur is marked and irregular.

(8) Development of the ischial tuberosity The pelvis of CS10 displays pronounced development in the ischial tuberosity where the tendons of the adductor magnus and biceps femoris muscles attach (Fig. 13.16). Bone modification to the ischial tuberosity is a response to repetitive use of the adductor magnus muscle used in pulling the hip inwards to the centerline of the body.

(9) Hypertrophied ligament attachment around the fovea capitis Finally, we would add to the above set of MSM evidence the presence of hypertrophied ligament attachments around the fovea capitis on the femoral heads (Fig. 13.17). This area represents the attachment of the ligamentum teres (foveal ligament) which tenses during abduction and outward rotation of the thigh. This feature

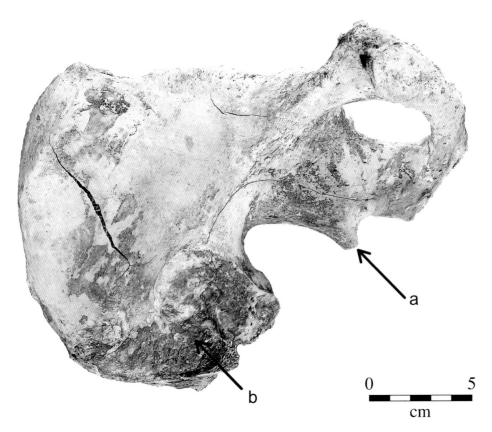

Fig. 13.15 CS10's robustly developed and elongated ischial spine (a) and pronounced areas of insertion of gluteus maximus on posterior ilium (b) left side shown.

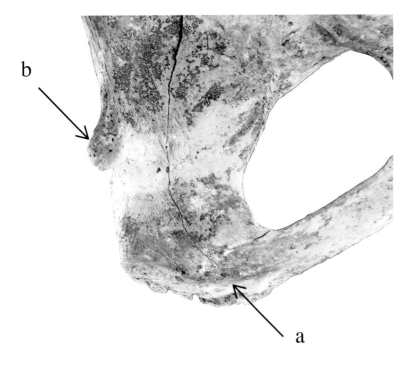

Fig. 13.16 The pelvis of CS10 shows strong development of the ischial tuberosity as shown in this detail (a), as well as robust extension of the ischial spines (b) posterior view of left side.

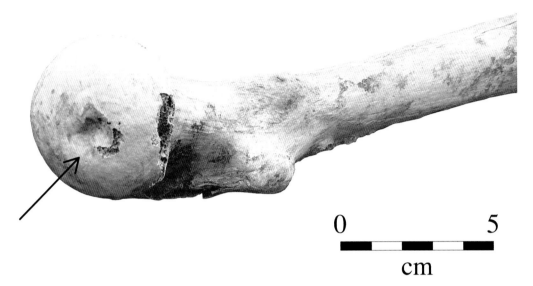

Fig. 13.17 The left femur of CS10 displays a hypertrophied ligament attachment of the foveal ligament.

0   5

cm

corroborates the wider set of muscular stressors to the pelvic and thigh muscles.

UPPER BODY

In addition to the stress markers on CS10's femora and pelvis, this man's upper humerus and scapula on his left side show alterations to the bone attachments by muscles in the arm and shoulder.

(1) Glenoid fossa and acromion of the left scapula There is a strongly developed muscle attachment evident in the area inferior to the glenoid fossa between the infraglenoid tubercle and the lateral border of the scapula. In this location a prominent bony ridge formed where the teres minor muscle attaches. This muscle is responsible for rotating the arm laterally. Additionally, the acromion displays strong muscle markings at the upper insertion for the deltoid and the insertion for the trapezius muscle (Fig. 13.18).

(2) Left humerus Echoing the evidence from the scapula, the left humerus of CS10 displays a prominent tuberosity at the attachment point for the deltoid (shoulder) muscle indicative of repetitive contraction of the deltoid muscle (Fig. 13.19). In order to develop these bone alterations, there must have been long-term asymmetric stress of the left humerus and scapula in CS10 brought about by some form of habitual physical activity.

This set of MSM evidence for the upper body fits with the indications we have already discussed showing that there were significant osteoarthritic changes to the left sternoclavicular joint of the manubrium (Fig. 13.20). A probable inference to be drawn is not just that the CS10 individual was left-handed, but that he used his left arm in repetitive, demanding physical activities that were expressed in a series of major modifications as well as, ultimately osteoarthritis.

ANTEMORTEM TRAUMA

CS10 displays two areas of possible antemortem trauma on his cranium and coccyx. There is no identified perimortem trauma.

(1) Temporal Fracture Blunt force, antemortem trauma to CS10's cranium was identified on the

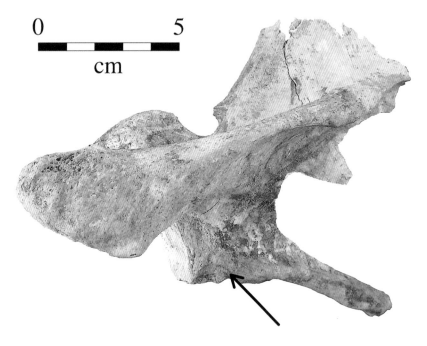

Fig. 13.18 CS10's left scapula with extra bone grown inferior to the glenoid fossa and enhanced muscle attachments on the acromion (not photographed in standard anatomical position).

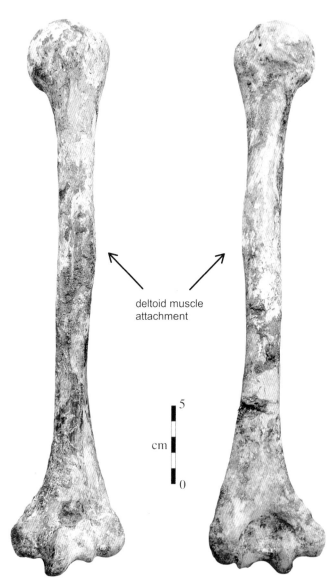

Fig. 13.19 Two views of the left humerus of CS10 showing development of the prominent tuberosity where the deltoid muscle attaches to the upper arm.

deltoid muscle attachment

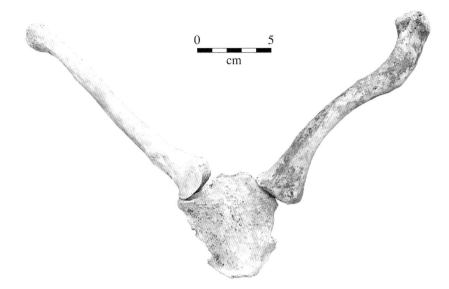

Fig. 13.20 The clavicles, manubrium and lower sternum body of CS10 showing the severe erosion of the left clavicular facet of the manubrium, associated with MSM evidence for his left arm (not photographed in standard anatomical position).

or landing forcefully on the tailbone. The fact that it healed asymmetrically suggests he continued to engage in physical activity that subjected the tailbone to disproportional force as it was healing. Bone remodeling of such a fracture can take years and the rate of healing is dependent on age and nutrition among other factors (Fatayerji and Eastell 2009:1203–1210). The presence of the bony callus suggests the broken tailbone had occurred during the final years of CS10's lifetime (see also discussion of Wedel and Galloway 2014:189).

DISCUSSION OF CS10 MSM AND TRAUMA

As discussed above, the pelvis and femora of the male individual from CS10 display many of the same diagnostic features as occur in the case of Seneb-Kay. The highly developed suite of bone attachments visible through the nine different features examined above shows extensive habitual use of: (1) the adductor magnus, (2) adductor longus, (3) biceps femoris, (4) gastrocnemius, (5) the gluteal muscles (medius and maximus). The development of these features stands out as being reflective of bone alteration responding to habitual physical activities engaged in by this individual. Here we propose that CS10 and Seneb-Kay shared a common physical regimen that resulted in this comparable ensemble of MSM in the hips and upper legs. While such observations would benefit from a wider comparative sample,

left temporal where a depressed area shows a fracture line with hinging effect and a sickle-shaped depressed fracture (Fig. 13.21). Because the bone was healing (bone apposition at the parietal notch), the trauma sustained by CS10 occurred at least a few months before his death. The location and nature of the impact area is undiagnostic as regards the cause.

(2) Coccyx CS10 suffered from a broken coccyx. The first coccygeal vertebra is fused to the sacrum and exhibits deformity. No other coccygeal vertebrae were recovered. The coccyx was not merely bruised but had been fractured and healed in a crooked position with deposition of a substantial hard bony callus around the fracture (Fig. 13.22). The coccyx was healed and the break must have occurred well in advance of his death, but the bony callus suggests the coccyx was still in the process of being remodeled by osteoclasts. This fracture could only have resulted from a significant blunt impact to his posterior region, most likely attributable to his falling

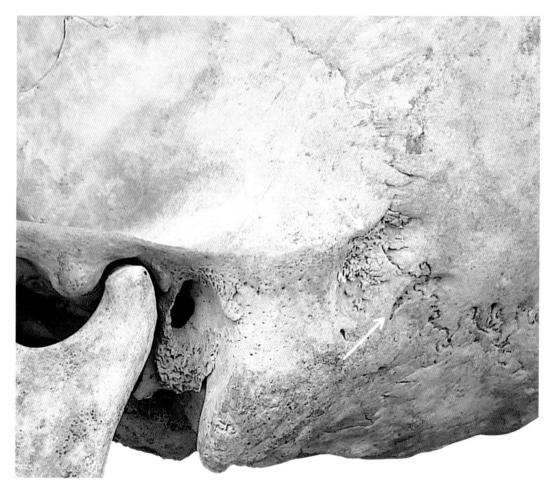

Fig. 13.21 Area of blunt force, antemortem trauma on the left temporal bone of CS10's cranium.

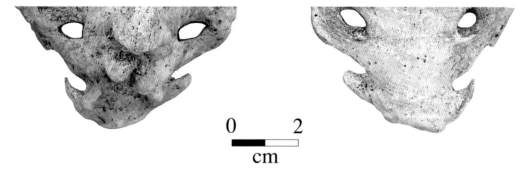

Fig. 13.22 CS10 had a fractured and asymmetrically healed coccyx (posterior and anterior views).

particularly a larger diachronic sample of skeletal individuals from Abydos itself, that data set is not currently available.

Nevertheless, as we have detailed in the discussion of Seneb-Kay's skeleton (Chapter 5) this set of features has been argued by a number of researchers to be indicative of habitual horse riding among historical populations in both the Near East and North America. While robust pelvic and upper leg development can certainly result from a variety of activities, the particular suite of features detailed here may well be indicative of the advent of horse riding and mastery at this particular stage in Egyptian history, particularly in association with the military class that we find increasingly prevalent in the textual record in the Second Intermediate Period.

Correlating with the lower body MSM evidence in CS10 is the evidence for severe stress resulting in osteoarthritis in the sacrum and lower back including the development of Schmorl's nodes in at least one of the vertebrae. CS10 was regularly subjecting his lower back to considerable stressors. While osteoarthritis in the spine is age dependent, and is often seen in skeletal populations in the Nile Valley and elsewhere as a result of habitual heavy labor and bearing heavy loads, this stands out in the case of CS10 as we are looking at an elite individual, a man who almost certainly ruled for part of his lifetime as a king. For an individual of such high social status, recurring heavy stress on the lower back is less likely to derive from habitual heavy labor. There may be an association with the MSM evidence and the osteoarthritis, potentially compounded by habitual equestrian activity as we have proposed for Seneb-Kay. Here we also note the additional piece of evidence supplied by the broken coccyx of CS10 which is likely to have derived from a serious fall. In sum we would propose a relationship between the MSM evidence on this body and features of the paleopathology and trauma visible on his skeleton. Implied here is a common physical regimen between CS10 and Seneb-Kay which may have included a military background with the particular set of physical activities concomitant with the parameters of martial training as practiced during the Second Intermediate Period. This possibility is further amplified when we turn to examine the MSM evidence from CS10's upper body

While the lower body of the CS10 individual indicates a comparable suite of muscular stressors to the bone modifications in Seneb-Kay (CS9), this individual displays a diagnostic set of upper body alterations that we do not see in the case of Seneb-Kay. Although the skeletal evidence indicates that both men were left-handed, CS10 regularly made much more rigorous and forceful use of his left arm. This was expressed in the pronounced development of the following suite of muscles of the left upper arm: (1) deltoid; (2) trapezius; (3) teres minor. This individual's upper left arm underwent not just robust muscular development but heavy usage in a way that does

not seem to be attributable to a normal range of upper body activity. Indeed, the extreme wear and even obliteration of the clavicular notch (making it contiguous with costal notch 1 of the left side of the manubrium) implies habitual, horizontal motion of the upper arm that stressed and eroded the sternoclavicular joint. Particularly in view of the high social status of CS10 and his nearly certain role as a king, such muscularity accompanied by extreme joint wear in this area offers evidence relevant to his long-term regimen of physical activities.

Given the asymmetrical development of these muscles we propose one distinct possibility is that the MSM reflects dedicated military activity associated with use of the left arm. A potential explanation for this robust development in the left arm may include long term training in the use of the sword or other bladed weaponry wielded in the dominant hand. However, in our opinion, the motions involved in sword action alone do not entirely explain the robusticity of this set of muscles. Another significant possibility is that the individual in CS10 underwent long-term training and practice as an archer due to the fact that the suite of muscles developed in CS10 are precisely those involved in archery (Axford 1995; Tihanyi et al. 2015). The bow is held in the non-dominant hand while the bowstring is drawn by the dominant hand: in the case of CS10, the left hand. The teres minor and deltoid muscles are principal among the humeral and scapular muscles used in pulling the bowstring and stabilizing the arm while taking aim in archery (Molnar 2006; Lin et al. 2010). Given that these muscles show such prominent development based on their insertion sites in this individual, bow pulling in archery appears to represent a good fit for the upper body MSM in CS10. Moreover, the severe erosion of the left sternoclavicular joint appears symptomatic of the repetitive horizontal motion in the clavicular area when one pulls back a bow.

The martial skills of Egyptian kings, particularly in archery is a prominent theme in royal iconography becoming extremely pervasive during Egypt's early New Kingdom, one to two centuries after the period of Seneb-Kay, CS10, and associated tombs at South Abydos. The ability of the king as an archer was often expressed a symbol of royal power, which did not necessarily correlate with actual martial abilities of the rulers in question. However, we have specific examples of Egyptian kings who underwent extensive, lifelong training in archery. The best-known case is King Amenhotep II of the 18th Dynasty whose texts and monuments celebrate the king's affinity for archery and his remarkable skill with the bow and arrow. This manifested itself both in demonstrations of his martial prowess as well as in actual military campaigning. Indeed, Amenhotep II (CG 61069: Smith 1912:36–38; Harris and Wente 1980:66–67, 210–211), was buried in his sarcophagus in the Valley of the Kings with a compound bow placed over the chest of his mummy (Loret 1898:91–112).

Bows in pharaonic Egypt include the "self" bow, composed of a single wood stave, primarily used during the eras prior to the Second Intermediate Period (Cartwright and Taylor 2008:77–83), as well as the "composite" or "compound" bows constructed of laminated wood to form a weapon that had to be drawn with greater force by the archer but which delivered much greater force to the bowstring (McLeod 1970:35–37; Western and McLeod 1995:77–94). The composite bow was a technological innovation introduced to Egypt from the Near East which we see incorporated into Egyptian military technology by the time of the early New Kingdom. Like the horse, chariot, and other innovations, the compound bow appears to have entered the Nile Valley during the Hyksos era and was rapidly adopted into Egyptian military practices in the Second Intermediate Period (Genz 2013:95–105; Pollastrini 2017:513–518).

Habitual martial activity using a bow of any type should be expected to develop the muscles of the upper part of the dominant arm and show itself in modifications to the corresponding bone attachments. The greater torsion and forces involved in use of a compound bow would further enhance the long-term muscle development and skeletal effects of habitual archery. It is an intriguing possibility that the lifetime of this individual corresponds with the period of the advent of new technologies that included use of the compound bow in the Nile Valley. For these reasons, we propose a significant possibility is that the CS10 individual displays indications of a professional military background with his body having responded to the physical aspects of the accompanying activities. We may further conclude that there is a reasonable possibility he was regularly engaged in two activities: horse riding and archery. Therefore, in several respects he skeletal evidence from CS10 complements the indications for the martial lifestyle and death in battle that we see in the case of Seneb-Kay. Seneb-Kay was unequivocally a king, and, based on the large size and design features of CS10, we can state that the occupant of CS10 was almost certainly a king who ruled over the same political entity as Seneb-Kay. Skeletal evidence lends weight to the conclusion that both men ascended to rulership from a military background. The possible historical and political context of these kings will be further examined in Part 4 of this volume.

THE CS8 INDIVIDUAL

Skeletal material recovered inside and adjacent to tomb CS8 is consistent with the evidence for the cemetery as a whole showing the use of the tombs for interments of single mature males. Principal evidence for the CS8 burial comes from the fragmented cranium and mandible. None of the long bones of this individual were recovered intact. Therefore, we are not able to present a fuller osteobiography for the man buried in tomb CS8. Based on stages of cranial suture fusion as indicated by Steele and Bramblett (1988) and dental wear (Smith 1984; Schmucker 1985), this male was at least 30 years of age (Table 13.3).

Table 13.3 Summary of skeletal attributes of CS8

Skeleton No.	Sex	Age (y)	% of Skeleton represented
CS8	Male, determined from cranium	At least 30, determined from cranium (significant closure of sutures), teeth (dental wear, no enamel on occlusal surface, dentin exposed)	7

TAPHONOMY

The dark coloration of the skull and mandible indicate that they remained underground for the most part since their deposition, likely re-covered by backfill after the point at which the tomb was first opened and robbed. A separation between the left and right parietal bones along the sagittal suture near bregma was a fresh break evidenced by the clean, light colored bone revealed in cross section and on the left edge of the break in contrast to the surrounding bone surfaces. This break was likely caused by a digging tool during excavation (Fig. 13.23).

DENTAL DISEASE

As occurs with Seneb-Kay (CS9) and the man buried in CS10, CS8 also has a deviated septum (Fig. 13.24). The deviation is towards the individual's left side. There is no evidence of any other trauma in the area of the nasal aperture of CS8, therefore, as with the other cases, we interpret the origin to be developmental.

CS8 provides additional evidence for the gritty diet of the individuals buried in Cemetery S, despite their evident high social status. Maxillary molars (M1 and 2 on both sides) exhibit wear up to Stage 6 (Schmucker 1985; Smith 1984). The mandibular molars also show evidence for long-term wear Stages 2–5 (Schmucker 1985; Smith 1984) and degeneration of the temporomandibular joint (Fig. 13.25) and the mandibular condyles. As we have seen with CS10, the stress exerted on and by the teeth that wore the tooth enamel down to the dentin also contributed to the osteoarthritis of the temporomandibular joint (flattening of the anterior surface of the fossa and flattening of the mandibular condyles; minimum to maximum

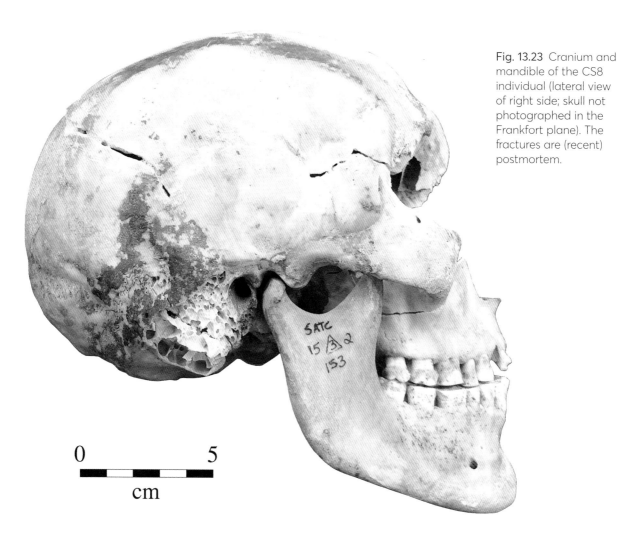

Fig. 13.23 Cranium and mandible of the CS8 individual (lateral view of right side; skull not photographed in the Frankfort plane). The fractures are (recent) postmortem.

0   5

cm

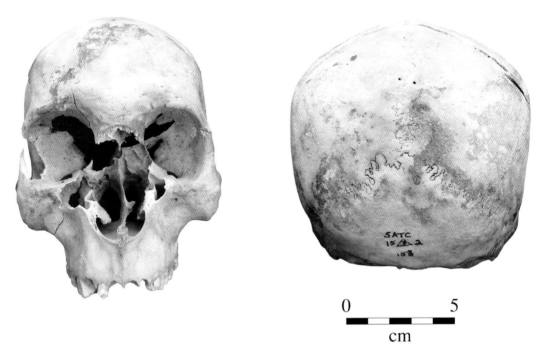

Fig. 13.24 Front and back of the CS8 cranium showing septal deviation (left) and the cranial sutures (right).

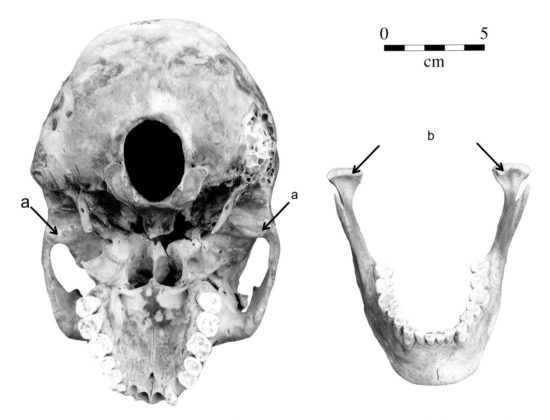

Fig. 13.25 Inferior view of the cranium and mandible of CS8 showing severe dental wear down to the dentin, flattening of the anterior border of the temporomandibular joint, glenoid fossa (a); and flattening of the condyles of the mandible (b).

expressions according to Rando and Wal-dron's (2012) criteria for diagnosing TMJ osteoarthritis.

A commonly observed dental disease in ancient peoples is calculus accumulation. The calculus observed for the individuals in the South Abydos skeletal sample is supragingival (i.e., above the gum), which is the more common type. The importance of calculus is found in its composition, as an indicator of diet, and in its buildup, as it can lead to periodontal disease characterized by alveolar recession of bone (uniform horizontal bone loss), exposure of the tooth roots, and porosity (Delgado-Darias et al. 2006; Forshaw 2009). Both CS8 and CS10 have as an indicator of periodontal disease the appearance of pitting on the alveolar bone caused by the resorption of the outer cortical plate, which exposed the underlying porous trabecular structure of the tooth. The progression of this condition was more developed in CS8 (Fig. 13.26). Had these individuals lived longer, this condition would have very likely resulted in tooth avulsion or displacement.

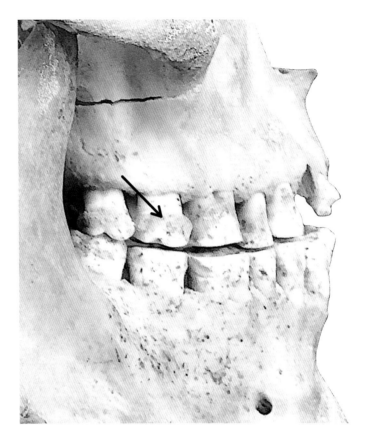

Fig. 13.26 Calculus deposition and the associated periodontal disease as indicated by alveolar recession on the CS8 individual.

Table 13.4 Summary of skeletal attributes of CS11.

Skeleton No.	Sex	Age (y)	% of Skeleton represented
CS11-1-2	Male, determined from robusticity of long bones available	At least 30, determined from long bones, epiphyseal lines fully fused	11

Table 13.5 Stature estimation for CS11 based on available long bone measurements (stature calculated from formulas for ancient Egyptian males provided by Raxter et al. 2008).

Bone	CS11-1-2	CS11-1-2 Stature	SEE	Range
Femur$_m$	2.257 (**44.3**) + 63.93=	163.91 cm	3.218	160.69–167.13
Radius$_m$	2.641 (**24.3**) + 100.91=	165.08 cm	3.731	161.35–168.81
Average / Range		164.95 cm		160.69–168.81

$_m$ = maximum length; SEE = standard of error estimates (Raxter et al. 2008)

THE CS11 INDIVIDUAL

The final burial for which a useful group of skel-etal remains were recovered is CS11. The tomb, the smallest in the main cluster, was heavily plundered and the primary concentration of skeletal remains were re-covered from debris in and adjacent to the inner end of the burial chamber. The recovered elements (Fig. 13.27) do not include the cranium. Consequently, the analysis of the CS11 individual is much more limited.

Most significantly—and consistent with the evidence for tombs CS8, CS9 (Seneb-Kay), and CS10—the burial in CS11 was a mature male (Table 13.4). The fusion of epiphyseal lines on the recovered femur indicate a man of 30+ years of age at time of death (fusion lines almost obliterated).

Estimation of stature (160.69–168.81 cm) is com-parable to the figures for the other individuals in the cemetery (Table 13.5). The surviving femur lacks the highly developed linea aspera and other musculo-skeletal stress markers present on the CS9 and CS10 individuals but is otherwise of comparable size and robusticity. Further analysis is unwarranted given the limited preservation of the CS11 burial.

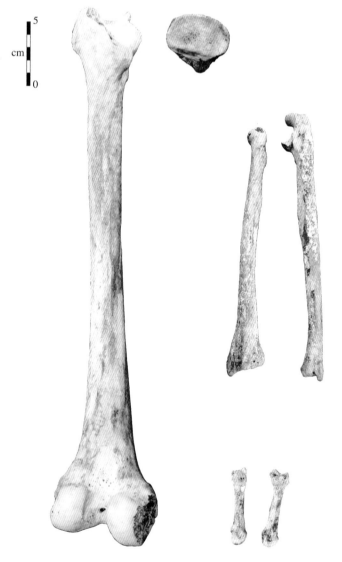

Fig. 13.27 Primary surviving elements of the CS11 individual including: femur, left side, posterior view (a), radius and ulna, left side posterior view (c–d); and metatarsals (e–f). (Elements not photographed in standard anatomical position.)

Part 4

Historical and Archaeological Synthesis

14

Seneb-Kay and the Abydos Dynasty*

The archaeological remains exposed during 2013–2016 at South Abydos show that the tradition of royal mortuary activity initiated under Senwosret III (ca. 1850 BCE) and extended during the reigns of three mid-13th Dynasty kings (probably Neferhotep I, Sahathor, and Sobekhotep IV, ca. 1750 BCE) was resumed during the later Second Intermediate Period with the addition of at least eight tombs to the site. Based on its painted wall decoration, the tomb of Seneb-Kay is the only one of this latter group of tombs that unequivocally belongs to a king. However, among the seven tombs, we see a tradition of royal funerary architecture that was derivative from the preceding 13th Dynasty royal tombs. Fragmentary remains of the burial assemblages hint at what would have been richly equipped tombs for the era. A pattern of single interments of mature males is consistent with the conclusion that all of these tombs were royal and belonged to kings who were close contemporaries of Woseribre Seneb-Kay. It appears probable that there were additional tombs that made use of the interior of the enclosures of the two 13th Dynasty tombs S9 and S10, but which were destroyed through the massive quarrying into those tombs' substructures during the late Roman and early Byzantine Periods. The indications are that the site represents a dynastic necropolis that included at least eight, and likely more, burials of Second Intermediate Period rulers.

The identification of the tomb of Seneb-Kay within a larger cemetery belonging to a group of kings of this same era at South Abydos provides crucial archaeological evidence relevant to a theory proposed first by Detlef Franke, and later expanded by Kim Ryholt, that the Thinite region was the center of an independent line of kings—an "Abydos Dynasty"—which emerged in the aftermath of the decline of the late Middle Kingdom state, contemporary with the Theban 16th Dynasty (Franke 1988:259; Ryholt 1997:163–166).[1] Evidence for the existence of the Abydos Dynasty was originally seen in stelae from Abydos commemorating three Second Intermediate Period kings: Wepwawetemsaf, Paentjeny, and Senaaib. These rulers are not attested through any evidence at Thebes. The meaning of the names Wepwawetemsaf and Paentjeny suggests these men had familial links with the Thinite region.[2] Additionally, analysis of the final surviving and badly-damaged column of the Turin Kinglist (Column 11) suggested that document contained an enumeration of a group of sixteen or more Second Intermediate Period kings who are distinct from the known 16th Dynasty Theban kings.

According to Ryholt's proposition, a power vacuum in Middle and Upper Egypt following the conquest of the 13th Dynasty capital, *Itj-Tawy*, by the Hyksos 15th Dynasty formed the catalyst for the development of two coeval dynasties, the Theban 16th Dynasty, and the (unnumbered) Abydos Dynasty. After a period of independence, these two dynasties succumbed to Hyksos military aggression. Based on its geographical position, the Abydos Dynasty may have met its demise first, later to be followed by the

* This chapter written by Josef Wegner.

16th Dynasty after a longer struggle. Ryholt speculated that the Abydos Dynasty may have survived for only a few decades (ca. 1650–1630 BCE), while the 16th Dynasty persisted for the better part of a century (ca. 1650–1580 BCE). After a brief period of Hyksos control in Upper Egypt, it was the revival of Theban independence in the form of the 17th Dynasty that developed into the well-known conflict between Thebes and Avaris. The political history of the Second Intermediate Period then culminated with the campaigns of Seqenenre-Tao, Kamose, and Ahmose (Vandersleyen 1971), and the reunification of Egypt that accompanied the Expulsion of the Hyksos during the reign of Nebpehtyre Ahmose.

Considerable doubt has been expressed by a number of Egyptologists on Ryholt's premise that the Thinite region may have maintained, even for a brief phase of time, territorial autonomy and an independent succession of kings apart from the Theban 16th Dynasty. In a detailed study of Abydene Second Intermediate Period stelae, Marcel Marée has argued that Kings Wepwawetemsaf and Paentjeny are not contemporaries of the 16th Dynasty but fall within the early 17th Dynasty and comprise members of the Theban royal succession (Marée 2010:241–282). James Allen, preferring to see all the rulers listed at the end of the Turin Kinglist as belonging to the Theban 16th and 17th Dynasties, has argued against the possibility that the document includes a separate compilation of rulers of the Abydos Dynasty (Allen 2010:1–10).

Apart from criticism of the evidence for a separate line of kings at Abydos, the most important qualification to Ryholt's theory lies in the strong indications that the rise of the Theban 16th Dynasty did not occur in response to a power vacuum following a Hyksos conquest of *Itj-Tawy* that ended the 13th Dynasty. As several scholars have observed, there is a compelling set of archaeological and historical data showing a substantial overlap between the last phase of the 13th Dynasty and the 16th Dynasty (Spalinger 2001:296–300; Bennett 2002:128–129; Polz and Seiler 2003:46–48; Allen 2010:1–10). The 13th Dynasty was likely ended by Hyksos expansion southwards to Memphis and the Fayum region but at a later point in time than the beginning of the 16th Dynasty. In the context of this chronological overlap, Alexander Ilin-Tomich has argued in favor of a direct evolution of the Theban state of the 16th

Dynasty from the late Middle Kingdom administrative entity known as the *tp-rsy*, the *Head of the South* (Ilin-Tomich 2014:158–161). The territory of the *tp-rsy* included the southern eight nomes of Egypt, from Elephantine (1st nome of Upper Egypt) to Thinis/Abydos (8th nome of Upper Egypt) with Thebes as its administrative center. Ilin-Tomich has suggested this entire territory detached from *Itj-Tawy* as a cohesive administrative unit, developing its own line of kings (the 16th Dynasty) who ruled the south contemporary with the last phase of the 13th Dynasty. In Ilin-Tomich's view, the Abydos Dynasty would have been neither necessary nor viable since Abydos itself had long been administratively part of the *Head of the South*.

Although it is notionally attractive that the administrative unit of the *tp-rsy* centered on Thebes broke away—geographically intact—from the weakening grasp of *Itj-Tawy*, can we assume that such a clean model fits with the realities of political developments during the phase of political and economic fragmentation encompassed by Egypt's Second Intermediate Period? Ultimately it remains unclear what historical events or combination of social and economic factors led to the secession of Upper Egypt during the final phase of the 13th Dynasty. Middle and Upper Egypt may not have broken away so neatly, nor in a state of internal political harmony, an issue we shall explore in the following two chapters.

The tombs of Seneb-Kay and the other seven probable kings at South Abydos now provide clear evidence for the fact that Abydos was being used as a burial ground during this same timeframe (ca. 1650–1600 BCE), by a substantial group of Second Intermediate Period rulers. Do the tombs of Seneb-Kay and the other men buried in the royal cemetery represent kings of the Theban 16th Dynasty who were buried at Abydos? Alternatively, are these men somehow to be attributed to the final stage of the 13th Dynasty, buried near more illustrious forebears of the 12th and middle 13th Dynasties? Or, do the South Abydos tombs provide evidence for the existence of an autonomous Abydos Dynasty that overlapped with both the 16th and end of the 13th Dynasties? In order to address these various possibilities, we turn firstly to examine the name of King Seneb-Kay and what it may tell us about the date and historical associations of this king.

THE NAME OF WOSERIBRE SENEB-KAY

Preserved in the decorated burial chamber of Seneb-Kay are the king's nomen, Seneb-Kay, and prenomen, Woseribre, along with a group of royal epithets: *nṯr nfr, nb tꜣwy, nb irt ḫt, ny-swt-bity*, *God-god, Lord of the Two-Lands, Lord of Ritual, King of Upper and Lower Egypt*. The tomb lacks use of the king's Horus name, Two-Ladies name, and Golden Horus name. All elements of the full five-fold royal titulary are rarely attested in the sparse monumental record for the Second Intermediate Period, although continued use of the full set of five names does occur during this era (Leprohon 2013:81–92). Presumably Seneb-Kay had other elements of the full royal titulary, but these were not recorded in the decoration of his burial chamber. The two identified names of the king open up several significant historical issues regarding his identity, historical placement, and dynastic associations.

THE NOMEN SENEB-KAY

Regarding the king's nomen, it is notable that no other attested examples of a male personal name *Snb-Kꜣy* exist. Grammatically the use of the word *snb, to be healthy,* fronting another word could logically be taken as an adjectival predicate as occurs in examples of compound names incorporating the *snb* element. However, the succeeding word *kꜣy* with double reed-leaf (*ii/y*), does not appear to be readable as a subject. Therefore, both through grammatical structure as well as the corpus of known personal names Seneb-Kay is unparalleled. Yet, the names *Snb*, and *Kꜣy*, individually are extremely common during the Middle Kingdom and Second Intermediate Period (Ranke 1935:312, 341). This raises the possibility that the name should be understood as two separate names combined in this single nomen.

One option is the compound name Seneb-Kay represents use of a filiative nomen to be read *Seneb's (son) Kay*. The individual would therefore properly be named Kay with his paternity embedded in the nomen. The sporadic use of filiative personal names has been argued in the case of royal nomina during the 13th Dynasty. Its use might be associated with

legitimation of descent in cases where a son succeeded his father on the throne (Ryholt 1997:207–208). In fact, the possibility for such a filiative nomen has been suggested separately in regard to the problematical nomen Seb-Kay which occurs on the ebony apotropaion from Abydos (CG 9433/JdE34988), which we attribute here to Seneb-Kay himself (discussed in detail below). Ryholt has attempted to place two kings, Seb and Kay, into the 13th Dynasty royal succession by reading this as a filiative nomen (Ryholt 1997:341). He linked Seb-Kay with the occurrence of a name Kay in the nomen Kay-Amenemhat (Amenemhat VII) and proposed the succession, (1) Seb, (2) Kay, (3) Amenemhat VII. He identified Seb and Kay as early 13th Dynasty kings (Ryholt 1990:110, 1997:219). The improbability of a succession of three generations of men within just a few years of rule has been noted (von Beckerath 1999:434; Schneider 2006:179). Schneider has argued for association of the name Seb-Kay on the Abydos apotropaion with Sobekhotep II. These suggestions all appear highly improbable in light of the discovery of Seneb-Kay's tomb at South Abydos and chronological evidence summarized here that place his reign during the later Second Intermediate Period.

Based on a wider survey of the occurrence of double names during the Middle Kingdom, Vernus has suggested that what might appear to be a practice of filiative naming is rather to be understood as use of two names both referring to a single individual (Vernus 1986). This system functions akin to a name and nickname, or other forms of doubled personal names that occur in many cultures (Vernus 1971:193–198). Instead of *Seneb's son Kay*, following the structure "A (who is known as) B," the nomen would be taken as *Seneb (known as) Kay*. Indeed, given the relative rarity of double names in royal nomina of the 13th Dynasty and Second Intermediate Period, this mode of naming appears more probable. Due to the extremely rapid succession patterns seen in the Second Intermediate Period, it would appear doubtful there was any strong impetus for statements of legitimation by means of filiative nomina. Indeed, instances of father to son royal succession are quite rare in the Second Intermediate Period and legitimation was effectively borne through other techniques.

In view of the scant historical data regarding the era in which Seneb-Kay reigned, it would be extremely useful if we could posit the succession of a king *Seneb* to his son, a king *Seneb's son Kay*. Indications for such a succession might, indeed, be argued on the basis of the possible position of Seneb-Kay's prenomen, Woseribre, in the Turin Kinglist, as we discuss further below. The occurrence in succession of two similarly structured prenomina, both following the pattern *Wsr-X-rᶜ*, could be viewed as an indication of familial succession in the dynasty to which Seneb-Kay belonged. However, we must acknowledge the limited evidence for the use of filiative nomina and the fact that the few examples where this might occur date to the early 13th Dynasty, rather than the later Second Intermediate Period. The occurrence of a filiative nomen appears relatively less likely, although the name clearly takes the form of a compound personal name composed of the two elements: Seneb and Kay. It is for that reason that we have chosen to render the nomen with hyphenation, "Seneb-Kay," rather than the alternative of a single name, "Senebkay."

THE PRENOMEN WOSERIBRE AND THE *WSR-X-Rᶜ* ENTRIES IN THE TURIN KINGLIST

Seneb-Kay's prenomen was *Wsr-ỉb-rᶜ*, Woseribre,[3] a name that provides a crucial piece of evidence towards considering his historical and dynastic associations. The name Woseribre does not survive anywhere in the Second Intermediate Period monumental record. However, two kings with prenomina using the structure *Wsr-X-rᶜ* occur among the Second Intermediate Period entries in the Turin Kinglist, suggesting the possibility that Woseribre Seneb-Kay was recorded in that document (Gardiner 1959: pl. 4). Here we discuss the king's prenomen and its possible occurrence in the Turin Kinglist as one line of evidence relevant to understanding the historical and political context of Seneb-Kay.

In the highly damaged Column 11 of the Turin Kinglist occurs a list of the kings of the Theban 16th Dynasty.[4] The relatively well-preserved Lines 1–15 of this column (continuing from the final line of the preceding Column 10) enumerate a group of nine Theban kings. These entries include known 16th Dynasty kings such as Nebiriau I and Nebiriau II, Sewoserenre Bebiankh, and Sekhemre-Shedwaset. There are six lost names for this sequence (Lines 10–15). These

missing names may account for some or all of a group of five other 16th Dynasty kings who are known from inscribed objects in the Theban region.[5] The final line of this grouping ends with a summation line (Line 15) following the format used for the ruler who precedes dynastic totals in the Turin Kinglist: *ỉr.n.f m nswyt 5 rnpwt, he made in the kingship 5 years.*

Below this final entry for the 16th Dynasty kings a new group of rulers begins. The first two of these (Lines 16–17) have similarly structured prenomens: *ny-swt-bỉty (Wsr-X-rᶜ), King of Upper and Lower Egypt, Woser-///re.* Here the fragment breaks away and only part of each name is preserved. Following the two *Wsr-X-rᶜ* kings occurs a long break after which Column 11 ends with its final lines at the bottom of the papyrus (Lines 26–31). Based on the fact that we have both the beginning and end of the column, and the line spacing (31 lines per column) is known from better preserved sections of the papyrus, there are eight missing lines in Column 11 (Lines 18–25). The heavily damaged entries at the base of the column include the partially preserved names of six kings along with preserved regnal lengths totaling 16–18 years (Fig. 14.1).

As we have seen above, in his 1997 study, *The Political Situation in Egypt during the Second Intermediate Period*, Ryholt presented the argument that the fragmentary entries in the Turin Canon, Lines 11/16 to 11/31, do not represent Theban 16th Dynasty kings but a separate regnal grouping, an unnumbered dynasty that did not survive into the system of numbered dynasties enshrined in Manetho's *Aegyptiaca* (Ryholt 1997:163–166). In developing this argument, Ryholt built on the earlier suggestion of Franke that there may have existed an independent group of minor kings based at Abydos during the Second Intermediate Period (Franke 1988:259). Attested only on monuments from Abydos, three kings, Sekhemre-Neferkhau Wepwawetemsaf, Sekhemre-khutawy Paentjeny, and Menkhaure Senaaib, could belong to this group of rulers. The names of two of them, Wepwawetemsaf and Paentjeny, have Abydene and Thinite associations (discussed further below) suggesting they may be rulers whose origins and power base centered on the Abydene rather than Theban region. Lack of evidence for their prenomina in the Turin Canon suggests that they might have occurred among the broken entries of Column 11. Since contemporaneous dynasties are recorded by necessity one after

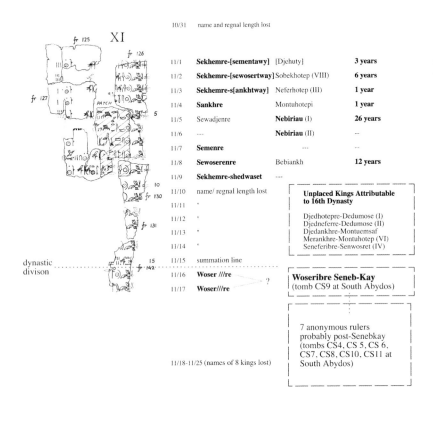

10/31	name and regnal length lost		
11/1	**Sekhemre-[sementawy]**	[Djehuty]	**3 years**
11/2	**Sekhemre-[sewosertway]**	Sobekhotep (VIII)	**6 years**
11/3	**Sekhemre-s[ankhtway]**	Neferhotep (III)	**1 year**
11/4	**Sankhre**	Montuhotepi	**1 year**
11/5	Sewadjenre	**Nebiriau (I)**	**26 years**
11/6	---	**Nebiriau (II)**	--
11/7	**Semenre**	---	--
11/8	**Sewoserenre**	Bebiankh	**12 years**
11/9	**Sekhemre-shedwaset**	---	
11/10	name/ regnal length lost		
11/11	"		
11/12	"		
11/13	"		
11/14	"		
11/15	summation line		
11/16	**Woser ///re**		
11/17	**Woser///re**	?	
11/18-11/25	(names of 8 kings lost)		

Unplaced Kings Attributable to 16th Dynasty

Djedhotepre-Dedumose (I)
Djedneferre-Dedumose (II)
Djedankhre-Montuemsaf
Merankhre-Montuhotep (VI)
Seneferibre-Senwosret (IV)

Woseribre Seneb-Kay
(tomb CS9 at South Abydos)

7 anonymous rulers probably post-Senebkay (tombs CS4, CS 5, CS 6, CS7, CS8, CS10, CS11 at South Abydos)

dynastic divison

11/26	///hebre	---	
11/27	name lost	---	**2 years**
11/28	name lost		**2 years**
11/29	name lost		**4 years**
11/30	///webenre	---	**3-4 years**
11/31	///webenre	---	**3-4 years**

column break in TC Vorlage

Fig. 14.1 Column 11 of the Turin Canon showing possible location of Woseribre Seneb-Kay.

16–17 (*Wsr-X-rꜥ*) or Lines 26–31 (including the two kings *///wbn-rꜥ*) correspond with the five 16th Dynasty kings attested through the monumental record. Furthermore, the five Theban 16th Dynasty kings known from the monumental record can all be accommodated by the six missing names that precede the 16th Dynasty summation line. This suggests all of the known Theban 16th Dynasty rulers are accounted for in sixteen lines of the Turin Kinglist 10/31 through 11/15.

Similar problems face the proposition that the 17th Dynasty rulers might be included in Column 11.[6] There are at least ten known kings belonging to the 17th Dynasty (Polz 2007:20–59). Yet, we have at least sixteen kings listed after the summation line for the 16th Dynasty and—as with the five missing 16th Dynasty kings—no indication among the surviving elements of the names that any of these correspond to rulers of the 17th Dynasty. These are a group of kings whose known titularies should be identifiable, even in the fragmentary entries surviving in Lines 16–17 and 26–31. While we must acknowledge the limitations inherent in the highly damaged nature of the document, all indications are that the Turin Kinglist includes a substantial number of names that do not

another in Egyptian dynastic histories such as the Turin Canon, the hypothesized Abydos Dynasty would presumably have been contemporary with or sequential to the Theban rulers of the 16th Dynasty that preceded it in Column 11.

Doubts have been expressed, both on the existence of the Abydos Dynasty (Marée 2010:275–277), as well as the nature of the royal names recorded in Column 11 of the Turin Canon. James Allen has suggested the entries in Column 11 are all to be attributed exclusively to the kings of the Theban 16th and 17th Dynasties, listed in succession in Column 11 and a now-missing Column 12 (Allen 2010:1–10). One of several problems confronting Allen's suggestion is that none of the fragmentary prenomina in Lines correspond with Theban rulers of the 16th to 17th Dynasty succession. As Ryholt had previously concluded, the indications are there is some other regnal grouping that must intervene between these two dynasties, and the 17th Dynasty list should form part of the now-missing Column 12.

With the discovery of the tomb of Woseribre Seneb-Kay, we now have a crucial new piece of evidence confirming the veracity of Column 11 of the Turin Kinglist: a king whose prenomen corresponds with names occurring after the summation line for the 16th Dynasty. Seneb-Kay's prenomen *Wsr-ib-rꜥ* follows the pattern of the two *Wsr-X-rꜥ* names in Column 11, Lines 16–17. Seneb-Kay might be one of these two kings, or his prenomen may be one that follows this same structure but occurs further down in the broken section of Column 11. If Woseribre Seneb-Kay is one of the two kings in Lines 16–17, this would imply that he dates relatively early in a sequence of some sixteen rulers recognized by the compiler of the Turin Kingslist and its earlier source document (the TC Vorlage). Such a chronological placement would seem to run counter to the inference from the tomb architecture at South Abydos (Chapter 12) that Seneb-Kay falls late in the group of eight tombs. However, the relatively cohesive nature of the architecture in the Second Intermediate Period tomb group as a whole makes fine-grained chronological conclusions tentative. The fundamental question emerges, do the regnal entries initiated with the two *Wsr-X-rꜥ* kings represent a distinct group of kings that may be equated with the tomb of Seneb-Kay and the seven additional burials at South Abydos? Let us turn to examine other evidence for the chronological placement of Seneb-Kay before returning to the issue of dynastic affiliation.

THE DATE OF SENEB-KAY: ARCHAEOLOGICAL AND ICONOGRAPHIC EVIDENCE

Fundamental to understanding the position of Seneb-Kay and the seven tombs at South Abydos are the chronological parameters of the king's lifetime and reign, and possible historical synchronisms that help to situate this ruler within the political history of the Second Intermediate Period. A variety of data

has emerged from the remains of the tomb and its decorative program which helps us to delineate the probable date of Seneb-Kay.

As we have examined earlier in this publication, a significant feature of Seneb-Kay's tomb is its reuse of a variety of materials for both the architecture as well as the tomb equipment. Reused architectural elements include the 11th Dynasty stela of Idudju-iker, and the probable reuse of a 13th Dynasty false door of one of the Sobekhotep kings as roofing slabs. An extensive series of mid- to late 13th Dynasty decorated chapel blocks form the bulk of the masonry for the burial chamber. The 13th Dynasty date of these chapel blocks as well as the Sobekhotep false door is paralleled in the cedar canopic chest fashioned from coffin boards bearing the blue-painted texts also naming a king Sobekhotep. Preserved elements of the chronologically diagnostic Coffin Text Spells 777–782 suggest this was one of the Sobekhotep kings of the mid- to late 13th Dynasty. Therefore, Seneb-Kay's canopic chest was assembled from repurposed coffin boards that had originated in a royal burial of the middle to late 13th Dynasty. The co-occurrence of the name Sobekhotep on the reused false door and the coffin boards suggests there was one particular earlier royal funerary complex that was targeted. Based on a variety of criteria this is likely to have been the tomb of Khaneferre Sobekhotep IV (who reigned ca. 1732–1720 BCE). There is a reasonable possibility that the adjacent 13th Dynasty tomb S10—the enclosure of which was itself reused as the location for Seneb-Kay's tomb—formed the source of this earlier royal material.

The phenomenon of reuse of elite and royal materials from the period of Sobekhotep IV is useful in providing a relative dynastic date for Seneb-Kay. Clearly a significant span of time must have elapsed to render 13th Dynasty materials—particularly royal funerary materials—a legitimate target for reuse. In both temporal and dynastic terms, this suggests a later Second Intermediate Period, or "post-13th Dynasty" date for Seneb-Kay. In particular, the possibility that Seneb-Kay himself might be a member of the 13th Dynasty (see for instance the opinion of Kemp, quoted by Quirke 2016:210) seems particularly improbable in light of the extensive appropriation of 13th Dynasty elite and royal materials. More significant than the approximate date range indicated by these reused materials are chronological parameters of the iconography of the texts and imagery in the burial chamber.

TRUNCATED HIEROGLYPHS

The texts in Seneb-Kay's burial chamber employ a variation on the late Middle Kingdom tradition of "incomplete" or truncated hieroglyphs. Appearing first in the late 12th Dynasty in the Memphite region, truncated hieroglyphs were used for the symbolic impairment of potentially threatening animal signs in inscriptions placed in proximity to the burial. Not attested in Upper Egypt during the late 12th and earlier 13th Dynasties, this tradition reemerged in the late 13th Dynasty and Second Intermediate Period in Upper Egypt. The phenomenon may reflect a transmission of Memphite court traditions to Upper Egypt in the mid- to late 13th Dynasties (Miniaci 2010a:113–134). However, as practiced during this final stage in Upper Egypt, the tradition appears to have become increasingly divorced from the original intent of reducing the threat of animal images in funerary texts. During the 16th and early 17th Dynasties the use of truncated hieroglyphs was extended to objects such as stelae used outside the setting of the burial assemblage. The actual signs subject to truncation were reduced and more sporadically applied. This decline in use of truncated hieroglyphs in Upper Egypt parallels the full development of the *rishi* coffin tradition in the 17th Dynasty and concomitant changes in burial traditions during that final stage of the Second Intermediate Period (ca. 1600–1550 BCE).

In the texts in Seneb-Kay's burial chamber, truncated hieroglyphs were applied in a mode consistent with the later stages of the practice in Upper Egypt. Truncation was used consistently for the *w*-chick hieroglyph, which is depicted with attenuated body and no legs. Two other signs show a subtle use of truncation. The *bity*-bee sign, that occurs in several locations has a shortened tail shown as a rounded element without the stinger that occurs in fully rendered versions of the glyph. Similarly, the *f*, horned viper, hieroglyph has a shortened tail that limits the snake in most cases to its head and the rounded midsection of the body. Notably, truncation does not occur in the case of the *d*-cobra, nor in the other bird sign, the *s3*-goose that occurs four times in the texts. One other hieroglyph that might have been shown truncated is the *m*-owl, but this sign does not occur in the surviving texts.[7]

The presence of truncated hieroglyphs, but the limited way they are applied, in Seneb-Kay's texts is consistent with evidence for the final stages of this tradition in Upper Egypt contemporary with the 16th to early 17th Dynasties. We see a close parallel to this mode of usage in the small stela of king Wepwawetemsaf from Abydos (discussed in detail below), where the *m*-owl in the king's nomen is truncated but the *s3* birds in the royal titulary are fully rendered. Among royal funerary objects comparable approaches to truncation occur in the scarab and canopic chest of the early 17th Dynasty king Sobekemsaf (likely Sewadjenre Sobekemsaf I), and the canopic chest of Sekhemre-Wepmaat Antef. These latter objects (dating ca. 1580–1570 BCE, following the scheme of Ryholt [1997:410]) form an approximate terminus for the chronological range of truncation, and the tradition survives in only a handful of additional instances beyond the period of the Theban Antef kings. The presence of truncated hieroglyphs therefore provides a useful, but not highly limited, dating criterion which generally situates Seneb-Kay in or contemporary with the Theban 16th or early 17th Dynasty. Chronologically diagnostic elements that may have a more limited temporal range occur in the figural decoration of the burial chamber as we now discuss.

ARTISTIC PARALLELS

Aside from stelae and portable elements of the funerary assemblage, the later Second Intermediate Period is attested through a rather modest corpus of decorated buildings. Despite the small surviving group of structures, there exist some significant parallels in the decoration of Seneb-Kay's burial chamber that establish valuable historical synchronisms for the reign of Seneb-Kay. One of the notable features of the burial chamber decoration is its lack of use of a grid system. As we have seen in Chapter 2, the primary areas to be decorated were framed in blocks delineated by black lines. The actual imagery was drawn free-hand using a light black line that was then superimposed by a thicker reddish-brown line and completed with in-fill of the polychrome elements.

Exactly the same approach occurs during the Second Intermediate Period in the tomb chapel of the governor of el-Kab, Sobeknakht II (el-Kab Tomb 10). Moreover, the style and treatment of the anatomical details of the human figures in the chapel of Sobeknakht II show more specific parallels with Seneb-Kay. An idiosyncratic feature of the depiction of the goddesses in Seneb-Kay's burial chamber is the use of a T-shaped nipple rendered in black, along with small stippled dots for the areolae of the goddesses' breasts. This element occurs clearly on both of the goddesses on the East Wall (Neith and Nut), as well as on the goddess with upraised arms on the North Wall (Isis or Nephthys). This same artistic convention occurs in the human figures, both female and male, in the decoration of Sobeknakht II at el-Kab, as well as in the closely contemporary tomb chapel of Horemkhauef at Hierakonpolis (Fig. 14.2).[8]

This distinctive mode of depicting the breast does not occur more widely in Second Intermediate Period funerary art suggesting it is not a general iconographic signature of the period, but one that may have relatively limited chronological and geographical range. One other attestation, albeit with a slightly less emphasized mode of representation, occurs on a painted stela, Turin Supplement 1281. Part of a group of stelae purchased in Upper Egypt by Ernesto Schiaparelli in 1901 (Del Vesco and Moiso 2017), this stela has no certain provenance though it may come from Gebelein, just south (40 km) of Thebes. This stela may indicate a geographical range for this stylistic feature outside of el-Kab (Fig. 14.3). The tomb of Seneb-Kay at Abydos now forms the northernmost attestation of this particular artistic trait.

The presence of the T-shaped nipple in the chapels of both Sobeknakht II and Horemkhauef is not surprising because, as W. V. Davies has established, they were decorated by the same master artist—Sedjemnetjeru—who left images and identifying texts of himself inside both structures (Davies 2001:119–112, 2010:223–240). Stylistically it appears that the chapel of Horemkhauef, which was completed posthumously, may represent an earlier project of Sedjemnetjeru, while decoration of the Sobeknakht II chapel occurred later in his career. The occurrence of this artistic convention in common with Sobeknakht II and Horemkhauef is chronologically significant because these two chapels provide a set of independent historical dating evidence that links them to 16th Dynasty regnal chronology. Analysis of the genealogical texts in the tomb of Sobeknakht II (Davies 2010:223–240), paired with the evidence of the Karnak Juridical Stela, demonstrate that Sobeknakht II's governorship of el-Kab occurred during the reigns of the middle 16th Dynasty kings Sewadjenre Nebiriau I and Sewoserenre Bebiankh.

The career of Horemkhaeuef of Hierakonpolis provides another historical synchronism through the content of his stela

1. Tomb of Seneb-Kay.

2. Tomb chapel of Sobeknakht II.

3. Tomb chapel of Sobeknakht II.

4. Tomb chapel of Horemkhauef.

Fig. 14.2 Artistic convention of the T-shaped nipple in the tomb of Seneb-Kay and chapels of Sobeknakht II at el-Kab (images 2–3 after Davies 2003b) and Horemkhauef (after Wrezinski 1927) at Hierakonpolis.

Fig. 14.3 Stela Turin Supplement 1281, from the 1901 Schiaparelli purchase (photo by Franco Lovera, courtesy of the Museo Egizio, Turin).

(MMA 35.5.55) originally set up in the courtyard of his Hierakonpolis tomb chapel (Fig. 14.4). The stela describes Horemkhauef's journey northwards to *Itj-Tawy* as part of his duties as first inspector of the priests of Horus of Nekhen (Hayes 1947:3–11). At *Itj-Tawy*, he received a new cult images of Horus and Isis from an (unnamed) king for installation in the temple at Hierakonpolis. This event appears to have occurred during the last stage of the 13th Dynasty and indicates a contemporaneity between the final rulers based at *Itj-Tawy* and the emergence of independent kings in Upper Egypt (Ilin-Tomich 2014:147–148).

Clearly the artistic convention of the T-shaped nipple is likely to have a period of use greater than just the timeframe represented by Sobeknakht II and Horemkhauef. However, we see no evidence for its use during the earlier or middle 13th Dynasty nor during the 17th Dynasty. It appears to be a chronologically limited, stylistic feature contemporary with the middle to late 16th Dynasty. Based on the extant examples, it provides a significant artistic indicator

that the tomb of Seneb-Kay falls in a timeframe contemporary with the middle to late 16th Dynasty.

THE WAND OF KING "SEB-KAY" AND TOMB D78 AT ABYDOS

In examining the historical context of Seneb-Kay a key piece of evidence occurs in the form of an inscribed wand excavated at Abydos during the 1899–1900 excavations of the Egyptian Research Account. In Tomb 78 in Cemetery D at North Abydos, Arthur Mace discovered a decorated wand made of ebony and bearing the name of a king "Seb-Kay" (Cairo Museum CG9433/JE34988: Fig. 14.5).[9] This object was found along with a limestone stela now in the Penn Museum (E9952) and an assemblage of pottery vessels, although the exact disposition of the individual artifacts was not recorded (Randall-MacIver and Mace 1902:92; and discussion of Quirke 2016:208–210).[10] The wand is decorated on one end with a long-eared feline or canine head. The primary surface is decorated with a series of apotropaic figures in raised relief. Between the animal-headed terminus and phyle of apotropaic figures occurs a text in three columns: *nṯr-nfr nb-tꜣwy sꜣ-Rꜥ (Sb-kꜣy) Ꜣst nṯrt mry*, "the Good god, Lord of the Two-Lands, Son of Re (Seb-Kay), beloved of the goddess Isis."

On the basis of this object, several scholars have attempted unconvincingly to place a king "Seb-Kay" or two sequential kings "Seb" and "Kay" within the regnal sequence of the 13th Dynasty. Ryholt posited the use of a filiative nomen and argued for the succession of three kings: a king Seb, a king Kay, and Amenemhat VII (Ryholt 1997:219). Also placing this king in the earlier 13th Dynasty, Schneider suggested that Seb-Kay may be a form of pet-name of Sobekhotep II (Schneider 2006:179). However, following the discovery of the tomb of Woseribre Seneb-Kay, it appears this wand is the sole-surviving object outside of his tomb that bears the name of Seneb-Kay. Although the name is written *Sb-kꜣy* (lacking the *n*), the format of the text is relatively crude and, we would suggest, temporally diagnostic of the later Second Intermediate Period rather than the earlier 13th Dynasty. The relatively narrow format of the cartouche containing the nomen leaves no room for even an attenuated *n*-hieroglyph and the element may have been omitted for graphic reasons. Therefore, it is highly probable the House, Neferuptah (Fig. 14.6). E9952 is a relatively roughly decorated example of the type and contrasts with better-executed examples dateable to the 12th and earlier 13th Dynasty. The carving style suggests a date at the very end of the 13th Dynasty or during the later Second Intermediate Period. Some of the specific artistic attributes of the stela are suggestive of a relatively late date. Here we may point to the close similarity in the figural style to the stelae in the Abydene stela workshop of the late 16th to early 17th Dynasty discussed by Marée. The use of attenuated *wedjat*-eyes (limited to just the eye and brow without the lower components) occurs in stelae of that group (Marée 2010: pls. 64, 72, 77–78). The tomb D78 stela appears to fall comfortably in the timeframe of the mid- to late 16th or earliest 17th Dynasty (see also discussion of Whelan 2016:285–338).

It is highly probable that the wand and stela belong to the same tomb owners, although the robbed state of D78 makes it possible there may have been mixing of objects from multiple contexts. Crucially in this regard, a decade after Mace's work in Cemetery D, Peet returned to this same area of Abydos, which lies on the north side of the low desert wadi approaching Umm el-Qa'ab (Cahail 2015:118–121). In the same area as Mace's Cemetery D, Peet continued excavations in an area that he now labeled Cemetery X. In the upper part of the fill of a disturbed shaft belonging to tomb X3, Peet recovered the remains of a 13th Dynasty painted wooden coffin (Peet 1914: 61, 123 and pls. 13 and 36). As we have discussed above (Chapter 6) in connection with the possible burial location of members of the family of Dedtu and Ibiau, the original decoration on this coffin belonged to a woman whose name likely reads: *ḥkrt-nswt Nfrtntrsỉ*, the *Royal Ornament, Nefretneteresi*.[11] These original texts include use of the chronologically diagnostic Coffin Texts Spells 777–785. However, the coffin had been usurped and later reused by a man: the *ỉtw n ṯt ḥḳȝ, Sbkḥtp*, whose name was added over that of the original owner. Almost certainly this *ỉtw n ṯt ḥḳȝ, Sbkḥtp* is the very same individual commemorated on the stela found along with the Se[ne]b-Kay wand in tomb D78. The coffin should have originated in the same tomb and presumably had been pulled out of context when the burial chamber of Sobekhotep was despoiled. The stela of Sobekhotep and Neferuptah may have fallen into the shaft from an aboveground chapel during the robbery process.

Fig. 14.4 The stela of Horemkhauef (MMA 35.5.55) from Hierakonpolis (photo courtesy of the Metropolitan Museum of Art).

that this wand bears a simplified writing of the name of Seneb-Kay. The context of its excavation a century ago opens a significant set of chronological and historical issues that affect our understanding of Seneb-Kay and his origins.

The stela recovered from the same tomb as the wand with the name of Seb-Kay is an *"ankh* stela," depicting a man and woman facing inwards flanking a central, recessed *ankh*, the loop of which perforates the stela (for the type see Hill 2010:227–247). The labels identify the male figure as *ỉtw n ṯt ḥḳȝ, Sbkḥtp*, the *Commander of the Crew of the Ruler, Sobekhotep*; and the woman as *ḥmt.f nbt-pr Nfrwptḥ, his wife the Lady of*

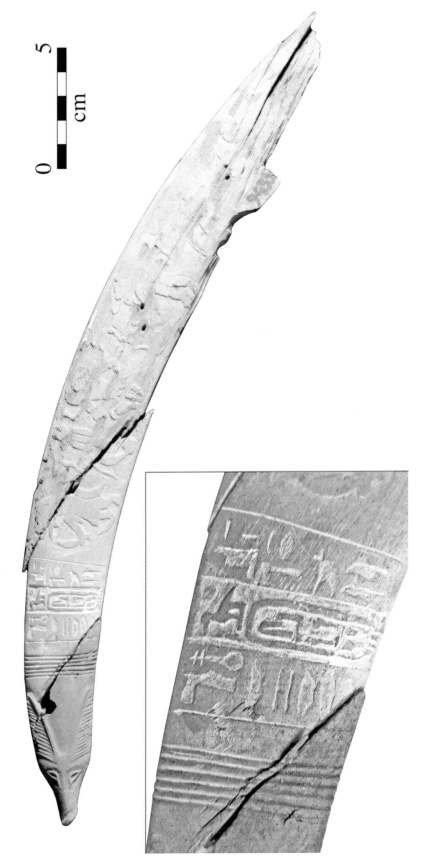

Fig. 14.5 The wand from Abydos tomb D78 (Cairo Museum, CG9433/JE34988, photo courtesy of Fred Vink).

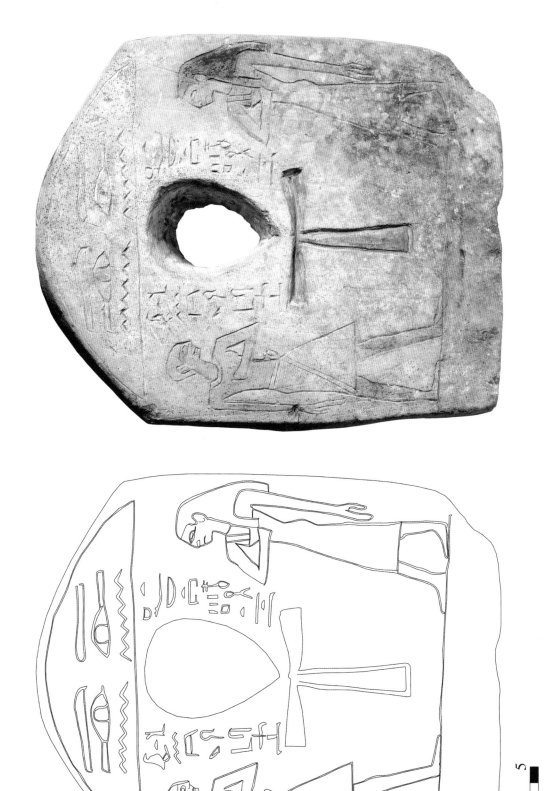

Fig. 14.6 Stela from Abydos tomb D78 (Penn Museum E9952).

These materials recovered from tombs D78/X3 at North Abydos are significant from several respects. The coffin of the *ꜣṯw n ṯt ḥkꜣ*, Sobekhotep shows a mode of reuse of a 13th Dynasty elite or royal coffin that closely parallels the reuse of cedar coffin boards of a king Sobekhotep to create the canopic chest of Seneb-Kay. Both of these coffins in their original state were decorated with the distinctive set of Coffin Text Spells 777–785 and date to the same approximate timeframe in the middle to late 13th Dynasty. In both cases, royal (King Sobekhotep) or elite (Nefretneteresi) tombs were despoiled with their contents being recycled by high-status individuals: a king (Seneb-Kay), and a military official (the *ꜣṯw n ṯt ḥkꜣ*, Sobekhotep).[12] The distinctive Second Intermediate Period style of the *ankh*-stela, along with the temporal parameters implied by reuse of a 13th Dynasty coffin suggests that Sobekhotep and his wife Neferuptah date to the same period as Seneb-Kay.[13] Consequently, the wand bearing the name of king Seb-Kay almost certainly belongs to these same individuals, was part of the contents of their tomb, and should be read as Se[ne]b-Kay.

In view of the pattern of reuse of 13th Dynasty coffins seen both in the burials of Seneb-Kay and the tomb of the *ꜣṯw n ṯt ḥkꜣ*, Sobekhotep, is it possible the wand itself was a repurposed artifact? It must be observed that the presence of a king's name on such an object is a conspicuous aberration. Attested texts on all other apotropaia provide the names of women and children along with protective spells and labels associated with the primary use of these objects in childbirth (see Altenmüller 1965; Quirke 2016:573–611). Moreover, the wand from tomb D78 displays a pronounced visual difference between the images and inscription. The wand is sculpted with a finely carved animal head on the terminus and divine images in raised relief. In contrast to these elements, the hieroglyphs composing the Se[ne]b-Kay label are comparatively roughly cut. The inscription occurs in three columns: two columns of incised hieroglyphs flanking the central column where the king's name was rendered in raised hieroglyphs. The overall style of the text departs conspicuously from the carving style seen in the rest of the wand's decoration. Although it does not appear that the text was added over some other inscription or image,[14] the difference in quality of the text and the rest of the carved imagery is clear. For that reason, we would suggest

that someone added the name of Se[ne]b-Kay secondarily to a wand that was produced earlier than that king's reign.

The Se[ne]b-Kay wand is the only known example of this type of object inscribed with the name of a king. The presence of a king's name on this artifact raises the crucial question of the relationship between Se[ne]b-Kay and the tomb owners, Sobekhotep and Neferuptah. Sobekhotep's title *ꜣṯw n ṯt ḥkꜣ*, *Commander of the Crew of the Ruler,* is a high-ranking military title used during the late Middle Kingdom and Second Intermediate Period. The title appears to denote a tier of commander connected with royal military forces (as expressed through use of the term *ḥkꜣ*) that, in terms of hierarchy, fell immediately below that of *imy-r mšꜥ*, *Overseer of the Army* or *General.* Its use appears to be associated with forces transported by boat on the Nile and has been discussed as having a naval connotation (Chevereau 1992:11–34), although military troops would have regularly made use of boats and the role of this type of commander was associated more with the military forces than the operations of the watercraft themselves (Quirke 2004:97–99). Therefore, the *ꜣṯw n ṯt ḥkꜣ*, Sobekhotep, was a high-ranking military official, and a man whose military career was closely contemporary with the reign of Woseribre Seneb-Kay.

From the physical analysis of Seneb-Kay's body (see above, Chapter 5) we have indications for his long-term involvement in martial activities, as well as his ultimate death in a military confrontation. The king's body strongly suggests he may have risen to rulership through a military career. Given its unique usage of the royal name, the presence of the Se[ne]b-Kay wand in the tomb of the commander Sobekhotep may reflect some form of close personal relationship between the two men. The occurrence of such an object in a tomb associated with a military commander dating to the same period as Seneb-Kay is unlikely to be a coincidence. It might have been bestowed as a royal favor or used in some way to commemorate service to Seneb-Kay. It might appear conceivable that the wand was decorated posthumously to memorialize service to a king who died in military campaigns that the *ꜣṯw n ṯt ḥkꜣ*, Sobekhotep, also participated in. However, if the Se[ne]b-Kay wand retained at this stage in the Second Intermediate Period the symbolic and functional associations of these objects with birth and rebirth, the artifact seems to imply a more intimate personal or familial connection between Seneb-Kay and the commander Sobekhotep and his wife Neferuptah.

An interesting and possibly significant feature of the Se[ne]b-Kay wand's text is that it connects the king with Isis: *nṯr-nfr nb-t3wy s3-Rᶜ (Sb-k3y) Ist nṯrt mry*, the *Good god, Lord of the Two-Lands, Son of Re (Seb-Kay), beloved of the goddess Isis*. Mention of Isis on a magical wand may well be connected with the principal function of these objects in birth rituals. The symbolic role of Isis as the mother of the reigning king suggests the connotation here lies in the mythology of Isis-Horus. Clearly, the addition of a king's name to this type of artifact must have occurred only later in life as Seneb-Kay's status as a king could not have been determined at the time of birth. The wand may have retrospectively commemorated his rise to rulership and particular personal connections with Sobekhotep and Neferuptah. The middle to late 16th Dynasty dating suggested above for the stela corresponds with the date indicated by the iconography in Seneb-Kay's burial chamber. Seneb-Kay, the *3ṯw n ṯt ḥk3*, Sobekhotep, and his wife, Neferuptah, appear to have been close contemporaries whose tombs were completed during a period of time coeval with the mid- to late 16th Dynasty. Given the nature of this object we may wonder whether Sobekhotep and Neferuptah might not be the parents of Seneb-Kay, a relationship that would explain the occurrence of the wand bearing his name in tomb D78.

As we have previously discussed, the king's nomen is unlikely to represent a filiative nomen and his descent from a father named Seneb can be reasonably excluded. Moreover, father to son succession is only rarely attested for the Second Intermediate Period and we can assume that Seneb-Kay's claim to power originated from other features of his family and social background. Seneb-Kay's descent from a military family, in this case possibly being the son of the *3ṯw n ṯt ḥk3*, Sobekhotep, would accord with the physical evidence for Seneb-Kay's background, as well as the broader implications from the skeletal remains of the CS10 individual's burial that at least one of the other men buried in the Second Intermediate Period cemetery at South Abydos also rose to rulership through virtue of his military background. Attribution of Seneb-Kay's origins to a local Abydene military family fits with the wider body of evidence for kingship during the Second Intermediate Period

in which rulers did not follow each other in strictly hereditary succession but rather were drawn from a mosaic of elite families.

While this identification of the *Commander of the Crew of the Ruler*, Sobekhotep, and his wife, the *Lady of the House*, Neferuptah, as the parents of Seneb-Kay remains a matter of speculation, there is a more fundamental inference to be made regarding the presence of the Se[ne]b-Kay wand at Abydos. Namely: the sole known artifact recording this king occurs at the very same site as his tomb. Just two kilometers separate Cemetery D, a site of elite funerary activity overlooking Umm el-Qa'ab, and the royal necropolis including Seneb-Kay's tomb that developed adjacent to the tomb complex of Senwosret III. Both his own tomb and the wand from tomb D78 provide strong indications for the Abydene and Thinite territorial associations of Seneb-Kay. It does not appear that following his death in battle Seneb-Kay's body was transferred to Abydos from some distant royal seat such as Thebes. The evidence of the wand and other elements from D78 are consistent with the conclusion that Seneb-Kay was a scion of a local elite family and that his burial at South Abydos reflects the base of his power in the Thinite region.

THE CASE FOR AN ABYDOS DYNASTY

The evidence we have summarized above for the chronological placement of Seneb-Kay as a contemporary of the Theban 16th Dynasty, ca. 1650–1600 BCE, paired with indications for his Thinite origins, likely descended from a local military family, now provide new points favoring the existence of an Abydos Dynasty. Prior to the discovery of the tomb of Seneb-Kay and the seven other Second Intermediate Period royal tombs at South Abydos, the rationale for the Abydos Dynasty rested on the fragmentary evidence of Column 11 in the Turin Kinglist and the existence of three Second Intermediate Period kings—Wepwawetemsaf, Paentjeny, and Senaaib—whose names and monuments from Abydos suggested they may have had local origins and a base of power centered in the Thinite region. Let us now review the evidence for these three kings and revisit the question of whether they might comprise members of the same dynastic grouping as Seneb-Kay. Could these kings be among the other individuals buried in the main cluster tombs at South Abydos?

WEPWAWETEMSAF

The stela of Wepwawetemsaf (British Museum EA 969) is the sole-surviving monument from a king whose nomen shows an explicit association with one of the principal deities of Abydos (Fig. 14.7). This king's prenomen, Sekhemre-Neferkhau, is distinctively Second Intermediate Period in format including use of the Sekhemre element which occurs in the prenomina of several of the 16th and early 17th Dynasty Theban kings. His nomen is a theophoric name composed of a statement involving the canine deity, Wepwawet, who is central to the Abydene Osiris cult: *Wpw3wt-m-s3.f*, literally *Wepwawet is his protection*. The structure of this name parallels other royal nomina of the Second Intermediate Period built around prominent deities such as the 16th Dynasty king

Montuemsaf, whose name embeds that of the Theban deity Montu, or the Sobekemsaf kings of the 17th Dynasty. Stela EA 969 shows the king before the deity with the label *dw3 Wpw3wt-R^c nb 3bdw, venerating Wepwawet-Re, Lord of Abydos*. The upper part contains the kings nomen and prenomen in a balanced arrangement beneath a winged sun-disk.

The dual occurrence of Wepwawet on this stela, both in the king's name as well as the divine recipient of royal devotion is notable. The form of Wepwawet seen here has been described as a syncretized form in which the deity is merged with Re (Bourriau 1988:72–73). Aside from EA 969 this particular form of the god occurs on five other stelae as well as a statue originating in Abydos and dating to the period from the Middle Kingdom to early New Kingdom.[15] The association with Re reflects the god's presence in the solar barque, a role also expressed in other epithets of Wepwawet. However, here we would observe that the name of the deity probably does not express a true syncretism but rather an association expressed through a direct genitive specifying Wepwawet in his station at the

0   5

cm

Fig. **14.7**   Stela of Wepwawetemsaf (British Museum, EA 969, photo courtesy of Marcel Marée, the British Museum).

prow of the solar barque: *Wepwawet of Re* (literally: the *Opener of the paths of Re*). If interpreted this way, Wepwawet-Re functioned in a similar way to other versions of the name of Wepwawet that embed geographical specificity or association with other gods.

The provenance of Wepwawetemsaf's stela from Abydos, as well as the link of the king's name with a prominent Abydene deity, led to the proposition of Franke and later Ryholt that Wepwawetemsaf might be one of an independent line of kings who ruled from Abydos during the Second Intermediate Period. More recently, Marée has argued for identifying Wepwawetemsaf as the immediate successor of the early 17th Dynasty king Sekhemre-Wahkhau Rahotep. Based on numerous stylistic and iconographic indications that link the Wepwawetemsaf stela with a larger stela of Rahotep (BM EA 833) also set up at Abydos, Marée suggests the two stelae derive from the same workshop and were either dedicated contemporaneously or in close succession (Marée 2010:261–266). He has proposed the regnal succession: Sekhemre-Wahkhau Rahotep; Sekhemre-Neferkhau Wepwawetemsaf; and Sekhemre-Wadjkhau Sobekemsaf for the beginning of the 17th Dynasty. While not denying the possibility that these kings may have had Thinite family connections, he situates them within the 16th–17th Dynasty Theban succession and uses that attribution to argue against Ryholt's postulate of an independent Abydos Dynasty.

One minor, but chronologically diagnostic, feature of the Wepwawetemsaf stela (and one that sets it apart from the Rahotep stela from the Osiris temple), occurs in the truncated form of the *m*-owl in the king's nomen. Truncated forms are not used for any of the other hieroglyphs and may have been selectively applied in this instance due to its presence within the cartouche. This mode of application is consistent with the patterns in use of truncated hieroglyphs that occur in the final stages of this practice. As we have noted above, the tradition persisted into the early 17th Dynasty and occurs during this timeframe on the canopic chests of a King Sobekemsaf (probably Sekhemre-Wadjkhau Sobekemsaf I), and Sekhemre-Wepmaat Antef (V). The occurrence of the truncated hieroglyph on the Wepwawetemsaf stela is consistent with the regnal placement that Marée has proposed. It is intriguing, however, that no use of truncated hieroglyphs occurs on the Rahotep stela that he suggests is so closely connected with that of Wepwawetemsaf.

PAENTJENY

A king whose nomen, or pre-coronation birthname, was *Pꜣ-n-Ṯny, The one of Thinis*, occurs on stela EA 630 from Abydos (Fig. 14.8). In a similar vein to their interpretation of the stela of Wepwawetemsaf, Franke followed by Ryholt have observed the name is explicitly Thinite in its associations and provides an indicator for the origins of this ruler in proximity to Abydos. Significantly his prenomen, Sekhemre-Khutawy, incorporates the Sekhemre element which occurs among several of the 16th and early 17th Dynasty Theban kings. Use of the Sekhemre element is a chronological indicator for the date of his reign within or contemporaneous with the 16th or early 17th Dynasties (see also suggestions of Siesse [2015:75–98], which are consistent with a late 16th to early 17th Dynasty date).

EA 630, the sole-surviving monument that names Paentjeny, was excavated by Petrie in 1902–1903 in the Osiris temple enclosure at Abydos. While inscribed with the king's titulary at the top, the stela depicts the *sꜣ-nswt Ḏḥwty-ꜥꜣ, King's Son, Djehuty-aa*, standing with arms raised facing the *ḥkrt-nswt Nfrw*, the *Royal Ornament, Neferu*. Although there is a chance the *sꜣ-nswt* here is actually a true son of Paentjeny, as Marée has observed, the honorific adaptation of this title for military officials indicates that Djehuty-aa was a high ranking military official shown here with his (probable) wife, Neferu, who bore the elite feminite title *ḥkrt-nswt*. This latter title is often associated with the wives of royal military officials during the Second Intermediate Period.

Marée has further proposed that this same Djehuty-aa was the principal owner of another stela, Brussels E.480 (Petrie 1903: pl. 30:5), a monument that commemorates several military officials including two bearing the title *ꜣṯw n ṯt ḥkꜣ*. The name of the primary stela owner, not entirely preserved but ending */////-ꜥꜣ*, could be the same Djehuty-aa. He has suggested that both stelae originated in the same context, possibly an offering chapel belonging to Djehuty-aa in or near the Osiris temple precinct.

In this case, the stela of Djehuty-aa naming king Paentjeny suggests the presence at Abydos of monuments relating to a group of military officials who were commemorated in association with that king. Based on similarities to his latest stylistic subgroup, Marée has proposed that Paentjeny was a close successor to

0 ___ 5
cm

Fig. 14.8 Stela of Djehuty-aa with titulary of King Paentjeny (British Museum, EA 630 photo courtesy of Marcel Marée, the British Museum).

Rahotep and Wepwawetemsaf but predated Sekhem-re-Wadjkhau Sobekemsaf (I). We would observe here, that aspects of the style of the Djeuty-aa stela accord closely with several earlier monuments dating to the 16th Dynasty. The use of the primary figure in raised relief within a sunk panel juxtaposed with an incised female figure is very similar to the stela of Horemkha-uef from Hierakonpolis discussed above. The juxtaposition of raised and sunk relief also occurs in the only surviving object attributable to King Seneb-Kay, the ebony wand discussed earlier in this chapter (see also Wegner 2017b:505–508). One other argument for placing Paentjeny as a Theban 17th Dynasty king might be use of the Sekhemre prefix which is such a common element during that period. However, this titulary element occurs also in the 16th Dynasty kings and should not be assumed to be an exclusive marker of kings ruling from Thebes. Despite Marée's arguments, it still appears possible that Paentjeny was a

close contemporary of Seneb-Kay and his primary base of power lay in the Thinite region rather than at Thebes. His conclusions regarding the date and Theban associations of Paentjeny appear to be less convincing than the case of Wepwawetemsaf. Nevertheless, even if we accept Marée's arguments for the placement of Paentjeny, there remains a third king among this group of rulers who may be suggested to be a close contemporary of Seneb-Kay and possible member of the Abydos Dynasty.

SENAAIB

King Senaaib is attested through a painted limestone stela (Cairo CG20517, Fig. 14.9). Originating from Mariette's work in the Kom es-Sultan (Mariette 1880: pl. 27; Lange and Schäfer 1908: no.20517; Malaise 1981:280), the stela records the Horus name

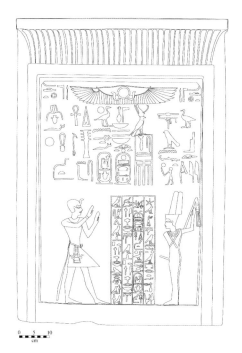

Fig. 14.9 *Stela of Senaaib (Cairo CG 20517, photograph by K. Cahail).*

(Sewadjtawy), prenomen (Menkhaure) and nomen (Senaaib) for this king (Ryholt 1997:392). The stela shows the king venerating the god Minhornakht. The deity stands on the right with Senaaib facing him with hands raised in adoration. The label above the deity reads, *Mnw-Ḥr-nḫt sꜣ Wsỉr mry, beloved of Minhornakht, son of Osiris.* The text between the two figures states: *dwꜣ Mnw-Ḥr-nḫt m prt.f nfrt ỉn nswt-bỉty (Mnḫꜣwrꜥ) dỉ ꜥnḫ ḏt sꜣ-Rꜥ n ḥt.f (Snꜥꜥỉb) ꜥnḫ ḏt ḏd.f ỉnḏ ḥr.k Mnw m ḥtp ỉnḏ ḥr.k Mnw Ḥr šms m ḥtp ỉnḏ ḥr.k Wsỉr-ḫntyỉmntỉw m ḥtp, Venerating Minhornakht during his beautiful procession by the King of Upper and Lower Egypt Menkhaure, given life forever, son of Re of his body, Senaaib, given life, he says: welcome to you Min in peace, welcome to you Minhor-shemes in peace, welcome Osiris-Khentiamentiu in peace.*

Although this king's name does not incorporate an explicit Abydene or Thinite reference as occurs with Wepwawetemsaf and Paentjeny, Franke followed by Ryholt have identified Senaaib as a local Abydene ruler through virtue of the Second Intermediate Period date of his stela, its Abydene provenance, and status as the sole-surviving monument of his reign, as well as its association with the local cult of Minhornakht, which emerged at Abydos during the 13th Dynasty. Contrasting with the titularies of Wepwawetemsaf and Paentjeny, Senaaib does not employ the distinctive 16th to 17th Dynasty Sekhemre prefix

in his prenomen. While there are certainly Theban rulers who employ other prenominal structures, this could suggest Senaaib does not lie in immediate chronological proximity to Rahotep, Wepwawetemsaf, and Paentjeny. The style of the painted stela of Senaaib certainly diverges from the artistic qualities that define the group of Abydene stelae of the late 16th to early 17th Dynasties discussed by Marée. We would suggest here that Senaaib's stela may date earlier than those of Wepwawetemsaf and Paentjeny and may chronologically be the closest royal monument at Abydos to the tomb of Seneb-Kay.

Here we would like to draw attention to the similarity in artistic idiom between the stela of Senaaib and the decoration in the burial chamber of Seneb-Kay. The overall style of the figures and use of blue-painted hieroglyphs on the stela show affinities with Seneb-Kay's tomb decoration. As with Seneb-Kay, there was no use of a grid system. Although there is no use of truncated hieroglyphs, as we see both in Seneb-Kay and the stela of Wepwawetemsaf, the style and somewhat irregular arrangement of the blue-painted hieroglyphs on Senaaib's stela are similar to those in Seneb-Kay's tomb. We might observe how the titulary and labels in the upper part of the stela are unframed while the text between king and deity, which include the king's speech, are independently bordered, reminiscent of the speech bands of the goddesses in Seneb-Kay's burial chamber. We may also observe the nearly identical technique in painting the winged sun-disk. The central circle of the disk was painted red inside a yellow outer band. The rounded ends of the feathers in the central, lower sections of the wings were also painted red providing the sun-disk with a red, horizontal lower "fringe" that contrasts with the light blue used for the feathers in both cases. Although these color conventions occur in other periods, the overall ensemble of stylistic similarities are suggestive of a close contemporaneity between Kings Senaaib and Seneb-Kay.

CHRONOLOGICAL PARAMETERS

The three kings discussed above—each known through just a single monument at Abydos—were proposed by Ryholt to be members of an independent Second Intermediate Period Abydene dynasty. As we have seen, however, the analysis of two of these kings suggests their chronological placement as successors to king Sekhemre-Wahkhau Rahotep, who appears to date relatively late in the Second Intermediate Period. Rahotep has been plausibly identified as the first king of the 17th Dynasty. Therefore, Rahotep and his possible successors Wepwawetemsaf and Paentjeny may date after the 16th and 17th Dynasty transition. The removal of Wepwawetemsaf and Paentjeny from the body of evidence for an independent Abydene line of kings, however, does not itself undermine the possible existence of a coeval dynasty at Abydos that was contemporary with the Theban 16th Dynasty. Senaaib remains a king for who there are no convincing links to the 16th or 17th Dynasties, and stylistic elements of his painted stela are suggestive of a date close in time to Seneb-Kay. Seneb-Kay himself through various chronological indicators, including artistic similarities with the chapel of Sobeknakht II at el-Kab, appears to be a contemporary of the middle to late 16th Dynasty. And, the other seven tombs attributable to kings at South Abydos appear to represent immediate predecessors or successors of Seneb-Kay.

With the removal of Wepwawetemsaf and Djehuty-aa from consideration the issue arises: do Seneb-Kay and the seven unknown kings buried at Abydos, as well as Senaaib, all represent members of the 16th Theban Dynasty? Can we explain the South Abydos necropolis as an Abydene burial ground used

by Theban rulers of the Second Intermediate Period? Let us turn to examine the chronological parameters for this dynasty.

Arguments against the existence of the Abydos Dynasty essentially espouse a unilinear political model in which a single, unified Upper Egyptian kingdom was created when the Theban region split away from the 13th Dynasty. The model assumes one regnal line, alternatively termed the "17th Dynasty" or the "16th and 17th Dynasties," forming a sequence spanning the period from the late 13th Dynasty through to the Expulsion of the Hyksos. However, there are serious chronological problems that confront the viability of such a unilinear model for the regnal history of the period under consideration here.

A combination of genealogical and chronological data establishes a temporal framework for the regnal and dynastic sequence of the late Second Intermediate Period in Upper Egypt. These data can be instructively compared with the numbers of attested rulers and extant data on regnal lengths. Historical evidence provided by the Juridical Stela and el-Kab inscriptions provides the basis for establishing the number of generations that elapsed between the final reigns of the 13th Dynasty and the beginning of the New Kingdom. As Chris Bennett has discussed, the probable generational distance between several key reigns—particularly Merhotepre of the 13th Dynasty and Nebiriau I of the 16th Dynasty—and the beginning of the 18th Dynasty forms the basis for a generational chronometer in which to situate the regnal history of Upper Egypt during the Second Intermediate Period (Bennett 2002:123–155, 2006:231–243). He has established the passage of six generations from Year 1 of Nebiriau I to the death of Renni of el-Kab during the reign of Amenhotep I. Although there is considerable leeway for conversion of generations to absolute years (Bennett 2006:240), this framework can also be defined in terms of the way the timeframe impinges on the chronology of the late Middle Kingdom and early 18th Dynasty. Bennett has estimated a period of 105 years between Year 1 of Nebiriau I and the accession of Ahmose. Other chronological models employ comparable totals for the period from the beginning of the 16th Dynasty to the reign of Ahmose (ca. 1650–1539 BCE; Schneider 2006:195–196).

It is not necessary here to enter into a discussion of the nuances of the chronological arguments, but let us adopt the 105-year figure as a reference point for assessing the viability of the unilinear regnal succession model. Within this period of slightly more than a century we must accommodate the known regnal lengths for the 16th Dynasty totaling 38 years (Nebiriau I and Bebiankh) and the 17th Dynasty totaling 14 years (Sobekemsaf I, Seqenenre Tao, and Kamose).[16] Additionally, we have the fragmentary reign lengths for the Column 11 kings on the Turin Kinglist (discussed above) totaling 14–16 years. A relatively small group of just ten kings account for 66 years leaving just 39 years remaining from the estimated timeframe of 105 years for all other rulers who are attested in the Turin Kinglist or known through the archaeological record.

This numerically uncounted group is sizeable including seven additional names for the 16th Dynasty entries in the Turin Kinglist,[17] as well as eleven names in the second half of Column 11 that do not have preserved regnal lengths. Additionally we have five Theban kings attested through inscriptional evidence who can be attributed to the 16th Dynasty,[18] as well as the three kings attested on stelae at Abydos whom Ryholt had attributed to the Abydos Dynasty.[19] Moreover, there are six additional 17th Dynasty kings for whom regnal lengths are not known.[20] To these kings we must now add Woseribre Seneb-Kay as well as, in all likelihood, the seven tombs in the Second Intermediate Period necropolis at South Abydos.

If we assume that the archaeologically attested 16th Dynasty kings, the three kings attested through stelae at Abydos, as well as the tombs of Seneb-Kay and the seven others at South Abydos are all kings included in the damaged sections of Turin Kinglist Column 11, we still achieve a daunting minimum of 25 kings whose reigns must be accommodated in this estimated 39 years based on Bennett's figure. This necessitates an average reign length of 1.5 years for these 25 kings.

The probability of so many these kings having such short reigns appears extremely low. Within this group, we have reigns of a number of significant 17th Dynasty rulers such as Senakhtenre-Ahmose and the three Antef kings, estimates for whose reigns are substantially longer than this low average. Particularly problematic is the fact that if they are analyzed as a group within the parameters of this timeframe, with the robust number of names before the 17th Dynasty, the time allocated to the nine Theban 17th Dynasty rulers leading up to accession of Nebpehtyre-Ahmose shrinks to a paltry two decades.

There are potential adjustments that might ameliorate this chronological problem. One possibility would be to entirely discount the longer regnal lengths for Nebiriau I (26 years) and Bebiankh (12 years) cited by the Turin Kinglist in order to accommodate a longer average for the remaining kings. Hypothetically, if these two kings were reduced to unknown reign lengths within the estimated 105-year timeframe from Year 1 of Nebiriau to Year 1 of Nebpehtyre-Ahmose we would still require a below 3-year average regnal length for the 25 unaccounted kings as well as Nebiriau I and Bebiankh.[21]

A second possibility would be to discount the relevance of the el-Kab genealogical evidence in order to lengthen the timeframe from Nebiriau I to Nebpehtyre-Ahmose. Certainly, the generational sequence that Bennett reconstructed based on the el-Kab genealogical data may be adjusted in terms of its translation into absolute years. However, lengthening this timeframe too much impinges considerably on the chronology of the late Middle Kingdom. It appears probable that with a 105-year timeframe between Nebiriau I and Ahmose there must already be a substantial overlap between the end of the 13th Dynasty and the emergent 16th Dynasty. On that basis, Bennett and others have argued for an overlap of the 16th ("early 17th Dynasty") with the final (post-Merneferre Ay) 13th Dynasty kings. With the sizeable number of Second Intermediate Period rulers that we need to accommodate, can we envision pushing the advent of the independent Theban 16th Dynasty yet further back in time so as to suggest a secession of Upper Egypt during the 13th Dynasty prior to Merneferre Ay?

There does not appear to be sufficient latitude in the chronological parameters to reasonably accommodate so many Upper Egyptian Second Intermediate Period kings within an exclusively unilinear Theban succession. A greater probability appears to be a phase of territorial fragmentation into multiple kingdoms that may have attended the final stages in the decline of 13th Dynasty power in Upper Egypt and its immediate aftermath. Indeed, based solely on these chronological constraints, and entirely separate from the archaeological evidence from South Abydos, other scholars have concluded that a political structure including multiple competing dynasties appears highly probable (Schneider 2006:196). This model appears to be consistent with the fact that we now have a royal necropolis at South Abydos that includes Seneb-Kay as well as at least seven additional kings who appear to have ruled from the same power base and over the same territory.

ABYDOS DYNASTY REDUX

The archaeological remains of the Second Intermediate Period necropolis at South Abydos provide strong evidence for a succession of kings who not only drew upon local resources and building materials, but who related in distinct ways to their 13th Dynasty predecessors. We have the intriguing cultural phenomenon of rulers who made use of the preexisting late Middle Kingdom funerary landscape for placement of their tombs, and whose builders employed architectural forms that were derivative from 13th Dynasty royal tomb prototypes. At the same time, they were involved in a form of state-supported robbery of the contents of those very same tombs, as well as reuse of funerary structures and burials of 13th Dynasty elites. These elements appear to be symptomatic of regional kings ruling within the circumscribed territorial and economic environment of the late Second Intermediate Period. While it is important to note that one prominent king of the Theban succession, Nebpehtyre Ahmose, built a mortuary complex at South Abydos, these Second Intermediate Period tombs, dating a century or more before, show no indications that they relate to Theban rulers who were transported from their hometown for burial at Abydos.

To this archaeological picture we may add the historical evidence that has been outlined in the preceding sections including the following salient points:

(1)   the extreme improbability that the known roster of Upper Egyptian kings attested for the late Second Intermediate Period can be accommodated in the approximate timeframe of somewhat over a century between the beginning of the 16th Dynasty and the reign of Ahmose.

(2)   the probable occurrence of at least two kings in Column 11 of the Turn Kinglist with the same prenominal structure (*Wsr-X-rꜥ*) as *Wsr-ib-rꜥ Snb-Kꜣy*.

(3)   the artistic parallels suggesting a close chronological proximity of the tomb of Seneb-Kay with the chapel of Sobeknakht II and Horemkhauef at el-Kab and Hierakonpolis.

(4)   the occurrence at Abydos of the wand bearing the name Seneb-Kay in the tomb attributed to the military commander Sobekhotep and his wife Neferuptah, whose funerary stelae may be dated also to the timeframe of the mid- to late 16th Dynasty.

The aggregate effect of this archaeological and historical data weighs heavily in favor of the existence of an independent line of Second Intermediate Period kings whose territory was centered in the Thinite region, and who made use of the royal necropolis at South Abydos. The term "Abydos Dynasty," as Ryholt had proposed prior to the discovery of Seneb-Kay, remains an appropriate designation for these rulers. This term does not presume the territorial scope of their kingdom, which may indeed have fluctuated significantly through time. Nor does it assume that Abydos proper was their main political center. The nome capital of Thinis located on the edge of the Nile presents the most probable site for the court of the Abydos Dynasty and a strategic center from which territory could have been controlled a significant distance both northwards and southwards. Although physical remains of the city have not yet been unearthed, textual and cemetery evidence shows that Thinis was, indeed, a major Upper Egyptian urban center with a highly developed administrative and economic framework (Brovarski 1986:475–486). If not on a par with Thebes in that same timeframe, Thinis certainly ranked within the top tier of urban centers in Middle and Upper Egypt.[22] The term "Thinite Dynasty" would form an appropriate alternative to the designation Abydos Dynasty (compare also the comments of Ryholt 1997:163).

In sum, based on multiple lines of consideration we can identify the Abydos Dynasty as forming a contemporaneous regnal line to the Theban 16th Dynasty. Ryholt (1997:202–203) originally speculated that the Abydos Dynasty was a short-lived kingdom that lasted perhaps two decades (ca. 1650–1630 BCE). While chronological evidence remains scant, in light of the eight known tombs at South Abydos, and the correspondence of the prenomina in the group

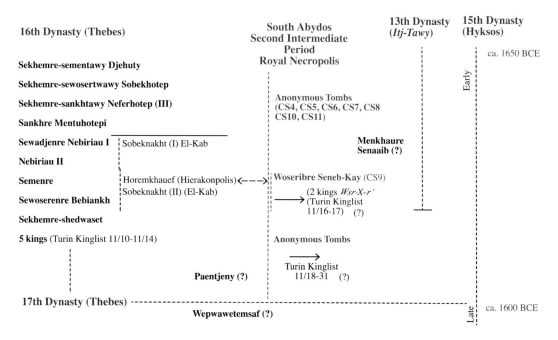

Fig. 14.10 Proposed synchronism between Seneb-Kay and the royal tombs at Abydos with the period of overlaps of the late 13th, early 15th, and 16th Dynasties, ca. 1650–1600 BCE.

of 16 kings in Turin Kinglist Column 11, we have a slightly firmer basis for commenting on the potential longevity of the Abydos Dynasty. Surviving regnal lengths for the Column 11 kings include entries for the last five names in Column 11, totaling 14–16 years. There are no figures for the preceding eleven kings including the two *Wsr*-X-*r*ʿ kings who initiate the sequence. Estimating an average regnal length of 3 years for these other eleven names easily yields a dynastic grouping with a total duration spanning half a century or more. Consequently, Ryholt's 20-year estimate for the length of the dynasty is likely to be too conservative. As we have commented above, the archaeological picture of the eight tombs at South Abydos also seems consistent with a series of royal burials over a period that exceeded two decades. The Abydos Dynasty is likely to represent a more substantial timeframe that paralleled the final phase of the 13th Dynasty, which persisted approximately to the reign of Nebiriau II (the period of Horemkhauef's journey to *Itj-Tawy*), as well as overlapping with much of the 16th Dynasty (Fig. 14.10).

Regarding the evolving territorial scope of the Abydos Dynasty, we remain hampered by the lack of data. Ryholt's proposition that these kings controlled territory as far north as Beni Hasan, 250 km north

of Abydos, was based on inclusion of Wepwawetemsaf as an Abydene ruler and the occurrence of a now-destroyed hieratic graffito naming that king in Tomb 2 at Beni Hasan (von Beckerath 1964:69; Ryholt 1997:165–166). If we accept Marée's identification of Wepwawetemsaf as an early 17th Dynasty ruler, then this argument loses validity and the northern extent of Thinite control becomes speculative. To the south, the evidence for the geographical limit of 16th Dynasty monuments and royal names to the area of Hu/Diospolis Parva remains a valid observation (Ryholt 1997:159–160), and we may propose a territorial boundary approximately in the area of Dendera.

Let us conclude this discussion with a comment on the implications of two coeval dynasties in Upper Egypt during the later Second Intermediate Period. Egyptologists have long struggled to understand the mechanics of kingship during the timeframe of the 13th through 17th Dynasties. With the numerous short reigns and evidence for transfer of kingship among multiple elite families, it is clear that traditional mode of father to son succession was not the dominant model for rulership in this era. Ideas such as circulating succession among elites as a mechanism for maintaining stability (Quirke 1991:123–140) or a kind of oligarchical system with selection of kings through acclamation by the elites have been proposed (Morenz 2010:293–320). For Upper Egypt, with such a robust number of kings represented through inscriptional evidence, as well as entries in the Turin Kinglist, the idea of a single line of succession runs contrary to the weight of the evidence. The men who ascended to the throne came from a shifting mosaic of elite lineages. Effectively, it appears likely that kingship was responding at some level to social conventions seen in other areas of the state system where, by the end of the 13th Dynasty, the highest-level powerholders were drawn not from the existing ranks of government, but rather from elite families (Shirley 2013:556–557).

Under such a social system, the emergence of multiple lines of rulership appears to be further accentuated. While such practices run counter to the core ideology of Egyptian kingship, where authority was vested in a single Horus-king, a system of this nature may have arisen as a pragmatic response to a variety of social and economic pressures. Division of kingship along multiple lines of succession may have involved cooperation and alliances between power-holders governing over different regions. However, it would also tend to create significant potential for regional rivalry and territorial conflict. Following this line of thought, Upper Egypt may have broken away from the control of *Itj-Tawy* through political changes that generated regional kings centered both in Thebes and Thinis-Abydos. Ultimately, within the numerous names that comprise the 13th and 14th Dynasties there may be potential for other regional lines of rulership during the Second Intermediate Period. Such a fundamentally fractured political situation would have presented a challenge to the compilers of documents like the Turin Kinglist and helps to explain some of the issues of interpretation associated with that document.

TERRITORIAL CONFLICT AND THE 16TH TO 17TH DYNASTY TRANSITION

As we have seen above, a cornerstone of Ryholt's political model for the Second Intermediate Period was the suggested impact of the Hyksos, firstly in ending the 13th Dynasty in *Itj-Tawy* and secondarily

the Abydos and Theban 16th Dynasties in the south. In this model, the demise of rule from *Itj-Tawy* created the impetus for the secession of Upper Egypt. The subsequent Hyksos invasion of Upper Egypt formed the chronological dividing line between the 16th and 17th Theban Dynasties. The first component of this model, the notion that the separation of Upper Egypt occurred in a power vacuum brought on by the Hyksos has been convincingly disproven. What of the second element of this model? Ryholt has argued that a major political division occurred when the Hyksos invaded and then withdrew from Upper Egypt, thereby creating the basis for the shift from the 16th to 17th Theban Dynasties. The new evidence provided by the body of King Seneb-Kay and the royal cemetery at South Abydos offers us new perspectives on this question.

In the Turin Kinglist and other ancient Egyptian historical records, dynasties were constructed not around the idea of familial succession but primarily around the concept of rulership emanating from specific geographical centers (Redford 1986). Given the numerous complexities of royal succession even within the most stable dynasties, discontinuities of the regnal sequence itself were of minor significance as compared to the broader issues of the location of political capital or scope of territory controlled. A core principal was the distinction between full unification of Upper and Lower Egypt, the ideal state of the *Sema-Tawy*, versus eras of fragmentation. Dynastic shifts appear to have been constructed primarily around these issues of territory and location of capital as illustrated by the division between the 17th and 18th Dynasties. No break in royal succession occurred with the accession of Ahmose at the end of the 17th Dynasty. Yet, the major territorial change involved in the Expulsion of the Hyksos and reunification of the country formed the basis for a dynastic division at that juncture.

Consequently, we would query whether a brief interregnum of Hyksos control in Upper Egypt is likely to have been recognized as an historical threshold of such importance to create two sequential Theban dynasties. As argued by Ryholt, this should only have been a transitory phase. However, it remains unclear whether this was accompanied by a break in the Theban royal succession or a reduction of Theban kings to nominal vassals of Hyksos overlords. The historical record presents no evidence for any disjunction or cessation of Theban rulers. An ongoing succession of Theban kings across this timeframe, even in the context of a short phase of suzerainty under Hyksos control, involves no substantive change in the scope of the Theban realm or its center of power. Due to this picture of cultural and political continuity, several scholars have dismissed the very basis for recognizing a change from the 16th to 17th (e.g., Miniaci 2011b:235–236). Nevertheless, von Beckerath, Ryholt, and others have presented a strong case that a major political shift was signaled in the historical tradition of a change from the 16th to 17th Dynasty, both based at Thebes.

More problematically, the evidence for a phase of direct Hyksos intervention in Upper Egypt remains debatable and with dubious chronological parameters. The idea that the Hyksos were a major enemy of Thebes at this stage has been inferred on the basis of textual sources in which the 16th Dynasty rulers project an aggressive, martial tone. The 16th Dynasty kings emphasized their role as military leaders who maintained the Theban realm against any and all opponents. This theme of defending Thebes can be read in royal titulary and epithets of the 16th Dynasty, such as the prenomen Sekhemre-Shedwaset, *The-might-of-Re-who-rescues-Thebes* (Ryholt 1997:156, 305–306), or Neferhotep III's epithets, *One beloved of his army*, and the *Guide of victorious Thebes* (Ryholt 1997:160). An overtly militaristic air occurs in the Gebelein stela of Dedumose II (Cairo CG 20533), where the king proclaims that he is *The good-god, beloved of Thebes, the one chosen by Horus who increases his [army], who has appeared like then lightening of the sun, who is acclaimed to kingship of both lands, the one who belongs to shouting* (Helck 1983:43–44; Morenz 2010:293–320).

Some of the texts present this royal role in opposition to foreign enemies and Ryholt has suggested that we glimpse indications for a lengthy, drawn-out conflict with the Hyksos that culminated with the defeat of Thebes at the end of the 16th Dynasty (Ryholt 1997:302–307). The Neferhotep III stela (Cairo JE59635, Vernus 1982:129–135) states the king to be: *sḫy nỉwt.f ḫprtỉ mꜥkꜣ sy ḥnꜥ ḫꜣswtyw, he who raises his city* (Thebes), *it having been sunk through strife with foreigners.* Here Ryholt has implied the term *ḫꜣswtyw, foreigners (lit: "hill-dwellers")*, refers specifically to the *ḥkꜣw ḫꜣswt*, Hyksos (Ryholt 1997:133–134). A similar bellicose tone occurs in the stelae of Montuhotepi from Karnak (Luxor CL 233 G), which discusses the

king's military achievements, including his success in *repelling the foreign lands* (Vernus 1989:140–161). Ryholt has speculated that the Hyksos military threat culminated towards the end of the 16th Dynasty when Dedumose II's predecessor, Dedumose I, might have sued for peace with the Hyksos, perhaps to be read into his titulary, *the peace of Ra is stable; he who brings peace; he who rescues the two lands,* as recorded on the Gebelein stela of the king's-son Khonsuemwaset (Barsanti 1908:1–2; el-Sayed 1979:167–207). Nowhere in these sources, is there any specification of the Hyksos as the principal enemy of Thebes. The *topos* of defeat of enemies is a generic one and may equally apply to the Nubian (Kerma) threat to Upper Egypt, which is actually more securely attested through textual and archaeological evidence.

Physical evidence that has been interpreted to show Hyksos dominion in Middle and Upper Egypt takes the form of monumental material transported to the Delta and reused at Tell el-Dabꞌa and later at Piramesse and Tanis (Ryholt 1997:133–135). Paralleling the case of the statuary and objects buried in the Kerma tumuli in Upper Nubia (see further below), the transport of monumental material could represent a type of plunder resulting from Hyksos victories in the south. Perhaps the most significant object in this line of argument is an early 12th Dynasty offering stand dedicated to *Montu, Lord of Waset* (Berlin 22487) that presumably originated in Thebes but which was later re-inscribed with the nomen of Apophis (Krauss 1993:27–28).

The principal indication for a phase of 15th Dynasty/Hyksos control that penetrated south of Thebes (Giveon 1983:155–161) are two inscribed blocks of the Hyksos kings Seuserre-Khan (an inscribed offering stand) and Auserre-Apophis (a door lintel) found in the Hathor temple at Gebelein (Porter and Moss 1937:163). Although some have suggested these blocks relate to a Hyksos fortress built at Gebelein (Redford 1997:119), Ryholt has argued the blocks indicate temple construction commissioned by Khyan and Apophis, thereby demonstrating that Gebelein lay within their realm. The comparatively undamaged quality of the Apophis lintel and location within the temple precinct would seem to run counter to suggestions for long distance transport as part of ship ballast (Ryholt 1997:135–136). Nevertheless, recent analysis has proposed later transport of the blocks to Gebelein as trophies of the Theban victory over the Hyksos

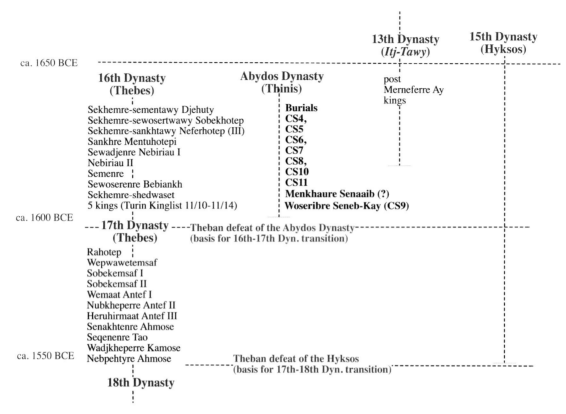

Fig. 14.11 Suggested dynastic structure of the late Second Intermediate Period with the 16th–17th Dynasty transition marked by defeat of Thinis and assumption of Theban rulership over the entirety of Upper Egypt.

as the end of the 17th Dynasty (Polz 2006:239–247, 2018:217–233). The Gebelein blocks present chronological complications since, if they reflect Hyksos control of the south from the reign of Khyan into the reign of Apophis, they might necessitate a longer phase of direct Hyksos domination than the brief Hyksos interregnum that Ryholt has proposed.[23]

Effectively, the textual references to the political opponents of the 16th Dynasty remain non-specific and could implicate other enemies—symbolic and real, both Egyptian and foreign—apart from the Hyksos. The physical evidence including the Gebelein blocks appears open to multiple lines of explanation. Transport of inscribed material within the Nile Valley need not directly mirror the geographical parameters of territorial expansion and military conquests. The argument that the Hyksos invaded and directly controlled Upper Egypt for any appreciable period of time remains viable but tenuous. And, as stated above, we have the fundamental question of whether a short-lived phase of Theban vassalage to the 15th Dynasty would be recognized by a dynastic division

superimposed by later chroniclers over the line of kings ruling from Thebes.

The evidence from South Abydos now supplies another possibility to be considered in the chronological patterning of the dynastic divisions that separate the 16th to 17th and 17th to 18th Dynasties. The dating evidence from Seneb-Kay's tomb along with tomb D78 containing the wand bearing his name are consistent with placement of this king contemporary with the middle to late 16th Dynasty. With the other seven tombs in the necropolis, as well as the possibility of additional now-missing tombs and a larger number of names attributable to this regnal grouping in the Turin Kinglist, we appear to have a line of rulers associated with the Thinite region that parallel much of the Theban 16th Dynasty, and who may have persisted as an independent kingdom up to the very end of the 16th Dynasty. The dynastic transition between the 16th and 17th Dynasty that Ryholt argued to correspond to a phase of Hyksos intervention in Upper Egypt might instead signal the defeat of the Abydos Dynasty and absorption of their territory into the Theban kingdom. This would be recognized as a major historical turning point when Thebes triumphed as the sole regnal line in Upper Egypt and was codified in the division between the 16th and 17th Dynasties (Fig. 14.11).

Much like the dynastic change from the 17th to 18th Dynasties that was constructed not based on any serious disjunction in royal succession but through the defeat of the 15th Dynasty and reunification of the country through Theban expansion into Hyksos territory (Polz 1998:219–231), so too the demise of the Abydos Dynasty and absorption of that kingdom's domain may have been recognized as a pivotal transition point in the political history and expansion of the Theban kingdom. Victory over the Abydos Dynasty by the Theban 16th Dynasty and the assumption of

Theban rule over the former Thinite territory would correspond with the end of the highly fragmented phase of the Second Intermediate Period when four regnal lines had vied for power. In this scenario the 13th Dynasty ended ca. 1675 BCE, contemporary with the middle of the 16th Dynasty, through Hyksos expansion southwards into Middle Egypt, while the Abydos Dynasty was defeated ca. 1600 BCE, through conflict with the Theban kingdom to its south. The transition between the 16th and 17th Dynasties was the point in time when the familiar, bipartite territorial division of Egypt into the Hyksos/15th Dynasty and the Theban 17th Dynasty formally emerged.

In discussing the territorial division between the Hyksos and Theban kingdoms it perhaps worthwhile to note that there could potentially be echoes of an

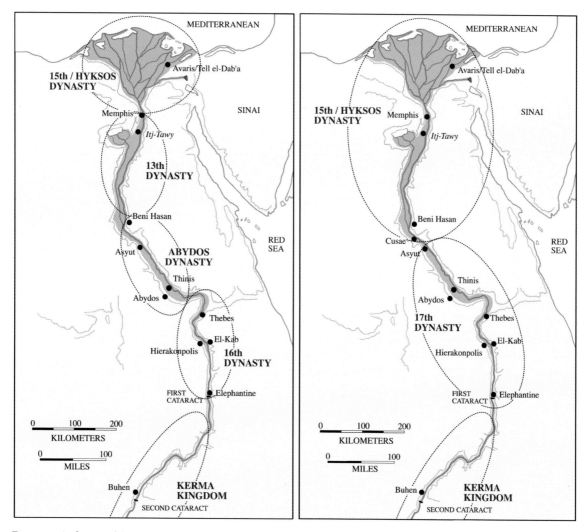

Fig. 14.12 Left: possible territorial divisions during the phase of the final decline of *Itj-Tawy* (ca. 1650–1600 BCE). Right: situation at the end of the Second Intermediate Period (ca. 1550 BCE).

earlier geographical imprint of the Abydos Dynasty within the territory controlled by the 17th Dynasty. Over the course of the 17th Dynasty, the frontier between the Hyksos and Thebans appears to have fluctuated in the region between Beni Hasan and Asyut. During the reign of Kamose, the First Kamose Stela records that the southern end of the Hyksos kingdom lay at Cusae, just north of Asyut. If we follow Marée's identification of King Wepwawetemsaf as brief-reigning successor to Rahotep, likely the first king of the 17th Dynasty, an indication of the extent of the Theban domain at that early stage may occur in the hieratic graffiti naming Wepwawetemsaf at Beni Hasan. If this reflects the northern end of Theban control, it is noteworthy that Beni Hasan lies only slightly north of Cusae and is closely consistent with the location of the frontier between the Hyksos and Theban kingdoms later during the reign of Kamose. The northern end of Theban territory at that early stage of the 17th Dynasty may have been largely contiguous with territory formerly controlled by the Abydos Dynasty that had now been incorporated into the Theban realm. On that basis, we may provisionally retain Ryholt's original suggestion that the Abydos Dynasty kings ruled over territory that extended approximately from the area of Dendera in the south to Beni Hasan in the north (Fig. 14.12).

Although addressing the geographical extent of territory held by the rulers of the Abydos Dynasty remains fundamentally beyond the surviving evidence, as we have examined throughout this chapter, the weight of that evidence indicates that Seneb-Kay lived and reigned during a phase of significant territorial division in Egypt. For the span of approximately half a century, the country was divided among four kingdoms. By the end of this era, the country had coalesced into two remaining kingdoms, the Hyksos and Theban polities. Let us now turn to examine the mystery of the violent death of Seneb-Kay and consider how the end of his dynasty may be involved in these territorial dynamics.

NOTES:

14.1 The Abydos Dynasty, which may have once been recorded in historical texts including the Ramesside compilation known as the Turin Kinglist, was eventually dropped from the royal canon and hence is an unnumbered dynasty.

14.2 Wepwawetemsaf literally means *Wepwawet is his protection*. Paentjeny means *The one of Thinis*,

compounded with the name of the city of Thinis, capital of the 8th nome of Upper Egypt.

14.3 The prenomen is one of the two names of Egyptian kings that occur inside the cartouche and is introduced by the title *ny-swt-bity*, *King of Upper and Lower Egypt* (Gardiner 1982:71–76; Leprohon 2013:7–19). Seneb-Kay would have had other elements of his titulary (Horus name, Golden-Horus name, and Two-Ladies name) that were not used in the decoration of his burial chamber. The prenomen is most frequently used in the Turin Kinglist although in some instances the nomen is used instead.

14.4 Some Egyptologists avoid the term 16th Dynasty, preferring instead a single Theban regnal sequence defined as 17th Dynasty (e.g., Bennett 2006:231–243, Miniaci 2011a:12–14). Here we follow the division separating an earlier Theban 16th Dynasty from a later 17th Dynasty and recognizing the likelihood that a political or territorial shift divides the two (see Ryholt 1997:151–162).

14.5 These five kings are, Djedhotepre-Dedumose (I), Djedneferre-Dedumose (II), Djedankhre-Montuemsaf, Merankhre-Menthotep (VI), and Seneferibre-Senwosret (IV). For these rulers see Ryholt (1997:151–162, 388–391).

14.6 The 17th Dynasty does not survive on the Turn Kinglist and presumably would have occurred on a missing Column 12. The dynastic tradition of the 17th Dynasty as a distinct regnal series from the 16th Dynasty is recorded in later kinglists including Manetho, which were compiled from earlier pharaonic sources.

14.7 Use of the *m*-owl was avoided through use of the horizontal biliteral sign for *im* (Gardiner Sign List Aa 13) in the one location where an *m* might have been used: in the name of the god Imseti.

14.8 The convention may also occur in the tomb of the *Commander of the Crew of the Ruler*, Bebi, at el-Kab (Davies and O'Connell 2009:52 and fig. 2) which is close in time to that of Sobeknakht II. It may also occur in the tomb chapel of Hormin (tomb 39 at el-Kab), but the published photographs and records for these other tombs are not clear enough to discern this detail.

14.9 Objects of this type are variably called "magical wands," "magical knives," "apotropaia" (Altenmüller 1965), or recently "birth tusks" (Quirke 2016:1–10). For ease of reference here we will use the more common designation of wand.

14.10 The wand and associated objects are discussed by Quirke (2016:208–210). Note that Quirke mistakenly states the stela to be in Glasgow, however, it is in the Egyptian collection of the Penn Museum (see also Hill 2010:235 and fig. 4; and Houser-Wegner 2014:50, fig. 21).

14.11 The reading of the original name has been discussed by Cahail (2015:119–121 and fig. 21).

14.12 The reuse of coffins is known from other periods of Egyptian history, see for example the well-documented studies by Kathlyn Cooney of Ramesside Period coffins (Cooney 2017:101–112). Noteworthy in the case of the *ꜣṯw n ṯt ḥkꜣ*, Sobekhotep, and King Seneb-Kay is repurposing of coffins by both high-status officials and kings. This phenomenon may be taken as a reflection of economic conditions of the period during which Seneb-Kay ruled as we consider elsewhere in this volume.

14.13 There are a significant number of objects including seals, a stela fragment from Abydos (Petrie 1902: pl. 60:4), and references in the Papyrus Boulaq 18 to men named Sobekhotep with the title *ꜣṯw n ṯt ḥkꜣ* (Chevereau 1992: no. 461; Stefanović 2006:88–89). Chevereau, followed by Stefanović, has grouped many of these together, reconstructing a family descent of the *ꜣṯw n ṯt ḥkꜣ*, Sobekhotep from an *ꜣṯw n ṯt ḥkꜣ*, Mentuhotep and mother Sat-Amun. However, it appears likely we have multiple different individuals represented spanning the 13th Dynasty and the Second Intermediate Period.

14.14 Fred Vink, who has examined the wand, stated that he has observed no indications the wand was recarved (personal communication). What appears more probable, however, is the addition of the text occurs over an empty section of a wand that originally bore no inscription.

14.15 These are Middle Kingdom stelae Tübingen 462; Cairo CG20089, CG20394, CG 20565, Statue Louvre A76; and stela Genf D.48 (see citations in Leitz 2003: (vol. II), 346).

14.16 Here again, we follow the division between a Theban 16th and 17th Dynasty as defined by Ryholt, rather than a single 17th Dynasty referring to this entire period as employed by Bennett and others.

14.17 Nebiriau II, Semenre, and the unnamed kings in the broken sections of TK 11/10–14.

14.18 Djedhotepre Dedumose I; Djedneferre Dedumose II; Djedankhre Mentuemsaf; Merankhre Montuhotep VI, and Seneferibre Senwosret IV.

14.19 Sekhemre-Neferkhau Wepwawetemsaf; Sekhemre-Khutawy Paentjeny; and Menkhaure Senaaib.

14.20 Sekhemre-Wahkhau Rahotep; Sekhemre-Shedtawy Sobekemsaf (II); Sekhemre-Wepmaat Antef; Nubkheperre Antef; Sekhemre-Heruhermaat Antef; and Senakhtenre Ahmose.

14.21 There would be then 77 years available for 27 kings making an average regnal length of 2.85 years.

14.22 Although there is a possibility that Thinis itself may have suffered an administrative decline during the Middle Kingdom and was replaced for a time by Abydos itself as capital of the 8th nome (Brovarski 1986:476).

14.23 The exact position and date of the Hyksos ruler Khyan remains debated. He is generally positioned as the immediate processor of Auserre Apophis with a reign ca. 1621–1581 BCE, contemporary with the transition between the 16th and 17th Theban Dynasties (Ryholt 1997:118–125). Recent suggestions for a much earlier dating (Moeller and Marouard 2011:87–121, 2018:173–197) do not accord well with the generally accepted direct succession between Khyan and Apophis (Aston 2018:15–56; Höflmayer 2018:143–171; Schneider 2018:277–285).

15

The Archaeology of Political Dissonance in Egypt's Second Intermediate Period*

The tomb and remnants of the burial of King Seneb-Kay at South Abydos present a unique set of evidence for the political and social context of his reign. The exact historical parameters of Seneb-Kay's lifetime, and those of the seven probable kings buried in the tombs in the main tomb cluster, remain open to discussion. However, at its most fundamental level Seneb-Kay's tomb is riddled with indications of the severe political discord that lies at the heart of Egypt's Second Intermediate Period. Let us briefly recap the primary evidence that has been presented throughout this volume.

The king's burial chamber was built from dismantled chapel blocks of the mid- to late 13th Dynasty commemorating the Theban family of Dedtu and his son Ibiau. Those men's identity had been viciously defaced by an extensive *damnatio memoriae* that bears the hallmarks of a political vendetta. Within Seneb-Kay's burial equipment, and providing a chronological parallel to the reused blocks, occurs the reuse of plundered 13th Dynasty elite and royal burial equipment. Seneb-Kay's canopic box was composed of reused cedar boards originating in the coffin of one of the Sobekhotep kings of the 13th Dynasty. Still preserving parts of its original textual corpus of Coffin Texts Spells 777–785, the coffin may be attributed with some degree of probability to Sobekhotep IV. These coffin boards appear to have originated in the adjacent tomb S10, part of the enclosure

of which Seneb-Kay's tomb builders also appropriated. Seneb-Kay's white-background outer sarcophagus was meticulously decorated with polychrome painted borders in an artistic mode that does not fit with the painted imagery inside his burial chamber, nor with the indications for the rapid completion of his tomb. That sarcophagus, too, may have been reused, again deriving from an elite burial context of the middle to late 13th Dynasty, and possibly from one of the family members of Dedtu and Ibiau whose chapel supplied the limestone for Seneb-Kay's burial chamber.

Seneb-Kay's own skeletal remains furnish overt indications for political and territorial conflict: a dramatic set of traumatic wounds that detail the violent death of this king in a military encounter. The battle-axe blows to his skull, including the full impression of the leading edge of a battle axe in the top of his cranium, appear attributable not merely to a violent death, but suggest the king may have died as the object of smiting, the classic pharaonic act of defeat of an enemy. Seneb-Kay's death appears likely to have occurred in combat with forces commanded by some other king. Moreover, the evidence for Seneb-Kay's death in battle appears to be associated with other evidence both from his own skeleton, and that of the individual buried in nearby tomb CS10, that these were kings who came to power from a military background and who spent much of their lives practicing

* This chapter written by Josef Wegner.

martial techniques. Musculoskeletal stress markers suggest a regimen of physical activities that may have included habitual equestrian activity for both men, as well as demanding, repetitive weapon use by the man buried in CS10. Muscle-use and wear patterns on the bones in CS10 implicate archery and training with a bow and arrow as a possible explanation. Both King Seneb-Kay and the CS10 individual may have been integrally involved in ongoing use of military technologies that had arrived in the Nile Valley contemporary with the Hyksos Period. These crucial new military practices include use of the domesticated horse as a means of rapid movement for military command and in association with the advent of chariot technology, which we see in full-scale use by the end of the 17th Dynasty. During this same timeframe, the compound bow was adapted into Egyptian military practices and thereafter was prominently used in battle by the pharaohs of the 18th and 19th Dynasties.

A somewhat puzzling, but suggestive set of historical evidence related to Seneb-Kay that provides further weight to these indications of his military background is the occurrence of the inscribed wand bearing his name in nearby Cemetery D at North Abydos. The Se[ne]b-Kay wand is presently the only object—apart from his own tomb and possibly the fragmentary entries in Column 11 of the Turin Kinglist—that testify to the historical existence of this king. The association of the wand with the burial of a military commander, the *Commander of the Crew of the Ruler*, Sobekhotep, and his wife Neferuptah, suggests some form of close relationship between Seneb-Kay and these people. Possibly Sobekhotep was a commander in Seneb-Kay's army, or Sobekhotep and his wife may be family members, or potentially the parents of this king. Whatever the exact relationship may have been we see further intimations of the military associations of Seneb-Kay.

At multiple levels we see reflections of extreme political dissonance reverberating through the material remains of Seneb-Kay's tomb. We would suggest that the tomb provides an index to the tensions and political violence that buffeted Egypt during the Second Intermediate Period. Even if we attempt to derive no more specific historical conclusions regarding the kingship of Seneb-Kay and the seven burials at South Abydos, the evidence is symptomatic of the political and social conditions of Upper Egypt in the timeframe ca. 1700 to 1600 BCE. However, given the

new evidence furnished by this royal necropolis at South Abydos, it does appear possible to build upon the discussion in the previous chapter and present suggestions regarding this evidence for political dissonance and how it may relate to the death of Seneb-Kay, as well as the proposition made above: that the defeat of the Abydos Dynasty by the rulers of Thebes might form the defining event that separates the 16th and 17th Theban Dynasties.

TERRITORIAL CONFLICT AND THE DEATH OF SENEB-KAY

The skeletal remains of Seneb-Kay and the individual—likely also a king—buried in tomb CS10 testify to the lives and social class of these men. These appear not to have been rulers who merely manipulated martial symbolism as way to legitimize their power. Rather, they were actively engaged in military activities and appear to have risen to power through their status within the military class of the Second Intermediate Period. They were "warrior kings" in the full sense of the term. The extensive set of traumatic injuries that detail the brutal death of Seneb-Kay in a military encounter present us with a signature of the scope of territorial conflict that affected Upper Egypt during this era and that drove this militarization of elite society and the kingship itself.

The violent death of Seneb-Kay predates the well-known example of King Seqenenre Tao who died in battle perhaps 50–75 years after Seneb-Kay. In the case of Seqenenre, the conflict between the Theban 17th Dynasty and the Hyksos is plausibly accepted both on the basis of the physical evidence, as well as the historical evidence for warfare with the Hyksos during his reign and those of his successors, Kamose and Ahmose. For Seneb-Kay, however, we are presented with a more challenging 3600-year old "cold case." Is it enough to simply document the fact that this king died in battle? Or, can we build upon the evidence to consider the territorial dynamics that led to his death. In view of the historical parameters for his reign, what potential political opponents might be implicated in Seneb-Kay's death in battle?

As we have considered above, the kings buried at South Abydos reigned during a period of pronounced territorial fragmentation in Egypt. During this time period, we have evidence for contemporaneous rulership of the 13th, 15th, 16th Dynasties, as well as the Thinite rulers of the Abydos Dynasty. Across this same timeframe occurred periodic incursions into Upper Egypt by forces allied with the rulers of the Nubian Kerma Kingdom. Any of these contemporaneous Egyptian dynasties or warfare associated with Nubian incursions present viable opponents that could explain the death of Seneb-Kay in battle. We can, however, weigh these various possibilities in terms of the evidence and consider the relative likelihood of these various candidates for the violent death of Seneb-Kay.

CONFLICT WITH THE 13TH DYNASTY

As now appears to be the case, during the final phase of the 13th Dynasty, Upper Egypt separated from the rule of *Itj-Tawy* and developed independent rulership. While Ilin-Tomich has argued in favor of a single Theban Kingdom, he has also suggested that one explanation for the aggressive tone and militarization of society seen in the 16th Dynasty lay in warfare against the south by the 13th Dynasty kings (Ilin-Tomich 2015:164–166). In the case of the division of Upper Egypt into two contemporaneous royal lines at Thebes and Thinis/Abydos, conflict with *Itj-Tawy* remains a viable scenario but with the likelihood that the Abydos Dynasty, not the Thebans, would have borne the brunt of any conflict with the kings of *Itj-Tawy*. The suggested extent of Thinite control extending northwards into Middle Egypt would have placed the Abydos Dynasty between the territory controlled by the 13th and 16th Dynasties and presumably the northern end of their realm directly abutted the southern limit of 13th Dynasty control.

In this regard, it is significant to note that one of the key historical synchronisms for the 16th Dynasty is the journey to *Itj-Tawy* of the priest of Horus of Nekhen, Horemkhauef. His trip to *Itj-Tawy* resulted in the acquisition of new cult images of Horus and Isis from an unnamed king for installation in the temple at Hierakonpolis. While such institutional connections with the rulers at *Itj-Tawy* may have occurred independent of any territorial conflict between the

13th and 16th Dynasties, it is interesting that we see no hint of political impediment to Horemkhauef's mission. One alternative to consider here is that a catalyst for the inception of the 16th Dynasty might not be the wholesale secession of the *Head of the South*, but the initial separation of a sizeable tract of territory that lay between *Itj-Tawy* and Thebes. If political forces arose leading to independence in the Thinite region, this would have precipitated autonomy of the Theban region and concomitant emergence of the 16th Dynasty, now geographically separated from *Itj-Tawy*. The 16th Dynasty may, in this case, have continued to evolve, centered around the administrative structures descended from the late Middle Kingdom as Ilin-Tomich has suggested. In such a model, an upstart dynasty centered in the Thinite region might have navigated a precarious existence between two potentially antagonistic dynasties, both on its northern and southern flanks.

At South Abydos, we see rather obvious signs of politically motivated animosities spanning several generations during the late 13th Dynasty and into the time of Seneb-Kay. While the *damnatio memoriae* against Dedtu and Ibiau is not likely to date to Seneb-Kay himself (the blocks for his tomb appear to have been culled from an already vandalized chapel), that phenomenon, paired with what appears to be an overt form of local state-supported tomb robbery of the 13th Dynasty royal burials at South Abydos, suggest a period of politically motivated vendetta against prominent 13th Dynasty figures. The Theban associations of the officials Dedtu and Ibiau, as well as their close familial links with the family of Kings Neferhotep I and Sobekhotep IV, hints at animosities among elite and royal power holders directed both southwards to Thebes and northwards to *Itj-Tawy*. These cultural phenomena could be rooted in a social and political context that included ongoing rivalry and conflict with the kings of the final phase of the 13th Dynasty. It appears plausible that Seneb-Kay might have died in armed confrontation with forces of the 13th Dynasty.

In order to accommodate conflict with the 13th Dynasty as an explanation for Seneb-Kay's death, this necessitates that he died relatively early in the period ca. 1650–1600 BCE, and prior to the final demise of the 13th Dynasty (which occurred ca. 1675 BCE contemporary with the reigns of Kings Nebiriau I–II). Such a placement would fit with the possible occurrence of his prenomen, Woseribre, as one of the first two *Wsr-X-rc* kings in Column 11 of the Turin Kinglist discussed in the previous chapter. However, some of the evidence we have reviewed above, including the iconography in the burial chamber and the D78 stela and burial equipment, appears to fit better with a relatively later date for Seneb-Kay at the end of the regnal sequence and close to the transition between the 16th and 17th Dynasties. Such a placement would put Seneb-Kay into a phase of time post-dating the end of the 13th Dynasty. In that case, other opponents would appear more likely.

HYKSOS MILITARY ACTIVITY IN UPPER EGYPT

In his historical model of Egypt's Second Intermediate Period, Ryholt proposed a dynastic sequence that would attribute the demise of an independent Abydos Dynasty to the Hyksos conquest of Upper Egypt. As we have seen above, this model hypothesized that the defeat of the 13th Dynasty based at *Itj-Tawy* created a power vacuum that spawned two contemporaneous dynasties, the 16th Dynasty at Thebes and the Abydos Dynasty. Ultimately Hyksos military actions reached Middle and Upper Egypt impacting both of these dynasties. Due to its geographical position verging on the expanding Hyksos territory, the Abydos Dynasty would initially have been more susceptible to Hyksos military pressure and may have succumbed relatively quickly to southward expansion of the 15th Dynasty.

Prior to the discovery of the Second Intermediate Period royal necropolis at South Abydos, Ryholt had speculated that the lack of evidence for royal tombs of the 16th Dynasty,[1] as well as the Abydos Dynasty could be attributed to Hyksos plundering of those burial grounds (Ryholt 1997:160, 165). Now, with the advantage of archaeological remains of eight probable kings' tombs at South Abydos, the evidence appears consistent with more typical practices of tomb robbery, rather than the wholesale plunder and destruction of a royal necropolis by a victorious military force. Alongside the uncertainties that surround interpretation of inscribed material that might reflect a Hyksos interregnum in Upper Egypt, the argument for the Hyksos as the primary agents who destroyed

the Abydos Dynasty remains doubtful. Nevertheless, the demise of the 13th Dynasty, ca. 1675 BCE, would have enlarged Hyksos territory southwards verging on the area controlled by the Thinite kings and may have led to an extended phase of conflict within Middle Egypt, whether or not the Hyksos ultimately invaded and took control of the south as a whole.

Consequently, territorial conflict with the Hyksos remains a viable explanation for the death of Seneb-Kay. Chronologically this would presumably fall in the period after the demise of the 13th Dynasty and would conform with the evidence favoring a date for Seneb-Kay contemporary with the latter half of the 16th Dynasty. However, we would conclude this discussion of warfare with the Hyksos as the cause of Seneb-Kay's death in battle by reiterating the observation discussed in Part I, that the weaponry involved in the death of Seneb-Kay, including the axe blade in the king's cranial Wound A do not fit with the most diagnostic of Hyksos weapons. While the Hyksos and allied forces in the Nile Valley likely made extensive use of the excurvate bladed battle-axe, there are no physical reasons to implicate the Hyksos specifically in the death of Seneb-Kay. It appears equally or perhaps more likely that Seneb-Kay's death occurred as part of territorial conflict centered in Upper Egypt with enemies originating from the south, either the Nubians or the Thebans.

NUBIAN INCURSIONS INTO UPPER AND MIDDLE EGYPT

A crucial iconographic dating feature that we have examined above for the tomb of King Seneb-Kay are idiosyncratic anatomical details of human figures that occur also in the tomb chapel of Sobeknakht (II) at el-Kab. The similarity of this element suggests a close chronological proximity between the reign of Seneb-Kay and Sobeknakht II, a man whose career can be dated to the middle to late 16th Dynasty. Significantly, the chapel of Sobeknakht II at el-Kab is a monument that also records a major Nubian incursion into Upper Egypt (Davies 2003a:3–6, 2003b:18–19). The partially preserved text in Sobeknakht's chapel records his role in repelling a military coalition that appears to have been initiated by the ruler of Kush but including other Nubian groups: ...*Kush*

Fig. 15.1 Initial section of the text of Sobeknakht at el-Kab describing an armed invasion instigated by Kush that penetrated into Upper Egypt (line drawing adapted after Davies 2003c:53).

came, aroused along his length, he had stirred up the tribes of Wawat, the [island-dwellers?] of Khenethennefer, the land of Punt, and the Medjau... (Fig. 15.1). The Nubian threat was countered when the Egyptians mustered forces *to fight the Nubians.* The encounter included an unnamed Egyptian king whom Sobeknakht welcomed *on account of the coming of his Person...to repel the looters...* Following the victory, there was a gathering attended by the king that culminated with dedications to Nekhbet of el-Kab (text translations, Davies 2003c:52–54).

While the account of Sobeknakht suggests this particular Nubian incursion was repulsed somewhere in the vicinity of el-Kab, there are both archaeological and textual indications that military actions emanating from Nubia were a persistent problem during the period. These raids appear to have included actions that reached further north into Middle Egypt. The transport of Egyptian objects south to Kerma and their burial in the royal tumuli of the Classic Kerma period suggests plundering that accompanied military forays northwards (Ryholt 1998:31–33). Material includes monuments taken from Elephantine and Upper Egyptian centers possibly including el-Kab itself. Originating from further north than Abydos, the Egyptian statuary reburied at Kerma includes figures of the nomarch Djefahapi and his wife Sennuwy (Tumulus KIII) from Asyut. If a correlation is made between the origin of the objects and the direct incursion by Kushite forces, the evidence may indicate Nubian ventures extending well north of Abydos (Valbelle 2004:176–183). Kushite military activity reaching into Middle Egypt would presumably have taken Nubian forces either directly through or along the margins of territory controlled by Seneb-Kay and his contemporaries.

The evidence for Nubian incursions into Upper and Middle Egypt during a period broadly contemporary with Seneb-Kay's reign opens up various scenarios for that king's involvement in such encounters. Seneb-Kay could have been involved in an Upper Egyptian alliance aimed at countering such a periodic threat, the type of encounter described in the Sobeknakht text at el-Kab. Seneb-Kay could have died in battle assisting some other ruler such as the Theban king during a major Nubian incursion. Physical indications on his body, as we have discussed in Chapter 5, suggest that his death occurred at some distance from his burial locale at Abydos. Therefore, conflict brought about by Kerma-led forces seems to be a viable context in which Seneb-Kay died, either assisting allied forces in defense of broader Upper Egyptian territory or leading the defense of his own realm if the invasion had penetrated into or through the Thinite region.

CONFLICT WITH THE THEBAN 16TH DYNASTY

In the previous chapter we have touched on the militaristic tenor of the 16th Dynasty and the possibility that this reflects a phase of territorial strife that impacted the Theban Kingdom. Indications of ongoing conflict are not limited to royal texts but are widely expressed in the titles and material culture of the period. Stelae and commemorative monuments contemporary with the 16th Dynasty reflect the prominence of military offices, broadly paralleling the physical evidence we have discussed above for Seneb-Kay and the CS10 burial at South Abydos.

Textual sources indicate a significant militarization of the elite levels of society in Upper Egypt (Grajetzki 2010b:310–311; Shirley 2013:566–569). Within the Theban sphere we may note the military personnel at sites like el-Kab where an astounding number of male family members of the governors Sobeknakht I and II held the military title *ꜣtw n ṯt ḥkꜣ*, *Commander of the Crew of the Ruler* (Stefanović 2006:86–88). Among prominent families with such military associations, royal connections were further expressed through the title *ḫkrt-nswt*, *Royal Ornament*, frequently held by the female family members.[2] Use of specific titles by this social class may reflect the political allegiances that bound military organization to the kingship.

Aspects of the material culture of the era corroborate the martial outlook of the 16th Dynasty. Weaponry including daggers and axe-heads bearing 16th Dynasty royal names may have commemorated military service to the king. Although weapons with royal names occur in other periods, the prominence of such objects in the limited corpus of the 16th Dynasty is notable. Among these we may mention daggers and axeheads bearing the names of Seuserenre Bebiankh, Montuemsaf and Seneferibre Senwosret IV (Kühnert-Eggebrecht 1969:29–30, 132). King Semenre, the probable successor to Nebiriau II, and a close contemporary of Seneb-Kay, is attested on a single artifact: a bronze axe-head (Petrie Museum UC30079). It is of at least passing interest that these blades are of

the same type and dimensions that created Wound A in the cranium of Seneb-Kay (Fig. 15.2).

We have already seen that some scholars have attributed the militaristic tone of 16th Dynasty royal texts to conflict with the Hyksos (Vernus 1982:134–135; Ryholt 1997:304–306) or tensions between Thebes and *Itj-Tawy* in the aftermath of the secession of Thebes (Ilin-Tomich 2014:164–166). Other authors have theorized that there may have been an ideological need for legitimization of rulership that led to a doctrine of Theban nationalism (Franke 1990:127–128) or exceptionalism (Vernus 1989:145–161; Morenz 2010:293–320). Additionally, the ongoing threat from Nubia may have contributed to the military traditions that characterize the era. However, if Upper and Middle Egypt existed through this period, not as a unified kingdom that had evolved directly from the *Head of the South*, but as a more complex political mosaic dominated by neighboring kingdoms in the Thinite and Theban regions, then we have significant potential for the periodic eruption of territorial conflict that is echoed in these royal records.

As Ryholt observed in his discussion of the 16th Dynasty, it is noteworthy that we have no known monuments at Abydos associated with the fourteen kings attributed to this succession of Theban rulers. While this could be explained by the limited monumental output and poor preservation of the era, based on the sizeable number of kings, this appears likely to form a valid index to the geographical limits of their

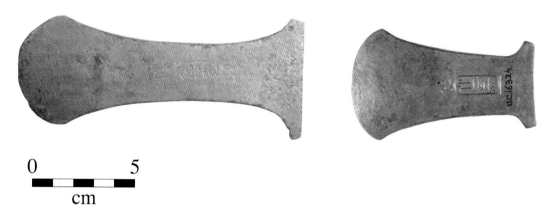

0   5

cm

Fig. 15.2 Examples of axe blades dated to the 16th Dynasty through their use of royal names. Left, axe blade with name of King Semenre (Petrie Museum, UC 30079); right, axe-blade attributed to Seneferibre Senwosret (Petrie Museum, UC 16324). Images courtesy of the Petrie Museum of Egyptian Archaeology.

authority. The first known king assumed to fall in the Theban succession with monuments at Abydos is Sekhemre-Wahkhau Rahotep, usually identified as the first or second ruler of the 17th Dynasty (Polz 2007:50–59). Stelae set up at Coptos and Abydos under Rahotep make references to recently ended conflict and temple reconstruction following damage that may be attributed to territorial strife (Ryholt 1997:309; Ilin-Tomich 2015:165–166). It seems remotely conceivable that the content of the Rahotep texts reflects the aftermath of a phase of Hyksos intervention in Upper Egypt. A more probable explanation may be that territorial conflict at this juncture had involved competing Upper Egyptian powers.

Consequently, the possibility that Seneb-Kay died as part of conflict between two rival Upper Egyptian kingdoms appears to be a significant possibility. It is plausible there were long standing tensions between the 16th Dynasty and rulers of the Abydos Dynasty that flared up periodically, or which primarily erupted towards the end of the 16th Dynasty at a point when the Theban Kingdom defeated and absorbed the erstwhile territory of the Abydos Dynasty. Given the uncertainty about the precise placement of his reign, Seneb-Kay may have died substantially before the late 16th Dynasty. As occurred later in the case of Seqenere Tao, the territorial integrity of the Abydos Dynasty itself may have survived his death in battle. However, given the extreme severity of his death, and the suggestion that he may have been dispatched through a formal smiting by an enemy king, we must legitimately wonder: what implications did Seneb-Kay's violent death have for the kingdom he ruled?

It appears possible the death of Seneb-Kay in some major military encounter marked the termination of the line of rulership to which he belonged. Could the death of Seneb-Kay have occurred in association with a final Theban victory over the kings of the Abydos Dynasty? In this case, we would have the remarkable potential for a correlation of the archaeological and anthropological evidence from South Abydos with the historical record for the late Second Intermediate Period. This territorial expansion of the Theban Kingdom and their assimilation of territory held until the end of the 16th Dynasty by the Thinite rulers may have provided the emergent 17th Dynasty kings that followed with a greatly expanded domain, and the physical and human capital with which to effectively challenge Hyksos control over northern Egypt. In this scenario, the death of Seneb-Kay could have been a watershed event in a military and political transition that unified the *Head of the South* under Theban control and, as such, was codified in later historical tradition by the shift from the 16th to 17th Dynasties.

FINAL THOUGHTS ON THE ABYDOS DYNASTY

Regarding the possible relationship between the 16th and 17th Dynasties and the group of kings buried at South Abydos there is an alternative possibility to consider. In reviewing the Second Intermediate Period rulers attributable to the Abydos Dynasty, we have touched on the evidence of several kings who appear to have Thinite associations but who arguably fall within the timeframe of the early 17th Dynasty. Following the analysis of Marée, two of the early 17th Dynasty kings, Paentjeny and Wepwawetemsaf (previously attributed by Franke and Ryholt to the Abydos Dynasty), appear to have Thinite familial associations. Additionally, their sole surviving monuments come from Abydos. If we ascribe the death of Seneb-Kay to conflict with the Theban Kingdom, then we must also account for the Thinite background of rulers slightly later in time that most scholars now attribute to the earliest years of the 17th Dynasty.

Perhaps the major transitional figure of this period is Sekhemre-Wahkhau Rahotep, often considered to be the first king of the 17th Dynasty (Polz 2007:50–59; Maree 2010:261–265). Extant monuments associated with Rahotep come not from Thebes but from Abydos and Coptos. Given the sparsely preserved monumental remains for this period, the small corpus of sources may provide only a partial reflection of the extent of Rahotep's domain. However, the lack of evidence from Thebes remains notable for this king and the occurrence of Rahotep's attested monuments at Abydos and Coptos may indicate that the territorial center of his power originated in the area north of Thebes extending from the Thinite though Coptite provinces (8th to 5th Upper Egyptian nomes). As noted above, and based on his stelae at the Min and Osiris temples (Blumenthal 1977:63–80; Ryholt 1997:168–172), Rahotep's reign may have included temple reconstruction that occurred in the aftermath of recently concluded military conflict.

Early 17th Dynasty stelae from Abydos dating to the reign of Rahotep and slightly thereafter record military officials and a garrison (*iwˁyt*) at Abydos that have been interpreted as an indication of Theban military buildup linked to the Hyksos conflict (Clère 1982:60–68; Franke 1985:175–176). However, this evidence might equally well suggest a developed military organization in the Thinite region that continued to evolve from the period of the Abydos Dynasty across the threshold into the early 17th Dynasty (Snape 1994:304–314). Moreover, if Rahotep was the father or predecessor of Wepwawetemsaf—as Marée has argued—then he too might easily have had Thinite origins. In this case, we may legitimately wonder: is the archaeological record providing hints at a crucial Thinite role in the emergent 17th Dynasty?

Certainly, the assumption that the Thebans must necessarily have defeated the Abydos Dynasty bears further scrutiny. It might be that the internecine conflict within Upper Egypt was resolved not through Theban ascendancy—as we have discussed above—but the reverse scenario. There is another viable option: the Thinite region with its succession of rulers like Woseribre Seneb-Kay drawn from the ranks of the military class may have itself have expanded southwards, reunifying the *Head of the South*,

and precipitating the dynastic division enshrined in the Turin Kinglist and later historical sources as the transition from the 16th to 17th Dynasty. The presumed Theban origins of Rahotep and the earliest 17th Dynasty kings may well be erroneous. The 17th Dynasty might have included kings emanating from the Thinite region. Perhaps the line of rulers classified here as the Abydos Dynasty represent forerunners to the 17th Dynasty whose primary achievement was reunifying the *Head of the South* (Fig. 15.3). Subsequent 17th Dynasty kings may have originated from both Thinis and Thebes before culminating in the well-documented familial succession from Seqenenre Tao through Ahmose.

The notion that the Abydos Dynasty was a weak regional power that was inevitably subject to destruction at the hands of either the Hyksos (Ryholt 1997:304), or a more powerful Theban Kingdom, may be fundamentally flawed. Despite the evident lack of resources, and severe economic problems that confronted Seneb-Kay and his contemporaries, the military capabilities of a kingdom struggling on multiple fronts may have propelled the martial spirit that emerges in the archaeological and textual records of this era. Alternatively, Seneb-Kay's death in battle may have been part of a longer conflict between rival powers in Upper Egypt that was resolved, not through a final moment of territorial conquest, but

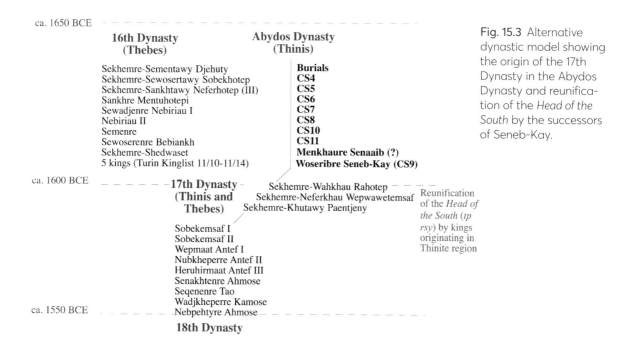

Fig. 15.3 Alternative dynastic model showing the origin of the 17th Dynasty in the Abydos Dynasty and reunification of the *Head of the South* by the successors of Seneb-Kay.

through some other means such as intermarriage of elite families, leading to the reconsolidation of the *Head of the South* under a single line of rulership.

Thebes and Thinis-Abydos appear to have been interwoven in more complex web of personal and political interaction at this stage in the Second Intermediate Period than extant evidence allows us to explain. However, if Seneb-Kay and the Abydos Dynasty are in some way forebears to the emergent 17th Dynasty succession, this would also allow us to view with fresh eyes one of the major monumental complexes of the later 17th Dynasty: the pyramid complex of Ahmose, along with the commemorative chapel of his grandmother, Queen Tetisheri. It may be no coincidence that the Ahmose complex was situated at South Abydos and not far from the earlier tombs of the Abydos Dynasty kings. Does the location of that complex reflect the perception of deeper familial and dynastic associations of Ahmose and the Theban 17th Dynasty with earlier kings at Abydos, extending back to the era of Woseribre Seneb-Kay?

Returning to the issue of Seneb-Kay's violent death, the various historical scenarios discussed above all provide viable explanations for the political and societal fissures that could have been involved what must have been a major event of the era. Given the scant historical data for the political dynamics of the period bridging the end of the 13th Dynasty and beginning of the Theban 17th Dynasty, it is difficult to eliminate any of these four primary possibilities—the final kings of the 13th Dynasty, the Hyksos 15th Dynasty, the Kerma Kingdom, or the Theban 16th Dynasty—as Seneb-Kay's primary opponent. Fundamentally, the evidence supplied by his tomb and his body, along with those of the seven additional burials in the royal cemetery at South Abydos, provide testimony to the severe territorial fragmentation, political discord, and economic decline that affected Upper Egypt during the later Second Intermediate Period. These tombs date within an era when Egypt was not only riven by four contemporaneous kingdoms but was threatened by the military capabilities of the Kerma Kingdom in Nubia. The conflicts of the era, which fed a dominant military culture, in combination with innovations in military technology that accompanied the Hyksos Period, are also to be witnessed in the physical record at South Abydos.

It is the very nature of Seneb-Kay's death, when viewed alongside the extensive indications for political discord embedded in his tomb, that suggests that the king was a casualty of territorial conflicts playing out within Middle and Upper Egypt. If Seneb-Kay's death is associated in some way with Theban military expansion into the territory of the Abydos Dynasty, his defeat may represent an important transitional moment helping to usher in the final stage of the Second Intermediate Period, which was characterized by the geographical expansion and resurgence of the Theban Kingdom. Alternatively, his death in battle may have been only a momentary setback for the Abydos Dynasty. Indeed, rather than precipitating the end of his kingdom it may have been an event that incited an increase in military activity leading kings of the Thinite region to expand southwards into Theban territory, eventually culminating in the reunification of Upper Egypt and the transition to the 17th Dynasty. The tomb of King Woseribre Seneb-Kay has opened a new window onto Egypt's Second Intermediate Period and presents us with a set of questions that can only be fully answered through archaeological evidence yet to be to recovered at Abydos or elsewhere in the Nile Valley.

NOTES:

15.1 Only one 16th Dynasty royal burial is known from the area of Dra Abu el-Naga at Western Thebes, that of Queen Montuhotep, wife of King Djehuty. Other 16th Dynasty royal tombs were presumably in the same region, but no remains have been identified. This may not be due to concerted destruction at the hands of Hyksos armies, but due to the relatively modest scale of royal burial structures of this period as now illustrated by the tombs at South Abydos.

15.2 Among holders of the title *ꜣṯw n ṯt ḥḳꜣ*, 70% of the women on the same monuments held the title *ḥkrt-nswt*, *Royal Ornament* (Stefanović 2006:7).

References

Abbas, J., Hamoud, K., Peleg, S., May, H., Masharawi, Y., Cohen, H., Peled, N., and Hershkovitz, I. 2011. Facet Joints Arthrosis in Normal and Stenotic Lumbar Spines. *Spine* 36(24): E1541–E1546.

Allen, James. 2010. The Second Intermediate Period in the Turin King-List. In *The Second Intermediate Period: Current Research, Future Prospects*, edited by M. Marée, 1–10. Peeters, Leuven.

Altenmüller, Hartwig. 1965. *Die Apotropaia und die Götter Mittelägyptens: eine typologische und religiongeschlichtliche Untersuchung der sogenannten "Zaubermesser" des Mittleren Reiches*, (I: Text; II: Katalog). Ludwig Maximilian Universität, Munich.

Andreu, Guillemette. 1991. Recherches sur la classe moyenne au Moyen Empire. In Schoske, Sylvia (ed.), *Akten des vierten Internationalen Ägyptologen Kongresses München 1985. Band 4: Geschichte, Verwaltungs- und Wirtschaftsgeschichte, Rechtsgeschichte, Nachbarkulturen. Studien zur Altägyptischen Kultur, Beihefte* 4. Hamburg, Buske: 15–26.

Andreu, Guilemette, Rutschowscaya, Marie-Hélène, and Ziegler, Christiane. 1997. *L'Égypte ancienne au Louvre*. Hachette, Paris.

Antolak, S.J., Hough, D.M., Pawlina, W., and R.J. Spinner. 2002. Anatomical Basis of Chronic Pelvic Pain Syndrome: The Ischial Spine and Pudendal Nerve Entrapment. *Medical Hypotheses* 59(3): 349–353.

Armelagos, G.J. and Van Gerven, D.P. 2003. A Century of Skeletal Biology and Paleopathology: Contrasts, Contradictions, and Conflicts. *American Anthropologist* 105(1): 53–64.

Armelagos, G.J., Sirak, K., Werkema, T., and Turner, B.L. 2014. Analysis of Nutritional Disease in Prehistory: The Search for Scurvy in Antiquity and Today. *International Journal of Paleopathology* 5: 9–17.

Arnold, Dieter. 2008. *Middle Kingdom Tomb Architecture at Lisht*. The Metropolitan Museum of Art Egyptian Expedition vol. 28. The Metropolitan Museum of Art, New York.

Aston, David A. 2018. How Early (and How Late) Can Khyan Really Be: An Essay Based on "Conventional Archaeological Methods." In *The Hyksos Ruler Khyan and the Early Second Intermediate Period in Egypt*, edited by Irene Forstner-Müller and Nadine Moeller, 15–56. Holzhausen, Vienna.

Awad, Hamza and Khaled Ahmed. 2003. Eine Stele des Mittleren Reiches im Louvre. *Göttinger Miszellen* 197: 43–48.

Axford R. 1995. *Archery Anatomy: An Introduction to Techniques for Improved Performance*. Souvenir, London.

Ayrton, Edward, Currelly, Charles, and Weigall, Arthur. 1904. *Abydos: Part III*. Egypt Exploration Fund, London.

Barsanti, Alexandre. 1908. Stèle inédite au nom du roi Radadouhotep Doudoumes. *Annales du Service des Antiquités de l'Égypte* 9: 1–2.

Barta, Winfried. 1968. *Aufbau und Bedeutung der altägyptischen Opferformel*. Ägyptologische Forschungen 24. J.J. Agustin, Glückstadt.

Bass, W. 2005. *Human Osteology*. Special Publication No. 2 of the Missouri Archaeological Society. Missouri Archaeological Society, Columbia, MO.

Bazin, Laure and Khaled el-Enany. 2010. La stèle d'un "chancelier du roi et prophète d'Amon" de la fin du Moyen Empire à Karnak (Caire JE 37507). *Cahiers de Karnak* 13: 1–23.

Beckerath, J. von 1999. Review: Ryholt, K.S.B. 1997. *The Political Situation in Egypt during the Second Intermediate Period c. 1800-1550 BC*. CNI Publications 20. *Archiv für Orientforschung*. The Carsten Niebuhr Institute of Near Eastern Studies, University of Copenhagen; Museum Tusculanum Press, Copenhagen: 46–47, 433–435.

Bennett, C.J. 1941. Growth of the *Htp-di-nsw* Formula in the Middle Kingdom. *Journal of Egyptian Archaeology* 27: 7–82.

Bennett, Chris. 2002. A Genealogical Chronology of the Seventeenth Dynasty. *JARCE* 39: 123–155.

———. 2006. Genealogy and Chronology of the Second Intermediate Period. Ägypten *und Levante* 16: 231–243.

Bennett, Deb. 1998. *Conquerors: The Roots of New World Horsemanship*. Amigo Publications, Lubbock, TX.

Berlev, Oleg. 1974. A Contemporary of King Sewah-en-re. *Journal of Egyptian Archaeology* 60: 106–113.

Berlev, Oleg and Hodjash, Svetlana. 1998. *Catalogue of the Monuments of Ancient Egypt: from the Museums of the Russian Federation Ukraine, Bielorussia, Caucasus, Middle Asia and the Baltic States*. Orbis Biblicus et Orientalis, Series Archaeologica 17. Vandenhoeck & Ruprecht, Friborg and Göttingen

Berman, Lawrence M. and Bohač, Kenneth. 1999. *Catalogue of Egyptian Art: the Cleveland Museum of Art*. Hudson Hill Press, New York.

Bibby, Miriam 2003. The Arrival of the Horse in Egypt: New Approaches and a Hypothesis. In *Current Research in Egyptology III*, edited by Rachel Ives, Daniel Lines, Christopher Naunton, and Nina Wahlberg, 13–18. Archaeopress, Oxford.

Bietak, M. and E. Strouhal. 1974. Die Todesumstände des Pharaos Seqenenre' (17. Dynastie): Vorbericht. *Annalen des Naturhistorischen Museums in Wien* 78: 29–52.

Blondiaux, J. 1994. A propos de la dame d'Hochfelden et de la pratique cavalière: discussion autour des sites fonctionnels fémoraux. *Actes des 6e journées anthropologiques (9–11 juin 1992), dossier de documentation archéologique*. 6: 97–109.

Blumenthal, Elke. 1977. Die Koptosstele des Königs Rahotep (London U.C. 14327). In *Ägypten und Kusch: Fritz Hintze zum 60. Geburtstag*, edited by Erika Endesfelder, Karl Heinz Priese, Walter Friedrich Reineke, and Steffen Wenig, 63–80. Akademie Verlag, Berlin.

Bochi, Patricia A. 1999. Death by Drama: The Ritual of *damnatio memoriae* in ancient Egypt. *Göttinger Miszellen* 171: 73–86.

Bourriau, Janine 1988. *Pharaohs and Mortals: Egyptian Art in the Middle Kingdom*. Cambridge University Press, Cambridge.

———. 2001. Change of Body Position in Egyptian Burials from the mid XIIth Dynasty until the Early XVIIIth Dynasty. In *Social Aspects of Funerary Culture in the Old and Middle Kingdoms: Proceedings of the International Symposium Held at Leiden University 6–7 June, 1996*, edited by Harco Willems, 1–20. Peeters, Leuven.

van den Brink, Edwin. 1982. *Tombs and Burial Customs at Tell el-Dab'a and their Cultural Relationship to Syria-Palestine during the Second Intermediate Period*. Veröffentlichungen der Institute für Afrikanistik und Ägyptologie der Universität Wien 23, Beiträge zur Ägyptologie 4. Afro-Pub, Vienna.

Brovarski, Edward. 1986. Thinis. In *Lexikon der Ägyptologie VI*, edited by W. Helck and E. Otto, 475–486. Verlag Otto Harrassowitz, Wiesbaden.

———. 2018. *Naga ed-Dêr in the First Intermediate Period*. Lockwood Press, Atlanta, Georgia.

Cahail, Kevin. 2014. In the Shadow of Osiris: Non-Royal Mortuary Landscapes at South Abydos during the Late Middle and New Kingdoms. Ph.D. diss., University of Pennsylvania.

———. 2015. A Family of Thirteenth Dynasty High Officials: New Evidence from South Abydos. *Journal of the American Research Center in Egypt* 51: 93–122.

———. 2019. The Earliest Attestation of the Late Egyptian *tw=j ḥr sḏm* Construction in the Second Intermediate Period Tomb of Seneb-Kay at South Abydos: Evidence of a Residence Sociolect? *Revue d'Égyptologie* 69: 15–34.

Cartwright, Caroline and Taylor, John H. 2008. Wooden Egyptian Archery Bows in the Collections of the British Museum. *Technical Research Bulletin, British Museum* 2: 77–83.

Casini, Emanuele, 2017. Remarks on Ancient Egyptian Cartonnage Mummy Masks from the late Old Kingdom to the End of the New Kingdom. In *Current Research in Egyptology 2016*, edited by Julia Chyla, Karolina Rosińska-Balik, Joanna Dębowska-Ludwin, and Carl Walsh, 56–73. Oxbow Books, Oxford.

Chevereau, Pierre-Marie. 1992. Contribution à la prosopographie des cadres militaires du Moyen Empire. *Revue d'égyptologie* 43: 11–34.

Clère, Jacques J. 1982. La stèle de Sânkhptaḥ. *Journal of Egyptian Archaeology* 68: 60–68.

Cooney, Kathlyn 2017. Coffin Reuse: Ritual Materialism in the Context of Scarcity. In *Proceedings of the First Vatican Conference 19–22 June 2013* 1, edited by Alessia Amenta and Hélène Guichard, 101–112. Edizioni Musei Vaticani, Città del Vaticano.

Crist, T.A. and Sorg. M.H. 2014. Adult Scurvy in New France: Samuel de Champlain's "Mal de la terre" at Saint Croix Island, 1604–1605. *International Journal of Paleopathology* 5: 95–105.

D'Auria, Sue, Lacovara, Peter, and Roehrig, Catherine (eds) 1988. *Mummies & Magic: The Funerary Arts of*

Ancient Egypt. Museum of Fine Arts, Boston.

Dar, H., Masharawi Y., Peleg, S., Steinberg, N., May, H., Medlej, B., Peled, N., and Hershkovitz, I. 2010. Schmorl's Nodes Distribution in the Human Spine and Its Possible Etiology. *European Spine Journal* 19(5): 670–675.

Daressy, Georges. 1893. Notes et remarques. *Recueil de travaux relatifs à la philologie et à l'archéologie égyptiennes et assyriennes* 14: 20–38, 165–185.

———. 1908. Le cercueil du roi Kames. *Annales du Service des Antiquités de l'Égypte* 9: 61–3, and pl. 9.

———. 1909. *Cercueils des cachettes royales.* Catalogue géneral des Antiquités Égyptiennes du Musée du Caire. Nos 61001–61044. Impr. de l'Insitut français d'archéologie orientale, Cairo.

Davies, Norman de Garis. 1901. *The Rock Tombs of Sheikh Saïd.* Egypt Exploration Fund, London.

———. 1920. *The Tomb of Antefoker, Vizier of Sesostris I and of his Wife, Senet* (no. 60). George Allen and Unwin, London.

Davies, W. Vivian. 1987. *Catalogue of Egyptian Antiquities in the British Museum VII. Tools and Weapons I, Axes.* British Museum Publications, London.

———. 2001. The Dynastic Tombs at Hierakonpolis: the Lower Group and the Artist Sedjemnetjeru. In *Colour and Painting in Ancient Egypt,* edited by W.V. Davies, 113–125. The British Museum Press, London.

———. 2003a. Sobeknakht of Elkab and the coming of Kush. *Egyptian Archaeology* 23: 3–6.

———. 2003b. Sobeknakht's Hidden Treasure. *British Museum Magazine* 46: 18–19.

———. 2003c. Kush in Egypt: A New Historical Inscription. *Sudan and Nubia* 7: 52–55.

———. 2010. Renseneb and Sobeknakht of El Kab: The Genealogical Data. In *The Second Intermediate Period: Current Research, Future Prospects,* edited by M. Marée, 223–240. Peeters, Leuven.

Davies, W.V. and O'Connell, Elizabeth. 2009. The British Museum Expedition to Elkab and Hagr Edfu, 2009. *British Museum Studies in Ancient Egypt and Sudan* 14: 51–72.

Del Vesco, Paolo and Moiso, Beppe (eds). 2017. *Missione Egitto 1903–1920: l'avventura archeologica M.A.I. raccontata.* Modena: Museo Egizio; Franco Cosimo Panini, Turin.

Delgado-Darias, T., Velasco-Vázquez, J., Arnay-De-La-Rosa, M., Martin-Rodriguez, E., and González-Reimers, E. 2006. Calculus, Periodontal Disease and Tooth Decay among the Prehispanic Population from Gran Canaria. *Journal of Archaeological Science.* 33(5): 663–670.

Dobie, Frank. 1952. *The Mustangs.* Little Brown and Company, Boston.

Dodson, Aidan. 1994. *The Canopic Equipment of the Kings of Egypt.* Kegan Paul International, London and New York.

———. 1998. A Funerary Mask in Durham and Mummy Adornment in the Late Second Intermediate Period and Early Eighteenth Dynasty. *Journal of Egyptian Archaeology* 84: 93–99.

———. 2011. Two Mummy-masks from the Dawn of the New Kingdom. In *Under the Potter's Tree: Studies on Ancient Egypt Presented to Janine Bourriau on the Occasion of her 70th Birthday,* edited by David Aston, Bettina Bader, Carla Gallorini, Paul Nicholson, and Sarah Buckingham, 333–347. Peeters, Leuven.

Drenkhahn, Rosemarie. 1976, Bemerkungen zu dem Titel *Xkr.t nswt. Studien zur Altägyptischen Kultur* 4: 59–67.

Eaton-Krauss, Marianne. 1990. The Coffins of Queen Ahhotep, Consort of Seqeni-en-re and Mother of Ahmose. *Chronique d'Égypte* 65: 195–205.

———. 2003. Encore: The Coffins of Ahhotep, Consort of Seqeni-en-Re and Mother of Ahmose. In *Ägypten-Münster: Kulturwissenschaftliche Studien zu Ägypten, dem Vorderen Orient und verwandten Gebieten,* edited by A.I. Blöbaum, J. Kahl, and S.D. Schweitzer, 75–89. Harrassowitz, Wiesbaden.

Erickson, J., Lee, D., and Bertram, J. 2000. Fourier Analysis of Acetabula Shape in Native American Arikara Populations before and after Acquisition of Horses. *American Journal of Physical Anthropology* 113: 473–480.

Erman, Adolf. 1919. *Reden, Rufe und Lieder auf Gräberbildern des Alten Reiches.* Verlag der Akademie der Wissenschaften in Kommission bei Georg Reimer, Berlin.

Fatayerji, Diana and Eastell, R. 2009. Age-Related Changes in Bone Turnover in Men. *Journal of Bone and Mineral Research* 14(7): 1203–1210.

Fischer, Henry George. 1996. A Shrine and Statue of the Thirteenth Dynasty. In *Egyptian Studies III: Varia Nova,* 123–139. The Metropolitan Museum, New York.

Forshaw, R.J. 2009. Dental Health and Disease in Ancient Egypt. *British Dental Journal* 206(8): 421–424.

Forstner-Müller, Irene. 2002. Tombs and Burial Customs at Tell el-Dab'a in Area A/II at the end of the MBIIA Period (Stratum F). In *The Middle Bronze Age in the Levant. Proceedings of an International Conference on MBIIA Ceramic Material in Vienna, 24–26 of January*

2001, Vienna, edited by M. Bietak, 153–184. Verlag der Österreichischen Akademie der Wissenschaften, Vienna.

Franke, Detlef. 1984a. Probleme der Arbeit mit altägyptisches Titeln des Mittleren Reiches. *Gottinger Miszellen* 83: 103–124.

———. 1984b. *Personendaten aus dem Mittleren Reich (20.–16. Jahrhundert v. Chr.): Dossiers 1–976.* Ägyptologische Abhandlungen 41. Harrassowitz, Wiesbaden.

———. 1985. An Important Family from Abydos of the Seventeenth Dynasty. *Journal of Egyptian Archaeology* 71: 175–176.

———. 1988. Zur Chronologie des Mittleren Reiches. Teil II: die sogenannte "Zweite Zwischenzeit" Altägyptens. *Orientalia* 57: 245–274.

———. 1990. Erste und Zweite Zwischenzeit-Ein Vergleich. *Zeitschift fur Ägyptische Sprache und Altertumskunde* 117: 119–129.

———. 2003. The Middle Kingdom Offering Formulas—A Challenge. *Journal of Egyptian Archaeology* 89: 39–57,

Frankfort, Henri. 1928. The Cemeteries at Abydos: Work of the Season 1925–26. *Journal of Egyptian Archaeology* 14: 235–245.

Gale, Rowena, Gasson, Peter, Hepper, Nigel, and Killen, Goffrey. 2000. Wood. In *Ancient Egyptian Materials and Technology*, edited by Paul Nicholson and Ian Shaw, 334–371. Cambridge University Press, Cambridge, UK.

Gardiner, Alan. 1959. *The Royal Canon of Turin.* The Griffith Institute, Ashmolean Museum, Oxford.

———. 1982 (reprint). *Egyptian Grammar: An Introduction to the Study of Hieroglyphs.* The Griffith Institute, Ashmolean Museum, Oxford.

Geisen, Christina. 2004a. *Die Totentexte des verschollenen Sarges der Königin Mentuhotep aus der 13. Dynastie: ein Textzeuge aus der Übergangszeit von den Sargtexten zum Totenbuch.* Studien zum Altägyptischen Totenbuch 8. Harrassowitz, Wiesbaden.

———. 2004b. Zur zeitlichen Einordnung des Königs Djehuti an das Ende der 13. Dynastie. *Studien zur Altägyptischen Kultur* 32: 149–157.

Genz, Hermann. 2013. The Introduction of the Light, Horse-Drawn Chariot and the Role of Archery in the Near East at the Transition from the Middle to the Late Bronze Ages: Is there a Connection? In *Chasing Chariots: Proceedings of the First International Chariot Conference* (Cairo 2012), edited by André J. Veldmeijer and Salima Ikram, 95–105. Sidestone, Leiden.

Giveon, Raphael. 1983. The Hyksos in the South. In *Fontes atque Pontes: Eine Festgabe fur Hellmut Brunner*, edited by M. Görg, 155–161. Harrassowitz, Wiesbaden.

Gleeson, Moll, Mayberger, E., Kariya, H., Skinner, L.-A., Wegner, J., Adams, M., and Zidan E. 2017. Conservation at Abydos: Past Practices and Future Possibilities. In *Engaging Conservation: Collaboration across Disciplines, edited by* Nina Owczarek, Molly Gleeson, and Lynn Grant, 57–64. Archetype Publications, London.

Graefe, Erhart. 2007. *Die Doppelgrabanlage "M" aus dem Mittleren Reich unter TT 196 im Tal el-Asasif in Theben-West.* Aegyptiaca Monasteriensia 5. Shaker, Aachen.

Grajetzki, Wolfram. 2000. *Die Höchsten Beamten der Ägyptischen Zentralverwaltung zur Zeit des Mittleren Reiches.* Achet, Schriften der Ägyptologie 2. Achet-Verlag, Berlin.

———. 2009. *Court Officials of the Egyptian Middle Kingdom.* Duckworth Egyptology, London.

———. 2010a. *The Coffin of Zemathor and other Rectangular Coffins of the Late Middle Kingdom and Second Intermediate Period.* Egyptology 15. Golden House Publications, London.

———. 2010b. Notes on Administration in the Second Intermediate Period. In *The Second Intermediate Period: Current Research, Future Prospects*, edited by M. Marée, 305–312. Uitgeverij Peeters, Leuven.

Gilbert, B. M. and McKern, T. W. 1973. The Method for Aging the Female Os Pubis." *American Journal of Physical Anthropology* 38:31–38.

Gray, L.P. 1978. Deviated Nasal Septum. Incidence and Etiology. *The Annals of Otology, Rhinology & Laryngology. Supplement.* 87 (Suppl 50): 3–20.

Guglielmi, Waltraud. 1973. *Reden, Rufe und Lieder auf altägyptischen Darstellungen der Landwirtschaft, Viezucht, des Fisch und Vogelsangs vom Mittleren Reich bis zur Spätzeit.* Tübinger Ägyptologische Beiträge 1. R. Habelt, Bonn.

Hafez, H.M., Woolgar J., Robbs J.V. 2001. Lower Extremity Arterial Injury: Results of 550 Cases and Review of Risk Factors Associated with Limb Loss. *J Vasc Surg.* 33: 1212–1219.

Haines, Francis. 1938a. Where Did the Plains Indians Get Their Horses?" *American Anthropologist* 40(1): 112–117.

———. 1938b. The Northward Spread of Horses among the Plains Indians. *American Anthropologist* 40(3): 429–437.

Hannig, Rainer. 2006. *Ägyptisches Wörterbuch II: Mittleres Reich und Zweite Zwischenzeit*, 2 vols. Hannig-Lexica 5; Kulturgeschichte der Antiken Welt 112. von Zabern, Mainz.

Harris, James E. and Wente, Edward. 1980. *An X-Ray Atlas of the Royal Mummies*. University of Chicago Press, Chicago and London.

Harvey, Stephen P. 1998. The Cults of King Ahmose at Abydos. Ph.D. diss., University of Pennsylvania, Ann Arbor: UMI.

———. 2004. New Evidence at Abydos for Ahmose's Funerary Cult. *Egyptian Archaeology* 24: 3–6.

Hayes, William C. 1947. Horemkha'uef of Nekhen and his Trip to It-Towe. *Journal of Egyptian Archaeology* 33: 3–11.

———. 1953. *The Scepter of Egypt: a Background for the Study of the Egyptian Antiquities in the Metropolitan Museum of Art, I. From the Earliest Times to the End of the Middle Kingdom*. Harper; Metropolitan Museum of Art, New York.

———. 1959. *The Scepter of Egypt: A Background for the Study of the Egyptian Antiquities in the Metropolitan Museum of Art II. The Hyksos Period and the New Kingdom (1675–1080 BC)*. Harvard University Press, for the Metropolitan Museum of Art, Cambridge, MA.

Hein, Irmgard and Satzinger, Helmut. 1993. *Stelen des Mittleren Reiches II, einschiesslich der I. und Zwischenzeit*. Corpus antiquitatum Aegyptiacarum, Kunsthistorisches Museum Wien 7. von Zabern, Mainz.

Helck, Wolfgang. 1983. *Historisch-biographische Texte der 2. Zwischenzeit und neue Texte der 18. Dynastie*, 2nd revised ed. Kleine ägyptische Texte [6 (1)]. Harrassowitz, Wiesbaden.

Herbich, Tomasz and Richards, Janet. 2006. The Loss and Rediscovery of the Vizier Iuu at Abydos: Magnetic Survey in the Middle Cemetery. In *Timelines, Studies in Honour of Manfred Bietak* 1, edited by Ernst Czerny, Irmgard Hein, Hermann Hunger, Dagmar Melman, and Angela Schwab, 141–149. Peeters, Departement Oosterse Studies, Leuven.

Hill, Jane. 2010. Window between Worlds: The Ankh as a Dominant Theme in Five Middle Kingdom Mortuary Monuments. In *Millions of Jubilees: Studies in Honor of David P. Silverman* I, edited by Z. Hawass and J. Houser Wegner, 227–247. Publ. du Conseil Suprême des Antiquitiés de l'Égypte, Cairo.

Hill, Jane, Rosado, Maria, and Wegner, J. 2017. The Abydos Dynasty: An Osteological Examination of Human Remains from the Second Intermediate Period Royal Cemetery. In *Proceedings of the XI International Congress of Egyptologists, Florence 23–30 August 2015*, edited by Maria Rosati and Maria Christina Guidotti, 276–282. Archaeopress, Oxford.

Hodges, D.C., 1991. Temporomandibular Joint Osteoarthritis in a British Skeletal Population. *American Journal of Physical Anthropology* 85(4): 367–377.

Höflmayer, Felix. 2018. An Early Date for Khyan and its Implications for Eastern Mediterranean Chronologies. In *The Hyksos Ruler Khyan and the Early Second Intermediate Period in Egypt*, ed, Irene Forstner-Müller and Nadine Moeller, 143–171. Holzhausen, Vienna.

Holladay, John. 1982. *Cities of the Delta, Part III/Tell el-Makhuta. Preliminary Report on the Wadi Tumilat Project 1978-1979*. Undena Publications, Malibu.

Houser-Wegner, Jennifer. 2014. Hidden Treasures: Abydos in the Basement. *Expedition* 56(1): 43–51.

Howard, D. 2014. *Bronze Age Military Equipment*. CPI Group, Croyden, UK.

Hugar, B.S., Harish, S., Chandra, Y.G., Praveen, S., and Jayanth, S.H. 2012. Study of Defense Injuries in Homicidal Deaths–An Autopsy Study. *Journal of Forensic and Legal Medicine* 19(4): 207–210.

Ikram, Salima and Dodson, Aidan. 1998. *The Mummy in Ancient Egypt: Equipping the Dead for Eternity*. Thames and Hudson, New York and London.

Ilin-Tomich, Alexander. 2011. Changes in the *Htp-dj-nsw* Formula in the Late Middle Kingdom and Second Intermediate Period. *Zeitschift fur Agyptische Studien* 138: 20–34,

———. 2014. The Theban Kingdom of Dynasty 16: Its Rise, Administration and Politics. *Journal of Egyptian History* 7: 143–193.

———. 2015. Theban Administration in the Late Middle Kingdom. *Zeitschrift für Ägyptische Sprache und Altertumskunde* 142(2): 120–153.

———. 2018. Female Titles Specific to Southern Upper Egypt in the Late Middle Kingdom and the Second Intermediate Period. *Bulletin of the Australian Centre for Egyptology* 26: 19–36.

Janaway, R.C., Percival, S.L., and Wilson A.S. 2009. Decomposition of Human Remains. In *Microbiology and Aging: Clinical Manifestations*, edited by S.L. Percival, 313–334. Springer, New York.

Jones, Dilwyn. 2000. *An Index of Ancient Egyptian Titles, Epithets, and Phrases of the Old Kingdom*. BAR International Series 866. Archaeopress, Oxford.

Jurmain, Robert, Cardoso, F.A., Henderson, C., and

Villotte, S. 2012. Bioarchaeology's Holy Grail: The Reconstruction of Activity. In Grauer, Al (ed.), *Companion to Paleopathology*, Blackwell, Oxford: 531–552.

Kalichman, L. and Hunter, D.J. 2007. Lumbar Facet Joint Osteoarthritis: A Review. *Seminars in Arthritis and Rheumatism* 37(2): 69–80.

Kaiser, Werner. 1983. Zu den msw-nswt der älteren Bilddarstellungen und der Bedeutung von rpwt. *Mitteilungen des Deutschen Archäologischen Instituts, Abteilung Kairo* 39: 261–296.

Kemp, Barry. 1968. The Osiris Temple at Abydos. *Mitteilungen des Deutchen Archäologischen Instituts Abteilung Kairo* 23: 138–155.

Killen, Geoffrey. 1994. *Egyptian Woodworking and Furniture*. Shire Egyptology 21. Shire, Princes Risborough.

Kitchen, Kenneth. 1961. An Unusual Stela from Abydos. *Journal of Egyptian Archaeology* 47: 10–18 and pls. 2–3.

————. 1962. Amenysonb in Liverpool and the Louvre. *Journal of Egyptian Archaeology* 48: 159–160.

Klemm, Rosemarie and Klemm, Dietrich. 1993. *Steine und Steinbrüche im Alten Ägypten*. Springer Verlag, Berlin.

Krauss, Rolf. 1993. Zur Problematik der Nubienpolitik Kamoses sowie der Hyksosherrschaft in Oberägypten. *Orientalia* 62: 17–29.

Krogman, W.M. and M.Y. Iscan. 1986. *The Human Skeleton in Forensic Medicine*. Charles C. Thomas, Springfield, IL.

Kühnert-Eggebrecht, Eva 1969. *Die Axt als Waffe und Werkzeug im alten Ägypten*. Münchner Ägyptologische Studien 15. Hessling, Berlin.

Lacau, Pierre. 1904. *Sarcophages antérieurs au Nouvel Empire*. Tome 1. Catalogue général des antiquités égyptiennes du Musée du Caire, nos. 28001–28086. Impr. de l'IFAO, Cairo.

————. 1906. *Sarcophages antérieurs au Nouvel Empire*. Tome 2. Catalogue général des antiquités égyptiennes du Musée du Caire, nos. 28087–28126. Impr. de l'IFAO, Cairo.

Lange, Hans O. and Schäfer, Heinrich. 1908. *Grab- und Denksteine des Mittleren Reiches II*. Catalogue général des antiquités égyptiennes du Musée du Caire 52. Reichsdruckerei, Berlin.

————. 1925. *Grab- und Denksteine des Mittleren Reiches III*. Catalogue général des antiquités égyptiennes du Musée du Caire 53. Reichsdruckerei, Berlin.

Lapp, Günther. 1993. *Typologie der Särge und Sargkammern von der 6. Bis 13. Dynastie*. SAGA 7. Heidelberger Verlag, Heidelberg.

Leek, F.F. 1972. Teeth and Bread in Ancient Egypt. *The Journal of Egyptian Archaeology* 58: 126–132.

Legrain, Georges. 1902. Le temple et les chapelles d'Osiris à Karnak. *Recueil de travaux relatifs à la philologie et à l'archéologie égyptiennes et assyriennes* 24: 208–214.

Leitz, Christian. 2003. *Lexikon der Ägyptischen Götter und Götterzeichnungen*. Peeters en Departement Oosterse Studies, Leuven and Dudley, MA.

Leprohon, Ronald. 2013. *The Great Name: Ancient Egyptian Royal Titulary*. Writings from the Ancient World 33. Society of Biblical Literature, Atlanta.

Lesko, Leonard H. 1979. *Index of the Spells on Egyptian Middle Kingdom Coffins and Related Documents*. B.C. Scribe, Berkeley.

Licata, M., Ronga, M., Cherubino, P., and Armocida, G. 2014. Different Types of Traumatic Lesions on Mediaeval Skeletons from Archaeological Sites in Varese (North Italy): Diagnosis on Ante Mortal Fractures Using Macroscopic, Radiological and CT Analysis. *Injury* 45(2): 457–459.

Lin, J., Hung, C., Yang, C-C., Chen, H., Chou, F., and Lu, T. 2010. Activation and Tremor of the Shoulder Muscles to the Demands of an Archery Task. *Journal of Sports Sciences*. 28(4): 415–421.

Loret, Victor. 1898. Les tombeaux de Thouthmis III et d'Amenophis II. *Bulletin de l'Institut égyptien* 3(9): 91–112.

Lovell, N.C. 1997. Trauma Analysis in Paleopathology. *American Journal of Physical Anthropology* 104(s25): 139–170.

Lüscher, B. 1990. *Untersuchugen zu ägyptischen Kanopenkasten. Vom Alten Reich bis zum Ende der Zweiten Zwischenzeit*. HÄB 31. Gerstenberg, Hildesheim.

Mace, Arthur and Winlock, Herbert. 1916. *The Tomb of Senebtisi at Lisht*. The Metropolitan Museum of Art Egyptian Expedition. Metropolitan Museum of Art, New York.

Malaise, Michel. 1981. Inventaire des stèles égyptiennes du Moyen Empire porteuses de représentations divines. *Studien zur Altägyptischen Kultur* 9: 259–283.

Marée, Marcel. 2010. A Sculpture Workshop at Abydos from the Late Sixteenth or Early Seventeenth Dynasty. In *The Second Intermediate Period: Current Research, Future Prospects*, edited by M. Marée, 275–277. Uitgeverij Peeters, Leuven.

Mariette, Auguste. 1880. *Catalogue général des monuments d'Abydos découverts pendant les fouilles de cette ville*. Imprimerie Nationale, Paris.

Mariotti V., Facchini, F., and Giovanna Belcastro. M. 2007. The Study of Entheses: Proposal of a Standardised Scoring Method for Twenty-three Entheses of the Postcranial Skeleton. *Collegium Antropologicum* 31(1): 291–313.

McCormack, Dawn. 2010. The Significance of Royal Funerary Architecture for the Study of the Thirteenth Dynasty. In *The Second Intermediate Period: Current Research, Future Prospects*, edited by M. Marée, 69–84. Uitgeverij Peeters, Leuven.

———. 2014. Fragments of a Difficult Era: Excavations of Tomb S9 at South Abydos. *Expedition* 56(1): 16–18.

McLeod, W. 1970. *Composite Bows from the Tomb of Tutankhamun*. Tutankhamun's Tomb Series III. Griffith Institute, Oxford.

Miniaci, Gianluca. 2006. Un Sobekemsaf da Dra Abu el-Naga. *Egitto e Vincino Oriente* 29: 75–87.

———. 2010a. The Incomplete Hieroglyphs System at the End of the Middle Kingdom. *Revue d'egyptologie* 61: 113–134.

———. 2010b. The Canopic Box of Khonswmes and the Transition from the Late Middle Kingdom to the Second Intermediate Period. *Egitto e Vicino Oriente* 33: 17ff.

———. 2011a. *Rishi Coffins and the Funerary Culture of Second Intermediate Period Egypt*. Egyptology 17. Golden House Publications, London.

———. 2011b. Through Change and Tradition: The Rise of Thebes during the Second Intermediate Period. In *Aegyptiaca et Coptica: Studi in onore di Sergio Pernigotti*, edited by P. Buzi, D. Picci and M. Zecchi, 235–249. BAR International Series 2264. Archaeoporess, Oxford.

———. 2018. Burial Equipment of Rishi Coffins and the Osmosis of the 'Rebirth Machine' at the end of the Middle Kingdom. In *Ancient Egyptian Coffins: Craft Traditions and Functionality*, edited by J.H. Taylor and M. Vandenbeusch, 247–274 . British Museum Publications on Egypt and Sudan 4. Peeters, Leuven.

Miniaci, Gianluca and Quirke, Stephen. 2008. Mariette at Dra Abu el-Naga and the Tomb of Neferhotep: A Mid 13th Dynasty Rishi Coffin (?). *Egitto e Vincino Oriente* 31: 5–25.

Moeller, Nadine and Marouard, Gregory. 2011. Discussion of Late Middle Kingdom and Early Second Intermediate Period History and Chronology in Relation to the Khayan Sealings from Tell Edfu. *Ägypten und Levante* 21: 87–121.

———. 2018. The Context of the Khyan Sealings from Tell Edfu and Further Implications for the Second Intermediate Period in Upper Egypt. In *The Hyksos Ruler Khyan and the Early Second Intermediate Period in Egypt*, edited by Irene Forstner-Müller and Nadine Moeller, 173–197. Holzhausen, Vienna.

Molen, Rami van der. 2005. *An Analytical Concordance of the Verb, the Negation, and the Syntax in Egyptian Coffin Texts*, 2 vols. Handbuch der Orientalistik, erste Abteilung: Der Nahe und Mittlere Osten 77. Brill, Leiden.

Molleson, T., and Blondiaux, J. 1994. Riders' Bones from Kish. *Cambridge Archaeological Journal* 4: 312–316.

Molnar, P. 2006. Tracing Prehistoric Activities: Musculoskeletal Stress Marker Analysis of a Stone-age Population on the Island of Gotland in the Baltic Sea. *Journal of Physical Anthropology* 219(1): 12–23.

Morenz, Ludwig D. 2010. Soldatenkönige, Königsakklamation und eine neue Göttin: zum Beginn des zweiten thebanischen Kleinstaates im 17. Jh. v. Chr. *Journal of Egyptian History* 3(2): 293–320.

Morgan. Jacques De.1895. *Fouilles à Dahchour: mars - juin 1894*. Vienne: Adolphe Holzhausen, Vienna.

Müller, Vera. 2018. Chronological Concepts for the Second Intermediate Period and their Implications for the Evaluation of its Material Culture. In *The Hyksos Ruler Khyan and the Early Second Intermediate Period in Egypt*, edited by Irene Forstner-Müller and Nadine Moeller, 199–216. Holzhausen, Vienna.

Munson Chapman, N.E. 1997. Evidence for Spanish Influence on Activity Induced Musculoskeletal Stress Markers at Pecos Pueblos. *International Journal of Ostearchaeolgy* 7: 497–506.

Newberry, Percy E. and F. Ll. Griffith. 1893–1900. *Beni Hasan*, 4 vols. Archaeological Survey of Egypt 1–2, 5, 7. Egypt Exploration Fund, London.

Niinimäki, S. 2012. The Relationship between Musculoskeletal Stress Markers and Biomechanical Properties of the Humeral Diaphysis. *American Journal of Physical Anthropology* 147(4): 618–628.

Nord, Del. 1970. *:krt-nswt* = "king's concubine"?. *Serapis* 2: 1–16.

O'Connor, David. 1985. The "Cenotaphs" of the Middle Kingdom at Abydos. In *Festschrift Mokhtar II*, edited by Gamal Eddin Mokhtar and Paule Posener-Kriéger, 161–177. Institut Français d'Archéologie Orientale, Cairo.

———. 1992. The Status of Early Egyptian Temples: An Alternative Theory. In *The Followers of Horus: Studies in Honor of Michael Allen Hoffman*, edited by

Barbara Adams and Renee Friedman, 83–98. Oxbow Monograph 22. Oxbow Books, Oxford.

Oppenheim, Adela; Arnold, Dorothea; Arnold, Dieter; and Yamamoto, Kei (eds). 2015. *Ancient Egypt Transformed: The Middle Kingdom*. Yale University Press, New Haven, London.

Ortner, D.J. 2003. *Identification of Pathological Conditions in Human Skeletal Remains*, 2nd ed. Academic, New York.

Ortner, D.J. and Putschar, W.G.J. 1981. *Identification of Pathological Conditions in Human Skeletal Remains*. Smithsonian Contributions to Anthropology, No. 28. Smithsonian Institute, Washington.

Parkinson, Richard and Quirke, Stephen. 1992. The Coffin of Prince Herunefer and the Early History of the *Book of the Dead*. In *Studies in Pharaonic Religion and Society in Honour of J. Gwyn Griffiths*, edited by Alan B. Lloyd, 37–51. Egypt Exploration Society, London.

Passalacqua, Nicholas. 2009. Forensic Age-at-Death Estimation from the Human Sacrum. *Journal of Forensic Sciences* 54 (2): 255–262.

Peden, Alexander J. 1994. *Egyptian Historical Inscriptions of the Twentieth Dynasty*. Paul Åstroms Förlag, Jonsered.

Peet, T. Eric. 1914. *The Cemeteries of Abydos. Volume II*. The Egypt Exploration Fund, London.

_____. 1930. *The Great Tomb Robberies of the Twentieth Egyptian Dynasty*, vols. I–II. The Clarendon Press, Oxford.

Peitzman, Andrew B., Schwab, C. William, Yealy, Donald M., Rhodes, Michael, and Fabian Timothy, C. 2012. *The Trauma Manual: Trauma and Acute Care Surgery*. Wolters Kluwer Health, Philadelphia, PA.

Petrie, William M.F. 1890. *Kahun, Gurob, and Hawara*. Kegan Paul, Trench, Trübner, and Co., London.

_____. 1902. *Abydos Part I*. Egypt Exploration Fund, 22nd memoir. Kegan Paul, Trench, Trübner, and Co., London.

_____. 1903. *Abydos Part II*. Egypt Exploration Fund, 24th memoir. Kegan Paul, Trench, Trübner, and Co., London.

Petrie, William M.F., Brunton, Guy and Murray, Margaret. 1923. *Lahun II*. British School of Archaeology in Egypt and Egyptian Research Account [33] (26th year). British School of Archaeology in Egypt; Bernard Quaritch, London.

Pieper, Max. 1929. *Die grosse Inschrift des Königs Neferhotep in Abydos: ein Beitrag zur ägyptischen Religions- und Literaturgeschichte*. Hinrichs, Leipzig.

Pollastrini, Alberto Maria 2017. Some Remarks on the Egyptian Reception of Foreign Military Technology during the 18th Dynasty: A Brief Survey of the Armour. In *Proceedings of the XI International Congress of Egyptologists, Florence*, ed, Gloria Rosati and Maria Cristina Guidotti, 513–518. Archaeopress, Oxford.

Polz, Daniel. 1998. Thebes und Avaris: zur "Vertreibung" der Hyksos. In *Stationen: Beiträge zur Kulturgeschichte Ägyptens, Rainer Stadelmann Gewidmet*, edited by H. Guksch and D. Polz, 219–231. Phillip von Zabern, Mainz.

_____. 2006. Die Hyksos-Blöcke aus Gebelên: zur Präsenz der Hyksos in Oberägypten. In Czerny, Ernst, Irmgard Hein, Hermann Hunger, Dagmar Melman, and Angela Schwab (eds), *Timelines: Studies in Honour of Manfred Bietak*. Orientalia Lovaniensia Analecta 149. Leuven: Peeters, Leuven: 239–247.

_____. 2007. *Der Beginn des Neuen Reiches: Zur Vorgeschichte einer Zeitenwende*. DAI Sonderschrift 31. Walter de Gruyter, Berlin.

_____. 2018. The Territorial Claim and the Political Role of the Theban State at the End of the Second Intermediate Period. In *The Hyksos Ruler Khyan and the Early Second Intermediate Period in Egypt*, edited by Irene Forstner-Müller and Nadine Moeller, 217–233. Holzhausen, Vienna.

Porter, Bertha and Moss, Rosalind. 1937. *Topographical Bibliography of Ancient Egyptian Hieroglyphic Texts, Reliefs, and Paintings V: Upper Egypt: Sites (Deir Rîfa to Aswân, excluding Thebes and the temples of Abydos, Dendera, Esna, Edfu, Kôm Ombo and Philae)*. Clarendon Press, Oxford.

_____. 1964. *Topographical Bibliography of Ancient Egyptian Hieroglyphic Texts, Reliefs, and Paintings I: the Theban Necropolis. Part 2: Royal Tombs and Smaller Cemeteries*, 2nd, revised and augmented ed. Oxford University Press; Griffith Institute, Oxford.

Porter, Robert. 2013. The Second Intermediate Period according to Edfu. *Göttinger Mizsellen* 239: 75–79.

Quirke, Stephen. 1990. *The Administration of Egypt in the Late Middle Kingdom: The Hieratic Documents*. SIA, New Malden.

_____. 1991. Royal Power in the 13th Dynasty. In Quirke, Stephen (ed.),Middle Kingdom Studies, SIA, New Malden: 123–139.

_____. 2004. *Titles and Bureaux of Egypt 1850–1700 BC*. Egyptology 1. Golden House Publications, London.

_____. 2016. *Birth Tusks: the Armoury of Health in Context—Egypt 1800 BC*. Middle Kingdom Studies 3.

Golden House Publications, London.

el-Rabi'i, Abdel-Méguid. 1977. Familles abydéniennes du Moyen Empire. *Chronique d'Égypte* 52(103): 13–21.

Randall-MacIver, David and Mace, Arthur. 1902. *El-Amrah and Abydos*. Egypt Exploration Fund, London.

Rando, C. and Waldron, T. 2012. TMJ Osteoarthritis: A New Approach to Diagnosis. *American Journal of Physical Anthropology* 148(1): 45–53.

Ranke, Hermann. 1935. *Die ägyptischen Personennamen. Band I: Verzeichnis der Namen*. J.J. Augustin, Glückstadt.

Raulwing, Peter and Clutton-Brock, Julia. 2009. The Buhen Horse: Fifty Years after its Discovery (1958–2008). *Journal of Egyptian History* 2(1): 1–106.

Raxter, M.H., Ruff, C.B., Azab, A., Erfan, M., Soliman, M., and El-Sawaf, A. 2008. Stature Estimation in Ancient Egyptians: A New Technique Based on Anatomical Reconstruction of Stature. *American Journal of Physical Anthropology* 136(2): 147–155.

Redford, Donald. 1986. *Pharaonic King-Lists, Annals and Day-Books*. Society for the Study of Egyptian Antiquities 4. Benben, Missisaugua, ON.

――――. 1997. Textual Sources for the Hyksos Period. In Oren, Eliezer D. (ed.), *The Hyksos: New Historical and Archaeological Perspectives*. University Museum Monograph 96. The University Museum, University of Pennsylvania, Philadelphia: 1–44.

Reinhard, K., Tieszen, L., Sandness, K.L., Beiningen, L.M., Miller, E., Ghazi, A.M., Miewald, C.E., and Barnum, S.V. 1994. Trade, Contact, and Female Health in Northeast Nebraska. In *In the Wake of Contact: Biological Responses to Conquest*, edited by Clark Larsen and George R. Milner, 63–74. Wiley-Liss, New York.

Reisner, George. 1967. *Canopics*. Catalogue général des antiquités égyptiennes du Musée du Caire. Nos. 4001–4740 and 4977–5033. Impr. de l'Institut français d'archéologie orientale, Cairo.

Richards, Janet. 2003. The Abydos Cemeteries in the Late Old Kingdom. In *Egyptology at the Dawn of the Twenty-First Century: Proceedings of the Eighth International Congress of Egyptologists* 1, edited by Zahi Hawass and Lyla Pinch Brock, 400–407. American University in Cairo Press, Cairo.

――――. 2005. *Society and Death in Ancient Egypt: Mortuary Landscapes of the Middle Kingdom*. Cambridge University Press, Cambridge, UK.

Rigault-Déon, Patricia. 2012. *Masques de Momies du Moyen Empire Égyptien: Les Decouvertes de Mirgissa*. Musee du Louvre, Paris.

Roksandic, M. and Armstrong, S.D. 2011. Using the Life History Model to Set the Stage(s) of Growth and Senescence in Bioarchaeology and Paleodemography. *American Journal of Physical Anthropology* 145(3): 337–347.

Rosati, Gloria. 2004. A Group of Middle Kingdom Stelae from El-Rizeiqat/El-Gebelein. *Studien zur Altägyptischen Kultur* 32: 333–349.

Rossel, Stine. 2007. The Development of Productive Subsistence Economies in the Nile Valley: Zooarchaeological Analysis of El-Mahâsna and South Abydos, Upper Egypt. Ph.D. diss. Harvard University, Cambridge, MA.

Ruff, C. 1994. Biomechanical analysis of Northern and Southern Plains Femora: Behavioral Implications. In *Skeletal Biology and the Great Plains: Migration, Warfare, Health and Subsistence*, edited by D. Owsley and R. Jantz, 235–246. Smithsonian Institute, Washington, DC.

Russmann, Edna. 2001. *Eternal Egypt: Masterworks of Ancient Art from the British Museum*, British Museum Press, London.

Ryholt, Kim. 1990. A Reconsideration of Some Royal Nomens of the Thirteenth Dynasty. *Göttinger Miszellen* 119: 101–113.

――――. 1997. *The Political Situation in Egypt during the Second Intermediate Period c. 1800–1550 B.C.* Carsten Niehbuhr Institute Publications 20. Museum Tusculanum Press, Copenhagen.

――――. 1998. A Statuette of Sobkhotep I from Kerma Tumulus X. *Cahiers de Recherches de l'Institut de Papyrologie et d'Égyptologie de Lille* 19: 31–33.

Sanchez, Gonzalo M. 2000. A Neurosurgeon's View of the Battle Reliefs of King Sety I: Aspects of Neurological Importance. *Journal of the American Research Center in Egypt* 37: 143–165.

Sandness, K. and Reinhard, K. 1992. Vertebral Pathology in Prehistoric and Historic Skeletons from Northeastern Nebraska. Plains Anthropologist 37(141): 299–309.

Sasada, Yukiko. 2013. An Alternative Theory for "Bitwear" Found on the Lower Second Premolar of the Buhen Horse. In *Chasing Chariots: Proceedings of the First International Chariot Conference* (Cairo 2012), edited by André J. Veldmeijer and Salima Ikram, 229–236. Sidestone, Leiden.

Säve-Söderbergh, Torgny. 1949. A Buhen Stela from the Second Intermediate Period. *Journal of Egyptian Archaeology* 35: 50–58.

el-Sayed, Ramadan. 1979. Quelques précisions sur l'histoire de la province d'Edfou à la 2e Période Intermédiaire (étude des stèles JE 38917 et 46988 du Musée du Caire). *Bulletin de l'Institut Français d'Archéologie Orientale* 79: 167–207.

Schiestl, Robert. 2008. Tomb Types and Layout of a Middle Bronze IIA Cemetery at Tell el-Dab'a, Area F/1. Egyptian and non-Egyptian Features. In *The Bronze Age in the Lebanon: Studies on the Archaeology and Chronology of Lebanon, Syria and Egypt*, edited by M. Bietak and E. Czerny, 243–256. Verlag der Österreichischen Akademie der Wissenschaften, Vienna.

_____. 2009. *Tell el-Dab'a XVIII: Die Palastnekropole von Tell el-Dab'a. Die Graber des Areals F/1 der Straten d/2 und d/1.* Verlag der Österreichischen Akademie der Wissenschaften, Vienna.

Schmucker, B.J. 1985. Dental Attrition: A Correlative Study of Dietary and Subsistence Patterns in California and New Mexico Indians. In *Health and Disease in the Prehistoric Southwest*, edited by C.F. Merbs and R.J. Miller, 275–323. Arizona State Univesity Archaeological University Paper No. 34. Dept. of Anthropology, Arizona State University, Tempe, AZ.

Schneider, Thomas. 1998. *Ausländer in Ägypten während des Mittleren Reiches und der Hyksoszeit. Teil 1: Die ausländischen Könige.* Ägypten und Altes Testament 42. Harrassowitz, Wiesbaden.

_____. 2006. The Relative Chronology of the Middle Kingdom and the Hyksos Period (Dyns. 12–17). In *Ancient Egyptian Chronology*, edited by E. Hornung, R. Krauss, and D. Warburton, 168–196. Brill, Leiden.

_____. 2018. Khyan's Place in History: A New Look at the Chronographic Tradition. In *The Hyksos Ruler Khyan and the Early Second Intermediate Period in Egypt*, Irene Forstner-Müller and Nadine Moeller, 277–285. Holzhausen Vienna.

Schulman, Alan. 1957. Egyptian Representations of Horsemen and Riding in the New Kingdom. *Journal of Near Eastern Studies* 16(4): 263–271.

_____. 1980. Chariots, Chariotry and the Hykos. *Journal of the Society for the Study of Egyptian Antiquities* 10: 105–153.

Shaw, Ian. 1999. *Egyptian Warfare and Weapons.* Shire Egyptology, Buckinghamshire, UK.

_____. 2001. Egyptians, Hyksos and Military Technology: Causes, Effects or Catalysts. In *The Social Context of Technological Change, Egypt and the Near East, 1650–1550 BC* edited by Andrew J. Shortland, 59–71. Oxbow, Oxford.

Shaw, Garry. 2009. The Death of King Seqenenre Tao. *Journal of the American Research Center in Egypt* 45: 159–176.

Shirley, J.J. 2013. Crisis and Restructuring of the State: from the Second Intermediate Period to the Advent of the Ramesses. In *Ancient Egyptian Administration*, edited by J.C. Moreno Garcia, 521–606. Brill, Leiden.

Siesse, Julien. 2015. Throne Names Patterns as a Clue for the Internal Chronology of the 13th to 17th Dynasties (Late Middle Kingdom and Second Intermediate Period). *Göttinger Miszellen* 246: 75–98.

Simpson, William K. 1974. *The Terrace of the Great God at Abydos: the Offering Chapels of Dynasties 12 and 13.* Publications of the Pennsylvania-Yale Expedition to Egypt 5. The Peabody Museum of Natural History of Yale University; The University of Pennsylvania Museum of Archaeology and Anthropology, New Haven and Philadelphia.

Smith, Grafton Elliot. 1912. *Cairo Catalogue Generale Nos. 61051–61100, The Royal Mummies.* Imprimerie de l'Institut français d'archéologie orientale, Cairo.

Smith, Grafton Elliot and Dawson, Warren R. 1924. *Egyptian Mummies.* George Allen & Unwin, London and New York.

Smith, B.H., 1984. Patterns of Molar Wear in Hunter-gatherers and Agriculturalists. *American Journal of Physical Anthropology* 63(1): 39–56.

Smither, Paul C. 1939. The Writing of *Htp-di-nsw* in the Middle and New Kingdoms. *Journal of Egyptian Archaeology* 25(1): 34–37.

Snape, Steven. 1994. Statues and Soldiers at Abydos in the Second Intermediate Period. In *The Unbroken Reed: Studies in the Culture and Heritage of Ancient Egypt in Honour of A.F. Shore*, edited by Christopher Eyre, Anthony Leahy, and Lisa M. Leahy, 304–314. Egypt Exploration Society, London.

Spalinger, Anthony. 1980. Remarks on the Family of Queen *Xc.s-nbw* and the Problem of Kingship in Dynasty XIII. *Revue d'Égyptologie* 32: 35–41.

_____. 2001. Review of K.S.B. Ryholt, The Political Situation in Egypt during the Second Intermediate Period, c. 1800–1550 B.C. *Journal of Near Eastern Studies* 60(4): 296–300.

Stefanović, Danijela. 2006. *The Holders of Regular Military Titles in the Period of the Middle Kingdom: Dossiers.* Egyptology 4. Golden House Publications, London.

_____. 2009. *The Non-Royal Regular Feminine Titles of the Middle Kingdom and Second Intermediate Period.* Golden House Publications, London.

Steele, D.G. and Bramblett, C.A. 1988. *The Anatomy and Biology of the Human Skeleton.* Texas A&M University Press, College Station, TX.

Stewart, T. D. *Essentials of Forensic Anthropology: Especially as Developed in the United States.* Charles C. Thomas, Springfield IL.

Taylor, John H. 1996. An Egyptian Mummy Mask in the British Museum: A New Date and Identification of the Owner. *Apollo* 144(413): 33–38.

———. 2001a. Patterns of Colouring on Ancient Egyptian Coffins from the New Kingdom to the Twenty-Sixth Dynasty: An Overview. In *Colour and Painting in Ancient Egypt,* edited by W.V. Davies, 164–181. British Museum Press, London.

———. 2001b. *Death and the Afterlife in Ancient Egypt.* British Museum Press, London.

Terada, M. 2010. An Examination of Proximal Tibia Anterior Shear Force and Neuromuscular Control in Individuals with Chronic Ankle Instability. Master's thesis, The University of Toledo, Toledo, OH.

Thongngarm, T. and McMurray, R.W., 2000. Osteoarthritis of the Sternoclavicular Joint. *Journal of Clinical Rheumatology* 6(5): 269–271.

Tihanyi, B., Bereczki, Z., Molnar, E., Berthon, W., Révész, L., Dutour, O., and Pálfi, G. 2015. Investigation of Hungarian Conquest Period (10th c. AD) Archery on the Basis of Activity-Induced Stress Markers on the Skeleton—Preliminary Results. *Acta Biologica Szegediensis* 59: 65–77.

Ubelaker, D.H. 1999. *Human Skeletal Remains: Excavation, Analysis, Interpretation.* Taraxacum, Washington, DC.

Valbelle, D. 2004. The Cultural Significance of Iconographic and Epigraphic Data found in the Kingdom of Kerma. In *Proceedings of the IXth International Conference on Nubian Studies (Boston 21–26 August 1998),* edited by T. Kendall, 176–183. Department of African-American Studies, Northeastern University, Boston.

Vandersleyen, Claude. 1971. *Les Guerres d'Amosis, Fondateur de la XVIIIe Dynastie,* Fondation Égyptologique Reine Élisabeth, Brussels.

Vernier, Émile. 1925. *Bijoux et Orfèvreries.* Catalogue Général des Antiquités Égyptiennes du Musée du Caire 80, nos. 42640–53171. Imprimerie de l'Institut français d'archéologie orientale, Cairo.

Vernus, Pascal. 1971. Noms propres juxtaposés au Moyen Empire. *Revue d'*Égyptologie 23: 193–198.

———. 1982. La stèle du roi Sekhemsankhtaouyrê Neferhotep Iykhernofret et la domination Hyksôs (stèle Caire JE 59635). *Annales du Service des Antiquités de l'Égypte* 68: 129–135.

———. 1986. *Le surnom au Moyen Empire: répertoire, procédés d'expression et structures de la double identité du début de la XIIe dynastie à la fin de la XVIIe dynastie.* Studia Pohl 13. Biblical Institute Press, Rome.

———. 1989. La stèle du pharaon Mntw-htpi à Karnak: un nouveau témoignage sur la situation politique et militaire au début de la D.P.I. *Revue d'Égyptologie* 40: 140–161.

Vila, André. 1976. Les masques funéraires. In *Mirgissa III-Les Nécropoles,* edited by J. Vercoutter, 151–268. Direction Génerale des Relations Culturelles, Scientifiques et Techniques; Centre National de la Recherche Scientifique. Paris.

Vogel, Carola. 2003. Fallen Heroes? Winlock's 'Slain Soldiers Reconsidered. *Journal of Egyptian Archaeology* 89: 239–245.

Wagner, M., Wu, X., Tarasov, P., Aisha, A., Ramsey, C.B., Schultz, M., Schmidt-Schultz, T., and Gresky, J. 2011. Radiocarbon-dated Archaeological Record of Early First Millennium B.C. Mounted Pastoralists in the Kunlun Mountains, China. *PNAS* 108(38): 15733–15738.

Walker, P.L., Bathurst, R.R., Richman, R., Gjerdrum, T., and Andrushko, V.A. 2009. The Causes of Porotic Hyperostosis and Cribra Orbitalia: A Reappraisal of the Iron-deficiency-anemia Hypothesis. *American Journal of Physical Anthropology* 139 (2): 109–125.

Ward, William. 1982. *Index of Egyptian Administrative and Religious Titles of the Middle Kingdom.* American University in Beirut Press, Beirut.

Wedel, Vicki and Galloway, Alison. 2014. *Broken Bones: Anthropological Analysis of Blunt Force Trauma,* 2nd ed. Charles Thomas Publisher, Springfield, IL.

Wegner, Josef. 2007. *The Mortuary Temple of Senwosret III at Abydos.* Publications of the Pennsylvania-Yale-Institute of Fine Arts Expedition, New Haven and Philadelphia.

———. 2009. The Tomb of Senwosret III at Abydos: Considerations on the Origins and Development of the Royal Amduat-Tomb. In *Archaism and Innovation: Studies in the Culture of Middle Kingdom Egypt,* edited by David P. Silverman, William Kelly Simpson, and Josef Wegner, 103–169. Publications of the Pennsylvania-Yale-Institute of Fine Arts Expedition, New Haven and Philadelphia.

———. 2014. Kings of Abydos: Solving an Ancient Egyptian Mystery. *Current World Archaeology* 64: 18–25.

————. 2015. A Royal Necropolis at South Abydos: New Light on Egypt's Second Intermediate Period. *Near Eastern Archaeology* 78(2): 68–78.

————. 2017a. A Royal Boat Burial and Watercraft Tableau of Egypt's 12th Dynasty (c.1850 BCE) at South Abydos. *International Journal of Nautical Archaeology* 46(1): 5–30.

————. 2017b. Raise Yourself Up: Mortuary Imagery in the Tomb of Woseribre Seneb-Kay. In *Company of Images: Modelling the Imaginary World of Middle Kingdom Egypt (2000–1500 BC)*, edited by G. Miniaci, M. Betrò, and S. Quirke, 479–511. Peeters, Leuven.

————. 2018a. Woseribre Seneb-Kay: A Newly Identified Upper Egyptian King of the Second Intermediate Period. In *The Hyksos Ruler Khyan and the Early Second Intermediate Period in Egypt: Problems and Priorities of Current Research*, edited by Irene Förstner-Muller and Nadine Moeller, 287–306. Holzhausen Verlag, Vienna.

————. 2018b. The Stela of Idudju-iker, Foremost-one of the Chiefs of Wawat, New Evidence on the Conquest of Thinis under Wahankh Antef II. *Revue d'Égyptologie* 68: 157–213.

————. 2020. Two Recently Discovered Burial Chambers of the 13th Dynasty at Abydos: Evidence for the Brother-Kings Sobekhotep IV and Sahathor. In *Festschrift for Zahi Hawass*, vol. 3. edited by Janice Kamrin et al., 1665–1681 . Charles University Press, Prague.

Wegner, Josef and Kevin Cahail. 2014. Ancient Reuse: The Discovery of a Royal Sarcophagus Chamber. *Expedition* 56(1): 19–23.

————. 2015. Royal Funerary Equipment of a King Sobekhotep at South Abydos: Evidence for the Tombs of Sobekhotep IV and Neferhotep I?. *Journal of the American Research Center in Egypt* 51: 123–164.

Western, A.C. and McLeod, W. 1995. Woods Used in Egyptian Bows and Arrows. *Journal of Egyptian Archaeology* 81: 77–94.

Whelan, Paul. 2016. On the Context and Conception of Two 'Trademark' Styles from Late Middle Kingdom Abydos. In *The World of Middle Kingdom Egypt (2000–1550 BC). Contributions on Archaeology, Art, Religion, and Written Sources*, Volume II, edited by G. Miniaci and W. Grajetzki, 285–338. Golden House Publications, London.

Wilkinson, Richard. 2011. Controlled Damage: The Mechanics and Micro-history of the *Damnatio Memoriae* Carried out in KV-23, the Tomb of Ay. *Journal of Egyptian History* 4(1): 129–147.

————. 2016. *Damnatio Memoriae* in the Valley of the Kings. In *The Oxford Handbook of the Valley of the Kings*, edited by Richard H. Wilkinson and Kent Weeks (eds), 335–346. Oxford University Press, Oxford.

Willems, Harco. 1988. *Chests of Life: A Study of the Typology and Conceptual Development of Middle Kingdom Standard Class Coffins*. Ex Oriente Lux, Leiden.

Williams, F.M.K., Manek, N.J., Sambrook, P.N., Spector, T.D., and Macgregor, A.J. 2007. Schmorl's Nodes: Common, Highly Heritable, and Related to Lumbar Disc Disease. *Arthritis Care & Research: Official Journal of the American College of Rheumatology* 57(5): 855–860.

Winlock, Herbert E. 1922. The Egyptian Expedition 1921–1922: Excavations at Thebes. *Bulletin of the Metropolitan Museum of Art* 17: 19–49.

————. 1945. *The Slain Soldiers of Neb-hepet-Re'-Mentu-Hotpe*. Publications of the Metropolitan Museum of Art Egyptian Expedition 16. The Metropolitan Museum of Art, New York.

Yoshimura, Sakuji. 2008. *Excavating in Egypt for 40 Years, Waseda University Expedition 1966–2006, A Special Exhibition in the Egyptian Museum, Cairo*. AKHT, Tokyo.

Zakrzewski, S.R. 2012. Dental Morphology, Dental Health and Its Social Implications. In *Prehistory of Northeastern Africa New Ideas and Discoveries*, edited by Jacek Kabaciński, Marek Chłodnicki, Michał Kobusiewicz, and Muzeum Archeologiczne w Poznaniu, 125–140. Studies in African Archaeology 11. Poznań Archaeological Museum, Heidelberg.